LEGAL STUDIES SERIES

BASIC LEGAL RESEARCH AND WRITING

Edward A. Nolfi
Attorney-at-Law
Akron, Ohio

Pamela R. Tepper, Esq.
Southeastern Paralegal Institute
Dallas, Texas

GLENCOE

Macmillan/McGraw–Hill

New York, New York
Columbus, Ohio
Mission Hills, California
Peoria, Illinois

Library of Congress Cataloging-in-Publication Data

Nolfi, Edward A., date.
[Basic legal research]
Basic legal research and writing / Edward A. Nolfi, Pamela R. Tepper.
p. cm.—(Legal studies series)
Originally issued as 2 separate works: Basic legal research / Edward A. Nolfi. © 1993, and Basic legal writing / Pamela R. Tepper. © 1992.
ISBN 0-02-801276-3 :
ISBN 0-02-801277-1 (includes software)
1. Legal research—United States. 2. Legal composition. I. Tepper, Pamela R., date. Basic legal writing. 1993. II. Series.
[KF240.N65 1993]
340'.072073—dc20 92-25750
CIP

Send all inquiries to:
GLENCOE DIVISION
Macmillan/McGraw-Hill
936 Eastwind Drive
Westerville, OH 43081

ISBN 0-02-801276-3
ISBN 0-02-801277-1 (includes software)

Printed in the United States of America.

1 2 3 4 5 6 7 8 9 POH 99 98 97 96 95 94 93 92

OTHER TITLES IN THE LEGAL STUDIES SERIES

Basic Law Office Management

Basic Legal Writing

Basic Legal Research

Basic Family Law

Introduction to Legal Assisting

Basic Civil Litigation

Defining the Law: A Basic Legal Dictionary

ABOUT THE AUTHORS

Edward A. Nolfi is a general practice attorney who has handled a wide variety of civil and criminal matters and has done legal research for a U.S. congressman. In 1988, he became Professor of Law at the Academy of Court Reporting in Akron, Ohio, and served in that position for three years. Earlier, during the mid-1980s, he was an associate editor with the Lawyers Co-operative Publishing Company.

Pamela R. Tepper currently teaches legal research and writing at the Southeastern Paralegal Institute and at Southern Methodist University in Dallas, Texas. She practices in the areas of corporate law, commercial litigation, probate, and juvenile law.

CONTENTS

Part Two

Researching Primary Authority

Part Three

Researching Secondary Authority

Part Four

Citing the Law

Part Five

Using Computers and Other Technologies

Part Six

Research Strategies

Section II Basic Legal Writing

PREFACE

The Text

This textbook is divided into two sections: Section I—Basic Legal Research, by Edward A. Nolfi, and Section II—Basic Legal Writing, by Pamela R. Tepper. The compilation provides both depth and breadth of coverage of these interrelated subjects. The student who has a knowledge of law books and experience with their use and who has *also* developed an ability to render arguments in forceful and lucid prose will be well prepared to enter today's competitive job market.

Organization

Section I, which contains 14 chapters, covers the following topics:

- The basics of legal research (Chapter 1)
- The principal sources of the law—cases, statutes, constitutions, court rules, and administrative regulations (Chapters 2 to 7)
- The publications used in legal research (Chapters 8 and 9)
- Citations and citators (Chapters 10 and 11)
- The high technology of legal research (Chapters 12 through 14)

Section II is composed of 13 chapters. Chapter 1 covers the basics of the American legal system. In Chapters 2 through 13 the student learns that:

- Decisions written by judges are not always models to be emulated
- The centuries-old traditions of the law are both a valued bond and a constraining hindrance to clear writing
- There are audiences to be identified, purposes to be defined, language to be chosen, arguments to be made
- There is a time for the adversarial and a time for the objective
- There are many different types of legal documents, from letters to memoranda to pleadings to briefs to contracts to wills
- Legal writing is both fraught with pitfalls and brimming with possibilities

The text also includes four appendixes, as follows:

- Appendix I contains the text of the U.S. Constitution
- Appendix II gives parallel volume references for the U.S. Supreme Court reporters, useful in the study of case law
- Appendix III gives selected references to law sources in the various states

- Appendix IV presents the Library of Congress Classification system used in most law libraries

The glossary following the appendixes contains key terms and definitions used in both Section I and Section II.

Design

Each chapter begins with a topic outline followed by a Commentary section that presents a sample situation in which the student is introduced to the information discussed in the chapter. Chapter objectives follow.

The text was designed to be user-friendly. The lined margins provide ample space for both instructors and students to make notes within each chapter. Key terms are boldfaced and defined at first use, with a list of these terms at the end of each chapter. Students are encouraged to write in this book, to complete the activities, and to keep this text at home or in the office as a handy reference guide.

Other Learning and Teaching Resources

The accompanying *Study Guide* is designed as a student support in the study and practice of legal research and writing. Performing the exercises will help the student achieve the objectives of the course. The *Study Guide* emphasizes skill building and application of that skill through exercises.

To facilitate the teaching and learning process, an *Instructor's Manual* accompanies this text. Included are model course syllabi for classes that meet on the quarter system and for those on semester schedules. In addition, there are answer keys to all review and discussion questions contained in the text, along with tests and answers for each chapter.

Computer-Assisted Legal Research Tutorial

The software component available with this textbook, *Computer Assisted Legal Research Tutorial,* is designed to instruct each student in using LEXIS and WESTLAW. The software covers basic principles of on-line bibliographic database searching, such as Boolean operators (AND and OR) and correcting over- and under-inclusion. The techniques used in each service are illustrated by escorting the student through specific search simulations. The simulations are off-line, eliminating connect-time charges and the need for a modem.

The software has been written to create and display screens, graphics, and instructional text windows. The tutorial includes a pulldown menu structure which is fully mouse-supported, though a mouse-supported system is not required to operate the software.

The software contains eight lessons which appear in a single scrolling list box. When the student logs onto the program, the Lessons menu scrollbar is positioned at the last lesson accessed. This allows the student to continue easily from where he or she left off.

The eight lessons in the CALR software are:

1. Introduction to CALR
2. Introduction to Searching
3. Searching LEXIS

4. LEXIS Advanced Search Techniques
5. Searching WESTLAW
6. WESTLAW Advanced Search Techniques
7. Shepard's
8. Legal Periodicals

Each lesson contains review questions, and the software will display and print a student report. This report lists the date, lesson name, number of questions answered, and score.

The software also features LEXIS and WESTLAW Search Planners which allow students to enter their search terms and connectors on a fill-in-the-blanks form. The software then displays the proper statement syntax for LEXIS or WESTLAW. The Planners are a valuable educational component in the software, and students will be able to use them separately from the tutorial. In this manner, the Planners will help students formulate their own searches while on the job.

Acknowledgments

The author wishes to acknowledge the contributions of the following reviewers, without whose efforts, suggestions, ideas, and insights this text would not be as valuable a tool as it is.

William R. Buckley, Esq., Assistant Professor, Paralegal Studies, College of Great Falls, Great Falls, MT

Susan Dunn, Esq., Coordinator of Legal Research and Writing, Adelphi University Lawyer's Assistant Program, West Hempstead, NY

David A. Dye, Esq., Coordinator, Legal Assistant Program, Missouri Western State College, St. Joseph, MO

Jeffrey A. Helewitz, Esq., Adjunct Faculty, Paralegal Programs at New York University, Queens College & Baruch College, New York, NY

Aletha L. Honsowitz, Esq., Lawyer/Librarian, Thomas M. Cooley Law School Library; CALR Instructor, Thomas M. Cooley Law School, Lansing, MI

Honorable Richard D. Huffman, Academic Coordinator, Evening Division, University of San Diego Lawyer's Assistant Program, San Diego, CA

Anne E. Kastle, Esq., Faculty, Legal Assistant Program, Edmonds Community College, Lynnwood, WA

Kathleen Mercer Reed, Esq., Instructor, Legal Assisting Technician Program, University of Toledo Community and Technical College, Toledo, OH

Julia O. Tryk Esq., Chair, Paralegal Program, Sawyer College of Business, Cleveland Heights, OH

Barbara J. Young, Esq., Academic Coordinator, Legal Assistant Studies, San Jose State University, San Jose, CA

Edward A. Nolfi
Pamela R. Tepper

SECTION I

BASIC

LEGAL RESEARCH

PART ONE

PRELIMINARY MATTERS

CHAPTER 1 Introduction to Legal Research

OUTLINE

COMMENTARY

Your child was born at City Hospital last week, and your father has given you $100 to open a bank account in your child's name. The clerk at the bank says you need a Social Security number to open the account. The clerk at the Social Security Administration says you need a birth certificate to get a number. The clerk at the Health Department says you can't get the birth certificate because City Hospital hasn't filed it yet. The clerk at City Hospital says it takes eight weeks to process the birth certificate, because it is necessary to get the doctor's signature. What are you going to do? Who are you going to believe? What is the law regarding birth certificates? How do you find out?

OBJECTIVES

In this chapter you will learn about the origins and nature of the U.S. legal system, the business of law publishing, and what ties them together: the need to do legal research. You will also learn about law books and law libraries. After reading this chapter, you should be able to:

1. Identify the origins of the U.S. legal system in English history.
2. Explain what the "common law" is.
3. Describe the basic structure of the U.S. legal system.
4. Understand the significance of "federalism" for legal research.

5. Understand the significance of the "separation of powers" for legal research.
6. Appreciate why master legal researchers know "who publishes what."
7. Explain why legal research is necessary.
8. Explain the purpose of legal research.
9. Distinguish "primary" authority from "secondary" authority.
10. Explain why law librarians avoid giving patrons *the* answer to legal questions.

1–1 The U.S. Legal System

It is evident that to do legal research you must have an adequate understanding of the legal system. It is also evident that to have an adequate understanding of the legal system, you must be able to recognize the law in all its forms. In short, you must know the "sources of the law."

The U.S. legal system is complex. We inherited the sophisticated legal system of medieval England, and, to avoid the tyranny of a king, modified it with the Constitution of the United States. As a result, to research U.S. law effectively, a legal researcher must know and appreciate a few fundamental facts, myths, and legends from world, English, and American history.

Law Is the Command of a Sovereign

What is the law? There are many answers to this question, and, together, the answers form our **jurisprudence,** a term used to describe both the philosophy of law and the law collectively. Indeed, one of the encyclopedias covering "all the law of America" is entitled *American Jurisprudence.* (See Chapter 8.) Fortunately, among all the answers, there is one that serves as a beacon for lawyers, law students, paralegals, and legal researchers of all kinds. To paraphrase the great English jurist Sir Edward Coke, *law is the command of a sovereign.*

What a command is, is easy to understand—someone telling you what you can or cannot do—but what is a sovereign? By definition, a **sovereign** is an entity with the power to command. The classic sovereign is the king. Who makes the laws, the commands, that people must follow? The classic answer, still true in many parts of the world today, is that the most powerful person, the one who can enforce obedience, is sovereign.

World history is replete with the conquests, crusades, and wars of men and women who have struggled to rule. These leaders have followed a variety of philosophies and religions. What is the taproot of the U.S. legal system? There is a specific time and place in world history to which it can be traced. The year is 1066 A.D., and the place is England.

Common-Law Origins

On Christmas Day, 1066, William the Conqueror was crowned King of England. It was the climax of the **Norman Conquest,** in which William, living on the Normandy coast of France, crossed the English Channel with his army and deposed the reigning king, Harold.

The Norman Conquest is significant because as sovereign, William exercised his powers in unprecedented ways. Unlike the previous kings of England, who allowed local disputes to be resolved by local officials, William decreed that he alone would resolve all disputes. Among other things, William declared that all of the land of England would be titled "of the King," and he parceled out the use of the land in exchange for services to his kingdom, establishing a system known as **feudalism.**

At first, William personally decided disputes all over England. He soon discovered, however, that he couldn't continue to do so, because he couldn't be in two places at once. He couldn't handle important national and international affairs in London, and at the same time be in Scotland to hear various disputes there. William therefore delegated some of his power to decide domestic disputes to representatives by giving them—the first **judges**—the power to decide disputes in his name, subject to his review.

The judges were given large territories to cover on horseback. Each judge would ride into a town and announce that he had come to decide disputes on behalf of the King. After hearing and deciding all the disputes in that town, he announced when he expected to return and rode on to the next town. Each judge went from town to town deciding disputes, "riding a circuit" around and back to the first town.

While on the road, these judges would often pass by each other. They would stop and invite each other to a roadside inn to talk about the cases they had decided. In discussing their cases, they discovered that each of them had, given a similar set of facts, decided the outcome of a case differently.

The judges realized that their comfortable jobs—riding around hearing and deciding cases on behalf of the King—were in jeopardy. They had observed that people have a sense of *simple justice:* that persons in like circumstances should be treated alike. If the peasants complained to the King that his judges were not treating them fairly, because they were not treating persons in like circumstances alike, the King would have their heads! The judges realized that more important than the merits of their individual decisions, their decisions as a whole had to be consistent from territory to territory, from circuit to circuit, across all of England.

The judges agreed to continue to meet regularly. They would keep a record of the facts they found in each case, their reasoning in deciding the case, and their decision. At the inn, they would report and study each other's cases. If they had a case that presented a similar fact pattern or issue, they would follow the reasoning and rule of law laid down by the judge in the case that had already been decided.

Following the rule established for the preceding similar case, the **precedent,** is known as the doctrine of ***stare decisis*** (Latin for "stand by that decided"). By following precedent, the rules of law made by judges in deciding actual cases, the judges, over time, made rules of law common to all of England, known as the **common law.** Restated, the common law is the law made by judges in deciding actual cases—a legal system emphasizing case law.

For example, the judges, not the King, made the "mailbox rule" of contracts: that if a contract offer invites acceptance by mail, a contract is created when the acceptance is mailed. Later judges followed the reasoning of the first judges to decide the issue: that the offeror who invites acceptance by mail should bear the risk of the acceptance being lost in the mail, and be bound by the contract, even if the offeror doesn't actually receive the acceptance.

By following the doctrine of *stare decisis,* the judges put some predictability into their decisions: they would follow the reasoning of the most similar past case, unless they decided that its reasoning would not apply.

Although, since 1066, the kings of England gradually lost most of their sovereign powers to the English legislature (i.e., the Parliament), for over 700 years there were two main sources of law in England: the commands of the king and the rules of law—the common law—made by judges. (See Figure 1–1.) The sovereignty of the king and the common law were carried to English colonies.

The Constitution of the United States

By the mid-1700s, the English had colonized the eastern coast of North America, displacing claims of sovereignty by the native American Indians. The colonists were subjects of the King of England and subject to the common law.

The American colonists, however, saw the tyranny inherent in the sovereignty of a king. They wanted to start new lives in America, yet they were controlled by a King who reigned over 3,000 miles away. Having little or no voice in their government, they were taxed, without representation, mostly for the benefit of the King. Finding this sovereignty intolerable, they revolted. On July 4, 1776, they declared their independence and fought until their colonies were recognized as sovereign states.

In 1787, delegates from the states met in Philadelphia to organize a powerful government to unite the states. Throughout the summer, the delegates, mostly lawyers trained in English law, debated various plans and political theories, and reached a consensus. The result was the Constitution of the United States. (See Figure 1–2 and Appendix I.)

Ratified on June 21, 1788, and put into effect on April 30, 1789, the **Constitution of the United States** is the fundamental law of the land. Two aspects of the Constitution, two aspects of **constitutional law,** are of great significance to the legal researcher: federalism and the separation of powers. Both were designed, in part, to prevent any one person from attaining the power, and the inevitable tyranny, of a king.

Federalism The preamble of the Constitution of the United States proclaims: "We the People of the United States . . . do ordain and establish this Constitution." Ultimate sovereignty was placed in the people, but immediately expressed in the Constitution. The Constitution created a new sovereign—the federal government of the United States of America. Under **federalism,** the federal government is a limited sovereign, having only the powers explicitly or implicitly granted it in the Constitution, primarily the powers granted the Congress in Article I, Section 8.

As the Tenth Amendment reflects, the states retained sovereignty over all powers not granted to the federal government. Thus, the person researching

Figure 1–1 The Medieval English Legal System

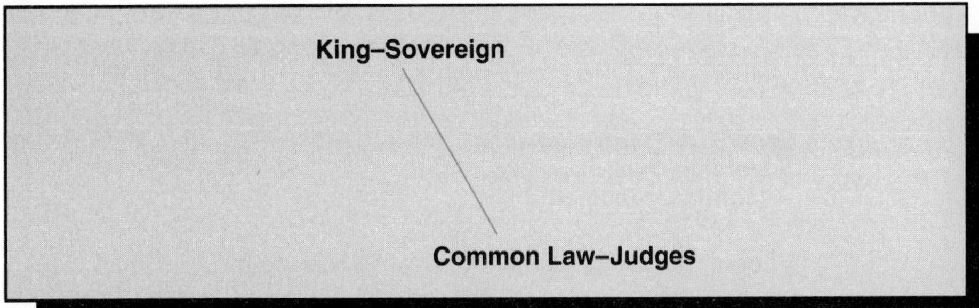

Figure 1–2 The Origins of the Constitution of the United States

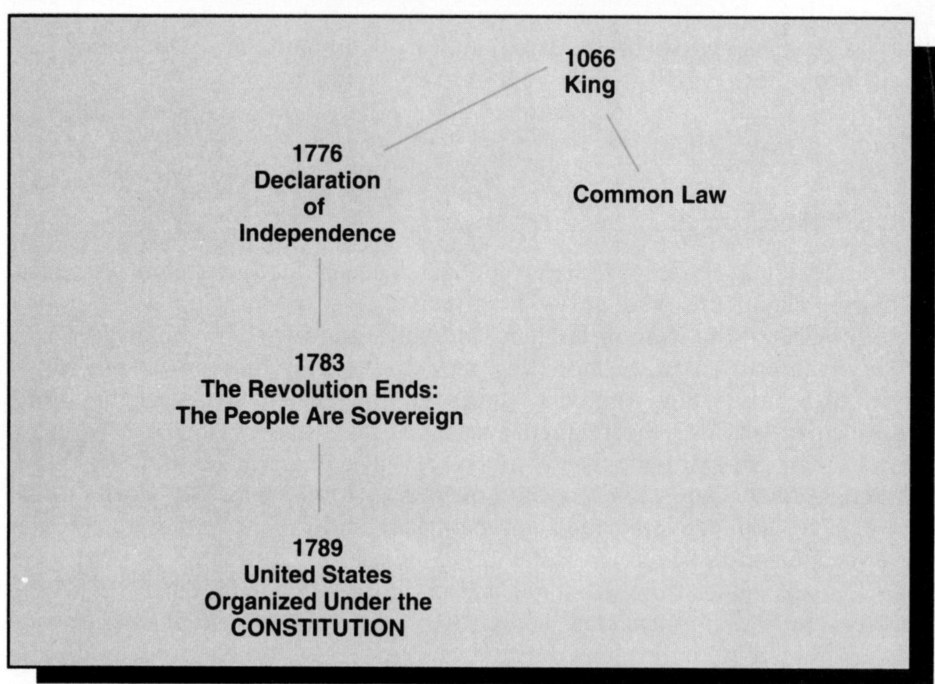

U.S. law must be aware that there are 51 sovereigns in the United States: the federal government (including the District of Columbia) and 50 state governments. (See Figure 1–3.) The first step in legal research is to determine if the subject to be researched is a matter of federal law or state law, and if state law, of what state.

Separation of Powers As Articles I, II, and III reflect, the powers of the federal government, under the Constitution, are divided into three branches: legislative, executive, and judicial. This division, maintained by checks and balances, is the **separation of powers.**

Under Article I, the **legislative** branch, headed by Congress, makes the law. The legislative branch makes new laws. When it passes a law, it makes a reality in the future. Indeed, the ***ex post facto*** ("after the fact") clauses of the Constitution prohibit criminal laws from having a retroactive effect. **Statutes** are

Figure 1–3 The Federalism Compromise

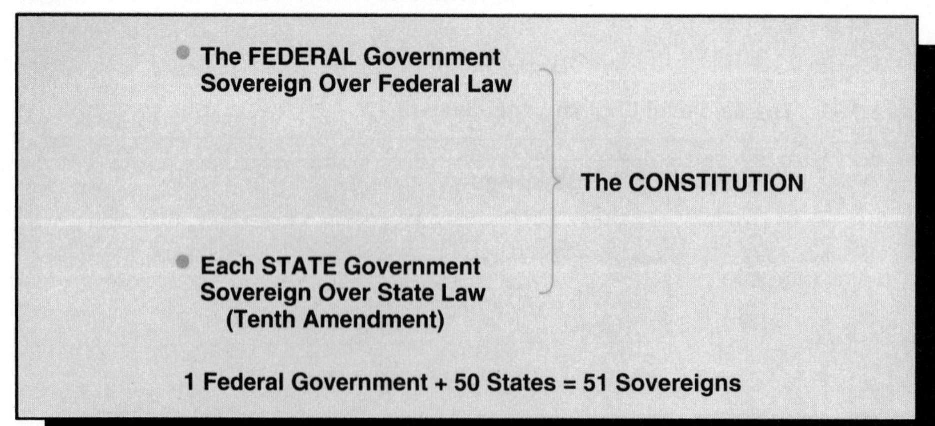

the laws the legislative branch makes, and law from the legislative branch is generally known as **statutory law.**

Under Article II, the **executive** branch, headed by the President, enforces the law. The executive branch sees that the laws are "faithfully executed." When the executive branch enforces a law, it is a reality in the present. To announce the exercise of a discretionary power, the executive may issue an **executive order.** The President, with the advice and consent of the Senate, also negotiates nation-binding agreements with foreign countries, known as **treaties.**

Under Article III, the **judicial** branch, headed by the Supreme Court, interprets the law. The judicial branch reviews the law, and makes law only in deciding actual legal controversies, known as **cases.** When the judicial branch interprets a law, its reality applies to events in the past, and a precedent is laid down for the future. Law from the judicial branch is generally known as **case law.**

Unstated in the Constitution, but understood by the lawyers at the time the Constitution was written and today, is the fact that the Constitution did not displace the common law of England and colonial America. Unless a federal or state constitution or statute changed the common law, U.S. judges continued, and continue today, to apply the common law, as developed in the United States since the American Revolution.

In addition, under the legislative and executive branches, **administrative agencies** have been created. Since the typical legislator or executive does not have sufficient expertise to regulate a specialized area of the law such as aviation or radio transmission, administrative agencies, such as the Federal Aviation Administration (FAA) and the Federal Communications Commission (FCC), have been created and staffed by experts in the field. Within their specialized area of the law, administrative agencies may perform analogous legislative, executive, and judicial functions by making, enforcing, and interpreting their own **regulations.** (See Figure 1–4.)

Although the Constitution does not require the states to establish separation

Figure 1–4 The Separation of Powers Compromise

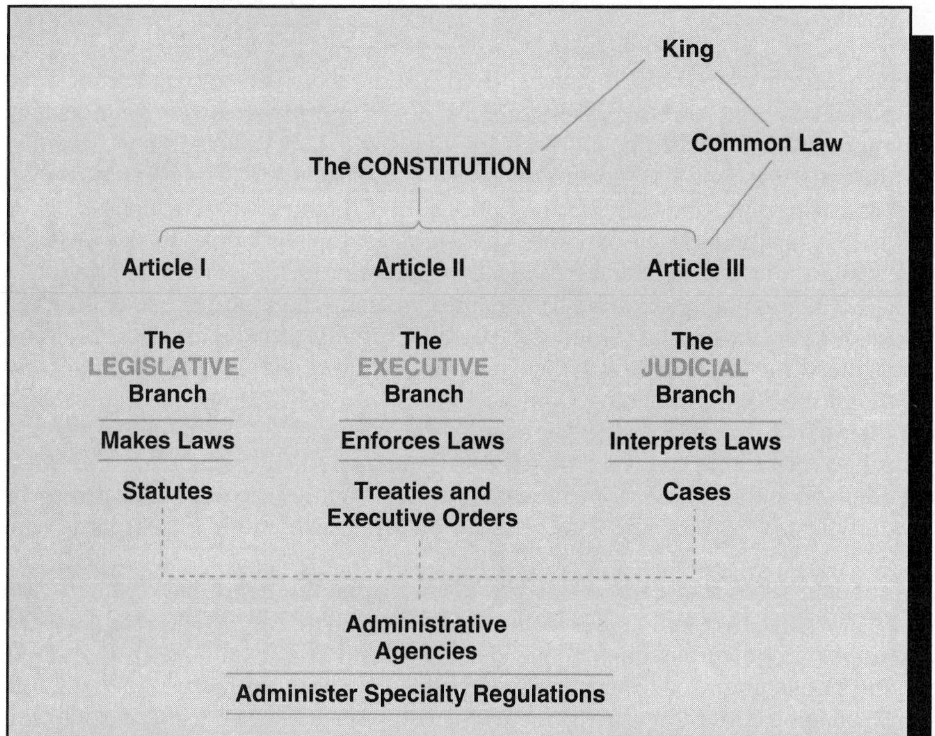

of powers in their constitutions, all the states have governments resembling the federal government. Thus, for the person researching U.S. law, there is another complexity. Not only are there 51 sovereigns, but each sovereign has its own constitution, three branches, and administrative agencies. In a real sense, then, there are 204 significant sources of law in the United States; 51 sovereigns, times four governmental units each: legislative, executive, and judicial branches, and administrative agencies.

1–2 The Business of Law Publishing

Who keeps track of the law coming from 51 sovereigns and the countless entities and subdivisions within them? The federal government and state governments publish some materials, but for a number of reasons, most legal publications are prepared by a private law publishing industry. First, the law in its various forms—statutes, cases, regulations, and the like—is public property, free to be published by anyone. Second, since private publishers are closer to, and more responsive to, the legal marketplace, they can get better products to the market quicker and at less cost than the government does. Third, private publishers may hire better writers and editors, invest more time and money, and advertise more effectively. Finally, private publishers have the incentive of making a profit.

Law Publishing in the United States

After the printing press was brought to England in the 1400s, it became practical to publish court decisions and other laws. However, in medieval England, and later in colonial America, law books were few and far between. Law publishing was not a major industry because the legal profession was not yet a major industry.

In the late 1800s, as the United States experienced the Industrial Revolution, the legal profession grew in stature. By the mid-1800s, U.S. courts had decided hundreds of thousands of cases, thereby developing their own common law. The number of decisions handed down by the U.S. courts grew steadily. Entrepreneurs saw the opportunity to sell "U.S. law" back to lawyers and other interested parties, and the U.S. law publishing industry was born.

In 1856, Hubert Howe Bancroft saw the need for law books in the growing West and founded the Bancroft-Whitney Company. In 1873, Frank Shepard had the idea of creating books that systematically listed when judges had cited other cases and founded the Frank Shepard Company. In 1876, John B. West recognized the need for the systematic publication of state court decisions and founded the West Publishing Company (West). In 1882, James E. Briggs found a better way to publish the decisions of the U.S. Supreme Court and established the Lawyers Co-operative Publishing Company (LCP). In 1887, Matthew Bender had the vision to publish practice-oriented materials written by acknowledged experts, and thus he founded Matthew Bender & Company. And so on.

The late 1800s and early 1900s saw fierce competition for market share and even lawsuits between major competitors. In particular, West established a monopoly in the publishing of court decisions, and LCP established a monopoly in the publishing of selected decisions with analysis. After West sued LCP in 1892, alleging copyright infringement, the companies became testy, if not bitter, rivals.

The Great Depression of the 1930s, and World War II in the 1940s, matured the law publishing industry. During the 1960s, 1970s, and 1980s, when the nation entered the "information age," the legal profession grew rapidly, and the established law publishers reaped the profits. Besides hundreds of thousands of pages of statutes and regulations, there are now over three million cases in U.S. case law, and the flood continues.

Today, the law publishing industry can be analogized to the rental car industry. The "Hertz" of the industry, the largest company and the established leader, is West Publishing Company (West), of St. Paul, Minnesota. The "Avis" is the former Lawyers Co-operative Publishing Company (LCP) of Rochester, New York, now the Lawyers Cooperative Publishing division of Thomson Legal Publishing Inc. (TLPI). TLPI includes LCP's former subsidiary, now a co-division, the Bancroft-Whitney Company of San Francisco, California, and LCP's former subsidiary, now a division of Thomson Professional Publishing, the Research Institute of America (RIA) of New York, New York. TLPI also includes the Clark Boardman Callaghan (CBC) division, a combination of the former Clark Boardman Co. Ltd. of New York, New York, and the former Callaghan & Company of Wilmette, Illinois. TLPI and Thomson Professional Publishing are subsidiaries of Thomson U.S. Inc.

At the heels of the leaders is a group of major competitors, the "Budget," "Dollar," and "Thrifty" types. These competitors include the Bureau of National Affairs, Inc. (BNA), of Washington, D.C.; Commerce Clearing House, Inc. (CCH), of Chicago, Illinois; Matthew Bender & Co. (MB) of New York, New York; Mead Data Central (MDC) of Dayton, Ohio, and its subsidiary The Michie Company (Michie) (pronounced Mickey) of Charlottesville, Virginia; Prentice-Hall Information Services (P-H), a division of Simon & Schuster, Inc., Paramus, New Jersey; and Shepard's/McGraw-Hill, Inc. (Shepard's), of Colorado Springs, Colorado.

There are also hundreds of smaller companies filling the gaps; e.g., Anderson Publishing Company of Cincinnati, Ohio; Banks-Baldwin Law Publishing Co. of Cleveland, Ohio; Business Laws, Inc., of Chesterland, Ohio; Foundation Press, Inc., of Westbury, New York; Little, Brown and Company of Boston, Massachusetts; Pike & Fischer, Inc., of Bethesda, Maryland; and many more.

Law publishing is a multimillion-dollar industry. West's sales are about half a billion dollars a year. In 1989, International Thomson Organization Ltd. purchased LCP for $810 million in cash, to acquire LCP's $200 million in yearly revenue. Several other companies are owned by giant media conglomerates and/or have nine-figure incomes.

Why Master Legal Researchers Know "Who Publishes What"

This book carefully identifies "who publishes what." Why should you care who publishes what? Aren't all law books the same? The answer is "No!"

Law publishing is highly competitive and profitable. Therefore, law publishers usually do not acknowledge their competitor's works in their publications, even if the competitor covers the same law source, no matter how useful such references might be to the legal researcher. Yet, to paraphrase William Mark McKinney, law publishers are human. They miss cases, exclude them, or include them but index them poorly. There is no such thing as a perfect law book. If you can't find what you are looking for in one publisher's book, you need to know the alternatives. You need to know the competitor's book that covers the same law source, so you can use it instead.

As you become experienced in legal research, you will find that different law publishers have different publishing styles: aggressive or cautious, comprehensive or selective, fast or thoughtful, self-supporting or thoroughly cross-referenced. You get more out of a publication when you understand the style it reflects.

Perhaps the best reason why you should know who publishes what is simply this: Every master in the art of legal research knows who published what.

1–3 The Purpose of Legal Research

There's a legal system, and a legal publishing industry to cover it, but why do legal research at all? What's the big deal? Doesn't the judge know all the law anyway? It can't be that complicated, can it?

Legal research is a big deal because the law is a big deal. The law is complicated, but legal research will allow you to cut through it and make effective arguments to the judge. Ethical codes and rules require legal professionals to be competent, and legal research ability is part of that competence.

The Court May Be Ignorant

One of the biggest misconceptions about the law is the notion that the courts know everything there is to know about the law. Courts are run by judges, who are human beings. No one has ever read and digested all of the millions of existing cases, statutes, regulations, and other sources of the law. Moreover, the law is always changing. It is so vast that no one person can ever know all of it. The best one can do is research the law, thoroughly.

Just because judges can't know everything, however, doesn't mean they don't know anything. Just as the average paralegal knows more law than the average layman, and the average lawyer knows more law than the average paralegal, so the average judge knows more law than the average lawyer, and so is worthy of respect. However, because judges don't know every law, they can be convinced by an effective argument. The wise advocate tactfully makes the judge aware of the law, to the advocate's—and the advocate's client's—advantage.

The Way to Win

What is the goal of legal research? It relates to the goal of any advocate in any case: to get the judge to say, *"You win."*

Stop and think. Why should a judge rule in your favor? *What is the strongest argument you can make to a judge?*

Recall what the first judges realized. Human beings have a sense of simple justice: *that persons in like circumstances should be treated alike.* The challenge is to make the judge's basic sense of justice work in your favor.

The strongest argument you can make to a judge begins with someone else. Someone else was once in circumstances—whether factually, legally, or both—just like yours. If that person went to court and the judge said that he won, you can argue simple justice: persons in like circumstances should be treated alike. That person was in circumstances like yours, and he won. Since he won, the judge should say you win, because persons in like circumstances should be treated alike.

Don't lose sight of the purpose of legal research: *to find a case like yours, where the person like you won.* That is the strongest argument you can make to a judge. It's the way to get the judge to say, "You win." (See Figure 1–5.)

What Aaron Burr Said About the Law

Aaron Burr said, "The law is what's boldly asserted and plausibly maintained." In every case, competent advocates boldly assert the law in their favor. The winner is the advocate who most plausibly maintains what he or she boldly asserts. The most plausible and maintainable assertion you can make is one backed by sound legal research. Tell the judge about the cases like yours, where people like you won. If your research is superior, the judge should conclude either that the cases you found are more like the case at hand than the cases your opponent found, where people like your opponent won, or that the cases cited are equally relevant, but more cases have gone your way. Either way, the judge should say, "You win."

Authority: Primary and Secondary

Law is not only commands argued about, it is also something decided and commanded anew by the sovereign. You should understand the difference between the law itself—firmly rooted in and established by the sovereign—and a mere "bold assertion" of the law, however plausibly maintained by a nonsovereign.

At its best, law is a bold assertion plausibly maintained because a sovereign said it. **Law** is the command of a sovereign. In the United States, no man,

Figure 1–5 Why Do Legal Research?

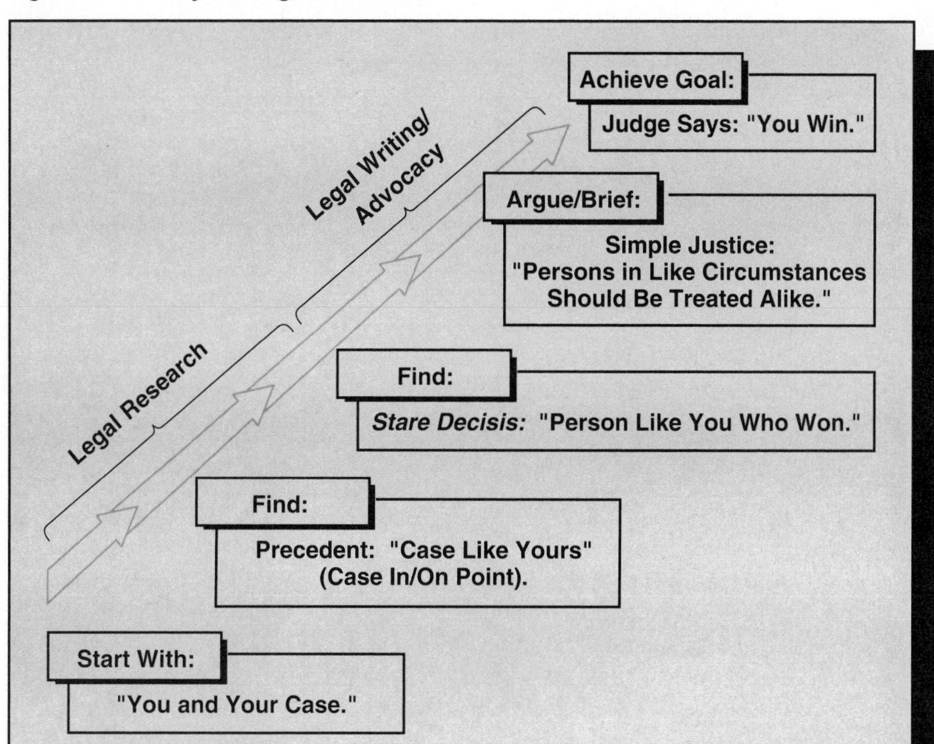

woman, or business is above the law. The Constitution of the United States is the supreme law of the land. As a result of federalism, law can come only from the federal government or from a state government. As a result of the separation of powers, law can come only from the appropriate branch or agency of the sovereign. Only what the appropriate branch or agency of the sovereign commands is the law.

The Constitution is the fundamental law. The legislature makes statutes. The executive issues executive orders. The courts decide cases. Administrative agencies regulate special areas of the law. These acts—the Constitution, statutes, executive orders, court decisions, and administrative regulations—are authoritative acts of the sovereign and are known as **primary authority.** Primary authority is the law itself.

Everything else is **secondary authority.** Everything else includes encyclopedias, law review articles, newspaper polls, personal opinions, company policies, and teacher's assertions.

Any assertion of the law, no matter how bold, made by someone who is not the appropriate representative of the sovereign, acting in that capacity, is not the law. It may be a fine expression of the law, it may explain the law and give it meaning, but it is not the law. (See Figure 1–6.)

Suppose you decide to put an item on layaway at a department store. The clerk says you must deposit 25% of the purchase price. You ask the clerk to accept 20% of the purchase price, which is all you have with you. The clerk snaps, "You must put 25% down, that's the law." Is it? Unless there is a statute, case, or regulation of the sovereign that says so, or a judge who will say so if you take the matter to court, it's not the law. The 25% requirement, however boldly asserted, is just a store *policy,* a guide to decision making, but not the law. The store, perhaps through the manager, could simply decide to change its policy and accept your 20% deposit, and no law would be broken.

Suppose your instructor tells you that you can't successfully be sued for negligence if you didn't proximately cause the harm, but the hurt person sues

Figure 1–6 Legal Authority: Primary and Secondary

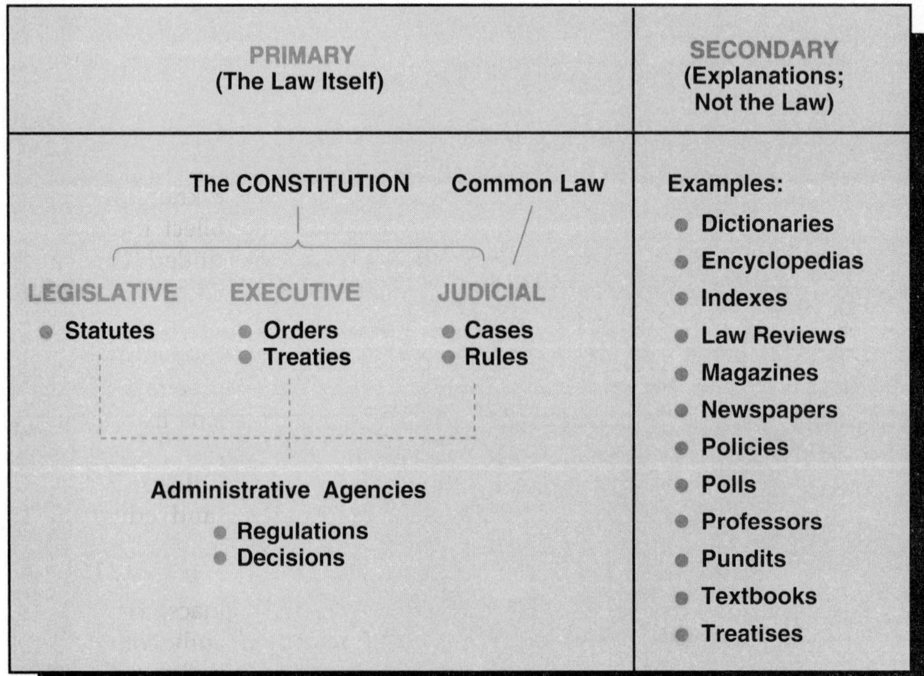

you anyway. The judge will not be impressed if you say: "My instructor said I can't lose." Your instructor is not a sovereign, nor is he the appropriate representative of a sovereign, acting in that capacity, for deciding negligence law. The judge will be impressed if you say something like: "Your honor, may I tell you about several cases like mine, where the persons like me won?"

Does secondary authority have any value? Yes. Courts consider primary authority first and foremost, but if the primary authority is unclear, or if there is no primary authority on the issue at hand, the courts will consider secondary authority. The law in a given circumstance may have been better expressed by a law book writer than by a representative of a sovereign. One might read a book, such as this one, because the author—a teacher—can explain the law better than any representative of a sovereign. In a law review article, a law professor may describe the best laws for the future and suggest a course for the development of those laws that a court would be wise to follow.

As a legal researcher, you must know how to research both primary authority and secondary authority. When you report the results of your research, however, cite to primary authority whenever and wherever possible. Primary authority is the law itself.

1–4 Law Books and Law Libraries

When people with no legal training enter a law library for the first time, they are awed and overwhelmed. They find themselves surrounded by row upon row of impressive-looking books lining the shelves. Earth-tone colors—lime, green, brown, tan, black, and blue—predominate, occasionally splashed with reds and maroons. The titles are mysterious—codes and coordinators; reporters and reviews; statutes and citators—and imposing.

This book explains those impressive-looking books. In particular, it introduces you to the jargon of legal research. Legal research terms are explained and used, because once you understand the jargon of legal research, you can, very often, judge a law book by its cover.

How to Judge a Law Book by Its Cover, and Other Parts

The title of a law book usually reflects its contents. Once you know the jargon, you know what's in the book. For example, books that collect the opinions written by judges are called **reports.** Thus, if you see a book entitled *United States Reports,* you can reasonably infer that it contains opinions written by the appellate judges, the **justices,** on the U.S. Supreme Court.

You should carefully examine every law book the first time you use it. If a book's title is not specific, examine the cover page. The cover page of the *South Western Reporter,* for example, indicates that it collects opinions from courts in Arkansas, Kentucky, Missouri, Tennessee, and Texas.

One part of a law book frequently neglected but well worth reading is the "foreword" or "preface." In prefaces, law book authors and editors often explain with great accuracy what is and what isn't in the book. Many law books have guides explaining how to use the book.

You should also examine tables of contents. Like almanacs, dictionaries, encyclopedias, and other reference books, law books frequently contain more information than you might at first expect. Many law books have two tables of

Rows of "Impressive-Looking" Law Books

Source: © *Doug Martin.*

contents: one that summarizes the book in breadth and one that outlines the book in depth.

You should be especially alert to law books containing tables of information, which are valuable tools for legal research. For example, some books covering federal law have "code" finding tables. If you know that your legal research problem involves a specific section of the *United States Code,* you can quickly find out if it is referred to in a given book by looking up that "code" section in the code-finding table for that book and consulting the references, if any, listed there.

You should also examine a law book's index. Most indexes are prepared directly from the text, so if a topic is in the index, it, or something about it, is in the book. If it's not in the index, it's probably not in the book. The quality of a book can often be determined by the depth and quality of its index.

Visit Law Libraries

Legal researchers do their best work in law libraries. Like all artists, you should develop a "professional curiosity" about your work. Just as musicians attend concerts and sculptors visit museums to gain more insight into their work, you should visit law libraries whenever possible. In exploring a law library, and in considering the opportunities for doing research there, you will inevitably increase your knowledge and sharpen your skills.

This is not to say, however, that it will be easy to get in. Most law libraries are private, members-only operations.

Most county or court law libraries were created for the use of the judges in that county or court. The judges decide who can use their library, and they usually limit use to attorneys in the local bar association and their employees.

Some law libraries are run by associations of attorneys that limit use to attorneys who are dues-paying members and their employees. Most law firms limit use of their libraries to their own partners, associates, and employees. Most law schools limit the use of their libraries to their own students and faculty.

Fortunately the situation is not as bleak as it may at first appear. Private libraries are gradually opening up their memberships to law and paralegal students. The main branches of many college and public libraries are increasing their law book collections, so you may find the law book you are looking for there. In addition, more and more legal material is being put on computer, accessible to any authorized user.

Your best bet, however, to get into a law library for free is to find the law libraries in your area that are members of the Federal Depository Library Program. (See Figure 1–7.) Under this program, the library gets copies of federal government publications at little or no cost. In return, by federal law, the library must be open to the public.

Even if a law library you wish to use is a Federal Depository Library, you may run into obstacles. Since most books in a law library require training for effective

Figure 1–7 Federal Depository Library Logo

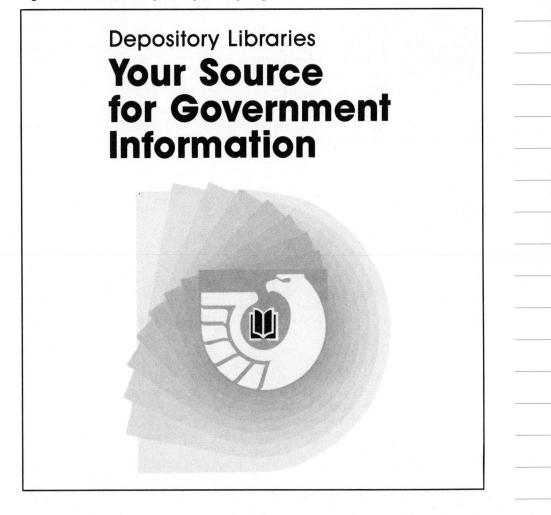

use, law librarians don't welcome the idea of having their doors open to everyone. Regular patrons of law libraries, trained in legal research, are generally quiet, responsible people who don't cause trouble.

For example, a state university law school library may be a Federal Depository Library. But the library may be on the second floor of the law school building and accessible only from within the building. There may be no first-floor signs to direct visitors to the entrance of the library or even mention its existence, let alone announce that it is open to the public.

Outside the entrance, there may be prominent signs indicating that the library is for the use of law school students and faculty only. Again, there may be nothing to indicate that the library is open to the public, except, perhaps, a small sign reading, "Visitors must register."

Inside the library, the desk clerks may question and discourage those who enter who do not look like they belong there. If visitors insist on staying, they are asked to register not just once, but every time they enter the library (which may be unconstitutional). In addition, some staff may refuse to assist patrons who are not law school students.

Thus, you may have to be a detective to find the library, and brave and tactful to get in. It is important that you act and dress appropriately, obey reasonable requests, and cultivate the impression that you belong there by your effective use of the library's resources.

Once librarians become used to your presence, they will be friendlier. If you need help finding what you are looking for, ask the reference librarian. If the librarian doesn't help you find exactly what you are looking for, the librarian's suggestions will usually lead you in the right direction, at least by getting you to think of a solution to your problem yourself.

There is one more thing that you should be aware of when you visit a law library. Law librarians are concerned that their reference advice not be construed as legal advice. Don't ask a law librarian to find "the" answer to your legal problem. That's what lawyers do. Law librarians know that people do not ordinarily ask legal questions out of idle curiosity, and they are wary of accusations of unauthorized law practice, or legal malpractice, being made against them. A law librarian can suggest sources for you to use, but you have to do the research yourself.

SUMMARY

1–1

Law is the command of a sovereign. The classic sovereign is the king. In the Norman Conquest of 1066 A.D., William the Conqueror became King of England. William appointed the first judges, who rode circuits in England. By following precedent, the judges made rules of law common to all of England, known as the common law. The common law is the law made by judges in deciding actual cases, and it was brought to America. In the United States, however, the U.S. Constitution is the supreme law of the land, and the federal government and each state are sovereign; thus, there are 51 sovereigns. The powers of the federal government are divided into three branches: legislative, executive, and judicial. The legislative branch makes the law in the form of statutes. The executive branch enforces the law. The judicial branch interprets the law and makes law—the common law—in deciding cases. Administrative agencies regulate specialized areas of the law.

1–2

Most legal publications are prepared by the private law publishing industry. Many law publishers were founded in the late 1800s. When the nation entered the "information age" in the 1900s, the established law publishers reaped the profits. The largest law publisher is West Publishing Company, of St. Paul, Minnesota. The next largest is the Lawyers Cooperative Publishing division of Thomson Legal Publishing Inc., Rochester, New York. There are several other major law publishers, and, together, they make up a multimillion-dollar industry. In view of the competitiveness of these publishers, good legal researchers know the importance of "who publishes what."

1–3

Courts are run by judges, who are human beings. To get the judge to say, "You win," the strongest argument you can make is that persons in like circumstances should be treated alike. The purpose of legal research, then, is to find a case like yours where the person like you won, and tactfully point it out to the judge. Legal research is how the law, boldly asserted, is plausibly maintained. It is important to distinguish primary authority, the law itself, from secondary authority. You must know how to research both, but when you report the results of your research, cite to primary sources whenever and wherever possible.

1–4

This text explains the books found in law libraries. Once you understand the jargon of legal research, you can, very often, judge a law book by its cover. You should check the title, the cover page, the table of contents, the preface, the tables, and the index. You should visit law libraries whenever possible. Most law libraries, however, are private, members-only operations. Thus, your best bet to get into a law library for free is to find the law libraries in your area that are members of the Federal Depository Library Program and, by federal law, must be open to the public. Act and dress appropriately, obey reasonable requests, and cultivate the impression that you belong by your effective use of the library's resources. Finally, be aware that law librarians are concerned that their reference advice not be construed as legal advice. A law librarian can suggest sources for you use, but you have to do the research yourself.

REVIEW

Key Terms

Before proceeding, review the key terms listed below to be sure you understand each one. If necessary, read over the corresponding section of the chapter. When you are ready to test your understanding, answer the Review Questions.

administrative agencies
case law
cases
common law
Constitution of the United States
constitutional law
executive
executive order
ex post facto
federalism
feudalism
judges
judicial
jurisprudence
justices
law
legislative
Norman Conquest
precedent
primary authority
regulations
reports
secondary authority
separation of powers
sovereign
stare decisis
statutes
statutory law
treaties

Questions for Review and Discussion

1. To what event in 1066 A.D. can the U.S. legal system be traced?
2. Who makes the "common law," and what does it have in common?
3. What is the fundamental law in the United States?
4. How many sovereigns are there in the United States?
5. How are the powers of the federal government divided?
6. Why do master legal researchers know "who publishes what"?
7. Why is legal research necessary?
8. What is the purpose of legal research?
9. Why is primary authority more important than secondary authority?
10. Why do law librarians avoid giving patrons "the" answer to legal questions?

Activities

1. Using an almanac, general encyclopedia, or history book, bone up on American history. Review the circumstances that lead to the writing of documents like the Declaration of Independence, the Constitution, and the Bill of Rights. Understand that the fundamentals of legal research come directly out of American history.
2. Develop the habit of knowing "who publishes what." Take the time to note the name of the publisher of each law book, which is usually found at the bottom of the spine of the book and at the bottom of the title page.
3. Find and visit the nearest law library that is a member of the Federal Depository Library Program. Although to most people the law is foreign and mysterious, to those who know where to look, the law is readily available. The law of the United States is probably the most recorded, organized, and analyzed body of knowledge in the world. Relatively speaking, it's almost as available as it could possibly be. Once you find the law, all you have to do is read it—carefully.

PART TWO

RESEARCHING PRIMARY AUTHORITY

CHAPTER 2 Case Law

OUTLINE

2–1 Judicial Power
- Court Sovereignty
- Legal Reasoning

2–2 Judicial Opinions
- Parts of an Opinion
- Types of Opinions

2–3 Judicial Reports
- Reported Opinions
- National Reporter System
- Federal Court Reports
- State Court Reports
- Unreported Opinions

COMMENTARY

While at the court house, filing suit against City Hospital, you see a notice announcing an opening for a "legal assistant/paralegal" for the City Law Department. Among the duties listed is "some legal research." After determining that City Hospital is privately owned, you apply for the job. During your interview the law director is impressed, but skeptical of your ability to do legal research. Nonetheless, you're hired, called in, and given your first assignment. The mayor wants to display a nativity scene in Central Park during the Christmas holiday season. The law director feels this would violate the establishment clause of the First Amendment, but a book the law director used in law school mentions a case, *Lynch v. Donnelly* [465 U.S. 668 (1984)], that allowed it. You are to locate the case and find out why the nativity scene was allowed in that case.

OBJECTIVES

In this chapter you will learn when the courts have power, how that power is exercised, and how the exercise of that power is explained by the courts in written opinions. Court opinions, the backbone of the common law, are found in a variety of books. After reading this chapter, you should be able to:

1. Accurately describe a court's power to make law.
2. Explain what the *ratio decidendi* of a case is.
3. Explain what the "holding" of a case is.
4. Identify the parts of a judicial opinion.
5. Understand the types of judicial opinions.
6. Describe the courts in a three-level court system.
7. Identify the federal reporters in the National Reporter System.

8. Recognize the regional reporters in the National Reporter System.
9. Identify major reporters outside the National Reporter System.
10. Understand the significance of "unreported" opinions.

2–1 Judicial Power

As discussed in Chapter 1, the U.S. legal system has roots in the common law. The common law is made and maintained by the courts. In a common-law system, the best argument you can make to a judge to win your case is that there was a case like yours where the person like you won.

Court Sovereignty

Under the Constitution of the United States and under state constitutions, the power to interpret the law is given to the courts. In a common-law system, where the doctrine of *stare decisis* is followed, the interpretations themselves become precedents for future cases. Thus, in a sense, the courts not only interpret the law, they also make the law.

It is important at this point not to lose sight of the constitutional separation of powers. The courts do not have sovereign power to simply "dream up" the law like the legislative branch. The courts have sovereign power only when they interpret the law. A court must be confronted with a legal controversy, a case, in order to exercise sovereign power. Only in interpreting the law to decide a case can a court make the law. The court makes precedent.

Not only must a court be confronted with a legal controversy to interpret and make law, it must also be confronted with an *actual* legal controversy. Courts do not hear hypothetical or pretended controversies. Unless an actual case is filed and an actual legal controversy exists, the courts are without power to act. Otherwise, the courts would be "dreaming up" the law like the legislature, which would be fundamentally illegal. A fundamentally illegal act is **unconstitutional.** (See Figure 2–1.)

An infamous case, *In re Copland* [66 Ohio App. 304, 33 N.E.2d 857 (Cuyahoga County Ct. App. 1940)], serves as a memorable example of the limits of judicial power. In *Copland,* the appellate court was asked to review the disbarment of a judge:

> who was found guilty of having written, and caused to be published in a legal journal, an opinion in a fictitious cause purporting to have been heard and decided by him when he well knew that its published report would be relied upon by lawyers and judges as the decision of a court in a litigated controversy.

The judge said:

> [I]t was his purpose to edify the Bench and Bar by his thesis published under the guise of an authentic court finding . . . [and that] he employed this means for the purpose of stating his personal views on a hypothetical legal question for the benefit of the legal professional and the exaltation of his ego [66 Ohio App. at 305, 306].

Maintaining the distinction between primary authority and secondary authority, the appellate court noted that the judge "by deception and concealment would foist his legal views upon his brethren as the judgment of a court of law," and said "[h]is effrontery in so doing is monstrously astounding." [66 Ohio App. at 305.]

Figure 2–1 The Judicial Branch

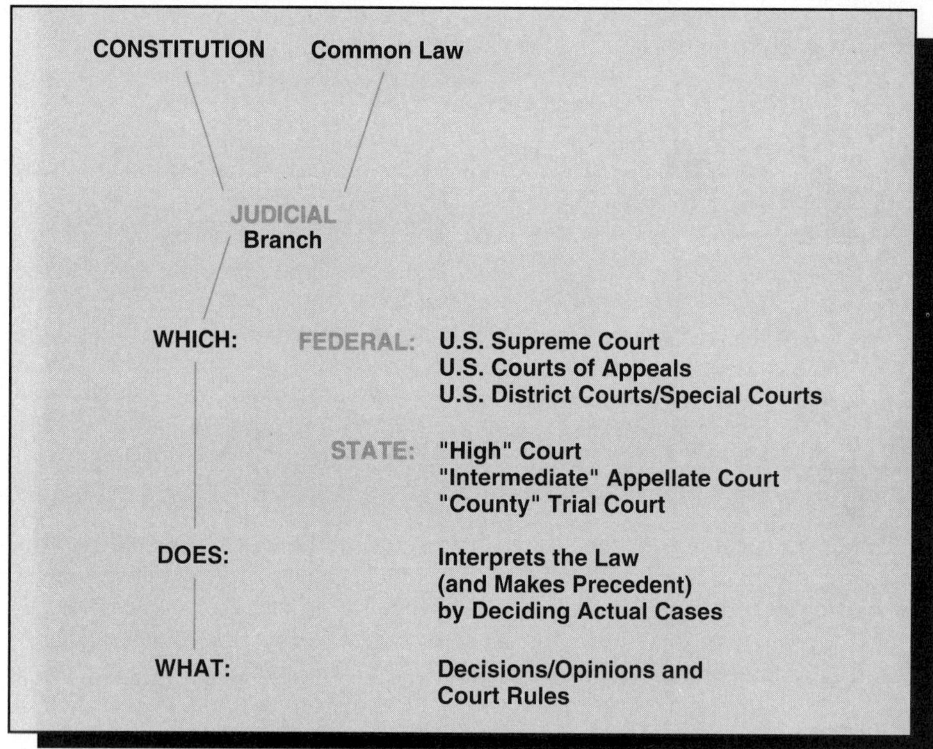

In upholding the disbarment of the judge, the appellate court took care to point out that it was acting appropriately within the law: "We have pursued the authorities for like situations. We find none and none are necessary." [66 Ohio App. at 307.] It was a deft declaration that the court, confronted by a real case, had dutifully searched for precedents under the doctrine of *stare decisis* and, finding none, exercised its sovereign power in its best judgment.

Legal Reasoning

In a common-law system, legal reasoning is often reasoning by analogy. When a court is called on to decide a case, it must compare the case to similar cases already decided and follow the most analogous case as precedent. Under the doctrine of *stare decisis,* if the court does not follow the precedent from the most analogous case, it must find a good reason for not doing so.

In deciding a case, a court is confronted with an actual legal controversy, known as the **case at bar.** Ordinarily, there is both a **plaintiff** (i.e., the person or legal entity that sought relief in the trial court) and a **defendant** (i.e., the person or legal entity responding to the plaintiff's claim). A plaintiff, especially a "plaintiff" expecting to be unopposed, may be termed a **petitioner,** and a defendant, especially a "defendant" opposing a petitioner, may be termed a **respondent.** The court must reason out the **decision,** the outcome of the case, declaring whether the plaintiff (or petitioner) wins or the defendant (or respondent) wins. A preliminary decision (e.g., a ruling on a motion) is known as an **order.** The final decision of a court entered into its records is its **judgment.** A determination of the rights and duties of the parties (e.g., in a divorce) is known as a **decree.** A judgment or decree is an **adjudication** of the case.

In deciding a legal controversy, a court usually weighs two types of authority: mandatory authority and persuasive authority. A court must follow **mandatory authority** (also referred to as **binding authority),** which consists of the laws properly enacted by its sovereign's legislature, and the law found in the opinions of its sovereign's next higher or highest court, if any. If mandatory authority is lacking in any way, a court may consider **persuasive authority,** which consists of nonmandatory court opinions within its sovereign, opinions by any other court tracing its origins to the Norman Conquest of 1066, and secondary authority.

The court must reason its way through the legal controversy and arrive at a decision. The basic technique, honed over the centuries, is for the court to determine the point on which the case will turn, known as the ***ratio decidendi,*** and, if necessary, make a **holding,** a rule of law, upon which to decide the case.

Let's consider an example. Suppose that a power failure causes the traffic light at an intersection to go out. Subsequently, two cars collide head-on, because both drivers, one driving on a two-lane highway and the other driving on a four-lane highway, each thought he had the legal right to proceed through the intersection. (See Figure 2–2.) If the drivers sue each other, how does the court decide who wins?

The parties and the court do legal research. If there is a previous case like this one, known as a **case in point,** it is a simple matter to decide who wins. If a court in a previous case held that at an intersection a driver must yield to the car on the driver's right, then the driver of the car on the right wins.

If there is no previous case like the case at bar, if it is a case without precedent, known as a **case of first impression,** the matter is much more complicated. Suppose that there was no "right-of-way" rule in the sovereign or that the legislature had said that right-of-way does not apply at an intersection with a traffic light. Then what?

If there is no previous case like the case at bar, the court must, nonetheless, analogize from the case, however distant, most like the case at bar. To make a

Figure 2–2 Intersection Example

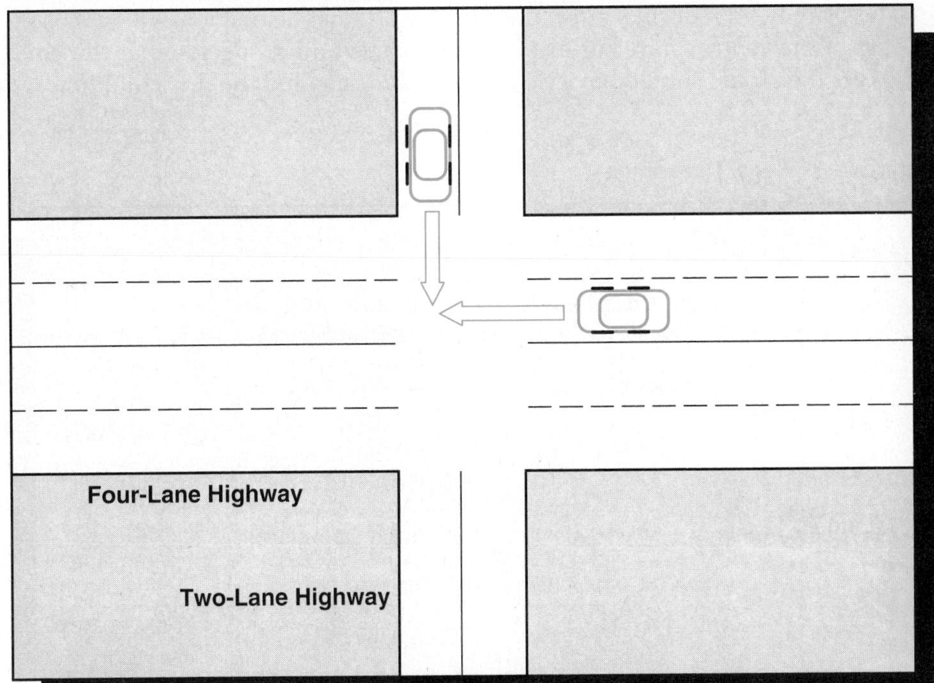

distinction that master legal researchers recognize, there is often a case **"on point"** that covers the issue implicitly, or by analogy, even if there is no case **"in point"** that covers the issue explicitly, or exactly.

Suppose that in an earlier railroad crossing case, a court had reasoned that the driver of a car must yield to a train because trains are bigger and heavier than cars, more difficult to stop, and, in a sense, a train's railroad is a "bigger" road than a car's highway. If the court in the case at bar decides that the relative size of the roads is the key to deciding which driver must yield at a highway intersection, that becomes the *ratio decidendi* of the case. Making a new rule of law for highway intersections, the court holds that in the event of a traffic light failure, the driver on the smaller highway must yield to the driver on the bigger highway. Following the new rule, the court "logically" decides that the driver on the four-lane highway wins.

Of course, this kind of reasoning by analogy is subject to argument. The court could have ruled that the smaller car must yield to the larger car or that the legislature meant the right-of-way rule to not apply only where there was an *operating* traffic light, and so on. The *ratio decidendi* of a case, the distinction made, is crucial. A different *ratio decidendi* will lead to a different holding and may result in a different decision in the case.

A court may also make extra comment in its opinion, not necessary to the decision, known as ***dicta*** (plural of ***dictum***). Not being necessary to the decision, *dicta* are only secondary authorities. Irrelevant comment (e.g., the judge mentioning that as she decided the case it was snowing outside) is known as ***obiter dicta.*** Serious comment, however, comment of importance to potential litigants, is known as **considered *dicta*** and has persuasive authority. For example, the court confronted with the highway intersection case might discuss how it would rule in a rail-rail crossing case. The comment is *dicta,* because it is not about the highway intersection case at bar, but it is serious comment because the court's discussion gives guidance to potential litigants in a future rail-rail crossing case. (See Figure 2–3.)

The nature of legal reasoning can also be understood with a nonlegal example. Suppose a parent must decide which of two children gets the last cookie in the cookie jar. How does the parent decide who eats the cookie?

The parent will decide after first making some distinction—a *ratio decidendi*—in the controversy. For example, the parent might decide that the child who eats the cookie should have clean hands and rule that the first child to wash

Figure 2–3 Legal Reasoning

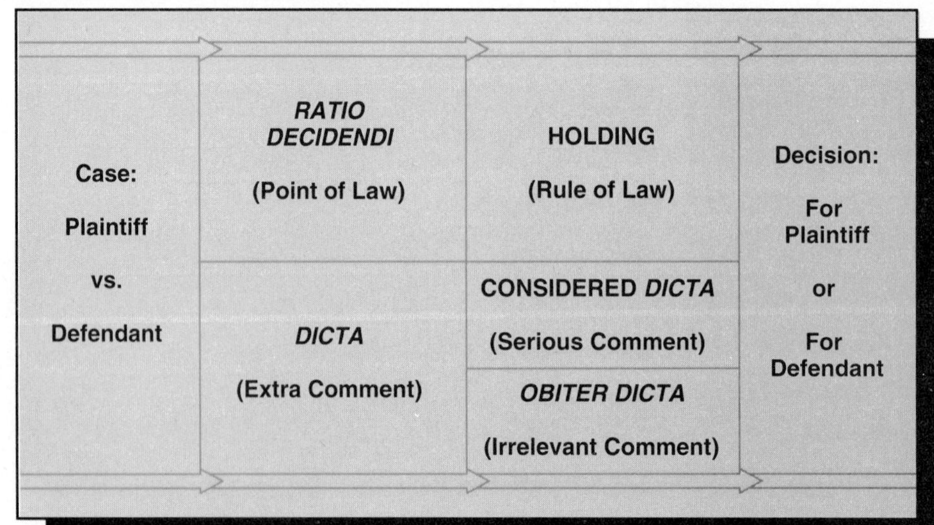

his hands gets the cookie. Or the parent might decide that the child who gets the cookie should first eat all her vegetables and rule that the first child to eat all her vegetables gets the cookie. Or the parent might decide that the children should be treated equally whenever possible and split the cookie in half. In any event, once a distinction is made, a rule can be formulated and a decision easily made. With a precedent established, it will be easier for the parent to decide later who gets the last piece of pie.

2–2 Judicial Opinions

When confronted with a legal controversy, a court has the power to decide who wins. In the course of reasoning out a decision, a court ordinarily develops a *ratio decidendi* and a holding, but, from the winner's point of view, there is no necessity for the court to explain its reasoning. The winner has achieved the goal: the judge said to the winner, "You win."

For the loser, however, a decision that "you lose" without explanation is not emotionally or intellectually satisfying. From the loser's point of view, simple justice requires that persons in like circumstances be treated alike, and the loser believes that in past cases most like his, the persons like him won. The loser wants to know why the judge disagreed. To feel that justice has been done, the loser must be able to see how the judge based the decision against him on other more analogous precedents.

Moreover, for other persons like the winner and loser, the decided case like theirs is a precedent. They want to understand why the winner won and to change their situation, if necessary, to assure themselves that they will win if their case goes to court in the future. In addition, other judges have an interest in understanding why the winner won in the event they must decide a case like that case.

Because of the need for a just explanation, and for the establishment of *ratio decidendi,* holdings, and precedent, it is customary for a court, especially an appellate court reviewing a lower court case, to explain its reasoning and its decision in writing. A court's written explanation of its decision is known as its **opinion.**

Parts of an Opinion

A published appellate judicial opinion customarily consists of the following parts, in the order discussed. (See the case illustrated in Figure 2–4.)

A published appellate judicial opinion begins with the title of the case. Cases are usually titled in the names of the lead parties. The plaintiff, or plaintiffs, are separated from the defendant, or defendants, by *v.* for *versus,* meaning against. Thus, if John Doe and Richard Roe sue Sammy Smith, the title of the case, abbreviated, is *Doe v. Smith.* In a few states, the case title is reversed if and when the defendant appeals.

In criminal cases, the plaintiff is the sovereign. Criminal cases are titled "United States of America" or "State of," "People of" or "Commonwealth of" a state, versus the defendant or defendants (e.g., "United States of America v. Oliver North" is cited *United States v. North).* In forfeiture cases, the case is titled in the name of the sovereign and the contraband seized (e.g., *One 1958 Plymouth Sedan v. Pennsylvania).*

Figure 2–4 Illustrative Case

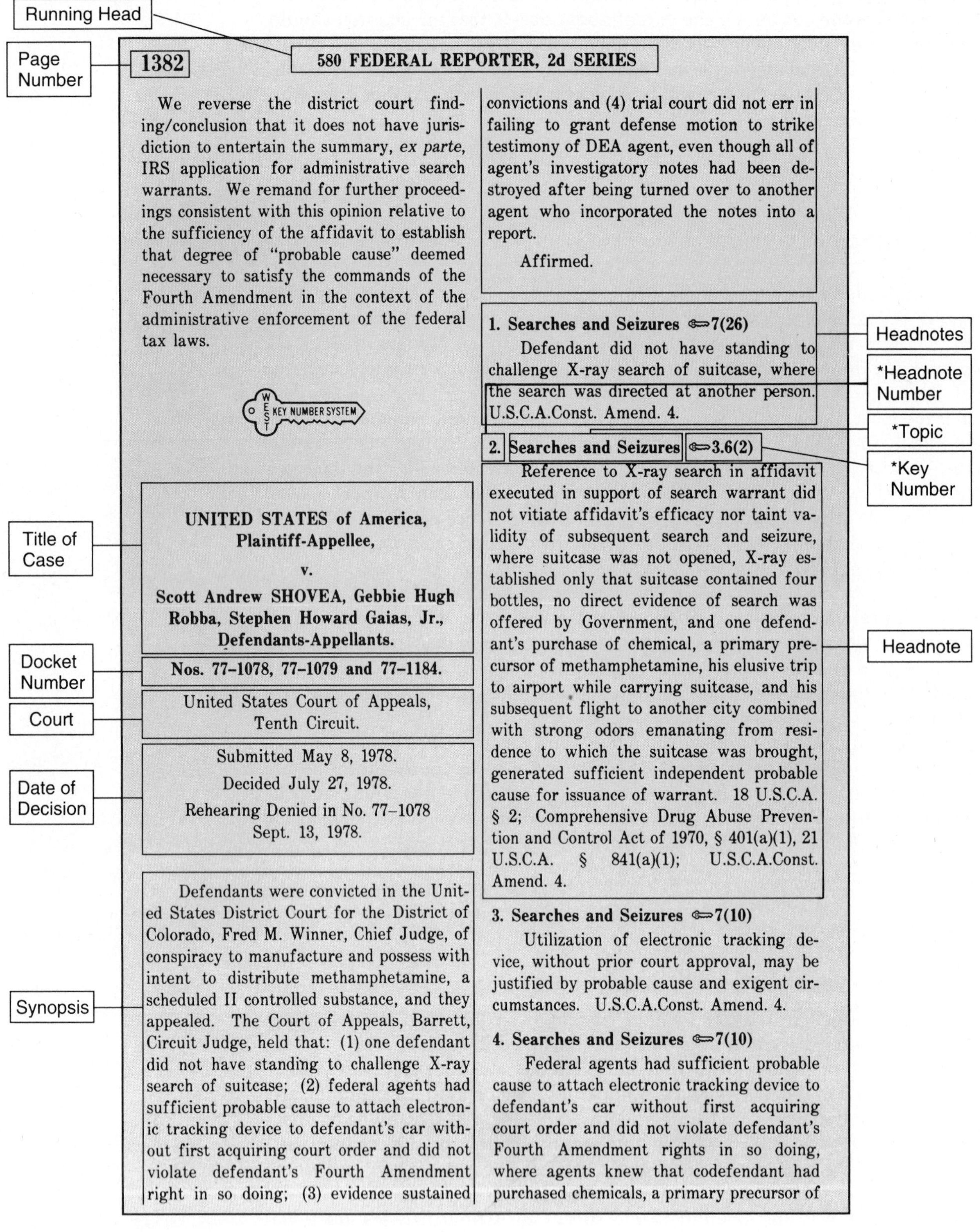

Running Head
Page Number
1382
580 FEDERAL REPORTER, 2d SERIES
We reverse the district court finding/conclusion that it does not have jurisdiction to entertain the summary, ex parte, IRS application for administrative search warrants. We remand for further proceedings consistent with this opinion relative to the sufficiency of the affidavit to establish that degree of "probable cause" deemed necessary to satisfy the commands of the Fourth Amendment in the context of the administrative enforcement of the federal tax laws.
WEST KEY NUMBER SYSTEM
Title of Case
UNITED STATES of America, Plaintiff-Appellee,
v.
Scott Andrew SHOVEA, Gebbie Hugh Robba, Stephen Howard Gaias, Jr., Defendants-Appellants.
Docket Number
Nos. 77-1078, 77-1079 and 77-1184.
Court
United States Court of Appeals, Tenth Circuit.
Date of Decision
Submitted May 8, 1978.
Decided July 27, 1978.
Rehearing Denied in No. 77-1078 Sept. 13, 1978.
Synopsis
Defendants were convicted in the United States District Court for the District of Colorado, Fred M. Winner, Chief Judge, of conspiracy to manufacture and possess with intent to distribute methamphetamine, a scheduled II controlled substance, and they appealed. The Court of Appeals, Barrett, Circuit Judge, held that: (1) one defendant did not have standing to challenge X-ray search of suitcase; (2) federal agents had sufficient probable cause to attach electronic tracking device to defendant's car without first acquiring court order and did not violate defendant's Fourth Amendment right in so doing; (3) evidence sustained convictions and (4) trial court did not err in failing to grant defense motion to strike testimony of DEA agent, even though all of agent's investigatory notes had been destroyed after being turned over to another agent who incorporated the notes into a report.
Affirmed.
Headnotes
*Headnote Number
*Topic
*Key Number
1. Searches and Seizures ⟹7(26)
Defendant did not have standing to challenge X-ray search of suitcase, where the search was directed at another person. U.S.C.A.Const. Amend. 4.
2. Searches and Seizures ⟹3.6(2)
Reference to X-ray search in affidavit executed in support of search warrant did not vitiate affidavit's efficacy nor taint validity of subsequent search and seizure, where suitcase was not opened, X-ray established only that suitcase contained four bottles, no direct evidence of search was offered by Government, and one defendant's purchase of chemical, a primary precursor of methamphetamine, his elusive trip to airport while carrying suitcase, and his subsequent flight to another city combined with strong odors emanating from residence to which the suitcase was brought, generated sufficient independent probable cause for issuance of warrant. 18 U.S.C.A. § 2; Comprehensive Drug Abuse Prevention and Control Act of 1970, § 401(a)(1), 21 U.S.C.A. § 841(a)(1); U.S.C.A.Const. Amend. 4.
Headnote
3. Searches and Seizures ⟹7(10)
Utilization of electronic tracking device, without prior court approval, may be justified by probable cause and exigent circumstances. U.S.C.A.Const. Amend. 4.
4. Searches and Seizures ⟹7(10)
Federal agents had sufficient probable cause to attach electronic tracking device to defendant's car without first acquiring court order and did not violate defendant's Fourth Amendment rights in so doing, where agents knew that codefendant had purchased chemicals, a primary precursor of

*See Chapter 3

Figure 2–4 cont.

UNITED STATES v. SHOVEA 1383

Cite as 580 F.2d 1382 (1978)

methamphetamine, and agents observed codefendant leave residence, carrying suitcase in careful manner, drive to airport in elusive manner, fly to another city where he was met by defendant and drive to defendant's residence. 18 U.S.C.A. § 2; Comprehensive Drug Abuse Prevention and Control Act of 1970, § 401(a)(1), 21 U.S.C.A. § 841(a)(1); U.S.C.A.Const. Amend. 4.

5. Criminal Law ⚿1144.13(3, 5)

On appeal from jury conviction, Court of Appeals must view evidence, both direct and circumstantial, and all reasonable inferences to be drawn therefrom in light most favorable to Government in determining its sufficiency.

6. Conspiracy ⚿47(12)

Evidence supported conviction of conspiracy to manufacture and possess with intent to distribute methamphetamine, a schedule II controlled substance. 18 U.S.C.A. § 2; Comprehensive Drug Abuse Prevention and Control Act of 1970, § 401(a)(1), 21 U.S.C.A. § 841(a)(1).

7. Criminal Law ⚿696(1)

Trial court did not err in failing to grant defense motion to strike testimony of DEA agent, although all of agent's investigatory notes had been destroyed after being turned over to another agent who incorporated the notes into a report.

8. Criminal Law ⚿1171.3

Although evidence did not support assistant United States attorney's closing argument that it was possibility that defendant had given another the idea to use fictitious name of defendant's employer in ordering chemical used to make controlled substance, since defendant's participation in conspiracy to manufacture was substantial, error, if present, was harmless. 18 U.S.C.A. § 2; Comprehensive Drug Abuse Prevention and Control Act of 1970, § 401(a)(1), 21 U.S.C.A. § 841(a)(1).

9. Criminal Law ⚿728(2)

Where defense was aware that comment unsupported by evidence was made in prosecution's closing argument, but defense attorney opted, as trial tactic, not to move court for corrective action at that time and the comment was relatively harmless, trial court properly refused to grant defendant's motion for mistrial.

Jonathan L. Olom, Denver, Colo. (Stanley H. Marks, Denver, Colo., on brief) for appellant Shovea.

Edward L. Kirkwood, Asst. Federal Public Defender, Denver, Colo. (Daniel J. Sears, Federal Public Defender, Denver, Colo., on brief) for appellants Robba and Gaias.

Edward W. Nottingham, Asst. U. S. Atty., Denver, Colo., for appellee (Joseph F. Dolan, U. S. Atty., Denver, Colo., with him on brief for Shovea and Robba, Cathlin Donnell, U. S. Atty., Denver, Colo. (Interim) with him on brief for Gaias).

Before BARRETT, and McKAY, Circuit Judges, and BRATTON, District Judge.*

BARRETT, Circuit Judge.

Scott Shovea (Shovea), Gebbie Robba (Robba) and Stephen Gaias (Gaias) appeal their jury convictions of conspiracy to manufacture and possess with intent to distribute methamphetamine, a schedule II controlled substance, in violation of 18 U.S.C.A. § 2 and 21 U.S.C.A. § 841(a)(1).

Appellants were originally indicted with Geoffrey Hungerford (Hungerford). At the commencement of the trial, the Government dismissed its charges against Hungerford. Thereafter, a mistrial was declared as to Gaias. The trial proceeded as to Shovea and Robba. They were convicted. Subsequent thereto, Gaias was tried individually and convicted. A detailed recitation of the pertinent facts should facilitate our review.

Gaias originally ordered a chemical, phenyl–2–proponone (p–2–p), a primary precursor of methamphetamine, from a New York chemical company under the name of "Jay Edwards." The order was submitted on behalf of "Royce International, 315

* Of the District of New Mexico, sitting by designation.

Figure 2–4 cont.

UNITED STATES v. SHOVEA **1391**

Cite as 580 F.2d 1382 (1978)

> In determining whether the "clear error" rule should be invoked, the entire record must be reviewed and considered. *Adams v. United States,* 375 F.2d 635 (10th Cir. 1967), cert. denied, 389 U.S. 880, 88 S.Ct. 117, 19 L.Ed.2d 173 (1967); *Jennings v. United States,* 364 F.2d 513 (10th Cir. 1966), *cert. denied,* 385 U.S. 1030, 87 S.Ct. 760, 17 L.Ed.2d 677 (1967). And in weighing whether there was a clear error the most significant factor to be considered is the strength of the case against the defendant. *United States v. Williams,* 445 F.2d 421 (10th Cir. 1971). The evidence against Stevens is substantial; the testimony concerning other stolen vehicles could not have had a significant effect in influencing the jury verdict. *Kotteakos v. United States,* 328 U.S. 750, 66 S.Ct. 1239, 90 L.Ed. 1557 (1946).
>
> 452 F.2d, at p. 635.

We hold that the prosecutor's comment did not give rise to clear error. Shovea's participation in the conspiracy was substantial. Error, if present, was harmless. In *United States v. Guerrero,* 517 F.2d 528 (10th Cir. 1975), we stated:

> We recently noted in *Young v. Anderson,* 513 F.2d 969 (10th Cir. 1975), citing to *Donnelly v. DeChristoforo,* 416 U.S. 637, 94 S.Ct. 1868, 40 L.Ed.2d 431 (1974):
>
> > . . . not every trial error or infirmity which might call for application of supervisory powers correspondingly constitutes a "failure to observe that fundamental fairness essential to the every concept of justice." *Lisenba v. California,* 314 U.S. 219, 236 [62 S.Ct. 280, 290, 86 L.Ed. 166] (1941).
>
> 416 U.S. 637, at 642, 94 S.Ct. 1868, at 1871, 40 L.Ed.2d 431.
>
> 517 F.2d, at p. 531.

See also: United States v. Hall, 536 F.2d 313 (10th Cir. 1976), *cert. denied,* 429 U.S. 919, 97 S.Ct. 313, 50 L.Ed.2d 285 (1976); *Sanchez v. Heggie,* 531 F.2d 964 (10th Cir. 1976); *cert. denied,* 429 U.S. 849, 97 S.Ct. 135, 50 L.Ed.2d 122 (1976).

[9] Shovea's trial attorney was aware that the comment was made. He opted, as a matter of trial tactic, not to move the court for corrective action at that time. Under these circumstances and in view of the relative harmless nature of the comment, the trial court properly refused to grant Shovea's motion for mistrial.

*Headnote Reference

(d), (e) and (f)

Shovea's remaining allegations of error do not merit further detailed discussion. The evidence obtained by the search following execution of the search warrant was proper, as discussed under Robba, *supra;* the trial court's instructions relating to possession were proper; and the Government's experts were properly qualified.

III.

Gaias' sole allegation of error is that the trial court erred in allowing in evidence that which the Government obtained by search and seizure at 3352 West Gill Place following the execution of the search warrant, since "that search warrant was substantially based upon a previous unconstitutional search of . . . [his] . . . suitcase." This contention is without merit. *See* Robba (a), *supra.*

WE AFFIRM.

Decision

*See Chapter 3

Source: Federal Reporter, Second Series, vol. 580 (St. Paul, MN: West Publishing Company, 1978), pp. 1382–1391. Reprinted with permission.

Not all cases are contested. Some cases, such as bankruptcy, probate, and guardianship cases, are simply titled *"In the Matter of (whatever)"* or, in Latin, *"In re (whatever)."* Some cases can be brought on the application of one party and may be titled *"Ex parte (whoever)."*

If a person can sue as a named plaintiff with a collateral benefit to the general public, the case title may begin *"State ex rel. (whoever v. whoever),"* indicating "State on the relation of the named plaintiff v. defendant." In maritime law, a case title may be simply the name of the affected ship (e.g., *The Titanic*).

The case title usually indicates who appealed, known as the **appellant** or **petitioner,** and who answered the appeal, known as the **appellee** or respondent. In some states a defendant-appellant may be known as the **plaintiff in error.**

Next, the court opinion contains the case's trial or appellate court docket number. The **docket number** is the court's serial number. There are two types of docket numbers. In most courts, the docket number indicates the year the case was filed and when it was filed in relation to the other cases filed that year. In abbreviations, the docket number may also indicate the month filed or the type of case (e.g., civil, criminal, or domestic relations). For example, "CV 92-3-120" might indicate "the 120th civil case filed in the third month of 1992." In some courts, the docket number indicates the sequence of filing from the day the court first opened for business. For example, "No. 12984" might mean "the 12,984th case filed in this court since it opened for business."

If necessary to avoid confusion, the opinion next states the name of the court deciding the case. The date of the decision is listed next, sometimes after the date the case was argued before the court.

Some publishers prepare a short paragraph summary of the entire case, known as the **synopsis** of the case, which appears next. Following that, most publishers prepare brief summaries of the major legal points made in the opinion, known as **headnotes,** because they are editor-made notations that appear before the court's opinion, often at the "head," or top, of the page. Also, the court, or a court employee known as the "Reporter of Decisions," may prepare an official summary or list of the major legal points in the opinion, known as the **syllabus.**

Next, the names (and sometimes the firms) of the attorneys who argued the case are listed. This information can be extremely valuable to a legal researcher because many attorneys, if asked, will share their advice, wisdom, insight—even research references—gained from actually litigating their case like yours.

The justices who decided the case are usually listed next. Note that the abbreviations C.J., JJ., and J. indicate "Chief Justice," "Justices," and "Justice," and are not abbreviations for the first name of a justice.

Next comes the opinion of the court, explaining the decision in the case. Most opinions begin with a brief overview of the case. The classic opinion then goes through the facts of the case in detail, the law that the court deemed applicable, the court's reasoning, and, finally, its decision.

An appellate court can make three kinds of decisions, in whole or in part, for or against the plaintiff, defendant, or both. The appellate court can **affirm,** which means it agrees with the decision of the lower court and that the party who won in the lower court wins. The appellate court can **reverse,** which means it disagrees with the decision of the lower court and that either the party who lost in the lower court wins **(reversal)** or the case itself is dismissed **(vacated).** Or, the appellate court can **remand,** which means it found that the proceedings in a lower court were not fair or complete, so it could not determine who should win and is therefore returning the case to lower court for a new decision to be made after a fair and complete proceeding.

Types of Opinions

An appellate court opinion may consist of several opinions. Appellate courts consist of panels of three to nine justices. Each justice may have his own reasoning for voting to decide a case one way or the other, and each justice may write an opinion explaining his reasoning for voting the way he did.

For example, the custom in the U.S. Supreme Court is for the Justices to hear a case and then to meet in a private conference to vote on and decide the case. If the Chief Justice is in the majority, the Chief Justice assigns one of the Justices in the majority to write the opinion of the Court. If the Chief Justice is not in the majority, the Senior Associate Justice in the majority assigns one of the Justices in the majority to write the opinion of the Court.

If the other Justices who agree with the decision agree with the reasoning written by the assigned Justice, they simply "join" in the opinion of the Court. If a majority of the Justices join together in the opinion of the Court, the opinion is known as a **majority opinion,** and it, along with the decision, is considered precedent. If a Justice agrees with the decision but does not fully agree with the opinion of the Court, the Justice may write a separate opinion, known as a **concurring opinion,** in which other Justices may join.

On occasion, a majority of the Justices may agree on a decision, but a majority is unable to agree on the reasoning. The opinion of the Court is then known as a **plurality opinion,** in which other Justices who agree with the decision may join.

A Justice who disagrees with the decision of the Court may write an opinion explaining the disagreement, known as a **dissenting opinion,** in which other Justices who disagree with the decision may join.

There are two other types of opinions. To signal unity (or to disguise differences), the majority agreeing with the decision may write a joint anonymous opinion, known as a ***per curiam*** ("by the court") **opinion.** If the court does not deem it necessary to write a full opinion, it may prepare a brief opinion, known as a **memorandum opinion.** Memorandum opinions are ordinarily used for the granting or denial of an application for a writ of *certiorari* (e.g., "cert. granted" or "cert. denied"). A **writ of *certiorari*** is the written order of an appellate court with discretionary jurisdiction (usually the highest court in a three-level court system) stating that it chooses to review a lower court decision and directing the lower court to produce its records for review.

2–3 Judicial Reports

Court opinions (technically, copies of court opinions) are collected and published in books known as **reports.** (See Figure 2–5.) A set of reports is known as a **reporter.** Not all opinions are published in reports, for a number of reasons, including the level of the court involved, discussed next. Unreported decisions and the danger of decisions flooding the U.S. legal system are discussed in the final part of this section.

The federal court system and most state court systems are three-level court systems. (See Figure 2–6.) Some states, having less legal business, have a two-level court system.

The first level in both systems consists of trial courts. The purpose of the trial court is to determine the facts and make the original application of the law. Evidence is presented to a fact finder, judge or jury, and after a verdict is reached, judgment is entered. In the vast majority of cases, the disagreement between the parties is much more a disagreement about the facts than a disagreement about the law. When a trial court applies the law as understood by

Figure 2–5 Case-Decision-Opinion-Report

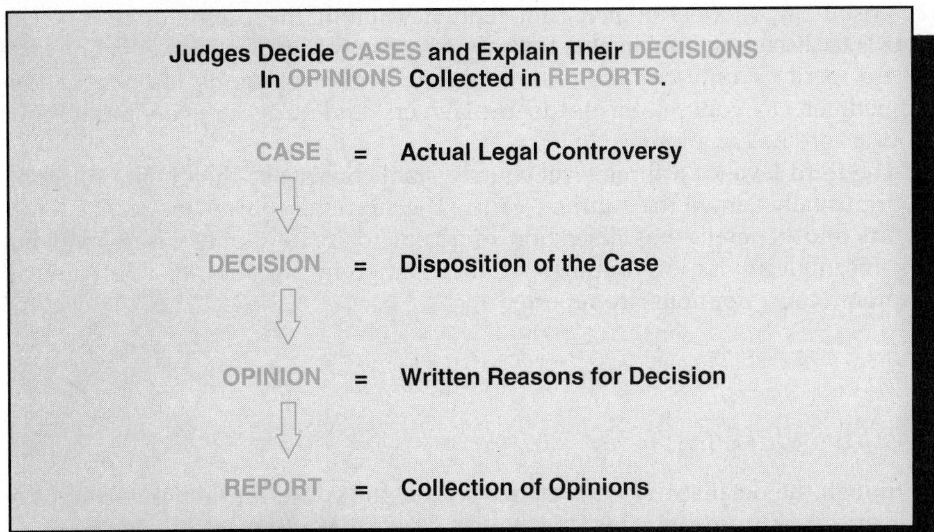

both parties, no new precedent is made. Since there is no new law to be found by researching such a case, they are generally not reported. Trial court opinions are reported only if the trial judge takes the time to write an opinion to explain a novel application of the law in an unusual or unusually significant case.

Judges Decide CASES and Explain Their DECISIONS
In OPINIONS Collected in REPORTS.
CASE = Actual Legal Controversy
DECISION = Disposition of the Case
OPINION = Written Reasons for Decision
REPORT = Collection of Opinions

The second and third levels of a three-level court system (combined in a two-level court system) consist of appellate courts. By reviewing the trial court record, weighing arguments presented in written briefs, and, if necessary, hearing oral argument, appellate courts review the decisions of the trial courts, and in so doing, determine whether the trial courts properly applied the law. Appellate court opinions are generally reported because their opinions must be researched in order to find the law.

The second level of a three-level court system consists of intermediate appellate courts. Generally, the parties to a trial have a right to appeal, to have the acts of the trial judge reviewed, because of the broad discretionary powers given to the trial judge. However, experience shows that many appeals to intermediate appellate courts are without merit. Whether the result of bitterness, confusion, desperation, ignorance, or simply a dramatic attempt to

Figure 2–6 Three-Level Court System

EXAMPLES		Federal Courts	Illinois Courts	New York Courts
Appellate Courts	"High," or "Supreme," Court	U.S. Supreme Court	Illinois Supreme Court	New York Court of Appeals
	Intermediate Appellate Court	U.S. Court of Appeals (by Circuit)	Illinois Appellate Court	Appellate Term, N.Y. Supreme Court
Trial Courts		U.S. District Court (by District)	Illinois Circuit Court	New York Supreme Court

establish a new precedent, parties often appeal even though the precedents are against them. There is an increasing tendency among the intermediate appellate courts to discourage publishers from reporting opinions in appeals having little or no merit, if only by not recommending certain opinions for publication. Sometimes, to conceal misdeeds by lawyers and judges, even meritorious appeals are not reported.

The third level of a three-level court system consists of the "high," or final, court, usually named the supreme court. The supreme court manages the lower courts and generally has discretion to accept for review only cases involving significant legal issues. Because of their inherent significance, virtually all supreme court opinions are reported.

Reported Opinions

Although the details vary with the sovereign, the court, and the publisher, the publication of court opinions does follow a general pattern.

Court opinions are released chronologically, as the courts decide the cases filed chronologically. The opinion is typed or printed and made part of the court's official record.

Because it is impractical for everyone interested in knowing the law to travel to every courthouse in the country to read every opinion in every court's official record, supreme courts (or the legislature) usually arrange for one government agency or private publisher to publish the **official reports** for the court system. The opinions, however, are not copyrightable. They are public records that anyone is free to publish. Opinions are often published without special authority in books known as **unofficial reports.** The only significance of the official version is that it controls if the unofficial version conflicts with the official version. Since publishers know that nobody would want to buy an inaccurate unofficial version, this rarely happens. "Unofficial" versions are carefully checked against the original and official versions, and they can, in fact, be more reliable than the "official" version. For example, when the editors of the Lawyers Cooperative Publishing Company (LCP) were preparing to reprint the company's unofficial *United States Supreme Court Reports, Lawyers' Edition* (L. Ed.) in 1905, they found many differences between the official records of the court and the court's "official" reports. On the advice of the court that the court records were "more official" than the "official" reports, the editors "reported from the records" to give lawyers the correct version.

If an individual court opinion is published separately, it is known as a **slip opinion.** Court opinions are first collected for reporters in temporary pamphlets, known as **advance sheets,** quickly assembled and distributed to customers to use until enough opinions have been released, and enough time has passed, for the publisher to be able to make a permanent bound volume. The advance sheets usually have the same pagination as the bound volume.

A reporter is a set of bound volumes that publish court opinions. When the features of a reporter change, or the marketing of the set changes, publishers sometimes start a new or higher numerical series of the reporter. For example, when West Publishing Company no longer reported U.S. District Court opinions in its *Federal Reporter* (F.), it started the *Federal Reporter, Second Series* (F.2d).

Court reports collect court opinions in a variety of combinations. Most reporters collect opinions by sovereign and court. LCP's *United States Supreme Court Reports, Lawyers' Edition, Second Series* (L. Ed. 2d), for example, collects the opinions of the U.S. Supreme Court. Some reporters collect opinions by geographic area or region. West's *South Eastern Reporter* (S.E.), for example, collects opinions from the southeastern states of Georgia, North Carolina, South Carolina, Virginia, and West Virginia. Some reporters collect opinions by subject. For example, *United States Tax Cases* (U.S.T.C.), published by Commerce Clearing House, Inc. (CCH), collects opinions in cases deciding federal tax law.

A bound reporter volume ordinarily contains several useful features. The full names and titles of the justices whose opinions appear in the volume may be listed. (See Figure 2–7.) If the bound volume is unofficial, there may be a cross-reference table showing where the official version of an opinion appears in the volume and vice versa. A table, in alphabetical order by case title, may indicate the opinions reported in the volume and the page on which they can be found. (See Figure 2–8.) Other tables may list and cross-reference statutes, court rules, and "words and phrases" interpreted by the opinions in the volume, and where those interpretations can be found. Finally, as will be discussed in Chapter 3, there may be a "digest" for the volume collecting by topic the legal points made in the opinions in the volume.

As we will learn in Chapter 10, reporters are customarily identified by conventional abbreviations, so that a particular opinion can be simply cited by volume number, reporter abbreviation, and page number. For example, the famous U.S. Supreme Court opinion in *Marbury v. Madison,* decided in 1803, can be found in the first volume published by reporter William Cranch, which became the fifth volume of the Government Printing Office's official reporter, the *United States Reporter,* wherein the opinion begins on page 137. It can also be found in the second volume of the *United States Supreme Courts Reports, Lawyers' Edition,* an unofficial reporter published by LCP, wherein the opinion begins on page 60. By custom, all of that can be said as follows: *Marbury v. Madison,* 5 U.S. (1 Cranch) 137, 2 L. Ed. 60 (1803). Being part of the jargon of legal research, reporter abbreviations are noted and used in this book wherever appropriate.

National Reporter System

As discussed in Chapter 1, law publishing was not a major industry in the United States through the early 1800s. Law books, published by local publishers widely scattered around the country, were scarce and did not systematically report the opinions of all appellate courts. The change started in 1879, in St. Paul, Minnesota.

In 1876, John B. and Horatio D. West began publishing a weekly newsletter for Minnesota attorneys that included all the opinions of the Supreme Court of Minnesota. Attorneys in neighboring states, who also received the newsletter, asked the West brothers to include opinions from their states in the newsletter. In 1879, the West brothers began publishing a new set of books, the *North Western Reporter* (N.W.), that included opinions from the states of Iowa, Michigan, Minnesota, Nebraska, North Dakota, South Dakota, and Wisconsin.

The *North Western Reporter* was a hit. It was the only complete and reliable source of appellate court opinions in the region. The concept was quickly applied in other parts of the country. By 1888, the West brothers, incorporated as West Publishing Company, had seven regional reporters covering the states (discussed below under "State Court Reports") and two federal reporters covering the federal courts (discussed below under "Federal Court Reports"), and had achieved a monopoly in publishing all of the appellate court opinions in the country. The system, known as the National Reporter System, remains, with a few additions, the backbone of legal research in the United States. Because of its national scope, the National Reporter System reporters are the most important for a legal researcher to be familiar with. A reference to a National Reporter System volume has meaning throughout the country.

Figure 2–7 Table of Judges

JUDGES
OF THE
FEDERAL COURTS

With Date of Appointment

DISTRICT OF COLUMBIA CIRCUIT

WARREN E. BURGER, Circuit Justice	6–23–69	Washington, D. C.

CIRCUIT JUDGES

SPOTTSWOOD W. ROBINSON, III, C. J.*	11– 3–66	Washington
J. SKELLY WRIGHT*	3–30–62	Washington
PATRICIA M. WALD	7–26–79	Washington
ABNER J. MIKVA	9–26–79	Washington
HARRY T. EDWARDS	2–20–80	Washington
RUTH BADER GINSBURG	6–18–80	Washington
ROBERT H. BORK	2–12–82	Washington
ANTONIN SCALIA	8–17–82	Washington
KENNETH W. STARR	9–20–83	Washington
LAURENCE H. SILBERMAN	10–28–85	Washington

SENIOR CIRCUIT JUDGES

DAVID L. BAZELON	2–10–50	Washington
JOHN A. DANAHER	3–31–54	West Hartford, Conn.
CARL MCGOWAN	3–27–63	Washington
GEORGE E. MACKINNON	5– 6–69	Washington
ROGER ROBB	5– 6–69	Washington
MALCOLM RICHARD WILKEY	2–25–70	Washington

DISTRICT JUDGES

AUBREY E. ROBINSON, Jr., C. J.	11– 3–66	Washington
GERHARD A. GESELL	12– 7–67	Washington
JOHN H. PRATT	6– 7–68	Washington
BARRINGTON D. PARKER	12–19–69	Washington
CHARLES R. RICHEY	5– 5–71	Washington
LOUIS F. OBERDORFER	11– 1–77	Washington
HAROLD H. GREENE	5–19–78	Washington
JOHN GARRETT PENN	3–23–79	Washington
JOYCE HENS GREEN	5–11–79	Washington
NORMA HOLLOWAY JOHNSON	5–12–80	Washington

* Former U. S. District Judge.

617 F.Supp. VII

Source: Federal Supplement, vol. 617 (St. Paul, MN: West Publishing Company, 1986), p. vii. Reprinted with permission.

Figure 2–8 Table of Cases

CASES REPORTED

ARRANGED UNDER THEIR RESPECTIVE CIRCUITS

DISTRICT OF COLUMBIA CIRCUIT

FIRST CIRCUIT

617 F.Supp. XLIII

Source: Federal Supplement, vol. 617 (St. Paul, MN: West Publishing Company, 1986), p. xliii. Reprinted with permission.

Federal Court Reports

The federal court system is a three-level court system with specialized courts.

The highest level in the federal court system, the court of last resort, is the U.S. Supreme Court, located, since 1800, in Washington, D.C. The Court assembled in 1790 in New York City, moved to Philadelphia later that year, and released its first opinions in 1792. A private individual, Alexander J. Dallas, who had published a volume of Pennsylvania state court reports, decided to report the opinions of the other "Pennsylvania" court. Covering the period from 1792 to 1800, Volumes 2, 3, and 4 of Dallas contained the first opinions of the Court. Dallas was succeeded by William Cranch and Henry Wheaton, and, beginning in 1828, a series of private individuals were hired to be the Court's official reporter: Richard Peters, Benjamin C. Howard, J. S. Black, and John William Wallace. The volumes of these early reporters were published by a variety of publishers.

In 1875, the reporter volumes compiled by individuals (known as **nominative reporters)** from Dallas to Wallace were renumbered sequentially and became Volumes 1–90 of the official *United States Reports* (U.S.), published by the U.S. Government Printing Office. (See Appendix II.) Advance sheets for *United States Reports* are available, but they are not published as fast as the advance sheets for the two unofficial reporters discussed next.

Two problems that were encountered with the early Supreme Court reports were availability and price. In 1882, James E. Briggs, attorney for a railroad, was practicing law with his son, William H. Briggs, and an associate, Ernest Hitchcock, in Newark, New York. Briggs needed access to the opinions of the U.S. Supreme Court but was tired of driving his buggy all the way to the library in Rochester (over 30 miles away) to review the opinions. Upon investigation, Briggs and his associates determined that because of the economies of mass production, if 2,500 lawyers subscribed in advance, the reports of the Supreme Court, then selling for as much as $15 per volume, could be published and sold at one dollar per volume.

Briggs and his associates sent out circulars asking lawyers if they would subscribe in advance to a Supreme Court reporter at one dollar per volume. They got back over 3,500 orders. The project was undertaken under the name of the Lawyers Co-operative Publishing Company, because lawyers, with their advance subscriptions, cooperated in the company's initial venture. Ironically, just three years later, Briggs, as president, moved the company to Rochester.

LCP's first publication was the *United States Supreme Court Reports, Lawyers' Edition* (L. Ed.), reporting the decisions of the court from 1792. In 1896, LCP added notations by Professor Walter Rose to the set, and L. Ed with "Rose's Notes" became the constitutional scholar's reporter. Over time, LCP's editors added their own commentary to the set, and, by 1957, under the guidance of Ernest Hugo Schopler, a second series was begun (L. Ed. 2d), regularly featuring in-depth collections of cases known as annotations. (See Chapter 4.) Advance sheets report cases until a bound volume can be published with annotations, a table of cases, and other similar editorial features. The bound volumes also include, where available, summaries of the briefs filed in each case. One advantage of L. Ed. 2d is its inclusion in LCP's Total Client Service Library. (See Chapter 4.)

The third principal source of the opinions of the U.S. Supreme Court is the *Supreme Court Reporter* (S. Ct.) published by West Publishing Company. The *Supreme Court Reporter* was begun in 1882, starting with Volume 106 of the official reports. (See Appendix II.) Advance sheets report cases until a bound volume can be published with a table of cases and other similar editorial features. One advantage of the *Supreme Court Reporter* is its inclusion in West's National Reporter System and West's Topic and Key Number digests. (See Chapter 3.)

The Supreme Court Reporters

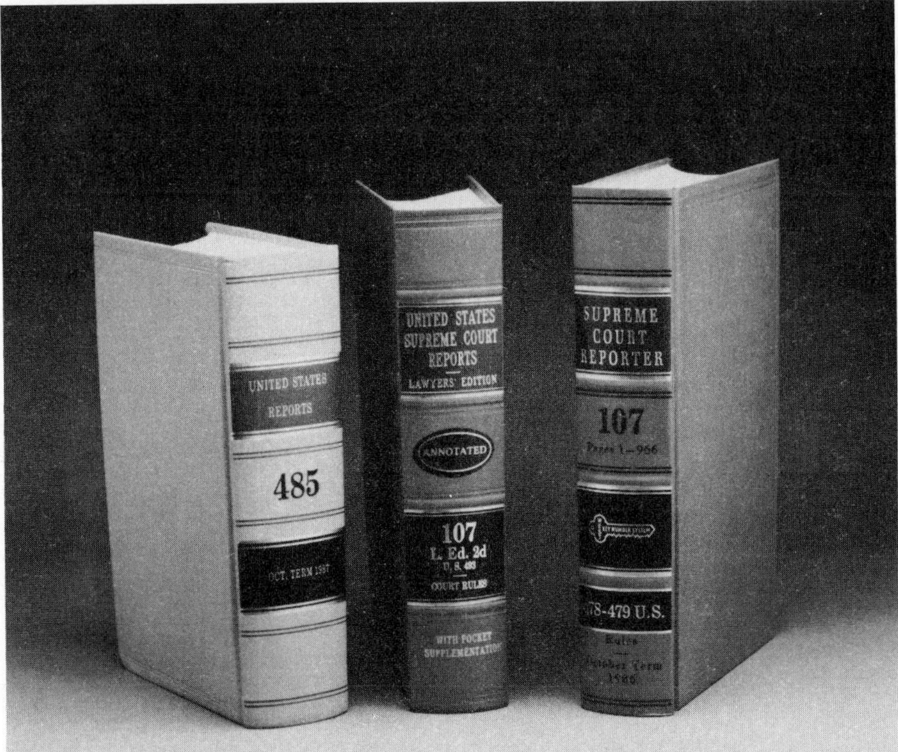

Source: © Doug Martin.

Both L. Ed. 2d and the *Supreme Court Reporter* indicate on their spines the volumes of the *United States Reports* covered in the volume. (See Appendix II.) Both L. Ed. 2d and the *Supreme Court Reporter* have in their volumes exact cross-reference tables to and from the *United States Reports.* Both L. Ed. 2d and the *Supreme Court Reporter* note with an asterisk and page number the pagination of the official reporter in the text of their report of the opinion, a device known as **star pagination,** so that any passage in L. Ed. 2d or in the *Supreme Court Reporter* can be cited to the *United States Reports.* One subtle distinction, that may be important to a legal researcher, can be made between the sets. The *Supreme Court Reporter* never cites L. Ed. 2d, whereas L. Ed. 2d's running heads give the three principal parallel cites for a United States Supreme Court case: *United States Reports* (U.S.), L. Ed. 2d, and the *Supreme Court Reporter.*

Two other publications, both emphasizing the speedy publication of Supreme Court opinions via weekly publication of slip opinions, are worthy of note. The Bureau of National Affairs (BNA) publishes *United States Law Week* (U.S.L.W.) and CCH publishes the *United States Supreme Court Bulletin* (S. Ct. Bull. [CCH]).

The opinions of the Supreme Court are also available on the LEXIS (GENFED;US file) and WESTLAW (SCT and SCT-OLD databases) computer-assisted legal research systems, which will be discussed in Chapter 12.

Most of the opinions of the lower federal courts are not officially reported. Fortunately, in 1880, West undertook the systematic unofficial publication of lower federal court opinions in units of its National Reporter System. First, however, to cover the 18,000 federal cases decided from 1789 to 1879, the cases were arranged alphabetically and numbered in that order, and published in a 31-volume set, *Federal Cases* (F. Cas.). The 31st volume contains cross-reference tables to the reporters in which the cases were originally reported.

In 1879, West began the federal portion of its National Reporter System with the *Federal Reporter* (F.), reporting, chronologically, until 1932, opinions designated for publication by the intermediate courts of appeals and selected trial court opinions from the district courts. In 1932, West began a new series, the *Federal Reporter, Second Series* (F.2d), to include only U.S. Court of Appeals opinions. West started a new unit of the National Reporter System, the *Federal Supplement* (F. Supp.), to report U.S. District Court opinions. (See Figure 2–9.) Advance sheets are published for F.2d and F. Supp. to report cases until a bound volume can be published.

The federal courts of appeals are divided into 11 multistate circuits, the District of Columbia Circuit, and the "Federal Circuit" created in 1982. (See Figure 2–10.) The U.S. Court of Appeals for the Federal Circuit took over the functions of the former U.S. Court of Patent Appeals and the appellate division of the former U.S. Court of Claims. Along with the opinions of the geographic circuit courts of appeals, F.2d now contains the opinions of the U.S. Court of Appeals for the Federal Circuit and the Temporary Emergency Court of Appeals. F.2d also lists decisions without a published opinion.

The opinions of the federal courts of appeals are also available on the LEXIS (GENFED;USAPP and other files) and WESTLAW (CTA, CTA-OLD, and other databases) computer-assisted legal research systems, to be discussed in Chapter 12.

In addition to district court opinions, F. Supp. now includes U.S. Claims Court (Cl. Ct.), Judicial Panel on Multidistrict Litigation (J.P.M.L.), and Special Court Regional Rail Reorganization Act (Regional Rail Reorg. Ct.) opinions.

West also publishes *Federal Rules Decisions* (F.R.D.), a collection of district court opinions not designated for publication, that, since 1939, involve the Federal Rules of Civil Procedure, or, since 1946, involve the Federal Rules of Criminal Procedure. LCP provides similar coverage in *Federal Rules Service* (Fed.

Figure 2–9 West's Leading Federal Reporters

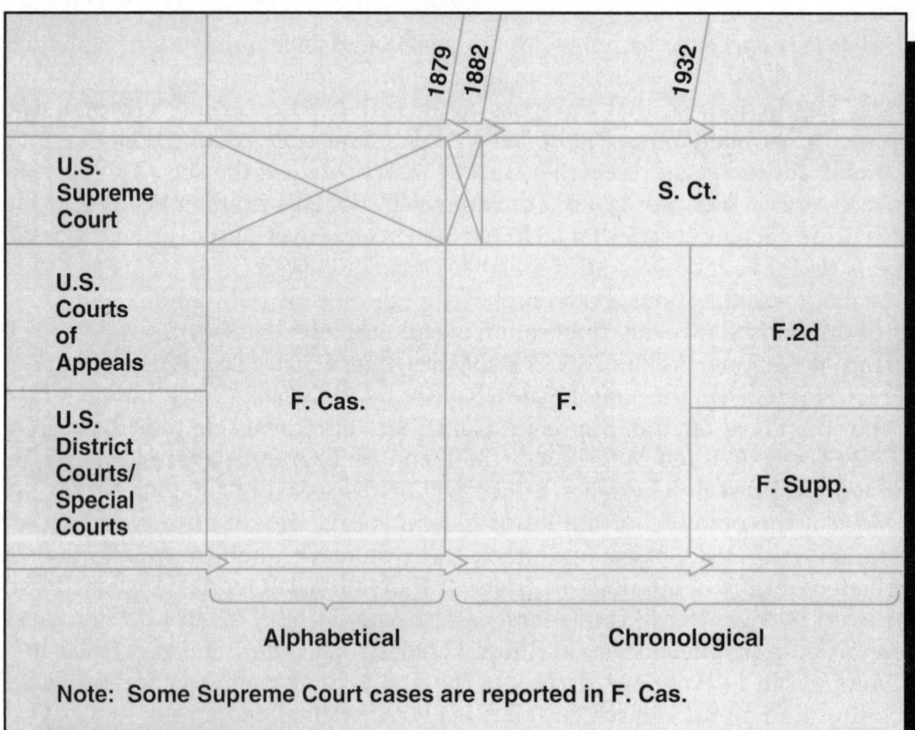

Figure 2–10 U.S. Federal Judicial Circuits

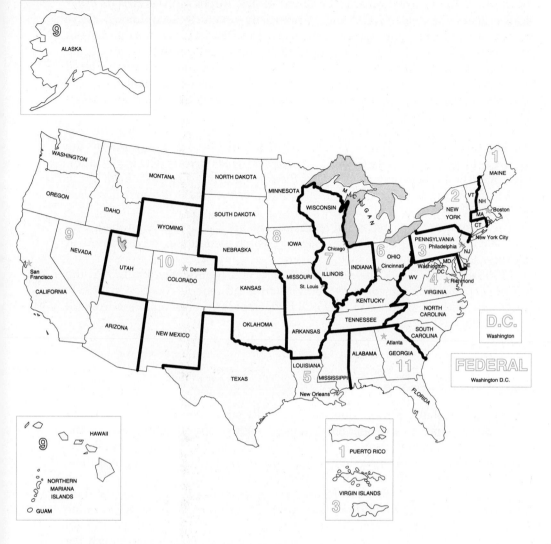

Source: Sample Pages (St. Paul, MN: West Publishing Company, 1986), p. 200. Reprinted with permission.

R. Serv.) and *Federal Rules Service, Second Series* (Fed. R. Serv. 2d) (formerly published by Callaghan & Company).

The opinions of the federal district courts are also available on the LEXIS (GENFED;DIST and other files) and WESTLAW (DCT, DCT-OLD, and other databases) computer-assisted legal research systems, which will be discussed in Chapter 12.

Beyond the reporters already discussed, there are a number of reporters currently covering the specialized federal courts.

Started in 1975, West's *Military Justice Reporter* (M.J.) reports opinions of the U.S. Court of Military Appeals, the various Courts of Military Review, and the Court of Veterans Appeals.

Started in 1979, West's *Bankruptcy Reporter* (Bankr.) reports opinions from the U.S. Bankruptcy Courts and other cases involving bankruptcy law not reported in F. Supp.

West's *United States Claims Court Reporter* (Cl. Ct.) reports opinions of the U.S. Claims Court since 1982, and opinions in cases on appeal from that court.

The Government Printing Office officially publishes the designated opinions of the U.S. Tax Court (formerly the Board of Tax Appeals) in its *Reports of the United States Tax Court* (T.C.). CCH unofficially covers these opinions, along with U.S. Supreme Court, Court of Appeals, and District Court tax opinions in its *United States Tax Cases* (U.S.T.C.). Prentice-Hall (P-H) unofficially covers the same courts in its *American Federal Tax Reports* (A.F.T.R.) and *American Federal Tax Reports, Second Series* (A.F.T.R.2d). CCH and P-H also each publish the Tax Court's undesignated opinions in a set entitled *Tax Court Memorandum Decisions* (T.C.M. [CCH]; T.C.M. [P-H]).

Finally, among federal reports, the Government Printing Office also officially publishes the opinions of the U.S. Court of International Trade (formerly the U.S. Customs Court) in its *Court of International Trade Reports* (Ct. Int'l Trade), also published officially in the *Customs Bulletin and Decisions* (Cust. B. & Dec.), which BNA unofficially covers in its *International Trade Reporter Decisions* (I.T.R.D. [BNA]).

The opinions of the specialized federal courts are also available on the LEXIS and WESTLAW computer-assisted legal research systems to be discussed in Chapter 12.

LEXIS and WESTLAW also cover the federal courts generally. On LEXIS, the GENFED;COURTS2 file contains opinions from all federal courts. On WESTLAW, the ALLFEDS and ALLFEDS-OLD databases contain opinions from all federal courts.

State Court Reports

The reports of state court opinions can be briefly summarized as follows. Every state, at one time or another, has arranged for the official publication of the opinions of its highest court, if not all appellate courts, by a local publisher. West's National Reporter System, which unofficially reports all the appellate court opinions of all the states in a regional or specialized reporter, has become so prevalent, however, that several states have eliminated one or more of their little-used official state reporters, and most of them recognize the appropriate unit of the National Reporter System for their state as their official reporter. In the larger states, there may also be a market for a local publisher to publish the state's court opinions unofficially. The variety of reports for a state can become bewildering.

For example, in 1911, E. A. Feazel of the Cleveland Law Library Association, writing in the *Law Library Journal*, lamented:

> This paper is to be neither a defense of, nor apology for the abominable system, or rather lack of system which has prevailed in reporting the decisions of Ohio courts, especially inferior courts, for the writer has never been connected with any of the publishing houses whose misguided enterprise is responsible for the present conditions, nor with the legislative branch of the state government with which is lodged the power to correct those conditions.
>
> The excuse for this paper is the fact that Ohio reports are so confusing that only a small percentage of Ohio lawyers understand them, coupled with a desire on the writer's part to be of some assistance in helping lawyers and librarians outside the state to comprehend the scope and relative value of the various series of reports. [Feazel, *Ohio Case Law*, 4 LAW LIBR. J. 2 (1911)]

Fortunately, over time, the situation in Ohio improved, and now it is almost simple. In 1982, Anderson Publishing Company (Anderson), which had published the unofficial *Ohio Opinions* (Ohio Op.), *Ohio Opinions, Second Series* (Ohio Op. 2d), and *Ohio Opinions, Third Series* (Ohio Op. 3d), became Ohio's official reporter and started a new set, *Ohio Official Reports*. The only complication with *Ohio Official Reports* is that the State's supreme court opinions are cited as if they were a continuation of the former official set, *Ohio State Reports;* court of appeals opinions are cited as if they were a continuation of the former official set, *Ohio Appellate Reports;* and other law courts are cited as if they were a continuation of the former official, *Ohio Miscellaneous.* Thus, opinions in *Ohio Official Reports* are cited to Ohio St. 3d, Ohio App. 3d, and Ohio Misc. 2d. A final twist occurred in 1991, when Anderson's contract expired, and West became Ohio's official reporter, taking over publication of *Ohio Official Reports.*

West's National Reporter System covers the states with seven regional reporters. (See Figure 2–11.) Starting in 1879 with the *North Western Reporter* (N.W., N.W.2d) covering Iowa, Michigan, Minnesota, Nebraska, North Dakota, South Dakota, and Wisconsin, West added the *Pacific Reporter* (P., P.2d) in 1883, now covering Alaska, Arizona, California, Colorado, Hawaii, Idaho, Kansas, Montana, Nevada, New Mexico, Oklahoma, Oregon, Utah, Washington, and Wyoming. In 1885, West added the *North Eastern Reporter* (N.E., N.E.2d), covering Illinois, Indiana, Massachusetts, New York, and Ohio, and the *Atlantic*

Figure 2–11 National Reporter System Map

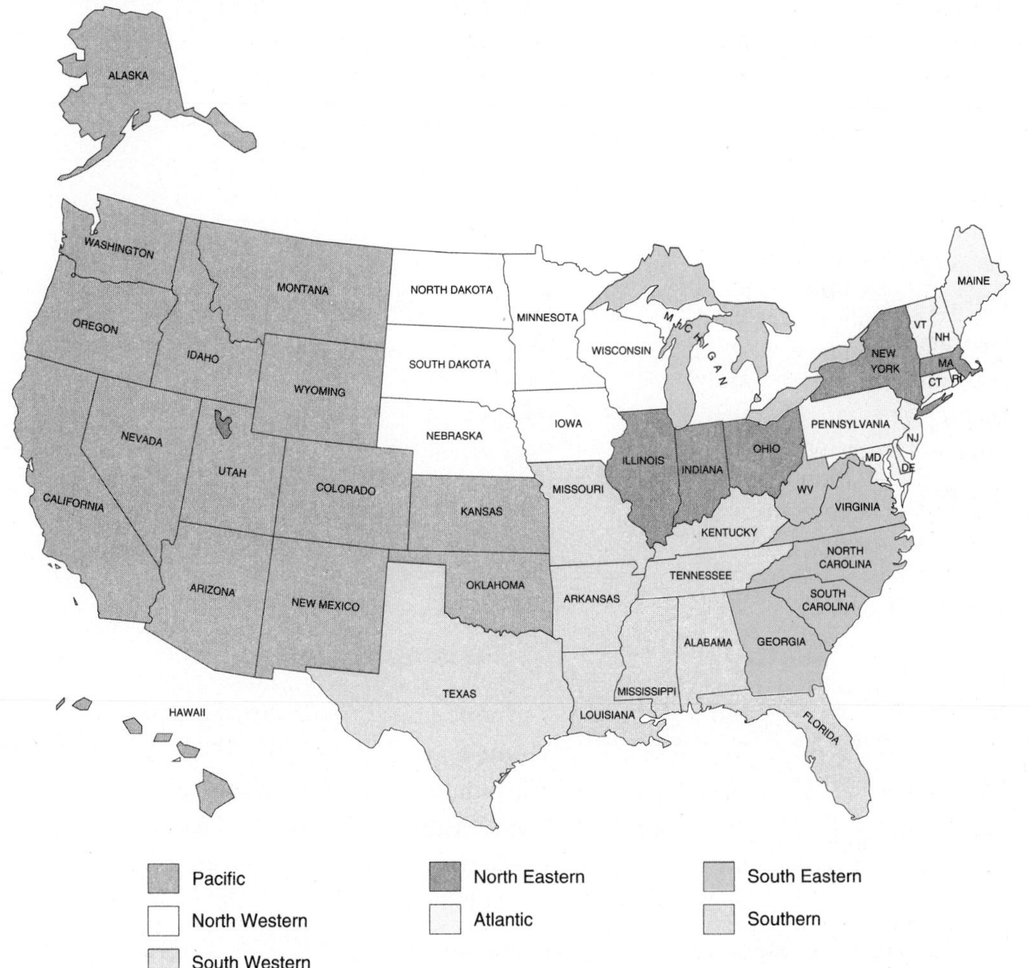

The National Reporter System also includes the Supreme Court Reporter, the Federal Reporter, the Federal Supplement, Federal Rules Decisions, West's Bankruptcy Reporter, the New York Supplement, West's California Reporter, West's Illinois Decisions, West's Military Justice Reporter, and the United States Claims Court Reporter.

Source: West's Law Finder (St. Paul, MN: West Publishing Company, 1990), p. 2. Reprinted with permission.

Reporter (A., A.2d), now covering Connecticut, Delaware, Maine, Maryland, New Hampshire, New Jersey, Pennsylvania, Rhode Island, Vermont, and the District of Columbia. In 1886, West added the *South Western Reporter* (S.W., S.W.2d), covering Arkansas, Kentucky, Missouri, Tennessee, and Texas. In 1887, West added the *Southern Reporter* (So., So. 2d), covering Alabama, Florida, Louisiana, and Mississippi, and the *South Eastern Reporter* (S.E., S.E.2d), covering Georgia, North Carolina, South Carolina, Virginia, and West Virginia. (See Figure 2–12.)

Recognizing the large amount of legal business in one of the nation's most populous states, in 1888, West added a specialized unit to the National Reporter System, the *New York Supplement* (N.Y.S., N.Y.S.2d) to cover New York. Similarly, in 1959, West added *West's California Reporter* (Cal. Rptr.) to cover California. And in 1976, West added *West's Illinois Decisions* to cover Illinois.

The abbreviation of the current official reporter, if any, for the highest court in each state, or the current National Reporter System reporter covering the state, is as follows:

State	*Reporter Abbreviation*	*State*	*Reporter Abbreviation*
Alabama	So. 2d	Montana	Mont.
Alaska	P.2d	Nebraska	Neb.
Arizona	Ariz.	Nevada	Nev.
Arkansas	Ark.	New Hampshire	N.H.
California	Cal. 3d	New Jersey	N.J.
Colorado	P.2d	New Mexico	N.M.
Connecticut	Conn.	New York	N.Y.2d
Delaware	A.2d	North Carolina	N.C.
Florida	So. 2d	North Dakota	N.W.2d
Georgia	Ga.	Ohio	Ohio St. 3d
Hawaii	Haw.	Oklahoma	P.2d
Idaho	Idaho	Oregon	Or.
Illinois	Ill. 2d	Pennsylvania	Pa.
Indiana	N.E.2d	Rhode Island	A.2d
Iowa	N.W.2d	South Carolina	S.C.
Kansas	Kan.	South Dakota	N.W.2d
Kentucky	S.W.2d	Tennessee	S.W.2d
Louisiana	So. 2d	Texas	S.W.2d
Maine	A.2d	Utah	P.2d
Maryland	Md.	Vermont	Vt.
Massachusetts	Mass.	Virginia	Va.
Michigan	Mich.	Washington	Wash. 2d
Minnesota	N.W. 2d	West Virginia	S.E. 2d
Mississippi	So. 2d	Wisconsin	Wis. 2d
Missouri	S.W. 2d	Wyoming	P. 2d

State court opinions are also available on the LEXIS and WESTLAW computer-assisted legal research systems, which will be discussed in Chapter 12. On LEXIS, the STATES;OMNI2 file contains court opinions from all the states, and the STATES;HIGHCT file contains opinions from the highest courts in all the states. On WESTLAW, the ALLSTATES and ALLSTATES-OLD databases contain court opinions from all the states, and the ATL, NE, NW, PAC, SE, and SO databases contain the opinions reported in the Atlantic, North Eastern,

Figure 2–12 States Covered in Specific West Regional Reporters

Regional Reporter	States Covered
Atlantic	Connecticut, Delaware, Maine, Maryland, New Hampshire, New Jersey, Pennsylvania, Rhode Island, Vermont; also District of Columbia
North Eastern	Illinois, Indiana, Massachusetts, New York, Ohio
North Western	Iowa, Michigan, Minnesota, Nebraska, North Dakota, South Dakota, Wisconsin
Pacific	Alaska, Arizona, California, Colorado, Hawaii, Idaho, Kansas, Montana, Nevada, New Mexico, Oklahoma, Oregon, Utah, Washington, Wyoming
South Eastern	Georgia, North Carolina, South Carolina, Virginia, West Virginia
South Western	Arkansas, Kentucky, Missouri, Tennessee, Texas
Southern	Alabama, Florida, Louisiana, Mississippi

North Western, Pacific, South Eastern, and Southern regional reporters, respectively. (See Appendix III for a collection of selected state law sources, including selected state-specific LEXIS files and WESTLAW databases.)

Unreported Opinions

Appellate courts, both intermediate and supreme, are becoming increasingly concerned about the burdens placed on the legal system by an ever-growing flood of appellate court opinions. There are now three million to four million reported cases in U.S. case law, and the number grows by more than 60,000 cases per year. Some argue that the information content of the average case has decreased to the point that the value to society of reporting every case is less than its cost in the forests cut down to make the paper to make the books and the valuable library and office space used to shelve it all.

Many appellate courts have sought to limit the number of their opinions that are reported. With increasing frequency, appellate courts are disposing of cases with memorandum opinions or without opinions. Most appellate courts require attorneys who cite unreported opinions (which should be considered only persuasive authority) to include a copy of the opinion in their briefs to the court. Some appellate courts have gone so far as to prohibit the citing of opinions in briefs where the opinions have not been specifically marked by the appellate court as being "for publication."

As a practical matter, legal researchers must try to find cases like theirs where the persons like them won even if those cases are unreported. Nothing tells the legal researcher what the law is on a topic better than the reasoned opinion of a court, whether or not that opinion is reported. If a copy must be obtained of the unreported case in order to cite it, so be it. Even if a court prohibits the citation of an unreported case, one would be foolish not to tactfully make an argument—based on the unreported case—known to have worked in the past.

So how does the legal researcher find unreported cases on a given topic? Beyond the methods that can also be used for finding reported cases (see Chapter 3), there are three principal methods.

First, some publishing companies, recognizing the importance of unreported opinions, publish summaries and indexes to unreported decisions. For example, in Ohio, the Banks-Baldwin Law Publishing Company publishes the *Ohio Appellate Decisions Index,* which notes the key issues and facts in each case. As the publisher's catalog notes, there are "nearly 8,000 decisions issued each year by Ohio's twelve District Courts of Appeals, less than 10% of which are officially reported." Summaries of unreported decisions may also be found in local bar association newsletters.

Second, most "unreported" opinions, by definition not published in books, have nonetheless been entered into computer databases. Unreported cases can be searched and found on both the LEXIS and WESTLAW computer-assisted legal research systems, to be discussed in Chapter 12.

Third, as a last resort, an "unknown" unreported opinion can sometimes be obtained from the court through a clerk familiar with the case.

SUMMARY

2–1

Under the Constitution of the United States and under state constitutions, the sovereign power to interpret the law, and in so doing make the law, is given to the courts. A court must be confronted with an *actual* legal controversy, a case, in order to exercise sovereign power. When a court is called on to decide a case, it must compare the case to similar cases already decided and follow the most analogous case as precedent. A court must follow mandatory authority, but it may consider persuasive authority. In making a decision, the court will determine the point on which the case will turn, known as the *ratio decidendi,* and, if necessary, make a holding, a rule of law, upon which to decide the case.

2–2

Because of need for a just explanation and for the establishment of *ratio decidendi,* holdings, and precedent, it is customary for a court, especially an appellate court reviewing a lower court case, to explain its reasoning and its decision in writing. A court's written explanation of its decision is known as its opinion. A published appellate judicial opinion customarily consists of the following parts: title of the case, docket number, name of court, date of decision, synopsis, headnotes, syllabus, attorneys' names, justices' names, overview of the case, the facts, the law, the court's reasoning, and the court's decision. The appellate court can affirm, which means it agrees with the decision of the lower court, it can reverse, which means it disagrees with the decision of the lower court, or it can remand, which means it found that the proceedings in a lower court were not fair or complete, and so it is returning the case to lower court. The types of opinions include the majority opinion, the concurring opinion, the plurality opinion, and the dissenting opinion, as well as the *per curiam* opinion, and the memorandum opinion.

2–3

Court opinions are collected and published in books known as reports. A set of reports is known as a reporter. Trial court opinions are reported only if the trial judge takes the time to write an opinion to explain a novel application of the law in an unusual or unusually significant case. Appellate court opinions are generally reported, because their opinions must be researched in order to find the law. Nevertheless, there is an increasing tendency among the intermediate appellate courts to discourage publishers from reporting opinions in appeals having little or no merit. Court opinions are released chronologically. Supreme courts will usually arrange for one government agency or private publisher to publish the official reports for the court system. However, opinions are often published without special authority in unofficial reports. Court reports collect court opinions in a variety of combinations, but most collect opinions by sovereign and court. A bound reporter volume ordinarily contains several useful features, including the full names and titles of the justices, cross-reference tables, alphabetical tables of cases, and tables of statutes construed. Of all the reporters, the National Reporter System reporters are the most important for a legal researcher to be familiar with. Currently, the United States Supreme Court is reported officially in the *United States Reports* (U.S.), published by the Government Printing Office. Unofficially, Supreme Court cases are reported in the *United States Supreme Court Reports, Lawyers' Edition, Second Series* (L. Ed. 2d), published by LCP and the *Supreme Court Reporter* (S. Ct.) published by West. Federal court of appeals cases are reported only in the *Federal Reporter, Second Series* (F.2d), published by West, and federal trial court opinions are reported in the *Federal Supplement* (F. Supp.) published by West. The specialized federal courts are covered by a variety of reporters. As for the state courts, every state, at one time or another, has arranged for the official publication of the opinions of its highest court, if not all appellate courts, by a local publisher. West's National Reporter System, which unofficially reports all the appellate court opinions of all the states in a regional or specialized reporter, has become so prevalent, however, that several states have eliminated one or more of their little-used official state reporters, and most of them recognize the appropriate unit of the National Reporter System for their state as their official reporter. The seven current regional reporters in the National Reporter System, each in their second series, are the *North Western Reporter* (N.W.2d), the *Pacific Reporter* (P.2d), the *North Eastern Reporter* (N.E.2d), the *Atlantic Reporter* (A.2d), the *South Western Reporter* (S.W.2d), the *Southern Reporter* (So. 2d), and the *South Eastern Reporter* (S.E.2d). There are now three million to four million reported cases in U.S. case law, and the number grows by more than 60,000 cases per year. In recent years, however, unreported cases outnumber reported cases by a wide margin.

REVIEW

Key Terms

Before proceeding, review the key terms listed below to be sure you understand each one. If necessary, read over the corresponding section of the chapter. When you are ready to test your understanding, answer the Review Questions.

adjudication
advance sheets
affirm
appellant
appellee
binding authority
case at bar
case in point
case of first impression
certiorari, writ of
concurring opinion
considered *dicta*
decision
decree
defendant
dicta, dictum
dissenting opinion
docket number
headnotes
holding
in point
judgment
majority opinion
mandatory authority
memorandum opinion
nominative reporters
obiter dicta
official reports
on point
opinion
order
per curiam opinion
persuasive authority
petitioner
plaintiff
plaintiff in error
plurality opinion
ratio decidendi
remand
reporter
reports
respondent
reversal
reverse
slip opinion
star pagination
syllabus
synopsis
unconstitutional
unofficial reports
vacated

Questions for Review and Discussion

1. What can a legislature do in making law that a court cannot do in making precedents?
2. What is the *ratio decidendi* of a case?
3. What is the "holding" of a case?
4. Are headnotes written by the court?
5. How is a plurality opinion different from a majority opinion?
6. How are appellate courts different from trial courts?

7. Name the current National Reporter System reporters that cover the U.S. Supreme Court, the U.S. Courts of Appeal, and the U.S. District Courts.
8. Name the seven regional reporters in the National Reporter System.
9. Name the reporter for the U.S. Supreme Court published by LCP.
10. How many "unreported" opinions are there?

Activities

1. Read through a recent opinion of the U.S. Supreme Court. Notice the Court's concern for detail in stating the facts, its citation of authority in stating the law, and its careful reasoning in reaching a decision.
2. Examine a recent opinion reported in the National Reporter System. Identify the parts of the opinion. Was there a dissenting opinion in the case?
3. Compare and contrast a volume of L. Ed. 2d with a volume of S. Ct. Did you find the cross-reference tables to the *United States Reports?*

CHAPTER 3 Case Finders

OUTLINE

COMMENTARY

After receiving your oral report about the *Lynch v. Donnelly* case and discussing your findings with the mayor, the law director asks you to prepare a memorandum on the subject of public religious displays. The law director wants you to find as many cases as you can and focus the memorandum on the facts of each case. Heading out of the office on the way to court, the law director mentions that "we" have only the state digest in the office, so you'll have to go down to the County Law Library to use federal digests. Before you realize it, the law director is gone. What digests are you going to use?

OBJECTIVES

In this chapter you will begin to learn how lawyers and legal researchers "find a case like yours where the person like you won." This chapter gives an overview of all the methods of finding cases, with an emphasis on searching specialized indexes known as digests. In particular, you will learn about the digest method of West Publishing Company. After reading this chapter, you should be able to:

1. Identify the essential parts of a case citation.
2. Describe how law students find cases when they begin law school.
3. Explain the purpose of a memorandum of law and its use in finding cases.
4. Recognize briefs as potential case finders.

5. Compare and contrast a digest with an index.
6. Explain "digest topics" and "key numbers."
7. Describe the digest method in detail.
8. Identify the units in the American Digest System.
9. Recognize the limitations of digests as case finders.
10. List the major case finders discussed in other chapters of this book.

3–1 Case Finders Generally

As discussed in Chapter 1, courts have power only to decide actual cases. Actual cases occur **chronologically,** in real-time sequence. As noted in Chapter 2, most reporters report cases chronologically as the courts decide them. Yet, as discussed in Chapter 1, the goal of legal research is to find cases like yours, where the person like you won. In other words, the goal of legal research is to find cases on your topic, or **topically.** If the cases are reported chronologically, how do you find them topically? This is the most fundamental problem in legal research. The solution is using a case finder.

There are two types of case finders: indexes and collections. The value of an index is that the publisher has taken the time to systematically record the location of cases by topic to speed up your research. The value of a collection is that the publisher has taken the time to arrange the cases by topic to reduce the amount of your research. The law's unique indexing case finder, the digest, is discussed in this chapter. The law's unique collection case finder, the annotation, will be discussed in Chapter 4.

Citations

As noted in Chapter 2, case reporters are customarily identified by conventional abbreviations. No matter what type of case finder you use, the reference to the location at which a case opinion may be found in a reporter is customarily given by a **citation** (or **cite**). The citation is usually a reference to the first page of the report of an opinion in a reporter, but it may also be a reference to a specific succeeding page of the opinion, known as a **jump cite** or **pinpoint cite.** Since an opinion may be reported in more than one reporter (e.g., in an official reporter and in an unofficial reporter), it may be found in more than one location. An alternate location reference for a case opinion is known as a **parallel citation** (or **parallel cite**).

As will be discussed in Chapter 10, there are a variety of styles for citing cases and other sources, but one convention is universal. Cases are always cited by volume number, reporter abbreviation, and page (or paragraph) number, in that order. For example, instead of referring to "the U.S. Supreme Court opinion in the case of Moore against the City of East Cleveland, decided in 1977, starting on page 494 of Volume 431 of the *United States Reports,* published by the U.S. Government Printing Office," the custom is to cite the case as follows: *Moore v. City of East Cleveland,* 431 U.S. 494 (1977). An example of a jump cite to the portion of the *Moore* opinion on page 497 of Volume 431 of the *United States Reports* would be as follows: *Moore v. City of East Cleveland,* 431 U.S. 494, 497 (1977). As an example of a citation including a parallel cite, instead of referring to "the New York Court of Appeals opinion in the case of Palsgraf against the Long Island Railroad Co., decided in 1928, starting on page 339 of Volume 248 of the *New York Reports,* and also starting on page 99 of Volume 162 of the *North Eastern Reporter,* the custom is to cite the case as follows: *Palsgraf v. Long Island Railroad Co.,* 248 N.Y. 339, 162 N.E. 99 (1928).

Giving conventional legal citations to legal authorities is important because of the distinction between primary authority and secondary authority. Unless you are an official representative of a part of a sovereign acting in that capacity (i.e., a legislator, executive, judge, or administrator), what you say about the law is not the law itself. It's not primary authority. It is, at best, only secondary authority. When you make a bold assertion about the law, a lawyer or legal researcher will want you to give at least one conventional reference to a primary authority, or a respected secondary authority, that also said so, or implied so. Then, if the lawyer or legal researcher has any doubt as to whether you have stated or interpreted the law accurately, he can look up your reference (made according to the style that will be discussed in Chapter 10) and decide for himself. Get in the habit of citing legal authority, especially primary authority, for your legal assertions.

Casebooks

The case finder lawyers first learn about in law school, and the case finder lawyers in practice most frequently forget about, is the law school casebook.

Most U.S. law schools claim to teach the law by the so-called Socratic method first introduced at Harvard Law School by Christopher Columbus Langdell in 1871. Teaching a course in contract law, Langdell provided his students with a book, now known as a **casebook,** containing a series of carefully selected cases on each topic he covered. Langdell had his students read the cases he collected in his book, then, in class, he carefully questioned them in order to teach them to discover for themselves the rules of law that could be found in the cases.

Langdell's teaching method caught on and became the standard in law schools across the nation. The method has been severely criticized at times, and properly so, because if not properly done, if the questioning is not carefully built around the student's knowledge, the students are tortured and not taught. Nevertheless, the method, in some form or another, has remained a part of the law school experience.

Because of the Socratic, or "casebook," method, professors and scholars at leading law schools have, over the years, written hundreds of casebooks for use in law school courses in almost every subject. What better way is there to find a case on your topic than to use the work of a scholar committed to studying the law? The only limit is that a given casebook may not cover your particular topic or the casebook may be more time-consuming to use than other case finders.

For example, three renowned professors of criminal law, Yale Kamisar, Wayne R. LaFave, and Jerold H. Israel, have co-authored *Modern Criminal Procedure: Cases, Comments and Questions,* published as part of the "American Casebook Series" by West Publishing Company (West). It is an excellent source of significant and instructive cases on the topics that have arisen in modern criminal procedure.

The principal publishers of casebooks are West, Foundation Press, and Little, Brown and Company. Casebooks may be purchased from the publisher or from a law school bookstore. Most lawyers keep at least some of their casebooks from

Casebooks

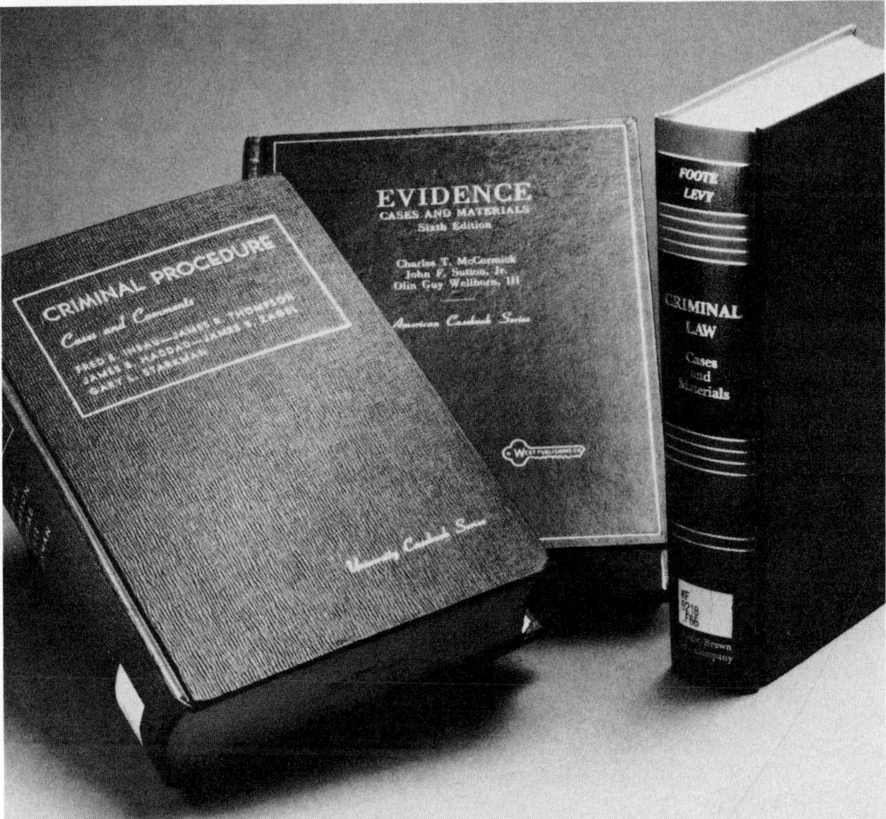

Source: © Doug Martin.

law school. Casebooks may also be found in law libraries according to the Library of Congress Classification system. (See Appendix IV.)

Lawyers

Like a professor or scholar, whose business is it to keep up to date on the law? The answer, of course, is a lawyer. By definition, a **lawyer** is a legal expert. The "average" lawyer has gone to law school, studied for a bar exam, performed legal research, given advice, and handled—through negotiations, hearings, trials, and appeals—a variety of cases. Another obvious and frequently forgotten potential case finder is the "average" lawyer.

Suppose you work in a large law firm and have been given an extensive legal research project. One way to get started is to ask the lawyers in the firm what they know about your topic. There is a good chance that somewhere in their past or in their law practice, at least one of them had a reason to become familiar with your topic. In fact, some lawyers, just to stay current in the law, read advance sheets religiously. Lawyers may, at times, astonish you with what they know "off the tops of their heads." They remember case names, cites, relevant books, their notes from a continuing education seminar, and other similar sources that they can and will refer you to. This information might have taken you hours to discover on your own or you might have missed some of it completely.

In short, lawyers are generally well-trained and experienced legal experts. Use their expertise to help you find your case.

Memorandums

In a well-run law office, the discoveries of the firm's lawyers and legal researchers may already be recorded and relevant to your topic. When a client comes into a law office for advice, it is a common and sensible practice for a lawyer to have the client's legal questions thoroughly researched before any "100%" advice is given.

The usual scenario is for a partner to pose the client's legal question to an associate or paralegal and to have the associate or paralegal research the question in detail. So as to not prejudice the research, the associate or paralegal is not told who in the fact pattern the partner represents.

The associate or paralegal is then directed to prepare a **memorandum of law,** a written discussion of a legal question, objectively reporting the law favoring each side in the fact pattern, as found after researching the topic. The "memo" may also include the researcher's opinion as to who, based on her research, she believes will win if the case goes to court. With a well-written memo in hand, a lawyer can confidently advise the client of the arguments pro and con and the likelihood of the client winning in court.

To avoid duplicating research that has already been done by someone else in the firm, well-run law offices keep a copy of every memorandum ever prepared by lawyers in their offices, indexed by topic. If you work in such a firm, you should check if your topic has already been researched and written up in a memo. If so, all you may have to do is update it.

Briefs

When a case is appealed, appellate courts ordinarily require the lawyers to present their arguments to the court in writing. A formal written argument to a court is known as a **brief.** A brief, as the name suggests, should be brief, because concise arguments are usually more powerful and persuasive than extended arguments. However, because lawyers often deal with complex legal issues and complicated fact patterns, a well-written brief may turn out to be quite lengthy.

Unlike a memorandum, which is objective in nature and intended to be used only within the firm, a brief is public advocacy. In a brief, lawyers argue their client's cause, putting forth the best arguments available for the client: cases like their client's where the person like their client won. Unlike a memorandum, a brief is filed with the court and available to the public. (See Figure 3–1.)

Libraries that serve appellate courts frequently collect the briefs and records filed in the cases before the court. In some states, the briefs and records are microfilmed and available in other libraries as well. If you know a case is relevant to your case, you can often find cases not only by reading the court's opinion, but also by reading the briefs filed by each party's lawyer in the case. You can find cases by using the work of a lawyer doing what a lawyer does best: arguing a client's cause.

3–2 Digests

Soon after West began publishing cases chronologically in the various units of the National Reporter System, its editors realized that lawyers and legal researchers needed a way of finding the cases reported by topic. Their solution was to create a specialized index of the reported cases and the rules of law found therein, known as a **digest.**

Figure 3-1 Excerpts From Two Briefs

Brief #1

IN THE UNITED STATES COURT OF APPEALS
SIXTH CIRCUIT
CINCINNATI, OHIO

JAMES A. TRAFICANT, JR.	)	
	)	
Petitioner/Appellant	)	
	)	CASE NO: 88-1271
-vs-	)	
	)	Tax Court
COMMISSIONER OF INTERNAL REVENUE SERVICE	)	No: 37845-84
	)	
Respondent/Appellee	)	

BRIEF OF PETITIONER/APPELLANT JAMES A. TRAFICANT, JR.

MATTHEW FEKETE
Attorney for Appellant
11 Overhill Road
Youngstown, Ohio 44512

WILLIAM S. ROSE, JR.,
Assistant Attorney General
Tax Division
c/o GARY R. ALLEN, CHIEF
Appellate Section, Tax Division
Department of Justice
P. O. Box 502
Washington, D.C. 20044

Figure 3–1 cont.

The Tax Court's reasoning is flawed. The Tax Court cites Helvering v. Mitchell, 303 U.S. 391 (1938). Helvering, at 303 U.S. 397, explains that ordinarily:

> "The difference in degree of the burden of proof in criminal and civil cases precludes application of the doctrine of res judicata. [In the case at bar, the] acquittal was 'merely . . . an adjudication that the proof was not sufficient to overcome all reasonable doubt of the guilt of the accused. '. . .That acquittal on a criminal charge is not a bar to a civil action by the Government, remedial in its nature, arising out of the same facts on which the criminal proceeding was based has long been settled."

Unfortunately for Petitioner, the Tax Court applied this rule without reason.

The criminal case was, by far, no ordinary case. The Petitioner, a public figure, without legal training, acting pro se, and opposed by the Justice Department of the United States, successfully vindicated himself from charges that he accepted bribes in violation of the Racketeer Influenced and Corrupt Organizations Act, 18 U.S.C. §1961 et seq, and charges that he willfully filed a false tax return in violation of §7206(1) of the Internal Revenue Code.

In an ordinary criminal case the jury receives general instructions on the burden of proof (i.e. the burden is on the prosecution to prove each element of the case beyond a reasonable doubt, and if the prosecution does not, the jury is to find for the defendant, whether or not he may be "innocent"). However, in Petitioner's case, Petitioner, a public figure, sought vindication from the charge that he had received a bribe. Acting pro se the Petitioner asked for and received from a judge a special instruction that the

Figure 3–1 cont.

jury was to determine whether or not there was a bribe, not merely whether there was "proof beyond a reasonable doubt" that there was a bribe. Accordingly, the judge specifically instructed the jury on issue of bribery:

> "Ladies and gentlemen of the jury, Count II of the indictment alleges the defendant knowingly signed and filed a false income tax return. If you find that the defendant did receive the bribes alleged in Count I of the indictment, you must consider whether he failed to report the bribes as income on his 1980 income tax return. Even if you find that there was no conspiracy, and that the defendant is not guilty of the RICO offense, you must consider the offense alleged in Count II of the indictment if you find that he accepted the bribes.
>
> However, if you find that the defendant did not receive the bribes alleged in Count I of the indictment, you shall find the defendant not guilty of Count II." [Emphasis Added; Criminal Transcript at p. 3369, lines 8-22. Quoted in Petitioner's Trial Brief, p. 40].

When the jury acquitted the Petitioner on all counts they did not determine "only that reasonable doubt existed that the accused was guilty of the offenses charged." The jury determined that there were no bribes.

Furthermore, the Tax Court ignored the remainder of the Supreme Court's analysis in Helvering v. Mitchell. On the very next page of the official reporter, at 303 U.S. 398, the Supreme Court declared:

> "Where the objective of the subsequent action is punishment, the acquittal is a bar, because to entertain the second proceeding for punishment would subject the defendant to double jeopardy; and double jeopardy is precluded by the Fifth Amendment whether the verdict was an acquittal or a conviction." [Emphasis Added].

That the objective of the subsequent Tax Court case was punishment is evident from the Tax Court's opinion.

Figure 3–1 cont.

Brief #2

IN THE UNITED STATES COURT OF APPEALS
FOR THE SIXTH CIRCUIT

No. 88-1271

JAMES A. TRAFICANT, JR.,
Petitioner-Appellant

v.

COMMISSIONER OF INTERNAL REVENUE,
Respondent-Appellee

ON APPEAL FROM THE DECISION OF THE
UNITED STATES TAX COURT

BRIEF FOR THE APPELLEE

STATEMENT OF THE ISSUES

1. Whether the Tax Court correctly found that taxpayer failed to report $108,000 on his 1980 income tax return and that the underpayment of tax was due to fraud within the meaning of Section 6653(b) of the Internal Revenue Code.

2. Whether the Tax Court abused its discretion in the following procedural rulings:

A. Refusing to permit taxpayer to act as a pro se co-counsel with his attorney before the Tax Court.

B. Limiting the scope of taxpayer's cross-examination as a result of taxpayer's Fifth Amendment claim.

C. Admitting into evidence the audio tapes of taxpayer's conversation at the Carabbias' home.

D. Declining taxpayer's motions to have the Tax Court judge disqualified.

Figure 3–1 cont.

TABLE OF AUTHORITIES

Figure 3–1 cont.

D. The Tax Court properly declined taxpayer's motions to have the Tax Court judge disqualified

Taxpayer claims (Br. 41-50) that Judge B. John Williams, the Tax Court judge who heard this case, was required to recuse himself from this case pursuant to 28 U.S.C. Section 455,[27] because his statements during a pre-trial hearing and his prior employment by the Government reveal bias in favor of the United States. To prevail on appeal, taxpayer must show that Judge Williams abused his discretion in failing to disqualify himself. Barksdale v. Emerick, 853 F. 2d 1359, 1361 (6th Cir. 1988). Taxpayer fails to demonstrate any abuse of discretion because these allegations of partiality are unsupported by the facts in this case.

It is well-established that a judge whose impartiality might reasonably be questioned must recuse himself from the trial. Barksdale v. Emerick, supra; Roberts v. Bailar, 625 F. 2d 125 (6th Cir. 1980). To be sufficient, a litigant's claims of judicial bias must contain specific facts and reasons; conclusory allegations and speculations are not sufficient. Action Realty Co. v. Will, 427 F. 2d 843 (7th Cir. 1970). The standard applied to those allegations is an objective one, i.e., recusal is necessary if "a reasonable person with knowledge of all the facts would conclude that the judge's impartiality might reasonably be

27 It is not clear whether 28 U.S.C. Section 455 applies to Tax Court judges since they are not defined as "judges of the United States." Compare 28 U.S.C. Section 451 with Section 7443 of the Internal Revenue Code (26 U.S.C.) (judges of the United States Tax Court serve for a fifteen-year term (although they may be reappointed) rather than serve during "good behavior"); cf., Sharon v. Commissioner, 66 T.C. 515, 533-534 (1978), aff'd 591 F. 2d 1273 (9th Cir. 1978), cert. denied, 442 U.S. 941 (1948). But in any event, regardless of the specific applicable statute, taxpayer's claims of prejudice are unsupported by the record.

Because digests are essentially indexes, they are not themselves cited as authority. Because digest paragraphs are summaries, cases found with digests should always be read before they are cited as authority.

How a Digest Is Like an Index

To appreciate what a digest is, you should first understand how an ordinary index is created and how it is used.

Indexes help where the topics within a text are presented in a varied or sequential order, like chronological order. Since it is impractical for researchers to read an entire book just to find one piece of information or to determine that the one piece of information is not in the book, an index allows researchers to go directly to the information desired without reading the whole book, or to quickly determine that the book, or a portion of it, does not contain the information they desire.

To create an ordinary index, the text to be indexed is read by an editor and divided up into key concepts, words, and phrases. As the editor notes all the key concepts, words, and phrases in a word or a few words known as **entries,** indenting subordinate concepts under major ones where appropriate, the editor records their location in the text by the page numbers at which they appear, known as **references.** The major entries, and then the subordinate entries beneath them, are then arranged alphabetically (in the order of the alphabet from A to Z) carrying the page references with the entries. In final editing, references to other entries, known as **cross-references,** are noted, and the index is complete.

To use an ordinary index, the researcher makes an educated guess as to the editor's choice of words for the major entry for the concept, word, or phrase sought in the text, and then, if appropriate, for the subordinate entry. If and when an appropriate entry is found, the researcher notes the page reference. The researcher then turns to the appropriate page and reads or scans the page until the desired concept, word, or phrase is found.

Case law research is analogous to researching a particular concept, word, or phrase in a large book. (See Figure 3–2.) The cases are reported chronologically, but a legal researcher like you wants to find cases only like yours. It is obviously impractical for you to read every case in every reporter every time you want to find a case like yours or to discover that there has been no case like yours. A digest is a specialized index that allows you to go directly to the case like yours without reading every case, or to quickly determine that there has been no case like yours.

West's editors prepare their digests in the process of preparing case opinions for publication in the National Reporter System. Each case opinion received for publication is read by an editor, who notes major portions of the opinion, usually whole sentences and paragraphs, that appear to be legally significant, because they appear to describe the rules of law being laid down or followed as precedent. The editor summarizes these points of law into **headnotes,** notations to be placed ahead of the judges' opinion in the reporter (and generally falling at the top or "head" of a page), and makes similar, if not identical, summaries to be the entries in the digest, referred to as **digests** or **digest paragraphs.** With each digest paragraph, the editor records the location of its source in the reporter by legal citation reference: the volume, reporter, and page.

West's editors do not arrange the headnotes and the digest paragraphs alphabetically. Instead, they are keyed to an outline of the law originally developed by their company in the 1890s. Headnotes, after being keyed to the outline, are numbered sequentially and remain ahead of the opinion in the

Figure 3–2 Finding Tools

	Organization	Entry	Reference
Ordinary Index	A–Z	Word or Phrase	Page Number
Digest	Outline	Paragraph	Citation (Volume–Reporter–Page)

reporter for each case. The paragraph origin in the text of the opinion for each headnote is indicated in the text by the headnote number in brackets (e.g., [5]). The digest paragraphs reflecting the headnotes are classified to the digest according to the outline.

Modified over the years, West's outline has seven main divisions: Persons, Property, Contracts, Torts, Crimes, Remedies, and Government. Each main division is divided into subdivisions, and the subdivisions are divided into **Topics,** which are the central divisions in the outline. There are more than 400 Topics in the outline. (See Figure 3–3.) Each Topic is then separately outlined according to the nature of the Topic, and the lines in the Topic outline are numbered sequentially. (See Figure 3–4.)

The numerical designation of a line in a Topic outline is known as a **Key Number.** Since there are Key Numbers under each Topic, a Key Number has no significance in itself. A Topic with a Key Number has a significance. If you can determine the Topic and Key Number combination or combinations for cases like yours, the "Key Number" will "unlock" the entry to the digest paragraphs summarizing the cases like yours in the digest. (See Figure 3–5.)

Using a digest is analogous to using an ordinary index, but more is involved. Instead of (1) alphabetically searching entries to (2) find a short entry giving you (3) a page reference to (4) turn to and search the text to check if the information you want is there, as you would with an ordinary index, the digest method is (1) conceptually searching an outline of the law to determine the appropriate Topic and Key Number combinations to (2) find a long entry (i.e., a digest paragraph under the appropriate Topic and Key Number combinations in a digest) giving you (3) a citation reference (volume, reporter, and page) to (4) select the right reporter, turn to the right page, and search the text to check if the case is a case like yours.

A Digest Walk-Through

Let's walk through an example, examining the digest method in more detail. (See Figure 3–6.) Suppose you want to find a case that ruled whether or not a cemetery plot was an "interest in land" such that a contract for the transfer of one would have to be in writing.

The first step in the digest method is to determine the appropriate Topic and Key Number combinations to be searched. One obvious approach to doing this is to become thoroughly familiar with West's outline of the law. Set out in Figure 3–3, the outline can be found in the front of any of West's digest volumes and in West's legal research pamphlet *West's Law Finder.* Ideally, you would recognize that a cemetery plot is a type of property, and thus the appropriate

Figure 3–3 West's Outline of the Law

OUTLINE OF THE LAW

Digest Topics arranged for your convenience by Seven Main Divisions of Law
For complete alphabetical list of Digest Topics, see Page XIII

---

1. PERSONS
2. PROPERTY
3. CONTRACTS
4. TORTS
5. CRIMES
6. REMEDIES
7. GOVERNMENT

1. PERSONS

RELATING TO NATURAL PERSONS IN GENERAL

Civil Rights
Dead Bodies
Death
Domicile
Drugs and Narcotics
Food
Health and Environment
Holidays
Intoxicating Liquors
Names
Poisons
Seals
Signatures
Sunday
Time
Weapons

PARTICULAR CLASSES OF NATURAL PERSONS

Absentees
Aliens
Chemical Dependents
Children Out-of-Wedlock
Citizens
Convicts
Indians
Infants
Mental Health
Paupers
Slaves
Spendthrifts

PERSONAL RELATIONS

Adoption
Attorney and Client
Employers' Liability
Executors and Administrators
Guardian and Ward
Husband and Wife
Labor Relations
Marriage
Master and Servant
Parent and Child
Principal and Agent
Workers' Compensation

ASSOCIATED AND ARTIFICIAL PERSONS

Associations
Beneficial Associations
Building and Loan Associations
Clubs
Colleges and Universities
Corporations
Exchanges
Joint-Stock Companies and Business Trusts
Partnership
Religious Societies

PARTICULAR OCCUPATIONS

Accountants
Agriculture
Auctions and Auctioneers
Aviation
Banks and Banking
Bridges

2 West's Fed Pr Dig 3d   VII   1—1

Figure 3–3 cont.

OUTLINE OF THE LAW

1. PERSONS—Cont'd

PARTICULAR OCCUPATIONS —Cont'd

Brokers
Canals
Carriers
Commerce
Consumer Credit
Consumer Protection
Credit Reporting Agencies
Detectives
Electricity
Explosives
Factors
Ferries
Gas
Hawkers and Peddlers
Innkeepers
Insurance
Licenses
Manufactures
Monopolies
Physicians and Surgeons
Pilots
Railroads
Seamen
Shipping
Steam
Telecommunications
Theaters and Shows
Towage
Turnpikes and Toll Roads
Urban Railroads
Warehousemen
Wharves

2. PROPERTY

NATURE, SUBJECTS, AND INCIDENTS OF OWNERSHIP IN GENERAL

Abandoned and Lost Property
Accession
Adjoining Landowners
Confusion of Goods
Improvements
Property

PARTICULAR SUBJECTS AND INCIDENTS OF OWNERSHIP

Animals
Annuities
Automobiles
Boundaries
Cemeteries
Common Lands
Copyrights and Intellectual Property
Crops
Fences
Fish
Fixtures
Franchises
Game
Good Will
Logs and Logging
Mines and Minerals
Navigable Waters
Party Walls
Patents
Public Lands
Trade Regulation
Waters and Water Courses
Woods and Forests

PARTICULAR CLASSES OF ESTATES OR INTERESTS IN PROPERTY

Charities
Condominium
Dower and Curtesy
Easements
Estates in Property
Joint Tenancy
Landlord and Tenant
Life Estates
Perpetuities
Powers
Remainders
Reversions
Tenancy in Common
Trusts

PARTICULAR MODES OF ACQUIRING OR TRANSFERRING PROPERTY

Abstracts of Title
Adverse Possession
Alteration of Instruments
Assignments
Chattel Mortgages
Conversion
Dedication
Deeds
Descent and Distribution
Escheat
Fraudulent Conveyances

VIII 1—2

Figure 3–3 cont.

OUTLINE OF THE LAW

2. PROPERTY—Cont'd

PARTICULAR MODES OF ACQUIRING OR TRANSFERRING PROPERTY—Cont'd

Gifts
Lost Instruments
Mortgages
Pledges
Secured Transactions
Wills

3. CONTRACTS

NATURE, REQUISITES, AND INCIDENTS OF AGREEMENTS IN GENERAL

Contracts
Customs and Usages
Frauds, Statute of
Interest
Usury

PARTICULAR CLASSES OF AGREEMENTS

Bailment
Bills and Notes
Bonds
Breach of Marriage Promise
Champerty and Maintenance
Compromise and Settlement
Covenants
Deposits and Escrows
Exchange of Property
Gaming
Guaranty
Implied and Constructive Contracts
Indemnity
Joint Adventures
Lotteries
Principal and Surety
Rewards
Sales
Subscriptions
Vendor and Purchaser

PARTICULAR CLASSES OF IMPLIED OR CONSTRUCTIVE CONTRACTS OR QUASI CONTRACTS

Account Stated
Contribution

PARTICULAR MODES OF DISCHARGING CONTRACTS

Novation
Payment
Release
Subrogation
Tender

4. TORTS

Assault and Battery
Collision
Conspiracy
False Imprisonment
Forcible Entry and Detainer
Fraud
Libel and Slander
Malicious Prosecution
Negligence
Nuisance
Products Liability
Seduction
Torts
Trespass
Trover and Conversion
Waste

5. CRIMES

Abduction
Abortion and Birth Control
Adulteration
Adultery
Affray
Arson
Bigamy
Blasphemy
Breach of the Peace
Bribery
Burglary
Common Scold
Compounding Offenses
Counterfeiting
Criminal Law
Disorderly Conduct
Disorderly House
Disturbance of Public Assemblage
Dueling
Embezzlement
Embracery
Escape
Extortion and Threats
False Personation

IX 1—3

Figure 3–3 cont.

OUTLINE OF THE LAW

5. CRIMES—Cont'd

False Pretenses
Fires
Forgery
Fornication
Homicide
Incest
Insurrection and Sedition
Kidnapping
Larceny
Lewdness
Malicious Mischief
Mayhem
Miscegenation
Neutrality Laws
Obscenity
Obstructing Justice
Perjury
Piracy
Prize Fighting
Prostitution
Rape
Receiving Stolen Goods
Rescue
Riot
Robbery
Sodomy
Suicide
Treason
Unlawful Assembly
Vagrancy

6. REMEDIES

REMEDIES BY ACT OR AGREEMENT OF PARTIES

Accord and Satisfaction
Arbitration
Submission of Controversy

REMEDIES BY POSSESSION OR NOTICE

Liens
Lis Pendens
Maritime Liens
Mechanics' Liens
Notice
Salvage

MEANS AND METHODS OF PROOF

Acknowledgment
Affidavits
Estoppel
Evidence
Oath
Records
Witnesses

CIVIL ACTIONS IN GENERAL

Action
Declaratory Judgment
Election of Remedies
Limitation of Actions
Parties
Set-Off and Counterclaim
Venue

PARTICULAR PROCEEDINGS IN CIVIL ACTIONS

Abatement and Revival
Appearance
Costs
Damages
Execution
Exemptions
Homestead
Judgment
Jury
Motions
Pleading
Process
Reference
Stipulations
Trial

PARTICULAR REMEDIES INCIDENT TO CIVIL ACTIONS

Arrest
Assistance, Writ of
Attachment
Bail
Deposits in Court
Garnishment
Injunction
Judicial Sales
Ne Exeat
Pretrial Procedure
Receivers
Recognizances
Sequestration
Undertakings

X

1—4

Figure 3–3 cont.

OUTLINE OF THE LAW

6. REMEDIES—Cont'd

PARTICULAR MODES OF REVIEW IN CIVIL ACTIONS

Appeal and Error
Audita Querela
Certiorari
Exceptions, Bill of
New Trial
Review

ACTIONS TO ESTABLISH OWNERSHIP OR RECOVER POSSESSION OF SPECIFIC PROPERTY

Detinue
Ejectment
Entry, Writ of
Interpleader
Possessory Warrant
Quieting Title
Real Actions
Replevin
Trespass to Try Title

FORMS OF ACTIONS FOR DEBTS OR DAMAGES

Account, Action on
Action on the Case
Assumpsit, Action of
Covenant, Action of
Debt, Action of

ACTIONS FOR PARTICULAR FORMS OR SPECIAL RELIEF

Account
Cancellation of Instruments
Debtor and Creditor
Divorce
Partition
Reformation of Instruments
Specific Performance

CIVIL PROCEEDINGS OTHER THAN ACTIONS

Habeas Corpus
Mandamus
Prohibition
Quo Warranto
Scire Facias
Supersedeas

SPECIAL CIVIL JURISDICTIONS AND PROCEDURE THEREIN

Admiralty
Bankruptcy
Equity
Federal Civil Procedure

PROCEEDINGS PECULIAR TO CRIMINAL CASES

Extradition and Detainers
Fines
Forfeitures
Grand Jury
Indictment and Information
Pardon and Parole
Penalties
Searches and Seizures

7. GOVERNMENT

POLITICAL BODIES AND DIVISIONS

Counties
District of Columbia
Municipal Corporations
States
Territories
Towns
United States

SYSTEMS AND SOURCES OF LAW

Administrative Law and Procedure
Common Law
Constitutional Law
International Law
Parliamentary Law
Statutes
Treaties

LEGISLATIVE AND EXECUTIVE POWERS AND FUNCTIONS

Bounties
Census
Customs Duties
Drains
Eminent Domain
Highways
Inspection
Internal Revenue
Levees and Flood Control

XI 1—5

Figure 3–3 cont.

OUTLINE OF THE LAW

7. GOVERNMENT—Cont'd

LEGISLATIVE AND EXECUTIVE POWERS AND FUNCTIONS—Cont'd

Pensions
Post Office
Private Roads
Public Contracts
Public Utilities
Schools
Securities Regulation
Social Security and Public Welfare
Taxation
Weights and Measures
Zoning and Planning

JUDICIAL POWERS AND FUNCTIONS, AND COURTS AND THEIR OFFICERS

Amicus Curiae
Clerks of Courts
Contempt
Court Commissioners
Courts
Federal Courts
Judges
Justices of the Peace
Removal of Cases
Reports
United States Magistrates

CIVIL SERVICE, OFFICERS, AND INSTITUTIONS

Ambassadors and Consuls
Asylums
Attorney General
Coroners
District and Prosecuting Attorneys
Elections
Hospitals
Newspapers
Notaries
Officers and Public Employees
Prisons
Reformatories
Registers of Deeds
Sheriffs and Constables
United States Marshals

MILITARY AND NAVAL SERVICE AND WAR

Armed Services
Military Justice
Militia
War and National Emergency

XII 1—6

Source: West's Federal Practice Digest 3d, vol. 2 (St. Paul, MN: West Publishing Company, 1984), pp. vii–xii. Reprinted permission.

Figure 3–4 Searches & Seizures Topic Outline

SEARCHES AND SEIZURES

SUBJECTS INCLUDED

Examination of persons or places for discovery of property stolen or otherwise unlawfully obtained or held, or of evidence of the commission of an offense

Taking into legal custody such property or proofs, or property forfeited for violation of law

Nature and scope of such remedies in general

Constitutional and statutory provisions relating to such searches and seizures

In what cases and to and against whom and in respect of what property they are allowed

Jurisdiction over and proceedings to obtain searches or seizures

Issuance, requisites and validity of search warrants and warrants for seizure, etc.

Execution of warrants, making searches and seizures, proceedings to enforce seizures, and disposition of property seized

Liabilities for wrongfully procuring or making searches or seizures

SUBJECTS EXCLUDED AND COVERED BY OTHER TOPICS

Arrest, searches incidental to, see ARREST

Evidence wrongfully obtained, see CRIMINAL LAW

Forfeiture for crime, grounds, see FORFEITURES and specific topics involving forfeitures

International law, operation as to seizures, see INTERNATIONAL LAW

Particular subjects, searches and seizures for enforcement of laws relating to, see CUSTOMS DUTIES, DRUGS AND NARCOTICS, GAMING, INTERNAL REVENUE, INTOXICATING LIQUORS, LOTTERIES

For detailed references to other topics, see Descriptive-Word Index

---

Analysis

69 West's Fed.Pr.Dig.2d—1

Figure 3–4 cont.

SEARCHES & SEIZURES

69 F P D 2d—2

⚷3.3. —— Search or seizure without warrant.—Continued.
 (8). Conduct constituting illegal search; curing illegality.
 (9). Determination of right to search without warrant.
3.4. —— Requisites and validity of warrants in general.
3.5. —— Proceedings for issuance of warrants in general.
3.6. —— Factual showing required for issuance.
 (1). Affidavit or complaint in general.
 (2). Probable or reasonable cause.
 (3). Hearsay, beliefs, conclusions and competency.
 (4). Search of buildings, premises or vehicles.
 (5). Search for articles.
3.7. —— Description of places, persons or things in affidavits or warrants.
3.8. —— Execution and return of warrants.
 (1). In general.
 (2). Places, persons or things within scope of warrant.
3.9. —— Contesting, quashing or vacating proceedings.
4. Seizure proceedings against property forfeited.
5. Disposition of property seized.
7. Unreasonable searches and seizures.
 (1). Constitutional rights and violation thereof in general.
 (2). Application of federal Constitution to states or state officers.
 (3). Application of federal Constitution to territorial officers.
 (4). Application of Constitution to acts of private persons.
 (5). Search warrants.
 (6). —— Issuance and validity.
 (7). —— Affidavits and complaints.
 (8). —— Description.
 (9). —— Execution of warrants.
 (10). Persons, places, and possessions protected from searches and seizures without warrant.
 (11). —— Aliens and enemies.
 (12). —— Arrested persons.
 (13). —— Bankrupts.
 (14). —— Convicts.
 (15). —— Corporations, and corporate officers and records.
 (16). —— Disorderly house.
 (17). —— Game.
 (18). —— Income tax returns.
 (19). —— Intoxicating liquors.
 (20). —— Narcotics or poisons.
 (21). —— Railroad equipment.
 (22). —— Safe deposit boxes.
 (23). —— Stenographer's notes of testimony.
 (24). —— Weapons.
 (25). —— Witnesses and persons compelled to produce evidence.
 (26). Persons entitled to raise question of violation of constitutional rights.
 (27). —— Waiver or consent.
 (28). —— Voluntary character of consent.
 (29). Presumptions and burden of proof.
8. Actions for wrongful search or seizure.
9. Review.

For detailed references to other topics, see Descriptive-Word Index

Source: West's Federal Practice Digest 2d, vol. 69 (St. Paul, MN: West Publishing Company, 1978), pp. 1–2. Reprinted with permission.

Figure 3–5 Searches & Seizures Digest Paragraphs

69 F P D 2d—533 **SEARCHES & SEIZURES ⚷7(10)**

For references to other topics, see Descriptive-Word Index

len articles therein were in plain view, and where plaintiff's wife consented to their seizure, search and seizure were not unreasonable, and defendants were not liable for damages. 42 U.S.C.A. § 1983; U.S.C.A.Const. Amend. 4.

Robbins v. Bryant, 349 F.Supp. 94, affirmed 474 F.2d 1342.

⚷7(10). Persons, places, and possessions protected from searches and seizures without warrant.

U.S.Cal. 1976. Sanctity of private dwellings is ordinarily afforded the most stringent Fourth Amendment protection; one's expectation of privacy in automobile and of freedom in its operation is significantly different from traditional expectation of privacy and freedom in one's residence. U.S.C.A.Const. Amend. 4.

U. S. v. Martinez-Fuerte, 96 S.Ct. 3074, 428 U.S. 543, 49 L.Ed.2d 1116, on remand 538 F.2d 858.

Decision of border patrol to locate checkpoint at San Clemente was reasonable in view of needs of law enforcement furthered by such location, high absolute number of apprehensions at such checkpoint, and fact that San Clemente was selected as location where San Diego-to-Los Angeles traffic was lightest, thereby minimizing interference with legitimate traffic. U.S.C.A.Const. Amend. 4.

U. S. v. Martinez-Fuerte, 96 S.Ct. 3074, 428 U.S. 543, 49 L.Ed.2d 1116, on remand 538 F.2d 858.

Principal protection of Fourth Amendment rights at checkpoints lies in appropriate limitations on scope of stop. U.S.C.A.Const. Amend. 4.

U. S. v. Martinez-Fuerte, 96 S.Ct. 3074, 428 U.S. 543, 49 L.Ed.2d 1116, on remand 538 F.2d 858.

U.S.Cal. 1974. Bank's keeping records of its customers pursuant to the Bank Secrecy Act does not constitute a "seizure," and inasmuch as access to the records is to be controlled by legal process, the record-keeping provisions did not give rise to an illegal search and seizure. U.S.C.A.Const. Amend. 4; 12 U.S.C.A. §§ 1730d, 1829b, 1951–1959.

California Bankers Ass'n v. Shultz, 94 S.Ct. 1494, 416 U.S. 21, 39 L.Ed.2d 812.

Regulations of Secretary of Treasury implementing the domestic reporting requirements of the Bank Secrecy Act abridge no Fourth Amendment right of the bank itself inasmuch as bank is a party to the transaction, and requirements for reporting information with respect to abnormally large transactions in currency were not unreasonable. U.S. C.A.Const. Amend. 5; Currency and Foreign Transactions Reporting Act, §§ 206, 222, 31 U.S.C.A. §§ 1055, 1082.

California Bankers Ass'n v. Shultz, 94 S.Ct. 1494, 416 U.S. 21, 39 L.Ed.2d 812.

U.S.Cal. 1967. What a person seeks to preserve as private, even in an area accessible to the public, may be constitutionally protected under Fourth Amendment. U.S.C.A.Const. Amend. 4.

Katz v. U. S., 88 S.Ct. 507, 389 U.S. 347, 19 L.Ed.2d 576.

A person in a telephone booth may rely upon protection of Fourth Amendment, and is entitled to assume that words he utters into mouthpiece will not be broadcast to the world. U.S.C.A.Const. Amend. 4.

Katz v. U. S., 88 S.Ct. 507, 389 U.S. 347, 19 L.Ed.2d 576.

Government's activities in electronically listening to and recording defendant's words spoken into telephone receiver in public telephone booth violated the privacy upon which defendant justifiably relied while using the telephone booth and thus constituted a "search and seizure" within Fourth Amendment, and fact that electronic device employed to achieve that end did not happen to penetrate the wall of the booth could have no constitutional significance. U.S.C.A.Const. Amend. 4.

Katz v. U. S., 88 S.Ct. 507, 389 U.S. 347, 19 L.Ed.2d 576.

Search and seizure, without prior judicial sanction and attendant safeguards, conducted by electronic surveillance by way of an electronic listening and recording device attached to outside of public telephone booth from which defendant had placed calls did not comply with constitutional standards, although, accepting account of government's actions as accurate, magistrate could constitutionally have authorized with appropriate safeguards the very limited search and seizure that government asserted in fact took place and although it was apparent that agents had acted with restraint. U.S.C.A.Const. Amend. 4.

Katz v. U. S., 88 S.Ct. 507, 389 U.S. 347, 19 L.Ed.2d 576.

U.S.Cal. 1967. Except in carefully defined classes of cases, search of private property without proper consent is unreasonable unless it has been authorized by valid search warrant. U.S.C.A.Const. Amend. 4.

Camara v. Municipal Court of City and County of San Francisco, 87 S.Ct. 1727, 387 U.S. 523, 18 L.Ed.2d 930.

Lessee of ground floor of apartment building had constitutional right to insist that city housing inspector obtain warrant to search his premises and could not constitutionally be convicted of violating city housing code by refusing to consent to warrantless inspection. U.S.C.A.Const. Amend. 4.

Camara v. Municipal Court of City and County of San Francisco, 87 S.Ct. 1727, 387 U.S. 523, 18 L.Ed.2d 930.

see United States Code Annotated

Source: West's Federal Practice Digest 2d, vol. 69 (St. Paul, MN: West Publishing Company, 1978), p. 533. Reprinted with permission.

Figure 3–6 The Digest Method

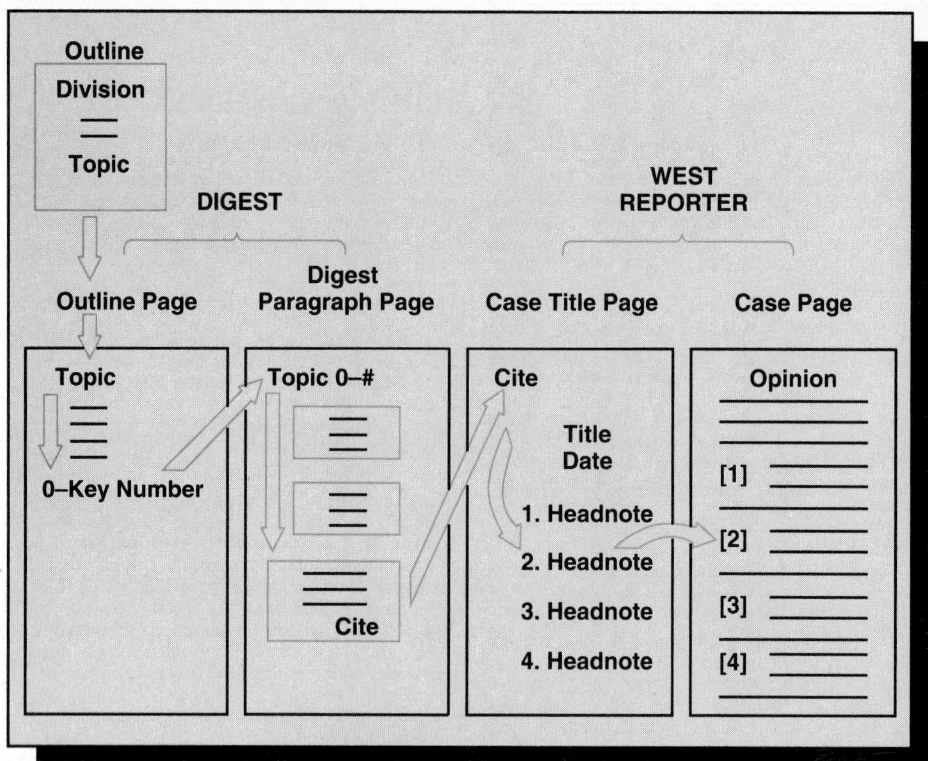

major division of the outline to search is "Property." Under the major division "Property," you would go to the subdivision "Particular Subjects and Incidents of Ownership." Under that subdivision, "Cemeteries" is the relevant Topic.

To view the outline of the Topic, you would find the first few pages of the Topic in the appropriate digest volume in the appropriate digest set, each set being organized alphabetically by topic. You would scan the outline of the Topic—Cemeteries—for a line such as "Cemetery plots as interests in land," and pick up the line's Key Number.

Another approach to finding Topics and Key Numbers is to use West's "Descriptive-Word Index" volumes for the appropriate digest set. (See Figure 3–7.) The index contains a variety of catch words as entries, with references to Topic and Key Number combinations, intended to allow researchers to find the best combination or combinations that will enable them to find cases like theirs.

If you have already found one case like yours, another approach is to use West's tables of cases for the appropriate digest set. These tables list the Topic and Key Number combinations in which digest paragraphs have been made for each case. These Topic and Key Number combinations can also be picked up directly from the headnotes in the report of the case like yours in the National Reporter System. This leads to yet another approach, which is, generally, to get suggested Topic and Key Number combination cross-references from other West publications.

West publishes an array of books, discussed generally in West's legal research pamphlet *West's Law Finder*, and most are tied together by Topic and Key Number references.

West publishes the National Reporter System, discussed in Chapter 2. The federal and specialized courts are covered by specialized reporters, and the

Figure 3–7 Descriptive-Word Index

89 F P D 2d—263 **ELECTRONIC**

References are to Digest Topics and Key Numbers

ELECTRONIC EAVESDROPPING—Cont'd
TAPE recorded telephone conversations—
Admissibility. Crim Law 394.3
Consent—
Induction coil, placing on extension. Crim Law 394.3
Voluntariness, government's special employee giving. Crim Law 680(1)
Interrogation without counsel. Crim Law 412.2(1)
Order of proof, voluntariness of consent. Crim Law 680(1)
Self-incrimination, compelling. Crim Law 393(1)
TAPE recordings—
Copies, admissibility. Crim Law 398(2)
Foreign language, playing to jury, interpreter translating. Crim Law 663
Government agent's telephone conversation with defendant, admissibility with agent's consent. Crim Law 394.3
Long distance telephone calls, placing without charge, investigating device for circumventing toll equipment. Crim Law 394.5(2)
Taking without taxpayer's knowledge, interviews with treasury agents. Crim Law 438
Transcripts for jury—
Convenience. Crim Law 663
Purpose, identification of speakers during deliberation. Crim Law 673(2)
TAX evasion case, transcripts containing attorney-client conversation, grand jury presentation warranting new trial. Crim Law 1189
TAX evasion prosecution, monitored conversations used in evidence. Crim Law 394.5(1)
TECHNICAL trespass—
Violating federal eavesdropping rule. Tel 491
TELEPHONE booth. Const Law 266
Conversation, violating privacy. Searches 7(10)
TELEPHONE company, monitoring own employees. Tel 495
TELEPHONE conversations—
Magnetic pickup device, sender's consent to use. Tel 495
Mother and daughter, separated husband recording. Tel 498
Party's consent, admissibility. Crim Law 394.3
TELEPHONE service—
Installation request not consent. Tel 495
TRANSMITTER planted on body of undercover agent, conversation between defendant and undercover agent—
Crim Law 394.3
Searches 7(10)
UNDERCOVER agent's conversation with illegal whiskey seller, admissibility. Crim Law 394.3
UNITED States courts—
State laws prohibiting, affect. Crim Law 394
UNREASONABLE search or seizure. Searches 7(1)
VENTILATING shaft by sheriff. Searches 7(1)

ELECTRONIC EAVESDROPPING DEVICES
LIBEL, article caption that divorce litigant got assistant of spouse's employee to sell out. Libel 50½

ELECTRONIC EQUIPMENT
PRINTED circuits, patents. Pat 323
RAIL shipments—
Character and value of goods, shipper's statement. Carr 110

ELECTRONIC FUNDS TRANSFER SYSTEMS
SAVINGS and loan association accounts, access of holders, status of systems as branch. B & L Assoc 24

ELECTRONIC LOCATION DEVICES
AIRCRAFT, attachment of device. Searches 1

ELECTRONIC MONITORING
HARMLESS error in admitting conversations overheard by. Crim Law 1169(1)

ELECTRONIC RECORDING DEVICES
DISCOVERY, make, model, and serial numbers. Crim Law 627.6(3)

ELECTRONIC SCANNED POSITIVES
SECONDARY boycott to persuade supplier to substitute photo-engraving method in printing industry, evidence. Labor 578

ELECTRONIC SURVEILLANCE
ACTING assistant attorney general, authorization of application before senate confirmation. Tel 496
AFFIDAVIT—
Wiretap denial, effectiveness as denial of illegal use of pen register. Gr Jury 36
AGGRIEVED person's right to suppress content of wire or oral communication illegally intercepted. Crim Law 394.5(2)
ASSERTION of possible illegal surveillance, sufficiency to require government to reply. Tel 496
ASSISTANT attorney general designated ad hoc to authorize application, wiretap evidence suppressed—
Crim Law 394.3
Tel 496
ATTORNEY general, good faith, omnibus crime control. Tel 498
ATTORNEY General authorizing in interest of national security. Searches 7(1)
BAD faith, application not identifying person other than suspect—
Crim Law 394.3
Tel 496
BEEPERS, placement on vehicle. Searches 7(10)
BERGER decision, applicability to cases pending when Mapp case was decided. Courts 100(1)
BUSINESS premises, forcible entry to install wiretap—
Searches 7(10)
Tel 496
COMPELLING disclosure to defendants of records of. Crim Law 627.8(1)
CONTEMPT, grand jury witness, representation not discussed over tapped line—
Crim Law 641.12(1)
Gr Jury 36
CONTINUOUS listening for thirty days, validity of statute authorizing—
Searches 7(1)
Tel 492
CONTRABAND, monitor installed after lawful seizure. Searches 7(10)
CONVERSATIONS overheard as inadmissible against owner of premises whether present or not. Crim Law 394.3
CONVERSATIONS recorded illegally, examining government logs to determine relevancy. Crim Law 627.7(4), 627.8(4)
COURT not to assume that statute prohibiting would be disregarded. Crim Law 322
COURT order, person authorizing application, government not truthfully identifying—
Crim Law 394.3
Tel 496
DEFENSE counsel's conversation, bail pending appeal from civil contempt commitment. Contempt 56
DEPOSITIONS, F.B.I. agent supervising surveillance. Fed Civ Proc 1415
DISCLOSURE motion, search of files and affidavit denying request for surveillance. Crim Law 627.8(1)

Source: West's Federal Practice Digest 2d, vol. 89 (St. Paul, MN: West Publishing Company, 1978), p. 263. Reprinted with permission.

state courts are covered by regional reporters. Headnotes with Topic and Key Number take you back and forth between court opinions and West's digests.

As discussed in this chapter, West's American Digest System, and other West digests, index the reporters. Searches of reporters and digests, including Topics and Key Numbers, can be made electronically on West's computer-assisted legal research system, WESTLAW, to be discussed in Chapter 12.

West's annotated federal code, *United States Code Annotated* (U.S.C.A.), to be discussed in Chapter 5, and West's national encyclopedia, *Corpus Juris Secundum* (C.J.S.), to be discussed in Chapter 8, each contain Topic and Key Number research references.

West also publishes *Black's Law Dictionary*, to be discussed in Chapter 8, and a wide variety of form books and textbooks to be discussed in Chapter 9. The most recent editions of West's one-volume treatises for students, known as hornbooks, include digest references.

After determining the appropriate Topic and Key Number combinations to search, the next step in the digest method is to search the appropriate digest sets under the appropriate Topic and Key Number combinations. Under each Topic and Key Number, you will find all the digest paragraphs classified to that Topic and Key Number combination from all the cases. Under some Topic and Key Number combinations, there are only a few of these fine-print summaries, which you can quickly read and review. Under other Topic and Key Number combinations, however, there may be hundreds of these fine-print summaries, which may take you hours to read and review.

If you find a summary that appears to indicate a case like yours, the next step in the digest method is to use the citation (volume-reporter-page) to find the case in the National Reporter System.

The next step is to select the appropriate reporter, turn to the appropriate page, and search the text to check if the case is a case like yours. Sometimes this can be quickly done by finding the headnotes with your Topic and Key Number combinations and using the bracketed headnote numbers in the text to locate the part of the opinion discussing your topic. Because digest paragraphs are summaries, however, you may find upon reading the case you have been referred to that it is not really a case like yours.

In going through these steps, a legal researcher must also be aware that most digests are supplemented by cumulative annual pocket parts.

West's American Digest System

West Publishing Company began preparing digests in 1890. The digest sets indexing the case opinions in all the various units of the National Reporter System are known as the American Digest System.

In the same way that West reported federal cases before the National Reporter System started, in a special reporter, *Federal Cases*, West digested the cases before it made its Topic and Key Number outline of the law in a special digest. This special digest, the *Century Digest*, covers the years 1658–1896.

Since 1897, West has published a series of digests according to its Topic and Key Number outline of the law. Each major digest covers a 10-year period and is known as a decennial digest. Because of the tremendous growth in case law in the past few decades, West has started, with the Ninth Decennial, to issue the "decennials" in five-year parts. Until the next decennial part is published, the most recent coverage is collected in a series known as the General Digest. Thus, the American Digest System, which currently contains over 400 volumes, includes the following sets:

1658–1896 Century Digest	1946–1956 Sixth Decennial
1897–1906 First Decennial	1956–1966 Seventh Decennial
1907–1916 Second Decennial	1966–1976 Eighth Decennial
1916–1926 Third Decennial	1976–1981 Ninth Decennial, Part 1
1926–1936 Fourth Decennial	1981–1986 Ninth Decennial, Part 2
1936–1946 Fifth Decennial	1986–1991 General Digest (7th Series)

Thus, to thoroughly search a topic from the present back to 1658, it is necessary to search in each of 11 sets under the appropriate Topic and Key Number combination, and, because it used a different numbering system, in the Century Digest under the appropriate number found in the cross-reference *Table of Key Numbers Section for Century Digest* found in West's First and Second Decennials.

Other Digests

Because of the massive size of the American Digest System, many legal researchers ignore the entire system and use West's special digests, digests published by Lawyers Cooperative Publishing (LCP), and other publications.

West publishes the information contained in the American Digest System in special digests. Except for the states of Delaware, Nevada, and Utah, West publishes a digest for every state. The state digests are much more focused, and so they are easier to use than the decennials. To search for case law in a given state, including decisions in federal cases from that state, search the state's digest under the appropriate Topic and Key Number combinations.

West also publishes regional digests covering some of the regional reporters in the National Reporter System. The digest paragraphs are arranged alphabetically by the states in the region. The regional digests currently published include the *Atlantic Digest, Second Series,* the *North Western Digest, Second Series,* the *Pacific Digest, Third Series,* and the *South Eastern Digest, Second Series.*

For federal cases, West currently publishes *West's Federal Practice Digest, 4th,* covering cases since December 1975. Under each Topic and Key Number combination, the digest paragraphs are arranged chronologically by court level for the Supreme Court and the Courts of Appeals, then alphabetically through the District Courts. In addition, under the Topic "Patents," Key Number 328, there is a numerical list of all patents adjudicated since December 1975, and under the Topic "Trade Regulations," Key Number 736, there is an alphabetical list of the trademarks and trade names adjudicated since December 1975.

West's Federal Practice Digest, 4th, completely replaces *West's Federal Practice Digest, 3d,* which covered cases from December 1975 into 1983. Federal cases before December 1975 are digested in the following sets:

1961–Nov. 1975	West's Federal Practice Digest, 2d
1939–1960	Modern Federal Practice
1789–1938	Federal Digest

As might be expected, West publishes a digest covering only the opinions of the U.S. Supreme Court, the *U.S. Supreme Court Digest.*

LCP also publishes a U.S. Supreme Court digest, the *Digest of United States Supreme Court Reports,* more commonly known by the title on the spine: *U.S. Supreme Court Digest, Lawyers' Edition.* Of course, LCP cannot use West's Topic and Key Number system. LCP's editors create unique headnotes for the opinions in L. Ed and L. Ed. 2d and classify them to their L. Ed Digest according to nearly 400 digest Titles of their own, similar to the titles in LCP's national

West's Federal Practice Digest, 4th

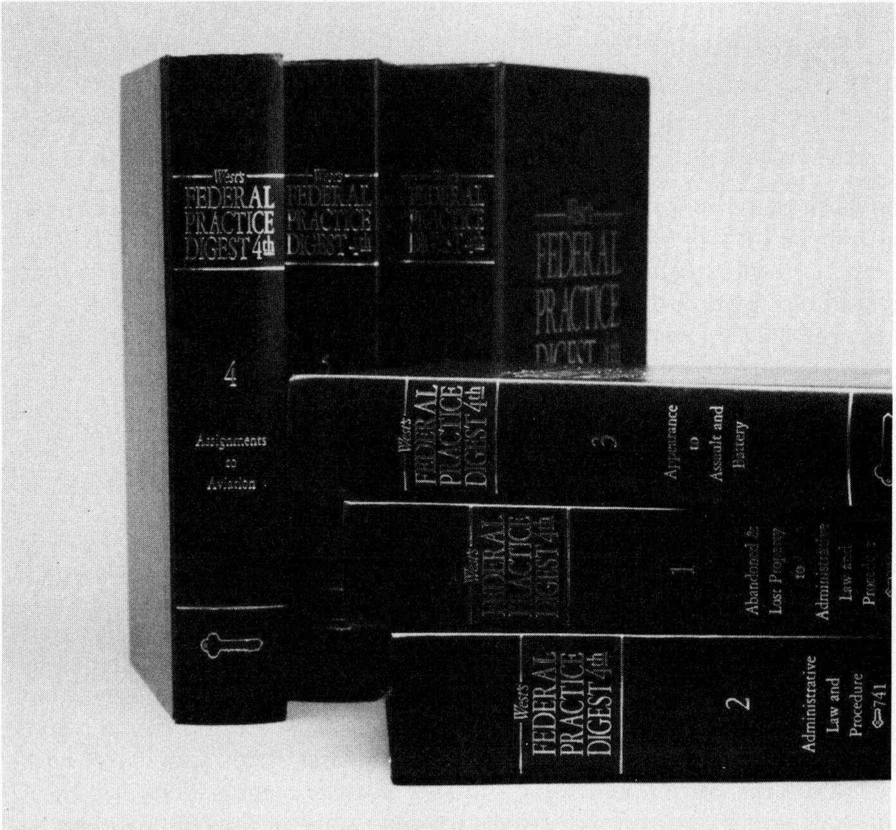

Source: © Doug Martin.

encyclopedia, *American Jurisprudence, Second Series.* (See Chapter 8.) Each digest Title is outlined according to the nature of the title, and each line is given a Section Number. (See Figure 3–8.)

The L. Ed. Digest also includes an extensive table of cases in several volumes, an index to L. Ed., L. Ed. 2d, and other annotations, and references to other parts of LCP's Total Client Service Library. (See Chapter 4.) LCP also publishes digests to cases and annotations in its various annotation series. (See Chapter 4.)

West also publishes digests for some of its specialized reporters, including *West's Bankruptcy Digest* and *West's Education Law Digest* along with the *Military Justice Digest* and the *U.S. Claims Court Digest.*

The Limitations of Digests

Digests have a number of limitations as case finders. In theory, you find the single West Topic and Key Number combination (or L. Ed. Title and Section Number combination), turn to the appropriate digest volume, and find all the cases like yours neatly summarized. In practice, there can be difficulties every step of the way.

It is not always a simple matter to find the appropriate Topic and Key Number (or Title and Section Number) combination. In the West digest search example used above, concerning cases that ruled whether or not a cemetery plot is an "interest in land" such that a contract for the transfer of one would have to be in writing, a researcher might just as logically try to search under the major

Figure 3–8 *U.S. Supreme Court Digest, Lawyers' Edition*

ACCORD AND SATISFACTION

Scope of Topic: This topic covers the general nature, requisites, and effect of agreements for the discharge of contracts, or settling a cause of action arising either from tort or contract, by substituting something else for such contract or cause of action.

Treated elsewhere are the compromise or settlement of disputed claims (see COMPROMISE AND SETTLEMENT); contracts whereby an old obligation is extinguished and a new one, between the same or different parties, substituted in its place (see NOVATION); and the relinquishment of rights or claims (see RELEASE). For matters as to procedure and proof, see such topics as APPEAL; EVIDENCE; PLEADING; etc.

[For fact-word approach see Word Index to this Digest]

§ 1 Generally.
§ 2 By part payment generally.
§ 3 —necessity and sufficiency of consideration.
§ 4 Unexecuted agreement.
§ 5 Effect of protest.

§ 1 Generally.

Research References

1 Am Jur 2d, Accord and Satisfaction §§ 1–4

ALR Digests: Accord and Satisfaction, § 1

Auto-Cite®—any case citation herein can be checked for form, parallel references, later history and annotation references through the Auto-Cite computer research system.

Where there is no unfairness, and all the facts are equally known to both sides, an adjustment by them is final and conclusive. Hager v Thompson, 1 Black 80,
17 L Ed 41

Courts will uphold adjustments of parties made in good faith and understanding. Brown v Spofford, 95 US 474,
24 L Ed 508

An accord and satisfaction requires the voluntary consent of the creditor. Wilmot v Mudge, 103 US 217,
26 L Ed 536

The common-law rule that actual payment of a debt of record cannot be pleaded in bar of an action to recover the debt has been changed by statute in both England and the United States and now an accord and satisfaction has the same effect. Bofinger v Tuyes, 120 US 198, 7 S Ct 529,
30 L Ed 649

A receipt in full, unless given in ignorance of its purport, or in circumstances constituting duress, is an acquittance in bar of any further demand. De Arnaud v United States, 151 US 483, 14 S Ct 374,
38 L Ed 244

An agreement that payment in United States currency should extinguish a larger amount due under a street-lighting contract estimated in Puerto Rican currency is binding where there was a bona fide dispute between the parties as to the medium of payment, the municipality insisting that it was Puerto Rican money, and the lighting company that it was current foreign money. San Juan v St. John's Gas Co. 195 US 510, 25 S Ct 108,
49 L Ed 299

§ 2 By part payment generally.

Research References

1 Am Jur 2d, Accord and Satisfaction §§ 6, 26, 33, 35

ALR Digests: Accord and Satisfaction, § 2

Cross References

Satisfaction of claim against government, see CLAIMS § 52.

Payment of a sum agreed upon in compromise of a decree appealed from constitutes an accord and satisfaction. Bofinger v Tuyes, 120 US 198, 7 S Ct 529,
30 L Ed 649

If there is a bona fide dispute as to the amount due from one person to another, or the amount is uncertain or unliquidated, a compromise and payment of a certain agreed sum as a satisfaction of the entire claim is

39

Source: U.S. Supreme Court Digest, Lawyers' Edition, vol. 1 (Rochester, NY: Lawyers Cooperative Publishing Co., 1984), p. 39. Reprinted with permission.

division "Contracts" instead of "Property," then under "Nature, Requisites, and Incidents of Agreements in General," and under the Topic "Frauds, Statute of," with a completely different Key Number. You may find that the cases like yours can be found under several different Topic and Key Number (or Title and Section Number) combinations.

In fact, as West Publishing Company founder John B. West discovered, his own editors sometimes disagreed about the "correct" classification of a case. Writing in the *Law Library Journal* West noted:

> The digester bound to a fixed classification soon finds himself sorely pressed to make certain cases "fit the classification." I remember three excellent digesters who spent an entire day in disagreeing as to whether seal fishery cases should be classified under the topic "Fish" or that of "Game" in the Digest Scheme. It is the old story of the camel's head in the tent. What seems at first a plausible pretext for forcing some novel case or new principle into a topic or subdivision to which it does not naturally belong, leads to hopeless confusion [West, *Multiplicity of Reports,* 2 LAW LIBR. J. 4 (1909)].

To keep up with changes in technology and the law, West has occasionally changed Topics and Key Numbers, including going to subdivided Key Numbers (e.g., a Key Number such as "37.15[2]"). This change can cause confusion, since a researcher going back in time must also trace the changes in the Topics and Key Numbers.

Again, once a legal researcher gets to a digest under a particular Topic and Key Number (or Title and Section Number), there may be hundreds of digest paragraphs to search. As to West's digests, the WESTLAW computer-assisted legal research system allows this search to be done electronically (see Chapter 12), but even electronic digest searches can be imperfect.

Finally, digest paragraphs, like headnotes, have been frequently called into question. An editor, in the rush to prepare headnotes for a reporter and digest paragraphs for a digest, may unavoidably miss significant points of law in the opinion, or misstate points, where the cases are read chronologically rather than topically. Moreover, headnotes and digest paragraphs, like the entries in an ordinary index, can be very superficial and give very little information or guidance.

Attorney Jesse Franklin Brumbaugh, as far back as his 1917 book *Legal Reasoning and Briefing* (Indianapolis: Bobbs-Merrill, 1917), noted these and other deficiencies in digests. He wrote:

> First the topical divisions may be so poorly chosen that the subject-matter is either not all covered, or there may result the most confusing overlapping. In such instances, unless the decisions are repeated, there may be all the way from one to a dozen places where good fishing may be had for the point desired. Furthermore, another blight of a peculiarly insidious type may follow from a careless classification of materials under the topics chosen. Presuming that excellent divisions into topics have been made, the entire field covered and the topics being mutually exclusive, still it does not follow that the material of the law will have been properly pigeonholed under the best topic. This will direct the searcher to cases that, while they may contain the point desired, were not decided upon this point and discuss it as merely incidental thereto, if not merely as dicta. The effect is to lead to false practice, the quoting of precedents not four-square to the proposition. It leads the hurried practitioner to use dictum for "The Law," and is all the more dangerous because so insidious an evil [p. 237].

Brumbaugh concluded that the worst feature of a digest is that it "involves such a tremendous waste of time on the part of the searcher in overcoming these logical discrepancies [p. 237]." He advised: "That set of books which supplies the lawyer with the case or cases which he desires in the simplest, quickest and most reliable manner is, other things being equal, the most valuable to him."

3–3 Other Case Finders

It is important to understand that there are many other case finders that are not discussed in detail in this chapter. The more you do legal research, the more you will come to realize that case citations are included in virtually every law book, and thus, *virtually every law book is a potential case finder.* Once you have a case cite, you have overcome the fundamental problem that cases are reported chronologically, but you want to find cases topically. The following sections briefly discuss other principal case finders and list the chapters in this book in which they are discussed in more detail.

A.L.R. Annotations

Partially in response to West's digest system, LCP developed a specialized series of collection case finders known as annotations. *American Law Reports* (A.L.R.) annotations will be discussed in Chapter 4.

Computer-Assisted Legal Research

Case reporters, case finders, and many other legal sources have been put on computer. Through word searching texts by computer, legal researchers can, in effect, make their own indexes of the source being searched. The two major computer-assisted legal research (CALR) systems, LEXIS and WESTLAW, will be discussed in Chapter 12.

Shepard's Citations

Shepard's Citations, a hybrid of case indexing and case collecting through tables of case cites, were developed to allow attorneys to check the status of cases as precedent, but they can also be used as imperfect case finders. *Shepard's Citations* will be discussed in Chapter 11.

Secondary Authority

Secondary authority includes everything that is not primary authority. Again, since case citations are included in virtually every law book, virtually every law book is a potential case finder. The principal secondary sources not otherwise discussed in this book will be discussed in Chapters 8 and 9.

SUMMARY

3–1

The fundamental problem in legal research is that cases are reported chronologically, but a legal researcher wants to find cases topically. The solution is to use a case finder; either an index or a collection. A case is customarily cited by its location in a reporter: volume-reporter-page. There are some obvious case finders that should not be ignored. Because of the Socratic, or "casebook," method, professors and scholars at leading law schools have, over the years, written hundreds of casebooks in almost every subject. Lawyers may astonish you with what they know "off the tops of their heads." In a well-run law firm, a memorandum of law, an in-house written discussion of a legal question, may already have been prepared. In the courthouse, you may find briefs, the formal written arguments filed with the court, in cases like yours.

3–2

West Publishing Company's solution to the fundamental legal research problem was to create a specialized index of the reported cases known as a digest. A digest allows you to go directly to the case like yours without reading every case or to quickly determine that there has been no case like yours. West prepares its digests in the process of preparing case opinions for publication in the National Reporter System. If you can determine the Topic and Key Number combination or combinations for cases like yours, the "Key Number" will "unlock" the entry to the digest paragraphs summarizing the cases like yours in the digest. West's digest sets indexing the case opinions in the various units of the National Reporter System are known as the American Digest System. Because of the massive size of the American Digest System, many legal researchers ignore the entire system and use special digests. West publishes a digest for almost every state, some regional digests, and federal digests, including the *U.S. Supreme Court Digest*. LCP publishes the *U.S. Supreme Court Digest, Lawyers' Edition*. Digests have a number of limitations as case finders, stemming from the difficulties inherent in classifying the law.

3–3

The more you do legal research, the more you will come to realize that case citations are included in virtually every law book. Thus, virtually every law book is a potential case finder. Besides casebooks, lawyers, memorandums, briefs, and digests, other case finders include annotations, computer-assisted legal research, *Shepard's Citations*, and other secondary sources.

REVIEW

Key Terms

Before proceeding, review the key terms listed below to be sure you understand each one. If necessary, read over the corresponding section of the chapter. When you are ready to test your understanding, answer the Review Questions.

brief
casebook
chronologically
citation
cite
cross-references
digest
digest paragraphs
digests
entries
headnotes
jump cite
Key Number
lawyer
memorandum of law

parallel citation
parallel cite
pinpoint cite
references
topically
Topics

Questions for Review and Discussion

1. What are the essential parts of a case citation?
2. What is a casebook?
3. Why is a memorandum of law prepared?
4. Why is a brief prepared?
5. How is a digest like an ordinary index?
6. Does a Key Number mean anything by itself?
7. What are the steps in the digest method?
8. Are state digests part of the American Digest System?
9. What are the limitations of digests as case finders?
10. What is true about almost every law book?

Activities

1. Go to a library that contains the entire American Digest System and examine some of its over 400 volumes. The entire set takes up many shelves or perhaps a whole wall. Realize that this is just the *index* to more than three million reported cases. Ponder just how much law is hidden, indeed, buried, in the cases.
2. Take some time to study West's outline of the law. Do you understand the divisions? Are they mutually exclusive? In particular, note the Topics. There's a good chance that you don't even know what some of the terms mean. Look them up in a law dictionary. (See Chapter 8.)
3. Examine LCP's digest Titles in the L. Ed. Digest. Compare them with West's Topics. As you perform legal research, as you learn more about the law, these Titles and Topics will become more familiar to you.

CHAPTER 4 Annotations

OUTLINE

COMMENTARY

You find the county library and are greeted at the door by the librarian. You introduce yourself and your position with the City Law Department and ask where the federal digests are located. The librarian says they are shelved on the left wall across from the A.L.R. You think: "A.L.R.?" Thinking you're puzzled about the location of the digests, the librarian says, "Let me show you." The librarian takes you to the digests, you say, "Thank you," the librarian leaves, but all the time you're wondering, can I find cases on public religious displays in A.L.R.?

OBJECTIVES

In this chapter you will learn about a system for finding cases based on searching collections of cases, known as annotations. Emphasis is placed on the *American Law Reports* (A.L.R.) system published by Lawyers Cooperative Publishing (LCP). After reading this chapter, you should be able to:

1. Recognize the purpose and use of annotations.
2. Compare and contrast annotations and digests.

3. Identify and use the various annotation series.
4. Judge the quality of the various annotation series.
5. Identify and use the various parts of an A.L.R. annotation.
6. Find A.L.R. annotations using the digest method.
7. Find A.L.R. annotations using the index method.
8. Find A.L.R. annotations using miscellaneous methods.
9. Identify and use A.L.R. supplementation.
10. Understand the limitations of A.L.R. in legal research.

4–1 Annotations Generally

Unlike a digest, which is a method of finding cases in a specialized index of the law, an **annotation** is a method of finding cases in a specialized collection of the law.

The word ***annotate*** means to note. A common scholarship technique is to annotate—to note, or to mark up—a book or text. When a passage makes an important point, needs explanation, or deserves comment, a scholar often records related points, explanations, and comments right in the margin. Having all the related points, explanations, and comments collected in one spot, it is easy to study the subject in detail. A scholar can easily find what he or she wants to know about a particular point using these notes.

Annotation, in its ordinary sense, is especially useful in the law. Legal researchers are usually seeking to find all the cases, explanations, and comments available on a particular point of law. If someone has already read, analyzed, and synthesized the relevant law, and put it into note form for you, your research is virtually complete. All you have to do is read the notes.

Where Annotations Came From

To understand the nature of annotations, it's important to understand their origin. The annotation method of finding cases developed from a complex blend of scholarship, fate, and experience.

In 1856, bookseller Hubert Howe Bancroft started his own publishing house in San Francisco, California. Bancroft's, selling books of all kinds, soon became the largest publishing house west of the Mississippi. In 1871, recognizing the need of western lawyers for access to case reports, and the difficulty of having reporter sets shipped from the East Coast, Bancroft published a *selective* reporter, *American Reports,* in 60 volumes. Bancroft's editors selected cases of general value and authority from all the states, decided from 1868 to 1887, and published them with brief notes discussing other similar cases.

American Reports was a hit. In 1878, in response to customer requests, Bancroft began to publish another set, *American Decisions,* to selectively report cases from 1760 to 1868, with brief notes. The set was completed in 1888 with publication of the 100th volume. The two sets, *American Decisions* and *American Reports,* covering U.S. case law from 1760 to 1887, began the Annotated Reports System.

In 1886, Bancroft merged with another San Francisco law book publisher, Summer Whitney, to form the Bancroft-Whitney Company (BW). In 1888, BW started a third selective reporter, *American State Reports,* containing more extensive annotations. The 140-volume set, completed in 1911, along with *American Decisions* and *American Reports,* formed the Trinity Series.

Meanwhile, back on the East Coast, in Northport, New York, the Edward Thomson Company (ET), organized in 1887, also recognized the inherent value of a selective reporter with extensive annotations, and in 1906, began publishing a 53-volume set, completed in 1918, entitled *American and English Annotated Cases.*

Upstate, in Rochester, New York, the Lawyers Co-operative Publishing Company (LCP), was also publishing a selective annotated reporter, *Lawyers' Reports Annotated* (L.R.A.). Started in 1888, and completed in three parts (First Series, 70 volumes, covering 1888–1905; New Series, 52 volumes, covering 1905–1914; and Third Unit, 24 volumes, covering 1914–1918), L.R.A. featured **exhaustive annotations** of selected cases, collecting every case on the point annotated.

L.R.A. started as a secondary publication. LCP's principal case-finding publication was to be a special digest designed to compete with West's American Digest System.

The editors at LCP recognized an inherent weakness in West's American Digest System: the reality of change and conflict. To get the West reporters out in a timely fashion, the West editors had to prepare headnotes for a case and classify them to the digests long before the true significance of the case, if any, was known. On one hand, the case might be reversed, discredited, or overruled by statute, or, on the other hand, the case might become a leading or landmark case or become significant in an area of law other than that to which it was originally classified. No matter how skilled the West headnote editor was, he was limited insofar as he read cases chronologically, rather than topically. To make a better digest, LCP editors were assigned to read West's reported cases by topic, rather than chronologically, in order to prepare and collect more accurate and meaningful digest paragraphs.

In 1888, LCP began publishing its digest, the *General Digest.* In 1892, West countered by filing a copyright infringement suit, claiming that Volume VII of the *General Digest* was pirated from West's headnotes and digests. In 1897, a federal appeals court, ruling that there was sufficient evidence that some LCP editors had systematically borrowed from the West's headnotes in preparing the *General Digest,* enjoined its publication, in part. [*West Publishing Co. v. Lawyers Co-operative Publishing Co.,* 79 F. 756 (2d Cir. 1897)].

To avoid copyright infringement claims, LCP published the *"New Series," General Digest, American and English, Annotated,* in 22 volumes, from 1897 to 1907. As noted in the preface to Volume 3, the digest was **"annotated"** with "careful editorial compilation of the authorities on important points raised by the decisions."

After its 1897 court victory, however, West scored a major psychological victory by publishing in its advance sheets sweeping headlines stating: "GENERAL DIGEST PIRATICAL." [*Lawyers Co-operative Publishing Co. v. West Publishing Co.,* 52 N.Y.S. 1120 (App. Div. 1898)]. After a bitter advertising campaign, LCP withdrew the *General Digest,* because a more profitable opportunity had come along.

LCP rediscovered L.R.A. By 1906, L.R.A. had become LCP's leading publication, and its *"New Series"* was launched. L.R.A. became LCP's special case finder prepared by reading cases topically.

On April 18, 1906, BW was struck by the San Francisco earthquake and fire. BW's factory and books of account were destroyed. Although, remarkably, most of BW's lawyer-customers paid their debts despite the fact that BW's proof had been destroyed, BW struggled to get back on its feet. In a gesture of friendship, LCP sent BW $5,000 in gold. As a result of LCP's moral and financial support, in 1909, LCP was able to negotiate an option to purchase 51% of BW's stock after 10 years.

Two joint ventures then paved the way for a unification of all the annotated reporters in the country.

In 1912, BW entered into a joint venture with ET to merge *American State Reports* into *American and English Annotated Cases.* From 1912 to 1918, they co-published 32 volumes of a new and improved set, *American Annotated Cases,* with extensive annotations.

In 1919, LCP made its move. LCP executed its option to purchase 51% of BW's stock, and it made BW a subsidiary. LCP-BW then entered into a joint venture with ET to merge *American Annotated Cases* and *Lawyers' Reports Annotated,* and co-publish the super-annotated set ***American Law Reports (A.L.R.).*** (See Figure 4–1.)

A.L.R. was a hit. It started with "the largest subscription list of any set of reports ever published" and added 4,000 new subscriptions in its first year. [26#3 Case & Com., back cover (Mar.-Apr. 1920).]

A.L.R. had a number of features. It had annotations covering all areas of law and covering every U.S. court. Printed in a new typeface, with a single annotation-finding digest system and a single supplement, A.L.R. was prepared by a team of LCP-BW-ET editors who averaged 15 years of law writing experience.

Figure 4–1 The Birth of A.L.R.

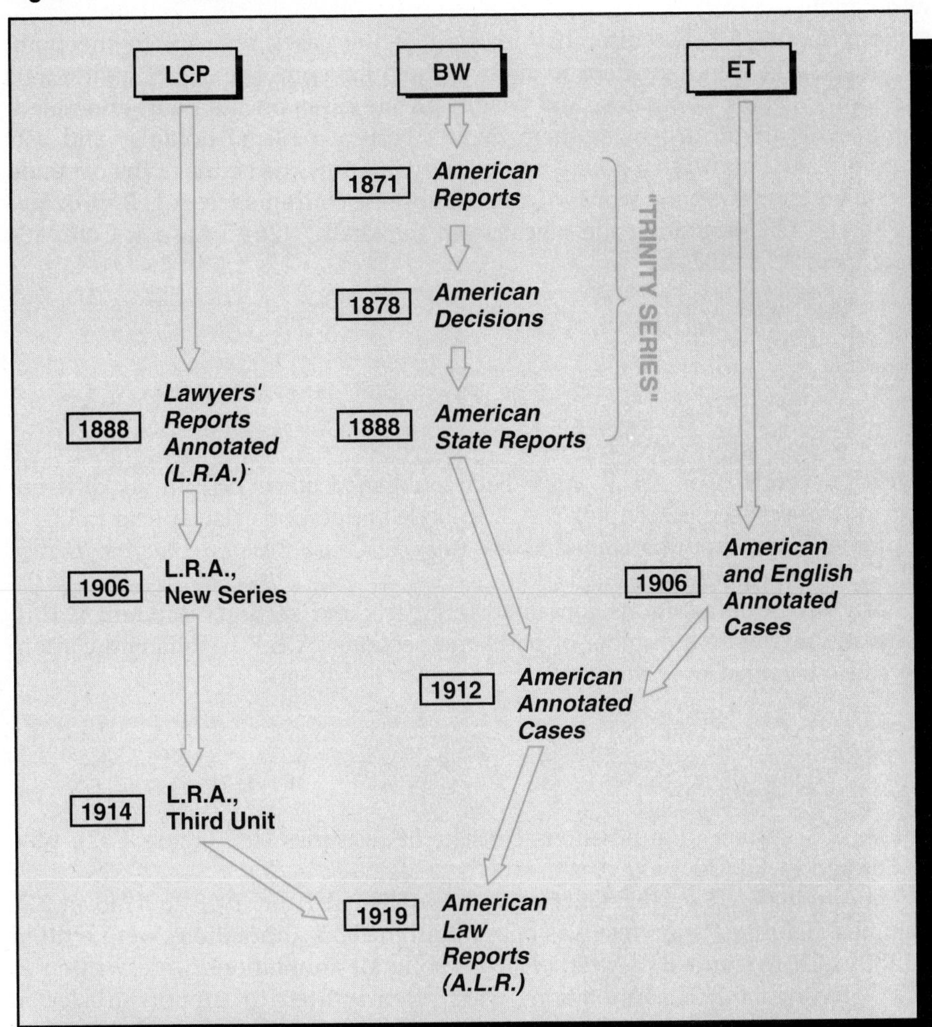

Finally, in the 1930s, during the height of the Great Depression, LCP-BW bought out ET's interest in A.L.R., and BW became a wholly owned subsidiary of LCP. The following sections discuss LCP's management of A.L.R. since then. (In 1989, LCP was sold to International Thomson Organization Ltd., and on December 31, 1990, became the Lawyers Cooperative Publishing division of Thomson Legal Publishing Inc.)

When to Use Annotations

Annotations are best used early in the legal research process. They are designed to be a fast method for finding case law. If an annotation exists on the point you are researching and you can find it, you may be taken right to the heart of your issue. An annotation is similar to a memorandum of law.

A.L.R. is a shortcut in two significant ways. First, A.L.R. is LCP's answer to West's Digest System. When you use an A.L.R. annotation, the A.L.R. editor has already done the West digest search for you. Even in a simple annotation, the A.L.R. editor searches all the relevant West Topics and Key Numbers. For example, in an annotation such as "Mausoleum as Nuisance," 1 A.L.R. 546, the A.L.R. editor searches the West digests under both the subject (Cemeteries), and the cause of action (Nuisance). It is not uncommon for an A.L.R. editor to search through 20 or more West Key Numbers in preparing an A.L.R. annotation.

Second, the A.L.R. editor has read all of the cases relevant to the point annotated and is in a position to analyze them for you. The A.L.R. editor sifts through, chooses, compares, and weighs all the cases on the point annotated, summarizes them, organizes them by fact pattern or legal holding, and lists them pro and con. With a good annotation, you know the status of the common law on your point. In the words of a state supreme court justice, A.L.R. provides the service of "separating the wheat from the chaff." [26#5 Case & Com. 134 (Aug.-Sept.-Oct. 1920).]

4–2 A.L.R. Annotations

Over 500 volumes of A.L.R. have been published since 1919 in six different series. As discussed in Chapter 2, A.L.R.-style annotations also appear in LCP's Supreme Court reporter *United States Supreme Court Reports, Lawyers' Edition* (L. Ed. and L. Ed. 2d).

Early A.L.R. annotations contained few parts and sections. Modern A.L.R. annotations contain a number of parts and sections. A.L.R.'s style and content have also changed over the years.

Series

The A.L.R. system of annotations consists of six series (see Figure 4–2), plus L. Ed. and L. Ed. 2d.

The original A.L.R. (First Series) was published from 1919 to 1948 in 175 volumes. Before ET's interest was bought out in 1935, annotations were written at both LCP-BW and ET. After 1935, virtually all annotations were written at LCP. Starting in 1936, annotations were often written to support articles in LCP's encyclopedia, *American Jurisprudence.* (See below and Chapter 8.) Over

Volumes of A.L.R.

Source: © Doug Martin

15,000 annotations were collected in A.L.R. (First Series), and its reputation grew year after year.

A.L.R. Second Series (A.L.R.2d) was published from 1948 to 1965 in 100 volumes. The principal reason for the new series was to give LCP salesmen a "new" book to sell. Minor editorial changes included a section-numbered scheme (outline) and an index preceding each long annotation. In the late 1950s, A.L.R.-style annotations were included in L. Ed., and, in L. Ed. 2d, they became a permanent feature.

A.L.R.2d was the heyday of A.L.R. A small group of editors wrote most of the annotations, and few limitations were placed on their writing. Many viewed each annotation as a Ph.D. thesis. Within the company, LCP editors were viewed as "creative law writers," with some displaying "genius."

A.L.R. Third Series (A.L.R.3d) was published from 1965 to 1980 in 100

Figure 4–2 A.L.R. Series

A.L.R. (1st)	1919–1948	175 Volumes
A.L.R.2d	1948–1965	100 Volumes
A.L.R.3d	1965–1980	100 Volumes
A.L.R. Fed.	1969–Present	Over 100 Volumes
A.L.R.4th	1980–1992	90 Volumes
A.L.R.5th	1992–Present	Several Volumes

volumes. A.L.R.3d reflected the subtle but definite shift in writing style from "great book" to "product." In the 1960s, LCP management put every department, including editorial, on a strict budget. A.L.R.3d added new features, such as a larger typeface for "improved readability" (which also reduced the number of annotations per volume) and a box of Total Client Service Library references (that "billboarded" other LCP products). Annotations were written at both LCP and BW.

To capture the tremendous growth of federal law during the 1960s, and to sell another book, LCP, since 1969, has put federal law annotations in a separate series: A.L.R. Federal (A.L.R. Fed.).

By 1974, all A.L.R. editors were required to follow a strict style and content rulebook. A narrow interpretation of relevancy was imposed. Commentary was limited to "practice pointers." The idea that A.L.R. annotations were Ph.D. theses was discarded. Instead, each A.L.R. annotation became a narrow, carefully budgeted, slice of law.

A.L.R. Fourth Series (A.L.R.4th) was published from 1980 to 1992, and the strict rulebook style is evident. By 1987, LCP removed the phrase "creative law writing" from its editor recruiting materials, and no editor was considered a genius.

In 1992, LCP started A.L.R. Fifth Series (A.L.R.5th) with several cosmetic changes, including expanded research references, West digest references, and extensive jurisdiction tables. Reported cases are collected at the end of each volume.

LCP also publishes subject-specific A.L.R. sets, such as *A.L.R. Medical Malpractice*, containing medical malpractice annotations.

Parts and Sections

Prior to A.L.R.5th, the modern A.L.R. annotation contained the following parts and sections. (See Figure 4–3.)

Preceding the annotation is the reported case. The reported case is an example of the point annotated. A.L.R. editors attempt to collect "leading" cases wherein the point annotated is a "major feature" of the case. The case is summarized, and headnotes are made and classified to the A.L.R. Digests (see below). When available, the briefs of counsel on appeal are summarized just before the opinion of the court.

In A.L.R.4th the reported case is a state case. In A.L.R. Fed., the reported case is a Court of Appeals, District Court, or other lower federal court case. In L. Ed. 2d the reported case is a U.S. Supreme Court case.

The annotation begins with a short title and the name of the purported author. Keep in mind that an annotation is a cooperative effort. The purported author is usually the editor who read all the cases and prepared the first rough draft, but if that editor has left LCP, the purported author may be a revising editor. In any event, a revising editor will frequently make substantial changes in the first editor's content and emphasis. The reported case materials are prepared by a third editor, the indexing materials are prepared by clerical assistants, and the supplementary materials are prepared by still other editors and clerical assistants.

The next part of the annotation is the **TCSL Box.** Cross-references to other units of the LCP's Total Client Service Library are listed.

After the TCSL Box is a detailed logical section-numbered outline known as a **scheme.** After standardized §§ 1 and 2, the subject is outlined beginning with § 3. The analysis may be legal, factual, or both, depending on the subject annotated.

The next part is a legal word and fact index of the annotation, followed by the

Figure 4–3 Sample Annotation

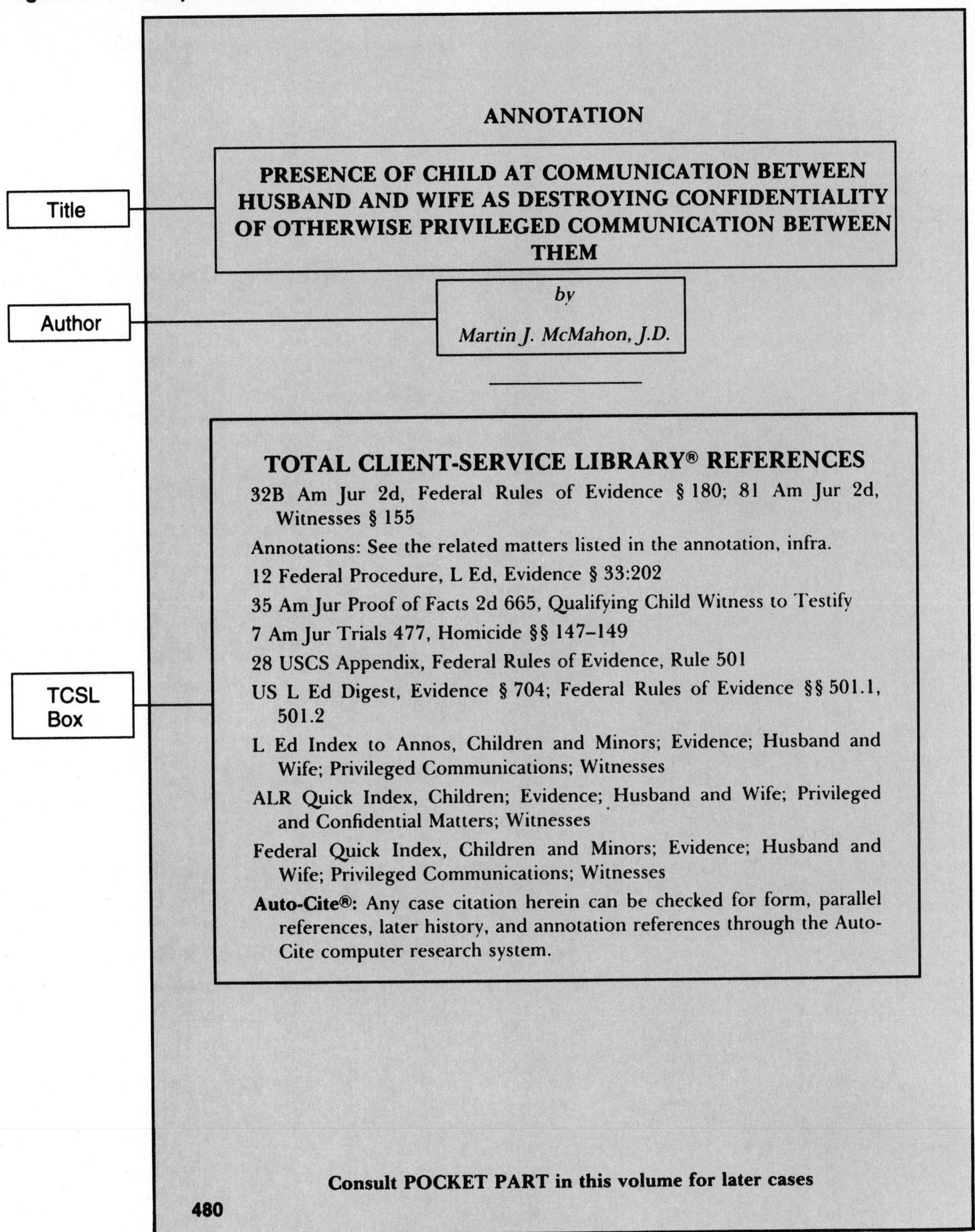

Title

Author

TCSL Box

ANNOTATION

PRESENCE OF CHILD AT COMMUNICATION BETWEEN HUSBAND AND WIFE AS DESTROYING CONFIDENTIALITY OF OTHERWISE PRIVILEGED COMMUNICATION BETWEEN THEM

by

Martin J. McMahon, J.D.

TOTAL CLIENT-SERVICE LIBRARY® REFERENCES

32B Am Jur 2d, Federal Rules of Evidence § 180; 81 Am Jur 2d, Witnesses § 155

Annotations: See the related matters listed in the annotation, infra.

12 Federal Procedure, L Ed, Evidence § 33:202

35 Am Jur Proof of Facts 2d 665, Qualifying Child Witness to Testify

7 Am Jur Trials 477, Homicide §§ 147–149

28 USCS Appendix, Federal Rules of Evidence, Rule 501

US L Ed Digest, Evidence § 704; Federal Rules of Evidence §§ 501.1, 501.2

L Ed Index to Annos, Children and Minors; Evidence; Husband and Wife; Privileged Communications; Witnesses

ALR Quick Index, Children; Evidence; Husband and Wife; Privileged and Confidential Matters; Witnesses

Federal Quick Index, Children and Minors; Evidence; Husband and Wife; Privileged Communications; Witnesses

Auto-Cite®: Any case citation herein can be checked for form, parallel references, later history, and annotation references through the Auto-Cite computer research system.

Consult POCKET PART in this volume for later cases

480

Figure 4–3 cont.

Presence of child at communication between husband and wife as destroying confidentiality of otherwise privileged communication between them

Scheme

INDEX

Index

Figure 4–3 cont.

Jur Table

TABLE OF JURISDICTIONS REPRESENTED
Consult POCKET PART in this volume for later cases

US: §§ 5, 7
Ill: §§ 2[b], 5
Ind: §§ 5, 7
Kan: §§ 6
Ky: §§ 6
Me: §§ 3, 4
Md: §§ 2[b], 7
Mass: §§ 2[b], 3-5, 8
Mo: §§ 4, 6
NY: §§ 5, 7
NC: §§ 2[b], 4
Pa: §§ 2[b], 7
RI: §§ 7
Tenn: §§ 5
Tex: §§ 6
Wash: §§ 7
W Va: §§ 5
Wyo: §§ 5

Scope

§ 1. Introduction

[a] Scope

This annotation collects and analyzes the state and federal cases in which the courts have discussed or decided whether, or under what circumstances, the presence of a child during a communication, verbal or nonverbal, between husband and wife vitiates the privilege against a spouse's testimony in opposition to the other spouse, on the ground that the child's presence destroys the otherwise confidential nature of the communication.

Since relevant statutes are included only to the extent that they are reflected in the reported cases within the scope of this annotation, the reader is advised to consult the latest enactments of pertinent jurisdictions.

Related Matters

[b] Related matters

Instructions to jury as to credibility of child's testimony in criminal case. 32 ALR4th 1196.

Applicability of marital privilege to written communication between spouses inadvertently obtained by third person. 32 ALR4th 1177.

Existence of spousal privilege where marriage was entered into for purpose of barring testimony. 13 ALR4th 1305.

Testimonial privilege for confidential communications between relatives other than husband and wife—state cases. 6 ALR4th 544.

Communication between unmarried couple living together as privileged. 4 ALR4th 422.

Spouse's betrayal or connivance as extending marital communications privilege to testimony of third person. 3 ALR4th 1104.

Effect, on competency to testify against spouse or on marital communication privilege, of separation or other marital instability short of absolute divorce. 98 ALR3d 1285.

Competency of one spouse to testify against other in prosecution for

482

Figure 4–3 cont.

offense against child of both or either. 93 ALR3d 1018.

Competency of one spouse to testify against other in prosecution for offense against third party as affected by fact that offense against spouse was involved in same transaction. 36 ALR3d 820.

Husband or wife as competent witness for or against co-offender with spouse. 90 ALR2d 648.

Calling or offering accused's spouse as witness for prosecution as prejudicial misconduct. 76 ALR2d 920.

Effect of divorce or annulment on competency of one former spouse as witness against other in criminal prosecution. 38 ALR2d 570.

Crimes against spouse within exception permitting testimony by one spouse against other in criminal prosecution. 11 ALR2d 646.

"Communications" within testimonial privilege of confidential communications between husband and wife as including knowledge derived from observation by one spouse of acts of other spouse. 10 ALR2d 1389.

Conversations between husband and wife relating to property or business as within rule excluding private communications between them. 4 ALR2d 835.

Marital privilege under Rule 501 of Federal Rules of Evidence. 46 ALR Fed 735.

Competency of one spouse to testify in federal criminal prosecution of other. 3 L Ed 2d 1607.

§ 2. Summary and comment

[a] Generally

Summary

Ordinarily, the fact that a conversation between husband and wife is overheard and understood by anyone, even a member of their family, vitiates the privilege against one spouse's testimony against the other (81 Am Jur 2d, Witnesses § 155).

The courts have generally held that the presence of a child, who was shown to have paid attention to the communication, destroyed the confidentiality of an otherwise privileged communication between husband and wife (§§ 3, 5, 7, infra). The presence of a child at such communication, the courts have held, did not destroy the spouses' confidentiality, however, where the child was not paying attention at the time of the communication (§§ 4, 8, infra).

In cases in which the children in question were 13 years of age or older, the courts have usually held that the presence of the children destroyed any spousal confidentiality, even though the children did not participate in the communication between their parents (§ 5, infra). However, it has been held that the presence of a teenaged child, who testified to her remembering the conversation between her parents, would not destroy the confidentiality of that conversation (§ 5, infra).

In cases involving the presence of children who were in their preteen years, the determination of whether confidentiality has been destroyed has depended largely on whether the children appeared to have been paying attention to the communications in question (§§ 3, 4, infra).

Without regard to the ages of the children who were present during spousal communications, the courts have generally held that confidentiality was destroyed where the child actually participated in the communications (§ 6, infra). In cases in which children did not participate in conversations between their parents, courts have usually held that, regardless of the children's ages, confidentiality was destroyed (§ 7, infra). The failure of such children to pay attention,

483

Figure 4–3 cont.

however, has been a ground for holding that the confidentiality of the parents' communication was not destroyed (§ 8, infra).

There appears to be a tendency of the courts, in early cases from the 19th century, to hold that the confidentiality of communications between husbands and wives was not destroyed by the presence of their children of ages in the 11- to 14-year-old category (§§ 4, 5, 7, infra), while in more recent cases, beginning in the 1920s, the courts have held that confidentiality was destroyed with respect to children in the same general age group (§§ 3, 5, infra).

Practice Pointers

[b] Practice pointers

Counsel is reminded that an objection to the admission of a conversation between husband and wife may be overruled on the ground of evidence that a child overheard and understood the communication.[1] Counsel is advised that it is generally a question of fact for the trial judge to determine whether the child in question was of sufficient intelligence to pay attention and to understand what was being said between the parents.[2]

In challenging the admission into evidence of a spousal communication, counsel is reminded that the challenging party has the burden of rebutting the presumption that statements between spouses are confidential.[3]

Even if there has been error in the admission of testimony by a spouse as to a privileged communication with the other spouse, counsel is advised that the error might not be held to be prejudicial where other witnesses testified to the same communication.[4]

Counsel who represents the spouses jointly, in seeking to introduce testimony as to conversations between the spouses, should try to establish separately the facts and circumstances from which the trier of fact may determine whether the presence of children rendered the spouses' communication admissible; counsel should not rely only on the phrasing of counsel's question to a witness spouse, asking whether there were any conversations between the spouses in the presence of their children.[5]

1. See, for example, Linnell v Linnell (1924) 249 **Mass** 51, 143 NE 813, where the court found that the daughter heard the conversation in question, in view of the fact that when she came into the room in which the husband and wife were conversing angrily, the daughter was crying.

2. See, for example, Freeman v Freeman (1921) 238 **Mass** 150, 130 NE 220, in which the trial judge admitted a conversation between husband and wife in the presence of their daughters, the eldest being 9 years old.

3. See People v Sanders (1982) 111 **Ill** App 3d 1, 66 Ill Dec 761, 443 NE2d 687, revd on other grounds 99 Ill 2d 262, 75 Ill Dec 682, 457 NE2d 1241, 39 ALR4th 471, on remand 127 Ill App 3d 471, 82 Ill Dec 753, 469 NE2d 287, in which the court stated that the presumption can be rebutted by the presence of children who are old enough to understand what is being said and who could possibly testify as to what they heard, or who participated in the marital communication itself.

4. See, for example, Master v Master (1960) 223 **Md** 618, 166 A2d 251, where the court held that any error in the admission of the wife's testimony by the trial court could hardly be held prejudicial after her two daughters testified to the same conversation.

5. See, for example, Amer Realty Co. v Spack (1932) 280 **Mass** 96, 181 NE 753, in which the court held that evidence of an alleged conversation between the defendant spouses was rightly excluded by the trial judge absent any testimony to

484

Figure 4–3 cont.

39 ALR4th MARITAL PRIVILEGE—PRESENCE OF CHILD § 3
39 ALR4th 480

Counsel is advised that, in addition to the rule that a spouse may not testify directly as a witness to a privileged communication, the reading of recorded conversations into the record has been held to constitute testimony of privileged communications, since the courts have refused to allow a spouse to utilize mechanical means of repeating the other spouse's words, thus accomplishing indirectly what the spouse could not do directly by disclosing the confidential communication.[6]

In the event that a child witness is to be used to testify to a conversation between the parents, counsel is advised that the question of whether a child witness is competent to testify can depend on such information as the child's age, grades in school, ability to differentiate between right and wrong, sense of moral obligation to speak the truth, and recollection of other events that took place at about the same time as the communication to which the child will testify.[7]

§ 3. Child 12 years or younger—where child did not participate in communication but paid attention to it

In the following cases, the confidentiality of otherwise privileged communications between husband and wife was held destroyed by the presence of children at the communications where the children, who were 12 years old or younger, were found to have paid attention to and to have understood the spousal communication, although they did not participate in it.

Introductory Paragraph

Affirming a decree of divorce in favor of a husband who brought an action against his wife on the grounds of cruel and abusive treatment, the court, in Linnell v Linnell (1924) 249 **Mass** 51, 143 NE 813, overruled the wife's exceptions to the admission of a conversation between her husband and herself where the husband had testified that his 10-year-old daughter was in the next room and that the door was open, the distance from one room to the other being 10 or 12 feet, "just across the hall." In view of the husband's further testimony that his wife's voice was extremely angry and excited, that afterwards the daughter came into the room in which the husband and wife were conversing, and that the daughter was crying, the court held that this evidence, if believed, warranted a finding that the daughter heard the conversation, which made it admissible.

Setout

Overruling the husband's exceptions to the trial court's rulings relating to evidence in a wife's action for divorce in which she charged her husband with cruel and abusive treatment, the court, in Freeman v Freeman (1921) 238 **Mass** 150, 130 NE 220, held that the trial court's admission of a conversation between the husband and wife in the presence of

establish the ages of the children who were alleged to have been present during the conversation, or other circumstances from which it could be determined whether any of the children possessed sufficient intelligence to pay attention to the conversation, if, in fact, any of them heard it.

6. For example, see Hicks v Hicks (1967) 271 **NC** 204, 155 SE2d 799 (wife did not know that her conversation with husband, in presence of their 8-year-old daughter, was being tape recorded); and Hunter v Hunter (1951) 169 **Pa** Super 498, 83 A2d 401 (husband's son by former marriage recorded conversations with wife pursuant to prearrangement between husband and son).

7. See 35 Am Jur Proof of Facts 2d 665, Qualifying Child Witness to Testify.

485

Source: American Law Reports, Fourth Series, vol. 39 (Rochester, NY: Lawyers Cooperative Publishing Co., 1985), pp. 480–485. Reprinted with permission.

"Table of Jurisdictions Represented." The **jur table** is useful in determining if the annotation cites any cases from a given state or federal circuit.

The most important part of the annotation is § 1[a] **Scope.** It states, with some specificity, the purported contents of the annotation. The scope statement may indicate that the annotation contains less than the title of the annotation might imply. To keep annotations artificially short, A.L.R. editors are usually prohibited from making reference to cases in the annotation that are not literally within the scope of the annotation as perceived by the revising editor, even though the revising editor may not have read all the cases. Moreover, doubts about problem cases are usually resolved in favor of exclusion, rather than inclusion.

Section 1[b], **Related matters,** is a list of similar, related annotations, along with a token sample of law articles and treatises on the point annotated. The quality of the related matters section indicates the quality of the coverage of the annotation system in your area of interest. If a statute or court rule is particularly relevant to the point annotated, a copy is included in a § 1[c].

Section 2, "Summary and comment," is a summary of the law found in the preparation of the annotation, but not a free commentary by the editor who read all the cases. Each statement is required to be supported by a citation to another part of the annotation or another outside source. Section 2[b], **Practice pointers,** contains "useful hints" on how to handle a case involving the point annotated.

Beginning with § 3, the cases are collected according to the scheme. Each section, or part of a section, begins with an introductory paragraph defining the type of cases to follow. Each case is then set out—sketched—in a paragraph known as a **setout.** If there are numerous repetitive cases, the case cites are merely listed with sample setouts. Since a setout is but a sketch of a case, it may not reflect the true nature of the case. Thus, cases found in A.L.R. should be read in full before being cited in a brief.

If an annotation contains only a few cases, it will not have a scheme, index, jurisdiction table, or numbered sections.

How an A.L.R. Annotation Is Prepared

Just as it's important to understand how a digest is prepared to begin to understand its limitations, it's important to understand how an annotation is prepared to begin to understand its limitations.

An A.L.R. annotation begins with topic selection. Selectors read current cases looking for emerging legal issues of interest to the average lawyer. The goal is to find an interesting case to lead a "hot" topic. If the expense of making an annotation on a given topic can be justified to LCP management, a selection memo is prepared for an editor.

The editor begins by making an exhaustive search of the subject, including secondary sources of all kinds. Rather than maintaining a massive law database, LCP has its editors separately research each annotation. The editor collects and reads all the relevant cases in, on, and around the point being annotated. While actual techniques vary, editors are instructed to read each case once, decide if it is explicitly on point, prepare setouts, then organize the setouts within a scheme. The rough draft is then edited by a revising editor to keep each annotation within the strict "rulebook" style. True commentary and creativity are thus kept to a minimum.

Again, an important part of the process is the A.L.R. editor's search of the West Digest System. West Topics and Key Numbers searched for each annotation are kept on file, along with other key sources searched, and the

Topics and Key Numbers are used as the basis for supplementing each annotation in the future.

4–3 A.L.R. Annotation Finders

While annotations are essentially finding tools, there are so many of them that there are finding tools to find annotations. There are several ways to find an A.L.R. annotation.

A.L.R. Indexes

Over the years, LCP published a complex series of "Word" and "Quick" indexes for A.L.R. annotations. Finally, in 1986, LCP simplified the matter somewhat with the publication of *Index to Annotations.* (See Figure 4–4.) *Index to Annotations,* a five-volume set, indexes all the annotations in A.L.R.2d, A.L.R.3d, A.L.R.4th, A.L.R. Fed., and L. Ed. 2d. To cut costs, A.L.R. (First Series) was not covered. A.L.R. (First Series) annotations are still indexed with the *A.L.R. First Series Quick Index.*

The A.L.R. indexes are known as "word-fact" indexes. To search for law relating to an automobile accident, for example, one can search traditional legal words like *negligence* and *due care,* along with fact words like *automobile* and *highway.* Under each entry are the appropriate annotation titles and their cites. (See Figure 4–5.)

The last (S–Z) volume of *Index to Annotations,* at page 757, also contains useful tables that show "where federal statutes, regulations, and court rules, uniform and model acts, restatements of law, and professional codes of ethics, are cited in annotations" in A.L.R.3d, A.L.R.4th, A.L.R. Fed., and L. Ed. 2d.

Each modern volume of A.L.R. also contains a "Subjects Annotated" volume index and a table of cases reported in the volume. Recent volumes also contain a table of contents.

Figure 4–4 A.L.R. "Quick" Indexes

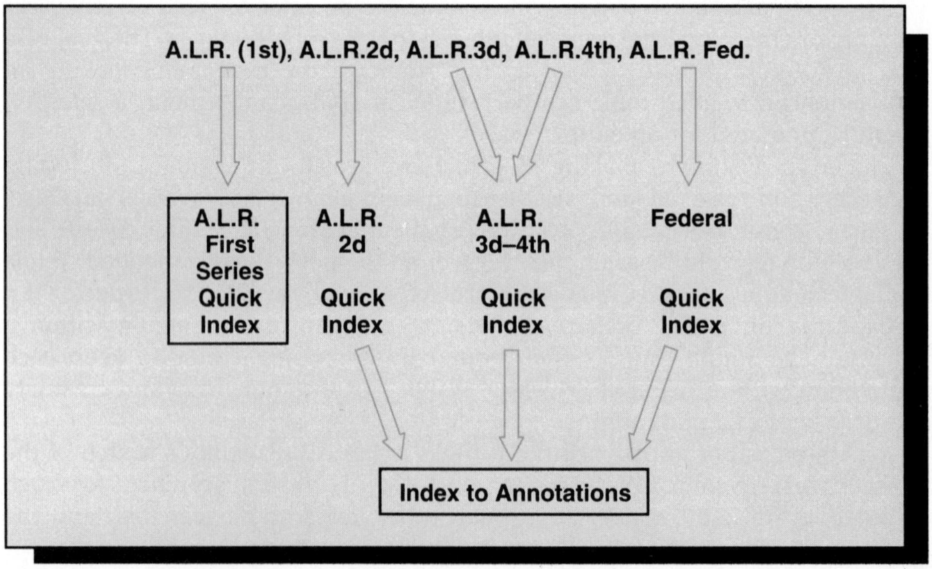

Figure 4–5 Index to Annotations

INDEX TO ANNOTATIONS

604 **Consult POCKET PART for Later Annotations**

Source: Index to Annotations, vol. S–Z (Rochester, NY: Lawyers Cooperative Publishing Co., 1986), p. 604. Reprinted with permission.

A.L.R. Digests

LCP publishes a digest for A.L.R. (First Series), a digest for A.L.R.2d, and a digest for A.L.R.3d, A.L.R.4th, and A.L.R. Fed. combined. (See Figure 4–6.) The law is classified under a few hundred topics. Under each topic are annotation titles and their cites, along with digest paragraphs prepared for the reported cases and their cites.

A.L.R. Help Line

LCP operates a toll-free number, 1-800-543-2068, which you may call to receive editorial assistance in locating annotations.

Total Client Service Library

Although L. Ed. was the first set of books published by LCP, the company's defining set, its backbone, is A.L.R. Just as each A.L.R. annotation is researched and written individually, without reference to a master outline, so each LCP publication is researched and written individually, without reference to a master outline. Just as LCP struggled to develop organizational tools—digests and indexes—for A.L.R. the company also struggled to develop a system of organization for its array of books.

A partial solution came in the mid-1930s. After preparing A.L.R. annotations for several years, some A.L.R. editors were sitting around at lunch one day discussing their work. One remarked that so many A.L.R. annotations had been written that an encyclopedia could be made out of them. The editor-in-chief overheard him and said, "Let's do it." As a result, in 1936, *American Jurisprudence* (Am. Jur.)—and later, *American Jurisprudence 2d* (Am. Jur. 2d)—was born. (See Chapter 8.)

Whereas A.L.R. provided a point-by-point treatment of the law, Am. Jur. provided an overview of the law, built on, and citing, among other things, A.L.R. annotations and the cases within A.L.R. annotations. As it turned out, some annotations had to be written to fill in gaps in coverage for the new encyclopedia, but the close relationship indicates why Am. Jur. 2d is an excellent tool for finding A.L.R. annotations.

From 1953 to 1964, LCP created a series of national form books, which will be discussed in Chapter 9. Each picked up the "Am Jur" moniker: *Am Jur Legal Forms* (1953) [and *Am Jur Legal Forms 2d* (1971)], *Am Jur Pleading and Practice Forms*

Figure 4–6 A.L.R. Digests

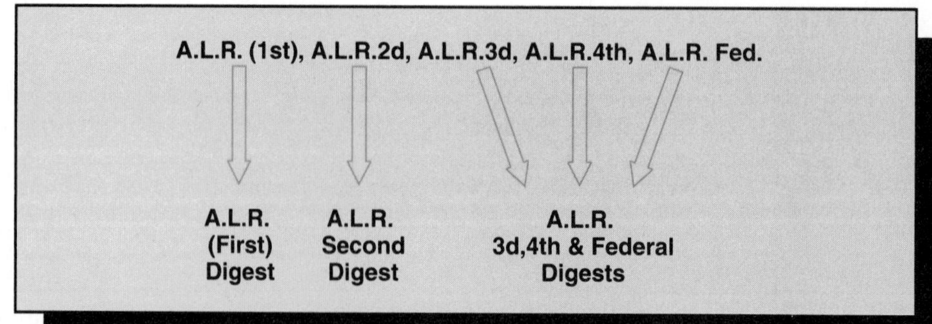

(1956) [now *Am Jur Pleading and Practice Forms, Revised* (1967)], *Am Jur Proof of Facts* (1959) [and *Am Jur Proof of Facts 2d* (1974)], and *Am Jur Trials* (1964).

Finding that lawyers liked buying "coordinated" books, in 1961 LCP's marketing department devised a slogan for LCP's national sets: the **Total Client Service Library** (TCSL). Every new national set LCP created was then made part of the TCSL, including among others, *A.L.R. Federal* (1969), *United States Code Service* (U.S.C.S.) (1972) (to be discussed in Chapter 5), *Federal Procedural Forms, Lawyers' Edition* (1975) (to be discussed in Chapter 9), *Bankruptcy Service, Lawyers' Edition* (1979), and *Federal Procedure, Lawyers' Edition* (1981) (to be discussed in Chapter 9). Auto-Cite (to be discussed in Chapter 11) was added in 1982.

LCP's editorial department supported the TCSL "coordination" claim by thoroughly cross-referencing each set in the TCSL with each other set in the TCSL, and in particular, with A.L.R. It is important to remember, however, that each is independently researched and written, and thus, as with A.L.R. itself, some law may fall through the cracks.

In 1986, LCP's indexing department took a step toward editorially coordinating LCP's books with the development of the *Thesaurus of Legal Fact Words and Concepts.* The thesaurus provides a "general model for an index." To the extent LCP indexers have followed it, there is now editorial coordination in the indexing of LCP books, including the A.L.R. *Index to Annotations.*

Case & Comment Magazine

In 1894, LCP started *Case & Comment,* "The Lawyers Magazine," to advertise L.R.A., and, in 1919, continued the idea by advertising A.L.R. *Case & Comment* contains practical articles for practicing lawyers, along with summaries of A.L.R.'s reported cases. At the end of each summary is the announcement "ALR . . . covers the point" and a citation to A.L.R.

Shepard's Citations

Shepard's Citations, which will be discussed in Chapter 11, includes cites to A.L.R. annotations.

Auto-Cite and LEXIS

To be discussed in Chapters 11 and 12, A.L.R. annotations can be found by Auto-Cite, and word-searched directly, using the LEXIS computer-assisted legal research system (ALR;ANNO file).

4–4 A.L.R. Annotation Supplementation

Cases are frequently decided after an A.L.R. annotation on the point has already been published. A.L.R. annotations are kept up to date by supplementary material that collects these "later cases." The method of supplementation has changed frequently over the years. (See Figure 4–7.)

Figure 4–7 A.L.R. Supplementation

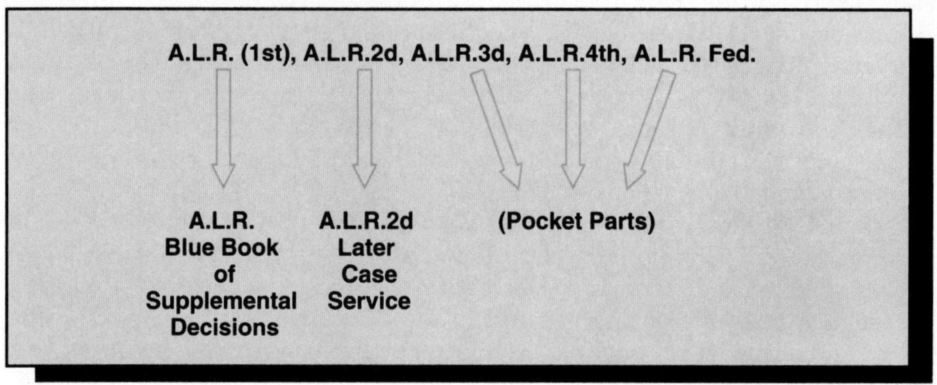

Blue Books

To supplement A.L.R. (First Series) annotations, LCP started publishing the *A.L.R. Blue Book of Supplemental Decisions*. The volumes in this set simply list cites to later cases on each annotation topic.

Later Case Service

To supplement A.L.R.2d annotations, LCP started publishing the *A.L.R. 2d Later Case Service*. Instead of simply listing cites to later cases on each annotation topic, each case is keyed to the appropriate section of the annotation supplemented.

Pocket Supplementation

To supplement A.L.R.3d, A.L.R.4th, and A.L.R. Fed., LCP now publishes annual cumulative pocket parts for each volume. Again, each case is keyed to the appropriate section of the annotation supplemented.

A.L.R. Latest Case Service

LCP operates a toll-free number, 1-800-225-7488, which you may call to get references to cases decided since the last A.L.R. supplement was published.

Annotation History Table

Another method used to keep annotations up to date is to issue superseding or supplementing annotations. If the subject matter of an annotation, or a part of it, has changed significantly, a **superseding annotation** may be prepared. The subject will be rewritten as if there were no annotation on the point. If there have been a lot of cases on an annotated point, but no fundamental changes, a **supplementing annotation** may be prepared. The new cases are discussed with reference to the original annotation.

To check if a particular annotation, or a part of it, has been superseded or supplemented, refer to the supplemental service for that series of annotations or to the Annotation History Table in the last (S–Z) volume of the *Index to*

Annotations. (See Figure 4–8.) To check if a particular annotation supersedes or supplements another annotation, refer to the scope section of the annotation.

4–5 The Limitations of A.L.R. Annotations

During the heyday of A.L.R., some A.L.R. editors saw themselves as the keepers of the common law. Marketing slogans like "All the case law on your point" were developed. Today, A.L.R. is simply an unusual case finder.

If your point is annotated, you may find more cases and quicker with an A.L.R. annotation than with West's digests. But, relatively speaking, less and less of U.S. case law is being annotated. A.L.R. annotations collect (and West's digests index) reported cases, but more and more of U.S. case law is going unreported. When there is no A.L.R. annotation on your point, you must turn to other sources. Moreover, even if there is an annotation on your point, it merely collects "in point" cases, without real commentary.

Figure 4-8 Annotation History Table

ANNOTATION HISTORY TABLE

This table lists annotations in all series of American Law Reports (ALR) and United States Supreme Court Reports, Lawyers Edition (L Ed) which have been superseded or supplemented by later annotations. Consult the pocket part in this volume for later history.

ALR (First Series)

1 ALR 148–149
Superseded 74 ALR2d 828

1 ALR 222–264
Subdiv VIII superseded 71 ALR2d 1140

1 ALR 329–331
Superseded 36 ALR2d 861

1 ALR 343–349
Superseded 51 ALR2d 1404

1 ALR 383–392
Superseded 13 ALR4th 1153

1 ALR 449–450
Superseded 28 ALR2d 662

1 ALR 546–547
Superseded 50 ALR2d 1324

1 ALR 834
Superseded 91 ALR2d 1344

1 ALR 861–878
Superseded 41 ALR2d 1213

1 ALR 884–892
Superseded, as to private easements, 25 ALR2d 1265

1 ALR 1163–1172
Superseded 28 ALR4th 482

1 ALR 1267–1277
Superseded 87 ALR2d 271

1 ALR 1368–1374
Superseded 46 ALR2d 1140

1 ALR 1528–1532
Superseded 13 ALR3d 42

1 ALR 1632–1634
Superseded 53 ALR2d 572

1 ALR 1688–1691
Superseded 99 ALR2d 7

2 ALR 6–36
Supplemented 49 ALR2d 982

2 ALR 61–67
Superseded 14 ALR3d 783

2 ALR 225–236
Supplemented 41 ALR2d 1263

2 ALR 287–293
Superseded 11 ALR4th 345

2 ALR 345–347
Superseded 44 ALR2d 1242

2 ALR 545–551
Superseded 54 ALR3d 9

2 ALR 579–582
Superseded 50 ALR2d 1161

2 ALR 592–593
Superseded 12 ALR3d 933

2 ALR 867–879
Superseded 25 ALR3d 941

2 ALR 1008–1014
Superseded 90 ALR2d 1210

2 ALR 1068
Superseded 6 ALR3d 1457

2 ALR 1368–1371
Superseded 56 ALR3d 1182

2 ALR 1376
Superseded 45 ALR2d 1296

2 ALR 1389–1390
Superseded 28 ALR3d 1344

2 ALR 1522–1526
Superseded 157 ALR 1359

2 ALR 1576–1579
Superseded 77 ALR2d 1182

3 ALR 242
Superseded 72 ALR2d 342

3 ALR 312–323
Superseded 24 ALR2d 194

3 ALR 610–612
Superseded 12 ALR2d 611

3 ALR 824–829
Superseded 13 ALR3d 848

3 ALR 833–844
Superseded 22 ALR3d 1346

3 ALR 902–928
Superseded 57 ALR3d 1083

3 ALR 1003–1021
Superseded 98 ALR3d 605

3 ALR 1096
Superseded 89 ALR3d 551

3 ALR 1104
Superseded 8 ALR4th 886

3 ALR 1109
Superseded 92 ALR2d 1009

3 ALR 1130–1145
Supplemented 41 ALR2d 739

3 ALR 1279–1282
Subdiv II superseded 100 ALR2d 227

3 ALR 1304–1306
Superseded 82 ALR2d 611

3 ALR 1385–1393
Superseded 92 ALR3d 623

Consult POCKET PART for Later Entries **1079**

Source: Index to Annotations, vol. S–Z (Rochester, NY: Lawyers Cooperative Publishing Co., 1986), p. 1079. Reprinted with permission.

SUMMARY

4–1

The annotation method of finding cases is based on finding cases in a specialized collection of law. If someone has already read, analyzed, and synthesized the relevant law for you, and put it into note form, your research is virtually complete. *American Law Reports* (A.L.R.) is the super-annotated set; LCP's special case finder is prepared by reading cases topically.

4–2

There are six series of A.L.R. annotations: A.L.R. (First Series), A.L.R.2d, A.L.R.3d, A.L.R.4th, A.L.R.5th, and A.L.R. Fed. L. Ed. and L. Ed. 2d also contain A.L.R.-style annotations. The reported cases serve as examples of the points annotated. Large annotations have a detailed logical section-numbered outline known as a *scheme.* When using a modern annotation, be aware of its scope statement and the fact that commentary and creativity have been artificially limited.

4–3

Annotations can be found with the *Index to Annotations* and the A.L.R. digests. References to annotations are also found in Total Client Service Library volumes (such as *American Jurisprudence*), in *Case & Comment* magazine, and in other sources.

4–4

Modern annotations are supplemented by pocket supplementation. To check if an annotation has been supplemented or superseded, consult the Annotation History Table in the last volume of the *Index to Annotations.*

4–5

A.L.R. is an unusual case finder. If your point is annotated, you may find more cases and quicker with an A.L.R. annotation than with West's digests.

REVIEW

Key Terms

Before proceeding, review the key terms listed below to be sure you understand each one. If necessary, read over the corresponding section of the chapter. When you are ready to test your understanding, answer the Review Questions.

American Law Reports (A.L.R.)
annotate
annotated
annotation
exhaustive annotations
jur table
Practice pointers
Related matters
scheme
Scope
setout
superseding annotation
supplementing annotation
TCSL Box
Total Client Service Library (TCSL)

Questions for Review and Discussion

1. What is the purpose and use of an annotation?
2. What are the differences between an annotation and a digest?
3. What are the current annotation series?
4. What series of A.L.R. was written by a small group of creative law writers, without rule books or artificial limitations of any kind?
5. What are the parts and sections of a modern A.L.R. annotation and what do they do?

6. What is the index for modern A.L.R. annotations?
7. What is the digest for modern A.L.R. annotations?
8. In what other ways can you find an A.L.R. annotation?
9. How are modern A.L.R. annotations supplemented?
10. Why might an A.L.R. annotation not contain "All the case law on your point," as advertised?

Activities

1. Read through several modern-schemed A.L.R. annotations, noting the structure of the annotation. Make sure you understand each part and section. Note how well the scheme outlines the topic. Find out if, and where, the A.L.R. editor has collected cases on opposite sides of the same issue.
2. Look up the word *annotate* in an ordinary dictionary. Decide how much an A.L.R. editor, in writing an A.L.R. annotation, annotates, in the ordinary sense of the word.
3. After completing this book, select a modern A.L.R. annotation and research the titled topic, on your own, without using the annotation. Compare your results with the annotation. Did you miss relevant cases found (or included) by the A.L.R. editor? Did you find relevant cases missed (or excluded) by the A.L.R. editor? Reread the title and scope of the annotation. Did the A.L.R. annotation contain what you expected to find, based on its title and scope?

NOTES

CHAPTER 5 Statutory Law

OUTLINE

5–1 Legislation
- Legislative History
- After a Bill Becomes Law

5–2 Federal Codes
- United States Code (U.S.C.)
- Annotated Codes
- United States Code Annotated (U.S.C.A.)
- United States Code Service (U.S.C.S.)
- The Limitations of Codes

5–3 State Codes

5–4 Local Codes

COMMENTARY

On your way back to the office after researching public religious displays, you learn that a train carrying hazardous materials has derailed near the center of the city. Tank cars are on fire, spewing poisonous smoke and gas, and several thousand residents have been forced to evacuate. When you get back to the office, you find the law director and everybody else watching the mayor's press conference on TV. The mayor is asked why trains carrying such hazardous cargo were allowed to pass through the city. The mayor says he doesn't know, but he's going to ask the law director to find out what the city can do about it. The law director tells you to put the public religious display project on hold. Instead, your assignment is to find out what federal laws apply to the transportation of hazardous materials and if they preempt (i.e., prohibit) any state or local law.

OBJECTIVES

In this chapter you will learn about the books that track the law made by the legislative branch. Emphasis is placed on federal legislation and its publication. After reading this chapter, you should be able to:

1. Define basic legislative terminology.
2. Understand the nature of legislative history.
3. Identify the official chronological source of federal legislation.
4. Explain how federal legislation is found topically.
5. Identify the official code of federal legislation.
6. Describe the benefits of an "annotated" code.
7. Recognize the indexes available for annotated codes.
8. Compare and contrast West's annotated code with LCP's annotated code.
9. Recognize the limitations of annotated codes.
10. Describe the usual features of state and local codes.

5–1 Legislation

The legislative branch of government makes the law. Unlike judges, who must be confronted with an actual legal controversy and interpret the law to make precedent, legislators simply "dream up" the law. The legislative branch makes **statutes,** and law from the legislative branch is known as **statutory law.** (See Figure 5–1.) The legislative process resulting in the making of a statute is known as **enactment.** Because the federal legislative process is illustrative of the legislative processes in the states, the federal legislative process is discussed in detail in this chapter.

Federal law is made in the sense of being "dreamed up" by Congress. Congress meets in two-year periods, each known as a **Congress,** with 1789–1790 as the 1st Congress and 1991–1992 as the 102nd Congress. The Twentieth Amendment, Section 2, of the Constitution of the United States, requires Congress to "assemble at least once in every year, and such meeting shall begin at noon on the 3d day of January, unless they shall by law appoint a different day." Accordingly, each Congress consists of a first and a second **session,** each approximately one year in length.

A proposed permanent law introduced in the House of Representatives or in the Senate is known as a **bill** (introduced with the words "Be it enacted"). Bills introduced in the House of Representatives during a Congress are numbered sequentially beginning with H.R. 1. Bills introduced in the Senate during a Congress are numbered sequentially beginning with S. 1.

In each house, bills are studied by committees. Public hearings may be held, after which the committees report their recommendations to the full house. Placed on the calendar, bills come up for debate, possible amendment, and a vote. Bills considered and passed by one house (each an **act;** each corrected, final, officially signed copy known as an **engrossed bill**) are sent to the other house for consideration and passage. Substantial differences between versions

Figure 5–1 The Legislative Branch

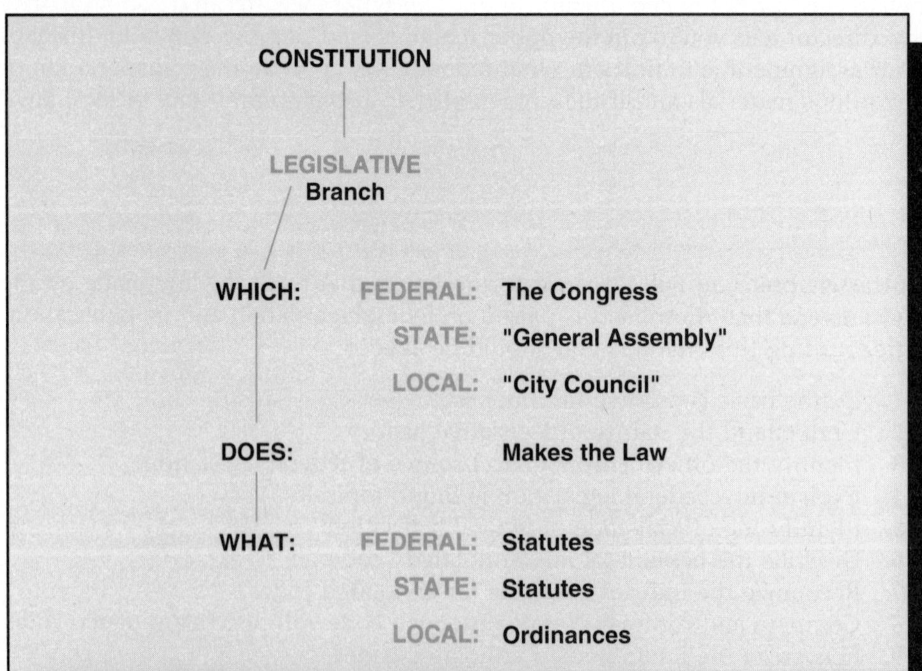

may be ironed out by a joint conference committee, followed by a vote in each house.

As specified by Article 1, Section 7, of the Constitution of the United States, bills that pass both houses (each corrected, final, officially signed copy on parchment known as an **enrolled bill**) are presented to the President for signature (approval), return without a signature **(veto),** timely nonreturn (abstention), or untimely nonreturn **(pocket veto).** A bill becomes law if the President signs it, if the President returns it within 10 days (Sunday excepted) and the veto is overridden by a two-thirds vote in each house, or if the President does not return it within 10 days (Sunday excepted) and the houses of Congress have not adjourned.

Bills not passed during a Congress must be reintroduced to be considered again for passage. Bills should be compared and contrasted with joint resolutions, concurrent resolutions, and simple resolutions.

A **joint resolution** (designated H.J. RES. or S.J. RES.) is a proposed temporary (time-oriented) law (introduced with the words "Be it resolved"), such as an extension of a law about to expire or a one-time expenditure. Joint resolutions are passed like bills, except that a proposed constitutional amendment must be passed by a two-thirds vote of each house and need not be presented to the President. (See Figure 5–2.)

A **concurrent resolution** (designated H. CON. RES. or S. CON. RES.) is a proposed *administrative* (not legislative) statement of Congress, such as an expression of congressional opinion or the creation of a joint committee, which must be passed by each house to become effective, but is not a law commanding all. Similarly, a **simple resolution** (designated H. RES. or S. RES.) is a proposed *administrative* (not legislative) statement of one house, such as an expression of the house's opinion or the creation of a committee, which must be passed to become effective, but is not a law commanding all.

Legislative History

The laws enacted by the legislature are subject to interpretation by the courts. While it is true that in interpreting a statute a court may consider **legislative history,** the committee reports, floor debates, and other information considered by the legislature in enacting a bill or joint resolution, this is ordinarily done only when the statute has never been interpreted by a court before. Most legal research texts bury this fact in a blizzard of information about the sources of legislative history.

If a statute has never been interpreted by a court before, a court may seek to determine the intent of the legislature in passing the law and apply the law in a manner consistent with that intent. But a court is not bound by legislative intent. A court is bound only by the wording of the statute if the statute is constitutional. More importantly, once a statute has been interpreted by a court, that interpretation becomes a precedent that does have persuasive, if not mandatory, authority. A court can be bound by another court's interpretation of a statute.

As a practical matter, then, the only time a legal researcher need research legislative history is if a court is deciding a case of first impression as to interpreting a statute. If the statute has already been interpreted, legislative history is usually discussed and determined, if at all, in the first few case opinions under the statute.

A detailed discussion of legislative history is beyond the scope of this book. In summary, legislative intent can be inferred from amendments, committee reports, debates, and hearings.

Figure 5–2 Sample Joint Resolution

Sixty-sixth Congress of the United States of America;

At the First Session,

Begun and held at the City of Washington on Monday, the nineteenth day of May, one thousand nine hundred and nineteen.

JOINT RESOLUTION

Proposing an amendment to the Constitution extending the right of suffrage to women.

Resolved by the Senate and House of Representatives of the United States of America in Congress assembled (two-thirds of each House concurring therein), That the following article is proposed as an amendment to the Constitution, which shall be valid to all intents and purposes as part of the Constitution when ratified by the legislatures of three-fourths of the several States.

"ARTICLE ———.

"The right of citizens of the United States to vote shall not be denied or abridged by the United States or by any State on account of sex.

"Congress shall have power to enforce this article by appropriate legislation."

Speaker of the House of Representatives.

Vice President of the United States and President of the Senate.

Legislative intent may be inferred by comparing the original version of a bill or joint resolution with any amendments and whether or not those amendments were enacted. The original version of a bill and its amendments can be found by working with the official record of Congress, the *Congressional Record*, and by checking the bill number in the *History of Bills and Resolutions* part of the *Congressional Record Index* for the appropriate session of Congress.

If passage of a bill or joint resolution is recommended by a committee, the committee usually writes a report explaining its recommendation. Legislative intent may be inferred from a committee report. West Publishing Company (West)'s *United States Code Congressional and Administrative News* (U.S. Code Cong. & Admin. News) publishes selected committee reports for significant enacted legislation.

A significant bill or joint resolution may be debated on the floor in each house of Congress. Legislative intent may be inferred from the debate, especially from statements by a sponsoring legislator about the scope of the legislation. Such statements can be found in the *Congressional Record* (Cong. Rec.).

The shortcut to all of this is to find a legislative history that has already been compiled. Sources that may help include *Sources of Compiled Legislative Histories*, Commerce Clearing House, Inc. (CCH)'s *Public Laws—Legislative Histories Microfiche*, and the Congressional Information Service, Inc. (CIS)'s *Legislative History Service*.

The most widely used indexes of legislative history are the *Congressional Information Service/Index* ("CIS Index") and the *CCH Congressional Index*.

Some legislative history materials have been put on the LEXIS and WESTLAW computer-assisted legal research systems, which will be discussed in Chapter 12.

Because of the nature of legislative history research, it is appropriate to obtain the assistance of a librarian familiar with the resources available in a given library. Similarly, "legislative history" on a current bill or joint resolution may be found by contacting the local office of your congressman or congresswoman, or one of your senators, and asking for assistance.

The only major difference between federal legislation and state legislation is the availability of legislative history. While state legislative history theoretically exists, sources of state legislative history are usually nonexistent. State committee reports and floor debates are rarely published. At best, a state legislative bureau (e.g., Ohio's Legislative Service Commission) may be able to provide summaries of proposed legislation. Legislative history may be limited to a drafting committee's commentary collected in the state's annotated code (discussed in section 5–3 below).

After a Bill Becomes Law

A bill or joint resolution that has become law during a particular session of the legislature is known as a **session law.** (See Figure 5–3.) Most laws apply to everyone, and each is known as a **public law.** During each Congress, public session laws are numbered sequentially beginning with Public Law No. 1 (Pub. L. No. 1). Some laws apply only to an individual or a few individuals, and each is known as a **private law.** During each Congress, private session laws are numbered sequentially beginning with Private Law No. 1 (Priv. L. No. 1).

A copy of a particular law passed during a session of the legislature is known as a **slip law.** Slip laws are collected and officially published in numerical order by the U.S. Government Printing Office in the *United States Statutes at Large*

Figure 5–3 Enactment of a Bill

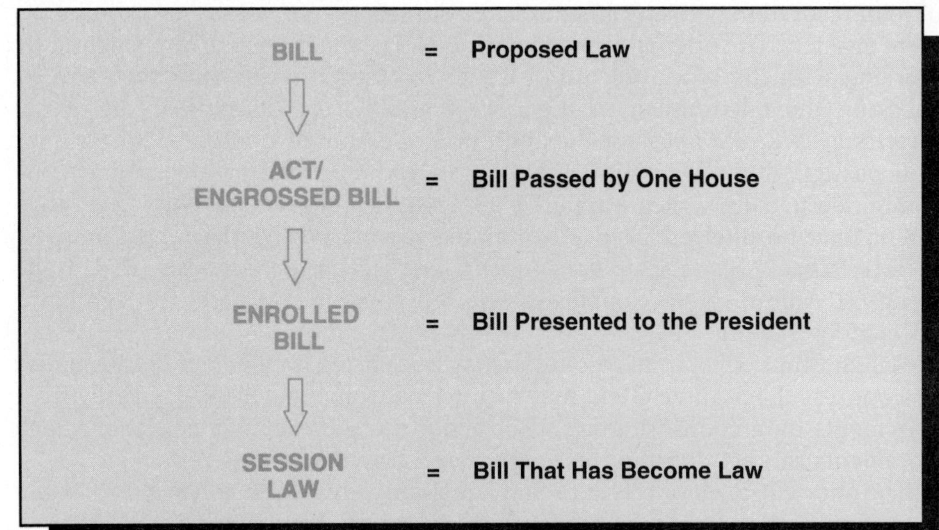

(Stat.). Slip laws are also published by West in U.S. Code Cong. & Admin. News (see Figure 5–4) and by Lawyers Cooperative Publishing (LCP) in its advance sheets to the *United States Code Service* (U.S.C.S.) (discussed in section 5–2 below).

The Stat. includes enacted bills, joint resolutions, and concurrent resolutions. Simple resolutions are included in the *Congressional Record.*

5–2 Federal Codes

The *United States Statutes at Large* (Stat.), published by the U.S. Government Printing Office, is the official chronological source of federal legislation. Legal researchers, however, want to find the law on a given topic. If statutes come out chronologically, how do you find them topically? The solution is to use a specialized collection. Since the number of pages of statutes issued each year is much less than the number of pages of case opinions, and legislation often expires, is repealed, or is later superseded, legislatures have undertaken to have all their permanent public statutes in force organized topically. Such a topical collection of statues is known as a **code.** The process of collecting permanent public statutes topically, adding amendments, and deleting expired, repealed, or superseded statutes, is known as **codification.**

The statutes of the U.S. government were first codified by commissioners in the *Revised Statutes of 1875.* The *Revised Statutes of 1875* was introduced as a bill, which also repealed the public laws then in *Statutes at Large.* With the bill's passage, the codification became **positive law,** the law "actually enacted."

However, this first codification, known as the first edition, was later discovered to contain errors and improper additions, and a second edition was authorized by Congress in 1878, but never enacted into positive law. The second codification was only ***prima facie*** (accepted on its face, but not irrebuttably) evidence of the law as actually enacted. The one official source again became *Statutes at Large.* Congress did not codify its statutes again until 1926.

Figure 5-4 Slip Law Published in *U.S. Code Congressional and Administrative News*

PUBLIC LAW 99-280 [S. 1282]; April 24, 1986

HEALTH SERVICES AMENDMENTS ACT OF 1986

For Legislative History of Act see Report for P.L. 99-280 in Legislative History Section, post.

An Act to amend the Public Health Service Act to revise and extend the programs of assistance for primary health care.

Be it enacted by the Senate and House of Representatives of the United States of America in Congress assembled,

Health Services Amendments Act of 1986.

SECTION 1. SHORT TITLE: REFERENCE TO ACT.

(a) SHORT TITLE.—This Act may be cited as the "Health Services Amendments Act of 1986". 42 USC 201 note.

(b) REFERENCE TO ACT.—Whenever in this Act an amendment or repeal is expressed in terms of an amendment to, or a repeal of, a section or other provision, the reference shall be considered to be made to a section or other provision of the Public Health Service Act. 42 USC 201 note.

SEC. 2. MEDICALLY UNDERSERVED POPULATIONS.

Section 330(b) (42 U.S.C. 254c(b)) is amended—

(1) by striking out the second, third, fourth, and fifth sentences of paragraph (3); and

(2) by adding at the end thereof the following:

"(4) In carrying out paragraph (3), the Secretary shall by regulation prescribe criteria for determining the specific shortages of personal health services of an area or population group. Such criteria shall— Regulations.

"(A) take into account comments received by the Secretary from the chief executive officer of a State and local officials in a State; and State and local governments.

"(B) include infant mortality in an area or population group, other factors indicative of the health status of a population group or residents of an area, the ability of the residents of an area or of a population group to pay for health services and their accessibility to them, and the availability of health professionals to residents of an area or to a population group. Children and youth.

"(5) The Secretary may not designate a medically underserved population in a State or terminate the designation of such a population unless, prior to such designation or termination, the Secretary provides reasonable notice and opportunity for comment and consults with— Prohibition. State and local governments.

"(A) the chief executive officer of such State;

"(B) local officials in such State; and

"(C) the State organization, if any, which represents a majority of community health centers in such State.

"(6) The Secretary may designate a medically underserved population that does not meet the criteria established under paragraph (4) if the chief executive officer of the State in which such population is located and local officials of such State recommend the designation of such population based on unusual local conditions which are a barrier to access to or the availability of personal health services.". State and local governments.

Page

100 STAT. 399

Volume of Statutes at large

Source: United States Code Congressional and Administrative News, vol. 4 (St. Paul: West Publishing Company, 1986), p. 1286. Reprinted with permission.

United States Code (U.S.C.)

In 1926, committees of the House and Senate collected the current laws in the *Revised Statutes of 1875* and the current laws in *Statutes at Large* since 1873, and created the *United States Code* (U.S.C.), published by the Government Printing Office. Since 1926, a new edition of U.S.C. has been issued every six years. Since 1932, cumulative supplements have been issued each intervening year. U.S.C. has a general index.

The U.S.C. officially collects federal statutes topically in 50 **titles.** In 1982, the Office of Law Revision Counsel was created to collect, restate, and revise the federal statutes one title at a time for enactment into positive law. The titles of U.S.C. and their status are as follows:

1. General Provisions [positive law]
2. The Congress
3. The President [positive law]
4. Flag and Seal, Seat of Government and the States [positive law]
5. Government Organization and Employees [positive law]
6. [Surety bonds] [superseded by Title 31]
7. Agriculture
8. Aliens and Nationality
9. Arbitration [positive law]
10. Armed Forces [positive law]
11. Bankruptcy [positive law]
12. Banks and Banking
13. Census [positive law]
14. Coast Guard [positive law]
15. Commerce and Trade
16. Conservation
17. Copyrights [positive law]
18. Crimes and Criminal Procedure [positive law]
19. Customs Duties
20. Education
21. Food and Drugs
22. Foreign Relations and Intercourse
23. Highways [positive law]
24. Hospitals and Asylums
25. Indians
26. Internal Revenue Code
27. Intoxicating Liquors
28. Judiciary and Judicial Procedure [positive law]
29. Labor
30. Mineral Lands and Mining
31. Money and Finance [positive law]
32. National Guard [positive law]
33. Navigation and Navigable Waters
34. [Navy] [superseded by Title 10]
35. Patents [positive law]
36. Patriotic Societies and Observations
37. Pay and Allowances of the Uniformed Services [positive law]
38. Veterans' Benefits [positive law]
39. Postal Service [positive law]
40. Public Buildings
41. Public Contracts
42. The Public Health and Welfare
43. Public Lands
44. Public Printing and Documents [positive law]
45. Railroads
46. Shipping [Subtitle II is positive law]
47. Telegraphs, Telephones, and Radiotelegraphs
48. Territories and Insular Possessions
49. Transportation [Subtitles I, II, and IV are positive law]
50. War and National Defense; and Appendix.

U.S.C. titles may be divided into subtitles. Titles or subtitles may be divided into chapters, which may be divided into subchapters. Chapters or subchapters may be divided into parts, which may be divided into subparts. Under each title, statutes are organized in **sections.** Sections (which may have letter additions) may be divided into subsections. Sections or subsections may be further divided into paragraphs, subparagraphs, sentences, and words.

For example, the word *business* in the tax statute that defines a "Subchapter S" corporation (i.e., a corporation that may be taxed like a partnership) is the nineteenth word in the only sentence in the first paragraph of the first subsection of § 1361, which falls in part I of Subchapter S of Chapter 1 of Subtitle A of Title 26 of the U.S.C. Going back:

1. Title 26: Internal Revenue Code of 1986 as amended.
2. Subtitle A: Income Taxes.
3. Chapter 1. Normal Taxes and Surtaxes.
4. Subchapter S. Tax Treatment of S Corporations and Their Shareholders.
5. Part I. In General.
6. Section 1361. S Corporation defined.
7. Subsection (a). S Corporation defined.
8. Paragraph 1. In general.
9. Only sentence.
10. Nineteenth word.

Statutes are cited by title number, code abbreviation, and section number. For example, the statute that makes it a federal crime to assassinate the President of the United States, Section 1751 of Title 18 of the U.S.C., is cited 18 U.S.C. § 1751. The "Subchapter S" definition discussed above would be cited 26 U.S.C. § 1361 (a)(1).

The concept of positive law is discussed in the U.S.C. at 1 U.S.C. § 204(a). It is important to note, however, that the courts have uniformly held that if there is a conflict in wording between the chronological Stat. and the topical U.S.C., the chronological version, the Stat., controls.

Annotated Codes

The official U.S.C., published by the U.S. Government Printing Office, lacks a few basic features of importance to legal researchers.

First, as a government publication, the U.S.C. is not always published in a timely manner. A statute may be enacted and not appear in the U.S.C. or in a U.S.C. supplement for several months.

Second, the U.S. Government Printing Office does not publish an array of law books on par with West or LCP. As a result, the U.S.C. does not provide useful cross-references to other law books.

Third, as discussed above, the laws enacted by the legislature are subject to interpretation by the courts. The U.S.C. does not include summaries of court opinions that have interpreted particular statutes.

Filling the void, West and LCP publish their own versions of the U.S.C., using the same title and section numbering system.

West publishes the *United States Code Annotated* (U.S.C.A.) and LCP publishes the *United States Code Service* (U.S.C.S.). (See Figure 5–5.) Each is an **annotated code,** containing case summaries of how the courts have interpreted each statute. Each federal annotated code is a multivolume set, with each title of the U.S.C. contained in one or more volumes of the set. Each statute is set out, followed by history notes, research references, and case summaries. The history notes usually include references to Public Law numbers and the Stat. Each federal annotated code is kept current by cumulative annual pocket parts and replacement volumes, as well as by a current service.

Unless a legal researcher already has a reference to a particular code section,

Figure 5–5 Federal Codes

Publisher	Title	Features
U.S. Government Printing Office	U.S.C.	Official; unannotated
West	U.S.C.A.	Unofficial; annotated
LCP	U.S.C.S.	Unofficial; annotated

NOTE: These federal codes all have same title and section numbering system.

the most common method of entry into a federal annotated code is through an index. Each federal annotated code has a general index for the set and a "volume index" (i.e., an index of just one title, found in the last volume of the set containing statutes from that title). Since the volume indexes are usually much more detailed than the general index, you should generally use the volume index if you know the title in which the statute you are looking for will be found.

It is interesting to note that the general index for the U.S.C. was prepared under contract by West and that the indexers at LCP used that public domain index in preparing LCP's general index of the federal code.

Examples of Volume Indexes

Source: © Doug Martin.

The next most common method of entry into a federal annotated code is to work with the tables of contents in the front of each volume and at the front of each chapter of a title.

As will be discussed in Chapter 12, the U.S.C. and both federal annotated codes may be searched by computer.

The U.S.C. and both federal annotated codes also contain tables showing where statutes in the Stat. may be found in the U.S.C., where a section can be found in a revised title, and other similar tables. Both federal annotated codes also contain tables of acts by popular names.

United States Code Annotated (U.S.C.A.)

Since 1927, West has published the *United States Code Annotated* (U.S.C.A.). The U.S.C.A. follows the format and language of the U.S.C., which, as discussed above, is only *prima facie* evidence of the law, unless the relevant title has been enacted into positive law.

The U.S.C.A., as a major West publication, lists Topic and Key Number research references for a statute, references to other West publications, and references to specific sections of the *Code of Federal Regulations* (C.F.R.) (to be discussed in Chapter 7). Following West's philosophy of comprehensive publishing, the set includes extensive case summaries, apparently drawn from

A Set of United States Code Annotated (U.S.C.A.)

Source: © Doug Martin.

headnotes in the National Reporter System and/or digest paragraphs from West's digests. The case summary section is entitled "Notes of Decisions." (See Figure 5–6.)

As will be discussed in Chapter 6, the U.S.C.A. also includes volumes covering the Constitution of the United States and federal court rules.

The U.S.C.A. can also be searched on the WESTLAW (USCA database) computer-assisted legal research system, to be discussed in Chapter 12.

United States Code Service (U.S.C.S.)

Since 1972, LCP has published the *United States Code Service* (U.S.C.S.). The U.S.C.S. follows the format of the U.S.C., but its text follows the language in the Stat., which, as discussed above, controls when there is a conflict with the U.S.C. The titles of the U.S.C. are conveniently listed on the inside front cover of each volume. The U.S.C.S. also includes advance sheets with cumulative tables and slip laws.

The U.S.C.S., as part of LCP's Total Client Service Library, lists research references to other LCP publications (especially A.L.R. annotations), references to law review articles (to be discussed in Chapter 9), and references to the *Code of Federal Regulations* (C.F.R.) (to be discussed in Chapter 7). Following a philosophy of selective publishing, LCP's editors prepare case summaries for the U.S.C.S., known as **casenotes,** only when a case appears to add something new to the law. LCP also frequently prepares casenotes for administrative decisions. The casenote section is entitled "Interpretive Notes and Decisions." (See Figure 5–7.)

As will be discussed in Chapter 6, the U.S.C.S. also includes volumes covering the Constitution of the United States and federal court rules.

The U.S.C.S. can also be searched on the LEXIS (GENFED;USCS file) computer-assisted legal research system, to be discussed in Chapter 12.

The Limitations of Codes

A legal researcher should bear in mind that like headnotes, digest paragraphs, and A.L.R. setouts, U.S.C.A. case summaries and U.S.C.S. casenotes are finding aids that do not always accurately reflect the detail of a case opinion. They are written in a competitive environment and usually give only the holding of a court without its reasoning.

Moreover, the recent flood of court decisions has affected casenoting. In 1986, to limit the number of casenotes being drawn for the U.S.C.S., LCP directed its casenoters to avoid casenoting U.S. District Court opinions.

5–3 State Codes

Just as the legislative process of the federal government is illustrative of the legislative processes in the states, the books covering the legislative branch of the federal government are illustrative of the books covering the legislative branches of the states.

In general, state legislatures meet in sessions. The session laws are published separately as slip laws and in official chronological collections similar to the Stat. (e.g., *Laws of Washington*). Again, since legal researchers need to find legislation

Figure 5-6 Excerpt From the U.S.C.A.

Note 10

10. Suppression of evidence

Where inspection of defendant's premises was conducted following issuance of inspection warrant under this section, inspection was limited to administrative inspection and was conducted in accordance with this section, any matters revealed by such inspection were not subject to suppression in criminal proceeding. U. S. v. Prendergast, D.C.Pa.1977, 436 F.Supp. 931, affirmed 585 F.2d 69.

Where subsequent statements made by defendant were directly related to information gathered by Drug Enforcement Agency compliance officers as result of illegal search of defendant's pharmacy, defendant was entitled to suppression of such statements. U. S. v. Enserro, D.C. N.Y.1975, 401 F.Supp. 460.

§ 881. Forfeitures

Property subject

(a) The following shall be subject to forfeiture to the United States and no property right shall exist in them:

(1) All controlled substances which have been manufactured, distributed, dispensed, or acquired in violation of this subchapter.

(2) All raw materials, products, and equipment of any kind which are used, or intended for use, in manufacturing, compounding, processing, delivering, importing, or exporting any controlled substance in violation of this subchapter.

(3) All property which is used, or intended for use, as a container for property described in paragraph (1) or (2).

(4) All conveyances, including aircraft, vehicles, or vessels, which are used, or are intended for use, to transport, or in any manner to facilitate the transportation, sale, receipt, possession, or concealment of property described in paragraph (1) or (2), except that—

(A) no conveyance used by any person as a common carrier in the transaction of business as a common carrier shall be forfeited under the provisions of this section unless it shall appear that the owner or other person in charge of such conveyance was a consenting party or privy to a violation of this subchapter or subchapter II of this chapter; and

(B) no conveyance shall be forfeited under the provisions of this section by reason of any act or omission established by the owner thereof to have been committed or omitted by any person other than such owner while such conveyance was unlawfully in the possession of a person other than the owner in violation of the criminal laws of the United States, or of any State.

(5) All books, records, and research, including formulas, microfilm, tapes, and data which are used, or intended for use, in violation of this subchapter.

(6) All moneys, negotiable instruments, securities, or other things of value furnished or intended to be furnished by any

624

Figure 5–6 cont.

person in exchange for a controlled substance in violation of this subchapter, all proceeds traceable to such an exchange, and all moneys, negotiable instruments, and securities used or intended to be used to facilitate any violation of this subchapter, except that no property shall be forfeited under this paragraph, to the extent of the interest of an owner, by reason of any act or omission established by that owner to have been committed or omitted without the knowledge or consent of that owner.

Seizure pursuant to Supplemental Rules for Certain Admiralty and Maritime Claims

(b) Any property subject to forfeiture to the United States under this subchapter may be seized by the Attorney General upon process issued pursuant to the Supplemental Rules for Certain Admiralty and Maritime Claims by any district court of the United States having jurisdiction over the property, except that seizure without such process may be made when—

(1) the seizure is incident to an arrest or a search under a search warrant or an inspection under an administrative inspection warrant;

(2) the property subject to seizure has been the subject of a prior judgment in favor of the United States in a criminal injunction or forfeiture proceeding under this subchapter;

(3) the Attorney General has probable cause to believe that the property is directly or indirectly dangerous to health or safety; or

(4) the Attorney General has probable cause to believe that the property has been used or is intended to be used in violation of this subchapter.

In the event of seizure pursuant to paragraph (3) or (4) of this subsection, proceedings under subsection (d) of this section shall be instituted promptly.

Custody of Attorney General

(c) Property taken or detained under this section shall not be repleviable, but shall be deemed to be in the custody of the Attorney General, subject only to the orders and decrees of the court or the official having jurisdiction thereof. Whenever property is seized under the provisions of this subchapter, the Attorney General may—

(1) place the property under seal;

(2) remove the property to a place designated by him; or

(3) require that the General Services Administration take custody of the property and remove it to an appropriate location for disposition in accordance with law.

Other laws and proceedings applicable

(d) The provisions of law relating to the seizure, summary and judicial forfeiture, and condemnation of property for violation of

Figure 5–6 cont.

the customs laws; the disposition of such property or the proceeds from the sale thereof; the remission or mitigation of such forfeitures; and the compromise of claims shall apply to seizures and forfeitures incurred, or alleged to have been incurred, under the provisions of this subchapter, insofar as applicable and not inconsistent with the provisions hereof; except that such duties as are imposed upon the customs officer or any other person with respect to the seizure and forfeiture of property under the customs laws shall be performed with respect to seizures and forfeitures of property under this subchapter by such officers, agents, or other persons as may be authorized or designated for that purpose by the Attorney General, except to the extent that such duties arise from seizures and forfeitures effected by any customs officer.

Disposition of forfeited property

(e) Whenever property is forfeited under this subchapter the Attorney General may—

(1) retain the property for official use;

(2) sell any forfeited property which is not required to be destroyed by law and which is not harmful to the public;

(3) require that the General Services Administration take custody of the property and remove it for disposition in accordance with law; or

(4) forward it to the Drug Enforcement Administration for disposition (including delivery for medical or scientific use to any Federal or State agency under regulations of the Attorney General).

The proceeds from any sale under paragraph (2) and any moneys forfeited under this subchapter shall be used to pay all proper expenses of the proceedings for forfeiture and sale including expenses of seizure, maintenance of custody, advertising, and court costs. The Attorney General shall forward to the Treasurer of the United States for deposit in the general fund of the United States Treasury any amounts of such moneys and proceeds remaining after payment of such expenses.

Forfeiture of schedule I substances

(f) All controlled substances in schedule I that are possessed, transferred, sold, or offered for sale in violation of the provisions of this subchapter shall be deemed contraband and seized and summarily forfeited to the United States. Similarly, all substances in schedule I, which are seized or come into the possession of the United States, the owners of which are unknown, shall be deemed contraband and summarily forfeited to the United States.

Plants

(g)(1) All species of plants from which controlled substances in schedules I and II may be derived which have been planted or cultivated in violation of this subchapter, or of which the owners or cul-

626

Figure 5–6 cont.

tivators are unknown, or which are wild growths, may be seized and summarily forfeited to the United States.

(2) The failure, upon demand by the Attorney General or his duly authorized agent, of the person in occupancy or in control of land or premises upon which such species of plants are growing or being stored, to produce an appropriate registration, or proof that he is the holder thereof, shall constitute authority for the seizure and forfeiture.

(3) The Attorney General, or his duly authorized agent, shall have authority to enter upon any lands, or into any dwelling pursuant to a search warrant, to cut, harvest, carry off, or destroy such plants. END!

Pub.L. 91–513, Title II, § 511, Oct. 27, 1970, 84 Stat. 1276; Pub.L. 95–633, Title III, § 301(a), Nov. 10, 1978, 92 Stat. 3777; Pub.L. 96–132, § 14, Nov. 30, 1979, 93 Stat. 1048. ~~and~~!

Historical Note

References in Text. "This subchapter", referred to in text, was in the original "this title" which is Title II of Pub.L. 91–513, Oct. 27, 1970, 84 Stat. 1242, and is popularly known as the "Controlled Substances Act". For complete classification of Title II to the Code, see Short Title note set out under section 801 of this title and Tables volume.

"Subchapter II of this chapter", referred to in subsec. (a)(4)(A), was in the original "title III", meaning Title III of Pub.L. 91–513, Oct. 27, 1970, 84 Stat. 1285. Part A of Title III comprises subchapter II of this chapter. For classification of Part B, consisting of sections 1101 to 1105 of Title III, see Tables volume.

The criminal laws of the United States, referred to in subsec. (a)(4)(B), are classified generally to Title 18, Crimes and Criminal Procedure.

The Supplemental Rules for Certain Admiralty and Maritime Claims, referred to in subsec. (b), are set out in Title 28, Judiciary and Judicial Procedure.

The customs laws, referred to in subsec. (d), are classified generally to Title 19, Customs Duties.

Schedules I and II, referred to in subsecs. (f) and (g)(1), are set out in section 812(c) of this title.

Codification. "Drug Enforcement Administration" was substituted for "Bureau of Narcotics and Dangerous Drugs" in subsec. (e)(4) to conform to congressional intent manifest in amendment of section 802(4) of this title by Pub.L. 96–132, § 16(a), Nov. 30, 1979, 93 Stat. 1049, now defining term "Drug Enforcement Administration" as used in this subchapter.

1979 Amendment. Subsec. (d). Pub.L. 96–132 substituted "The provisions" for "All provisions", and struck out "and the award of compensation to informers in respect of such forfeitures" following "compromise of claims".

1978 Amendment. Subsec. (a)(6). Pub.L. 95–633, § 301(1), added par. (6).

Subsec. (e). Pub.L. 95–633, § 301(a)(2), (3), struck out of cl. (2) provisions relating to use of proceeds of sale and added provision relating to the forwarding by the Attorney General of money and proceeds remaining after payment of expenses.

Effective Date. Section effective Oct. 27, 1970, see section 704(b) of Pub.L. 91–513, set out as an Effective Date note under section 801 of this title.

Legislative History. For legislative history and purpose of Pub.L. 91–513, see 1970 U.S.Code Cong. and Adm. News, p. 4566. See, also, Pub.L. 95–633, 1978 U.S. Code Cong. and Adm.News, p. 9496; Pub. L. 96–132, 1979 U.S.Code Cong and Adm. News, p. 2003.

Cross References

Contraband articles, including narcotic drugs, seizure and forfeiture of carriers transporting, see section 781 et seq. of Title 49, Transportation.
Narcotic drug defined, see section 787 of Title 49.

627

Figure 5–6 cont.

21 § 881 FOOD AND DRUGS Ch. 13
Note 1

Library References

Drugs and Narcotics ⚷191. C.J.S. Drugs and Narcotics § 141.

West's Federal Forms

Forfeiture proceedings, see § 5891 et seq.
Judgment of condemnation, forfeiture and destruction, see § 4543.
Process in admiralty, see § 11271 et seq.

Code of Federal Regulations

Administrative policies, practices, and procedures, see 21 CFR 1316.01 et seq.
Inspection, search, and seizure, see 19 CFR 162.0 et seq.

Notes of Decisions

---

1. Constitutionality

This section, section 1595a of Title 19, and section 781 of Title 49 are not unconstitutional in failing to provide a prior hearing before seizure of the property. U. S. v. One 1973 Volvo, D.C.Tex.1974, 377 F.Supp. 810.

2. Construction

Provisions of subsec. (d) of this section relating to remission of forfeited vehicles should be liberally construed to effectuate remission. U. S. v. One 1976 Buick Skylark, 2-Door Coupe, Vehicle Identification No. 4W27C6K148647, D.C.Colo.1978, 453 F.Supp. 639.

This section authorizing seizure of derivative contraband articles, which are not intrinsically illegal in character, but derive their contraband status only from their association with criminal activity, must be strictly construed. U. S. v. One 1972 Datsun, Vehicle Identification No. LB1100355950, D.C.N.H.1974, 378 F.Supp. 1200.

3. Construction with other laws

Warrant requirement of this section would not be read into section 1595a of Title 19. U. S. v. One 1972 Chevrolet Nova, C.A.Mass.1977, 560 F.2d 464.

Forfeiture proceedings arising out of drug offenses are governed by same provisions as apply to customs forfeitures under section 1595 et seq. of Title 19. U. S. v. One Motor Yacht Named Mercury, C.A.R.I.1975, 527 F.2d 1112.

628

Source: United States Code Annotated, vol. 21 (St. Paul, MN: West Publishing Company, 1981), pp. 624–628. Reprinted with permission.

A Set of United States Code Service (U.S.C.S.)

Source: © Doug Martin.

topically, an official topical code is authorized in each state (e.g., *Revised Code of Washington*), which may or may not be positive law. The code is usually available in an annotated form (e.g., *Revised Code of Washington Annotated*). (See Appendix III.)

Again, unless a legal researcher already has a reference to a particular code section, the most common method of entry into a state annotated code is through an index. For example, in Ohio, each state annotated code has a general index for the set and more-detailed volume indexes for each title.

The codes set out each statute, followed by history notes, research references, and case summaries. Tables usually correlate earlier and later versions of the code. State codes also generally include some type of legislative service as a source of recent legislation.

To be discussed in Chapter 6, state codes generally also include volumes covering the state constitution and court rules.

Interestingly, there is no one book that collects the statutes of all the states. Some looseleaf services, which will be discussed in Chapter 7, contain comparative charts, and the *Martindale-Hubbell Law Directory,* which will be discussed in Chapter 8, includes a "law digests" volume comparing various state laws; but no one book collects the text of the law from each state. However, all statutes databases can be searched on the LEXIS and WESTLAW computer-assisted legal research systems, to be discussed in Chapter 12.

Under Article I, Section 10, Clause 3, of the Constitution of the United States,

Figure 5–7 Excerpt From the U.S.C.S.

ENFORCEMENT OF VOTING RIGHTS **42 USCS § 1973e**

CROSS REFERENCES

This section is referred to in 42 USCS §§ 1973a, 1973b, 1973i, 1973k.

RESEARCH GUIDE

Federal Procedure L Ed:
Elections and Elective Franchise, Fed Proc, L Ed §§ 28:81, 83, 109.

Am Jur:
16A Am Jur 2d, Constitutional Law § 655.
25 Am Jur 2d, Elections § 57.

INTERPRETIVE NOTES AND DECISIONS

42 USCS § 1973d(b) is constitutional, as it does not exceed authority granted to Congress by § 2 of Fifteenth Amendment; moreover, assignment of federal examiners does not violate Due Process Clause in precluding judicial review of administrative findings because right to due process applies only to persons and not to states. South Carolina v Katzenbach (1966) 383 US 301, 15 L Ed 2d 769, 86 S Ct 803.

§ 1973e. Examination of applicants for registration

(a) Form of application; requisite allegation of nonregistration. The examiners for each political subdivision shall, at such places as the Civil Service Commission [Director of the Office of Personnel Management] shall by regulation designate, examine applicants concerning their qualifications for voting. An application to an examiner shall be in such form as the Commission [Director] may require and shall contain allegations that the applicant is not otherwise registered to vote.

(b) Placement of eligible voters on official lists; transmittal of lists. Any person whom the examiner finds, in accordance with instructions received under section 9(b) [42 USCS § 1973g(b)], to have the qualifications prescribed by State law not inconsistent with the Constitution and laws of the United States shall promptly be placed on a list of eligible voters. A challenge to such listing may be made in accordance with section 9(a) [42 USCS § 1973g(a)] and shall not be the basis for a prosecution under section 12 of this Act [42 USCS § 1973j]. The examiner shall certify and transmit such list, and any supplements as appropriate, at least once a month, to the offices of the appropriate election officials, with copies to the Attorney General and the attorney general of the State, and any such lists and supplements thereto transmitted during the month shall be available for public inspection on the last business day of the month and in any event not later than the forty-fifth day prior to any election. The appropriate State or local election official shall place such names on the official voting list. Any person whose name appears on the examiner's list shall be entitled and allowed to vote in the election district of his residence unless and until the appropriate election officials shall have been notified that such person has been removed from such list in accordance with subsection

213

Figure 5–7 cont.

(d): Provided, That no person shall be entitled to vote in any election by virtue of this Act unless his name shall have been certified and transmitted on such a list to the offices of the appropriate election officials at least forty-five days prior to such election.

(c) Certificate of eligibility. The examiner shall issue to each person whose name appears on such a list a certificate evidencing his eligibility to vote.

(d) Removal of names from list by examiners. A person whose name appears on such a list shall be removed therefrom by an examiner if (1) such person has been successfully challenged in accordance with the procedure prescribed in section 9 [42 USCS § 1973g], or (2) he has been determined by an examiner to have lost his eligibility to vote under State law not inconsistent with the Constitution and the laws of the United States.

(Aug. 6, 1965, P. L. 89-110, Title I, § 7, 79 Stat. 440; June 22, 1970, P. L. 91-285, § 2, 84 Stat. 314.)

HISTORY; ANCILLARY LAWS AND DIRECTIVES

References in text:

"This Act", referred to in this section, is Act Aug. 6, 1965, P. L. 89-110, 79 Stat. 437, which appears generally as 42 USCS §§ 1973a et seq. For full classification of such Act, consult USCS Tables volumes.

Explanatory notes:

The bracketed words "Director of the Office of Personnel Management" and "Director" are inserted in subsec. (a) of this section on the authority of Reorg. Plan No. 2 of 1978, 43 Fed. Reg. 36037, 92 Stat. 3784, which appears as 5 USCS § 1101 note, which transferred all functions vested by statute in the Civil Service Commission, except as otherwise specified, to the Director of the Office of Personnel Management effective Jan. 1, 1979, as provided by Ex. Or. No. 12107 of Dec. 28, 1978, § 1-102, 44 Fed. Reg. 1055, which appears as 5 USCS § 1101 note.

Redesignation:

This section. formerly part of Act Aug. 6, 1965, P. L. 89-110 was redesignated as part of Title I of such Act by Act June 22, 1970, P. L. 91-285, § 2, 84 Stat. 314.

CODE OF FEDERAL REGULATIONS

Office of Personnel Management, Voting Rights Program, 45 CFR Part 801.

CROSS REFERENCES

This section is referred to in 42 USCS § 1973j.

RESEARCH GUIDE

Federal Procedure L Ed:

Elections and Elective Franchise, Fed Proc, L Ed §§ 28:70, 82, 84, 87, 103.

214

Figure 5–7 cont.

Am Jur:
16A Am Jur 2d, Constitutional Law § 655.
25 Am Jur 2d, Elections § 115.

Annotations:
Diluting effect of minorities' votes by adoption of particular election plan, or gerrymandering of election district, as violation of equal protection clause of Federal Constitution. 27 ALR Fed 29.

INTERPRETIVE NOTES AND DECISIONS

42 USCS § 1973e is constitutional, as it does not exceed authority granted to Congress by § 2 of Fifteenth Amendment. South Carolina v Katzenbach (1966) 383 US 301, 15 L Ed 2d 769, 86 S Ct 803.

Fact that Congress directs—in 42 USCS § 1973e—that voting examiners follow state law gives state court jurisdiction to enjoin examiners from acting contrary to state law, and administrative remedy provided in 42 USCS § 1973g applies only to questions of individual applicants' compliance with qualifications required and not to questions of what qualifications should be. Perez v Rhiddlehoover (1965, ED La) 247 F Supp 65.

Holder of federal certificate of eligibility to vote is not required to go to Mississippi registrar's office and sign oath in registration book, because eligibility to vote is determined as of the time of application to be registered, and this Act is self-executing once the applicant is listed and the certificate of eligibility is issued. United States v Mississippi (1966, SD Miss) 256 F Supp 344.

§ 1973f. Observers at elections; assignment; duties; reports

Whenever an examiner is serving under this Act in any political subdivision, the Civil Service Commission [Director of the Office of Personnel Management] may assign, at the request of the Attorney General, one or more persons, who may be officers of the United States, (1) to enter and attend at any place for holding an election in such subdivision for the purpose of observing whether persons who are entitled to vote are being permitted to vote, and (2) to enter and attend at any place for tabulating the votes cast at any election held in such subdivision for the purpose of observing whether votes cast by persons entitled to vote are being properly tabulated. Such persons so assigned shall report to an examiner appointed for such political subdivision, to the Attorney General, and if the appointment of examiners has been authorized pursuant to section 3(a) [42 USCS § 1973a(a)], to the court.

(Aug. 6, 1965, P. L. 89-110, Title I, § 8, 79 Stat. 441; June 22, 1970, P. L. 91-285, § 2, 84 Stat. 314.)

HISTORY; ANCILLARY LAWS AND DIRECTIVES

References in text:
"This Act", referred to in this section, is Act Aug. 6, 1965, P. L. 89-110, 79 Stat. 437, which appears generally as 42 USCS §§ 1973a et seq. For full classification of such Act, consult USCS Tables volumes.

Explanatory notes:
The bracketed words "Director of the Office of Personnel Management" are inserted in this section on the authority of Reorg. Plan No. 2 of 1978, 43 Fed. Reg. 36037, 92 Stat. 3784, which appears as 5 USCS

215

Source: United States Code Service, Title 42, Sections 1861–1982 (Rochester, NY: Lawyers Cooperative Publishing Co., 1986), pp. 213–215. Reprinted with permission.

states may enter into interstate compacts (e.g., to resolve boundary disputes or to create a port authority) with the consent of Congress. The text of an interstate compact can be located in the session laws of the respective sovereigns (congressional consent in the *United States Statutes at Large*). The text may also be located in the annotated codes of the respective states. Cases interpreting interstate compacts are digested under *States* Key Number 6 in West digests and under *States* Section Number 22 in the L. Ed. Digest.

5–4 Local Codes

Local governments exist only after the appropriate sovereign's legislature passes an **enabling act** allowing or creating the local government. The enabling act, along with the sovereign's constitution, gives the local government its power. When a local governmental body, such as a city council, legislates, it makes an **ordinance.** Ordinances may be collected topically in a code.

The codified ordinances of a local government are usually published by small private publishers. It can be difficult, if not impossible, to locate a copy of a local government's code outside the territory of the local government. If a copy is not available at the local law or public library, a legal researcher may have no choice but to review the code in the local government's offices.

Local codes are rarely annotated. However, local codes, especially local traffic laws, often mimic the state's statutes. When this is so, the state's annotated code may be consulted for case authority interpreting the statute/ordinance.

If the desired ordinance cannot be located in the local code by working the table of contents, you may find that the local code has a general index you can search.

SUMMARY

5–1

The legislative branch of government makes statutes. Federal law is made in the sense of being "dreamed up" by Congress. A proposed permanent law introduced in the House of Representatives or in the Senate is known as a bill. A bill that passes both houses is presented to the President and becomes law if the President signs it, if the President returns it within 10 days (Sunday excepted) and the veto is overridden by a two-thirds vote in each house, or if the President does not return it within 10 days (Sunday excepted) and the houses of Congress have not adjourned. Bills should be compared and contrasted with joint resolutions, concurrent resolutions, and simple resolutions. The laws enacted by the legislature are subject to interpretation by the courts. As a practical matter, the only time a legal researcher need research legislative history is if a court is deciding a case of first impression as to interpreting a statute. Legislative intent can be inferred from amendments, committee reports, debates, and hearings. While state legislative history theoretically exists, sources of state legislative history are usually nonexistent. Slip laws are collected and officially published in chronological order by the U.S. Government Printing Office in the *United States Statutes at Large* (Stat.).

5–2

Statutes come out chronologically, but they may be found topically with a specialized collection known as a code. The process of collecting permanent public statutes topically, adding amendments, and deleting expired, repealed, or superseded statutes is known as codification. The *United States Code* (U.S.C.) officially collects federal statutes topically in 50 titles. Titles may be divided into subtitles, chapters, subchapters, parts, and subparts. Under each title, statutes are organized into sections. Sections may be divided into subsections, paragraphs, subparagraphs, sentences, and words. Statutes are cited by title number, code abbreviation, and section number. The U.S.C. does not provide useful cross-references to other law books, and it does not include summaries of court opinions that have interpreted particular statutes. West and LCP each publish a federal annotated code. Each is a multivolume set, with each title of the U.S.C. contained in one or more volumes of the set. Each statute is set out, followed by history notes, research references, and case summaries. Each federal annotated code is kept current by cumulative annual pocket parts and replacement volumes, as well as a current service. Each has a general index and volume indexes for each title. West publishes the *United States Code Annotated* (U.S.C.A.), which lists Topic and Key Number research references for a statute, along with other references to West publications. LCP publishes the *United States Code Service* (U.S.C.S.), which lists research references to A.L.R. annotations and other LCP publications. A legal researcher should bear in mind that like headnotes, digest paragraphs, and A.L.R. setouts, casenotes are finding aids that do not always accurately reflect the detail of a case opinion or even refer you to every case.

5–3

Like the federal legislature, state legislatures meet in sessions. The session laws are published separately as slip laws, in official chronological collections, and in official topical codes, usually in annotated form. The most common method of entry into a state annotated code is through an index. The codes set out each statute, followed by history notes, research references, and case summaries. There is no one book that collects the statutes of all the states.

5–4

Local governments exist only after the legislature of the appropriate sovereign passes an enabling act allowing or creating the local government. When a local governmental body, such as a city council, legislates, it makes an ordinance. Ordinances may be collected topically in a code. The codified ordinances of a local government are usually published by small private publishers. A legal researcher often has no choice but to review the code in the local government's offices.

REVIEW

Key Terms

Before proceeding, review the key terms listed below to be sure you understand each one. If necessary, read over the corresponding section of the chapter. When you are ready to test your understanding, answer the Review Questions.

act
annotated code
bill
casenotes
code
codification
concurrent resolution
Congress
enabling act
enactment
engrossed bill
enrolled bill
joint resolution
legislative history
ordinance
pocket veto
positive law
prima facie
private law
public law
sections
session
session law
simple resolution
slip law
statutes
statutory law
titles
veto

Questions for Review and Discussion

1. What is the difference between a bill, a joint resolution, a concurrent resolution, and a simple resolution?
2. When do you need to research legislative history?
3. What is the official chronological source of federal legislation?
4. What is codification?
5. What is the official code of federal legislation?
6. What are the benefits of an annotated code?
7. How are the federal annotated codes indexed?
8. What research references does the U.S.C.A. have that the U.S.C.S. doesn't have? What research references does the U.S.C.S. have that the U.S.C.A. doesn't have?
9. Why shouldn't you cite a casenote in a brief?
10. Is there an annotated code for your state?

Activities

1. Go to a library that contains West's *United States Code Congressional and Administrative News* (U.S. Code Cong. & Admin. News). Pick out a recent volume. Examine some of the laws that have passed Congress. Develop a sense of the magnitude of man's quest for order under law.
2. Review a statute in LCP's *United States Code Service* (U.S.C.S.). Read the material printed just after the statute. "P.L." is referring you to "Public Law" whatever. "Stat." is referring you to *United States Statutes at Large.* Read through the history of the statute. If you feel like you understand some of it, you're on the right track.
3. If you can, visit Capitol Hill in Washington, D.C., or your state capitol. Visit the chambers of each house, and the offices of your local representatives. If you can't go to Washington, D.C., visit the local office of your congressional representative. Understand that you have a voice in the federal legislature and in your state legislature. Recognize the importance of exercising your right to vote.

CHAPTER 6 Constitutional Law, Court Rules, and Other Promulgations

NOTES

OUTLINE

6–1 Constitutional Law
- Federal Constitution
- Annotated Constitutions
- State and Local Constitutions

6–2 Court Rules
- Annotated Court Rules

6–3 Treaties

COMMENTARY

In your research of the federal laws that apply to the transportation of hazardous materials and the issue of preemption, you see references to the supremacy clause of the Constitution of the United States. Your mind is full of questions. Where is the supremacy clause in the Constitution? What exactly does it state? How have the courts interpreted it in other kinds of cases? Is preemption in your case typical or atypical?

OBJECTIVES

In this chapter you will learn about the sources of law under the Constitution and under the legislative, executive, and judicial branches of government, other than case law, statutory law, and administrative law. After reading this chapter, you should be able to:

1. Recognize the nature of constitutional law.
2. Identify sources of the text of the Constitution.
3. Identify the official version of the Constitution.
4. Identify the annotated sources of the Constitution.
5. Find the text of state constitutions.
6. Understand the nature of court rules.
7. List the different kinds of court rules.
8. Identify the annotated sources of the federal court rules.
9. Find state court rules.
10. Find treaties and executive orders.

6–1 Constitutional Law

The documents that form a government are known as that government's **charter.** In a loose sense, documents such as the Declaration of Independence and the Federalist Papers are part of the charter of the United States of America. In a strict sense, the charter of the United States of America is its written fundamental law, its **constitution,** the Constitution of the United States. Law directly derived from this fundamental document is known as **constitutional law.** (See Figure 6–1.)

Federal Constitution

Law is the command of a sovereign, and in the United States of America the people are sovereign. As the **preamble**—the introductory statement of legal intent—states, the people "to form a more perfect Union, establish Justice, insure domestic Tranquillity, provide for the common defence, promote the general Welfare, and secure the Blessings of Liberty" have exercised their power through the Constitution of the United States. As Article VI, Clause 2, of the Constitution provides, the Constitution, federal laws made pursuant to it, and treaties made under it, are the supreme law of the land. The Constitution returns some powers to the people, including the power to amend the Constitution and the power to vote.

The Constitution was drafted at the Constitutional Convention held in Philadelphia in the summer of 1787. Signed by 39 delegates on September 17, 1787, the Constitution became effective, by its terms, when it was ratified by the ninth state, which was New Hampshire, on June 21, 1788. The federal government began operating under the Constitution on April 30, 1789.

The Constitution is organized into articles, sections, and clauses. Articles I, II, and III cover the branches of the federal government. Article I covers the legislative branch; Article II covers the executive branch; and Article III covers the judicial branch. Article IV covers the states. Article V covers the amendment process. Articles VI and VII cover miscellaneous matters.

Figure 6–1 Constitutional Law

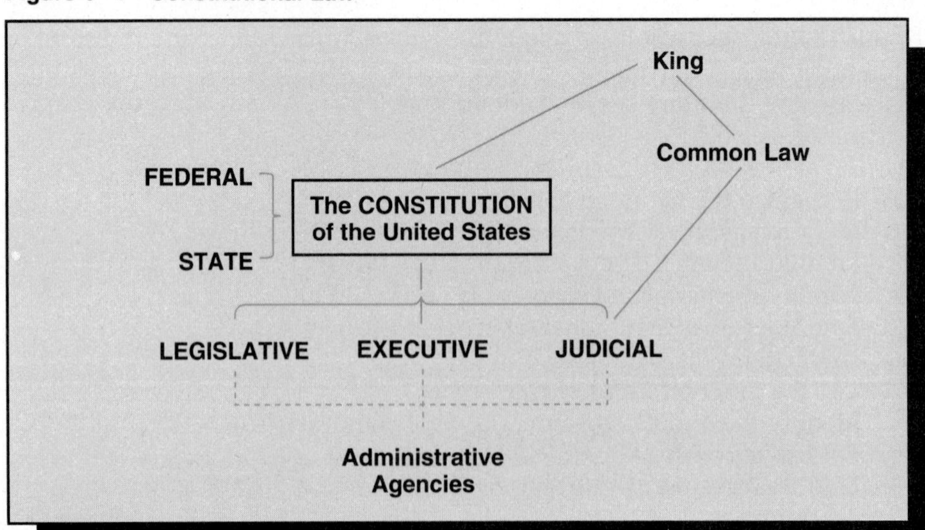

There have been 27 amendments (technically, additional articles) to the Constitution. The first 10 amendments, ratified by three-fourths of the states on December 15, 1791, are known as the **Bill of Rights.** The twenty-seventh was certified on May 18, 1992.

The Constitution is the most widely available law in the United States. The text is routinely reproduced in almanacs, encyclopedias, and dictionaries, especially law dictionaries. The text is also found in law, history, and political science texts, and in patriotic pamphlets and prints. Ironically, few people have ever read the Constitution from beginning to end. This fundamental document, important to legal researchers because it explains the structure of the government and the sources of law, is reproduced in Appendix I.

What is the official version of the Constitution of the United States? The answer is *the* Constitution of the United States, on parchment, under glass, bathed in helium, and lowered nightly into a vault below the floor of the Exhibition Hall Rotunda of the National Archives on Constitution Avenue in Washington, D.C.

Annotated Constitutions

Under the doctrine of **judicial review,** the clauses of the Constitution, like statutes, are subject to interpretation by the courts, particularly by the U.S. Supreme Court. In fact, since the Constitution was designed to be a flexible general guide for the government, it is subject to more interpretation than a

The Constitution of the United States at the National Archives

Source: © Paul Conklin.

statute, which, by design, is usually quite specific. Legal researchers usually need to refer to an **annotated constitution,** a version of the Constitution containing case summaries of how the courts have interpreted the Constitution.

Three annotated constitutions are preferred by most legal researchers for researching constitutional law. The most readily available annotated constitutions are the *United States Code Annotated* (U.S.C.A.) and the *United States Code Service* (U.S.C.S.); both were discussed with regard to statutes in Chapter 5. Both sets have volumes in which each clause of the Constitution is set out, followed by the usual code treatment: history notes, research references, and case summaries. The U.S.C.A., published by West Publishing Company (West), gives digest Topic and Key Number references. The U.S.C.S., published by Lawyers Cooperative Publishing (LCP), gives *American Law Reports* (A.L.R.) annotation references. Both sets may be entered by a volume index, and both sets are kept current by cumulative annual pocket parts and a current service.

The third source, much less widely available, is a one-volume annotated constitution entitled *The Constitution of the United States of America.* Published pursuant to a congressional resolution (see 2 U.S.C. § 168), it is prepared by the Congressional Research Service of the Library of Congress. Significant cases are weaved into the analysis following each clause.

Other sources of case authority and interpretation concerning the Constitution can be found in a variety of publications. As discussed in Chapter 3, both West and LCP publish digests covering the Supreme Court. As discussed in Chapter 4, LCP publishes annotations, particularly in *United States Supreme Court Reports, Second Lawyers' Edition* (L. Ed. 2d), that cover points ruled on by the Supreme Court. As discussed in Chapter 9, there are numerous treatises and periodicals covering legal issues of all kinds, including constitutional law.

State and Local Constitutions

As the people as a whole have for the federal government, the people of each state, as sovereign, have **promulgated** (made official and public) a constitution to be the fundamental law for their state. Just as the federal constitution can be found with a federal annotated code, state constitutions are usually found with their state annotated code, either as a separate volume or in an appendix. For example, Anderson Publishing Company publishes the Ohio Constitution, annotated, in an appendix volume to its *Page's Ohio Revised Code Annotated.* Again, an annotated version includes case summaries of how the courts have interpreted the constitution. Often cross-references are provided to similar constitutional provisions in other states and in the federal constitution, so a legal researcher can research case interpretations in other states as persuasive authority. Like codes, entry into an annotated state constitution may be made through a general or a volume index.

Another source of state constitutions is a three-volume set, *Constitutions of the United States: National and State,* prepared by the Columbia University Legislative Drafting Research Fund.

The fundamental law of a local government agency is usually known as its **charter.** Like local ordinances, a legal researcher may have no choice but to review the local charter in the local government's offices.

6–2 Court Rules

As discussed in Chapter 2, the courts have the power to decide real cases. Insofar as the sovereign's constitution and statutes (not unconstitutional) empower and direct the judicial process, the courts are bound to follow them. However, if no constitutional clauses or statutes direct the judicial process, the judicial branch has inherent power to promulgate its own rules governing its own activities in deciding cases. It is common for high-level courts to govern the lower courts and to establish uniform procedures through a system of court rules. (See Figure 6–2.)

For example, suppose your local county courthouse opens at 8:30 a.m. Why is it 8:30 a.m. instead of, say, 9:00 a.m.? The Constitution of the United States does not provide when state courts must open for the day. The state constitution probably does not provide when the state's courts must open for the day. The state statutes probably do not provide when the state's courts must open for the day. Since the court must open sometime to decide cases, and the relevant constitutions and statutes don't provide a time, the state courts then have inherent authority to set the opening time by rule. If the high or supreme court does not set the time, then an intermediate court might set the time. If not, the matter will be left to the discretion of the local trial judges. If they enter a rule on the public journal of the court, that's the time. If they don't, the matter will be left to the discretion of the individual judge.

Who makes the rules governing the filing of a civil lawsuit in a U.S. District Court? The U.S. Supreme Court does, but not because of inherent power. The Constitution provides twice, in Article I, Section 8, and in Article III, Section 1, that Congress has the power to create the lower federal courts. This is the legislative branch's check on the power of the judicial branch provided by the framers of the Constitution. Under Title 28 of the *United States Code* (U.S.C.), Congress has created the lower federal courts, but, under 28 U.S.C. § 2072, Congress has delegated to the Supreme Court the authority to make rules of procedure for the District Courts. Who makes the rules of procedure for cases before the Supreme Court? The Supreme Court. Since the Constitution is silent on the matter, the Supreme Court has inherent power and authority to make its own rules.

There are rules covering virtually every procedural act possible in the judicial branch. There are rules of civil procedure, criminal procedure, evidence (trial procedure), and appellate procedure and practice. There are rules of juvenile procedure, traffic court, claims court, and bankruptcy. There are rules governing

Figure 6–2 Court Rules

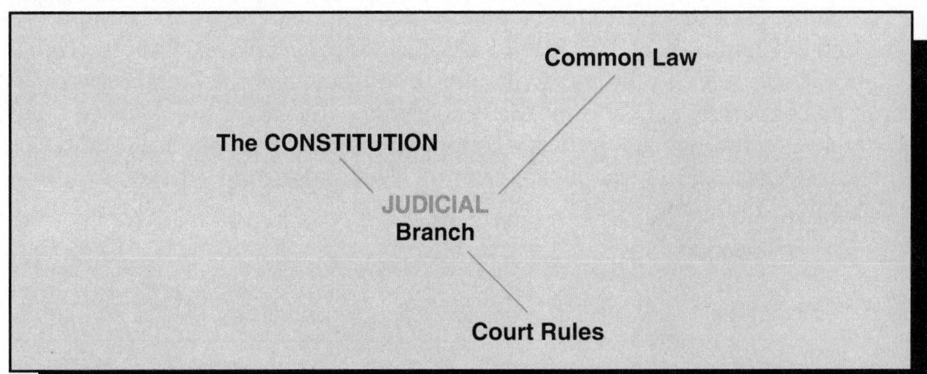

attorneys, judges, admission to the bar, grievances, and discipline. There are "codes" of rules regarding ethics and judicial conduct. The rules may be local, or, most often, rules of superintendence (general applicability).

Major publishers often publish court rules in pamphlet form. West, for example, publishes the rules of most states, including the federal courts in the state, in pamphlets titled by the state, "Rules of Court," year, and volume (e.g., *Michigan Rules of Court—1992—Federal*).

Publishers also publish pamphlets covering specific areas of law, which include the relevant statutes and court rules. West, for example, publishes the *Federal Criminal Code and Rules,* covering the relevant portions Titles 18, 21, 28, and 46 of the U.S.C., and the Federal Rules of Criminal Procedure, Rules Governing Section 2254 Cases, Rules of Procedure for the Trial of Misdemeanors Before United States Magistrates, Federal Rules of Evidence, Federal Rules of Appellate Procedure, and Rules of the Supreme Court.

Annotated Court Rules

Like constitutional clauses, court rules are subject to interpretation by the courts, and in particular, by the court that promulgated them. Thus, a legal researcher may need to refer to an annotated version of the court rules, a version of the court rules containing case summaries of how the courts have interpreted the court rules.

Just as an annotated constitution can be found with a federal annotated code, annotated federal court rules are found with a federal code, either in a separate volume or at the end of the volume of the relevant title. The principal federal annotated codes—the U.S.C.A. and the U.S.C.S.—were discussed with regard to statutes in Chapter 5. The U.S.C.S. covers federal rules in special "Court Rules" volumes.

The U.S.C.A. follows the relevant title method, locating, for example, the Federal Rules of Criminal Procedure at the end of Title 18, and the Federal Rules of Civil Procedure at the end of Title 28. In both sets, each rule is followed by the usual code treatment: history notes, research references, and case summaries. The U.S.C.A., published by West, gives digest Topic and Key Number references. The U.S.C.S., published by LCP, gives A.L.R. annotation references. Again, both sets may be entered by a volume index, and both sets are kept current by cumulative annual pocket parts and a current service.

Just as annotated federal court rules can be found with a federal annotated code, annotated state court rules are usually found with their state annotated code, either in a separate volume or at the end of the volume of the relevant title.

Other sources of case authority and interpretation concerning court rules can be found in a variety of publications. As discussed in Chapter 2, West publishes *Federal Rules Decisions* (F.R.D.) as part of its National Reporter System. As discussed in Chapter 3, LCP's *United States Supreme Court Digest, Lawyers' Edition* contains court rules volumes. LCP also publishes *Federal Rules Service.* As discussed in Chapter 4, LCP publishes annotations that cover points ruled on by the courts, including court rules. To be discussed in Chapter 9, there are numerous treatises and form books covering legal matters of all kinds, including those arising under court rules.

6–3 Treaties

As mentioned in Chapter 1, a nation-binding agreement with a foreign country is known as a **treaty.** Treaties are part of the rules governing sovereign countries by their consent, the law of nations, known as **international law.** Article II,

Court Rules Volumes of the U.S.C.S.

Source: © Doug Martin.

Section 2, Clause 2, of the Constitution of the United States provides that the President "shall have Power, by and with the Advice and Consent of the Senate, to make Treaties; provided two-thirds of the Senators present concur." If the President makes an agreement with a foreign country, but does not seek the advice and consent of the Senate, it is known as an **executive agreement.** The President may abide by an executive agreement, but his successor may ignore it, since it is, by definition, not nation-binding.

Article VI, Clause 2, of the Constitution of the United States provides that along with the Constitution and the laws made pursuant to it, "all Treaties made, or which shall be made, under the Authority of the United States, shall be the supreme Law of the Land; and the Judges in every State shall be bound thereby, any Thing in the Constitution or laws of any State to the Contrary notwithstanding." As the supreme law of the land, treaties affect everyone.

Treaties have been published in a variety of publications. Currently, all treaties and executive agreements in which the United States is a party are published as pamphlets in the *Treaties and Other International Acts Series* (T.I.A.S.), bound in volumes as *United States Treaties and Other International Agreements* (U.S.T.), each published pursuant to 1 U.S.C. § 112a by the U.S. Department of State. They are indexed by the *United States Treaties and Other International Agreements Cumulative Index.* Treaties and executive agreements are also published in *United States Statutes at Large* (Stat.) by the U.S. Government Printing Office.

Treaties in Force is an annual publication of the U.S. Department of State. It can be used, along with the monthly *Department of State Bulletin* and its monthly and annual indexes, to determine the current status of a treaty or executive agreement. *Treaties in Force* lists all currently effective treaties and executive agreements by country and by subject.

Some treaty publications cover particular subjects. Commerce Clearing House Inc. (CCH) publishes *Commerce Clearing House, Tax Treaties,* which covers treaties involving tax law. C. Kappler's *Indian Affairs, Laws and Treaties* covers treaties involving Indian tribes.

Like constitutional clauses and court rules, treaties are subject to interpretation by the courts. Thus, a legal researcher may need to refer to an annotated version of a treaty. LCP's annotated code, U.S.C.S., includes volumes of treaties by year of ratification, with casenotes.

SUMMARY

6–1

The charter of the United States of America is its written fundamental law, the Constitution of the United States. In the United States the people are sovereign, and they exercise their power through the Constitution. The Constitution, organized into articles, sections, and clauses, now includes 26 amendments. The clauses of the Constitution are subject to interpretation by the courts. The most readily available annotated constitutions are the constitutional volumes of the *United States Code Annotated* (U.S.C.A.) and the *United States Code Service* (U.S.C.S.). Both set out each clause of the Constitution, followed by history notes, research references, and case summaries. Both sets may be entered by a volume index. Just as the federal constitution can be found with a federal annotated code, state constitutions are usually found with their state annotated code.

6–2

If no constitutional clauses or statutes direct the judicial process, the judicial branch has inherent power to promulgate its own rules governing its own activities in deciding cases. It is common for high-level courts to govern the lower courts and to establish uniform procedures through a system of court rules. There are rules covering virtually every procedural act possible in the judicial branch. Major publishers often publish court rules in pamphlet form. Court rules are subject to interpretation by the courts, and so a legal researcher may need to refer to an annotated version. Annotated federal court rules are found with the annotated federal codes, either in a separate volume or at the end of the volume of the relevant title. Annotated state court rules are usually found with their annotated state code.

6–3

A nation-binding agreement with a foreign country is known as a treaty. If the President makes an agreement with a foreign country, but does not seek the advice and consent of the Senate, it is known as an executive agreement. Treaties have been published in a variety of publications. Currently, all treaties and executive agreements in which the United States is a party are published in *Treaties and Other International Acts Series* (T.I.A.S.) and in *United States Statutes at Large* (Stat.). *Treaties in Force* can be used, along with the *Department of State Bulletin,* to determine the current status of a treaty or an executive agreement. Treaties are subject to interpretation by the courts. *United States Code Service* (U.S.C.S.) includes volumes of treaties with casenotes.

REVIEW

Key Terms

Before proceeding, review the key terms listed below to be sure you understand each one. If necessary, read over the corresponding section of the chapter. When you are ready to test your understanding, answer the Review Questions.

annotated constitution
Bill of Rights
charter
constitution
constitutional law
executive agreement
international law
judicial review
preamble
promulgated
treaty

Questions for Review and Discussion

1. What is the fundamental law?
2. Do you have a source of the text of

the Constitution of the United States at home?

3. Where is the original Constitution of the United States?
4. Why would you use an annotated federal code to study a clause of the Constitution?
5. Where would you expect to find the text of your state constitution?
6. Where do the courts get the power to make court rules?
7. Name some of the different kinds of court rules.
8. Why would you use an annotated federal code to study a federal court rule?
9. Where would you expect to find your state's rules of civil procedure?
10. What book would you use to find out if a treaty is still in force?

Activities

1. Despite its fundamental importance, few people have ever read the Constitution of the United States from beginning to end. If you haven't, do so now. Turn to Appendix I for a copy of the complete text.
2. Find and read your state constitution. What are your constitutional rights under state law?
3. Find and read the two most-cited rules of court, the Federal Rules of Civil Procedure and the Federal Rules of Evidence. Note, however, that the most important rules of all may be the various appellate court rules. Appellate courts will throw out your appeal if you don't strictly comply with their rules. Before you appeal, *always* read, study, and follow the appropriate appellate court rules.

NOTES

CHAPTER 7 Administrative Law

OUTLINE

7–1 Administrative Agencies and Executive Departments
- Administrative Regulations
- Administrative Codes
- Administrative Orders and Executive Orders
- Administrative Decisions
- Attorney General Opinions

7–2 Looseleaf Services
- Tax Services

COMMENTARY

In your research of the federal laws that apply to the transportation of hazardous materials and the issue of preemption, you see references to the *Federal Register*, for example, 47 Fed. Reg. 51991 (1982), and to the *Code of Federal Regulations*, for example, 49 C.F.R. § 171 (1985). You are intrigued. To what extent does the U.S. Department of Transportation regulate the transportation of hazardous materials?

OBJECTIVES

In this chapter you will learn about sources of law subordinate to, but important as, law from the legislative, executive, or judicial branches. Emphasis is placed on the federal executive departments and independent agencies. After reading this chapter, you should be able to:

1. Understand why administrative agencies were created.
2. Compare and contrast administrative agencies and executive departments.
3. Understand basic administrative rulemaking.
4. Find regulations chronologically.
5. Find regulations topically.
6. Compare and contrast administrative and executive orders.
7. Recognize administrative decisions.
8. Recognize the nature and use of looseleaf services.
9. Identify the basic features of looseleaf services.
10. Identify the major federal tax services.

7–1 Administrative Agencies and Executive Departments

As a practical matter, as technology advances and society grows more complex, a sovereign's legislative, executive, and judicial branches become increasingly unable to manage all the details of government. The gaps are filled and the details are managed by the branches of government creating specialized governmental entities, known in the broad sense as **administrative agencies.**

For example, when the transmission and reception of electromagnetic radiation, radio, were developed in the early 1900s, few, if any, of the federal government's legislators, executives, or judges had sufficient expertise in electronics or physics to be able to govern its development. When the nation's first commercial radio station, KDKA in Pittsburgh, Pennsylvania, went "on the air" in 1920, the average legislator, executive, or judge did not foresee that someday there would be hundreds of radio stations across the country and countless radio-wave transmitting devices (e.g., automatic garage door openers) with potentially conflicting signals, causing "interference" with each other. When the need to govern the details of radio became apparent, such as the need to assign stations to particular frequencies of amplitude modulation (AM) or frequency modulation (FM), the legislature acted by creating a body of experts to manage the problem.

Under its constitutional authority to regulate interstate commerce, Congress, with the Federal Communications Act of 1934, created an independent agency, the Federal Communications Commission (FCC), to manage radio communications. The FCC grants radio station licenses, assigns frequencies, and is responsible for tracking down and stopping unauthorized radio broadcasts. One requirement of the FCC is familiar to almost everyone. Licensed broadcast stations must identify themselves on the air at least once every hour ("station identification").

In the narrow sense, an **administrative agency** is an "independent agency," a governmental entity distinct from the three branches of government, created to independently govern a limited specialized area of the law. (See Figure 7–1.) Since an administrative agency is distinct from the three branches of government, it has to answer only to the three branches of government in a formal way. For example, if the National Labor Relations Board (NLRB) wants to order a particular company committing an unfair labor practice against a union to reinstate a particular employee with back pay, it need not ask for specific permission from any of the three branches of government to do so. The legislature has already granted general authority to do so in the National Labor

Figure 7–1 Administrative Agencies

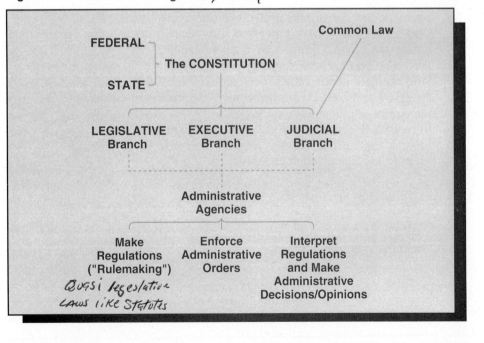

Relations Act, the executive has already appointed members to the NLRB with the power to do so, and the judiciary will enforce the orders of the NLRB to do so that the judiciary interprets to be within the mandate of the act.

Under the executive branch of government, groups of specialists may be organized to assist the executive in carrying out the functions of the executive branch. Among administrative agencies in the broad sense, these organizations are known as **executive departments.** (See Figure 7–2.) The heads of executive departments do not run entities distinct from the executive branch, and so they must answer to the executive both formally and informally. For example, if the Secretary of the Department of Defense wants to eliminate a major weapon system, it must be with the approval of the executive, the President, who is the commander in chief. Similar "executive departments" may also be created under the legislative branch (e.g., the General Accounting Office and the Library of Congress) and are known as **legislative departments.**

The technical distinction between administrative agencies and executive departments has been blurred in two ways. First, administrative agencies and executive departments are generally required by the sovereign to follow similar operating procedures. In the federal government, for example, each must follow the Administrative Procedure Act, which requires them to notify the public of proposed rule changes, hold public hearings, and the like. Second, the names given to the various administrative agencies and executive departments are often confusingly similar, yet widely varied.

An administrative agency, or a part of it, may be called, among other things, an administration, agency, authority, board, bureau, commission, corporation, department, division, foundation, office, or service. For example, local weather reports, watches, and warnings originate from offices of the National Weather Service (NWS), which is part of the National Oceanographic and Atmospheric Administration (NOAA), which is part of the U.S. Department of Commerce, which is, of course, an executive department of the President.

Usually the best way to sort out "who's who" is to consult an almanac, encyclopedia, directory, or manual. For the federal government, an extremely

Figure 7–2 The Executive Branch

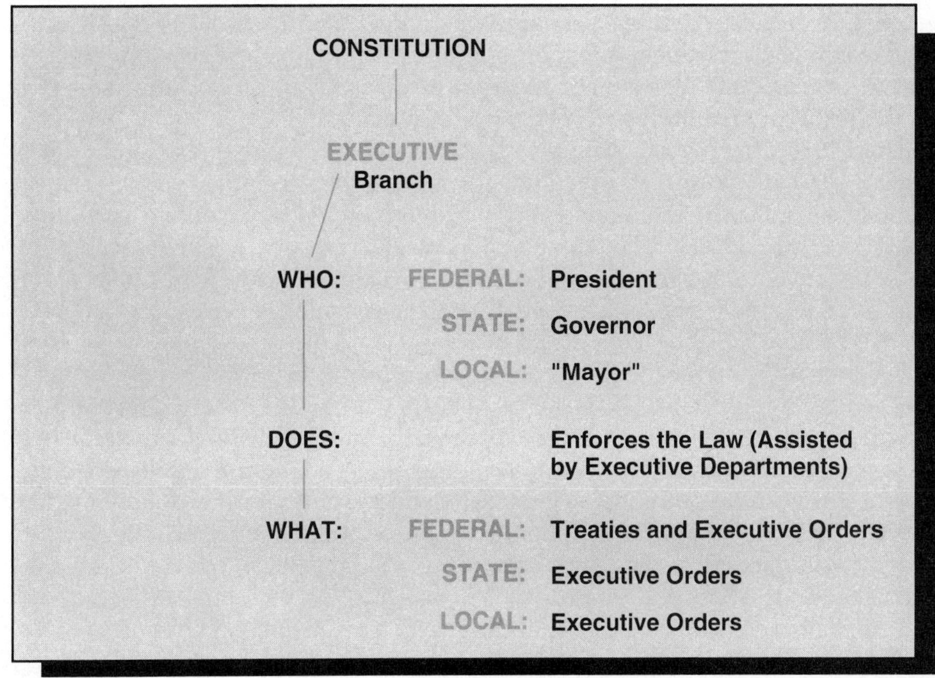

useful text is the *U.S. Government Manual* prepared annually by the National Archives. The *U.S. Government Manual* is a "road map" to the federal government. Each entity in the federal government is covered, with emphasis on the executive departments and independent agencies. Each entity and its function are described in a concise narrative, usually with citations to its statutory source of authority. The names and functions of the major officials are also listed. (See Figure 7–3.)

The *U.S. Government Manual* includes several useful indexes and tables. Appendix A lists agencies that have been abolished, or whose powers have been transferred and to where they have been transferred (e.g., the powers of the former Materials Transportation Bureau [MTB] of the Department of Transportation [DOT] are now exercised by the Office of Hazardous Materials Transportation [OHMT]). Appendix B is the famous "alphabet soup" table listing the acronyms for all the governmental agencies (e.g., CIA, FAA, FBI, NRC) and what they stand for (i.e., Central Intelligence Agency, Federal Aviation Administration, Federal Bureau of Investigation, Nuclear Regulatory Commission, respectively). (See Figure 7–4.) Appendix C contains governmental organizational charts.

Monitor Publishing Co. publishes several "Yellow Book" directories for the federal government. The *Federal Yellow Book,* for example, is described by the company as the "who's who in federal departments and agencies."

There are now hundreds of administrative agencies in the federal and state governments. Insofar as the number of administrative agencies is an accurate reflection of the complexity of society and its technological advances, it is evident that we live in a very complex, technologically advanced society.

Administrative Regulations

Like the sovereign's legislature, administrative agencies may "dream up" laws, so long as they are within the scope of the authority, the specialized area of law, given to the administrative agency by the legislature. To reflect the difference between the broad powers of the legislative branch and the limited powers of an administrative agency, however, the terminology is different. Whereas a legislature enacts statutes, an administrative agency issues **regulations.** Whereas a legislature legislates, an administrative agency **regulates.** Whereas statutes are made as the result of a legislature's enactment, regulations are made as the result of an administrative agency's **rulemaking.**

Until 1936, there was no official source for federal regulations. Ignorance of federal regulations and the resulting confusion were rampant. The situation came to a head in the infamous Supreme Court case *Panama Refining Co. v. Ryan* [293 U.S. 388 (1935)]. The Panama Refining Company was prosecuted for violating an administrative regulation, and the case reached the Supreme Court on appeal before it was discovered that the regulation in question had been revoked before the prosecution had begun.

To clear up some of the ignorance and confusion, in 1936, Congress passed the Federal Register Act [49 Stat. 500, 44 U.S.C. § 1504 et seq.]. The National Archives was given the duty of preparing and publishing (through the Government Printing Office) the *Federal Register* (Fed. Reg.). Published daily, except on Saturdays, Sundays, or legal holidays and the day following, the *Federal Register* is the official chronological source of federal regulations. For any federal administrative regulation or ruling to have legal effect, it must be published in the *Federal Register.*

Each daily *Federal Register* is about the size of a magazine, and bound volumes of the set are truly massive. The pages of the set are numbered consecutively

Figure 7–3 Excerpt From the *U.S. Government Manual*

POSTAL RATE COMMISSION

1333 H Street NW., Washington, DC 20268–0001
Phone, 202-789-6800

Chairman	Janet D. Steiger
Special Assistant	Maureen Drummy
Legal Adviser to the Chairman	Gerald E. Cerasale
Vice Chairman	Patti Birge Tyson
Special Assistant	W. Lawrence Graves
Commissioner	Henry R. Folsom
Special Assistant	(vacancy)
Commissioner	John W. Crutcher
Special Assistant	Leonard Merewitz
Commissioner	W.H. Trey LeBlanc III
Special Assistant	Jennafer W. Moreland
Chief Administrative Officer and Secretary	Charles L. Clapp
General Counsel	David F. Stover
Assistant General Counsel	Stephen L. Sharfman
Director, Office of Technical Analysis and Planning	Robert Cohen
Assistant Director, Office of Technical Analysis and Planning	Charles C. McBride
Director, Office of the Consumer Advocate	Stephen A. Gold
Personnel Officer	Cyril J. Pittack

[For the Postal Rate Commission statement of organization, see the *Code of Federal Regulations*, Title 39, Part 3002]

The major responsibility of the Postal Rate Commission is to submit recommended decisions to the United States Postal Service on postage rates and fees and mail classifications. In addition, the Commission may issue advisory opinions to the Postal Service on proposed nationwide changes in postal services; initiate studies and submit recommendations for changes in the mail classification schedule; and receive, study, and issue recommended decisions or public reports to the Postal Service on complaints received from the mailing public as to postage rates, postal classifications, postal services on a substantially nationwide basis, and the closing or consolidation of small post offices.

The Postal Rate Commission is an independent agency created by the Postal Reorganization Act (39 U.S.C. 3601–3604), as amended.

The Postal Rate Commission promulgates rules and regulations and establishes procedures and takes other actions necessary to carry out its functions and obligations. Acting upon requests from the United States Postal Service, or on its own initiative, the Commission recommends to the Board of Governors of the United States Postal Service changes in rates or fees in each class of mail or type of service. It submits recommended decisions on establishing or changing the mail classification schedule, and holds such hearings on the record as are required by law and are necessary to arrive at sound and fair recommendations. The Commission has appellate jurisdiction to review Postal Service determinations to close or consolidate small post offices.

Sources of Information

Employment The Commission's programs require attorneys, economists, statisticians, accountants, industrial engineers, marketing specialists, and administrative and clerical personnel. Requests for employment information should be directed to the Personnel Officer.

Reading Room Facilities for inspection and copying of records that are available to the public are located in Suite 300, 1333 H Street NW., Washington, DC. The room is open from 8 a.m. to 4:30 p.m., Monday through Friday, except legal holidays.

Rules of Practice and Procedure The Postal Rate Commission's Rules of Practice and Procedure governing the conduct of proceedings before the Commission may be found in part 3001 of title 39 of the *Code of Federal Regulations.*

For further information, contact the Secretary, Postal Rate Commission, 1333 H Street NW., Washington, DC 20268–0001. Phone, 202-789-6840.

Source: United States Government Manual, 1988–1989 ed. (Washington, DC: United States Government Printing Office), pp. 666–667.

Figure 7–4 Excerpt From the *U.S. Government Manual,* Appendix B

APPENDIX B: Commonly Used Abbreviations and Acronyms

ABMC	American Battle Monuments Commission
ACDA	United States Arms Control and Disarmament Agency
ACUS	Administrative Conference of the United States
ACYF	Administration for Children, Youth, and Families
ADAMHA	Alcohol, Drug Abuse, and Mental Health Administration
ADB	Asian Development Bank
ADD	Administration on Developmental Disabilities
ADEA	Age Discrimination in Employment Act
AEDS	Atomic Energy Detection System
AFBCMR	Air Force Review Board for Correction of Military Records
AFCARA	Air Force Civilian Appellate Review Agency
AFDB	African Development Bank
AFDC	Aid to Families with Dependent Children
AFDF	African Development Fund
AFIS	American Forces Information Service
AFPC	Armed Forces Policy Council
AFPPS	American Forces Press and Publications Service
AFRRI	Armed Forces Radiobiology Research Institute
AFRTS	Armed Forces Radio and Television Service
AFSC	Armed Forces Staff College
AGRICOLA	Agricultural OnLine Access
AID	Agency for International Development
AMS	Agricultural Marketing Service
Amtrak	National Railroad Passenger Corporation
ANA	Administration for Native Americans
AOA	Administration on Aging
APHIS	Animal and Plant Health Inspection Service
ARC	Appalachian Regional Commission
ARS	Agricultural Research Service
ASCS	Agricultural Stabilization and Conservation Service
ATSDR	Agency for Toxic Substances and Disease Registry
BEA	Bureau of Economic Analysis
BIA	Bureau of Indian Affairs
BIB	Board for International Broadcasting
BJA	Bureau of Justice Assistance
BJS	Bureau of Justice Statistics
BLM	Bureau of Land Management
BLMRCP	Bureau of Labor-Management Relations and Cooperative Programs
BLS	Bureau of Labor Statistics
BPA	Bonneville Power Administration
BSC's	Business Service Centers
CBO	Congressional Budget Office
CCC	Commodity Credit Corporation
CCEA	Cabinet Council on Economic Affairs
CCR	Commission on Civil Rights

Source: United States Government Manual, 1988–1989 ed. (Washington, DC: United States Government Printing Office), p. 785.

throughout the year and run into five figures. (See Figure 7–5.) Weekly, quarterly, and annual indexes are issued, but they are not cumulative. Seizing the publishing opportunity, the Congressional Information Service publishes the *CIS Federal Register Index,* which is cumulative.

The text of the *Federal Register* since July 1, 1980, is also available on the LEXIS (GENFED;FEDREG file) and WESTLAW (FR database) computer-assisted legal research systems, which will be discussed in Chapter 12.

State administrative regulations are rarely published chronologically.

Sample Issues of the *Federal Register* (Fed. Reg.)

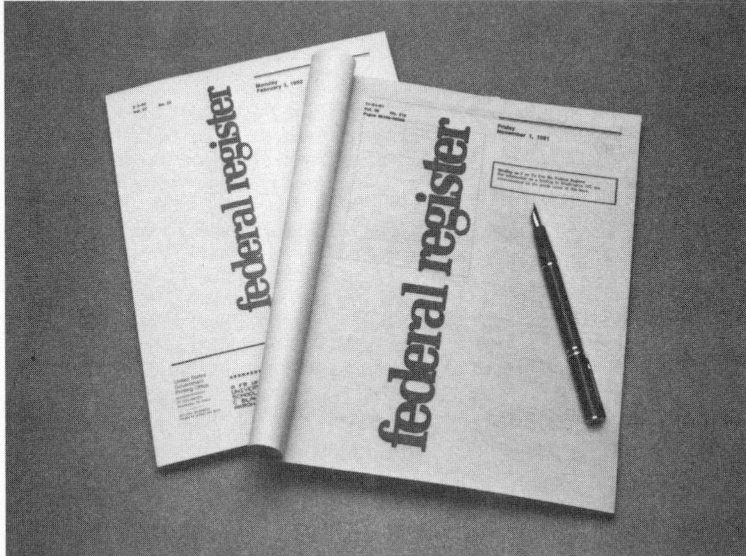

Source: © Doug Martin.

Administrative Codes

Just as statutes made by legislatures are collected topically in books called codes, regulations made by administrative agencies are also collected topically in books also called codes, or more specifically, **administrative codes.** As with the codification of statutes, the codification of regulations adds amending regulations to regulations currently in force and removes expired, repealed, or superseded regulations.

The official administrative code of the federal government, the topical collection of federal regulations, is the *Code of Federal Regulations* (C.F.R.), prepared and published (through the Government Printing Office) by the National Archives under the Federal Register Act. The C.F.R. is published in pamphlets in 50 titles generally parallel to the 50 titles of the *United States Code* (U.S.C.). The covers of the pamphlets are white and another color. To keep the code up to date, approximately one-quarter of the pamphlets are replaced each calendar quarter. The covers of the new year's pamphlets are white and a color contrasting from the previous year's color (e.g., 1990 was blue; 1991 was maroon).

To bring a pamphlet of C.F.R. up to date, one must consult the *Federal Register.* A monthly pamphlet, *LSA: List of CFR Sections Affected*, lists regulatory changes made since a particular title pamphlet was last published. The *Federal Register* also has a list "CFR Parts Affected" cumulated on the last day of each month, and cumulated daily back to the last day of the previous month.

The C.F.R. includes an annual index volume. Its entries are coordinated with the Office of the Federal Register's *Thesaurus of Indexing Terms* developed in 1980 (see 45 Fed. Reg. 2998, Jan. 15, 1980). The index also includes tables in a "Finding Aids" section.

The text of the C.F.R. is also available on the LEXIS (GENFED;CFR file) and WESTLAW (CFR database) computer-assisted legal research systems, to be discussed in Chapter 12.

If there is a conflict in language between the *Federal Register* and C.F.R., the *Federal Register* version controls.

Figure 7–5 Excerpt From the *Federal Register* (Fed. Reg.)

27872 Federal Register / Vol. 56, No. 116 / Monday, June 17, 1991 / Rules and Regulations

DEPARTMENT OF TRANSPORTATION

Research and Special Programs Administration

49 CFR Parts 107, 173, 178, and 180

[Docket No. HM-183, 183A; Amdt. Nos. 107-20, 173-212, 178-89, 180-2]

RIN 2137-AA42

Requirements for Cargo Tanks; Corrections

AGENCY: Research and Special Programs Administration (RSPA), DOT.

ACTION: Final rule; corrections and revisions.

SUMMARY: This amendment makes corrections and clarifying revisions to certain requirements pertaining to cargo tank motor vehicles in the Hazardous Materials Regulations (HMR, 49 CFR parts 171–180). These requirements were adopted in a final rule issued under Docket Nos. HM–183/183A (June 12, 1989, 54 FR 24982; May 22, 1990, 55 FR 21035; September 7, 1990, 55 FR 37028). The changes contained in this amendment will impose no new requirements on persons subject to the HMR.

EFFECTIVE DATE: June 17, 1991.

FOR FURTHER INFORMATION CONTACT:

Charles Hochman, telephone (202) 366–4545, Office of Hazardous Materials Technology, or Hattie Mitchell, telephone (202) 366–4488, Office of Hazardous Materials Standards, Research and Special Programs Administration, U.S. Department of Transportation, 400 Seventh Street SW., Washington, DC 20590–0001;

or

Richard Singer, telephone (202) 366–2994, Office of Motor Carriers, Federal Highway Administration, U.S. Department of Transportation, 400 Seventh Street SW., Washington, DC 20590–0001.

SUPPLEMENTARY INFORMATION: This document corrects typographical errors, omissions, and discrepancies to requirements in the HMR pertaining to cargo tank motor vehicles. Additionally, in response to inquiries received by RSPA concerning the clarity of particular requirements, changes are made which should reduce uncertainties. These changes impose no new requirements on persons subject to the HMR.

Because the amendments adopted herein clarify and correct certain provisions in the HMR, relieve certain restrictions in those regulations, and impose no new regulatory burden on any person, notice and public procedure are unnecessary. For these same reasons, these amendments are being made effective without the usual 30-day delay following publication.

The following is a section-by-section review of the amendments.

Section 107.504

The second sentence of § 172.504(c) implies that only those persons registered under the provisions of § 172.502(f) are eligible to renew their registrations. This error is corrected by changing "§ 172.502(f)" to "§ 172.502".

Section 173.33

RSPA has received several requests for clarification of the requirements contained in **§ 173.33(a)(2)**. The intent of this section is to prevent the transportation of two or more materials in the same cargo tank motor vehicle which, if mixed, would cause a vehicle fire, tank rupture or the release of acutely toxic vapors. An example of materials which would be prohibited are nitric acid and fuel oil. It was not intended to prevent the shipment of materials which if mixed would produce a moderate exothermic reaction that would not start a fire, rupture the tank or release acutely toxic vapors.

For hazardous materials offered for transportation in a cargo tank motor vehicle supplied by the motor carrier, § 173.22(a)(2) was revised in the September 7, 1990 amendment to clarify that shippers' responsibilities extend to the requirements in part 173 but not to the continuing requalification requirements contained in part 180. Section 173.33(a)(3) contains a requirement that, when the prescribed periodic retest or reinspection under subpart E of part 180 is past due, a specification cargo tank motor vehicle may not be filled and offered for transportation until the retest or reinspection has been successfully completed. Hazardous materials are often loaded at bulk loading facilities in cargo tank motor vehicles supplied by the motor carrier without the offeror in attendance. In these instances, verification of a carrier's compliance with part 180 is not possible. To alleviate this discrepancy, paragraph (a)(3) is revised to reflect that this requirement does not apply to an offeror in situations where the cargo tank is supplied by the motor carrier.

Paragraphs (c)(4) and (d)(1) contain criteria for the continued use of certain cargo tanks manufactured prior to December 31, 1990. Included are cargo tanks marked with a design pressure rather than a Maximum Allowable Working Pressure (MAWP), and cargo tanks fitted with non-reclosing pressure relief devices. The December 31, 1990 date should have been adjusted to coincide with the last date on which a cargo tank may be marked or certified to the MC specifications in effect on December 30, 1990. Accordingly in paragraphs (c)(4) and (d)(1), the date "December 31, 1990" is revised to read "August 31, 1993". In paragraph (c)(2), the December 31, 1990 date for requiring a cargo tank to be marked or remarked with an MAWP or design pressure in accordance with § 180.405(k) remains unchanged.

Many hazardous material liquids transported in cargo tanks are required to be completely blanketed with an inert gas, (e.g., see §§ 173.190 and 173.247a). To clarify the intent of the requirements of paragraph (d)(2), the wording "in its gaseous state" is revised to read "with a gas pad".

Formerly, § 173.33 contained various provisions pertaining to commodities, cargo tank design, qualification, maintenance and use of cargo tanks. Under HM–183/183A, these provisions were placed elsewhere in parts 173, 178 and 180, as appropriate. It has been brought to RSPA's attention that several provisions placed in the MC 331 specification, i.e. in §§ 178.337–1(e), 178.337–9 (b) and (d), and 178.337–15, also apply to existing MC 330 cargo tanks, and that Parts 173 and 180 contain no references to apply those requirements to MC 330 cargo tanks. RSPA plans to address reinstating these provisions for MC 330 cargo tanks in a rulemaking proposal in the near future.

Sections 173.245–17.374

In § 173.245, authorization for the use of DOT 406 cargo tanks was inadvertently omitted in the introductory text to paragraph (a)(29). This omission is corrected.

Also in the September amendment, §§ 172.101 and 173.154 were amended by increasing the concentration cut-off point for ammonium nitrate solution from "containing not less than 15% water" to "containing 35% or less water". RSPA stated in the preamble discussion that the entry for "Ammonium nitrate solution" was being revised to reflect that ammonium nitrate solutions with "35% or less water" do not meet the definition of an oxidizer. This statement should have read that such solutions with "over 35% water" do not meet the definition of an oxidizer. Also, in Docket HM–181 (December 21, 1990; 55 FR 52584), § 172.101 Hazardous Materials Table, special provision B5 to the entry "Ammonium nitrate, liquid (hot concentrated solution)" refers to

Code of Federal Regulations (C.F.R.)

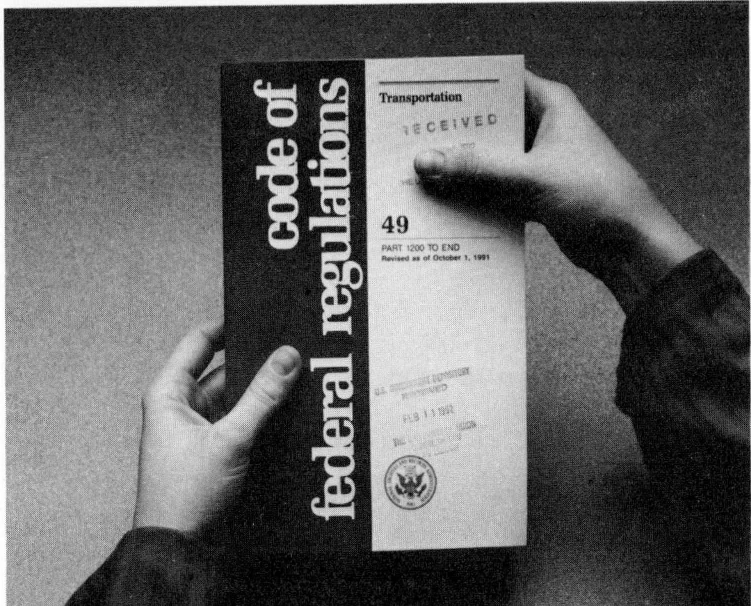

Source: © Doug Martin.

State administrative regulations are often published topically in state administrative codes. (See Appendix III.) Often a free copy of current codified regulations can be obtained simply by calling or writing the relevant agency.

Administrative Orders and Executive Orders

When the administrator of an administrative agency formally exercises discretionary "executive" power, the administrator makes an **administrative order.** When the executive of the executive branch formally exercises discretionary executive power, the executive makes an **executive order.** For example, Congress has given the President the discretion to suspend trade with a foreign country for 30 days without congressional consent. If the President wants to exercise the discretion to suspend trade with a foreign country for 30 days, the President does so by issuing an executive order. By custom, executive orders having no continuing legal effect, such as declaring a certain day to be "National Whatever Day," are known as **proclamations.** Presidential documents can be found in a variety of sources. The Office of Federal Register sources include the *Federal Register,* Title 3 of the C.F.R., the *Codification of Presidential Proclamations and Executive Orders,* and the *Weekly Compilation of Presidential Documents,* the latter including lists of laws approved, nominations, and other material released by the White House. Proclamations and executive orders are also found in *United States Code Congressional and Administrative News* (U.S. Code Cong. & Admin. News) and in advance pamphlets to the *United States Code Service* (U.S.C.S.). Proclamations also appear in *United States Statutes at Large* (Stat.).

State administrative and executive orders are rarely published, but they are in some states (e.g., Michigan).

Administrative Decisions

Since there may be a continuing need to interpret administrative regulations, many administrative agencies exercise judicial-like functions. For example, the Office of Hearings and Appeals of the Social Security Administration hears disputes concerning whether a person is disabled enough to be entitled to Social Security disability benefits. The "judge" in an administrative hearing is known as an **administrative law judge.** The administrative law judge's decision may be explained in an **administrative decision.**

Administrative decisions may or may not be appealed to the courts, depending on the subject matter involved. For example, decisions of the federal government's Employees' Compensation Appeals Board are not appealable to the courts because the board interprets a voluntary compensation act, the Federal Employee's Compensation Act, and not a liability act, such as the Federal Employers' Liability Act.

Like judicial opinions, administrative decisions are published in reports. The Government Printing Office publishes federal administrative decisions of various agencies in a variety of specialized reporters. These Government Printing Office publications are usually available at major federal depository libraries. Decisions of major federal administrative agencies are also published, usually in looseleaf form, by private publishers. State administrative decisions, except in the areas of tax law and workers' compensation, are rarely published.

Attorney General Opinions

An **attorney general** is the chief lawyer for a sovereign. The attorney general gives legal advice to officials in the executive branch, especially about the proper operation of governmental entities and agencies. When an executive official asks the attorney general for advice, it is a common practice, especially in the various states, for the attorney general to answer with a formal written opinion: an official memorandum of law.

Although the opinion of an attorney general is official, it is essentially advice and so is not considered primary authority. However, the opinions of attorneys general are ordinarily followed by governmental officials, and so they are considered very persuasive authority.

The opinions of the attorneys general are usually published by the appropriate sovereign. Many are also available on the LEXIS (e.g., GENFED;USAG file) and WESTLAW (e.g., USAG database) computer-assisted legal research systems, which will be discussed in Chapter 12. They are usually annotated in the sovereign's annotated codes. Citations to opinions of attorneys general are also cited in *Shepard's Citations,* to be discussed in Chapter 11.

7–2 Looseleaf Services

A **looseleaf service** is a law publication, usually a set of books, issued in notebook form.

Until recently, the law was published in notebook form only where the law was so complex and changed so rapidly that it was impractical to publish it in the permanent bound volumes or in permanent bound volumes with pocket supplements. The advantage of a looseleaf service, that the publisher could keep the service up to date simply by periodically issuing new or replacement

Looseleaf Services

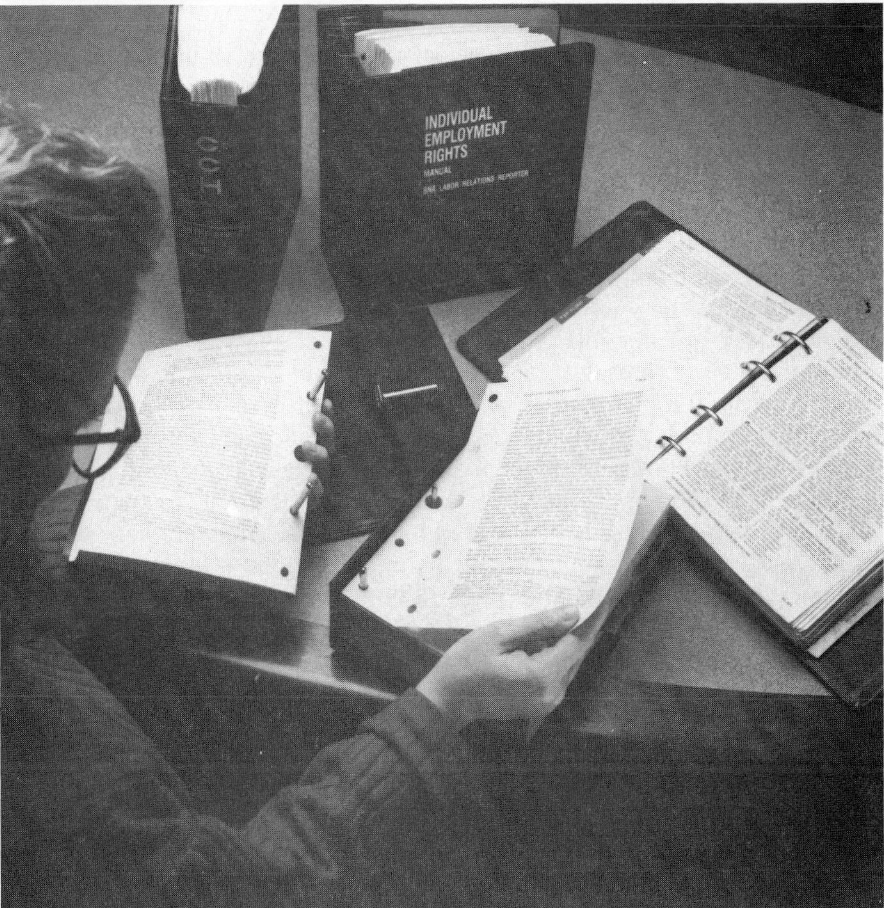

Source: © Doug Martin.

pages to be inserted into the set, was compatible with the need to keep up with the complex nature of, and rapid changes in, the law.

Recently, however, some publishers have shifted to publishing in notebook form simply because it is cheaper for them to do so. In 1986, for example, the Lawyers Co-operative Publishing Company (LCP) started several publications as looseleaf services, rather than as a set of bound volumes, in part because it had acquired the ability to make notebooks at its own manufacturing plant. Moreover, some publishers simply prefer to offer their supplementation in looseleaf form. Sometimes, instead of issuing individual replacement pages, publishers issue whole replacement sections, thereby making the updating of the looseleaf service quicker, simpler, and more convenient.

Understand that in the age of computer databases, the value of the permanent bound volume has declined. Information in a computer database, properly backed up, is almost as permanent as the information in a bound volume. When information is in a computer database it can be searched electronically, and it doesn't take up nearly as much shelf space as information in a book. Today, the importance of printed material is more in its readability than in its permanency, and in terms of readability, a looseleaf service is just as readable as a bound volume.

Still, most looseleaf services are published for complex and rapidly changing areas of the law, and the law that is most complex (involving specialized areas of the law), and changes most rapidly, is administrative law. In addition, most looseleaf services tend to cover areas of the law dealing with money, where the practitioners of the law tend to be those who can afford to pay for an up-to-date notebook service. As a result, most looseleaf services cover tax and business law.

Most of the major national looseleaf services are published by one of four major private publishers: Bureau of National Affairs, Inc. (BNA); Commerce Clearing House, Inc. (CCH); Prentice-Hall Information Services (P-H), a division of Simon & Schuster, Inc.; and Research Institute of America (RIA). There are looseleaf services available in almost every conceivable tax and business-related area of the law, including income tax, estate tax, pensions, securities, labor law, employment discrimination law, and the like. Looseleaf services can usually be located in law libraries according to the Library of Congress Classification system discussed in Appendix IV.

Almost every major looseleaf service begins with a section explaining how to use the set, including summaries of the contents, indexes, tables, and other available finding aids. Most looseleaf services are organized according to sections or paragraph numbers, which are relatively permanent, rather than by page number. There are page numbers, but they are there only to keep track of the pages in the set. Pages may be added to the set, but they are kept under a particular section or paragraph number by adding letters after page numbers (e.g., a page 12A to be added after page 12 but before page 13).

One excellent feature of a looseleaf service is the ease in which the publisher can bring together in one place all the sources of law, primary and secondary, on a particular subject, even while the law is changing. Instead of a researcher having to look in one book for a statute, another for a regulation, another for a textbook discussion, and another for a case opinion, a looseleaf service can be designed to bring all of this information together on a particular topic in consecutive pages of the notebook. Whether there are major or minor changes, a replacement page can be sent to the customer.

Looseleaf services ordinarily contain the text of the statutes, legislative history, and regulations concerning a particular topic, along with a text discussion, tables, and indexes. Sometimes there is a "current developments" section that includes the most recent material available that the publisher has not had sufficient time to edit into the main text and provide the replacement pages.

Tax Services

The complexity of tax law is well known, as is its political nature, making it subject to frequent changes and revisions. Thus, tax law is ideally suited to treatment in looseleaf services. Accordingly, the three major federal tax looseleaf services deserve special mention.

CCH publishes the *Standard Federal Tax Reporter.* It is organized in the format of the Internal Revenue Code (26 U.S.C.). After each code section, relevant regulations are presented, followed by a text discussion of the topic of the code section, followed by case summaries. CCH supports its commitment to tax law by publishing a general tax case reporter, *United States Tax Cases* (U.S.T.C.), and a reporter of U.S. Tax Court memorandum opinions, *Tax Court Memorandum Decisions* (T.C.M.). CCH also publishes a tax handbook, *U.S. Master Tax Guide,* keyed to the *Standard Federal Tax Reporter.*

RIA publishes the 35-volume *Federal Tax Coordinator 2d.* Rather than following the Internal Revenue Code section by section, RIA has broken down the law by topic. Major topic headings are lettered from A to V, with each federal code section and regulation reprinted by topic in the appropriate volume. The text is broken down into paragraphs cited by letter heading and paragraph number (e.g., V-2118). There are multiple finding aids for the set, including a topical index, and finding tables from the Internal Revenue Code, regulations, rulings, and cases. A companion set, *Tax Action Coordinator,* includes a tax analysis of legal forms and a complete set of tax forms. RIA also publishes a two-volume streamlined set, *Tax Guide,* and a tax handbook, the *Master Federal Tax Manual,* keyed to the *Federal Tax Coordinator 2d.* The entire RIA editorial staff consists of tax attorneys and accountants, who seek to write RIA services in "clear business English."

P-H publishes *Federal Taxes 2d.* Whereas P-H's first tax service was organized around the Internal Revenue Code (26 U.S.C.), like CCH's *Standard Federal Tax Reporter, Federal Taxes 2d* is broken down by topic, similar to RIA's *Federal Tax Coordinator 2d.* P-H supports its commitment to tax law by publishing a general tax case reporter, the *American Federal Tax Reports 2d* (A.F.T.R.2d) and a reporter of U.S. Tax Court memorandum opinions, *Memorandum Decisions of the Tax Court* (T.C.M.).

SUMMARY

7–1

The details of government are increasingly being managed by specialized governmental entities known as administrative agencies. Technically, an administrative agency is an "independent agency," a governmental entity distinct from the three branches of government, created to independently govern a limited specialized area of the law, which only has to answer to the three branches of government in a formal way. Executive departments are groups of specialists organized to assist the executive in carrying out the functions of the executive branch. The heads of executive departments must answer to the executive both formally and informally. An administrative agency, or a part of it, may be called, among other things, an administration, agency, authority, board, bureau, commission, corporation, department, division, foundation, office, or service. Usually the best way to sort out "who's who" is to consult an almanac, encyclopedia, or government directory or manual. For the federal government, a useful text is the *U.S. Government Manual,* which includes several useful indexes and tables. Appendix B is the famous "alphabet soup" table listing the acronyms for all the governmental agencies and what they stand for. An administrative agency issues regulations. The *Federal Register* (Fed. Reg.) is the official chronological source of federal regulations. Regulations made by administrative agencies are collected topically in books known as codes. The official topical collection of federal regulations is the *Code of Federal Regulations* (C.F.R.). When the executive of the executive branch formally exercises discretionary executive power, the executive makes an executive order. Executive orders having no continuing legal effect are known as proclamations. Presidential documents can be found in a variety of sources. Many administrative agencies exercise judicial-like functions. An administrative law judge's decision may be explained in an administrative decision. Administrative decisions may or may not be appealed to the courts, depending on the subject matter involved. Administrative decisions are published in reports.

7–2

A looseleaf service is a law publication, usually a set of books, issued in notebook form. Until recently, the law was published in notebook form only where the law was so complex and changed so rapidly that it was impractical to publish it in the permanent bound volumes or in permanent bound volumes with pocket supplements. Recently, however, some publishers have shifted to publishing in notebook form simply because it is cheaper for them to do so. Most looseleaf services are published for complex and rapidly changing areas of the law, and the law that is most complex (involving specialized areas of the law), and changes most rapidly, is administrative law. Most looseleaf services cover tax and business law. There are looseleaf services available in almost every conceivable tax and business-related area of the law. Most looseleaf services are organized according to sections or paragraph numbers, which are relatively permanent, rather than by page number. There are page numbers, but they are there only to keep track of the pages in the set. One feature of a looseleaf service is that it brings together in one place all the sources of law, primary and secondary, on a particular subject, even while the law is changing. Looseleaf services ordinarily contain the text of the statutes, legislative history, and regulations concerning a particular topic, along with a text discussion, tables, and indexes. Tax law is ideally suited to treatment in looseleaf services. The three major federal tax looseleaf services are CCH's *Standard Federal Tax Reporter,* RIA's *Federal Tax Coordinator 2d,* and Prentice-Hall's *Federal Taxes 2d.*

REVIEW

Key Terms

Before proceeding, review the key terms listed below to be sure you understand each one. If necessary, read over the corresponding section of the chapter. When you are ready to test your understanding, answer the Review Questions.

administrative agencies
administrative agency
administrative codes
administrative decision
administrative law judge
administrative order
attorney general
executive departments
executive order
legislative departments
looseleaf service
proclamations
regulates
regulations
rulemaking

Questions for Review and Discussion

1. Why are administrative agencies created?
2. How is an independent administrative agency different from an executive department?
3. What is the process called of making a regulation?
4. What is the official chronological source of federal regulations?
5. What is the official topical source of federal regulations?
6. How is a proclamation different from other executive orders?
7. What is an administrative law judge's written reasons for his or her decision called?
8. What, essentially, is a looseleaf service?
9. Why is a looseleaf better than a statutory code, an administrative code, a textbook, and a case reporter?
10. What are the major federal tax services?

Activities

1. Select a volume of U.S.C.A. or U.S.C.S., look up a statute, and find a cross-reference to C.F.R. Find the appropriate C.F.R. pamphlet and look up the C.F.R. reference. Notice how the regulations in C.F.R. are much more detailed than the statutes on the same topic.
2. Browse the aisles of your local law library and look for looseleaf services. How many does the library have? Is there an assortment, on a variety of topics? Do you feel that the collection is adequate and appropriate for your needs?
3. Thoroughly examine a major tax service, such as RIA's *Federal Tax Coordinator 2d.* Read the instructions on the use of the set. Do you understand each part, index, and table? Do you agree that basic tax research is not as difficult as it first appears?

PART THREE

RESEARCHING SECONDARY AUTHORITY

NOTES

CHAPTER 8 General Works

OUTLINE

8–1 Encyclopedias
Guide to American Law
Corpus Juris Secundum
American Jurisprudence 2d
State Encyclopedias
Law Outlines
8–2 Dictionaries
Black's Law Dictionary
Ballentine's Law Dictionary
Gifis' *Law Dictionary*
Other Dictionaries
8–3 Directories
Martindale-Hubbell Law Directory
Other National Directories
State, Local, and Specialized Directories

COMMENTARY

After completing your research of the federal laws that apply to the transportation of hazardous materials and the issue of preemption, you return to your preparation of a memorandum on public religious displays. But first, you want to get more background information on First Amendment law because you find the subject fascinating. What books can you turn to for an overview? Are there any books that explain words like *sedition* and phrases like "clear and present danger"?

OBJECTIVES

In this chapter you will learn about the general secondary sources of the law. These reference books are often used as a starting point for research in an unfamiliar area of the law, as a tool for legal self-study, or as a source of information about a particular lawyer or law firm. After reading this chapter, you should be able to:

1. Begin legal research in an unfamiliar area of the law.
2. Use *Corpus Juris Secundum* (C.J.S.).
3. Use *American Jurisprudence 2d* (Am. Jur. 2d).
4. Identify any legal encyclopedia for your state.
5. Understand the status of commercial law outlines.
6. Understand the poor quality of law dictionaries.
7. Recognize the benefits of *Black's Law Dictionary*.

8. Recognize the benefits of *Ballentine's Law Dictionary.*
9. Recognize the benefits of Gifis' *Law Dictionary.*
10. Use national and state legal directories.

8–1 Encyclopedias

An **encyclopedia** is a comprehensive work that covers all of the subjects within a particular branch of knowledge (or all branches of knowledge). While an encyclopedia covers all of a branch of knowledge and includes some detail, it is essentially a summary that does not include everything. An encyclopedia does not replace all other books on a given subject, it just ties them together.

A famous saying about the law, variously attributed, is that "the law is a seamless web." This is true in two senses. First, the law of property overlaps the law of contracts, which overlaps the law of torts, which overlaps criminal law, and so on. Second, the various forms of sovereign commands (from case opinions, to statutes, and back to court rules) mesh with each other to form "the" law. It has always been the dream of legal researchers to be able to read one text statement of the law bringing it all together. West Publishing Company (West) and Lawyers Cooperative Publishing (LCP) publish three national encyclopedias covering all of U.S. law: *Guide to American Law, Corpus Juris Secundum* (C.J.S.), and *American Jurisprudence 2d* (Am. Jur. 2d).

***Guide to American Law*, C.J.S., and Am. Jur. 2d**

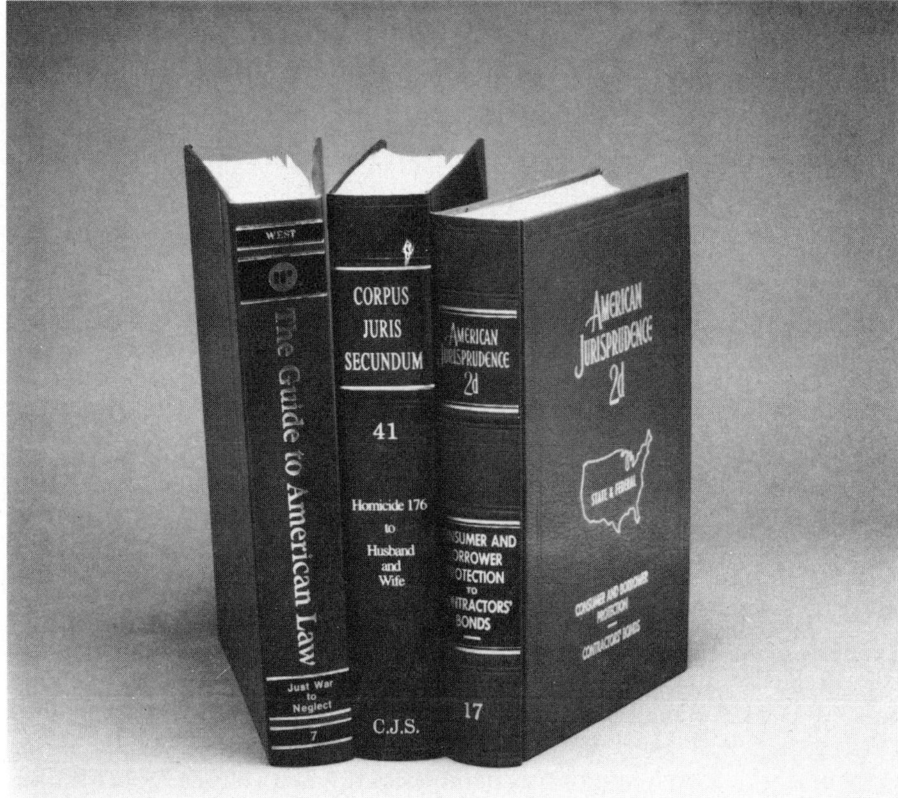

Source: © Doug Martin.

Guide to American Law

West publishes the "World Book" A-to-Z encyclopedia of the law, *Guide to American Law.* Written for lawyers and nonlawyers alike, the 12-volume set covers each legal subject in an easy-to-read style, but with formal legal citations. Unique among legal encyclopedias, *Guide to American Law* contains biographies of famous persons in the law, articles about famous cases and movements, and articles about governmental bodies and other legal organizations. (See Figure 8–1.) If, for example, you want to find out when the American Bar Association was founded, you could find the answer in *Guide to American Law.* If you have no idea where to start when researching a new topic, use this underrated general legal encyclopedia.

Corpus Juris Secundum

West's original encyclopedia for lawyers and legal researchers was *Corpus Juris* (C.J.), first published in 1936. Famous because a volume of the set sat on Perry Mason's desk in the opening of the classic television program, the title means "the body of the law."

In the late 1950s, West began publishing a modern version of the set, *Corpus Juris Secundum* (C.J.S.), the title meaning "the body of the law, second." Containing over 100 thick bound volumes, C.J.S. attempts to cover "the body" of U.S. law from its inception. The coverage includes federal law and, insofar as it can be stated generally, state law. Following West's philosophy of comprehensive law publishing, the text is supported by footnotes that purportedly include citations to every reported case on the point covered. (See Figure 8–2.) However, since 1961, C.J.S. has also included cross-references to West Topic and Key Numbers for each encyclopedia topic, so additional cases can be found using the West digests. C.J.S. is supplemented by replacement volumes as needed and annual cumulative pocket parts.

As an A-to-Z encyclopedia, C.J.S. can be entered by finding the volume with the appropriate topic, reviewing the topic outline at the beginning of the topic, then locating the desired section by its section number. The most common method of entry into C.J.S., however, is through an index. There are both a general index for the set and "volume" indexes for each topic, which are found in the last volume of the set containing that topic. Since the volume indexes are usually much more detailed than the general index, you should generally use the volume index if you know the topic you want to search.

American Jurisprudence 2d

LCP's original encyclopedia for lawyers and legal researchers was *Ruling Case Law,* started in 1914. In 1936, using *American Law Reports* (A.L.R.) annotations as a major resource, LCP began *American Jurisprudence* (Am. Jur.), the title meaning "all the law of America." Described as "[a] thoroughly modern statement of the American law in concise quotable text" [22 A.B.A. J. 363 (1936)], Am. Jur. was conceived as LCP's analytical source to the law in breadth, complementing A.L.R., its analytical source to the law in depth.

A bit of legal research humor was immortalized when volume 16 of Am. Jur. was shipped in November 1938. Indicating the topics covered in the volume, the spine proclaimed "Death to Diplomatic Officers." A whimsical advertisement in

Figure 8–1 Excerpt From *Guide to American Law*

The 1964 amendments also provided financing for the construction of the Capitol Page school in Washington, D.C.

The National Defense Education Act program is administered by the Department of Education.

NATIONAL DISTRICT ATTORNEYS ASSOCIATION The National District Attorneys Association was established in 1950, according to the association, "in direct response to the growth of organized crime and the increasing difficulty in monitoring interstate crime. Simply stated, its objective was to stem these undesirable elements through nation-wide exertion of prosecutional influence." Toward that end, the association sponsors regional institutes for prosecutors and enforcement officers; carries out educational and economic surveys of members; operates a placement service; and disseminates information on developments in criminal justice and civil liberties. Other activities include the awarding of scholarships, the preparation of amicus curiae briefs, and semiannual meetings. The members of the association include prosecutors and assistant prosecutors. The association maintains the following committees: Civil Function of a Prosecuting Attorney; Judicial Interpretation; Legislative Liaison; Planning and Research; and Prosecution Management. The association publishes *The Prosecutor* (bimonthly), a directory (annually), manuals, pamphlets, briefs of criminal and civil cases, and other materials.

NATIONAL ECONOMIC DEVELOPMENT LAW CENTER The National Economic Development Law Center was formed in 1969 to assist legal services attorneys working in economic development law, Community Economic Development Corporations (CDCs) funded by the Community Services Administration, and other organizations concerned with economic development. The center provides planning, training, research, and education services to concerned organizations in the hopes of promoting a uniform and comprehensive approach to community economic development policy. In addition to services provided directly, the center serves as a liaison with local, state, and Federal policy workers, recommending administrative, legal, and legislative proposals in response to community development needs. The center provides counseling and representation to development organizations in connection with funding, business transactions, tax exemptions, security offerings, and comprehensive planning. Other services include seminars and workshops on legal and tax issues. The center publishes *Economic Development Law Center Report* (bimonthly).

NATIONAL EMPLOYMENT LAW PROJECT The National Employment Law Project was initiated in 1969 to stimulate legal reform in areas relating to employment problems of the poor, such as employment discrimination, employment for the handicapped, public works programs, the Comprehensive Employment Training Act (CETA) (29 U.S.C.A. § 801 et seq.), compulsory welfare work requirements, unemployment insurance, and pension rights. In addition to the promotion of employment law reform through legal, legislative, and administrative advocacy, the project sponsors specialized seminars and maintains a library. Its publications include *Employment Law News* (quarterly), *Manual for Title VII Litigation, Legal Services Guide to Federal Unemployment,* and other materials related to employment law.

NATIONAL ENVIRONMENTAL POLICY ACT □ Federal legislation (42 U.S.C.A. § 4331 et seq.) that proclaimed a nationwide policy directed toward the protection and preservation of the environment. □

Among its provisions, the National Environmental Policy Act (NEPA) requires that every Federal agency submit an environmental impact statement with every legislative recommendation or program proposing major projects that will most likely affect the quality of the surrounding environment. If the Environmental Protection Agency, created pursuant to NEPA's mandate to safeguard the environment, determines that the intended project would adversely affect the environment, it can refuse to approve the project until steps are taken to minimize its effects. See also, entry on Environmental Law and Joseph L. Sax's essay on Environmental Law.

The earth we abuse and the living things we kill will, in the end, take their revenge; for in exploiting their presence we are diminishing our future.

MARYA MANNES

NATIONAL FOUNDATION ON THE ARTS AND THE HUMANITIES The general purpose of the National Foundation on the Arts and Humanities is to encourage and support national progress in the humanities and the arts.

Source: Guide to American Law, vol. 7 (St. Paul: West Publishing Company, 1984), p. 417. Reprinted with permission.

Figure 8–2 Excerpt From *Corpus Juris Secundum* (C.J.S.)

§§ 141-142 NEGLIGENCE 65A C. J. S.

jury, but is merely of dull mind, is chargeable with the same degree of care for his personal safety as one of brighter intellect.[5]

§ 142. Persons under Physical Disability

Rule **A person under any physical disability is required to exercise ordinary care to avoid injury, and if he fails to do so, and such failure contributes proximately to the injury, he is guilty of contributory negligence.**

Library References

Negligence ⚷86.

A person laboring under any physical disability increasing his liability to injury must nevertheless exercise ordinary care to avoid injury;[6] and if he fails to exercise that degree of care, and such failure contributes proximately to cause his injury, he is guilty of contributory negligence.[7] Such a person is not required to exercise a higher degree of care to that end than is required of a person under no disability;[8] ordinary care is all that is required.[9]

However, in determining whether such a person exercised ordinary care for his own safety, his disability is a circumstance to be considered.[10] Thus, while it has been said that ordinary care is such care as an ordinarily prudent person with the same disability would exercise under the same or similar circumstances,[11] it has also been held that it may be incumbent on one with a physical disability to put forth a greater degree of effort than would otherwise be necessary in order to attain that standard of care which is required of everyone.[12]

Blind persons and persons with defective vision. The fact that a person is wholly or partially blind does not relieve him of the duty to exercise ordinary care for his own safety;[13] and if he fails to exercise such care, and his failure to do so contributes proximately to cause his injury, he is guilty of contributory negligence.[14] It is not negligence as a matter of law for a blind person to be present in a public place[15] or to walk unattended on a public street.[16] In the absence of knowledge to the contrary, actual or imputed, such a person may assume that he is not exposed to, or threatened by, injury which can come to him only from a breach of the duty which others owe to avoid injury to him.[17]

5. Ala.—Worthington v. Mencer, 11 So. 72, 96 Ala. 310, 17 L.R.A. 407.
45 C.J. p 995 note 54.

6. Iowa.—**Corpus Juris Secundum cited in** Tisserat v. Peters, 99 N.W. 2d 924, 926, 251 Iowa 250.
Mass.—Keith v. Worcester, etc., R. Co., 82 N.E. 680, 196 Mass. 478, 14 L.R.A.,N.S., 648.
N.J.—Berger v. Shapiro, 152 A.2d 20, 30 N.J 89.
Karmazin v. Pennsylvania R. Co., 196 A.2d 803, 82 N.J.Super. 123, rehearing denied 198 A.2d 97, 82 N.J. Super. 435.
45 C.J. p 995 note 56.
Care required to avoid injury to person under physical disability see supra § 12.

Knowledge of danger

(1) Old woman of frail and slight physique suing for injuries resulting from fall sustained when salesman in provision, fruit, and vegetable market slightly brushed woman's elbow or arm must be charged with knowledge of her physical condition and of the risk she incurred in stationing herself so near to salesman that an ordinary movement on his part might jeopardize her safety.
Cal.—Ury v. Fredkin's Markets, 79 P.2d 749, 26 C.A.2d 501.

(2) Person whose faculties of observation are temporarily suspended as regards a dangerous condition is virtually in the same mental position as one who has never acquired knowledge of such condition.
Kan.—Cox v. City of Coffeyville, 110 P.2d 772, 153 Kan. 392.

7. Tenn.—Felton v. Horner, 37 S.W. 696, 97 Tenn. 579.
45 C.J. p 995 note 57.
Failure of passengers on trains to have an attendant as contributory negligence see Carriers § 776 a.

8. Cal.—Jones v. Bayley, 122 P.2d 293, 49 C.A.2d 647.
Me.—McCullough v. Lalumiere, 166 A.2d 702, 156 Me. 479.
S.C.—**Corpus Juris Secundum cited in** Conner v. Farmers and Merchants Bank, 132 S.E.2d 385, 392, 243 S.C. 132.
45 C.J. p 996 note 58.

9. Cal.—Jones v. Bayley, 122 P.2d 293, 49 C.A.2d 647.
S.C.—Conner v. Farmers and Merchants Bank, 132 S.E.2d 385, 243 S.C. 132.
45 C.J. p 996 note 59.

10. Conn.—Goodman v. Norwalk Jewish Center, Inc., 139 A.2d 812, 145 Conn. 146.
Mass.—Keith v. Worcester, etc., R. Co., 82 N.E. 680, 196 Mass. 478, 14 L.R.A.,N.S., 648.
45 C.J. p 996 note 60.

11. Cal.—Conjorsky v. Murray, 287 P.2d 505, 135 C.A.2d 478—Jones v. Bayley, 122 P.2d 293, 49 C.A.2d 647.
Conn.—Goodman v. Norwalk Jewish Center, Inc., 139 A.2d 812, 145 Conn. 146.
Me.—Ham v. Lewiston, 47 A. 548, 94 Me. 265.
S.C.—**Corpus Juris Secundum cited in** Conner v. Farmers and Merchants Bank, 132 S.E.2d 385, 392, 243 S.C. 132.

12. U.S.—Darter v. Greenville Community Hotel Corp., C.A.S.C., 301 F.2d 70.
Cal.—Jones v. Bayley, 122 P.2d 293, 49 C.A.2d 647—Armstrong v. Day, 284 P. 1083, 103 C.A. 465.
Me.—McCullough v. Lalumiere, 166 A.2d 702, 156 Me. 479.
Neb.—Trumbley v. Moore, 39 N.W.2d 613, 151 Neb. 780.
45 C.J. p 996 note 62.

Requirement stated in terms of degree of care

In some cases the text requirement has been stated in terms of a commensurately greater degree of care.
U.S.—Darter v. Greenville Community Hotel Corporation, C.A.S.C., 301 F.2d 70.

13. Cal.—**Corpus Juris Secundum cited in** Krause v. Apodaca, 186 C.A.2d 413, 9 Cal.Rptr. 10, 12.
Iowa.—Balcom v. Independence, 160 N.W. 305, 178 Iowa 685, L.R.A.1917C 120.
Pa.—Davis v. Feinstein, 88 A.2d 695, 370 Pa. 449.
45 C.J. p 996 note 64.
Care required to avoid injury to blind person see supra § 12.

14. Pa.—Karl v. Juniata County, 56 A. 78, 206 Pa. 633.
45 C.J. p 996 note 65.

15. N.Y.—Harris v. Uebelhoer, 75 N.Y. 169.

16. Or.—Weinstein v. Wheeler, 271 P. 733, 127 Or. 406, 62 A.L.R. 574.

17. Tenn.—**Corpus Juris cited in** East Tennessee Light & Power Co.

172

Source: Corpus Juris Secundum, vol. 65A (St. Paul: West Publishing Company, 1966), p. 172. Reprinted with permission.

the *American Bar Association Journal* mused: "Were we thinking of Munich? No—Only of every-day law." [25 A.B.A. J. 263 (1939).]

Planned by LCP editor Alfred W. Gans, who had worked on Am. Jur. from its inception, the modern *American Jurisprudence 2d* (Am. Jur. 2d) was begun in 1962. Containing over 80 volumes, Am. Jur. 2d, like C.J.S., covers federal law and, insofar as it can be stated generally, state law. However, following LCP's philosophy of selective law publishing, the text is supported by footnotes that purportedly include citations to only selected leading or landmark cases on the point covered. (See Figure 8–3.) Footnotes are also made to statutory sources and to A.L.R. annotations. Topics also begin with cross-references to other units of the Total Client Service Library. Am. Jur. 2d, like C.J.S., is supplemented by replacement volumes as needed and annual cumulative pocket parts, except for the federal tax volumes, which are prepared annually by the Research Institute of America (RIA).

As an A-to-Z encyclopedia, Am. Jur. 2d can be entered by finding the volume with the appropriate topic, reviewing the topic outline at the beginning of that topic, then locating the desired section by its section number. The most common method of entry into Am. Jur. 2d, however, is through an index. There are both a general index for the set and "volume" indexes for each topic, which are found in the last volume of the set containing that topic. Again, since the volume indexes are usually much more detailed than the general index, you should generally use the volume index if you know the topic you want to search.

Am. Jur. 2d includes a separate volume entitled *Table of Statutes and Rules Cited,* which allows a researcher of a federal statute or rule to find the Am. Jur. 2d topic and section number, if any, in which it is cited. The Am. Jur. 2d *New Topic Service,* as its name implies, contains new topics not yet incorporated into the main volumes. The one-volume Am. Jur. 2d *Desk Book,* created as a marketing tool, is a general legal almanac. Other than a list of Am. Jur. 2d topics, the *Desk Book* contains an odd collection of information, including historical documents, ethical codes, bar admission standards, uniform laws, financial tables, reporter abbreviations, and Latin phrases.

LCP also sells a separate student textbook, *Summary of American Law,* which is keyed to and summarizes Am. Jur. 2d. The first edition was prepared in 1947 (for Am. Jur.) by LCP editor Robert T. Kimbrough, with later editions by George L. Clark (1974) and Martin Weinstein (1988).

In the mid-1980s, LCP set out to modernize Am. Jur. 2d and its state encyclopedias. The editors of new and revised topics were encouraged to cite more modern cases in the supporting footnotes. However, to cut costs, LCP instructed some of its editors *not* to take the time to update material used from earlier versions. Thus, even in new and revised topics, some footnotes cite old cases.

Another aspect of LCP's modernization can be gleaned from an October 1987 advertising mailer:

> The contemporary topics in Ohio Jur 3d are grouped together under "problem areas." This eliminates searching through several volumes for one answer. For example, "Creditors' Rights and Remedies" gathers information from the areas of attachments, garnishment, civil arrest, fraudulent conveyances, and insolvency. And related matters are brought to your attention . . . automatically. It's an approach designed for the practitioner and not the professor.

State Encyclopedias

In states with a sufficient customer base to make publication of an encyclopedia feasible, there are state encyclopedias. West publishes encyclopedia sets in the

Figure 8-3 Excerpt From *American Jurisprudence 2d* (Am. Jur. 2d)

49 Am Jur 2d LANDLORD AND TENANT § 761

XXI. DUTIES AND LIABILITIES OF LANDLORD AS TO CONDITION, USE, REPAIR, AND IMPROVEMENT

A. IN GENERAL

§ 761. Generally; effect of want of title.

With respect to the duties and liabilities of the landlord as to condition, use, repair, and improvement, it is important to distinguish between his responsibility to the tenant and persons on the premises in the right of the tenant[19] and his responsibility to other third persons such as trespassers,[20] persons on the demised premises[1] or other premises with the consent of the landlord,[2] or persons on adjoining or nearby premises[3] and persons on the highway or street.[4] It is also important to distinguish between the landlord's responsibility as to the demised premises,[5] his responsibility as to other premises owned and possessed by him,[6] and his responsibility as to other premises owned, but not possessed, by him.[7] Another important consideration is whether he has made any special express or implied agreement as to condition, use, repair, or improvement.[8]

The general rule that one who assumes to be the owner of real property and, as such, assumes to control and manage it, cannot escape liability for injuries resulting from its defective condition, by showing want of title in himself,[9] has been applied to one who acts as landlord.[10] Accordingly, one in possession and control of real estate may be liable for injury to a tenant through failure to make repairs, although he does not have the legal title.[11] Thus, if an alleged landlord, by his conduct in dealing with the property and by his knowledge and transactions in reference to it, so acted that it could be fairly said that he assumed the duties and responsibilities of a landlord, it could be found that he was in fact the landlord with a landlord's usual liabilities, although he did not have legal title to the property

19. §§ 767 et seq., infra.

20. § 762, infra.

1. § 763, infra.

2. §§ 799 et seq., infra.

3. §§ 898 et seq., infra.

4. See 39 Am Jur 2d, HIGHWAY, STREETS, AND BRIDGES §§ 369, 370, 499, 502, 521, 522, 537, 544.

5. §§ 767 et seq., infra.

6. §§ 799 et seq., 803, infra.

7. § 804, infra.

8. §§ 828 et seq., infra.

9. See NEGLIGENCE (1st ed § 95).

10. Ziulkowski v Kolodziej, 119 **Conn** 230, 175 A 780, 96 ALR 1065; Skolnick v East Boston Sav. Bank, 307 **Mass** 1, 29 NE2d 585, 130 ALR 1519; Lindsey v Leighton, 150 **Mass** 285, 22 NE 901; Bannigan v Woodbury, 158 **Mich** 206, 122 NW 531 (in which it was held that an administrator lawfully in possession and control of a building belonging to the estate was personally liable for injuries sustained by a pedestrian on the adjoining sidewalk as a result of being struck by glass falling from a window negligently permitted to become unsafe).

Annotation: 96 ALR 1068, s. 130 ALR 1525.

11. Ziulkowski v Kolodziej, 119 **Conn** 230, 175 A 780, 96 ALR 1065, wherein it appeared that an intestate's widow, on the death of her husband, assumed possession and control for herself and her children of a three-family house owned by the intestate, collecting rents and making some repairs; and that while she was so in control and before her appointment as administratrix, one of the tenants was injured by falling on a common stairway because of its defective condition, and the court held that the widow was liable for the tenant's injuries although she was not in control as administratrix.

In Lindsey v Leighton, 150 **Mass** 285, 22 NE 901, it was held that one who assumed to be the owner of real estate the title to which was in his wife, and leased it as owner, could not escape liability for injuries sustained by the tenant by reason of the defective condition of the property, by showing want of title in himself.

68

Source: American Jurisprudence 2d, vol. 49 (Rochester, NY: Lawyers Co-operative Publishing Co., 1970), p. 68. Reprinted with permission.

style of C.J.S. for Illinois, Maryland, and Michigan. LCP publishes encyclopedia sets in the style of Am. Jur. 2d for California, Florida, New York, Ohio, and Texas. Although a state encyclopedia can be quite specific as to the law of a given topic, you should remember that as an encyclopedia, it is a summary secondary source of the law. As such, it should never be cited as if it were a primary authority.

Law Outlines

While an encyclopedia is a narrative summary, an **outline** is a summary showing the pattern of subordination of one thought to another. As discussed in Chapter 3, most law schools use the casebook method. Under this method, law students read cases and are encouraged to prepare for exams by outlining what they have learned. Commercially prepared law outlines are frowned upon and carry about as much weight as Cliff's Notes do with the typical high school English teacher. Because of this attitude, you should never cite a commercial law outline as either primary or secondary authority.

Nevertheless, commercial law outlines, like legal encyclopedias, summarize the law and cite cases and other legal materials in support. Many law students find through the grapevine that they can learn the fundamentals of the law effectively by reading and studying commercial law outlines. They're the books that everyone knows about, buys, and uses, but nobody talks about.

One publisher of a complete series of law outlines is Emanuel Law Outlines, Inc., founded by a *cum laude* graduate of Harvard Law School, Steven L. Emanuel. Emanuel law outlines feature an easy, read-like-a-book writing style, concise summaries of significant cases, and numerous examples, all set in large, easy-to-read type. In the 1988–1989 academic year, Emanuel sold nearly 100,000 law outlines. Emanuel also sells the Smith's Review Series, formerly published by West.

There are many other sets of commercial law outlines. They include Gilbert Law Summaries, Legalines, Ryan Law Capsules, Sum & Substance, and West's Black Letter Series. There are also guides to law school casebooks known as **canned briefs,** since each major case is preanalyzed ("canned") for the reader. The major canned-brief series are Casenote Legal Briefs and Cambridge Law Study Aids.

Law outlines and canned briefs are often sold in law school bookstores and are generally available by mail from the Chicago Law Book Company of Chicago, Illinois, The Law Annex at Harvard Book Stores, Inc., of Cambridge, Massachusetts, and the Law Distributors of Gardena, California.

8–2 Dictionaries

A **dictionary** is a book containing an alphabetical list of words, along with information about each word, usually including its spelling, pronunciation, **etymology** (word origin), **definitions** (meanings), forms, and uses. A **law dictionary** is a book containing a list of words unique to the legal profession, words often used by the legal profession (e.g., Latin phrases), and ordinary words with a legal meaning.

The two leading law dictionaries are published by the two largest law publishers: *Black's Law Dictionary* by West and *Ballentine's Law Dictionary* by LCP. Both dictionaries were originally prepared over 75 years ago: *Black's* in 1891, and *Ballentine's* in 1916.

Black's Law Dictionary and Ballentine's Law Dictionary

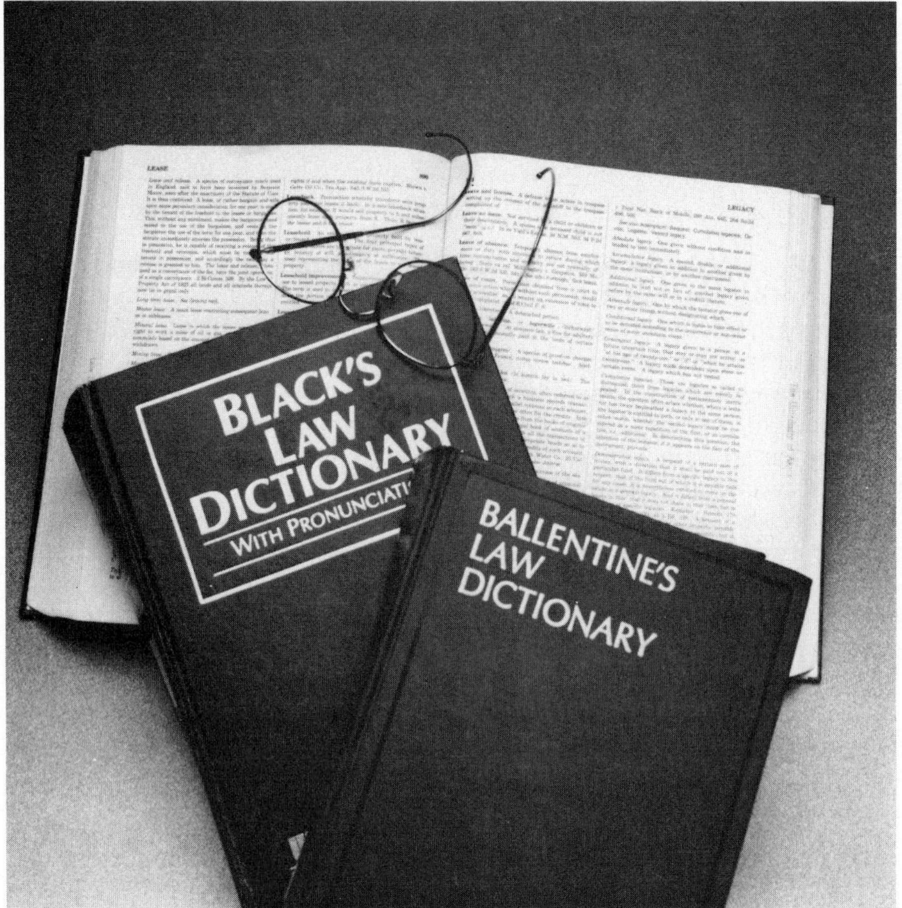

Source: © Doug Martin.

Because of their age and dated word lists, *Black's* and *Ballentine's* have become the objects of increasing derision within the legal profession. In 1985, Robert D. White took aim at *Black's Law Dictionary* with a satirical book entitled *White's Law Dictionary* (NY: Warner Books, Inc., 1985). The cover of *White's Law Dictionary* defines *Black's Law Dictionary* as "an overlarge medieval legal lexicon. Preeminent in the field, until superseded by this book." As White explains:

> Lawyers say words are their stock in trade. If so, they are burdened by an excess of inventory. Consider a volume which by default has held primacy among legal lexicons since its original publication in 1891: *Black's Law Dictionary*.
>
> The preface to *Black's* states that the latest edition includes 10,000 entries. Let's examine some of those 10,000.
>
> A random perusal turns up *zemindar*. You think, "Wow, I really didn't know that one. Good thing I have *Black's*." Its definition? "In Hindu Law, Landkeeper." You sigh a breath of relief; thank God your ignorance of zemindars didn't come up in public.
>
> Flipping back to the beginning, you see:
>
> > *A* The first letter in the English and most other alphabets derived from the Roman or Latin alphabet, which was one of several ancient Italian alphabets derived from the Greek, which was an adaptation of the Phoenician.
>
> Amazing. Just the other day you were wondering if that wasn't adapted from the Phoenician.

Come on, Mr. Black, what gives?

Do we really need a sixty-seven-word definition of "wrongful act," including a citation to a decision of the Illinois Court of Appeals? You couldn't leave it at "something one shouldn't do?"

How about "*Apt* Fit; suitable; appropriate"? Do I see a little padding to get the total up to 10,000?

And "*Cerebellum* Lower portion of brain below back of cerebrum concerned with muscular coordination and body equilibrium"—aren't we poaching a wee bit on another profession's turf? [p. viii–ix.]

White could have just as easily attacked *Ballentine's Law Dictionary.* Among its 30,000 terms is *zingara,* meaning "[a]ny female in a band of gypsies." It also defines the letter *A,* gives a 350-word definition for *accident,* and defines words such as *weather* and *umbilical cord.*

The problem with both *Black's* and *Ballentine's,* and virtually all other law dictionaries, is that they are not citation-based. A **citation-based** dictionary, the standard among general dictionaries, is created by collecting a fair sample of actual uses of each word in context **(citations),** allowing the editor of the dictionary to authoritatively determine whether the word is current or archaic and its "correct" spelling, etymology, meaning, and usage. The current law dictionaries simply do not include etymologies or citation-based authoritative definitions, and archaic words are rarely identified or eliminated.

Law dictionaries are substandard because of economics. The legal market has not been deemed large enough for a private publisher to profitably commit the resources necessary to create a citation-based law dictionary, although both West and LCP have the resources to do so. In 1989, the University of Texas School of Law and the Oxford University Press announced their plan to produce a citation-based law dictionary entitled the *Oxford Law Dictionary,* but the project has been abandoned.

Black's Law Dictionary

Despite its limitations, *Black's Law Dictionary* remains the most cited, most respected, and best-selling dictionary for the legal profession. It was originally prepared in 1891 (as *A Dictionary of the Law*) by Henry Campbell Black, the author of an obscure series of law treatises. Since then, *Black's* has been published in seven editions, dated 1910, 1933, 1951, 1957, 1968, 1979, and 1990. After Black's death, revisions were made by the publisher's editorial staff.

The major features of *Black's* include pronunciations for selected entries, selected citations to cases, a table of abbreviations, the Constitution of the United States, a time chart of the U.S. Supreme Court, an organizational chart of the U.S. government, and a table of British regnal years.

Black's is available in its standard edition (the basic hard-cover version), a deluxe edition (a more expensive version with a fancy cover and thumb-hole tabs), and an abridged edition (a shorter, cheaper soft-cover version). *Black's* is also available on the WESTLAW (DI database) computer-assisted legal research system, to be discussed in Chapter 12.

West also publishes a set of word-books combining elements of the National Reporter System and West's digest system: *Words and Phrases.* When a case opinion appears to judicially define a word or phrase, a headnote is drawn from the definition. These headnotes are collected in the manner of a digest, under the appropriate words and phrases listed from A to Z. *Words and Phrases* allows you to look up a word or phrase and to read digest paragraphs summarizing judicial definitions of that word or phrase. (See Figure 8–4.) The set is supplemented by annual cumulative pocket parts. Modern volumes of the

Figure 8–4 Excerpt From West's *Words and Phrases*

RES IPSA LOQUITUR

Injuries from breaking or explosion of bottle—Cont'd

v. Garrett, Tex.Civ.App., 143 S.W.2d 1020, 1022, 1023.

In action for injuries sustained by plaintiff, who was engaged in cold drink business, when bottled soft drink exploded and piece of glass bottle struck plaintiff, even if "res ipsa loquitur doctrine" was applicable, plaintiff was not entitled to judgment simply because jury found that plaintiff suffered damages in a given sum, where defendant's evidence was sufficient to make jury question of defendant's negligence, since the finding of extent of plaintiff's injuries was not a finding of negligence by defendant. Alagood v. Coca Cola Bottling Co., Tex.Civ.App., 135 S.W.2d 1056, 1060, 1061.

Where plaintiff, who operated a restaurant, was injured when a bottle of carbonated beverage manufactured and bottled by defendant exploded while plaintiff was putting bottle in an icebox after a case of beverage had been brought to restaurant by defendant's employee, the doctrine of "res ipsa loquitur" was applicable, and doctrine of "unavoidable accident" did not apply to relieve defendant from liability for injuries, notwithstanding that bottle was in plaintiff's possession and control at time of explosion. Bradley v. Conway Springs Bottling Co., 118 P.2d 601, 603, 605, 154 Kan. 282.

Where plaintiff in action for injuries against manufacturer of bottled beverages proved that plaintiff was taking a bottle of beverage from an ice box furnished plaintiff by manufacturer and had pulled bottle a few inches above top of water in box when bottle exploded causing fragments of glass to strike plaintiff and that bottle was purchased from manufacturer on day preceding explosion and was not frozen or knocked against other bottles or sides of box as it was being pulled from water before explosion, the doctrine of "res ipsa loquitur" was applicable, and plaintiff established a "prima facie case" of negligence against manufacturer. Lanza v. De Ridder Coca Cola Bottling Co., La.App., 3 So.2d 217, 218.

Where doctrine of "res ipsa loquitur" was otherwise applicable in action against manufacturer of beverages for injuries sustained when a bottle of beverage exploded, application of doctrine was not excluded or limited because plaintiff failed to produce bottle for examination by manufacturer, especially where bottle had burst into fragments and there was no evidence that plaintiff willfully failed to preserve and produce remains thereof. Lanza v. De Ridder Coca Cola Bottling Co., La.App., 3 So.2d 217, 218.

Injuries from consumption of beverage, food or candy, etc.

"Res ipsa loquitur" doctrine was not applicable to sustain recovery against manufacturer and bottler for injuries sustained in explosion of bottle of beer which was not within bottler's exclusive control for several days preceding explosion, in absence of evidence of reasonably discoverable defect in bottle, where proof of any such defect by means of fragments of bottle in his possession was available to person injured. Curley v. Ruppert, 71 N.Y.S.2d 578, 580.

In action against bottler for injuries caused by explosion of bottle of carbonated water, evidence not showing that bottle between time it left possession of bottler and when it came into possession of plaintiff who bought it in a store, that it was not subjected to any condition that would tend to bring about the explosion was insufficient to warrant verdict for plaintiff under "res ipsa loquitur doctrine". Kees v. Canada Dry Ginger Ale, 199 S.W.2d 76, 77, 79, 239 Mo.App. 1080.

Doctrine applicable where abnormal condition of soft drink was due to fermentation, caused by defective sealing of bottle. White v. Coca-Cola Bottling Co., La.App., 16 So.2d 579, 582.

In action against dairy company for injuries allegedly sustained from paint in milk, doctrine of "res ipsa loquitur" was applicable. Welter v. Bowman Dairy Co., 47 N.E.2d 739, 762, 318 Ill.App. 305.

In an action for damages for personal injuries resulting from consumption of a bottled beverage, the plaintiff may not rely on doctrine of "res ipsa loquitur." Tickle v. Hobgood, 4 S.E.2d 444, 445, 216 N.C. 221.

In action against a bottling company to recover for damages allegedly resulting from drinking bottled beverage containing noxious substance, the doctrine of "res ipsa loquitur" is inapplicable. Evans v. Charlotte Pepsi-Cola Bottling Co., 6 S.E.2d 510, 511, 216 N.C. 716.

In action by consumer against manufacturer for injuries allegedly caused by a fish

555

Source: Words and Phrases, vol. 37 (St. Paul: West Publishing Company, 1965), p. 555. Reprinted with permission.

National Reporter System also include a "Words and Phrases" section derived from the cases in those volumes.

Ballentine's Law Dictionary

Despite its limitations, *Ballentine's Law Dictionary* continues to be a major dictionary for the legal profession. Originally prepared in 1916 by James A. Ballentine, Assistant Professor of Law at the University of California and Dean of the San Francisco Law School, *Ballentine's* has had five printings and three editions: 1916 and 1923—first edition, 1930 and 1948–second edition, and 1969—third edition. The third edition was edited by LCP editor William S. Anderson.

The major features of *Ballentine's* include pronunciations for selected entries, selected citations to cases, and selected citations to *United States Supreme Court Reports, Lawyers' Edition* (L. Ed.), A.L.R., and Am. Jur.

Gifis' *Law Dictionary*

The most practical, readable, and useful law dictionary currently published is Gifis' *Law Dictionary*, published by Barron's Educational Series, Inc. Originally prepared in 1975 by Steven H. Gifis, Associate Professor of Law at the Rutgers School of Law, Gifis' *Law Dictionary* is now in its second edition, published in 1984.

The major feature of this law dictionary is Gifis' careful selection of entries to include modern legal words and ancient legal words still in use, and to exclude archaic legal words. (See Figure 8–5.) Other features include the cross-references of entries with their use in other definitions, pronunciations for selected entries, selected citations to cases, the Constitution of the United States, the ABA Model Code of Professional Responsibility, and the ABA Model Rules of Professional Conduct. Perhaps most important, this law dictionary is reasonably priced.

Other Dictionaries

Many other law dictionaries have been published. They include West's *Bouvier's Law Dictionary* (1914); Datinder S. Sodhi's *The Attorney's Pocket Dictionary* (1981), published by Law and Business Publications Inc.; William Statsky's *Legal Thesaurus/Dictionary* (1985), published by West; and Wesley Gilmer, Jr.'s *The Law Dictionary* (1986), published by Anderson Publishing Co.

There are also legal **thesauri** (books of words and their synonyms and near synonyms). These include *Cochran's Law Lexicon* (1973), Burton's *Legal Thesaurus* (1980), and Statsky's *Legal Thesaurus/Dictionary* (1985).

8–3 Directories

A **directory** is a list of names and certain other information, such as addresses, telephone numbers, and the like. A **legal directory** is a guide to lawyers, law firms, and/or governmental agencies.

Legal directories are often used to find and select lawyers admitted to practice in another state or in another jurisdiction. This is necessary because no

Figure 8–5 Excerpt From Gifis' *Law Dictionary*

SEDITION 431 SEGREGATION

ests that arise by operation of law.

The clearest examples of security interests are the **mortgage,** the **pledge** and the **conditional sale.** The mortgage involves the situation wherein the mortgagor gives the mortgagee a security interest in a specific asset, which is usually real property. The pledge deals with the situation wherein the creditor takes possession of the property. The conditional sale involves the situation wherein the seller gives credit and takes a security interest. The Uniform Commercial Code ignores differences of form and treats all secured interests in personal property simply as "security interests." See U.C.C. §9-102. Compare **security deposit.**

PURCHASE-MONEY SECURITY INTEREST one "taken or retained by the seller of the **collateral** to secure all or part of its price; or is one taken by a person who, by making advances or incurring an obligation, gives value in order to enable the debtor to acquire rights in or the use of collateral if such value is in fact so used." U.C.C. §9-107.

SEDITION illegal action tending to cause the disruption and overthrow of the government. The United States had enacted an Alien and Sedition Act as early as 1798. Sedition acts were also enacted during World War I, prohibiting types of communication advocating the overthrow of the government. In 1919, the Supreme Court held that seditious communications could be punished consistent with the First Amendment, if they presented a **clear and present danger** of bringing about an evil (violence) which the government had a right to prevent. See 249 U.S. 47.

The state governments also have the power to prevent harmful sedition. See 254 U.S. 325. However, the states cannot punish sedition against the United States where Congress has already **preempted** legislation in this area by "occupying the field" with legislation of its own. See 350 U.S. 497. See **treason.**

SEDITIOUS LIBEL in English law a misdemeanor involving the publishing of any words or document, with a seditious intention. "A seditious intention means an intention to bring into contempt or excite disaffection against the government or to promote feelings of ill will between the classes. If the seditious statement is published, the publisher is guilty of a seditious libel." Black, Constitutional Law 543 (2d ed. 1897). The law of seditious libel is now severely circumscribed in **the United States** by the **First Amendment** to the Constitution. See **freedom** [FREEDOM OF PRESS]; [FREEDOM OF SPEECH].

SEDUCTION "[i]nducing a chaste, unmarried woman, by means of temptation, deception, acts, flattery, or a promise of marriage, to engage in sexual intercourse." 151 So. 2d 752, 757. A woman may also entice a man to commit sexual intercourse. 138 So. 2. Force is not an **element** of "seduction." At common law, seduction merely created a **civil** liability and in some states the woman could recover **damages** for her seduction. In states where seduction is now a criminal offense, the chastity or reputation of chastity of the victim prior to seduction may be essential for conviction. See 18 U.S.C. §2198; Model Penal Code §213.3. Other states have barred actions for seduction. See N.Y. Civ. Rights L. §80a. Perkins & Boyce, Criminal Law 462 (3d ed. 1982). See **fornication.** Compare **rape.**

SEGREGATION to set apart; the separation of some persons or things from others. 170 S.E. 189, 191. For instance, a contract may require a party to keep certain funds segregated so that they will

Source: Steven H. Gifis, *Law Dictionary,* 2nd ed. (New York: Barron's Educational Series, Inc., 1984), p. 431. Reprinted with permission.

lawyer is admitted to practice in every state, or can in every jurisdiction, and clients may have legal problems that extend into other states and jurisdictions. Legal directories are also used to find correct addresses for, and certain information about, other lawyers. Moreover, legal directories are effective job-hunting tools, particularly if you are seeking a position in another state.

Martindale-Hubbell Law Directory

The long-established leading national law directory is the *Martindale-Hubbell Law Directory,* published annually by the Martindale-Hubbell division of Reed Publishing (USA) Inc. The directory is a multivolume set, arranged in alphabetical order by state. Since 1990, *Martindale-Hubbell* is also available for purchase on CD-ROM. It is also available on the LEXIS computer-assisted legal research system, to be discussed in Chapter 12.

Each volume of *Martindale-Hubbell* contains two parts. The first part, containing relatively few pages, purports to list all the lawyers in a given state, arranged alphabetically by city of practice, then by last name and first name. The information provided in this part includes birth date, bar admission date, college attended, and law school attended. Where Martindale-Hubbell has received confidential recommendations, a lawyer may be given a rating, the highest being *av,* meaning *a,* very high legal ability; and *v,* very high faithful adherence to ethical standards. Lawyers are listed in the first part at no cost.

The second part, containing most of the pages, consists of paid advertisements. Arranged by city of practice, then by sole practitioner or law firm, the information provided in this part includes addresses, telephone and fax numbers, areas of practice, biographies, and representative clients.

Martindale-Hubbell also includes, in separate volumes, "Law Digests" that summarize the laws of the various states, the laws of many foreign countries (including Canada and Canadian provinces), and other useful information (e.g., summaries of U.S. copyright, patent, and trademark laws). The state law digests, written by law firms in the respective states, are excellent starting points for researching the law in each state.

Martindale-Hubbell Law Directory

Source: © Doug Martin.

Other National Directories

There are several other national directories of lawyers, and two have unique formats.

Marquis Who's Who, Macmillan Directory Division, publishes *Who's Who in American Law.* The sixth edition was published in 1989. As its preface states, *Who's Who in American Law* "provides biographical information on approximately 27,600 lawyers and professions in law-related areas, including, among others, judges, legal educators, law librarians, legal historians, and social scientists."

West is developing, and has on-line, *West's Legal Directory.* Part of the WESTLAW computer-assisted legal research system, which will be discussed in Chapter 12, *West's Legal Directory* is an on-line database (WLD). For each attorney, there is a basic attorney profile (including address and telephone number, bar admissions, and areas of practice) and a professional profile (including birth date, education, representative clients, and foreign language ability).

State, Local, and Specialized Directories

Legal directories for several states and regions are published by the Legal Directories Publishing Company, Inc., of Dallas, Texas. The directories include alphabetical lists of attorneys statewide, an alphabetical list of law firms statewide, and an attorney list by county and city.

Local legal directories are also published by local bar associations and other publishers. In Ohio, for example, Anderson Publishing Company publishes the multivolume *Profiles of Ohio Lawyers.*

There are countless specialized directories, ranging from the *Congressional Directory* to the Association of American Law Schools' *Directory of Law Teachers* (for law school teachers). Some are available on the LEXIS and WESTLAW computer-assisted legal research systems, to be discussed in Chapter 12.

SUMMARY

8–1

It has always been the dream of legal researchers to be able to read one text statement of the law bringing it all together. Written for both lawyers and nonlawyers alike, West publishes the easy-to-read A-to-Z encyclopedia of the law, *Guide to American Law.* West's current encyclopedia for lawyers and legal researchers is *Corpus Juris Secundum* (C.J.S.), the title meaning "the body of the law, second." Following West's philosophy of "comprehensive" law publishing, the text in C.J.S. is supported by footnotes that purportedly include citations to every reported case on the point covered. C.J.S. also includes cross-references to West Topic and Key Numbers. The most common entry into C.J.S. is through the general index or a volume index. LCP's current encyclopedia for lawyers and legal researchers is *American Jurisprudence 2d* (Am. Jur. 2d), the title meaning "all the law of America, second." Am. Jur. 2d, like C.J.S., covers federal law and, insofar as it can be stated generally, state law. Following LCP's philosophy of "selective" law publishing, the Am. Jur. 2d text is supported by footnotes that purportedly include citations to only selected leading or landmark cases on the point covered and to A.L.R. annotations. The most common entry into Am. Jur. 2d is through the general index or a volume index. Am. Jur. 2d includes *Table of Statutes and Rules Cited, New Topic Service,* and a desk book. LCP also sells a separate student textbook, *Summary of American Law,* which is keyed to and summarizes Am. Jur. 2d. Some states have a state encyclopedia. Although they should never be cited as either primary or secondary authority, many law students find that they can effectively learn the fundamentals of the law by reading and studying commercial law outlines, including Emanuel law outlines, Gilbert Law Summaries, Legalines, Ryan Law Capsules, Sum & Substance, and West's Black Letter Series.

8–2

The two leading law dictionaries are *Black's Law Dictionary* and *Ballentine's Law Dictionary.* Because of their dated word lists, both are being increasingly derided within the legal profession. The problem with both *Black's* and *Ballentine's,* and virtually all other law dictionaries, is that they are not citation-based. Despite its limitations, *Black's* remains the most cited, most respected, and best-selling dictionary for the legal profession. West's *Words and Phrases* allows you to read digest paragraphs summarizing judicial definitions of particular words or phrases. Despite its limitations, *Ballentine's Law Dictionary* continues to be a major dictionary for the legal profession. The most practical, readable, and useful law dictionary currently published is the *Law Dictionary* (second edition) by Steven H. Gifis. It excludes archaic legal words and is reasonably priced.

8–3

Legal directories are often used to find and select lawyers admitted to practice in another state or in another jurisdiction, and to find correct addresses for, and certain information about, other lawyers. They are also effective job-hunting tools. The long-established leading national law directory is *Martindale-Hubbell Law Directory.* Lawyers are listed in the first part at no cost, whereas the second part contains paid advertisements. Marquis Who's Who publishes *Who's Who in American Law.* West is developing, and has on-line, *West's Legal Directory,* an on-line database. Legal directories for several states and regions are published by the Legal Directories Publishing Company, Inc.

REVIEW

Key Terms

Before proceeding, review the key terms listed below to be sure you understand each one. If necessary, read over the corresponding section of the chapter. When you are ready to test your understanding, answer the Review Questions.

canned briefs
citation-based
citations
definitions
dictionary
directory
encyclopedia
etymology
law dictionary
legal directory
outline
thesauri

Questions for Review and Discussion

1. Where would you begin research about a legal topic if you had no idea what it was about (e.g., Admiralty)?
2. What is West's national encyclopedia?
3. What is LCP's national encyclopedia?
4. Is there a legal encyclopedia for your state?
5. Why should you never cite a commercial law outline?
6. What quality do virtually all law dictionaries lack?
7. Why would you cite a definition from *Black's Law Dictionary* in a brief?
8. Why would you cite a definition from *Ballentine's Law Dictionary* in a brief?
9. Why would a student want to buy Gifis' *Law Dictionary?*
10. What is the leading long-established national legal directory?

Activities

1. Find the list of Am. Jur. 2d topics in the Am. Jur. 2d *Desk Book.* Select a topic and find it in the main set. Read a few pages and examine the footnotes. Find the volume index for the topic and compare it with the general index for the set. Are you confident that you can find and read about almost anything in the law in just a few minutes?
2. Compare Gifis' *Law Dictionary* with *Black's* or *Ballentine's.* Do you agree that Gifis' is a better value, or do you prefer *Black's* or *Ballentine's?* Compare your favorite with a good general "college" dictionary, such as the *Ninth New Collegiate Dictionary* by Merriam-Webster Inc. Do you think someone could publish a better law dictionary than those currently on the market?
3. Find the name of a lawyer you know in *Martindale-Hubbell Law Directory.* Can you find it in both the general listing and the advertising section? Why or why not?

CHAPTER 9 Specialized Works

OUTLINE

COMMENTARY

As you continue to research public religious displays, and First Amendment law generally, you continue to find the subject fascinating. It occurs to you that others may have found the subject fascinating as well. You wonder if any scholars have ever written a book on constitutional law. You wonder if a scholarly article has ever been written on public religious displays. What specialized sources can you find?

OBJECTIVES

In this chapter you will learn about most of the specialized secondary sources of the law. Emphasis is placed on textbooks, form books, and periodicals. After reading this chapter, you should be able to:

1. Compare and contrast textbooks and treatises.
2. Explain what a "hornbook" is.
3. Define "restatement."
4. Compare and contrast legal forms, and pleading and practice forms.
5. Identify and use national legal form sets.
6. Identify and use national pleading and practice form sets.
7. Recognize trial and practice books.
8. Explain what a "law review" is.
9. Recognize national legal magazines.
10. Identify national legal newspapers.

9–1 Textbooks and Treatises

A **textbook** contains the principles of a given subject, thus it is useful in the study of that subject. Most nonfiction books contain at least some of the principles of a given subject, and so may be loosely termed textbooks.

A **treatise** is a systematic scholarly discussion, or "treatment," of the principles of a given subject; thus it is especially useful in the study of that subject. Since most legal textbooks are written in a systematic form by legal professionals for legal professionals, they are generally known as treatises. Legal treatises contain references to case opinions, statutes, and other primary and secondary sources of the law. They may be critical (suggesting what the law should be), interpretative (explaining the law as it is), or expository (enumerating the sources of the law), or a combination of each type.

There are thousands of legal textbooks and treatises, and they cover virtually every legal subject. They may be published in either single volumes or multivolume sets. They may be published either in bound volumes or as a looseleaf service. (See Chapter 7.) Textbooks and treatises usually include the features of an ordinary book, such as a table of contents, the main body in chapters, and an index. Textbooks and treatises also usually include "legal" features, such as a table of cases cited, organization by section number, and pocket parts or other supplementation. Textbooks and treatises usually cover a

Treatises

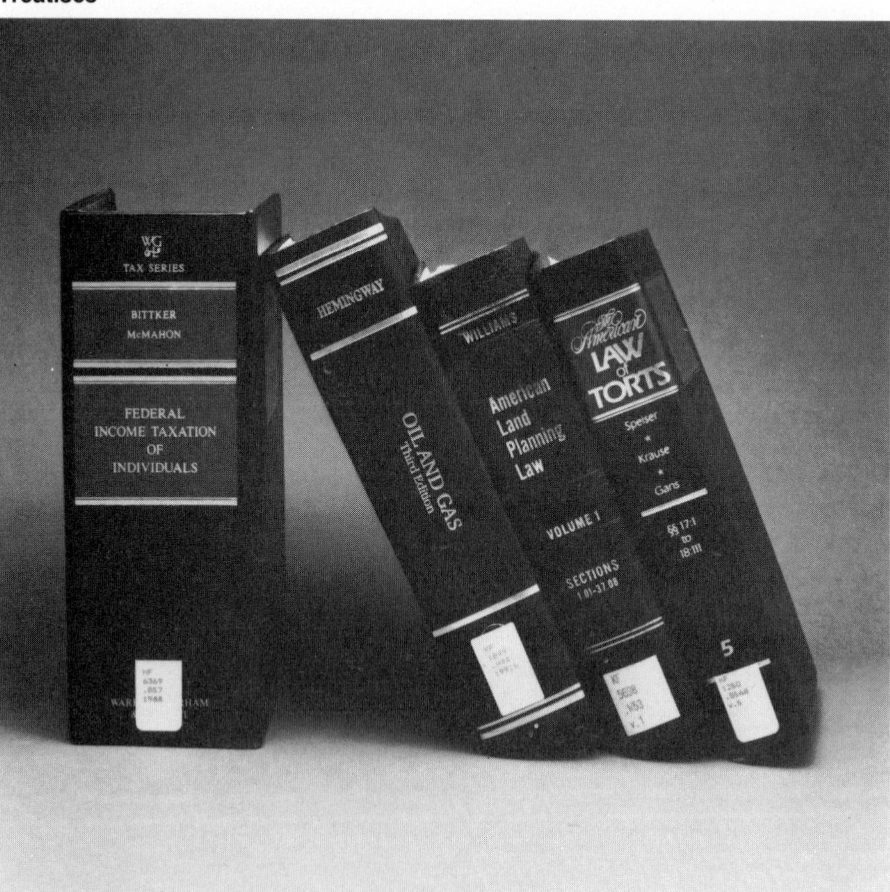

Source: © Doug Martin.

subject in more detail than an encyclopedia, outline, periodical, or other secondary source.

In most law libraries, textbooks and treatises are shelved together according to the Library of Congress Classification. (See Figure 9–1 and Appendix IV.) Since there are so many different textbooks and treatises, you have to check what is available in your local law library.

Although there is no formal classification of textbooks and treatises beyond the Library of Congress Classification system, textbooks and treatises may be grouped by their purpose for publication.

Many textbooks and treatises are written for practicing lawyers and paralegals. Examples include *The American Law of Torts* (Rochester, NY: LCP, 1983–1987), by Stuart M. Speiser, Charles F. Krause, and Alfred W. Gans; *Nimmer on Copyright* (New York: Matthew Bender, 1963), by Melville B. Nimmer; *The Paralegal Resource Manual* (Cincinnati: Anderson Publishing Co., 1989), by Charles P. Nemeth; *Pattern Deposition Checklists*, 2nd ed. (Rochester, NY: LCP, 1984), by Douglas Danner; and *Trademarks and Unfair Competition*, 2nd ed. (Rochester, NY: LCP, 1984), by J. Thomas McCarthy.

Some textbooks and treatises are written for scholarly purposes, such as *Jurisprudence: The Philosophy and Method of the Law* (Cambridge, MA: Harvard University Press, 1962), by Edgar Bodenheimer; and *The Language of the Law* (Boston: Little, Brown and Co., 1963), by David Mellinkoff.

Most textbooks and treatises, however, are written for educational purposes. Along with casebooks, discussed in Chapter 3, and continuing legal education seminar outlines, examples include *Business Law: With UCC Applications*, 7th ed. (Westerville, OH: the Glencoe Division of Macmillan/McGraw-Hill School

Figure 9–1 Example of a Treatise Shelf Directory

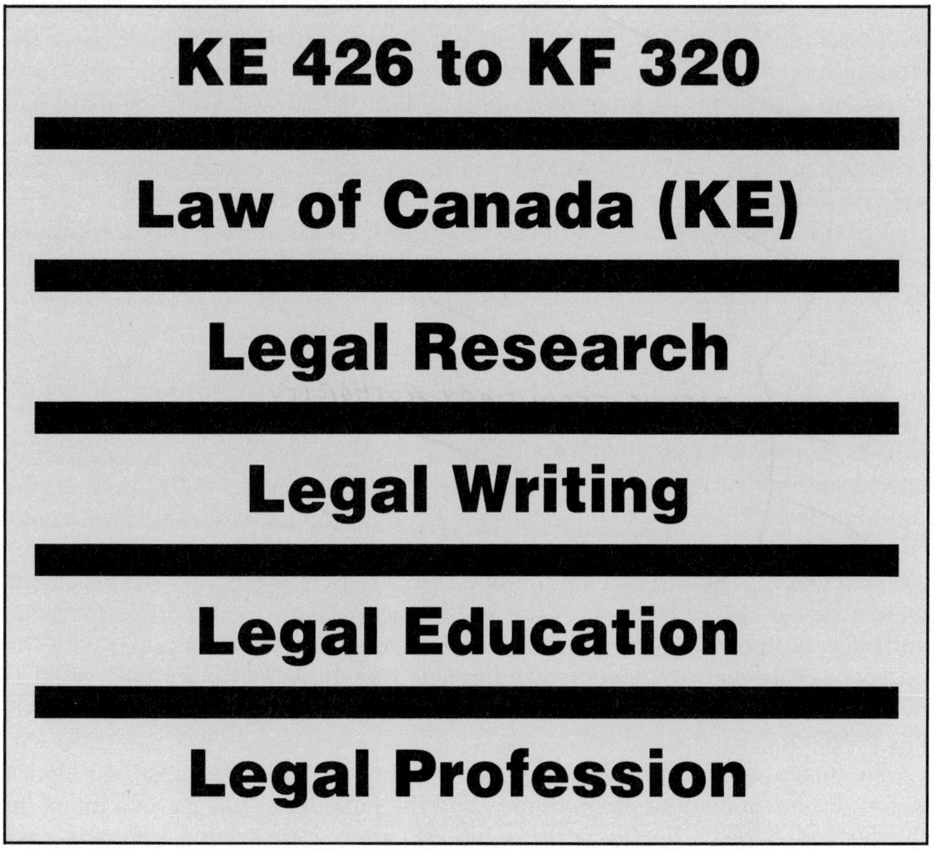

KE 426 to KF 320

Law of Canada (KE)

Legal Research

Legal Writing

Legal Education

Legal Profession

Publishing Co., 1989), by Gordon W. Brown, Edward E. Byers, and Mary Ann Lawlor; *Fundamentals of Criminal Advocacy* (Rochester, NY: LCP, 1974), by F. Lee Bailey and Henry B. Rothblatt; and *Real Estate and the Law* (Westerville, OH: the Glencoe Division of Macmillan/McGraw-Hill School Publishing Co., 1982), by Robert N. Corley, Peter J. Shedd, and Charles F. Floyd.

Hornbooks and Nutshells

Named after teaching tablets with handles used from the late 1400s to the middle 1700s (i.e., a sheet of paper protected by a sheet of translucent horn), **hornbooks** are today a series of one-volume, student-oriented treatises published by the West Publishing Company (West). Hornbooks generally cover basic legal subjects, such as criminal law, evidence, and property. (See Figure 9–2.) The authors are generally law professors renowned as experts in their field.

Among hornbooks, the most famous and influential was probably William L. Prosser's *Handbook of the Law of Torts* 4th ed. (1971). Often cited in briefs and court opinions, Prosser's text trained a generation of lawyers in the law of torts, to the point that a lawyer's "innate" ability to find a legal theory under which to sue is a national stereotype. Charles T. McCormick's *Law of Evidence*, 2nd ed. (1972) was another leading hornbook. *Corbin on Contracts* (1952) also deserves special mention. Many people believe that the character Professor Kingsfield in the movie and television series *The Paper Chase* was based on its author, Yale Law School professor Arthur Linton Corbin.

West's hornbooks are true treatises, and expensive. Realizing that there is a market for a wider range of less expensive textbooks than the hornbook series, West also publishes an "accurate, brief, convenient" series of paperback textbooks "priced for student budgets" known as **nutshells.** Named after the student's perpetual dream of putting an entire subject "in a nutshell" (like one's cranium), a nutshell, focusing on essentials and citing less law, costs about half of what a hornbook costs. Nutshells cover both basic subjects (e.g., criminal law, evidence, and property) and esoteric subjects (e.g., injunctions, insurance, and military law).

A list of West hornbooks and nutshells is printed on the pages preceding the title page of any nutshell.

Restatements

In 1923, a group of judges, lawyers, and law professors founded the American Law Institute (ALI), an organization dedicated to the simplification of the common law. This was to be achieved by preparing a clear and systematic exposition of the common law as if it were a codified statutory code, known as a **restatement,** prepared by expert "reporters." From 1923 to 1944, restatements were adopted and published for the laws of agency, contracts, property, torts, and several other subjects, but they never became authorities on a par with the decisions of the courts as originally intended. They have been frequently cited as persuasive authority, however, and since 1952, a second series of restatements has been adopted and published.

The current set of restatements may be determined from the latest ALI *Annual Report.* Each restatement has an index, and the First Series has its own index. In the Second Series, the "Reporter's Notes" after each section contains case citations. There may also be references to West's digest system and annotations

Figure 9–2 Excerpt From a Hornbook

ing. The mere fact that the publication was not privileged because it was inaccurately and negligently made does not mean of course that under present law the plaintiff would recover. The plaintiff, as a public official, or public figure, or private person, would have to establish the kind of fault on the part of the defendant with respect to the truth or falsity of the alleged defamatory imputation made about the plaintiff in the proceeding as is constitutionally required.

WESTLAW REFERENCES

digest(qualified /5 privilege* immunity /s defam! slander! libel!)

qualified /5 privilege* immunity /p defam! slander! libel! /p constitution! unconstitution!

Interest of Publisher

topic(237) /p selfdefense selfprotection

237k46

Interest of Others

restatement /s torts +5 603

libel! slander! defam! /p limited qualified /5 privilege /s profession**

restatement /s torts /5 595 596

Common Interest

digest(defam! libel! slander! /p "common interest*")

237k51(4)

Communications of One Who May Act in the Public Interest

libel! slander! defam! /p "public interest" /s qualified /s immunity privilege

237k51(5)

digest(libel! slander! defam! /p public /p "fair comment")

Abuse of Qualified Privilege Regarding Private Publication of Private Matters

opinion(abus! misus! /s qualified conditional /s privilege immunity)

"private defamation"

Burden of Proof—Court and Jury

digest(defam! slander! libel! /p "burden of proof")

defam! slander! libel! /p burden /4 proof proving /s defense privilege* immunity

Report of Public Proceedings—A Special Type of Privilege

defam! slander! libel! /p public legislative executive council committee /7 proceeding* meeting* /s report!

fair** accurate** correct** /s report! /s public legislative executive council committee /s proceeding* meeting* /p libel! slander! defam!

The Constitution Privilege

negligen! /s publish! publication! /p defam! libel! slander! /p constitution! unconstitution!

§ 116. Truth and Other Defenses

Truth or Justification

To create liability for defamation, there must be publication of matter that is both defamatory and false.[1] The well-settled common law rule prior to decisions by the United States Supreme Court related to the constitutional privilege to defame was that truth is an affirmative defense which the defendant must plead and prove. Thus, under the common law rule, the defamatory statement is regarded as false unless the defendant proves truth. It has been said that meeting the constitutional requirements regarding the necessity for proof of at least negligence with respect to the truth or falsity of a defamatory statement makes it necessary for the plaintiff to allege and prove the falsity of the communication.[2] The basis for this position is that the Supreme Court of the United States, in holding that the plaintiff must establish some kind of fault with respect to the issue of truth or falsity, has by implication allocated the issue of falsity to the plaintiff. But there can be two answers to this. In the first place, the constitutional privilege to defame may not extend to defamatory utterances privately made about private persons.[3] In the second place, there is no inconsistency in assuming falsity until defendant publisher proves otherwise and requiring the plaintiff to prove negligence or recklessness with respect to the truth or falsity of the imputation. There is, in other words, nothing inconsistent about requiring the defendant to prove truth if absolute protection is to be provided for a

§ 116

1. Second Restatement of Torts, § 581A, Comment *a.* leads to more in

2. See, Second Restatement of Torts, § 613, Comment *j;* Eldredge, The Law of Defamation, 1978, Sec. 63; Morris on Torts, Second edition, 1980, p. 350.

3. See § 113.

Figure 9–2 cont.

the defense of truth, and formerly these rules were carried to ridiculous extremes,[28] but it is now generally agreed that it is not necessary to prove the literal truth of the accusation in every detail, and that it is sufficient to show that the imputation is substantially true,[29] or, as it is often put, to justify the "gist," the "sting," or the "substantial truth" of the defamation.[30] Thus an accusation that the mayor of a town has wasted $80,000 of the taxpayers' money has been held to be justified by proof that he wasted $17,500, since there is no more opprobrium attached to the greater amount.[31] If, however, the defendant adds to the facts stated an opinion or comment of his own, the comment must be justified as a proper one in the light of the facts proved.[32]

The defense of truth frequently is a hazardous venture for the defendant, since if he fails to sustain it the jury may be permitted to find that he has reiterated the defamation, and to consider the fact in aggravation of the damages.[33] The modern cases, however, have tended quite properly to recognize that the defendant is entitled to present an honest defense without being penalized, and have limited such aggravation to cases where it appears that the defense was entered in bad faith, without evidence to support it.[34]

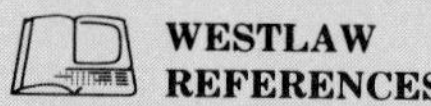
WESTLAW REFERENCES

Truth or Justification

digest(defam! libel! slander! /s truth /s defense)

defam! libel! slander! /p commonlaw /p burden /5 proof proving

Truth

justification /s libel! slander! defam!

truth /s justification /s libel! slander! defam!

§ 116A. Damages and Matters in Mitigation

Damages which may be recovered in an action for defamation are: (1) compensatory or actual, which may be either (a) general or (b) special; (2) punitive or exemplary; and (3) nominal.[1]

Downs v. Hawley, 1873, 112 Mass. 237; Sun Printing & Publishing Association v. Schenck, 2d Cir. 1900, 98 F. 925; Kilian v. Doubleday & Co., 1951, 367 Pa. 117, 79 A.2d 657.

27. Gardner v. Self, 1852, 15 Mo. 480; Buckner v. Spaulding, 1891, 127 Ind. 229, 26 N.E. 792; Pallet v. Sargent, 1858, 36 N.H. 496; Haddock v. Naughton, 1893, 74 Hun 390, 26 N.Y.S. 455. Cf. Stewart v. Enterprise Co., Tex.Civ.App.1965, 393 S.W.2d 372, refused n.r.e., appeal after remand 439 S.W.2d 674, refused n.r.e. (two accusations, truth of only one proved).

28. See for example Swann v. Rary, Ind.1833, 3 Blackf. 298 (two hogs and one); Sharpe v. Stephenson, 1851, 34 N.C. (12 Ired.) 348 (time and place); cf. Coffin v. Brown, 1901, 94 Md. 190, 50 A. 567 (time and place). See Courtney, Absurdities of the Law of Slander and Libel, 1902, 36 Am.L.Rev. 552, 561–564.

29. Alexander v. North Eastern R. Co., 1865, 6 B. & S. 340, 122 Eng.Rep. 1221; Zoll v. Allen, S.D.N.Y.1950, 93 F.Supp. 95; Florida Publishing Co. v. Lee, 1918, 76 Fla. 405, 80 So. 245; McGuire v. Vaughan, 1896, 106 Mich. 280, 64 N.W. 44; Skrocki v. Stahl, 1910, 14 Cal. App. 1, 110 P. 957.

30. Edwards v. Bell, 1824, 1 Bing. 403, 130 Eng. Rep. 162; Bell Publishing Co. v. Garrett Engineering Co., Tex.Civ.App.1941, 154 S.W.2d 885, affirmed 141 Tex. 51, 170 S.W.2d 197.

31. Fort Worth Press Co. v. Davis, Tex.Civ.App. 1936, 96 S.W.2d 416. Cf. Smith v. Byrd, 1955, 225 Miss. 331, 83 So.2d 172 (statement that sheriff shot a man justified by proof that sheriff was acting in concert with deputy who shot him).

32. Cooper v. Lawson, 1838, 8 Ad. & El. 746, 112 Eng.Rep. 1020; Commercial Publishing Co. v. Smith, 6th Cir. 1907, 149 F. 704; cf. Morrison v. Harmer, 1837, 3 Bing.N.C. 759, 132 Eng.Rep. 603.

33. Will v. Press Publishing Co., 1932, 309 Pa. 539, 164 A. 621; Coffin v. Brown, 1901, 94 Md. 190, 50 A. 567; Krulic v. Petcoff, 1913, 122 Minn. 517, 142 N.W. 897; Hall v. Edwards, 1942, 138 Me. 231, 23 A.2d 889 (with other evidence of malice). See Note, 1958, 56 Mich.L.Rev. 659.

In Domchick v. Greenbelt Consumer Services, 1952, 200 Md. 36, 87 A.2d 831, it was held that pleading truth makes a prima facie case as to malice. In Shumate v. Johnson Publishing Co., 1956, 139 Cal.App.2d 121, 293 P.2d 531, a publisher who verified a pleading of truth was held subject to punitive damages, although he was out of the state and took no other part.

34. Webb v. Gray, 1913, 181 Ala. 408, 62 So. 194; Fodor v. Fuchs, 1910, 79 N.J.L. 529, 76 A. 1081; Willard v. Press Publishing Co., 1900, 52 App.Div. 448, 65 N.Y.S. 73; Las Vegas Sun, Inc. v. Franklin, 1958, 74 Nev. 282, 329 P.2d 867; Snyder v. Fatherly, 1930, 153 Va. 762, 151 S.E. 149.

§ 116A

1. See, Stidham v. Wachtel, Del.1941, 2 Terry 327, 21 A.2d 282; Dobbs, Remedies, 1973, Sec. 7.2, pp. 513–523.

216

Source: Prosser & Keeton, *Torts,* 5th ed. (St. Paul: West Publishing Company, 1984), p. 839. Reprinted with permission.

Sample of West Hornbooks and Nutshells

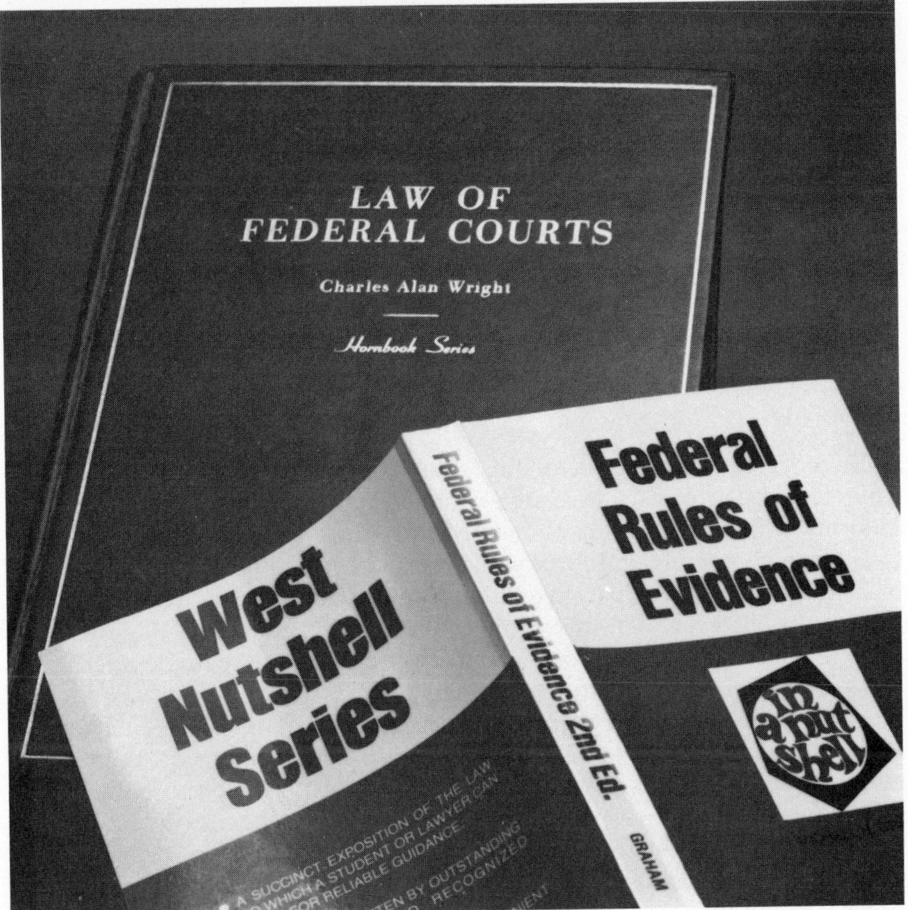

Source: © Doug Martin.

to the *American Law Reports* (A.L.R.). The *Restatement in the Courts* collects summaries of cases citing a restatement.

Uniform Laws

Some uniformity has been achieved in state statutory law through the work of the National Conference of Commissioners on Uniform State Laws, created in 1912. Following up on a recommendation by the American Bar Association, each state and the District of Columbia have appointed commissioners who meet once a year to review drafts of proposed uniform laws. If the commissioners find a proposed uniform law is desirable and practical, they promote its passage by their state legislature. Approved uniform laws are published in the commissioners' annual handbook and in West's *Uniform Laws Annotated, Master Edition.*

For example, ALI worked with the National Conference of Commissioners on Uniform State Laws to draft and promote the most pervasive uniform law to be substantially enacted in all 50 states and the District of Columbia: the Uniform Commercial Code (U.C.C.). As a result, the state laws of sales, negotiable instruments, and secured transactions are almost identical throughout the country.

9–2 Form Books

Lawyers and paralegals use **form books,** collections of sample legal documents used by other lawyers and paralegals to help them prepare documents for clients. Most form books also include checklists, and case, statute, and other cross-references, which are very helpful in preparing legal documents. However, while form books are excellent sources of ideas for how to handle a legal matter, you should *never* blindly follow a form. The law must always be individualized for the client. Most legal professionals agree with the statement: "I never saw a form that didn't need to be fixed."

Legal Forms

Samples of legally effective documents—such as contracts, deeds, and wills—are known as **legal forms.** There are several legal form books, some devoted to legal forms in general and others devoted to a single subject or jurisdiction.

One leading general legal form set is *American Jurisprudence Legal Forms 2d,* published by Lawyers Cooperative Publishing (LCP). Covering over 100 topics, the set is a collection of forms actually used in practice. (See Figure 9–3.) Cross-referenced with LCP's Total Client Service Library, the appropriate form can be found using the set's index volumes.

West also publishes an excellent general legal form set: *West's Legal Forms, 2d.* The set is divided into 11 topical units authored by experienced experts. In a guide to the set, West lists the following features: "expert authors; summary of contents for each volume; detailed table of contents; general background information; text analysis of subject matter; forms for information gathering; drafting checklists; basic and comprehensive forms; alternative provisions; comments to specific forms; tax considerations; federal laws; references to model acts and uniform laws; library references (including Key Numbers and C.J.S.); automation of form drafting; 'plain language' forms; indexes and tables; and updating."

Matthew Bender & Company, Inc. (MB), also publishes an excellent general legal form set: *Current Legal Forms With Tax Analysis,* originally prepared by Jacob Rabkin and Mark H. Johnson. The major feature of "Rabkin and Johnson" is its emphasis on the tax aspects of legal transactions represented by the legal forms involved.

Along with other national legal form books, there are also legal form books covering particular states. MB is the leader, publishing a "Transaction Guide" for each of several different states and regions.

The competition in form books can be intense. In Ohio, for example, there are four general legal form sets to choose from: Anderson Publishing Company's *Couse's Ohio Form Book;* Banks-Baldwin Law Publishing Company's *Baldwin's Ohio Legal Forms;* MB's *Ohio Transaction Guide—Legal Forms;* and LCP's *Ohio Forms: Legal and Business.*

Pleading and Practice Forms

Samples of documents used in actually litigating a case—such as complaints, answers, replies, interrogatories, motions, and judgments—are known as **pleading and practice forms.** Again, there are several pleading and practice form books; some are devoted to pleading and practice forms in general and others are devoted to a single subject or jurisdiction.

Figure 9–3 Excerpt From *American Jurisprudence Legal Forms 2d*

ASSIGNMENT FOR CREDITORS § 26:113

C. Release of Assignor

§ 26:111 Scope of division

The forms collected in this division consist of various clauses pertaining to releases by creditors that can be considered in connection with an assignment for the benefit of creditors. Included are federal tax references and text references for use in drafting such forms.

§ 26:112 Acceptance by creditors as release

Acceptance under this assignment by the creditors of __1____ *[debtor]* shall be taken and deemed as a complete payment by and release of __2____ *[debtor]* from the payment of any further sums to any existing creditor, except such part thereof as may be realized out of the net proceeds of the sale of the properties herein conveyed and of the money coming into assignee's hands by virtue of this assignment.

☑ **Notes on Use:**

Text reference: For discussion of provision according priority of payment to releasing creditors, see 6 Am Jur 2d, Assignments for Benefit of Creditors § 52.

§ 26:113 Creditor's release

Agreement made __1____, 19_2_, between __3____, of __4____ *[address]*, City of __5____, County of __6____, State of __7____, herein referred to as creditor, and __8____, of __9____ *[address]*, City of __10____, County of __11____, State of __12____, herein referred to as assignor.

Inasmuch as assignor, by a certain assignment, dated __13____, 19_14_, conveyed, assigned, transferred, and set over to __15____, of __16____ *[address]*, City of __17____, County of __18____, State of __19____, as assignee, all property and effects of every kind and description, real, personal, and mixed, of assignor (except as was exempt from levy and sale under execution) for the benefit of the creditors of assignor; and

The trust imposed by the assignment has been duly executed according to law by the assignee therein appointed, and the proceeds of the property, estate and effects mentioned in that assignment duly applied to the payment of the claims of the creditors of assignor, according to law, and creditor received __20____ *[number]* respective __21____ [share *or* shares] of the proceeds of that estate, according to the amount of __22____ *[number]* respective claims against assignor; and assignee has duly accounted,

The parties agree as follows:

In consideration of the premises, and in consideration of __23____ Dollars ($____), in hand paid by assignor, the receipt of which is acknowledged, creditor releases and discharges assignor from all further liability to or on

(For Tax Notes and Notes on Use of form, see end of form)

2 Am Jur Legal Forms 2d 607

Figure 9–3 cont.

account of any and all claims and demands whatsoever that the creditor had against assignor at the time of the making of the assignment, as aforesaid.

Creditor, for himself and his heirs, executors and administrators, agrees that from the date of this release, he will have and claim no further right, benefit, or interest in, to, or in respect of any and all claims or demands of whatever kind that he may have had against assignor at the time of the making of the assignment.

In witness whereof, I have executed this release at __24______ *[designate place of execution]* the day and year first above written.

[Signature]

[Acknowledgment]

☑ **Tax Note:**

For discussion of tax consequences of an agreement in cancellation of a bad debt, see FEDERAL TAX GUIDE TO LEGAL FORMS, Cancellation of Indebtedness ¶ 1505.

☑ **Notes on Use:**

Text reference: For discussion of relinquishment of release provision as validating assignment, see 6 AM JUR 2d, Assignments for Benefit of Creditors § 54.

Cross reference: For forms of acknowledgments, see ACKNOWLEDGMENTS (Ch 7).

V. ADMINISTRATION OF ESTATE

§ 26:121 Scope of division

The material in this division consists of forms pertaining to the administration of the assignor's estate, together with federal tax references, text references, and annotations for use in drafting the instruments.

§ 26:122 Notice to assignee of preferred claim—For labor

State of __1______
County of __2______
To: __3______, assignee of __4______ *[debtor]*, and to whom it may concern.

I, __5______, the undersigned, being first duly sworn, say:

1. __6______ *[Debtor]*, who on __7______, 19_8_, executed a general assignment for the benefit of creditors to __9______ *[assignee]* now is, and was at

(For Tax Notes and Notes on Use of form, see end of form)

Source: Am Jur Legal Forms 2d, vol. 2 (Rochester, NY: Lawyers Co-operative Publishing Co., 1971), p. 607. Reprinted with permission.

One leading set of general pleading and practice forms is LCP's *American Jurisprudence Pleading and Practice Forms Revised.* LCP also publishes an excellent pair of guides to federal pleading and practice (including practice before federal administrative agencies): a textbook set, *Federal Procedure, Lawyers' Edition*, and a form book set, *Federal Procedural Forms, Lawyers' Edition*. The pair anchor what LCP advertised in 1991 as its federal "family," including *United States Supreme Court Reports, Lawyers' Edition, Second Series* (L. Ed. 2d), A.L.R. Fed., *United States Code Service* (U.S.C.S.), and several other federal law publications. These sets can be entered through the general index for each set.

There are several other guides to federal procedure. West publishes *West's Federal Practice Manual* and *West's Federal Forms.* MB publishes *Moore's Federal Practice* and *Bender's Federal Practice Forms.* MB also publishes *Bender's Forms of Discovery* and several state pleading and practice form books.

Again, the competition in form books can be intense. In Ohio, for example, there are three general pleading and practice form sets to choose from: Anderson Publishing Company's *Anderson's Ohio Civil Practice With Forms*, Banks-Baldwin Law Publishing Company's *Baldwin's Ohio Civil Practice*, and MB's *Ohio Forms of Pleading and Practice.*

Trial and Practice Books

Books that guide a lawyer or a paralegal through the proof of contentions at trial, often with samples of litigation aids and trial testimony, are known as **trial and practice books.** LCP publishes two unique trial and practice sets: *American*

LCP's *Federal Procedure, Lawyers' Edition*, and *Federal Procedural Forms, Lawyers' Edition*

Source: © Doug Martin.

Jurisprudence Proof of Facts 2d and *American Jurisprudence Trials. American Jurisprudence Proof of Facts 2d* includes checklists for the proof of crucial facts in depositions and trials, and sample questions and answers to use in doing so. (See Figure 9–4.) *American Jurisprudence Trials,* after six volumes of general trial practice advice, is a collection of advice on how to try over 200 different kinds of cases, from airplane crashes to exploding gas tanks, from lawyers who have taken such cases to court. Each of these trial and practice guides has a general index for the set.

Trial and practice books blur into textbooks and treatises. There are several excellent guides to trial practice. For example, MB publishes the *Art of Advocacy* series, including *Preparation of the Case, Discovery, Settlement, Jury Selection, Opening Statement, Documentary Evidence, Direct Examination, Cross-Examination of Medical Experts, Cross-Examination of Non-Medical Experts, Summation,* and *Appeals.* LCP publishes the *Federal Trial Handbook 2d,* by Robert S. Hunter, and a series of state trial handbooks. An excellent state trial handbook, *Trial Handbook for Ohio Lawyers, Second Edition,* was put together for LCP by former Judge Richard M. Markus.

9–3 Periodicals

A **periodical** is a work that is published at regular intervals. Whereas reporters (discussed in Chapter 2) are published at regular intervals because cases occur chronologically, periodicals are published at regular intervals by the publisher's design. A.L.R. (discussed in Chapter 4) qualifies as a periodical, since the reported cases are not always reported in chronological order.

In the same way that ordinary periodicals are excellent sources of market information, recent scholarship, and current events, legal periodicals are excellent sources of information about the legal market, legal scholarship, and legal events. Specialty periodicals are also available to help keep the specialists up to date in their areas of specialty. Periodicals are also useful for historical research—to find out what people knew and what people were thinking at any given time.

Most of the periodicals in the following discussion are available on either or both the LEXIS and WESTLAW computer-assisted legal research systems, to be discussed in Chapter 12.

Law Reviews

A scholarly periodical published by a law school is known as a **law review.** Law reviews generally contain articles written by law professors, prominent practitioners, or outstanding students (known as **comments**), and short book, case, or subject reviews (known as **notes**).

A quality law review article, as an excellent critical commentary, may be treated by a court as persuasive authority. Because it may lead to the development of a new field of law or turn an established field of law in a new direction, it may have a significant and substantial effect on the law. Some lawyers, however, believe that most law review articles are nothing but academic drivel.

Virtually every law school publishes a law review. Most cover the law in general, but some stress the law of the state where the school is located.

Some law schools publish more than one review. One covers the law

Figure 9–4 Excerpt From *American Jurisprudence Proof of Facts 2d*

SUITABILITY OF WORK **1-613** **§ 16**

III. PROOF THAT WAGE AND SKILL LEVELS ARE INADEQUATE

A. Elements of Proof

§ 15. Guide and checklist

The following facts and circumstances, among others, tend to establish that the offer of employment that the claimant refused was unsuitable for him because it failed to utilize his existing skills and because the offered wage was inadequate:

- ☐ Claimant's existing skill and wage levels [§ 16]
- ☐ Circumstances of unemployment [§ 17]
  —Claimant unemployed through no fault of his own [§ 17]
- ☐ Duration of unemployment [§ 17]
- ☐ Offer of employment to claimant [§ 18]
- ☐ Investigation of offer [§ 18]
  —Comparison with existing skill and wage levels [§ 18]
- ☐ Refusal of offer because below existing skill and wage levels [§ 19]
- ☐ Availability for work at customary skill and wage levels [§ 20]
- ☐ Reasonable prospects of obtaining local work at customary skill and wage levels [§ 21]

B. Testimony of Claimant

§ 16. Existing skill level and earnings record

Q. Please state your name and address.

A. My name is ____________. I live at ____________.

Q. What is your occupation?

A. I an a tool and die maker.

Q. Are you working now?

A. No, I'm unemployed.

Q. Where were you last employed as a tool and die maker?

A. At ____________.

Q. Could you describe what you did there?

A. I worked in the machine shop, on construction and maintenance of tools, and calibrating them, also making dies that they use in their forging and stamping operations. Sometimes I had

1 POF 2d **635**

Figure 9–4 cont.

to do layout work and assembly work, fitting machines together.

Q. Was this considered skilled labor?
A. Yes, it's considered highly skilled work.

Q. How long did you work there?
A. For .... years.

Q. Were you a tool and die maker all that time?
A. Yes.

Q. How much were you making?
A. At the time I was laid off, $2.90 an hour.

Q. Was that the most you ever made?
A. No, for a while before that I made $3.15 an hour.

☐ **Note: Suitability of pay cut.** In determining the suitability of offered employment involving a pay cut, both the relative amount of the reduction and the absolute amount of the offered wage may be relevant. For example, a cut of 20 percent may be unsuitable for a person whose original wage was barely above subsistence level, but acceptable for someone whose previous wage was much higher. Therefore, to provide a clear illustration of a wage reduction that was deemed unsuitable under the circumstances presented, figures from an actual case have been used. See Re Troutman 264 NC 289, 141 SE2d 613. The claimant in that case became unemployed in 1964.

Q. What happened to cause a reduction?
A. The company shut down for a while back in 19...., because there wasn't any work, and when they reopened they had to lower the wage levels.

Q. Were you rehired at $2.90 an hour?
A. No, I was rehired at $2.60, then worked my way up.

Q. How long were you working at $2.90 an hour before you became unemployed?
A. .... months.

§ 17. Circumstances of unemployment

Q. What happened to make you unemployed this time?
A. The company cut back its operations and laid off a lot of people, including me.

Source: Am Jur Proof of Facts 2d, Vol. 1 (Rochester, NY: Lawyers Co-operative Publishing Co., 1974), p. 635. Reprinted with permission.

Sample Law Reviews

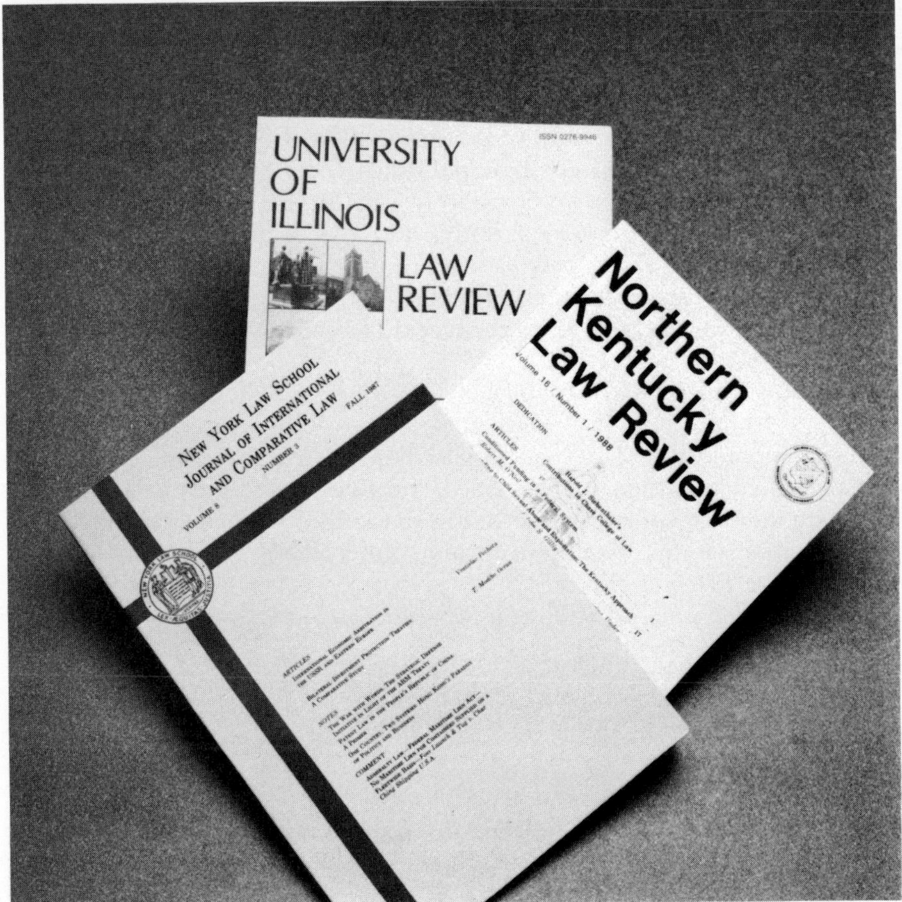

Source: © Doug Martin.

in general and the rest cover a specialized subject, such as environmental law or international law.

Law reviews are usually edited by law students as an academic exercise. Students research topics and check the work of outside authors and each other. Because the students invited to work on a law review usually have high grade point averages or demonstrated writing ability, serving on a law review is usually considered an honor. However, "law review" does not always mean "excellence." The author is aware of an incident in which a law student declined an invitation to join the law review at his school because the student editors could not articulate any purpose or goal for the law review other than the self-adulation of its members.

Law Journals

A **law journal** is a legal periodical emphasizing current events; if published by a bar association, it is usually known as a **bar journal.** They are legal magazines, supported in part by advertising that gives the readers market information. These journals keep legal professionals informed about current legal events and trends.

The leading national legal magazine is the American Bar Association's *ABA Journal* (A.B.A. J.). Self-described as "the lawyer's magazine" and "an independent, thoughtful and inquiring observer of the law and the legal profession," A.B.A. J. is a monthly "edited for members of the American Bar Association." Along with the feature articles, A.B.A. J. regularly includes a message from the ABA president, letters, news, the Supreme Court Report, trends in the law, books, classified advertising, and legal "war" stories. (See Figure 9–5.)

Specialty sections of the American Bar Association also publish journals. For example, the section on Business Law publishes *The Business Lawyer* quarterly and *The Business Lawyer Update* bi-monthly; the section on General Practice publishes *The Compleat Lawyer* quarterly; and the section on Law Practice Management publishes *Legal Economics* eight times a year.

Most state bar associations also publish journals. The Ohio State Bar Association, for example, publishes the weekly *Ohio State Bar Association Report* containing legislative reports, classified advertising, court rule changes, and official advance sheets. It also publishes *Ohio Lawyer,* a monthly journal with articles.

Many large county and city bar associations also publish journals. Local journals usually emphasize local activities, court decisions, and current events.

There are hundreds of journals covering specialized subjects, published by a variety of organizations. Examples include the *Catholic Lawyer,* the *Practical Lawyer,* and the *Practical Tax Lawyer.* Two journals cover the subject of legal research: *Law Library Journal* and *Legal Reference Services Quarterly.*

Newsletters

As they come down in scale and scope, legal journals blur into newsletters. Some formal governmental publications are published in newsletter form. The Internal Revenue Service (IRS), for example, publishes a weekly *Internal Revenue Bulletin* (I.R.B.), cumulated yearly in a *Cumulative Bulletin* (C.B.). The IRS's district directors publish *Tax Practitioner Newsletter,* which is distributed to tax practitioners in their districts. State newsletters are also published, such as *The Ohio State Tax Report,* published by the Ohio Department of Taxation, and the *State Public Defender Report,* published by the Ohio Public Defender.

Countless newsletters are published by private publishers. For example, Boardroom Reports, Inc., publishes the monthly *Tax HOTline,* featuring inside information from tax lawyers, accountants, and former IRS agents.

Newspapers

The national weekly legal newspapers are the *National Law Journal* and the *Legal Times* (formerly the *Legal Times of Washington*). *The American Lawyer* is a national monthly newspaper.

In major metropolitan areas, there are local legal newspapers. Examples include the *Los Angeles Daily Journal* and the *New York Law Journal.*

Periodical Indexes

The only practical way to find an article in a periodical that is no longer current is through an index. There are two principal general legal periodical indexes.

For many years, H. W. Wilson Company has been known for its general *Index to Periodicals.* In 1961, H. W. Wilson Company purchased the *Index to Legal Periodicals* from the American Association of Law Libraries. Covering the period

Figure 9–5 Excerpt From the American Bar Association *ABA Journal*

Attorney Discipline

Do we need an ethical rule restricting sexual relations with clients?

Simultaneously bedding and representing clients, Arnie Becker of "L.A. Law" has popularized an image of lawyers that many in the profession find disturbing. In response to increasing lawsuits, members of the Illinois and California bars have attempted to specifically prohibit attorneys from coercing and demanding sex of clients, while the American Academy of Matrimonial Lawyers has adopted an advisory standard.

The issue of regulating this activity is a complex one, says Susan Michmerhuizen of the American Bar Association's Center for Professional Responsibility: "Horror stories abound, and yet it's a difficult situation to reach under existing ethical rules."

Chicago lawyer Cornelia Honchar Tuite argues that a separate rule regulating sexual relations with clients is necessary to set clear standards for behavior. She believes that it could be reasonably tailored to distinguish romantic liaisons from dangerous ones.

Her colleague, Chicago trial lawyer Philip Corboy, believes that existing rules offer adequate protection. He doubts that yet another rule will deter the truly unethical attorney.

Yes: Put It in Writing

BY CORNELIA HONCHAR TUITE

Among the goals of the Model Rules of Professional Conduct is the comprehensive delineation of lawyers' fiduciary duties to clients—duties of trust, confidence and fair dealing.

Common sense says we should not gouge our clients, use confidentially obtained information for financial or professional gain, or counsel clients in any future criminal conduct.

Yet, the Model Rules specifically prohibit such conduct for several reasons: 1) to make a lawyer's duties clear, establishing a profession-wide baseline of proper behavior, below which no lawyer can fall with impunity; 2) to determine who may practice law, since it is a privilege, not a right; and 3) to inform the public of its rights and expectations.

The Rules function as much as a policy statement about the values of the American justice system as a disciplinary framework. In this context, should sexual relations with clients be ethically regulated? Yes.

A failure to regulate this sensitive aspect of a trusting relationship would mean we hold a client's money (given to us as fiduciaries) more valuable than the intangible, but far more precious, emotional trust our clients give us in trying times of their lives.

What we choose or decline to regulate is the litmus test of our values. What is wrong with recognizing the worth of emotional trust or with imposing the same fiduciary duties on intangible as well as tangible client valuables? Certainly, misappropriation of a $100 check pales in significance with charges that lawyers demand sex in return for representation.

Can anyone who values individual dignity honestly argue that a lawyer who sexually exploits a client meets a baseline standard of a profession resting on the same terrain of special public trust with the ministry and medicine?

We do not condone sexual exploitation by ministers or doctors; how can we, as lawyers, fail to say we, too, reject it?

I find no currency in arguments that common sense and general principles of misconduct, fitness to practice or bans on attorney-client conflict of interest provide a sufficient disciplinary mechanism to sanction those lawyers who sexually abuse their clients.

The Case for Specificity

Model Rule 1.8(d) bars lawyers from negotiating book contracts with clients before the representation's conclusion. About 99 percent of American lawyers never face this prospect, yet the potential conflict of interest prompted this rule's adoption. If we specifically regulate book contracts, how can we refuse to prohibit specifically the sexual exploitation of clients? What logic says regulate one, but not the other?

Similarly, under Rule 1.8(a) lawyers cannot enter business transactions with clients without written, full disclosure; the existence of fair, reasonable terms; and giving the client an opportunity to seek independent advice. Again, the inherent problems of conflicts of interest, impairment of the lawyer's judgment by self-interest, and potential breach of trust underlie this specific prohibition.

A carefully tailored, reasonable rule prohibiting client sexual exploitation during a representation would define the prohibited conduct so disciplinary agencies would have an established burden of proof and protect lawyers from spurious claims.

Currently, most lawyers are disciplined under general misconduct provisions, raising the potential for uneven application of the Rules, and the decided cases generally offer little guidance.

Most importantly, a rule articulates the profession's values, its abhorrence of sexual exploitation, its commitment to fiduciary duty in emotional as well as in business transactions, book contracts and safe-keeping of tangible assets. We must clearly state that sexual exploitation breaches client trust. The absence of a rule implies we do not believe it.

The law's primary goals are the protection of human worth and dignity. The law governing lawyers should echo those same goals. ■

Source: ABA Journal, Oct. 1970 (Chicago: American Bar Association), p. 46. Reprinted with permission.

from 1908 to the present, the *Index to Legal Periodicals* is published monthly (except September) and includes articles in over 500 periodicals deemed to have permanent reference value. The index is primarily by subject, with secondary indexing by author. The *Index to Legal Periodicals* is also available in many law libraries on the Wilsondisc CD-ROM system, and on the LEXIS (LAWREF; LGLIND and LEXREF;LGLIND files) and WESTLAW (LRI database) computer-assisted legal research systems, to be discussed in Chapter 12.

In 1980, the Information Access Corporation began to put out two indexes published with the assistance of an Advisory Committee of the American Association of Law Libraries: *Current Law Index* and *Legal Resource Index.* The *Current Law Index* indexes over 700 permanent legal periodicals by author, title, and other indexes. The *Legal Resource Index* is the computerized and microfilmed version of the *Current Law Index.* In addition to the coverage of the *Current Law Index,* the *Legal Resource Index* covers legal newspapers and other similar sources. The *Legal Resource Index* is also available in many law libraries as the LegalTrac database on the InfoTrac CD-ROM system, and on the LEXIS (LAWREF; LGLIND and LEXREF;LGLIND files), WESTLAW (LRI database), and DIALOG computer-assisted legal research systems, to be discussed in Chapter 12.

There are numerous specialized legal periodical indexes. Check with your local law library to see what is available there.

SUMMARY

9–1

The principles of a given legal subject can be found in a textbook or a treatise. There are thousands of legal textbooks and treatises, and they cover virtually every legal subject. They may be published in either single volumes or multivolume sets. Textbooks and treatises usually include the features of an ordinary book (e.g., a table of contents, the main body in chapters, and an index) and legal features (e.g., a table of cases cited, organization by section number, and pocket parts or other supplementation). In most law libraries, textbooks and treatises are shelved together according to the Library of Congress Classification system. Hornbooks are a series of one-volume, student-oriented treatises. Nutshells focus on essentials and cite less law. Restatements restate the common law as if it were a statutory code.

9–2

Lawyers and paralegals use form books—collections of sample legal documents used by other lawyers and paralegals—to help them prepare documents for clients. Most form books also include checklists, and case, statute, and other cross-references that are very helpful in preparation of legal documents. Samples of legally effective documents, such as contracts, deeds, and wills, are known as legal forms. There are several legal form books, some devoted to legal forms in general, and others devoted to a single subject or jurisdiction. National general legal form sets include *American Jurisprudence Legal Forms 2d* and *West's Legal Forms, 2d.* Samples of documents used in actually litigating a case—such as complaints, answers, replies, interrogatories, motions, and judgments—are known as pleading and practice forms. There are several guides to federal procedure. Books that guide a lawyer or paralegal through the proof of contentions at trial, often with samples of litigation aids and trial testimony, are known as trial and practice books.

9–3

A periodical is a work published at regular intervals. Legal periodicals are excellent sources of information about the legal market, legal scholarship, and legal events. A scholarly periodical published by a law school is known as a law review. A quality law review article may be treated by a court as persuasive authority. Virtually every law school publishes a law review. A law journal is a legal periodical emphasizing current events; if published by a bar association, it is usually known as a bar journal. The leading national legal magazine is the American Bar Association's *ABA Journal* (A.B.A. J.). Specialty sections of the American Bar Association also publish journals, as do most state bar associations. Some formal governmental publications are published in newsletter form. Countless newsletters are published by private publishers. The national legal weekly newspapers are the *National Law Journal* and the *Legal Times.* The only practical way to find an article in a periodical that is no longer current is through an index. There are two principal general legal periodical indexes: the *Index to Legal Periodicals,* published by the H. W. Wilson Company, which is also available on the Wilsondisc CD-ROM system; and the *Current Law Index/Legal Resource Index,* published by the Information Access Corporation, which is also available as the LegalTrac database on the InfoTrac CD-ROM system.

REVIEW

Key Terms

Before proceeding, review the key terms listed below to be sure you understand each one. If necessary, read over the corresponding section of the chapter. When you are ready to test your understanding, answer the Review Questions.

bar journal
comments
form books
hornbooks
law journal
law review
legal forms
notes
nutshells
periodical
pleading and practice forms
restatement
textbook
treatise
trial and practice books

Questions for Review and Discussion

1. When does a textbook become a treatise?
2. What is a hornbook?
3. What is a restatement?
4. What is the difference between a legal form and a pleading and practice form?
5. Where can you find legal forms?
6. Where can you find pleading and practice forms?
7. Who uses *American Jurisprudence Trials?*
8. How important are law reviews?
9. What is the leading national legal magazine?
10. What is the *National Law Journal?*

Activities

1. Read through a chapter of a West hornbook. Was the subject of the chapter explained to your satisfaction? Would you ever use a hornbook as a case finder?
2. Imagine that you are drafting the articles of incorporation for a non-profit corporation, and use the form books available to you. Which form books were most helpful? Would your answer be different if you were drafting a purchase agreement for the sale of a business?
3. Examine the law review of the law school closest to your home. How practical are the articles? Read through an article. Did you learn anything you couldn't have found out yourself?

PART FOUR

CITING THE LAW

Chapter 10
A Uniform System of Citation

Chapter 11
Shepard's Citations and Other Citators

CHAPTER 10 A Uniform System of Citation

OUTLINE

10–1 Citation Style
The Bluebook: A Uniform System of Citation
Other Systems of Citation
10–2 Technical Rules
Citing Cases
Citing Statutes
Citing Other Primary Sources
Citing Secondary Sources
Computer-Assisted Citation Style
10–3 Citation Requirements

COMMENTARY

The law director, impressed with the breadth and depth of your research into public religious displays, reminds you that you must put your research down in writing by the end of next week. As you start to write your memorandum, you realize that you must cite authority for all the legal propositions you make. And as a professional, you want your work to be in the proper form and style. You remember seeing a copy of *The Bluebook: A Uniform System of Citation* on the law director's desk.

OBJECTIVES

In this chapter you will learn about the conventions for citing legal materials. Emphasis is placed on *The Bluebook: A Uniform System of Citation*. After reading this chapter, you should be able to:

1. Understand the importance of *The Bluebook: A Uniform System of Citation*.
2. Identify and use *The Bluebook: A Uniform System of Citation*.
3. Identify other systems of citation.
4. Properly cite case names.
5. Properly cite case reporters.
6. Properly cite deciding courts.
7. Properly cite decision dates.
8. Properly cite statutes.
9. Properly cite constitutions, court rules, and administrative regulations.
10. Properly cite books and periodicals.

10–1 Citation Style

No matter how well you perform legal research, if you can't communicate your results to others, most of your time and effort will be wasted. It's not enough that you've found cases like yours (or other law) where the person like you won. You must be able to communicate that fact to the decision maker involved. In court, the judge will want you to prove your case, if only to make it easy for the judge to decide in your favor. The judge will expect you to **cite,** to point out the location of legal authority for, the law that supports your case. With your cites (i.e., your references to legal authority) in hand, the judge can compare the originals of what you've found with what, if anything, your opponent has found, and then make a decision.

As a matter of style, however, if you always cite legal materials in full (e.g., the annotation "Standing to sue for copyright infringement under 17 U.S.C.S. § 501(b)," by Edward A. Nolfi, J.D., found at page 509 of volume 82 of *American Law Reports, Federal,* published by the Lawyers Co-operative Publishing Company of Rochester, New York, in 1987), your reader would soon become overwhelmed by the citations, and the law for which you cite the legal materials will be obscured. For brevity and clarity, it is much more efficient to cite legal materials in an abbreviated form (e.g., Edward A. Nolfi, Annotation, *Standing to sue for copyright infringement under 17 U.S.C.S. § 501(b),* 82 A.L.R. Fed. 509 (1987) or simply 82 ALR Fed. 509), and that is the custom.

The only question is **citation style:** how legal materials should be abbreviated to avoid reader confusion. Without a uniform system of citation style, there might be confusion if the same or different abbreviations are used for the same or different publications covering the same or different law. For example, "M.C.A." might indicate the Annotated Code of Maryland, Mississippi, or Montana.

The question of citation style has never been answered comprehensively and authoritatively by the command of a sovereign, probably because of the complexity of the task. For the most part, there is no citation style required by law. Instead, there is a widely followed system developed by the editors of the East Coast Ivy League law school law reviews, and other systems developed by major law publishers.

The Bluebook: A Uniform System of Citation

The leading system of citation style is *The Bluebook: A Uniform System of Citation,* 15th ed. (1991), compiled by the editors of the *Columbia Law Review,* the *Harvard Law Review,* the *University of Pennsylvania Law Review,* and *The Yale Law Journal,* and published by the Harvard Law Review Association, 1511 Massachusetts Avenue, Cambridge, MA 02138. A spiral-bound book with a blue cover, *The Bluebook: A Uniform System of Citation* is often referred to as ***The Bluebook,*** and the citation style it suggests is often referred to as **Bluebook style.** Some people incorrectly refer to the book as the "Harvard Blue Book" or the "Harvard Citator" but, as the editors explain on page vii, the book is titled the *Bluebook* and subtitled *A Uniform System of Citation.*

The Bluebook expresses an appropriate citation style for law review articles and other legal writing, including appellate briefs. As the back cover indicates, *The Bluebook* consists of an introduction, practitioners' notes, general rules of citation style, specialized rules, tables and abbreviations, and an index. For the most part, *The Bluebook* is a reference book, not a textbook.

The Bluebook: A Uniform System of Citation

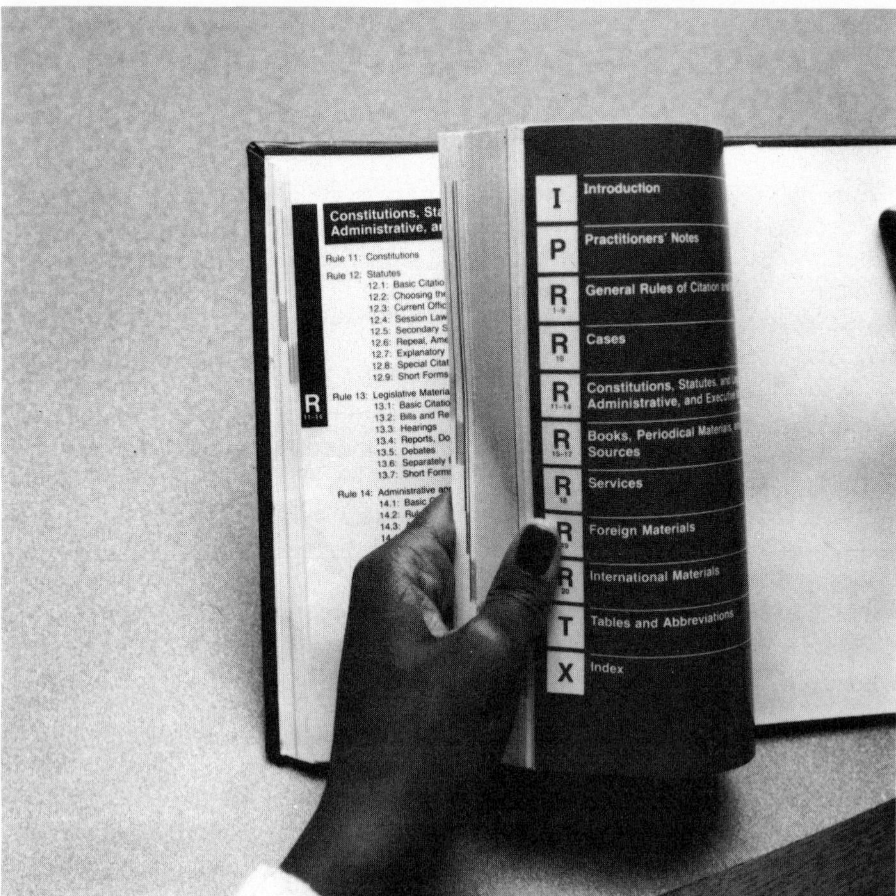

Source: © Doug Martin.

The Bluebook rules, full of exceptions and inexplicable conventions, display some favoritism toward particular publishers and publications. These rules have long been criticized as being complex, complicated, confusing, and vague, but they do reflect the tremendous variety of legal sources available in the United States and around the world. Other books have been published to explain Bluebook style, including C. Edward Good, *Citing & Typing the Law: A Guide to Legal Citation & Style* (Charlottesville: Legal Education Ltd., 1987); Elaine C. Maier, *How to Prepare a Legal Citation* (Woodbury, NY: Barron's Educational Series, Inc., 1986); and Alan L. Dworsky, *User's Guide to A Uniform System of Citation: The Cure for the Bluebook Blues* (Littleton, CO: Fred B. Rothman & Co., 1988); but some find these books to be as complicated, confusing, or vague as *The Bluebook* they seek to explain.

For the most part, there is no law requiring Bluebook style. In fact, as we shall see in the final section of this chapter, there are some laws that direct you not to follow Bluebook style. While Bluebook style is the customary standard for briefs, law review articles, and other legal writings, if there is no requirement to the contrary (e.g., an instructor's requirement or a court rule) and you're not preparing the final draft of a legal writing, it is not absolutely necessary to use Bluebook style. Nevertheless, it is good practice, both literally and figuratively, to use Bluebook style whenever possible.

Other Systems of Citation

Many people wonder why all law books do not use the same citation style. Since there is no comprehensive citation style required by law, major law publishers have been able to adopt their own citation styles for competitive reasons.

At West Publishing Company (West), for example, National Reporter System volumes suggest a citation style for the reported cases in the running head. But these cites do not give parallel cites to non-West reporters. Moreover, citations in *Corpus Juris Secundum* (C.J.S.), usually to West reporters, do not include dates, so to formally cite a case found in C.J.S. you must refer to the West reporter for the date of the case.

Lawyers Cooperative Publishing (LCP) also leaves dates out of its encyclopedia *American Jurisprudence 2d,* which frequently cites *American Law Reports* (A.L.R.). LCP claims this is done to save space, even though its cites often contain long strings of parallel citations. LCP's modern citation style (e.g., Miller v Robinson (1966) 241 Md 335, 216 A2d 743, 17 ALR3d 1425) minimizes the number of periods and spaces in the citation in order to save memory space in the company's computers, and thereby save money. Underscoring and italics are avoided to save production costs.

To be discussed in Chapter 11, Shepard's/McGraw-Hill, Inc., has developed and maintained its own system of citation and symbols in order to pack into each column and each page of its *Shepard's Citations* as much information as possible.

Unfortunately, under the circumstances, many legal researchers follow the citation style of the material they happen to be using and attempt to convert it into Bluebook style when they prepare their final draft.

10–2 Technical Rules

While Bluebook style is, for the most part, not required by law, it is the style that a legal researcher must know. Most courts do not explicitly require it, but most judges expect a legal professional's briefs and other legal writings to substantially conform to Bluebook style. It's a badge of competence. The judge will be impressed if, based on the style used in the brief, the author was once a member of a law review, or could have been.

This "badge-of-competence" attitude is pervasive in the legal profession. Most legal research and writing instructors require Bluebook style to be followed in all academic work. That is appropriate and commendable. But some have taken this attitude too far: they *define* sound legal research by its legal citation style. Sound research is proved by citing sound authority. If you cite poor authority properly, all you prove is that you can properly cite unsound research.

The following discussion covers the basic elements of Bluebook style for the simplest and most common citations. It is designed to be easily recalled so that in a pinch, you can quickly and confidently prepare briefs that substantially conform to Bluebook style. To strictly follow Bluebook style, however, carefully study *The Bluebook* or a *Bluebook* guide.

Citing Cases

Cases are usually cited by an underscored abbreviated case title, volume-reporter-page citations, court identification (if necessary), and year of decision. (See Figure 10–1 and *Bluebook* Rule 10.)

Figure 10–1 Citing a Case

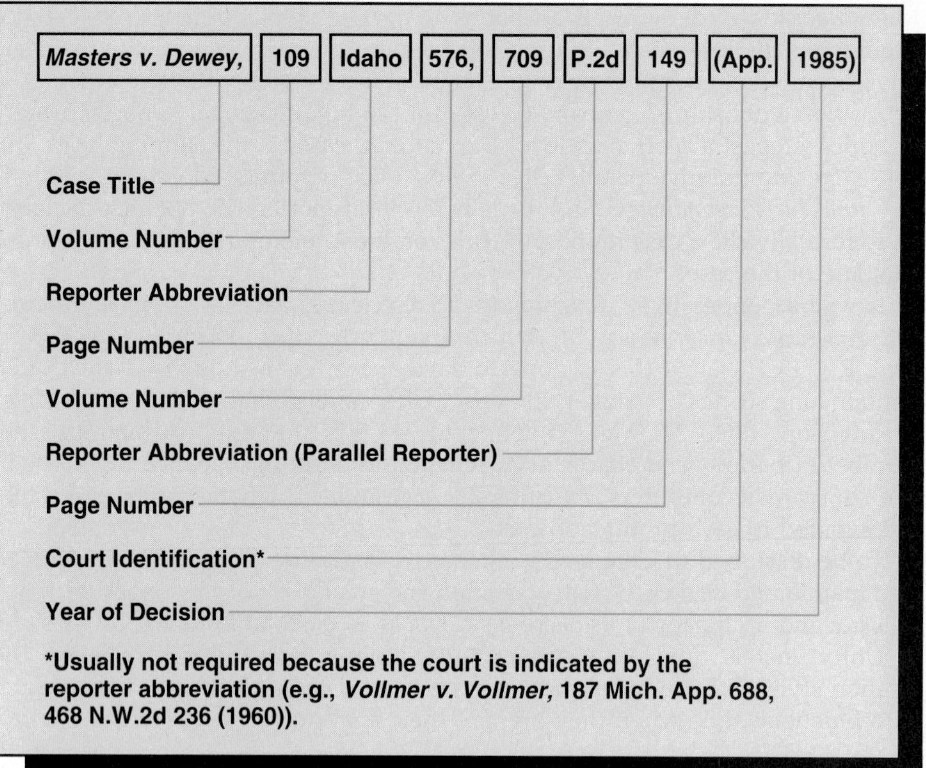

Case titles are abbreviated versions of the full name of the case, usually the last name of the first named plaintiff, followed by a space, the letter *v* and a period, a space, then the last name of the first named defendant, all underscored. Thus, Robert Smith suing John Doe, Jane Doe, and Richard Roe, comes out *"Smith v. Doe."* Use appropriate abbreviations (see *Bluebook* Table T.6), but spell out all essential terms of a name or title (e.g., *"Red Lion Broadcasting Co. v. FCC"*) and eliminate redundant abbreviations (e.g., omit *Inc.* from *ABC Co., Inc.*). *State, People,* or *Commonwealth* is sufficient to identify a state in a case from that state's state courts. For the federal government, use *United States.* If the cite is used in a formally printed publication, put the case title in italics instead of underscoring it.

Separate the case title from the reporter citations with a comma and a space. What follows is the volume number of the official reporter (if any), a space, the proper abbreviation of the official reporter, a space, and the page number of the first page of the case report in the official reporter (e.g., *New York Times Co. v. Sullivan,* 376 U.S. 254). If the volume number or page number is currently unknown, insert an underscore blank in place of the unknown number (e.g., ______ U.S. ______).

Except when citing an officially reported U.S. Supreme Court case in a formal brief (strict Bluebook style requires you to cite only to U.S., but a researcher may appreciate having the parallel cites), follow the official cite of the case (if any) with the appropriate unofficial cite(s) (if any). That is, follow the official cite (if any) with a comma, a space, the volume number of the unofficial reporter, a space, the proper abbreviation of the unofficial reporter, a space, and the page number of the first page in the unofficial reporter, continuing likewise until all unofficial cites are listed (e.g., *New York Times Co. v. Sullivan,* 376 U.S. 254, 84 S. Ct. 710, 11 L. Ed. 2d 686) (strict Bluebook style: *New York Times Co. v. Sullivan,* 376 U.S. 254).

After the last reporter citation, put a space, then the year of decision in parentheses (e.g., *New York Times Co. v. Sullivan,* 376 U.S. 254, 84 S. Ct. 710, 11 L. Ed. 2d 686 (1964)) (strict Bluebook style: *New York Times Co. v. Sullivan,* 376 U.S. 254 (1964)). If the citation is to a reporter that covers only one court, or if the particular court can be identified or presumed from the reporters cited (e.g., *Ricketts v. Scothorn,* 59 Neb. 51, 77 N.W. 365 (1898)), the case citation is complete.

However, if the citation is to a reporter that covers more than one court (such as a regional or intermediate appellate court reporter), you should indicate in an appropriate abbreviated form, within the parentheses and before the date, the particular court being cited (e.g., *Mitchell v. C.C. Sanitation Co.,* 430 S.W.2d 933 (Tex. Civ. App. 1968) or *McCormick & Co. v. Childers,* 468 F.2d 757 (4th Cir. 1972)).

With regard to the use of spaces in case names, reporter abbreviations, and court identification, note that single-letter abbreviations (and "2d"-like abbreviations) are not spaced (e.g., N.E.2d), except next to multiletter abbreviations (e.g., F. Supp.), which have a space before and after the multiletter abbreviation (e.g., Cir. Ct. App.).

Citing Statutes

Statutes are usually cited by title number, code abbreviation, section number, and year of publication (See Figure 10–2 and *Bluebook* Rule 12.) Statutes may also be cited by a "statutes at large" reference.

Statutes may be cited to either official or unofficial codes. A proper citation to a federal statute can be as simple as "42 U.S.C. § 1983 (1982)." The essential cite consists of the title number, space, code abbreviation, space, section symbol (i.e., §) or "sec.," space, and section number. After a space, the year of publication is added in parentheses to identify the proper version of the statute. If the statute is in a supplement, that should be indicated within the parentheses and before the date (e.g., 5 U.S.C.A. § 654 (West Supp. 1979)). If desired, the popular name of the statute can be given before the code reference (e.g., National Environmental Policy Act of 1969, § 102, 42 U.S.C. § 4332 (1982)). If necessary, a federal statute may also be cited to the session law (e.g., National Environmental Policy Act of 1969, Pub. L. No. 91–190, 83 Stat. 852 (1970)).

State statutes are usually cited to state codes, beginning with the state code

Figure 10–2 Citing a Statute

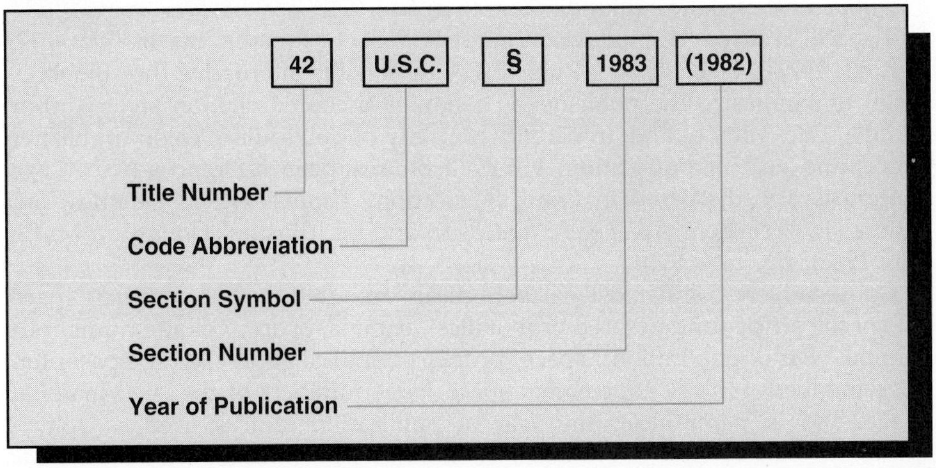

42 U.S.C. § 1983 (1982)

- Title Number — 42
- Code Abbreviation — U.S.C.
- Section Symbol — §
- Section Number — 1983
- Year of Publication — (1982)

abbreviation, the combination title and section number, and year of publication (e.g., Colo. Rev. Stat. § 24–3–204 (1973)). (See Appendix III.)

Citing Other Primary Sources

Constitutions are cited by sovereign abbreviation, space, "Const." and space, followed by the subdivision cited (e.g., U.S. Const. art. I, sec. 7, para. 2, cl. IV). Use "amend." to cite an amendment (e.g., U.S. Const. amend. IV). (See *Bluebook* Rule 11.)

Court rules are cited by the proper abbreviation for the rules, space, and rule number (e.g., Fed. R. Civ. P. 60(b)). (See *Bluebook* Rule 12.8.3.)

Administrative regulations are usually cited like a statute to the appropriate administrative code (e.g., 45 C.F.R. § 405 (1978)). If a federal administrative regulation is not in C.F.R., cite to the *Federal Register* (e.g., 48 Fed. Reg. 760 (1983)). A federal executive order is cited by "Exec. Order No." and space, order number, comma, space, and a cite to its location in C.F.R., or else in the *Federal Register* (e.g., Exec. Order No. 13,902, 3 C.F.R. 205 (1979)). (See *Bluebook* Rule 14.)

Citing Secondary Sources

Although primary authority is preferred over secondary authority, secondary authority may be cited.

Annotations in *American Law Reports* (A.L.R.) are cited by the author's full name, comma, space, "Annotation" and comma, space, the title of the annotation (underscored or in italics), comma, space, volume number, space, proper annotation series abbreviation, space, page number (of the annotation, not the reported case), space, and year of publication in parentheses (e.g., Colleen R. Courtade, Annotation, *Application of Functionality Doctrine Under § 43(a) of Lanham Act (15 U.S.C.S. § 1125(a),* 78 A.L.R. Fed. 712 (1986)). (See *Bluebook* Rule 16.5.5.)

Legal encyclopedias are cited by volume number, space, proper abbreviation, space, topic title (underscored or in italics), space, section symbol and section number, space, and year of publication in parentheses (e.g., 21 Am. Jur. 2d *Bailments* § 3 (1975)). (See *Bluebook* Rule 15.7.)

Textbooks, treatises, and other nonfiction books are cited by volume number (if more than one), author, comma, space, title of the book (underscored or in italics), space, section and/or page (or paragraph) number (if necessary), space, and in parentheses the edition (if more than one; "2d" or whatever, space, "ed." and space) and year of publication (e.g., William L. Prosser, *Law of Torts* § 122 (4th ed. 1972)). (See *Bluebook* Rule 15.) A reasonable alternative (not Bluebook style) to emphasize the publisher is generally accepted citation style: author, comma, title, edition, and, in parentheses, city of publication, colon, publisher, space, and year of publication, followed by any page references (e.g., Legal citation is also discussed in Frank S. Gordon, Thomas M. S. Hemnes, and Charles E. Weinstein, *The Legal Word Book,* 2nd ed. (Boston: Houghton Mifflin Co., 1982), pp. 149–168).

Consecutively paginated legal periodicals are cited author, comma, space, title of the article (underscored or in italics), comma, space, volume number (or if none, year of publication), space, proper periodical abbreviation, space, first page number of the issue, comma, space, page numbers of the cited material, space, and in parentheses the year of publication (unless used as volume number) (e.g., Patricia J. Williams, *Alchemical Notes: Reconstructed Ideals From*

Deconstructed Rights, 22 Harv. C.R.-C.L. Rev. 401, 407 (1987)). (See *Bluebook* Rule 16.2.)

Nonconsecutively paginated legal periodicals are cited author, comma, space, title of the article (underscored or in italics), comma, space, proper periodical abbreviation, comma, space, date of issue, comma, space, "at" and space, first page number of the issue, comma, space, page numbers of the cited material (e.g., Barbara Ward, *Progress for a Small Planet,* Harv. Bus. Rev., Sept.-Oct. 1979, at 89, 90). (See *Bluebook* Rule 16.3.)

Computer-Assisted Citation Style

Jurisoft, a division of Mead Data Central, Inc., sells *CheckRite* software, which checks citations in word-processing documents for proper Bluebook style. Paralegals are frequently delegated the task of shepardizing case citations in briefs and checking them for proper Bluebook style. (See Chapter 11.)

10–3 Citation Requirements

Before citing material in a brief, you should check the applicable court rules and statutes for any matters of citation style required by law. As *The Bluebook* advises: "The practitioner should also be aware that many courts have their own rules of citation that may differ in some respects from *The Bluebook* (p. 11)."

For example, a lawyer or paralegal preparing a brief for the Ohio Court of Appeals for the First Judicial District (Hamilton County, including Cincinnati), should refer to Local Rule 6, which addresses the "Form and Content of Appellate Briefs." Part D(1) provides:

> a. All citations to reported Ohio cases in briefs or memoranda shall recite the date, volume and page of the official Ohio report and the parallel citation, where the same exists, to the Northeastern Reporter, e.g., W.T. Grant Co. v. Lindley (1977), 50 Ohio St.2d 7, 361 N.E.2d 454; State v. Durham (1976), 49 Ohio App.2d 231, 360 N.E.2d 743; State v. Gastown, Inc. (1975), 40 Ohio Misc. 29, 360 N.E.2d 970.
> b. All citations to the United States Supreme Court cases in briefs or memoranda shall cite the date, volume and page of the official report and parallel citation to the Supreme Court Reporter, e.g. Jones v. United States (1960), 362 U.S. 257, 80 S.Ct. 725.

Citing the date first and giving a citation to an unofficial U.S. Supreme Court reporter are not Bluebook style, but they are part of the style required in briefs filed with the Ohio Court of Appeals for the First Judicial District.

The Ohio Supreme Court also follows the "date-up-front" convention, since its court rule examples follow that style, but there is no rule that explicitly requires this. The Ohio Supreme Court also prefers the "R.C." abbreviation for citations to the Ohio Revised Code, as explicitly permitted by the Ohio General Assembly in R.C. 1.01.

In the state of Michigan, the *Michigan Uniform System of Citation* "provides a comprehensive scheme for citation of authority in documents filed with or issued by Michigan courts."

Again, check the applicable court rules and statutes for special citation requirements, if any, before you submit your brief.

SUMMARY

10–1

In court, the judge expects you to cite the law that supports your case. For brevity and clarity, legal materials are cited in an abbreviated form. The leading system of citation style is *The Bluebook: A Uniform System of Citation*, 15th edition (1991). It is also known as *The Bluebook,* and the citation style it suggests is known as Bluebook style. For the most part, no law requires Bluebook style. Nevertheless, it is good practice to use Bluebook style unless there is a requirement to the contrary. Since there is no comprehensive citation style required by law, major law publishers have adopted their own style for competitive reasons.

10–2

Although most courts do not explicitly require it, most judges and most legal research and writing instructors expect a legal professional's briefs and other writings to substantially conform to Bluebook style. Cases are usually cited by an underscored abbreviated case title, volume-reporter-page citations, court identification (if necessary), and year of decision. If the cite is being used in a formally printed publication, put the case title in italics instead of underscoring it. Statutes are usually cited by title number, code abbreviation, section number, and year of publication. Constitutions are cited by sovereign abbreviation, space, "Const." and space, followed by the subdivision cited. Court rules are cited by the proper abbreviation for the rules, space, and rule number. Administrative regulations are usually cited like a statute to the appropriate administrative code. A.L.R. annotations are cited by the author's full name, comma, space, "Annotation" and comma, space, the title of the annotation (underscored or in italics), comma, space, volume number, space, proper annotation series abbreviation, space, page number (of the annotation, not reported case), space, and year of publication in parentheses. Legal encyclopedias are cited by volume number, space, proper abbreviation, space, topic title (underscored or in italics), space, section symbol and section number, space, and year of publication in parentheses. Textbooks, treatises, and other nonfiction books are cited by volume number (if more than one), author, comma, space, title of the book (underscored or in italics), space, section and/or page (or paragraph) number (if necessary), space, and in parentheses the edition (if more than one; "2d" or whatever, space, "ed." and space) and year of publication. Consecutively paginated legal periodicals are cited author, comma, space, title of the article (underscored or in italics), comma, space, volume number (or if none, year of publication), space, proper periodical abbreviation, space, first page number of the issue, comma, space, page numbers of the cited material, space, and in parentheses the year of publication (unless used as volume number). Nonconsecutively paginated legal periodicals are cited author, comma, space, title of the article (underscored or in italics), comma, space, proper periodical abbreviation, comma, space, date of issue, comma, space, "at" and space, first page number of the issue, comma, space, page numbers of the cited material.

10–3

Before citing any material in a brief, you should check the applicable court rules and statutes for any matters of citation style required by law.

REVIEW

Key Terms

Before proceeding, review the key terms listed below to be sure you understand each one. If necessary, read over the corresponding section of the chapter. When you are ready to test your understanding, answer the Review Questions.

The Bluebook
Bluebook style
citation style
cite

Questions for Review and Discussion

1. Why does the legal profession need a uniform system of citation style?
2. Why is it incorrect to speak of the "Harvard Citator"?
3. Why do legal publishers use different citation styles?
4. If there is more than one plaintiff or defendant, how do you abbreviate the case name?
5. Why do you need to know which reporters are official and which are unofficial?
6. In a case citation, what is put in the parentheses before the year of decision?
7. Is it true that if the year in a case citation is the year of decision, then the year in a statute citation is the year of enactment?
8. How are federal statutes and state statutes cited?
9. How are constitutions, court rules, and administrative regulations cited?
10. What information do you need to cite a law treatise?

Activities

1. Examine the citation style used in a modern A.L.R. annotation. Is it easier to follow than Bluebook style? Is it more efficient? Which style do you prefer?
2. Study the tables in part T of *The Bluebook*. Part T is an excellent checklist of the primary sources of U.S. law.
3. Check the applicable court rules and statutes in your state for matters of citation style required by law.

CHAPTER 11 *Shepard's Citations* and Other Citators

OUTLINE

11–1 *Shepard's Citations*
- Using *Shepard's* as a Case Reviewer
- Using *Shepard's* as a Case Finder
- *Shepard's* on LEXIS or WESTLAW

11–2 Other Citators
- Parallel Cites
- Auto-Cite
- Insta-Cite
- LEXIS or WESTLAW as a Citator

COMMENTARY

As you near completion of your memorandum on public religious displays, focusing on *Lynch v. Donnelly*, 465 U.S. 668 (1984), you discover another case dealing with public religious displays, *Allegheny County v. ACLU*, 492 U.S. 573 (1989), in a constitutional law treatise. The fact that you almost missed this important case, decided after *Lynch*, shocks you. You think how embarrassing it would have been if you had made such an error and it was exposed. Is there a way to avoid such an embarrassment?

OBJECTIVES

In this chapter you will learn about systems for checking the validity of case precedents and finding parallel citations. Emphasis is placed on *Shepard's Citations* published by Shepard's/McGraw-Hill, Inc. After reading this chapter, you should be able to:

1. Resist being deceived by human nature while performing legal research.
2. Resist being deceived by time while performing legal research.
3. Identify the greatest embarrassment in advocacy and legal research.
4. Find parallel citations using *Shepard's Citations*.
5. Find the appropriate volumes and pamphlets of *Shepard's Citations* for a particular search.
6. Use *Shepard's Citations* as a case reviewer.
7. Use *Shepard's Citations* as a case finder.
8. Find parallel citations using cross-reference books.
9. Identify the origins and use of Auto-Cite.
10. Identify the origins and use of Insta-Cite.

11–1 *Shepard's Citations*

As discussed in Chapter 1, the purpose of legal research is to find a case like yours where the person like you won. Finding cases is discussed in Chapters 2, 3, and 4. Of course, your best "case" could turn out to be a statute, regulation, or other primary law, or a secondary source, as discussed in Chapters 5 to 9. Cite your "case" to the judge in the style discussed in Chapter 10, argue simple justice ("persons in like circumstances should be treated alike"), and you can't lose. Or can you?

It is important to realize that there are two powerful forces that are always at work: human nature and time. Acting alone or in concert, these forces can deceive any legal researcher, no matter how experienced.

As discussed in Chapter 1, there is no perfect law book. It is human nature to seize on the first thing that meets one's expectations, even though it may not be the truth. It takes a lot of mental work to be objective, much more than most people imagine. A lot of people are "checkmated" while they dream of checkmating their opponent.

A law book editor, working in a competitive environment under time pressure and other stresses, may unwittingly cut corners. The law book editor may seize on and write, or be instructed to seize on and write, something not 100% accurate. A legal researcher, also working in a competitive environment under time pressure and other stresses, may also unwittingly cut corners. The legal researcher, eager to find a case like his where the person like him won, may seize on and cite the inaccurate statement without checking it out. As a result, the legal researcher can lose the case to a more careful and objective opponent.

Even if the law book editor and the legal researcher have been careful, honest, humble, and objective, the case can still be lost because of the march of time. As discussed in Chapter 1, the law is always changing. Using a recently published law book, the legal researcher finds a case like the legal researcher's, where the person like the legal researcher won, and argues it to the court. His opponent rises and agrees that the case cited is like the case at bar, but notes that the legal researcher's case was reversed on appeal, and so the person like the opponent ultimately won. The court agrees, and finds for the opponent. The legal researcher has experienced the greatest embarrassment in advocacy: *unwittingly arguing the opponent's case.*

A legal researcher can lose by unwittingly citing and arguing **bad law:** overruled (or otherwise discredited) precedent. Bad law is precedent without authority. Precedent can lose its value in a number of ways. A precedent may be overruled by a higher court (or by a statute). A court may overrule its own precedent. Or a precedent may be left alone to die, whether distinguished away by other courts, overwhelmed by contrary precedent, or simply forgotten. Courts have the power to declare precedents out of date, and they frequently do. It is the insidious power of the march of time.

In 1873, an Illinois law book salesman, Frank Shepard, gave some thought to the nature of law books and precedent, and how the value of a precedent is altered over time by later case precedent. Although he was not a lawyer, Shepard observed that some lawyers made notes in the margins of their law books when they became aware of later cases that altered the precedential value of a reported case. Shepard realized that the idea was sound, but that no practicing lawyer would have the time to keep such a system up to date. There were thousands of cases published each year in a variety of reporters and keeping up with it all would be a full-time job. Shepard decided that he would provide the service, and he founded his own company to do so.

Shepard started small. He began to read all the reports of the Illinois courts.

He carefully noted every time an earlier case was cited by a later case. He printed his notes for each case on gummed slips and sold them to lawyers, instructing them to paste them in the margins of their reports at the cited case. It was a hit. Shepard expanded into other states, hired several assistants, and changed the format of the service to book form. *Shepard's Citations* quickly became a standard legal research tool.

After Shepard died in 1900, his business was incorporated and transferred to New York City. In 1947, the company was moved to Colorado Springs, Colorado, and, in 1966, it was acquired by and became a division of McGraw-Hill, Inc. *Shepard's* current publisher is thus Shepard's/McGraw-Hill, Inc.

Shepard's leads a group of books and other media that list citations, which are known as **citators.** In listing parallel cites, citators list cites to a target case, known as the **cited case.** In listing cites of cases that make reference to a target case, citators list referring cases, known as **citing cases.**

Shepard's is a book of tables uniquely listing all the citing cases for a cited case. Under each cited case (volume number and reporter noted in the running head; page number noted in boldface between dashes in the tables), the cites of the citing cases are listed by volume number, Shepard's reporter abbreviation, and page number. (See Figures 11–1 and 11–2.) In the first listing for the cited case, parallel citations are listed in parentheses immediately following the page number heading. Note that *Shepard's* cryptic reporter abbreviations are not Bluebook style, and so they should not be used in formal legal writing.

When legal researchers **shepardize** a case, they review all the citing cases for a cited case to make sure the cited case is not bad law or to help find other cases like the cited case. When legal researchers shepardize a brief or other legal writing, they review all the cases cited in the brief or other legal writing to make

Shepard's Citations

Source: © Doug Martin.

Figure 11–1 Example of a *Shepard's Citations* Page

UNITED STATES SUPREME COURT REPORTS — Vol. 485

Cir. 11
920F2d791
Cir. Fed.
905F2d[1]384
e918F2d[1]163
Colo
757P2d1073
NY
142NYAD97
535NYS2d
[464
FAP§6.03

– 271 –
(99LE296)
(108SC1133)
s481US1068
s806F2d928
126FRD590
133FRD80
Cir. D.C.
Dk DC
91-3255
866F2d[2]1520
925F2d[1]453
Cir. 1
867F2d[1]722
876F2d256
907F2d[1]213
928F2d475
d931F2d[1]144
762FS426
767FS[1]1164
Cir. 2
844F2d55
853F2d80
864F2d1
f882F2d[1]685
f889F2d[1]452
924F2d[1]453
928F2d[2]73
e937F2d[1]747
689FS[1]352
769FS518
Cir. 3
f846F2d197
846F2d[2]199
f846F2d[1]913
851F2d619
862F2d443
866F2d[1]623
867F2d[1]1464
f869F2d[1]196
e885F2d[1]105
f885F2d[1]1151
887F2d[1]1218
j887F2d1229
903F2d236
910F2d[1]1165
919F2d230
920F2d[1]1131
920F2d[1]1153
932F2d[1]205
933F2d[1]1175
87BRW350
Cir. 4
854F2d[1]680
e867F2d[1]812
875F2d73
Cir. 5
854F2d[1]741
f864F2d403
f864F2d[1]404
867F2d1519

e867F2d[1]1520
f878F2d905
899F2d[2]367
Cir. 6
846F2d1035
866F2d[1]156
920F2d[1]1272
f934F2d1396
f940F2d999
d941F2d472
716FS309
Cir. 7
f846F2d[1]1141
847F2d[1]1287
f847F2d1288
848F2d760
848F2d[1]772
852F2d267
854F2d154
d879F2d1406
j879F2d1419
879F2d1560
892F2d[1]573
931F2d[1]433
690FS714
719FS1461
Cir. 8
859F2d[1]81
872F2d265
f872F2d266
882F2d[2]301
897F2d341
f897F2d[1]342
727FS[2]523
Cir. 9
879F2d664
882F2d1416
f885F2d[1]526
f926F2d[1]862
926F2d893
938F2d[1]1039
119BRW775
Cir. 10
j850F2d646
f902F2d[2]1495
Cir. 11
e849F2d[1]1391
f854F2d[1]1275
d858F2d[2]650
872F2d358
917F2d1546
918F2d[2]144
f750FS[1]1130
Cir. Fed.
854F2d464
f889F2d[1]1079
f940F2d643
Ala
558So2d359
Ariz
161Az379
778P2d1275
DC
566A2d35
Md
320Md213
320Md633
577A2d45
579A2d279
ND
427NW101
433NW205
Okla
805P2d662

Tex
776SW245
801SW927
FAP§2.06

– 293 –
(99LE316)
(108SC1145)
s801F2d228
s627FS923
58USLW
[4681
Cir. D.C.
900F2d[1]274
Cir. 1
865F2d[1]401
j865F2d423
935F2d[1]352
j935F2d360
728FS[1]832
751FS[1]287
f108BRW[1]869
Cir. 2
f894F2d[1]576
928F2d1275
712FS15
Cir. 3
d Dk 3
91-3085
j Dk 3
91-3085
d902F2d1120
903F2d[1]950
916F2d[1]906
d942F2d[1]847
j942F2d859
f714FS741
755FS1308
Cir. 4
905F2d722
745FS[1]315
Cir. 5
f897F2d779
911F2d1002
761FS[1]439
Cir. 6
887F2d1299
f887F2d[1]1301
909F2d932
919F2d41
f689FS[1]737
e718FS[1]625
747FS[1]404
Cir. 7
756FS[1]1146
Cir. 8
j940F2d374
e754FS[1]145
Cir. 9
757FS[1]1114
Cir. 10
748FS[1]1481
757FS1201
Cir. 11
716FS597
6FCCR4476
Ala
554So2d930
Calif
215CA3d62
231CA3d905
263CaR455
283CaR253
285CaR346

Fla
563So2d702
Ind
550NE86
Mass
31MaA497
407Mas565
555NE204
Me
581A2d803
Mich
443NW136
Minn
450NW606
ND
427NW309
NJ
121NJ77
125NJ134
577A2d1243
592A2d1185
NY
163NYAD
[600
558NYS2d
[974
Tex
798SW896
805SW506

– 312 –
(99LE333)
(108SC1157)
s479US1083
s798F2d1450
cc704FS5
j486US483
486US897
487US479
j487US495
j58USLW
[4444
58USLW
[4745
j58USLW
[5020
j59USLW
[4461
j59USLW
[4754
124FRD346
Cir. D.C.
d847F2d904
851F2d375
852F2d1343
j935F2d1333
Cir. 2
j891F2d1031
j903F2d166
d915F2d63
930F2d208
938F2d1543
753FS441
761FS230
Cir. 3
747FS1527
763FS137
Cir. 4
745FS327
Cir. 5
889F2d576
Cir. 7
845F2d147
Cir. 8
e897F2d924

j897F2d927
728FS1419
Cir. 9
898F2d1390
908F2d421
f731FS419
754FS784
Cir. 10
729FS1289
Cir. 11
j867F2d1349
f765FS1071
29MJ115
29MJ132

First
Cir. 2
d686FS[1]80

O'Connor 1st
491US[1]412
Cir. D.C.
919F2d[2]151
919F2d[1]152
f726FS[2]873
742FS[1]1194
746FS[1]196
746FS[1]216
Cir. 1
683FS[2]297
743FS[2]100
Cir. 2
d686FS[1]80
689FS[2]126
Cir. 4
907F2d[1]444
Cir. 6
d896F2d[1]199
923F2d[1]473
Cir. 8
935F2d[1]955
723FS[1]1352
726FS[1]1191
Cir. 9
847F2d[1]512
914F2d[2]1228
Cir. 10
f687FS[1]543
Cir. 11
748FS[2]1525

O'Connor 2nd
Cir. D.C.
731FS[1]1129
Cir. 2
742FS[1]1260
Cir. 6
d896F2d[1]199
f730FS[1]85
Cir. 11
765FS[10]710

Brennan
Cir. 6
d896F2d[1]199

———

Calif
229CA3d982
232CA3d431
47C3d486
764P2d1067
253CaR690
280CaR404
283CaR701
DC
573A2d1309
581A2d351
581A2d355
585A2d1347
Fla
538So2d460
Ga
260Ga671
260Ga679
398SE549
398SE555
Md
318Md447
318Md473
569A2d609
569A2d622
Mich
434Mch47
434Mch433
455NW19
455NW44
Minn
460NW16
Miss
552So2d824
NY
532NYS2d
[818
570NYS2d
[434
Ohio
61OA3d251
572NE731
Ore
306Ore187
759P2d249
Tenn
802SW212
Tex
755SW94
800SW307
806SW548
Va
406SE399
Wash
111Wsh2d29
759P2d369
Wis
145Wis2d41
152Wis2d513
426NW336
449NW857

– 340 –
(99LE357)
(108SC1173)
s482US913
s807F2d65
f485US973
Cir. 4
f846F2d[1]6
Cir. 5
f844F2d226
f844F2d[1]228
Cir. 7
872F2d1024
d96TCt444

f96TCt444
Wis
157Wis2d8
458NW816

– 351 –
(99LE368)
(108SC1179)
s481US1047
485US710
Cir. D.C.
907F2d1178
Cir. 2
867F2d[1]752
Cir. 3
859F2d[1]2
865F2d[1]58
Cir. 5
j901F2d62
Cir. 6
882F2d[1]1080
Cir. 7
f925F2d[1]1067
684FS[1]990
ClCt
16ClC[1]82
DC
585A2d156
586A2d694
Ga
261Ga12
401SE715
Mich
435Mch561
435Mch570
460NW202
460NW206
3PPR(9)14

– 360 –
(99LE380)
(108SC1184)
s481US1036
s648FS1234
s648FS1241
486US461
487US16
487US[2]458
58USLW
[4411
Cir. D.C.
d887F2d[1]292
f887F2d[2]293
j887F2d303
746FS[1]195
746FS[2]195
758FS12
Cir. 1
f916F2d[2]747
925F2d503
743FS102
Cir. 2
895F2d[1]65
905F2d[1]635
915F2d[1]63
690FS[1]1273
690FS[2]1273
f733FS[1]636
735FS1145
e735FS[1]1146
Cir. 3
j845F2d1211
725FS[1]235
768FS[2]159

Cir. 4
926F2d[2]366
737FS[1]953
Cir. 6
f854F2d[1]827
922F2d341
928F2d[2]209
Cir. 7
847F2d[2]1220
Cir. 8
753FS[2]800
Cir. 9
761FS101
Cir. 10
d687FS[1]543
d687FS[2]543
Colo
758P2d1370
758P2d1386
Md
315Md287
554A2d383
PR
1990JTS48
f1990JTS48

– 386 –
(99LE402)
(108SC1200)
s479US1083
Cir. 9
853F2d638
928F2d[1]865
Cir. Fed.
932F2d927

– 388 –
(99LE450)
(108SC1201)
s482US124
s488US808
s490US1044

– 395 –
(99LE455)
(108SC1204)
s484US895
s290Ark47
Ark
s716SW755
cc748SW668
Cir. 2
d898F2d[1]327
909F2d[1]73
715FS1273
Cir. 8
d940F2d
[[1]1185
j940F2d1186
d743FS[1]681
d759FS[1]573
Cir. 9
f878F2d265
Ariz
162Az593
785P2d113
Ark
296Ark277
753SW866
Colo
769P2d1059
Ind
531NE233
NH
131NH97
Continued

241

Source: Shepard's United States Citations, Case Edition, vol. 6 (Colorado Springs, CO: Shepard's/McGraw-Hill, Inc., 1984), p. 241. Reprinted with permission.

Figure 11–2 Excerpt of *Shepard's* Reporter Abbreviations

ABBREVIATIONS—REPORTS

AA–Antitrust Adviser, Third Edition (Shepard's, 1987)
AABA–Atwood & Brewster, Antitrust and American Business Abroad (Shepard's, 1981)
A2d–Atlantic Reporter, Second Series
Ab–Abstracts
AB–American Bankruptcy Reports
ABA–American Bar Association Journal
ABA(2)–American Bar Association Journal, Part 2
AbD–Abbott's Court of Appeals Decisions (N.Y.)
AbN–Abstracts, New Series
ABn–American Bankruptcy Reports, New Series
AbP–Abbott's Practice Reports (N.Y.)
AbPn–Abbott's Practice Reports, New Series (N.Y.)
AC–American Annotated Cases
AD–American Decisions
ADC–Appeal Cases, District of Columbia Reports
Add–Addison's Reports (Pa.)
Advo–Givens, Advocacy (Shepard's, 1985)
AE(2)–Acret, Architects and Engineers, Second Edition (Shepard's, 1984)
AE(2s)–Acret, Architects and Engineers, Second Edition, Supplement (Shepard's, 1984)
AEn–Buck, Alternative Energy (Shepard's, 1982)
AFW–Newberg, Attorney Fee Awards (Shepard's, 1987)
AgD–Eglit, Age Discrimination (Shepard's, 1982)
AgL–Davidson, Agricultural Law (Shepard's, 1981)
AGSS–Laritz, Attorney Guide to Social Security Disability Claims (Shepard's, 1986)
Aik–Aiken's Reports (Vt.)
AL–Turley, Aviation Litigation (Shepard's, 1986)
Æ2–American Law Reports, Second Series
Æ3–American Law Reports, Third Series
Æ4–American Law Reports, Fourth Series
Ala–Alabama Supreme Court Reports
AlA–Alabama Appellate Court Reports
Alk–Alaska Reports
Allen–Allen's Reports (Mass.)
ÆR–American Law Reports
ÆRF–American Law Reports, Federal
AMP–Bauernfeind, Income Taxation: Accounting Methods and Periods (Shepard's, 1983)
AN–Abbott's New Cases (N.Y.)
AntNP–Anthon's Nisi Prius Cases (N.Y.)
AOA–Anderson's Ohio Appellate Unreported Decisions
AR–American Reports
ARAP–Analytical Review: A Guide to Analytical Procedures (Shepard's, 1988)
ARD–Application for Review Decisions
Ark–Arkansas Reports
ARm–O'Reilly, Administrative Rulemaking (Shepard's, 1983)
AS–American State Reports
At–Atlantic Reporter
AtSN–Attorney Sanctions Newsletter (Shepard's)
Az–Arizona Reports
AzA–Arizona Court of Appeals Reports
Bar–Barbour's Supreme Court Reports (N.Y.)
BCh–Barbour's Chancery Reports (N.Y.)
Binn–Binney's Reports (Pa.)
Blackf–Blackford's Reports (Ind.)
Bland–Bland's Chancery Reports (Md.)
Bos–Bosworth's Reports (N.Y.)
Boy–Boyce's Reports (Del.)
BP–Drake & Mullins, Bankruptcy Practice (Shepard's, 1980)
BP(2)–Drake, Bankruptcy Practice, Second Edition (Shepard's, 1990)
Bradb–Bradbury's Pleading & Practice Reports (N.Y.)
Bradf–Bradford's Surrogate's Court Reports (N.Y.)
Bray–Brayton's Reports (Vt.)
Breese–Breese's Reports (Ill.)
BRW–Bankruptcy Reporter (West)
BTA–United States Board of Tax Appeals Reports
BTCL–Givens, Business Torts and Competitor Litigation (Shepard's, 1989)
Bur–Burnett's Reports (Wis.)
C2d–California Supreme Court Reports, Second Series
C3d–California Supreme Court Reports, Third Series

viii

Source: Shepard's United States Citations, Statute Edition, vol. 4 (Colorado Springs, CO: Shepard's/McGraw-Hill, Inc., 1986), p. viii. Reprinted with permission.

sure the brief or other legal writing does not cite bad law or to help find other cases like the case cited to use in a reply or a revision.

There are *Shepard's* sets covering virtually every set of court reports published in the United States, including every major unit of the National Reporter System. Note, however, that a *Shepard's* covering a particular state's reporters lists only citing cases from that state or cases originating in the federal courts in that state.

For the U.S. Supreme Court, for example, Shepard's/McGraw-Hill, Inc., publishes the *Shepard's United States Citations* (Case Edition) set. There are tables for the three major Supreme Court reporters—one for cites to *United States Reports* (U.S.), one for cites to *United States Supreme Court Reports, Lawyers' Edition* (L. Ed.), and *Lawyers' Edition, Second Series* (L. Ed. 2d), and one for cites to *Supreme Court Reporter* (S. Ct.)—running through several bound volumes and pamphlets covering different periods of time.

Suppose in June 1991, for example, you wanted to see the complete list of cites made to 450 U.S. 24. To limit the number of volumes and pamphlets you have to look through to make the complete list of cites for a cited case, Shepard's/McGraw-Hill, Inc., periodically publishes comprehensive bound volumes and pamphlets. However, in June 1991, the complete list of cites for 450 U.S. 24 happens to be in the maximum number of bound volumes (3) and pamphlets (3).

As of June 1991, the last major comprehensive bound volume covering 450 U.S. was published in 1984, covering cites to 409–458 U.S. (and parallel cites) from the date of the cited case to 1984. The next comprehensive volume covering 450 U.S., a "Supplement," was published in 1986, covering cites to 404–467 U.S. from 1984–1986. The next comprehensive volume covering 450 U.S., another "Supplement," was published in 1988, covering cites to 438–463 U.S. from 1986–1988.

To cover the six-month periods after major comprehensive bound volumes and "Supplements," Shepard's/McGraw-Hill, Inc., publishes yellow comprehensive pamphlets in January and July. To cover three-month periods after yellow comprehensive pamphlets (or after the latest bound volume but before the first yellow pamphlet), Shepard's/McGraw-Hill, Inc., publishes red comprehensive pamphlets in May and November. To cover periods after red comprehensive pamphlets (or after the latest yellow pamphlet or bound volume but before the first red pamphlet), Shepard's/McGraw-Hill, Inc., also publishes white "Advance Sheet" pamphlets.

In June 1991, the pamphlets covering 450 U.S. 24 included a yellow pamphlet published in January 1991, a red pamphlet published in May 1991, and a white "Advance Sheet" pamphlet published in June 1991.

Because some people find the comprehensive volume and pamphlet system confusing, and because the volumes and pamphlets can be easily misshelved by the uninformed, Shepard's/McGraw-Hill, Inc., publishes a list entitled "What Your Library Should Contain" on the cover of each pamphlet. (See Figure 11–3.) It is a good practice to consult this list, as necessary, before you begin to shepardize a case.

Although *Shepard's* was originally designed to list all the citing cases for a cited case, Shepard's/McGraw-Hill, Inc., has added to the concept. As the title page of each *Shepard's* volume indicates for the cited cases in the volume, *Shepard's* may also list other citing legal materials, such as A.L.R. annotations and law reviews, for a cited case. A **statute edition** lists all the citing cases for a particular statute or ordinance. *Shepard's United States Citations* (Statute Edition), for example, lists all the citing cases for a particular section of the *United States Code*. Constitutions, treatises, court rules, selected administrative decisions, and patents listed by patent number, copyrights listed by title of the copyrighted work, and trademarks listed alphabetically can also be shepardized.

Figure 11–3 Example of "What Your Library Should Contain"

Shepard's United States Citations

SEMIANNUAL SUPPLEMENT (IN TWO PARTS)
CASES PART 1A

IMPORTANT NOTICE

A 1990-1991 Hardbound Supplement for Shepard's United States Citations, Cases will be published in December, 1991 and delivered by January 31, 1992.

WHAT YOUR LIBRARY SHOULD CONTAIN
PART 1, CASES
BEFORE YOU RECEIVE THE 1990-1991 HARDBOUND SUPPLEMENT, RETAIN THE FOLLOWING:

1988 Bound Volumes (Vols. 1A, 1B, 1C, 2A, 2B, 2C)*
1984 Bound Volumes (Vols. 3, 4, 5, 6)*
1984-1986 Bound Supplement (Vols. 7A and 7B)*
1986-1988 Bound Supplement (Vols. 8, 9, 10, 11, 12)*
1988-1990 Bound Supplement (Vols. 13, 14, 15, 16, 17)*
**Supplemented with:*
–July, 1991 Semiannual Cumulative Supplement Vol. 90 No. 2 (Parts 1A and 1B)
–Sept., 1991 Cumulative Supplement Vol. 90 No. 4 (Part 1)
–Nov., 1991 Cumulative Supplement Vol. 90 No. 6 (Part 1)
–Jan., 1992 Semiannual Cumulative Supplement Vol. 90 No. 8 (Parts 1A and 1B)

AFTER YOU RECEIVE THE 1990-1991 HARDBOUND SUPPLEMENT, RETAIN THE FOLLOWING:

Bound Volumes and Bound Supplements same as above
1990-1991 Bound Supplement (Vols. 18 and 19)*
**Supplemented with:*
–Jan., 1992 Semiannual Cumulative Supplement Vol. 90 No. 8 (Parts 1A and 1B)

PART 2, STATUTES

Please refer to the current supplement cover for Part 2, Statutes.

Source: Shepard's United States Citations, Semiannual Supplement July (1991), Cases Part 1A, vol. 90., No 2 (Colorado Springs, CO: Shepard's/McGraw-Hill, Inc., 1991), front cover. Reprinted with permission.

Shepard's/McGraw-Hill, Inc., also publishes other publications and subject-specific *Shepard's*. Publication examples include *Code of Federal Regulations* (Citations), *Law Review Citations*, *Professional Responsibility Citations* (covering the American Bar Association *Code of Professional Responsibility* and *Code of Judicial Conduct*), and *Restatement Citations*. Subject examples include *Bankruptcy Citations*, *Federal Labor Law Citations*, *Federal Tax Citations*, *Military Justice Citations*, and *Uniform Commercial Code Citations*.

Using *Shepard's* as a Case Reviewer

Frank Shepard conceived of his book as a case reviewer. He listed all the citing cases for a cited case, so a legal researcher could make sure the cited case was not bad law (i.e., make sure it was "still" **good law** and to what extent). Over time, Shepard and his successors developed a system of analysis abbreviations, listed in the front of each volume, to add to the bare list of citing cases, to help the legal researcher quickly review the cited case, and to do so in a refined way. (See Figure 11–4.)

Shepard and his successors noted that there are two general types of citing cases. Often the "citing" case is really a later history of the cited case itself; the same case on appeal or remand. "History of Case" abbreviations—such as *a* for "same case affirmed on appeal," *m* for "same case modified on appeal," and *r* for "same case reversed on appeal"—have been added as appropriate to the citing references for the cited case.

Most often the citing case is a true citing case; that is, another case citing the cited case, perhaps as precedent. "Treatment of Case" abbreviations—such as *c* for the "decision or reasoning in cited case criticized," *d* for the citing case that "distinguished" itself from the cited case, and *f* for the citing case that "followed" the cited case as "controlling"—have been added as appropriate to the citing references for the cited case.

Although the analysis abbreviations help you to quickly review a cited case, remember they are not perfect, and can't be, because there is no perfect law book. Analysis abbreviations are generally added only when they are supported by the express language of the citing case. If a citing case implicitly criticizes the cited case, no analysis abbreviation appears to indicate that. Since the analysis is a literal one-time judgment expressed in summary form, you should always read the relevant cases. Moreover, *Shepard's* cannot be used in any direct way to determine if a case precedent has been overruled by statute.

One weakness inherent in *Shepard's* results from the fact that the cited case may deal with several points of law. It is not always clear for what point of law (if any) in the cited case the citing case referred to the cited case. Thus, it is not always clear for which point of law (if any) in the cited case the analysis abbreviation applies. To address this problem, modern *Shepard's* citing references include, to the extent possible, a superior figure (an "exponent") to the left of the page number. The superior figure indicates the headnote or syllabus paragraph of the *cited case* that states the point of law about which the *citing case* referred to the cited case.

In reviewing a case with *Shepard's*, remember that *Shepard's* lists only all citing cases for a cited case. Two case opinions can discuss the same point of law, but nothing requires the judge drafting the later opinion to cite the earlier case. The judge may not even be aware of the earlier case. Moreover, a case precedent can be "followed" or "overruled"—indirectly—by a noncting case.

You should also realize that a statute edition of *Shepard's* cannot be used directly as a case reviewer because a "statute edition" collects all the citing cases

Figure 11–4 Example of *Shepard's* Abbreviations

ABBREVIATIONS—ANALYSIS

History of Case

a	(affirmed)	Same case affirmed on rehearing.
cc	(connected case)	Different case from case cited but arising out of same subject matter or intimately connected therewith.
m	(modified)	Same case modified on rehearing.
r	(reversed)	Same case reversed on rehearing.
s	(same case)	Same case as case cited.
S	(superseded)	Substitution for former opinion.
v	(vacated)	Same case vacated.
US	cert den	Certiorari denied by U.S. Supreme Court.
US	cert dis	Certiorari dismissed by U.S. Supreme Court.
US	reh den	Rehearing denied by U.S. Supreme Court.
US	reh dis	Rehearing dismissed by U.S. Supreme Court.
US	app pndg	Appeal pending before the U.S. Supreme Court.

Treatment of Case

c	(criticised)	Soundness of decision or reasoning in cited case criticised for reasons given.
d	(distinguished)	Case at bar different either in law or fact from case cited for reasons given.
e	(explained)	Statement of import of decision in cited case. Not merely a restatement of the facts.
f	(followed)	Cited as controlling.
h	(harmonized)	Apparent inconsistency explained and shown not to exist.
j	(dissenting opinion)	Citation in dissenting opinion.
L	(limited)	Refusal to extend decision of cited case beyond precise issues involved.
o	(overruled)	Ruling in cited case expressly overruled.
p	(parallel)	Citing case substantially alike or on all fours with cited case in its law or facts.
q	(questioned)	Soundness of decision or reasoning in cited case questioned.

ABBREVIATIONS—COURTS

Cir. Fed.–U.S. Court of Appeals, Federal Circuit
Cir (number)–U.S. Court of Appeals Circuit (number)
CIT–United States Court of International Trade
CCPA–Court of Customs and Patent Appeals
Cl Ct–Claims Court (U.S.)
Ct Cl–Court of Claims Reports (U.S.)
Cu Ct–Customs Court Decisions
DC–District of Columbia
EC or ECA–Temporary Emergency Court of Appeals
ML–Judicial Panel on Multidistrict Litigation
RRR–Special Court Regional Rail Reorganization Act of 1973

xix

Source: Shepard's United States Citations, Case Edition, vol. 6 (Colorado Springs, CO: Shepard's/McGraw-Hill, Inc., 1984), pp. xix. Reprinted with permission.

for a statute or ordinance, and not for a case. Statute editions of *Shepard's* are excellent case finders, however, as discussed in the next part.

Using *Shepard's* as a Case Finder

Although *Shepard's* was designed as a case reviewer, it is frequently used as an imperfect case finder to help find other cases like the cited case. *Shepard's* lists all the citing cases for a case. There may be hundreds of cases that have cited a given cited case. Note, however, that the court deciding the citing case may cite the cited case for a number of reasons. Sometimes there's a legal significance; sometimes it's a coincidence. *Shepard's* perpetuates all citations of legal authority: the great, the good, the bad, and the ugly.

You can assume that 50% of the citing cases listed in *Shepard's* for a cited case like yours are also cases like yours. If you have found a case that you know is exactly like, or similar to, your case, you can shepardize it, and check out each case listed as a citing case. About 50% of the time—more if you're lucky, less if you're not—the citing case will be like yours. Because *Shepard's* systematically lists all the citing cases for a cited case, no editorial judgment is involved. You can often find cases like yours using *Shepard's* that didn't make it into an annotation, digest, encyclopedia, or other law book, because they didn't have to meet stricter editorial standards.

Unlike a case citing another case, when a case cites a statute it is highly probable that the statute is important to the case. You can assume that 75% of the citing cases listed in *Shepard's* statute edition for a cited statute like your case are also cases like yours. Because *Shepard's* statute edition systematically lists all the citing cases for a cited statute or ordinance, no editorial judgment is involved. You can often find cases like yours using *Shepard's* statute edition that didn't make it into an annotated code or other law book, because they didn't have to meet stricter editorial standards.

Again, *Shepard's* is an imperfect case finder. You have to consider your chances of success. *Shepard's* may list hundreds of citing cases for a cited case like yours, and about 50% will *not* be cases like yours. In a given case, using *Shepard's* as a case finder may not be worth the time and effort involved.

Shepard's on LEXIS or WESTLAW

Selected *Shepard's Citations* are available on the LEXIS (SHEP command) and WESTLAW (SH command) computer-assisted legal research systems, to be discussed in the next chapter. The principal advantage of using *Shepard's* on-line is that the bound volume and pamphlet lists of citing cases are automatically merged for each cited case. In addition, analysis abbreviations are spelled out in *Shepard's* on-line, and you can quickly retrieve a citing case from the computer-assisted legal research system.

11–2 Other Citators

While *Shepard's Citations* uniquely lists all the citing cases for a cited case, there are other useful citators that simply list parallel citations for a cited case and/or list all the cites to a single case as it has made its way through the court system.

The path a legal controversy has taken through the court system is known as its **case history.**

Parallel Cites

As discussed in the previous chapter, it is necessary to find the appropriate parallel cites to a case, if any, to properly cite the case in Bluebook style. There are often more practical reasons for finding a parallel cite. Law libraries, particularly law firm libraries, do not always contain the same sets of books. As a result, you must be able to find and use alternative sources. For example, in the early stages of your research you may have only the cite to a case in a state reporter, but need to find the case in the West regional reporter, or you may have only the cite to the case in the West regional reporter, but need to find the case in a state reporter.

Until computers were commonly used in legal research (see Auto-Cite and Insta-Cite discussed below), the most common way to get back and forth between state reporters and the National Reporter System was to use West's *National Reporter Blue Book* (not to be confused with *The Bluebook: A Uniform System of Citation*) and the appropriate West's state "Blue and White Book."

The *National Reporter Blue Book,* as its name suggests, is a blue book. Its tables list state citations for each state and give for each the parallel citations in the National Reporter System. The state "Blue and White Book" (e.g., *Ohio Blue and White*), as its name suggests, is a blue and white book. The blue pages repeat the parallel citation information found in the *National Reporter Blue Book* for that state. The white pages have tables that list the National Reporter citations for the state and give for each the parallel citations in the state reporters.

Besides *Shepard's,* other historic methods of finding parallel cites included searching tables of cases in volumes and digests, checking for cross-reference tables in volumes, thumbing through running heads, and other trickery. These methods are now overshadowed by two computer case history citators: Auto-Cite and Insta-Cite.

Auto-Cite

The first commercial computer case history citator was Auto-Cite, introduced directly to the public by the Lawyers Co-operative Publishing Co. (LCP) in 1982. Its origins date back to the preparation of *Lawyers' Reports Annotated* (L.R.A.) from 1888–1918, and include a citation service once offered by the company at no charge.

In 1913, LCP began "The Co-op. Citation Bureau" to help promote L.R.A. A legal researcher could send a case cite to LCP and LCP would return, at no charge, by mail or "telegraph collect" (1) the citations to "All the cases which have ever cited that case," (2) where, if at all, the case was reported in a "leading selected case series" (such as LCP's L.R.A.), and (3) where, if at all, the case was cited in an L.R.A. annotation, insofar as all of the above had already been found by LCP editors in preparing L.R.A. and other texts. The "Citation Bureau" was based on a card file of approximately 1.4 million cards on which LCP editors had checked and noted the histories of cases before citing them in L.R.A.

The free "Citation Bureau" faded out of existence, but as L.R.A. became A.L.R., LCP editors continued to keep case history file cards. Of course, until 1977, LCP never saw the need to publish the cards, because A.L.R. theoretically contained all its case analysis. Theoretically, A.L.R. readers did not need

Shepard's, because A.L.R. editors picked up the value of case precedents reading all the on-point cases in the course of preparing annotations. Instead of a few analysis abbreviations, A.L.R. provided a detailed narrative analytical treatment of all the case law on the point annotated, with complete case summaries set out for all relevant cites.

As will be discussed in the next chapter, by 1977, LCP was looking for a way to get into "electronic publishing." The pages of LCP's books were then being composed by computer, and the company had begun to look into computerizing other aspects of the manufacturing process. One aspect was editorial "testing." A clerical staff assisted LCP editors in checking the validity of cases cited in LCP publications using the LCP's case history collection. LCP decided to computerize its "testing" department. The new computer system was known as Auto-Cite (Automated Citation Testing Service).

In 1977, LCP entered into talks with Mead Data Central, publisher of the LEXIS computer-assisted legal research system. On January 22, 1979, the companies signed a royalty agreement whereby LCP's Auto-Cite system would be provided to LEXIS subscribers. LEXIS had already demonstrated that information could be economically entered into a computer database, and with the development of personal computers, acoustic couplers (a device in which a telephone receiver can be inserted), and modems, customers could be linked to an electronic publisher over telephone lines.

By 1982, LCP had collected nearly four million case histories. LCP decided to once again provide "testing" services not only to its own editors and LEXIS subscribers, but to its own customers as well, this time for a fee.

Auto-Cite allows the user to make an electronic citation search. Enter a cite by volume, reporter abbreviation, and page, and Auto-Cite displays the full citation to the case, including title, court (if necessary), date, parallel cites, references in A.L.R. annotations, and case history citations, all in an easy-to-read "sentence."

Auto-Cite is *not*, however, the same as *Shepard's*. *Shepard's* has all the citing cases for a cited case, and so is useful in both case review and case finding. *Shepard's* covers both the history and the treatment of a cited case. Auto-Cite covers only the history of the cited case and leaves case reviewing and case finding to A.L.R.

Auto-Cite has three main features: citation verification, parallel case referencing, and A.L.R. referencing.

Other than a check of citation information (e.g., the title of the case; the year of decision), the citation verification of Auto-Cite extends only to a determination of whether a case has become bad law as a result of its own history in the courts (e.g., reversed by a higher court). Auto-Cite's citation verification is not a determination of whether the case has become bad law as a result of its treatment by other courts, unless another case explicitly states that the cited case was affected by another case (an "as stated in" reference). Otherwise, the treatment of a case by other courts is still left to A.L.R. Auto-Cite does have an advantage over *Shepard's* in that its collection of case history information is all in one place.

Auto-Cite also has an advantage over *Shepard's* with regard to parallel citations. Auto-Cite displays collect in one place parallel cites for both the cited case and the history cases. To find the history case parallel cites in *Shepard's*, you have to make separate searches.

Auto-Cite also has some slight advantages over *Shepard's* in citing A.L.R. annotations. *Shepard's* gives only volume-series-page cites to citing annotations, and the annotations themselves are not shepardized. Auto-Cite includes full A.L.R. titles and section number references for citing annotations, and it returns cites to related annotations if an annotation cite is entered.

Auto-Cite also has greater coverage, in terms of both breadth (number) and depth (reach back in time), of case reporters and administrative decisions than its competitor, Insta-Cite (discussed below), including an extensive coverage of the Bureau of National Affairs (BNA), Commerce Clearing House (CCH), and other non-West reporters, in addition to those included in West's National Reporter System.

As discussed in the next chapter, direct access to Auto-Cite from LCP ceased on April 1, 1991, after a 10-year run. Thus, again, Auto-Cite is available only to LCP editors and LEXIS subscribers. LEXIS subscribers can also purchase *CheckCite* software from Jurisoft, a division of Mead Data Central, Inc., to automatically use Auto-Cite and *Shepard's* to check citations in a word-processing document on their personal computers.

Insta-Cite

As discussed in the next chapter, Insta-Cite, introduced in 1983, was West's WESTLAW response to Auto-Cite on LEXIS. Compared with Auto-Cite's history dating back to the 1800s, West created Insta-Cite from scratch, for purely competitive reasons.

Similar to Auto-Cite, Insta-Cite has three main features: case history, parallel citations, and citation verification. Insta-Cite's case history is case history: the ability to determine whether a case has become bad law as a result of its own history in the courts. Insta-Cite's parallel citations emphasize parallel citations to units of the National Reporter System. Insta-Cite's citation verification is simply case information (title, year of decision, etc.). While Insta-Cite includes citations to A.L.R. reported cases, it does not include citations to A.L.R. annotations.

Insta-Cite also has more current coverage of case reporters than its competitor, Auto-Cite, because Insta-Cite principally covers the National Reporter System, and West obviously has access to its own reporters before its competitors.

Insta-Cite is available only on the WESTLAW computer-assisted legal research system, to be discussed in the next chapter. WESTLAW subscribers can also purchase *WestCheck* software to automatically use Insta-Cite, *Shepard's*, and Shepard's Preview (to be discussed in the next chapter) to check citations in word-processing documents on their personal computers.

LEXIS or WESTLAW as a Citator

As discussed in the next chapter, LEXIS or WESTLAW can be used as a citator by using the cited case's cite as a word search for citing cases.

SUMMARY

11–1

It takes a lot of mental work to be objective. Because of human nature, a legal researcher may seize on and cite the inaccurate statement without checking it out. Because of the march of time, a legal researcher may suffer the greatest embarrassment in advocacy: unwittingly arguing the opponent's case. Bad law is precedent without authority. Starting in 1873, Frank Shepard provided the service of systematically noting every time an earlier case was cited by a later case. *Shepard's Citations* quickly became a standard legal research tool, leading a group of books and other media known as citators. In listing parallel cites, citators list cites to a target case, known as the *cited case.* In listing cites of cases that refer to a target case, citators list referring cases, known as *citing cases. Shepard's* is a book of tables uniquely listing all the citing cases for a cited case. When legal researchers shepardize a case, they review all the citing cases for a cited case to make sure the cited case is not bad law or to help find other cases like the cited case. There are *Shepard's* sets covering virtually every set of court reports published in the United States, including every major unit of the National Reporter System. A statute edition lists all the citing cases for a particular statute or ordinance. A legal researcher using *Shepard's* can review all the citing cases for a cited case. With help from analysis abbreviations for case history and treatment, the legal researcher can determine whether the cited case is bad law. A legal researcher can also use *Shepard's* as an imperfect case finder to find other cases like the cited case. Selected *Shepard's Citations* are available on the LEXIS and WESTLAW computer-assisted legal research services.

11–2

Until Auto-Cite and Insta-Cite were developed, the most common way to get back and forth between state reporters and the National Reporter System was to use West's *National Reporter Blue Book* and the appropriate West's state "Blue and White Book." The first commercial computer case history citator was Auto-Cite, introduced directly to the public by LCP in 1982. Auto-Cite allows the user to make an electronic citation search. Enter a cite by volume, reporter abbreviation, and page, and Auto-Cite displays the full citation to the case, including title, court (if necessary), date, parallel cites, references in A.L.R. annotations, and case history citations, all in an easy-to-read "sentence." Auto-Cite has three main features: citation verification, parallel case referencing, and A.L.R. referencing. Other than a check of citation information, the citation verification of Auto-Cite extends only to a determination of whether a case has become bad law as a result of its own history in the courts (e.g., reversed by a higher court). Since April 1, 1991, Auto-Cite is available only on the LEXIS computer-assisted legal research system. LEXIS subscribers can purchase *CheckCite* software to automatically use Auto-Cite and *Shepard's* to check citations in a word-processing document on their personal computer. Insta-Cite is West's WESTLAW response to Auto-Cite on LEXIS. Similar to Auto-Cite, Insta-Cite has three main features: case history, parallel citations, and citation verification. Insta-Cite's citation verification is simply case information. Insta-Cite is available only on the WESTLAW computer-assisted legal research system. WESTLAW subscribers can purchase *WestCheck* software to automatically use Insta-Cite, *Shepard's,* and Shepard's Preview to check citations in a word-processing document on their personal computer. In addition, LEXIS or WESTLAW can be used as a citator by using the cited case cite itself as a word search for citing cases.

REVIEW

Key Terms

Before proceeding, review the key terms listed below to be sure you understand each one. If necessary, read over the corresponding section of the chapter. When you are ready to test your understanding, answer the Review Questions.

bad law
case history
citators
cited case
citing cases
good law
Shepard's
shepardize
statute edition

Questions for Review and Discussion

1. Why is it hard for human beings to be objective while performing legal research?
2. Why should you hesitate to cite a case you found in a 20-year-old law book?
3. What is the greatest embarrassment in advocacy?
4. Where are parallel citations located in *Shepard's?*
5. What important feature of *Shepard's* do you find on the cover of its pamphlets?
6. What are *Shepard's* analysis abbreviations for?
7. Why is *Shepard's* an "imperfect" case finder?
8. What are West's state "Blue and White" books used for?
9. What are the main features of Auto-Cite?
10. What are the main features of Insta-Cite?

Activities

1. Locate the *Shepard's* sets in your local law library. Referring to the "What Your Library Should Contain" information on the covers of the pamphlets, determine if all the pamphlets have been properly shelved. Have superseded volumes and pamphlets been properly removed?
2. Shepardize a U.S. Supreme Court case decided in the 1960s. How many cases did you find?
3. If you dare, completely shepardize a U.S. Supreme Court case. That is, shepardize the case, then shepardize each of the cases you found. After eliminating duplicates, how many cites did you find? Are you impressed, overwhelmed, or both?

PART FIVE

USING COMPUTERS AND OTHER TECHNOLOGIES

CHAPTER 12 Computer-Assisted Legal Research

OUTLINE

COMMENTARY

The mayor and law director are pleased with your memorandum. By following your "advice," the diverse public religious display the city erects, balanced by nonreligious elements, survives the Christmas holiday season without objection. Now, you are hit by a "bolt from the blue." The U.S. senator from your state has died and the governor has appointed the mayor to fill the Senate seat. You are asked to join the new senator's staff in Washington, D.C., and you accept. The senator becomes a member of the Judiciary Committee just before the President nominates a U.S. Court of Appeals judge to be the next Associate Justice of the Supreme Court. Your assignment is to find all of the judge's opinions, analyze them for any unexplained changes or contradictions, and prepare the senator for the judge's testimony before the committee.

OBJECTIVES

In this chapter you will learn about the use of computer-modem technology to aid in the search of legal materials. Emphasis is placed on the two leading computer-assisted legal research systems: LEXIS and WESTLAW. After reading this chapter, you should be able to:

1. Describe the events preceding the discovery of CALR.
2. Understand the logic of a computer word search.
3. Describe the events since the discovery of CALR.
4. Describe the organization and use of LEXIS.
5. List the principal advantages of using LEXIS.
6. Describe the organization and use of WESTLAW.
7. List the principal advantages of using WESTLAW.
8. Recognize CALR systems other than LEXIS and WESTLAW.

9. Describe the advantages of CALR.
10. Describe the disadvantages of CALR.

12–1 Understanding Computer-Assisted Legal Research

Computer-assisted legal research (CALR) is the use of computer-modem systems to automate the search of legal materials as an aid in legal research. The search is made upon a collection of information placed in the computer's memory, known as a **database.**

The Data Corporation's Concordance

In 1965, Ohio State Bar Association executives became interested in developing a CALR system for Ohio lawyers. In 1966, a computer software company, Data Corporation of Beavercreek, Ohio, learned of the project and offered to build it. In 1977, a nonprofit corporation, Ohio Bar Automated Research (OBAR), was formed. OBAR entered into a contract with Data Corporation to build the system, also named OBAR. Ohio law was entered into Data Corporation's computer, and search software (a modification of software previously created for the Air Force called Central) was developed. The software allowed the user to make a **word search,** a computer search of the words likely to have been used to describe the information sought. Although OBAR could perform some searches faster and better than they could be performed manually, the system was slow, unreliable, and limited in scope. Since neither OBAR nor Data Corporation had sufficient funds to make additional changes, the project appeared doomed.

The project gained new life, however, in 1969, when Data Corporation was purchased by Mead Corporation (Mead) of Dayton, Ohio. Mead, a billion-dollar paper and forest products company, made the purchase in order to acquire a new printing process. The word search software just happened to come with the package. In 1970, Mead formed a subsidiary, Mead Data Central (MDC), to take over the OBAR project, and bought out OBAR corporation's interest.

The heart of MDC's system is a computer-generated **concordance,** an index of words. Unlike an ordinary index, which refers a reader to the location of concepts in a book by short entries and page references, a concordance is a literal alphabetical listing of the principal words of a book, with precise references to where in the book each word is used.

Many concordances, for example, have been made for the Bible. If biblical researchers want to find where the word *light* is used in the Bible, they can look the word up in a concordance for precise references by chapter and verse.

Most significant for legal research, however, is the fact that a concordance can be used to find relational concepts. For example, if you want to read about the biblical relationship between *mercy* and *sacrifice,* you can use a concordance to find a reference the words have in common. Since words are ordinarily used for the concepts they stand for, a convergence of those words likely involves a convergence of their concepts as well.

As cases and other documents are loaded on MDC's computer, the computer builds a concordance. While loading cases, the computer notes, for example, that the word *death* appears in the 15th case as the 89th word, in the 31st case as the 25th word, and in the 55th case as 17th word. The computer also notes that the word *penalty* appears in the 23rd case as the 40th word, in the 31st case as the 75th word, in the 55th case as the 20th word, in the 93th case as the 64th word, and so on. It is then relatively simple for a legal researcher trying to find "death penalty" cases to ask the computer—with its lightning-fast math, search, and sort capabilities—to compare the references to the words *death* (15–89, 31–25, 55–17) and *penalty* (23–40, 31–75, 55–20, 93–64) and return the full text of the cases in which both words appear (31 and 55), or the portion of the text where the word *death* appears within five words of the word *penalty* (case 55, from word 17 to word 20).

It is important to understand how CALR word searching is unique. Instead of using an existing index, digest, or annotation, CALR word searching allows legal researchers to make their own index of the material searched.

The system depends on the assumption that the words the judge used in a given opinion correspond to what the case is about and that a legal researcher can make educated guesses about what words the judge used in describing the case and their relationships in the opinion. The computer takes the legal researcher's words and the relationships, and searches its concordance. If the legal researcher makes good educated guesses and the desired words and relationships exist in cases in the database, the system returns the cases like the legal researcher's where the person like the researcher won.

The software MDC developed is **user-friendly** (easy to use). Once you are in the appropriate case file, if you want to search for the words *death* and *penalty* in the same case, all you have to do is type *death* and *penalty* and hit the enter key.

MDC had custom computer terminals and printers manufactured, and by 1973, the commercially viable system was ready to be put **on-line** (accessible by a modem-equipped computer using telephone lines).

Computer-Assisted Legal Research Takes Off

In April 1973, MDC introduced the LEXIS computer-assisted legal research system, and "electronic" law publishing was born. LEXIS was a pseudo-acronym (LEgal X Information Service?), based on market research indicating people had a favorable reaction to names with an *X* (e.g., Exxon). Lacking a door-to-door sales force, LEXIS was slow to catch on, but wherever it was sold, it was a hit.

Since the database originally included New York and Ohio cases, LEXIS was initially marketed in New York and Ohio. MDC rushed to add cases from other states because every time it did, it found more customers. By 1976, MDC had added a federal library, cases from several states, and thousands of users. As LEXIS grew, MDC grew, and the profits were plowed back into the system. MDC hired scores of data entry people to work around-the-clock. By 1979, LEXIS had the full text of almost every case—state and federal—on-line. In 1979, MDC continued its growth by starting NEXIS, a computer-assisted research system for news and business information.

West Publishing Company (West) was caught off-guard. For the first time in decades, West's monopoly over a lawyer's access to case law was broken. Like West, MDC had the cases too. And MDC had something West didn't: a computer system for the computer age.

West competed with MDC the only way it could: it poured money into the development of its own CALR system. To catch up with LEXIS' growing database, West created its own around-the-clock data entry department. In 1975, West introduced WESTLAW.

The original WESTLAW contained only West's case summaries (e.g., synopses and headnotes). It wasn't until July 1977 that West announced its intention to include the full text of all cases in its database. However, WESTLAW began to distinguish itself from LEXIS, since only WESTLAW contained both the full text of cases and West's case summaries.

For West, it was vitally important that WESTLAW succeed. For MDC, it was equally important that LEXIS maintain its advantage. The competition became intense. Each company looked for new features to distinguish its service, and each company tried to match any features added by its competitor.

For example, West began to make the same argument that the Lawyers Co-operative Publishing Company (LCP) had always made against West. LCP argued that although West had the cases, LCP had the analysis in A.L.R. Now West argued that although LEXIS had the cases on computer, WESTLAW had the analysis on computer. As early as 1978, West advertised its case summaries on WESTLAW with the slogan "Full Text Plus." West argued that a word search might not pick up a case in LEXIS, which contained only the opinions, because the court might not use the words searched, but the words might be in the West case summary, leading to the discovery of the case. For example, a judge might draft an opinion in a death penalty case, but not use the words *death penalty* in the opinion. However, a headnote for the case might indicate that it was a death penalty case. If a legal researcher was searching "death penalty" on LEXIS and WESTLAW, the argument went, the legal researcher would find the case with WESTLAW but not with LEXIS.

Meanwhile, LCP executives became concerned. It was clear that the future of law publishing was in *electronic publishing,* and LCP wasn't in the game. As discussed in the last chapter, LCP developed a computer citation system, Auto-Cite, and offered it to the general public in 1982. Noting that Auto-Cite gave citations to *American Law Reports* (A.L.R.) annotations, an LCP editor quipped: "We've put A.L.R. into CALR."

MDC executives anticipated the need to have a comeback to West's Full Text Plus campaign. In 1979, after two years of talks with LCP executives, LCP agreed to put Auto-Cite on LEXIS. To press its Full Text Plus advantage, West had to counter Auto-Cite on LEXIS. West poured money into the development of its own computer citation service, and in 1983, Insta-Cite, discussed in Chapter 11, was born. With Insta-Cite to answer Auto-Cite, West was again on the offensive.

In 1984, LEXIS remained in the lead. Nevertheless, MDC needed another comeback to West's persistent Full Text Plus campaign. MDC needed to add case analysis to LEXIS that West couldn't counter. LCP needed something to counter Insta-Cite on WESTLAW, and access to cases on computer.

In 1985, MDC and LCP made another agreement: a joint venture. MDC and LCP cooperated in putting A.L.R. (except First Series) on LEXIS. MDC got the leading book of case analysis, A.L.R., on LEXIS. LCP formed an "electronic" subsidiary, Veracorp, to sell Veralex (in Latin: "truth word"), consisting of Auto-Cite, A.L.R. on-line, and access to the cases on LEXIS, each accessible by **citation search** (i.e., entering a citation).

Introduced in February 1986, A.L.R. on LEXIS was a hit for MDC, which advertised the fact with full-page advertisements in national publications. LEXIS was set up so that in any combined file search of federal case law or state case law, A.L.R. would also automatically be searched. The implicit argument was that A.L.R. annotations were better than West's case summaries.

Veralex, introduced in January 1986 by LCP's Veracorp, was targeted at small and medium-sized firms. It had limited success. Many users did not understand or appreciate the citation search format. Without word search capability, Veralex was dwarfed by LEXIS and WESTLAW. A second agreement, in which LCP traded access to its sales force for access to LEXIS itself, led to the creation of Veralex 2. It failed. In 1991, Veralex 2 ceased operation, ending direct access to Auto-Cite as well.

Entering the 1990s, the competition between West and MDC balanced out.

Entering the 1990s, the competition between West and MDC balanced out. LEXIS has advantages over WESTLAW, and WESTLAW has advantages over LEXIS. LCP remains in the market with its production of Auto-Cite and A.L.R. for LEXIS.

12–2 LEXIS

Discussing every aspect and feature of LEXIS is beyond the scope of this textbook; however, the publisher has developed CALR tutorial software to accompany this text that provides instruction in searching LEXIS and reinforces the concepts presented on the following pages. You should also know that Mead Data Central publishes a number of excellent guides to using LEXIS, including the pamphlet *Learning LEXIS: A Handbook for Modern Legal Research* and the newsletter "LEXIS Brief."

You should carefully study this chapter and use the software that accompanies this text, as well as referring to Mead Data Central's LEXIS guides and the latest *Library Contents and Alphabetical List*, before accessing LEXIS on a subscriber line.

In summary, subscribers can access LEXIS through a dedicated UBIQ terminal or personal computer 24 hours-a-day (except Sunday). Using a modem, the user is connected with the MDC computer in Dayton, Ohio. At the

LEXIS/NEXIS

"Welcome to LEXIS" screen, the user transmits an identification number. After entering client information, the user selects the part of the database to search. The LEXIS database is divided into "services," "libraries," "files," "documents," "segments," and "words." A search is made by entering the desired terms and alternatives, along with **connectors** (codes to indicate the desired logical and numerical relationships among the terms). The results can be displayed in full, with the "key words in context" **(kwic),** or as a list of citations. The search can be modified as desired. Cases can be checked with Auto-Cite and *Shepard's.* Cases and statutes can be viewed via their citations using "LEXSEE" and "LEXSTAT" commands. There are a variety of options for printing search results. LEXIS also features "Dot Commands" (e.g., .kw) and "SHORT CUT," allowing the user to make a series of commands in one step, to speed through the usual command-return sequences.

The principal advantage of using LEXIS is the size of its database. LEXIS/NEXIS is the largest commercially available full-text computer database in the world. It has over 85 million documents available for reading and research.

In 1990, several hundred LEXIS files that were unavailable on WESTLAW were available on MDC. LEXIS is the sole source of several non-West publications, including many published by LCP. Only LEXIS provides access to the nation's most complete case-history citation service, Auto-Cite, and the leading book of case analysis (A.L.R.).

12–3 WESTLAW

Discussing every aspect and feature of WESTLAW is beyond the scope of this textbook; however, the publisher has developed CALR tutorial software to accompany this text that provides instruction in searching WESTLAW and reinforces the concepts presented on the following pages. You should also know that West publishes a number of excellent guides to using WESTLAW, including the pamphlet *Introductory Guide to Legal Research* and the newsletter "Password."

You should carefully study this chapter and use the software that accompanies this text, as well as referring to West's guides and the latest *Database List,* before accessing WESTLAW on a subscriber line.

In summary, WESTLAW can be accessed by subscribers through a WALT (West's Automated Law Terminal) or a personal computer 24 hours a day (except Sunday). Using a modem, the user is connected with the West computer in St. Paul, Minnesota. At the WESTLAW "logo" screen, the user transmits an identification number. After entering client information, the user selects the part of the database to search. The WESTLAW database is divided into "services," "databases," "documents," "fields," and words. A word search (i.e., **query**) is made by entering the desired terms and alternatives, along with connectors. The results can be browsed by page **(page mode)** or by search term **(term mode),** or a list of citations can be displayed. Cases can be checked with Insta-Cite, *Shepard's,* or Shepard's Preview (discussed below). Cases and statutes can be viewed via their citations using the "Find" service. There are many options for printing search results. WESTLAW also features EZ ACCESS, a slower but easier-to-use menu-driven version of WESTLAW.

The principal advantage of using WESTLAW is the ability to make computerized digest searches by searching West's case summaries on-line. Along with Insta-Cite and Star Paging, WESTLAW also features West publications like *Black's Law Dictionary* and *United States Code Annotated* (U.S.C.A.). In addition, the Shepard's Preview service on WESTLAW provides the most recent *Shepard's*

WESTLAW

Source: © Doug Martin.

citations for cases in the National Reporter System before their publication by Shepard's/McGraw-Hill, Inc., in bound volumes and pamphlets. WESTLAW's Quick-Cite updates Shepard's Preview by automatically using WESTLAW as a citator.

12–4 Other Databases

LEXIS and WESTLAW are unusual in providing full-text data accessible by word search. Other computer database systems generally provide abstracted information accessible by citation, list, or index. Some of the systems available independently of LEXIS and WESTLAW are mentioned in the following paragraphs.

DIALOG, "the world's largest card catalog," is prepared by Dialog Information Services Inc., a subsidiary of the Lockheed Corporation. Along with the Congressional Research Service, DIALOG's coverage includes business information, copyrights, engineering, medicine, patents and trademarks, science, and other subjects. DIALOG can also be accessed through WESTLAW.

ELISS, the Electronic Legislative Search Service prepared by Commerce Clearing House (CCH), contains up-to-date federal and state legislative information.

FLITE (Federal Legal Information Through Electronics) and JURIS (Justice Retrieval and Inquiry System) are systems available to employees of the federal government.

PHINet, the Prentice-Hall Information Network, was a full-text collection of Prentice-Hall's comprehensive tax and pension publications. PHINet is now part of TAXRIA.

12–5 The Advantages and Disadvantages of Computer-Assisted Legal Research

CALR has a number of advantages over research in books. The user may save money by being charged only for what is needed. CALR can eliminate the need for printed sources (unless they are cheaper in print) and save shelf space. Information on CALR is more current, doesn't physically deteriorate, and can be accessed from a variety of locations.

The principal advantage of CALR is the ability to perform a computer word search. Computer word searching is great when searching for uniquely identifiable information (e.g., a docket number) that must be found quickly and that cannot, as a practical matter, be found another way. For example, suppose you are getting married tomorrow to a person with an unusual name. Before you "tie the knot," you want to find out if your spouse-to-be has ever been involved in a court case, and why. You can use CALR to word search the name of your spouse-to-be. You may find, in an unreported opinion from a state court thousands of miles away, that your spouse-to-be successfully appealed a conviction on a "technicality." Such a search would, as a practical matter, be impossible without the word search capability of CALR.

On the other hand, CALR can be useless when you are searching for information described in common terms, involving sophisticated analysis. For example, if you search for exceptions to the rule that an acquittal in a criminal case does not collaterally estop (preclude) litigating the same issues in a civil case, and search the words *acquittal, civil, criminal, collateral,* and *estoppel,* in different relationships, you will find hundreds of irrelevant cases. In such a situation, where sentences are more important than words, you need to use a source organized, written, and indexed by human beings who understand the issue and exercise judgment. A search of *American Jurisprudence, Second* (Am. Jur. 2d), for example, would lead you to 46 Am. Jur. 2d, *Judgments* § 618 entitled "Denial of doctrine; exceptions and limitations," and the cases cited therein.

The problem is that computer word searches are "extremely literal." The computer merely searches a concordance. It works on the assumption that the user can make educated guesses about what words the writer of a document used in describing the concepts the researcher wants to find. Even an educated user can guess wrong, and the less educated the user, the poorer the guess.

Synonymous words are a major problem. If users search for the word *doctor,* they will get all the "doctor" cases, but they won't get all the "physician" cases unless they search for the word *physician* as well. One person can be described in several different ways (e.g., attorney, author, father, genius, guardian, lawyer, man, plaintiff, professor, teacher, uncle, victim, witness).

Another problem is ambiguity. Because words can have several denotations and connotations, word searches often lead to irrelevant, even comical, results. A researcher looking for a person named *John* may find a case involving a bathroom. One story involves a products liability lawyer who was searching for cases involving the female hormone drug diethylstilbestrol, commonly known as DES. He searched "DES" in an "all states" database. He found hundreds of cases—none involving the drug DES—from Des Moines, Iowa.

Because of ambiguity, include date restrictions in your searches wherever you can. If you know what you're looking for happened in 1990, a search restricted to 1990 avoids retrieving irrelevant results from other years. Similarly, if what you are looking for will be found in a particular LEXIS "segment" or WESTLAW "field" (e.g., case title or judge-author), just search that segment or field.

Another problem involves the nature of the computer systems. If you make an identical word search in both LEXIS and WESTLAW, you will not always get the same result. You will find that each system's database contains typographical errors. The errors may be errors repeated from the original document or that occur as a result of errors in data entry. If a searcher is looking for one word spelled one way and that word has been misspelled, the system will not return the case containing that word. West has tried to make a positive feature out of this by correcting typos made by the court on WESTLAW. MDC, taking the view that the opinion of the court is the opinion of the court and that its editors are not above the law, does not correct typos made by the court on LEXIS.

There are other reasons an identical word search in LEXIS and WESTLAW will not always get the same result. Each system automatically searches for certain plurals and equivalencies (e.g., *child* also retrieves *children*) and excludes commonly used words (called ***noise words*** in LEXIS, ***stop words*** in WESTLAW), such as *as, be, and,* and *the.* While the programming is similar, the words included or excluded by each system, and the system's operation, are not identical. For example, in a **proximity search** (i.e., is one word within a specified number of words from another) LEXIS does not count noise words, but WESTLAW does count stop words.

Another significant limitation of CALR is the cost. Word search systems are expensive. While schools can obtain the use of LEXIS and WESTLAW at discount prices (allowing students to use the services for free), in the real world you have to pay for it. Although the different systems have different pricing structures and charges, the average researcher making typical searches on LEXIS or WESTLAW can expect to pay over $200 per hour. Because of the cost, it is foolish to do any more reading than necessary while using CALR.

Other disadvantages to CALR include the fact that CALR systems generally do not contain historical materials, that determining what the CALR systems contain requires effort, and that CALR systems generally require considerable training and practice for effective use. Unreasonable resistance also exists to computer use by some people, especially among those born before the computer age. They are simply more familiar with, and prefer to use, books.

Understand that CALR has many advantages over books as a finding tool, but very few advantages over books as a reading tool. As a finding tool, CALR is a wonder and a joy. It is errorless, tireless, and incredibly fast. As a reading tool, it is a headache; sometimes literally so.

Under existing technology, computer monitors cannot be economically made to display sharp black figures on a white background (like a book). Black and white provides maximum contrast for greatest reading ease. On the other hand, looking at the glowing letters on a glare-filled screen causes most people to squint and strain, and eventually gives them a headache.

With the typical CALR display, you can view only a small part of a given document at a given time. For example, a screen of text on WESTLAW covers less than half of a page in a West reporter. Since you can see two pages of a book when it is open in front of you, a screen of WESTLAW covers less than a quarter of what you can see in a book. Although a CALR system may let you search through a result, you cannot scan it as if it were printed in a book.

Understand that while CALR was a great invention, books were too. Books continue to be a great invention. They collect a large amount of information in a single place. They're reasonably permanent, easy to carry, easy to handle, easy to use, and easy on the eyes. They don't use electricity or need special programming, and they usually don't break if you drop them. You can thumb through them, dog-ear them, and mark them up. Books are an incredible bargain. Buy a book and you can use it as often as you want, as long as you want, and wherever you want, at no additional cost, other than storage.

At present, the ideal use of CALR is to carefully prepare an effective search strategy before you start (West publishes "Query Planner" forms for this purpose). When you're ready, go on-line, quickly make your search, print the results, and get off. Study your results off-line. This procedure allows you to take advantage of the unique power of CALR—to make a computer word search—without bankrupting you or your employer. In general, use books as a reading tool and CALR as a finding tool, and you will do fine.

SUMMARY

12–1

Computer-assisted legal research (CALR) is the use of computer-modem systems to automate the search of legal materials as an aid in legal research. In 1973, Mead Data Central (MDC) of Dayton, Ohio, came on the scene with the first commercial CALR system, LEXIS. Featuring word search software based on a concordance, LEXIS was a hit, allowing researchers to make their own indexes of the material searched. WESTLAW was introduced in 1975. It took a long time for WESTLAW to catch up to LEXIS. However, WESTLAW began to distinguish itself from LEXIS, since only WESTLAW allowed a search of both the full text of cases and West's case summaries, advertised by West as "Full Text Plus." When LCP created the citation history service Auto-Cite in the late 1970s, Mead put it on LEXIS, forcing West to create its own citation history service, Insta-Cite, to put on WESTLAW. In 1985, MDC and LCP cooperated in putting A.L.R. on LEXIS. Entering the 1990s, the competition between West and MDC has balanced out. LEXIS has some advantages over WESTLAW, and WESTLAW has some advantages over LEXIS. LCP remains in the market with its production of Auto-Cite and A.L.R. for LEXIS.

12–2

The publisher of this text has developed CALR tutorial software that provides instruction in searching LEXIS. MDC publishes excellent guides to using LEXIS, including the pamphlet *Learning LEXIS: A Handbook for Modern Legal Research.* You should carefully study MDC's guides including the latest *Library Contents and Alphabetical List*, as well as use the software accompanying this text, before using LEXIS. The principal advantage of using LEXIS is that LEXIS/NEXIS is the largest commercially available full-text computer database in the world. LEXIS has several hundred files not available on WESTLAW, and it is the sole source of several non-West publications, including many published by LCP.

12–3

The publisher of this text has developed CALR tutorial software that provides instruction in searching WESTLAW. West publishes excellent guides to using WESTLAW, including the pamphlet *Introductory Guide to Legal Research.* You should carefully study West's guides including the latest *Database List*, as well as use the software accompanying this text, before using WESTLAW. The principal advantage of using WESTLAW is the ability to make a computer digest search by searching West's case summaries online.

12–4

CALR systems available independently of LEXIS and WESTLAW include DIALOG, ELISS, FLITE, JURIS, and TAXRIA.

12–5

CALR has several advantages over research in books. CALR can eliminate the need for printed sources and save shelf space. Information on CALR is more current, doesn't physically deteriorate, and can be accessed from a variety of locations. The principal advantage of CALR is the ability to perform a computer word search. Computer word searching is great if you are searching for uniquely identifiable information that must be found quickly and that cannot, as a practical matter, be found in any other way. However, CALR can be useless when you are searching for information described in common terms, involving sophisticated analysis. Computer word searches are "extremely literal." Synonyms are a major problem, as is ambiguity. If a searcher is looking for a particular word spelled in a particular way and that word has been misspelled, the system will not return the case containing that word. While their programming is similar, the words included or excluded by each system, and the systems' operation, are not identical. The average researcher making typical searches on LEXIS or WESTLAW will be expected to pay over $200 per hour.

Other disadvantages to CALR include the fact that CALR systems generally do not contain historical materials, that determining what the CALR systems do contain requires some effort, and that CALR systems generally require considerable training and practice for effective use. CALR has many advantages over books as a finding tool, but very few advantages over books as a reading tool. While CALR was a great invention, books were also a great invention, and continue to be a great invention. Books collect a large amount of information in a single place, and they are reasonably permanent, easy to use, and easy on the eyes. Once you buy a book, you can use it as much as you want, wherever and whenever you want, at no additional cost, other than storage. The ideal use of CALR is to carefully prepare an effective search strategy before you start. When you're ready, go on-line, quickly make your search, print the results, and get off. Study your results off-line. Take advantage of the power of CALR without bankrupting you or your employer. Use books as a reading tool and CALR as a finding tool.

REVIEW

Key Terms

Before proceeding, review the key terms listed below to be sure you understand each one. If necessary, read over the corresponding section of the chapter. When you are ready to test your understanding, answer the Review Questions.

citation search
computer-assisted legal research (CALR)
concordance
connectors
database
kwic
noise words
on-line
page mode
proximity search
query
stop words
term mode
user-friendly
word search

Questions for Review and Discussion

1. How did LCP compete with West before CALR?
2. How does LEXIS search millions of pages of text without searching all of it each time a user makes a search request?
3. What role did Auto-Cite, Veralex, and Veralex 2 play in the competition between LEXIS and WESTLAW?
4. What MDC publications explain the use of LEXIS?
5. What is the principal advantage of using LEXIS?
6. What West publications explain the use of WESTLAW?
7. What is the principal advantage of using WESTLAW?
8. What is DIALOG?
9. What are some of the advantages of using CALR?
10. What are some of the disadvantages of using CALR?

Activities

1. Obtain information about LEXIS from MDC. If at all possible, get LEXIS training. At a minimum, observe a trained user using LEXIS.
2. Obtain information about WESTLAW from West. If at all possible, get WESTLAW training. At a minimum, observe a trained user using WESTLAW.
3. Look up LEXIS and WESTLAW in the index to *The Bluebook: A Uniform System of Citation* (15th ed). Both entries guide you to page 68 and Rule 10.8.1(b). Note that a citation to LEXIS or WESTLAW is required only when a case is unreported.

CHAPTER 13 Microforms, Floppy Disks, CD-ROM, and Computer-Organized Legal Research

OUTLINE

13–1 Microforms
13–2 Floppy Disks
13–3 CD-ROM
13–4 Computer-Organized Legal Research
- Searching and Sorting a Database
- Word Processing
- The Advantages of Information on Computer
- COLR Products

COMMENTARY

After making effective searches on LEXIS and WESTLAW, you have collected all of the judge's opinions and are ready to begin to analyze them for any unexplained changes or contradictions. Can this be done in a systematic way? Can technology help? What about that computer sitting in front of you?

OBJECTIVES

In this chapter you will learn about the use of technology, other than computer-modem systems, to aid in the search for legal materials and to organize the results of legal research. Emphasis is placed on the power of searching and sorting a computer database. After reading this chapter, you should be able to:

1. Recognize the use of microforms in legal research.
2. Recognize the use of floppy disks in legal research.
3. Recognize the use of CD-ROM in legal research.
4. Describe the effect created when information is organized.
5. Distinguish COLR from CALR.
6. Compare and contrast COLR and litigation support.
7. Explain how COLR puts "new" information at a legal researcher's fingertips.
8. Use basic database terminology.
9. List the advantages of having information on computer.
10. Recognize the use of COLR products in legal research.

13–1 Microforms

Computer-modem technology is not the only way that technology has been used to aid in the search of legal materials. When law books began to overflow their shelves, lawyers, librarians, and other law office managers began to explore ways to solve the problem. Firms renting space in downtown office buildings, paying rent by the square foot, were particularly interested in cutting overhead by reducing the amount of space taken up by their books.

Although law publishers were not about to stop selling books, they did begin to recognize the problem. The Lawyers Co-operative Publishing Company (LCP) was the leader, until it got burned. In 1939, an LCP advertisement (45#2 Case & Com., inside back cover [Oct. 1939]) pointed out that LCP's selective annotated reporter, *American Law Reports* (A.L.R.), provided the benefit of "Economy of Space." In 1952, LCP ads bluntly declared that A.L.R. "saves you shelf space." Then, in 1955, LCP announced Microlex.

Microlex was a product of the Microlex Corporation, a joint venture of LCP and the inventor of a microprint process, Sidney Teiser. In 1950, market research indicated that some firms were not purchasing LCP sets because they didn't have enough space for them. Believing that **microforms,** the reproduction of printed matter in greatly reduced size, was the wave of the future, LCP poured money into Microlex. A.L.R., *United States Supreme Court Reports, Lawyers' Edition* (L. Ed.), and *Lawyers' Reports Annotated* (L.R.A.) were put on **microfiche,** file-card-sized sheets of film containing miniature pictures of printed pages. "Microlex Editions" contained 200 printed pages per card.

To the horror of LCP executives, Microlex was an Edsel-like flop. Microlex Corporation could not develop an adequate magnifier/reader for the cards, and only a few hundred sets were ever sold. Inconvenient to use, Microlex was also ahead of its time. Saving space alone wasn't enough to make lawyers give up the advantages of books. Cutting heavy losses, LCP dismantled the operation.

Adequate readers of microfiche and **microfilm** (reels or cassettes of film containing miniature pictures of printed pages) have since been developed, but they remain bulky and inconvenient. Space is a more important consideration than ever, but microforms are not frequently used outside of library research.

Microforms are a common source of the briefs and records of federal and state appellate courts. Microforms are also a common source of governmental documents and records. More than half of the documents published by the Government Printing Office are available in microform. Check with your local law library to find out what microforms are available there.

Only a few major publications are published in microform. Since 1973, West has published an "Ultra Fiche Edition" of the entire First Series of the National Reporter System, along with selected Second Series volumes. In 1985, LCP quietly announced the availability of A.L.R. and A.L.R.2d on microfiche. All of these microforms are designed to provide access to out-of-print volumes.

13–2 Floppy Disks

Out of the computer technology of the 1980s came the ordinary floppy disk. One floppy disk can contain hundreds of pages of information. Using a personal computer, a researcher can make a computer search of the information on disk and download or print it, without the time pressure and expense of a computer-modem system. Disks can be marketed like a book, a periodical

Microfiche

Source: © Doug Martin.

subscription, or a home video. Indeed, the only advantage a computer-modem system has over disks is the ability to access current "time-sensitive" information, such as a slip opinion or market quote. If information is not that time-sensitive, it can be put on disk.

Floppy disk publishing is in its infancy. Only a few legal publications have appeared on floppy disk. Commerce Clearing House (CCH) offers its *Master Tax Guide* on floppy disk (for transfer to the user's hard disk). As explained in a CCH advertising mailer:

> All information can be accessed instantly by key word or phrase searching, walking through subject menus or using a combination of the two. Also, a lightning-quick LINK command lets you leap from any paragraph reference within the text or topical index to the paragraph itself. Once there, a RELATE command brings up a list of related documents.

In a similar manner, Tax Analysts of Arlington, Virginia, publishes *The Internal Revenue Code on Diskette.*

A publisher of college educational material, South-Western Publishing Co., offers *The Legal Tutor on Contracts* and *The Legal Tutor on Sales* on floppy disk. In addition, the LEXIS simulation *Learning LEXIS: A Computer-based Training Course* and the WESTLAW simulation *PC WESTrain II* are offered on floppy disk.

Floppy Disk

Source: The Image Bank/Jeffrey M. Spielman.

13–3 CD-ROM

The "hot" technology of the 1990s is high-density **CD-ROM** (compact disk with read-only memory). One CD-ROM can contain thousands of pages of information. As with ordinary floppy disks, a researcher using a personal computer equipped with a CD-ROM reader can make a computer search of the

CD-ROM

Source: The Image Bank/J. Brousseau.

information on the disk and download or print it, without the time pressure and expense of a computer-modem system.

As with ordinary floppy disks, CD-ROM publishing is in its infancy. The first major legal publication on CD-ROM, circa 1986, was the Information Access Corporation's LegalTrac system. As discussed in Chapter 9, LegalTrac is the *Legal Resource Index* on CD-ROM.

In 1988, West began publication of "CD-ROM Libraries," including *Bankruptcy Library, Delaware Corporation Law Library, Federal Civil Practice Library, Federal Tax Library,* and *Government Contracts Library.* The *Federal Tax Library* includes the Bureau of National Affairs' (BNA) *Tax Management* portfolios.

In 1990, Martindale-Hubbell announced the *Martindale-Hubbell Law Directory on CD-ROM.* The Michie Company published *New Mexico Statutes Annotated* on CD-ROM, and in 1991, it published the *Code of Virginia* on CD-ROM.

In 1991, Matthew Bender & Co., Inc., announced the publication of its "Search Master" compact disk libraries, including *Collier Bankruptcy, Intellectual Property, Business Law, Federal Practice, Tax, Personal Injury, California Practice,* and *Texas Practice.*

13–4 Computer-Organized Legal Research

While computers can be used to search for legal materials as an aid in legal research, they can also be used to organize the information found. When the information found is organized, there is a **synergistic** ("a whole greater than the sum of its parts") effect. Information is created that is not available from any other source.

The purpose of this section is to identify and label this synergistic effect, an inherent aspect of legal research, as magnified by the use of computers. **Computer-organized legal research (COLR)** is hereby defined as the use of computers to automate the organization of the search results as an aid in legal research.

Litigation paralegals will recognize COLR as being analogous to litigation support. **Litigation support** involves the organization of case information, particularly from discovery, to aid an attorney in the trial of a case. Several litigation support computer software packages are available that are specifically designed for that purpose.

For example, a litigation paralegal might be asked to **digest** (extract significant information from) a deposition transcript. The paralegal, perhaps using a computer program, will index and (if desired) summarize the testimony of a particular witness, so that a busy attorney can quickly locate and review what the witness said about any given subject. This is particularly important if the attorney plans to use the deposition to rebut the testimony of a witness at trial.

The deposition digest may reveal things nobody realized; things nobody had put together before. Early in the deposition the witness said she was at "A" at 11 p.m. Later in the deposition the witness said she was at "B" at 11 p.m. Putting this testimony together, the paralegal provides the lawyer with a "juicy" fact: the witness said she was in two different places at the same time. The digest might also reveal a pattern of "forgetfulness" indicating that the witness didn't talk about what she was doing from 11 p.m. to midnight, and so on.

It is important to recognize that *but for* the creation of the digest, it is unlikely the discovered facts would have been available from any other source. The discovered facts would have been buried in the deposition.

Similarly, COLR is finding information like the legal researcher's from the results of an initial search to find cases like the legal researcher's where the person like the legal researcher won. COLR puts "new" information, discovered information, at the legal researcher's fingertips. COLR comes after CALR, but before and during legal writing.

Searching and Sorting a Database

As noted in Chapter 12, a computer search is made upon a collection of information placed in its memory, known as a database. In this loose sense, a **database** is any collection of information capable of being searched by a computer, no matter how disorganized that information is.

In this chapter the term *database* is used in its technical sense, as a collection of information specially organized for rapid search and retrieval. In such a database, information is organized into defined categories known as **fields.** The variable items in the database, known as **records,** contain the categorical information for each item. (See Figure 13–1.)

A simple example of a database is a telephone book. The fields are name, address, and telephone number. The records are the listed subscribers: Andrews, John, at 123 Main Street with the number 987–6543; Bacon, Richard, at 987 Market Avenue with the number 123–4567; and so on, alphabetically by last name. The telephone book is a database because it is specially organized (in fields and alphabetically by last name) for the rapid search and retrieval of someone's telephone number by his or her name.

Figure 13–1 Databases

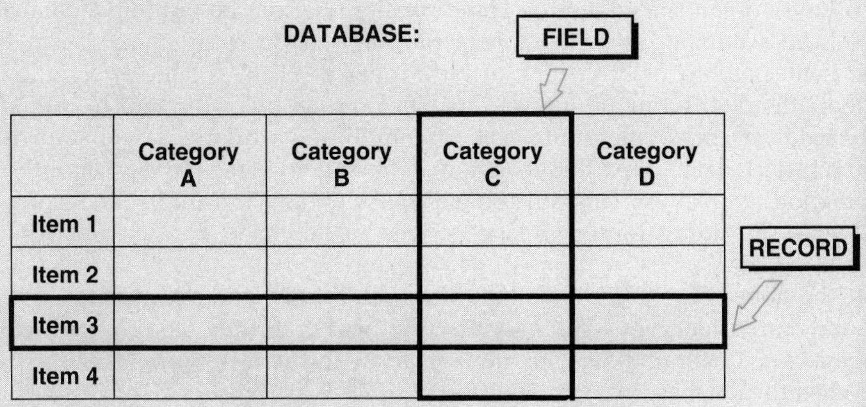

DATABASE:

FIELD (Category C column)

	Category A	Category B	Category C	Category D
Item 1				
Item 2				
Item 3				
Item 4				

RECORD (Item 3 row)

DATABASE EXAMPLE:
Vehicles in the Fleet

	Year	Make	Model	Mileage
#1	1988	Chevy	Cavalier	51,000
#2	1991	Honda	Civic	15,000
#3	1991	Ford	Pick-up	37,000
#4	1992	Chevy	Pick-up	16,000

Because a telephone book is not a computer database, it is difficult to search its information in unintended ways. It is difficult, for example, to find the address for a telephone number (e.g., the way 911 operators send ambulances to the scene of an accident).

When the information in a telephone book is put on computer, it becomes a relatively simple matter to have the computer quickly search for the telephone number in the telephone field, then pick up the address from the address field of the desired record.

While a computer can search for a desired record by searching for information in the record, the computer's awesome power is the ability to quickly **sort** (put in alphanumeric order) records by a given field. Thus, the computer could sort the records by the telephone number field, allowing a human (like a computer) to quickly search for the telephone number in the telephone number field, then pick up the address from the address field of the desired record.

Moreover, multiple sorts can be made of the records by different fields to organize the records by category in whatever priority is desired. For example, a sort by telephone number field, then by address field, and finally by name field, will return the database to its original arrangement: by name, then by address, and finally by telephone number.

Suppose you work for a large law firm and you want to predict which associates are going to make partner because you want to work with a rising star. You can make an educated guess by making a database. A knowledge of Lotus 1–2–3 or any other software that allows you to create your own database now comes in handy.

Suppose there are 30 partners and 15 associates, and that for the last 30 years the firm has published a **house organ** (an in-house periodical) announcing, among other things, all new associates with their biographies and all promotions to partner, including the new partner's activities in the firm.

A house organ is a gold mine of information that can be put into a database. You have a number of fields of personal information to organize: last name, first name, month of birth, day of birth, year of birth, college attended, law school attended, name of spouse, hobbies, and so on. Now add to the database fields of employment information: month of start date, day of start date, year of start date, department assigned to, supervising partner, months to promotion, and so on. Dust off the old house organs and fill in the records of everyone, including former associates who never made partner and left the firm.

If the house organ left something out, you'll have a blank field to fill. Ask around. For instance, Ms. Hill's secretary knows her birthday. Be observant. Mr. Thomas just celebrated his 25th anniversary with the firm, and so on.

When the database is complete, start sorting. Want a list of attorneys by age? Sort by day of birth, month of birth, year of birth. Want a list of attorneys by seniority? Sort by day of start date, month of start date, year of start date. Want to find out about that "Bob" your friend mentioned, who works in the litigation department? Sort by name and department.

Keep sorting and checking your records and you'll discover a lot of things. If associates don't make partner within five years, they never do. All the partners in the corporate department play golf. All the associates promoted to partner in two years or less either had Mr. Johnson for a supervisor or attended the local state university. Fascinating information, valuable information, found in a simple database.

The techniques described above can be applied to legal research. As you search legal materials, you can enter the information you find into a database. The database will lead you to the discovery of additional information.

A case law database, for example, could include such fields as citation, court,

court level, date, type of case, type of plaintiff, type of defendant, winner, key fact, second fact, *ratio decidendi,* holding, and so on. Sorting the database, you could quickly determine, for example, if a banker was ever held liable, and under what circumstances. You could quickly determine if the plaintiff had ever won a case in California, and so on.

COLR varies greatly with the needs of the researcher. The bigger the research project, the more it makes sense to build a database. Experiment. Be creative. If you succeed, you'll be far ahead of the competition.

Word Processing

One of the most common uses of a computer is for **word processing,** which includes the electronic display, correction, and revision of text before printing. Word processing improves writing because the ability to make quick revisions encourages revision, which is the heart of writing. Word processing can also improve legal research.

Professional word-processing software, such as WordPerfect, includes the search and sorting power discussed above, and may also include the ability to program a series of commands and keyboard strokes known in WordPerfect as a **macro.** Macros can automate portions of the legal research and writing process.

For example, a legal researcher can use word processing to prepare a list of sources to be preliminarily searched and to record the results. Case citations listed in the results can be extracted, duplicate citations can be eliminated, and the remaining citations can be expanded to include parallel citations and case history. The list of case citations can also be sorted by court level for effective reading and numbered in sequence.

As the cases are read, information from the cases can be referenced to the case list, and an outline can be made (and altered as necessary) for the legal writing being prepared. Citations found within the cases can be checked against the citations the legal researcher had already found, to ensure accuracy and completeness. A macro can automatically prepare a rough draft by reading the outline and calling case citations and case information from other documents. Of course, word processing can be used to revise the rough draft and create a final version of the legal writing being prepared.

Again, COLR varies greatly with the needs of the researcher. The bigger the research project, the more it makes sense to use word processing. Experiment. Be creative. If you succeed, you'll be far ahead of the competition.

The Advantages of Information on Computer

The more you use COLR, the more you will realize the advantages of having information on a computer. Information on a computer can be copied, deleted, formatted, merged, moved, printed, reformatted, replaced, revised, searched, sorted, and spell checked, among other things.

Develop the habit of putting as much information on a computer as you can. The only exception is "fast" facts (such as a telephone number given in a radio or television advertisement) for which you only have enough time to jot down notes on paper. Even then, you will probably want to record the notes on a computer as soon as possible.

COLR Products

For the most part, COLR is something you design yourself, using general computer software like Lotus 1–2–3 and WordPerfect. However, a few commercial "COLR" software products do exist. More will come in the future.

Anderson Publishing Co. sells a legal document creation system known as *Lawriter*. The software allows the user to merge client information with legal forms found in forms modules in the computer's memory. The available forms modules include *Couse's Ohio Will Forms, Couse's Ohio Incorporation Forms,* and *Personal Injury Settlement Forms.* The software also allows the user to alter text databases to create custom documents. The text databases include Ohio court rules and *Ohio Jury Instructions, Software Version.*

Jurisoft, a division of Mead Data Central, Inc., sells *FullAuthority* software that finds cites in a word-processing document and automatically builds a table of authorities.

SUMMARY

13–1

In 1950, market research indicated that some firms were not purchasing LCP sets because they didn't have enough space for them. Believing that microforms, the reproduction of printed matter in greatly reduced size, was the wave of the future, LCP poured money into "Microlex Editions" of A.L.R., L. Ed., and L.R.A. on microfiche, in 1955. However, Microlex flopped. Inconvenient to use, Microlex was also ahead of its time. Saving space alone wasn't enough to make lawyers give up the advantages of books. Microform readers remain bulky and inconvenient. Although space is now a more important consideration than ever, microforms are not often used outside of law library research. Microforms are a common source of the briefs and records of federal and state appellate courts. Microforms are also a common source of governmental documents and records. West publishes an "Ultra Fiche Edition" of the National Reporter System, and LCP publishes A.L.R. and A.L.R.2d on microfiche, all designed to provide access to out-of-print volumes.

13–2

One floppy disk can contain hundreds of pages of information. Using a personal computer, a researcher can make a computer search of the information on disk, and download or print it, without the time pressure and expense of a computer-modem system. If information is not time-sensitive, it can be put on disk. Only a few legal publications have appeared on floppy disk. CCH offers its *Master Tax Guide* on floppy disk. Both the LEXIS simulation and the WESTLAW simulation are offered on floppy disk.

13–3

The "hot" technology for the 1990s is high-density CD-ROM. One CD-ROM disk can contain thousands of pages of information. As with ordinary floppy disks, CD-ROM publishing is in its infancy. The first major legal publication on disk, circa 1986, was the Information Access Corporation's *Legal Trac* system. In 1989, West announced the publication of "CD-ROM Libraries." In 1990, Martindale-Hubbell announced the *Martindale-Hubbell Law Directory on CD-ROM.* In 1991, Matthew Bender announced the publication of its "Search Master" compact disk libraries.

13–4

When information is organized, there is a synergistic effect. Information is created that is not available from any other source. Computer-organized legal research (COLR) is the use of computers to automate the organization of the search results as an aid in legal research. COLR is analogous to litigation support. COLR is putting together information that would have been buried in the results of the initial search. COLR comes after CALR, but before and during legal writing. In the technical sense, a database is a collection of information specially organized for rapid search and retrieval. Information is organized into defined categories known as *fields.* Variable items in the database, records, contain the categorical information for each item. While a computer can search for a desired record by searching for information in the record, the computer's awesome power is the ability to quickly sort records by a given field. Multiple sorts can be made of the records by different fields to organize the records by category in whatever priority is desired. As you search legal materials, you can enter the information you find into a database. The database will lead you to the discovery of additional information. The bigger the research project, the more it makes sense to build a database. One of the most common uses of a computer is for word processing, which includes the electronic display, correction, and revision of text before printing. Word processing can also improve legal research. Macros can automate portions of the legal research process. COLR varies greatly with the needs of the researcher. The bigger the research project, the more it makes sense to use word processing. Information on a computer can be copied, deleted, formatted, merged, moved, printed, reformatted, replaced, revised, searched, sorted, and spell checked, among other things. A few commercial COLR products exist. Anderson Publishing Co. sells a legal document creation system known as *Lawriter*. Jurisoft sells *FullAuthority* software that finds cites in a word-processing document and automatically builds a table of authorities.

REVIEW

Key Terms

Before proceeding, review the key terms listed below to be sure you understand each one. If necessary, read over the corresponding section of the chapter. When you are ready to test your understanding, answer the Review Questions.

CD-ROM
computer-organized legal research (COLR)
database
digest
fields
house organ
litigation support
macro
microfiche
microfilm
microforms
records
sort
synergistic
word processing

Questions for Review and Discussion

1. What major publications are available in microform?
2. Can you name a publication available on floppy disk?
3. What was the first major publication available on CD-ROM?
4. What is a synergistic effect?
5. How is COLR different from CALR?
6. How is COLR analogous to litigation support?
7. How does COLR put "new" information at a legal researcher's fingertips?
8. What are database fields?
9. What are the advantages of having information on computer?
10. Can you name a COLR product?

Activities

1. Learn to type (keyboard). The principal way COLR users enter data into a computer, both today and for the foreseeable future, is through a typewriter-like keyboard. The ability to type (keyboard) is one of the most useful skills you can have and a practical necessity for COLR.
2. Learn to use professional spreadsheet software, such as Lotus 1–2–3. Learn to set up a database and use the sort commands. Use your abilities to find out what you want to know.
3. Learn to use professional word-processing software like WordPerfect. Learn how to create "macros" to speed your way through your work.

PART SIX

RESEARCH STRATEGIES

CHAPTER 14 Legal Research Strategies

OUTLINE

14–1 Ready for Legal Research
- Get the Facts
- Analyze the Facts

14–2 Basic Search Strategy
- Select the Sovereign
- Search Mandatory "Statutory" Authority
- Search Mandatory Case Authority
- Search Persuasive Case Authority
- Search Persuasive Secondary Authority

14–3 Basic Search Procedure
- Find the Law
- Read the Law
- Review the Law
- Stop the Search

14–4 Comprehensive Search Strategy
- Background and Citations
- Quick Read and Outline
- Second Read and First Draft
- Review and Final Draft

14–5 Limited Search Strategies
- Instant Answers

14–6 Mastering Legal Research

COMMENTARY

Just as the Judiciary Committee's work is winding down and it appears that the judge will be confirmed, a crisis occurs. A law professor has come forward to allege that the judge sexually harassed her 10 years ago when they worked together at a federal agency. The judge vehemently denies the allegation. The senator asks you to find out absolutely everything you can about the law of sexual harassment, for obvious reasons.

OBJECTIVES

In this chapter you will learn to organize your knowledge of Chapters 1 to 13 into effective legal research strategies. Emphasis is placed on the basic strategy of searching mandatory "statutory" authority, mandatory case authority, persuasive case authority, and persuasive secondary authority. After reading this chapter you should be able to:

1. Outline the materials used in legal research.
2. Recognize the importance of getting the facts.

3. Develop appropriate entry terms.
4. Describe search strategy.
5. Describe search methods.
6. Read and analyze the results of a search.
7. Stop a search when it is reasonably complete.
8. Perform a comprehensive search.
9. Perform a limited search.
10. Master legal research.

14–1 Ready for Legal Research

If you have read and studied this book through Chapter 13, you are ready to do legal research. Like Daniel in the movie *The Karate Kid,* you've learned all the fundamentals, even if you don't realize it yet.

This book develops the subject of legal research from a **bibliographic** approach, emphasizing detailed descriptions of the various books used. When bibliographic books describe a particular book among others, they explain the purpose of the book: why it exists. When you know the purpose of the book, you ought to know *when* to use it: for its purpose. When bibliographic books describe a particular book, they explain the structure of the book: how it is organized. When you know the structure of the book, you ought to know *how* to use it: by its structure.

By now you've acquired a good deal of background knowledge and insight. You've experienced the jargon of legal research in context. You've developed an understanding of the purpose and structure of law books and other media. You've also seen the limitations of law books and other media, a valuable "negative image," a warning of dangers and pitfalls, bringing the positive image, the true purpose and structure, into sharp focus. In this final chapter, you get the benefit of experience: strategies with which to apply the tactics already learned.

Take a moment to consider, to outline, all the tactics available to you in achieving your goal of finding a case (or other law) like yours where the person like you won. Billions of dollars, centuries of human effort, and waves of technology have combined to create a vast array of law books and other media that you can use. The law of the United States is probably the most recorded, organized, and analyzed body of knowledge in the world.

Researching federal law? All the primary sources are covered. The Constitution of the United States, the statutes of Congress, and court rules can be located in U.S.C.A., U.S.C.S., and other sources. Administrative regulations can be located in the *Federal Register,* C.F.R., and other sources. Supreme Court opinions can be located in U.S., L. Ed. & L. Ed. 2d, S. Ct., and other sources. Lower court opinions are located in F.2d, F. Supp., and other sources. Need help? Consider all the secondary sources. To get an overview, read Am. Jur. 2d, C.J.S., treatises, and other sources. To find more cases, use federal digests, A.L.R. Fed., and other sources. And whatever you do, don't forget looseleaf services, form books, law reviews, *Shepard's,* Auto-Cite, Insta-Cite, LEXIS, WESTLAW, and other sources.

Researching state law? There is a similar array: state codes, state administrative codes, official state reporters, National Reporter System regional reporters, state digests, A.L.R., and other sources.

As a legal researcher you can "stand on the shoulders" of judges, justices, lawyers, and law professors, and all other legal writers, authors, and editors in order to find a case (or other law) like yours where the person like you won to use to win your case.

Get the Facts

Of course, your vast knowledge of legal research sources is useless if you don't know what you are looking for. As the old saying goes, "If you don't know where you are going, any road will take you there." If you are doing legal research and suddenly don't know what to do next, there is a good chance you forgot what you were looking for. Refresh your memory and go on, renewed in the understanding that a necessary part of legal research is to gather the facts about the case you are researching, both before you begin and as needed along the way.

Analyze the Facts

After you have gathered the facts (or have been given the facts as an assignment), you must analyze them. You must identify the legal issues that need to be researched and the relative importance of each issue. You must come up with the terms you will use as entry points in digests, indexes, and tables of contents, or in a computer word search.

Your ability to analyze the facts will increase with experience. The more law you know and the more familiar you become with law books and other media, the easier it will be to identify the legal issues that need to be researched and their relative importance, along with appropriate terms to use as entry points.

One well-known rule of thumb for analyzing fact patterns, and for generating entry terms, is the "TAPP Rule" used by indexers at the Lawyers Cooperative Publishing Company (LCP). The **TAPP Rule** is that legal researchers should be able find the law they are looking for by looking up terms representing the thing, act, person, or place involved in the case. For example, if an automobile is damaged when it hits a hole in a parking lot, a researcher should be able to find the relevant law by looking up things like "automobile" or "vehicle," acts like "maintenance" or "negligence," persons like "driver" or "property owner," and places like "parking lot" or even "hole."

There are several similar rules of thumb. Writing in J. Myron Jacobstein and Roy M. Mersky's *Fundamentals of Legal Research,* 5th ed. (Westbury, NY: Foundation Press, 1990), on page 16, Steven M. Barkan suggests the "TARP Rule," consisting of the "*Thing* or subject matter," the "Cause of *action* or ground of defense," the "*Relief* sought," and the "*Persons* or *parties* involved." Forgoing a catchy acronym, West Publishing Company (West) in its *West's Law Finder* (1991), on p. 18, and its *Sample Pages,* 3rd ed. (1986), on pp. vii–viii, suggests the following analysis: "Parties," "Places and Things," "Basis of Action or Issue," "Defense," and "Relief Sought."

The types of legal issues that arise, and their relative importance, generally mirror the litigation process. Does the court have jurisdiction? Has the statute of limitations run? Have all other procedural requirements been met? Does the plaintiff have a sound theory on which to sue? Does the defendant have a sound defense? Were the rules of evidence followed at trial? What relief is appropriate?

Many researchers find it useful to write out each issue they are researching in a complete sentence.

In collecting appropriate entry terms for a search in a variety of sources, consider synonyms and near synonyms (e.g., apartment, dwelling, home, homestead, house, residence, unit), understanding that your issue may be organized and indexed differently in different sources. William P. Statsky, in his *Legal Research and Writing: Some Starting Points,* 3rd ed. (St. Paul, MN: West

Publishing Co., 1986), on pp. 98–101, recommends the routine word-associating of each major term you identify around a "cartwheel" of broader terms, narrower terms, synonyms, antonyms, "closely related terms," procedural terms, agencies and courts, and "long shots."

When the facts and issues are reasonably clear, and appropriate entry terms have come to mind, you are ready to find the law.

14–2 Basic Search Strategy

The basic legal research strategy for each issue has five overlapping phases or steps: (1) select the sovereign, (2) search mandatory "statutory" authority ("statutes in the sovereign"), (3) search mandatory case authority ("cases in the sovereign"), (4) search persuasive case authority ("cases in other sovereigns"), and (5) search persuasive secondary authority. (See Figure 14–1.)

Select the Sovereign

The first step is to determine whether the issue is a matter of federal law or state law, and if of state law, of what state.

Because law is the command of a sovereign, you must first select the appropriate sovereign's law to search. And as a practical matter, most law books cover either federal law or state law, or the law of a particular state. By selecting the appropriate sovereign's law to search, you avoid the mistake of searching another sovereign's law as mandatory authority.

Determining whether the issue is a matter of federal law or of state law is not always easy. Indeed, some issues may involve both federal law and state law.

Figure 14–1 Basic Search Strategy

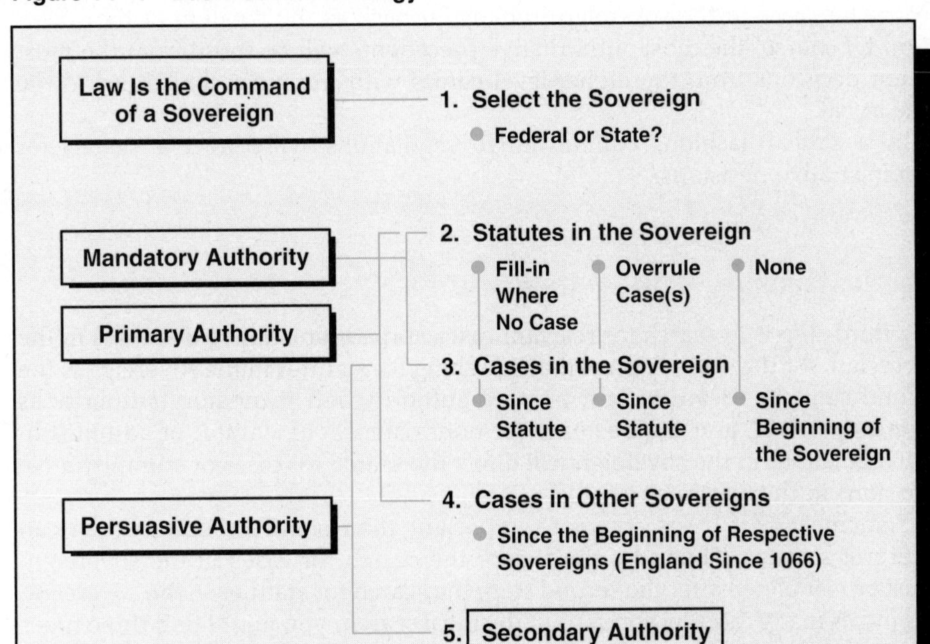

With experience, you will develop the knack of recognizing which is which.

In general, federal law is law that relates to the Constitution of the United States, the federal government, or the powers granted to Congress in Article I, Section 8. State laws cover everything else. One twist is that the Constitution of the United States and the decisions of the U.S. Supreme Court interpreting the Constitution of the United States are, via the supremacy clause, mandatory authority for the states. When in doubt, search both federal law and state law.

Search Mandatory "Statutory" Authority

The second step is to search for relevant constitutional provisions, statutes, administrative regulations, and court rules in the appropriate sovereign, and any relevant federal treaties. Unless your issue is of constitutional import, involves a court rule, or is affected by a treaty, as a practical matter you need search only for statutes in the sovereign. An enabling statute, or a cross-reference in an annotated code, should indicate the existence of any relevant administrative regulations. If you expect to find constitutional provisions, court rules, treaties, or administrative regulations, search for them.

There are at least three reasons why searching for statutes in the sovereign is the second step: (1) you want to find primary authority—the law itself—as soon as possible; (2) you want to find mandatory authority—the law that must be followed within the sovereign—as soon as possible; and (3) the existence (or nonexistence) of statutes on your issue will direct the next step: the search for cases in the sovereign.

Remember that statutes are usually enacted either to fill in where there is no case precedent or to overrule existing case precedent. If the statute fills in where there was no case precedent, you only need to search for cases in the sovereign from the date of the statute (obviously). Likewise, if the statute overruled existing case precedent, you know that precedent is bad law, and, again, you only need to search for cases in the sovereign from the date of the statute. Moreover, if there is a statute in the sovereign, the case summaries in an annotated code will help you to find relevant cases in the sovereign from the date of the statute. If there is no statute in the sovereign, you know you must search for cases in the sovereign from as far back as the creation of the sovereign. Of course, the most authoritative precedents will be those from the most recent decisions from the higher-level courts with the most similarities to the case at bar.

In a similar fashion, administrative regulations will direct a search for administrative decisions.

Search Mandatory Case Authority

The third step is to search for relevant cases and administrative decisions in the sovereign, for the same reasons that searching for statutes in the sovereign is the second step. You want to find primary authority and mandatory authority as soon as possible, and the existence (or nonexistence) of statutes or administrative regulations in the sovereign will direct the search for cases or administrative decisions in the sovereign.

Remember that cases are more important than statutes because they can interpret statutes. Thus, the third step, the search for cases in the sovereign, must be completed after the second step, the search for statutes in the sovereign.

Find as many cases as you can. In the ideal search, you might find three types of cases to cite in support of your case: the landmark case, the leading case, and the local case. The **landmark case** is the first significant case, often the case of first impression for your issue, decided in your favor. The **leading case,** which may also be the landmark case, is the case opinion that reads like an A.L.R. annotation or treatise, laying out all the precedent on your issue, pro and con, and deciding in your favor. The **local case** is the most recent case from your local jurisdiction decided in your favor, pointing out that your local jurisdiction follows the precedent established by the landmark case and reaffirmed by the leading case.

The third step, the search for cases in the sovereign, completes the search for mandatory authority. Remember that *dicta,* dissenting opinions, and precedent from equal or lower courts are not mandatory authority, but may be considered persuasive authority. Thus, insofar as the third step—the search for cases in the sovereign—discovers *dicta,* dissenting opinions, and precedent from equal or lower courts, it begins the fourth step, the search for persuasive case authority.

Search Persuasive Case Authority

If sufficient authority has not been found after the third step, the fourth step is to search for the remaining persuasive primary authority: the common law at large. The fourth step is to search for relevant cases in other jurisdictions and sovereigns that trace their origin to the Norman Conquest in 1066, as far back as the creation of that other sovereign, or, in the case of English law, as far back as the Norman Conquest in 1066. The most authoritative precedents will be those from the most recent cases from the higher-level courts with the most similarities to the case at bar.

Remember that statutes in other sovereigns are not considered persuasive authority because other sovereigns' legislatures can "dream up" whatever law they want. However, the existence of similar statutes in other sovereigns may support a policy argument based on the existence of a nationwide pattern or a trend.

The fourth step, the search for cases in the other sovereigns, completes the search for primary authority.

Search Persuasive Secondary Authority

If sufficient authority has not been found after the fourth step, the fifth step is to search for the remaining persuasive authority: secondary authority. Among secondary authorities, the most authoritative are well-reasoned law review articles and treatises, but, by definition, a court may be persuaded by other persuasive secondary authorities as well. For example, A.L.R.'s claim to fame is as the nation's most-cited law book (not simply a reporter). Nonlegal texts may also be cited. In fact, when courts decide a case of first impression, they may cite almost anything that supports their decision.

14–3 Basic Search Procedure

The basic legal research procedure is to find the law, read the law, review the law, and stop the search.

Find the Law

The most stressful task of a legal researcher is to go into the library (or get on-line) and, under time pressure, actually find the law desired in books and other media, based on the basic legal research strategy.

There are four basic methods of finding the law in a particular law book or in law books generally: the topic method, the case method, the statute method, and the index method. (See Figure 14–2.) The use of these methods requires cleverness, creativity, and patience.

The **topic method** can be used if you know the topic you want to search. It involves a search of the law book's table of contents, if any, and going to all references. In addition, scan the text for your topic. The "known topic" method is best used by experienced researchers who are confident they know exactly what they are looking for.

A basic strategy search using the topic method begins with the selection of the appropriate title and section of the sovereign's annotated code to check for statutes in the sovereign and to pick up cases from the case summaries. Cases are found by selecting the appropriate topics in the appropriate digest and using the A.L.R. Digest method of locating A.L.R. annotations.

Using CALR, the topic method allows the user to search a specialized database. Using LEXIS, A.L.R. annotations can be searched by topic, by searching A.L.R. titles and scope sections. Using WESTLAW, specific West digest Topics and Key Numbers can be searched.

The **case method** can be used if you know at least one case like yours (e.g., it is cited in your opponent's brief) and you want to search for more. This method involves a search of the law book's table of cases, if any, and going to the references. If you know only the popular name of the case, use a table of cases by popular names to convert it to a citation or search the name by CALR. Knowing the importance of cases in U.S. law, the "known case" method is a favorite of professional researchers.

A basic strategy search using the case method begins by checking the statutes cited in the case and in the sovereign's annotated code, and picking up cases from the case summaries. Cases can be found by picking up digest Topics and Key Numbers from the headnotes for the case and using Auto-Cite to locate A.L.R. annotations. And, of course, looking for cases from a case cite just "cries out" for shepardizing the case, using *Shepard's* as an imperfect case finder.

Using CALR, the case method allows the user to use *Shepard's* electronically or to use the CALR system as a citator. Using LEXIS, A.L.R. annotations can be searched by finding the case within an annotation. Using WESTLAW, Shepard's Preview can also be searched.

The **statute method** can be used if you know at least one statute like yours (e.g., it is cited in your opponent's brief) and you want to search for more law. This method involves a search of the law book's code finding table, if any, and going to the references. If you know only the popular name of the statute, use a table of statutes by popular names to convert it to a citation or search the name by CALR. Remember that many annotated codes give cross-references to related statutes within the sovereign and to comparative statutes from other sovereigns.

A basic strategy search using the statute method begins with a check of the statute in the sovereign's annotated code. Cases can be found by picking up the case summaries for the statute. If available for the sovereign's statutes, you can also shepardize the statute, using *Shepard's* as an imperfect case finder.

Using CALR, the statute method calls for the use of the CALR system as a citator.

The **index method** involves using your entry terms to search the law book's index, if any, and going to the references. If there is no index, use your entry terms to search the law book's table of contents, if any, and go to all references.

Figure 14–2 Methods of Finding the Law

	TOPIC METHOD (Table of Contents)	**CASE METHOD** (Known Relevant Case)	**STATUTE METHOD** (Known Relevant Statute)	**INDEX METHOD** (Entry Terms)
Statutes via Codes	Search appropriate title and contents	Search statutes cited in the case	Search the known relevant statute	Search the indexes
Cases via Digests	Search appropriate Topic from Outline	Search Topics and Key Numbers in the case	Search appropriate Topic from Outline	Search Descriptive Word Indexes
Cases via A.L.R.	Search A.L.R. digests	Auto-Cite on LEXIS or annotation (if any) following case in A.L.R.	Use code finding table for U.S.C., and search A.L.R. Digests	Search *Index to Annotations* and *A.L.R. First Series Quick Index*
Cases via *Shepard's*		Shepardize the case using *Shepard's* as an imperfect case finder	Shepardize the statute (if available) as an imperfect case finder	
Cases via LEXIS	Search specialized database and A.L.R. by title and scope	Shepardize, and use LEXIS as a citator, including for A.L.R.	Use LEXIS as a citator	Word search (including A.L.R.)
Cases via WESTLAW	Search specialized database and West Topics and Key Numbers	Shepardize, Shepard's Preview, Quick-Cite, and WESTLAW as a citator	Use Quick-Cite, and WESTLAW as a citator	Word search (including West's case summaries)

When in doubt, or as a double check, always use the "descriptive word or fact"/index method.

A basic strategy search using the index method begins with a search of the indexes of the sovereign's annotated code to check for statutes in the sovereign and to pick up cases from the case summaries. Cases can be found by searching the descriptive word indexes in digests to find the appropriate Topics and Key

Numbers in the appropriate digest, and using the *Index to Annotations* and *A.L.R First Series Quick Index* method of locating A.L.R. annotations.

Using CALR, the index method is the classic word search, allowing you to create your own index of the material searched. In addition to cases found by searching the full text of the opinions, LEXIS can pick up cases caught by A.L.R. annotations and WESTLAW can pick up cases caught by West's case summaries.

Of course, by now you realize that all of these methods overlap each other. In executing the basic strategy, you can use any method, or any combination of methods, to get the job done. Also remember that if one publisher's products aren't helping you in a given search, switch to the competitor's products. No law book is perfect, so you have to know the alternatives.

Read the Law

As a legal researcher, your most intellectual task comes after finding the law. You must carefully read and analyze *all* of the law you have found to determine just how relevant it is to your case. You must read the law both literally, as it is actually written, and figuratively, as it might be construed.

Every case you have found must be read in order to evaluate how similar it is to your case, including to what extent the case might be analogized to your case. Similarly, you must read every statute that you found to evaluate how similar each statute is to your case. This includes evaluating the extent of the legislature's intent in enacting the statute to include your case.

You must sort through all the law, noting anything that might be relevant and discarding the rest. If it's relevant, you must decide if it will help your case or hurt it, and to what degree. The ability to read and analyze the law "separates the contenders from the pretenders." Legal researchers extract gems from legal minds.

Review the Law

As discussed in Chapter 11, the powerful forces of human nature and time can deceive any legal researcher, no matter how experienced. The law that is found and read must also be reviewed to make sure that it is correct and up to date. New material generated by a review must also be found, read, and reviewed.

If a legal source has a supplement, such as a "developments" section, pamphlet, or pocket part, you must check it every time you use the source. Make it a habit. Check the supplement.

The importance of checking the supplement cannot be overstated. Legal research is required, in part, because the law changes. The main body or bound volume of a source may be several years out of date and overdue for replacement. The thicker the supplement, the greater the likelihood of disaster if you don't check it.

Often a researcher is looking for exactly what the supplement contains: the latest law on the subject. To impress students with the importance of checking the supplement, some legal research instructors give assignments in which every correct answer is found in the supplement.

As discussed in Chapter 11, the importance of reviewing cases cited in a memorandum or a brief—to make sure that the cases cited are not bad law—cannot be overstated. Use *Shepard's*, Auto-Cite, and Insta-Cite as much as possible. Don't let the person judging your work or your opponent catch a mistake that you should have caught. You should also check your opponent's work for mistakes that can be cited to your advantage.

Supplement in the Form of Pocket Part

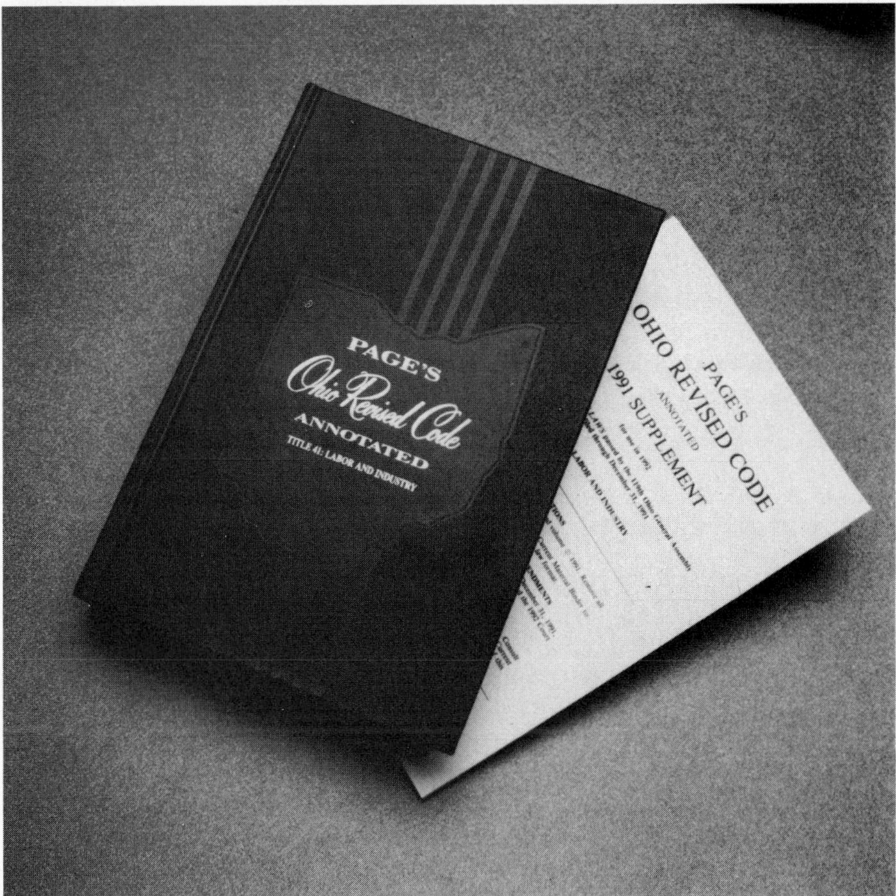

Source: © Doug Martin.

Stop the Search

A question that often arises in legal research is when to stop. "When you are done" is not always a satisfactory answer because it can be hard to know when you're done. Sometimes you search, but you can't find what you're looking for. Is it because what you're looking for isn't there or because you couldn't find it?

The practical answer is that legal research takes time, and time is money. At some point, you can't afford *not* to stop. There is no sense in doing $1,000 worth of research on a $500 case. In a world in which the typical personal injury lawyer collects a contingent fee of 33% of the money recovered, in one out of two cases of equal earning potential, the lawyer who wants to pay bills and make a profit *cannot possibly* afford legal research costing more than 16.5% of the money expected to be recovered. The practical limit, reduced by the lawyer's bills and profit, is much less.

Nevertheless, you must be wary of seizing on the first thing that meets your expectations. You have to learn how to be patient and objective, and strong enough to accept bad news, if that is what you find. When in doubt about stopping your search, don't. But if your search has become repetitive, such that you are merely going in circles, then stop.

Maybe the best answer is to think of yourself as the legal detective you are. You search through law books and other media for clues that will lead you to the answer to your problem. As you collect clues, you should progress toward the answer to your problem. You must believe that after a thorough search, the clues will shed light on, and focus on, a suspect. If a suspect is in sight, continue the search. If no suspect is in sight, stop the search.

14–4 Comprehensive Search Strategy

On occasion, situations arise where money is no object. A life or lifestyle is on the line, and for whatever reason, fame (e.g., the Supreme Court has granted *certiorari*) or fortune (e.g., the client is rich) allows you to make an **exhaustive search,** a search through every source. This section briefly discusses a strategy to use when you are asked to find out everything you can about a given topic.

Background and Citations

Begin by preparing a legal pad (or a COLR system) to keep a record of your search. The record fields should include "source," "other source," "other source searched," and "case cites." (See Figure 14–3.)

Begin by searching secondary sources for background information and for every apparently relevant cite. You can start anywhere. Record every source you search in the "source" field. If that source refers to another secondary source, record that other source in the "other source" field. When the source cites

Figure 14–3 Search Record

Source	Other Source	Other Source Searched	Case Cites

primary authority other than cases, also record that other source's cite in the "other source" field. Whenever the source cites a case, record the cite in the "case cites" field.

Work your way through every secondary source available to you. If there are competitive sources on the same topic (e.g., an Am. Jur. 2d article and a C.J.S. article), search *both*. It may seem redundant, and to a large extent it will be, but you want to make sure you capture all the other sources and case cites uniquely found in each source. As you are searching, make sure that you have searched every "other source" as a source, by checking off every "other source" in the appropriate "other source searched" field.

Continue by searching every available noncase primary source as a source, checking off each "other source" as appropriate. Eventually you will have searched every secondary source and every noncase primary source. Moreover, you can be confident that you searched every noncase source because you checked off every noncase source cited by a secondary source or a noncase primary source.

Having read all the secondary sources and noncase primary sources relevant to your problem, you will be well prepared to read and understand the most important law: the cases. You will also have a very long list of case cites.

Before reading the apparently relevant cases, you must process your list of case cites. Go through the list (or have your COLR system go through the list) and eliminate all the duplicate cites. Sort (or have your COLR system sort) the cites chronologically by court level and jurisdiction.

"Chronologically by court level" means, for example, that the first federal case cite will be for the oldest U.S. Supreme Court case, followed by the next-oldest case, and so on, down to the most recent case. Next is the oldest court of appeals case, the next-oldest, and so on, followed by district court cases. By "jurisdiction" means, for example, that all the First Circuit cases are grouped together, followed by all the Second Circuit cases, and so on.

Reading cases by court level, like searching statutes before cases, will save you time and effort. If, on a particular issue, a higher court has reversed a lower court, you know that the lower court precedent on that issue is bad law. And even if the higher court has affirmed the lower court, the higher court's opinion is more authoritative than the lower court's. If the higher court's opinion is more comprehensive than the lower court's opinion, it may not even be necessary to read the lower court's opinion. Of course, if the lower court has decided an issue or has provided information not touched on by the higher court, the lower court's opinion is authoritative and must be read.

The cases are read chronologically by jurisdiction to easily capture and understand the historical development of the law in each jurisdiction. Some researchers read the cases in reverse chronological order to catch when courts reverse themselves, but that advantage is outweighed by having a historical understanding of the reversal.

Quick Read and Outline

After your list of case cites is processed, quickly skim through all the cases, understanding that your list of cites is just a list of apparently relevant cases. As you skim through the cases, you will find that many are irrelevant to your problem. Quickly note them for what they are worth and discard them. For each case relevant to your problem, quickly record the reasons why on your list (or on your COLR system).

When you have completed your quick read of the cases, you will have a complete record of every case relevant to your problem and why. Sort the whys, and you can make a good tentative outline of what you have found for a memorandum or brief. Do so.

Second Read and First Draft

With your case list and outline in hand, read the relevant cases again, slowly and carefully, looking for every nuance in every detail, to extract the gems. Sift and sort and analyze, as you write down what you have found in your first draft, according to your outline.

Part of the genius of this strategy is that as you carefully read the cases, you can check (or use your COLR system to check) if you've found everything cited in each and every case. You'll discover that cases frequently cite law that was not found, and could not be found, in any other source. The unsupported claim of first-year law school professors turns out to be true: *the law is in the cases.* That's why you should research everything you find in a case.

Review and Final Draft

After the second reading you will have a complete first draft according to your tentative outline. Review it, revise it, and put it in proper form, and you will have your final draft. Both your legal research and your legal writing will be complete.

14–5 Limited Search Strategies

Most legal research—everyday legal research—is a limited quick search for specific information. The search strategy is simple and obvious. Search the appropriate sources for the appropriate information.

Examples of quick searches could be given endlessly. Looking for the text of U.S. Supreme Court case *Roe v. Wade?* You could use the L. Ed. Digest's Table of Cases to find the L. Ed. 2d cite, and use L. Ed. 2d to look up the case. Want to find out, for federal tax purposes, when the meals provided by an employer can be excluded from the employee's income? You could search the index for Title 26 of U.S.C.A., or a looseleaf federal tax service, for the appropriate code section. What days are legal holidays in your state? Use the index to your state's statutory code to find the appropriate code section, and look it up. How has a given word or phrase been legally defined? Examine West's *Words and Phrases,* and so on.

Instant Answers

In a crunch, reasonably reliable answers can be found by quickly searching secondary sources, and perhaps using CALR. Well-written A.L.R. annotations, encyclopedias, treatises, and law review articles can be reasonably reliable sources.

For example, if you want to know why Congress created the U.S. Court of Veterans Appeals (see 38 U.S.C. § 4051 et seq.) in 1988, you might guess that there was a law review article written about it somewhere. A search of LegalTrac under the topic "Veterans" would quickly lead you to several articles, including an excellent article by the Chair of the Veterans' Law Committee of the Federal Bar Association, Barton F. Stichman. [Barton F. Stichman, *The Veterans' Judicial Review Act of 1988: Congress Introduces Courts and Attorneys to Veterans' Benefits Proceedings*, 41 Admin. L. Rev. 365 (1989).]

Of course, the danger in making quick searches for instant answers is that it can become a sloppy habit, leading to malpractice. Beware of people who quote from legal encyclopedias without any supporting cases. Don't forget the difference between primary authority and secondary authority.

14–6 Mastering Legal Research

Many students are surprised to discover that legal research is a skill. Like any other skill, it can be mastered with knowledge and disciplined self-critical practice. The old story about the man who asked a conductor for directions to Carnegie Hall, but was mistaken for a promising young musician, applies here. "How do you get to Carnegie Hall?" he asked. The answer: "Practice, practice, practice."

You cannot earn a black belt in legal research. No matter what you have done in your life, someone will question your credentials. The only real reward is self-satisfaction. Only you will know when you have mastered legal research.

You have mastered legal research when you walk into a law library and take the right book off the shelf without even thinking about it.

You have mastered legal research when, if you are right-handed, you automatically take a book off the shelf with your left hand, so you can flip the pages with your right hand, or vice versa.

You have mastered legal research when you are comfortable with every legal source and can give each the credit, and the criticism, due.

You have mastered legal research when you are comfortable with every strategy and method of legal research and can use whatever strategy and method, or combination of strategies and methods, appropriate to get the job done.

You have mastered legal research when you can find whatever you are looking for, unless it's not there. If it's not there, you have mastered legal research when you have the confidence to say, "I have looked, and it's not there."

In short, you have mastered legal research when you have mastered the *art* of legal research.

As the captain told his crew in the movie *Away All Boats:* "Good luck, and good hunting."

Source: Reprinted with special permission of King Features Syndicate.

SUMMARY

14–1

If you have read and studied this book through Chapter 13, you are ready to do legal research. By this final chapter, you are given the benefit of experience: strategies with which to apply the tactics already learned. As a legal researcher, you can "stand on the shoulders" of justices, judges, lawyers, and law professors, and all other legal writers, authors, and editors, to find a case (or other law) like yours where the person like you won. Of course, your vast knowledge of legal research sources is useless if you don't know what you are looking for. If you are doing legal research and suddenly don't know what to do next, there is a good chance you forgot what you were looking for. After you have gathered the facts (or have been given the facts as an assignment), you must analyze them. You must identify the legal issues that need to be researched and the relative importance of each issue. You must come up with the terms you will use as entry points in digests, indexes, and tables of contents, or in a computer word search. The types of legal issues that arise, and their relative importance, generally mirror the litigation process. When the facts and issues are reasonably clear, and appropriate entry terms have come to mind, you are ready to find the law.

14–2

The basic legal research strategy for each issue has five overlapping phases or steps: (1) select the sovereign, (2) search mandatory "statutory" authority ("statutes in the sovereign"), (3) search mandatory case authority ("cases in the sovereign"), (4) search persuasive case authority ("cases in other sovereigns"), and (5) search persuasive secondary authority. The first step is to determine whether the issue is a matter of federal law or state law, and if of state law, of what state. One twist is that the Constitution of the United States and the decisions of the U.S. Supreme Court interpreting the Constitution of the United States are, via the supremacy clause, mandatory authority for the states. The second step is to search for relevant constitutional provisions, statutes, administrative regulations, and court rules in the appropriate sovereign, and any relevant federal treaties. There are three reasons why searching for statutes in the sovereign is the second step: (1) you want to find primary authority; (2) you want to find mandatory authority; and (3) the existence (or nonexistence) of statutes on your issue will direct the third step: the search for cases and administrative decisions in the sovereign. Find as many cases as you can, including landmark cases, leading cases, and local cases. Remember that *dicta*, dissenting opinions, and precedent from equal or lower courts are not mandatory authority, although they may be considered persuasive authority. If sufficient authority has not been found after the third step, the fourth step is to search for the remaining persuasive primary authority: relevant cases in other sovereigns that trace their origin to the Norman Conquest in 1066, as far back as the creation of that other sovereign, or, in the case of English law, as far back as the Norman Conquest in 1066. If sufficient authority has not been found after the fourth step, the fifth step is to search for the remaining persuasive authority: secondary authority.

14–3

The basic legal research procedure is to find the law, read the law, review the law, and stop the search. There are four basic methods of finding the law in a particular law book or in law books generally: the topic method, the case method, the statute method, and the index method. The topic method is used if you know the topic you want to search. It involves a search of the law book's table of contents, if any, and going to all references. The case method is used if you know at least one case like yours and you want to search for more. It involves a search of the law book's table of cases, if any, and going to the references. The statute method is used if you know at least one statute like yours and you want to search for more law. It involves a search of the law book's code finding table, if any, and going to the references. The index method involves using your entry terms to search the law book's index, if any, and going to the references. When in doubt, or as a double check, always use the index method. Using CALR, the index method is the classic word search. It allows you to create your own index of the material searched. In executing the basic strategy, you, as a legal researcher, can use any method, or any combination of methods, to get the job done. The law found must be carefully read and analyzed. You must sort through all the law, noting anything that might be relevant, and discard the rest. Legal researchers extract gems from legal minds. The law that is found and read must also be reviewed to make sure that it is correct and up to date. New material generated by a review must also be found, read, and reviewed. The importance of checking the supplement and of reviewing cites in a memorandum or brief to make sure that the cases cited are not bad law cannot be overstated. Stop when you are done, understanding that at some point, you can't afford not to stop. Nevertheless, you must be wary of seizing on the first thing that meets your expectations. Think of yourself as the legal detective that you are. As you collect clues, you should progress toward the answer to your problem. If a suspect is in sight, continue the search. If no suspect is in sight, stop the search.

14–4

On occasion, situations will arise allowing you to make an exhaustive search. Begin by searching secondary sources for background information and for every apparently relevant cite. Record every source you search. If that source refers to another secondary source, record that other source. When the source cites primary authority other than cases, also record that. Whenever the source cites a case, record the cite. Work your way through every available secondary source and noncase primary source as a source, checking off each "other source" as appropriate. Before reading the apparently relevant cases, eliminate all the duplicate cites and sort the remaining cites chronologically by court level and by jurisdiction. Quickly skim through all the cases. You will find that many are irrelevant to your problem. Quickly note them for what they are worth and discard them. For each case relevant to your problem, quickly record the reasons why. When you have completed your quick read of the cases, sort the whys, and make a tentative outline of what you have found. With your case list and outline in hand, read the relevant cases again, slowly and carefully, looking for every nuance in every detail, to extract the gems. Sift and sort and analyze, as you write down what you have found in your first draft, according to your outline. You'll discover that cases frequently cite law that couldn't be found in any other source; that the law is in the cases. Review your first draft, revise it as necessary, and you will have your final draft.

14–5

Most legal research—everyday legal research—is a limited quick search for specific information. The search strategy is simple and obvious. Search the appropriate sources for the appropriate information. In a crunch, reasonably reliable answers can be found by quickly searching secondary sources. The danger in making quick searches for instant answers is that it can become a sloppy habit, leading to malpractice. Don't forget the difference between primary authority and secondary authority.

14–6

Legal research is skill that can be mastered with knowledge and disciplined self-critical practice. You have mastered legal research when you walk into a law library and take the right book off the shelf without even thinking about it; when you are comfortable with every legal source; and when you are comfortable with every strategy and every method of legal research. You have mastered legal research when you can find whatever you are looking for, unless it's not there and you have the confidence to say, "I have looked, and it's not there." You have mastered legal research when you have mastered the *art* of legal research.

REVIEW

Key Terms

Before proceeding, review the key terms listed below to be sure you understand each one. If necessary, read over the corresponding section of the chapter. When you are ready to test your understanding, answer the Review Questions.

bibliographic
case method
exhaustive search
index method
landmark case
leading case
local case
statute method
TAPP Rule
topic method

Questions for Review and Discussion

1. What are the principal sources of federal case law?
2. What can happen if you do legal research before you have all the facts?
3. What is the importance of the "TAPP Rule" and other similar rules of thumb?
4. What should you search first, cases or statutes? Why?
5. What methods can you use to find the law in law books?
6. How should the results of a search be read and analyzed?
7. When should you stop a search?
8. How do you make a comprehensive search?
9. What danger is there in making a limited search?
10. How do you know when you have mastered legal research?

Activities

1. Practice. Make legal research a habit. Whenever you catch yourself saying, "I wonder," find out the answer.
2. As a matter of professional curiosity, compare and contrast other books on legal research. Look for mistakes. Look for faulty organization. Look for bias and prejudice. Decide which authors have thoroughly thought through the process of legal research, and follow their advice.
3. Share your knowledge of legal research with others. Extract their gems and discard their mistakes. Never stop learning.

SECTION II

BASIC

LEGAL WRITING

CHAPTER 1 The American Legal System

OUTLINE

1–1 The Sources of American Law
- Constitutional Law
- Common Law
- Statutory Law
- Administrative Law

1–2 Classifications of the Law
- Civil Law
- Criminal Law
- Procedural Law
- Substantive Law

1–3 The Court System
- Jurisdiction
- Federal Court System
- State Court Systems

1–4 Practical Considerations

COMMENTARY

You have just reviewed a case presented to your attorney. The case involves a claim by a man who allegedly has been discriminated against because of his age. You believe that this case involves a constitutionally protected right. Your attorney wants to know whether this is a federal or state court case. The court in which the case will be judged depends upon the nature of the claim. Knowing what law applies and which is the appropriate court under our legal system is important in the evaluation of cases presented. Understanding the interworkings of the American court system is fundamental.

OBJECTIVES

In Chapter 1 you will learn about the structure of the American legal system. After completing this chapter, you will be able to:

1. Distinguish between the four sources of American law.
2. Differentiate between civil law and criminal law.
3. Distinguish between legal and equitable remedies.
4. Explain how procedural law differs from substantive law.
5. Recognize the differences in levels of court jurisdiction.
6. Outline the structure of the federal court system.
7. Outline the structure of the state court system.
8. Recognize the initial steps that a paralegal must take when presented with a new case.

1–1 The Sources of American Law

Although the Constitution of the United States is the supreme law of the land, it is only one of many sources of American law. In addition to the Constitution, American law comprises common law, statutes, and administrative rules and regulations.

Constitutional Law

The law that interprets the Constitution of the United States and enforces rights under the Constitution is classified as **Constitutional law.** All issues relating to the Articles to the Constitution and the subsequent amendments form the basis for judicial examination of the Constitution. The judicial branch and, more specifically under Article III, the Supreme Court are vested with judicial power under the Constitution. Article III provides in part:

> Section 1. The judicial power of the United States shall be vested in one Supreme Court, and in such inferior courts as the Congress may from time to time ordain and establish.

No other branch of government has the power to review the Constitution or other laws of the federal and state governments. This is known as the doctrine of **judicial review.** The power of judicial review was established in the landmark case of *Marbury v. Madison,* 5 U.S. (1 Cranch) 137 (1803), wherein the Supreme Court established the power of the judicial branch of government to review actions and decisions made by the executive and legislative branches and to determine the constitutionality of those actions. The ability of a court to review the actions of the other branches of government is the heart of the American legal system and is instrumental to the development of its laws.

Common Law

The **common law** is that law created from the customs and habits of people when no written laws existed. Its development came about as judges examined disputes between parties and made decisions based upon what was customary in that place and what was believed to be fair and equitable. The only guidance that the judges had were the people and times themselves and the opinions of or decisions made by other judges in the past.

As the common law developed, so did the need to record the decisions being made. The recorded decisions are commonly referred to as **case law.** Case law developed from the strictures of the common law in England and is the system used by courts today. Since judges needed guidance in evaluating current situations based on previous decisions and the related legal principles, the doctrine of *stare decisis* and precedent emerged.

Stare Decisis According to the doctrine of ***stare decisis*** ("let the decision stand"), once a court has set down a legal principle applicable to a certain set of facts, judges will follow that principle in future cases, when the facts are the same or substantially similar. The doctrine establishes stability and consistency in our legal system, for without the doctrine of *stare decisis,* the system would be chaotic and arbitrary. It is important to note that the doctrine of *stare decisis* is not carved in stone. As case law develops and changes, some decisions lose their controlling effect because of changing social values or amendments to statutes and constitutions.

Precedent Included under the principle of *stare decisis* is the concept of **precedent.** A precedent sets a legal standard that may be followed by a court in a situation in which similar facts pertain. Whether the decision is a binding or a persuasive precedent will depend upon the origin of a court decision. **Binding precedent** must be followed by a court, whereas **persuasive precedent** need not be followed by a court. Decisions from the highest court in Massachusetts on a certain legal principle would be binding on all lower courts of that state. However, a decision in Maine or any other state on an undecided legal principle in Massachusetts would only be persuasive in a Massachusetts court. The exception is that decisions from the U.S. Supreme Court are binding for all state and federal courts. A precedent acts as a legal guide in determining which law to apply to a client's problem. It sets the standards in our society, and it ensures a degree of fairness of judgment by our courts.

Statutory Law

Laws passed by a legislature to regulate the conduct of citizens are called **statutes.** Under the American legal system at the federal level, Congress passes statutes that are signed by the President of the United States. States can pass laws through their state legislatures to be signed by their respective governors. The laws passed must conform to the U.S. Constitution and that state's constitution, or they risk being declared void by the judicial branch. Laws passed by cities and towns are often called **ordinances** and are considered a form of statute. The laws passed by city, town, state, and federal governments create the body of law known as **statutory law.**

Uniform Laws The laws passed by the states pertain only to the specific state in which they were enacted. This may pose problems when statutes from different states have different solutions for the same problem. Because of the high degree of mobility in our society, confusion may arise among citizens because of the variation of statutes from one state to another. In response to this situation, legal scholars created ***uniform laws*** as a universal standard of law in certain subject areas. In 1891 the National Conference of Commissioners on Uniform State Laws was formed in response to the growing need for uniformity of jurisprudence in our states. The conference meets annually to propose uniform laws, which may be accepted or rejected by the state legislatures. Unless a uniform law is adopted by a state, it has no legal effect in a state. Many states adopt modified versions of the uniform laws. The most widely adopted uniform law is the *Uniform Commercial Code,* adopted in whole or in part in every state, as well as in Washington, D.C., and the Virgin Islands. Other examples of widely recognized uniform laws are the Uniform Partnership Act and the Uniform Child Custody Jurisdiction Act.

Administrative Law

In response to our government's growth and to the social programs of the New Deal Era, Congress and the Executive Branch expanded **administrative law** to administer governmental programs through agencies. An **agency** is a governmental entity that has the power to make rules, regulate conduct, and adjudicate violations of agency rules and regulations. Administrative law is unique in that, as a result of the delegation of power from the federal and state governments, agencies perform many functions of the three branches of government: Agencies may legislate by making rules and regulations, agencies may supervise compliance with the regulations by acting as an executive power, and agencies may render decisions the way a court does—through adjudication.

Since, in the early stages of development the agencies' power went virtually unchecked, Congress passed a statute in 1946 which set standards according to which agencies must act. The statute is called the Administrative Procedure Act, 5 U.S.C. §§ 551 *et seq.*, which is divided into four areas known as the Freedom of Information Act, the Privacy Act, the Governmental Sunshine Act, and the Regulatory Flexibility Act. The Administrative Procedure Act provides for public awareness of agency rule making, procedural safeguards in an agency, adjudication, and procedures for gaining agency information. Under the Administrative Procedure Act, agencies regulate and supervise the activities of federal agencies such as the Environmental Protection Agency and the Federal Aviation Association, subject to compliance with the U.S. Constitution.

Most states have administrative regulations which oversee their agencies through acts similar to the Administrative Procedure Act. Each state act is different and should be consulted for state-specific administrative laws. Typical state administrative agencies are a state's unemployment commission, its teachers' association, and its welfare agencies.

1–2 Classifications of the Law

Although some people believe that "law is what the judge says it is," a **law** is a binding rule of conduct prescribed by elected representatives the violation of which may lead to a punishment, a penalty, or a sanction. Also, law provides for legal remedies for violations of legal rights and establishes a system through which legal disputes may be resolved. Law can be divided into two distinct areas, civil law and criminal law, and it can be further divided into procedural law and substantive law.

Civil Law

The law that resolves disputes between parties is referred to as **civil law.** Civil law involves such areas as tort law, contract law, and property law. In civil law, an individual brings a legal action, called a **lawsuit,** to request compensation for the wrongful acts of another party. The compensation is commonly referred to as a remedy. A **remedy** is the compensation awarded, as the result of a lawsuit, to a party by the court for the wrongful act of another party. A remedy can be either a legal remedy or an equitable remedy. Typically, a **legal remedy** is compensation in the form of money. The awarding of money for the actual loss suffered by a party's wrongdoing is called **compensatory damages.** The underlying theory of compensatory damages is to make the aggrieved or "harmed" party whole again. The intended result of compensatory damages is to place the aggrieved party in as good a position as before the occurrence of the wrongdoing.

Another type of money damage is **nominal damages.** This is sometimes referred to as "token damages." Nominal damages are awarded when an injured party has not been able to prove the substantial damage claimed. With nominal damages, therefore, the wrongful act is acknowledged with minimal financial compensation.

When the court determines that the acts of the wrongdoer were done intentionally or maliciously, the court may award monetary damages in excess of the actual damages; these are known as **punitive damages** or **exemplary damages.** This type of damage award is used sparingly and only in extreme cases. Such damages are often regulated by statute.

Remedies based upon principles of fairness and justice are called **equitable remedies.** This type of remedy is given only when monetary damages are inadequate or cannot be determined by the court. One common equitable remedy is an **injunction,** which may order an individual to refrain from doing an act or may direct someone to perform an act. An example of a situation when an injunction may be requested is in a divorce case when one spouse is prevented from depleting the marital assets to the harm of the other spouse.

Another typical equitable remedy is **specific performance,** which is an order of the court to perform an act which had been contractually promised. Suppose that you have found the perfect house and you are about to complete the sale when the seller, for no valid reason, decides against the sale. The court could order the sale of the house and have the seller specifically perform on the contract, thereby forcing the performance of the agreement. Consequently, equity ensures fairness.

Criminal Law

The body of law that deals with wrongful acts committed by an individual against society is known as **criminal law.** Normally, our state and federal legislatures define criminal law and acts that violate society's standards. Crimes, therefore, are offenses committed by people for which society, through our legislatures, imposes a punishment that may take the form of imprisonment, fines, and in some instances, death. A crime may be classified as either a **misdemeanor** or a **felony.**

Misdemeanor Of the two types of crimes, the less serious ones are known as misdemeanors and are punishable by a fine or imprisonment, or both, for a period of time not to exceed one year. Examples of common misdemeanors are assault and battery, shoplifting, malicious mischief, public intoxication, and disorderly conduct.

Felony The more serious crime is a felony, which is punishable by a prison sentence of at least one year; in some states punishment may be as severe as the death penalty. Felonies include murder, arson, rape, and armed robbery. Whether a crime is deemed a misdemeanor or a felony will be based upon the character of the punishment under the statute imposing the punishment.

Criminal Statutes State legislatures have passed criminal codes that regulate the conduct of its citizens. These state codes determine which crimes will be misdemeanors or felonies and what the punishment for committing the offenses will be. Because all state statutes are different, an offense in one state may not be an offense in another. Table 1–1 gives examples of civil and criminal law.

Procedural Law

Lawyers are trained to know how to proceed with their cases. They must know when to bring a lawsuit, how to respond to a lawsuit, and against whom they should direct their lawsuit. What guides lawyers in practice is **procedural law.** Procedural law dictates the steps that must be followed in the litigation process. The guide for procedure in civil law is the Rules of Civil Procedure. The procedural rules used in the federal system are called the Federal Rules of Civil Procedure. These rules control the tenor of the lawsuit at the federal level. During the 1930s, a committee appointed by the U.S. Supreme Court developed the rules of procedure. Each state has its own rules of procedure as well. Although some states have different procedures, the most widely adapted rules of procedure are the Federal Rules of Civil Procedure. The companion to the Federal Rules of Civil Procedure is the Federal Rules of Criminal Procedure, which are the procedural rules used in criminal matters. As with the civil rules, states have adopted rules of criminal procedure to follow in criminal cases.

Substantive Law

In contrast to procedural law, which defines the process, **substantive law** establishes the rules that apply when the rights of parties have been violated. Substantive law regulates the conduct of parties and determines the legal consequences in light of this conduct. When one party breaks a contract or hits another party with a baseball bat, the law that will resolve the dispute is the substantive law. Substantive law characterizes the law and sets parameters for a society's conduct.

Table 1–1 Civil and Criminal Law

Civil Law	Criminal Law
Contract Law	**Misdemeanor Offenses**
Warranties	Assault
Sale of goods	Disorderly conduct
Specific performance	Loitering
Restitution	Public intoxication
Tort Law	**Felony Offenses**
Deceptive trade	Arson
Defamation	Burglary
Fraud	Homicide
Invasion of privacy	Larceny (grand)
Misrepresentation	Robbery
Negligence	
Trade secrets	
Property Law	
Landlord tenant	
Environmental	
Water rights	
Condominiums	

1–3 The Court System

A **court** is a legal forum in which disputes among individuals, business entities, and governments are resolved. It is also a forum within which the state prosecutes criminal law violators. Courts hear controversies and pronounce a result called a **decision** or a **judgment.** The judgment may be rendered by a judge or a jury. A court can hear only cases that it is empowered to hear through a grant of authority by either a constitution or a statute.

Jurisdiction

The authority of a court to hear and decide cases is called its **jurisdiction.** In order for a court to hear a case, it must have both personal jurisdiction and subject matter jurisdiction over the parties or property in the case. **Personal jurisdiction** is the court's authority to render a decision against parties within a geographical territory. Notwithstanding the Supreme Court, federal and state courts can hear lawsuits only between persons within their boundaries or within their designated jurisdictions. **Subject matter jurisdiction** is the authority of a court to hear a certain type of controversy. When a court has the power to decide issues between parties and to render a final decision, the court is said to have subject matter jurisdiction over the case. For example, a court may be able to hear only divorce cases and not criminal cases, probate cases, or tax cases. A court can decide only those cases for which it has jurisdiction and on topics which it has the power to hear.

Jurisdiction can be broken down into five additional categories. The power of a court to hear a case from the beginning of a lawsuit to the end of a trial is known as **original jurisdiction. General jurisdiction** is the court's authority to hear *all* types of controversies, both civil and criminal. In contrast, some courts are empowered to hear only certain controversies. When only one court can hear the controversy, the court has what is called **exclusive jurisdiction.** Courts may have limited authority to hear cases; this is known as **limited jurisdiction.** Usually a federal or state statute will carve out an area of restrictive authority for a court. Probate courts, juvenile courts, and bankruptcy courts are just a few courts that have limited jurisdiction in the cases that come before them.

It is important to recognize that a court may have limited jurisdiction but not exclusive jurisdiction. This suggests that more than one court can hear the same type of case. When two or more courts are empowered to hear the same type of controversy, they have **concurrent jurisdiction.** For example, a state court as well as a federal court may have the power to hear a case involving unfair labor practices. The attorney will choose the court for tactical reasons, even though both courts have the authority to hear the case.

The final type of jurisdiction is **appellate jurisdiction.** A court empowered to review an inferior court's decision for errors of law has appellate jurisdiction. Normally, when the losing party in the trial court requests an appeals court to examine the decision of the trial court, the losing party is doing what is called invoking the appeals court's appellate jurisdiction. In summary, under our legal system, a court must have the power to hear a case, decide the issues before it, and bind its decision on the parties involved.

Federal Court System

The federal court system is limited by the U.S. Constitution as to the cases that it can hear. A federal court can hear cases involving the Constitution, treaties, federal statutes, and controversies between citizens of different states. A federal question is one that usually deals exclusively with federal issues. Federal question jurisdiction may focus on antitrust, bankruptcy, or immigration issues.

Another type of federal jurisdiction, which involves conflicts between parties from different states or different countries, is called **diversity jurisdiction.** Diversity jurisdiction is quite different from federal question jurisdiction in that it involves disputes between citizens of different states or between citizens of a state and foreign citizens or governments. Diversity jurisdiction was delegated to federal courts on the theory that state courts might favor their own residents over nonresidents. Another reason for diversity jurisdiction is the inconvenience and hardship for the out-of-state party being sued. For diversity jurisdiction the citizens must be from different states and the amount in controversy must be over $50,000.

Unless federal courts have exclusive jurisdiction to hear a case, as in cases involving bankruptcy, federal antitrust violations, and federal criminal prosecutions, either a federal or a state court may hear the case.

There are three levels of courts in the federal court system: the trial court, the appellate court, and the U.S. Supreme Court. Under Article III of the U.S. Constitution, Congress is authorized to create such "inferior" courts as it deems necessary. With this grant of power, Congress established a trial court (U.S. District Court), an appeals court (U.S. Circuit Courts of Appeals), and the U.S. Supreme Court, the highest court in the land.

U.S. District Courts The lowest court level in the federal system is called the **Federal District Court,** or **U.S. District Court.** This is normally a party's initial forum for a lawsuit in federal court. Federal district courts are divided into judicial districts, each state having at least one U.S. District Court. Some states, such as New York and Texas, have four districts, whereas other states, such as Missouri and Indiana, have two.

Most federal cases begin in the U.S. District Court, which are courts of original jurisdiction. For a case to be filed in U.S. District Court, it must meet the filing prerequisites, such as a federal question or a diversity of jurisdiction. If these prerequisites cannot be met, the case does not qualify for filing in a federal court.

U.S. Courts of Appeals Under the federal court system, an intermediate court of review, known as the **U.S. Court of Appeals,** exists. The country is divided into thirteen courts of appeals, with the states grouped into geographical regions called **circuits.** The circuits usually contain at least three states; for example, the seventh circuit contains Indiana, Illinois, and Wisconsin. The tenth circuit has six states—Wyoming, Utah, Colorado, Kansas, New Mexico, and Oklahoma. The District of Columbia has its own appellate court, called the U.S. Court of Appeals for the District of Columbia. Table 1–2 provides a listing of the federal circuits.

The thirteenth circuit court has limited jurisdiction for federal appeals cases. This court hears cases from the Court of International Trade, the U.S. Claims Court, the International Trade Commission, and specialized administrative offices, such as patent and trademark offices, and is known as the U.S. Court of Appeals for the Federal Circuit.

U.S. Supreme Court The highest court under both the federal system and the state system is the **U.S. Supreme Court.** Created by our Constitution, this is the

Table 1–2 Federal Circuit Courts

First Circuit	Eighth Circuit
Maine	North Dakota
New Hampshire	South Dakota
Massachusetts	Nebraska
Rhode Island	Minnesota
Puerto Rico	Iowa
Second Circuit	Missouri
Vermont	Arkansas
New York	**Ninth Circuit**
Connecticut	Washington
Third Circuit	Oregon
New Jersey	California
Pennsylvania	Nevada
Delaware	Arizona
Virgin Islands	Idaho
Fourth Circuit	Montana
West Virginia	Alaska
Virginia	Hawaii
North Carolina	Northern Mariana Islands
South Carolina	Guam
Maryland	**Tenth Circuit**
Fifth Circuit	Wyoming
Texas	Utah
Louisiana	Colorado
Mississippi	Kansas
Sixth Circuit	New Mexico
Michigan	Oklahoma
Ohio	**Eleventh Circuit**
Kentucky	Alabama
Tennessee	Georgia
Seventh Circuit	Florida
Wisconsin	**Twelfth Circuit**
Illinois	Washington, D.C.
Indiana	**Thirteenth Circuit**
	Federal Washington, D.C.

court of last resort for federal courts and state supreme courts. The Constitution mandates that the Supreme Court hear cases involving our ambassadors, public ministers, or consuls and those in which a state is a party. The Supreme Court also hears conflicts between states. Article III of the Constitution sets out the powers of the Supreme Court.

The Supreme Court consists of nine justices, one of whom, the Chief Justice, presides primarily over arguments to the Court, Court deliberations on cases, and administrative matters. The Justices are appointed by the President of the United States and are confirmed by the Senate. A Justice receives a lifetime appointment.

Although some cases have a mandatory right of appeal to the Supreme Court, most cases are heard by the court if a **writ of *certiorari*** is issued. The writ orders the lower court records to be produced to the highest court for review and examination. The granting of a writ is discretionary with the Court and is normally granted only when a constitutional right is involved or when an issue affects a large segment of the population. In addition, when there is conflict among the federal district or circuit courts on the manner in which certain law should be applied, the Court may grant a writ. Figure 1–1 depicts the structure of the court system.

Figure 1–1 Federal and State Court Systems.

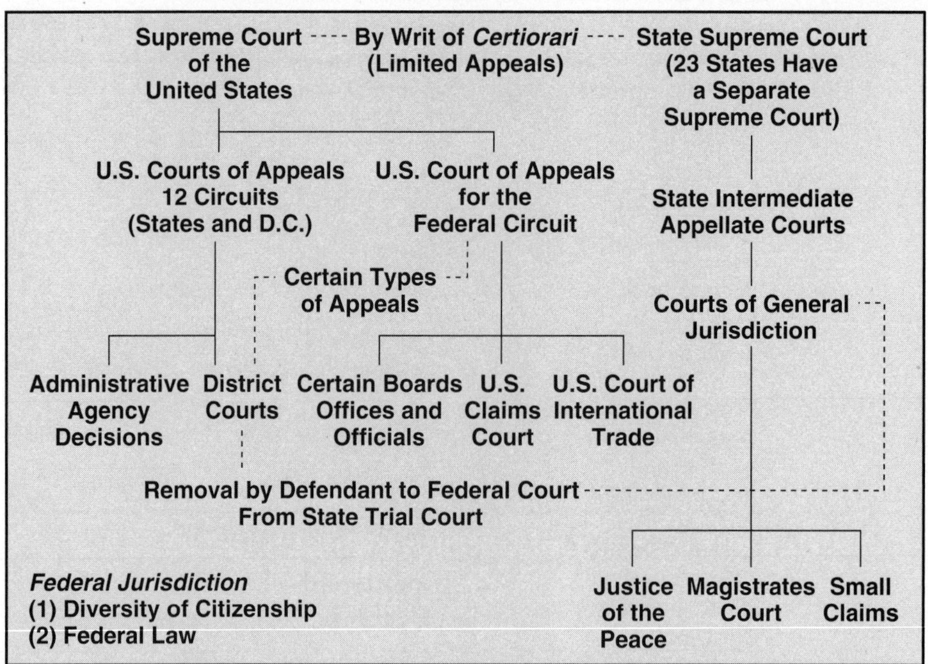

Source: Gordon Brown et al., *Business Law with UCC Applications,* 7th ed., Macmillan/McGraw-Hill, 1989.

State Court Systems

Each state has its own court structure. The common thread among the state court systems is that there are trial courts and appeals courts, but their names and areas of jurisdiction may differ greatly.

State Trial Courts The courts where most controversies are filed are known as state trial courts. Trial courts usually have the power to hear all cases and are courts of general jurisdiction. Their names range from district court to common pleas court to, as in New York, the supreme court. The jurisdiction of some trial courts is limited according to the types of cases they can hear. More specialized trial courts, such as juvenile, probate, and domestic relations, hear only cases involving certain subjects. Cases involving counties or cities and their citizens with private disputes are often heard by county courts or municipal courts. The determination of which court will hear the case depends upon the subject matter of the dispute, such as whether a local ordinance is involved. The lowest trial courts in most states are small claims courts or justice of the peace courts, which hear cases involving controversies over minimal amounts of money, usually somewhere between $500 and $5000.

State Intermediate Appellate Courts Some state court systems have an intermediate appeals court which reviews decisions from a lower court, usually a trial court. These cases are usually heard before a panel of three judges. Appeals courts generally review a lower court decision based upon the current legal principles in the jurisdiction and normally do not create new legal principles. (The exception is when the state's highest court has not rendered a decision in an area such as the legality of surrogacy.) Consequently, an appeals court may agree with the lower court decision, in which instance it is said to affirm the case. It may disagree with a lower court and reverse the case, or it may order the case back to trial, which is called remand. Normally, the term *remand* is used with the term *reverse;* the expression often used is *reversed and remanded.* The action taken must conform to the accepted legal principles of that jurisdiction. Some states, such as New Hampshire, Mississippi, and Utah, do not have an intermediate appeals court. The name of an appeals court will depend on the state, but in most instances, it is called the court of appeals.

State Supreme Courts A state's highest and final level of appeal is usually referred to as the supreme court. Most state supreme courts consist of a panel of three to nine justices who hear lawyers argue the case orally. The issues before the court involve points of law which are reviewed from decisions in lower courts. Generally, a state's supreme court renders final decisions subject only to limited review by the U.S. Supreme Court when a federal issue or constitutional right is involved. Not all states use the term *supreme court.* For example, in New York the highest court in the state is called the New York Court of Appeals, and in Texas there are two high courts addressing civil and criminal matters, called the Texas Supreme Court and the Texas Criminal Court of Appeals, respectively.

1–4 Practical Considerations

As a paralegal, you must be able to evaluate a number of considerations with your attorney when a case is presented to you. First, you must be able to assist in determining the type of area of law in question. Then, you must be able to assist in determining which court has the power to hear the case and the extent of a chosen court's jurisdiction. Finally, you must be able to assist in determining which law is applicable in the case and to decide what procedures are necessary for you to begin. Table 1–3 highlights some practical points to consider before filing a case.

Let's use the facts of the Commentary and determine which court would be appropriate. Since the claim involves an age discrimination claim, the court that would hear the claim would be federal. Not only is discrimination forbidden under the U.S. Constitution, but a federal statute [34 U.S.C. § 1 *et seq.*] also forbids age discrimination. Consequently, the federal court and the federal rules of civil procedure would govern this case.

Once the structure of the legal system has been mastered, learning where to find the law and the decisions rendered by the courts is important. The search begins in the law library.

Table 1–3 Preliminary Considerations for Filing a Lawsuit

1. Identify the court that has the jurisdiction to hear your case.
2. Determine with whom you should file your case in either federal or state court. You may have more than one choice.
3. Find the appropriate procedures in your jurisdiction for commencing the lawsuit.
4. Determine the applicable substantive law for your case.
5. Always consult with your attorney about your recommendations, and let your attorney and the client make the final decisions.

SUMMARY

1–1

The sources of American law are the U.S. Constitution, common law, statutes, and administrative regulations law. The principles of *stare decisis* and precedent developed from the written common law and case law. Both concepts dictate that a court use past case decisions in making decisions on current cases that are the same or substantially similar.

1–2

The law can be classified into distinct categories. Civil law is based upon wrongs committed by individuals against private citizens, and criminal law is based on wrongs committed by individuals against society. Procedural law is the practical guide to litigation, and substantive law directs what law should be applied by a court to resolve the issues before it.

1–3

A court must have the power to hear a case. This power is called jurisdiction. Jurisdiction may be original, general, exclusive, limited, or concurrent. Appellate jurisdiction is the power to review a lower court decision. There are two court systems in the United States: the federal court system and the state court system. A federal district court is limited to cases concerning the U.S. Constitution, a federal statute, or parties from different states. The federal court system consists of the U.S. District Court, the U.S. Court of Appeals, and the highest court, the U.S. Supreme Court. The state court systems vary. All states have a trial court and a court of final review.

1–4

In evaluating a case, a paralegal must be able to assist in determining the law, the jurisdiction of the court, and the appropriate court to hear the case. The paralegal must also assist in deciding how to proceed and in determining the appropriate substantive law in a case before filing the case in the appropriate court.

REVIEW

Key Terms

Before proceeding, review the key terms listed below to be sure you understand each one. If necessary, read over the corresponding section of the chapter. When you are ready to test your understanding, answer the Review Questions.

administrative law
agency
appellate jurisdiction
binding precedent
case law
circuits
civil law
common law
compensatory damages
concurrent jurisdiction
Constitutional law
court
criminal law
decision
diversity jurisdiction
equitable remedies
exclusive jurisdiction
exemplary damages
Federal District Court
felony
general jurisdiction
injunction
judgment
judicial review
jurisdiction
law
lawsuit
legal remedy
limited jurisdiction
misdemeanor
nominal damages
ordinances
original jurisdiction
personal jurisdiction
persuasive precedent

precedent
procedural law
punitive damages
remedy
specific performance
stare decisis
statutes
statutory law
subject matter jurisdiction
substantive law
uniform laws
U.S. Court of Appeals
U.S. District Court
U.S. Supreme Court
writ of *certiorari*

Questions for Review and Discussion

1. Define the sources of American law.
2. How did the concept of *stare decisis* develop?
3. What are the classifications of law, and how are they distinguished?
4. What is a legal remedy?
5. What does the term *jurisdiction* mean?
6. List two types of federal jurisdiction and give examples of each.
7. How is the federal court system set up?
8. Name two common factors in the state and federal court systems.

Activities

1. Outline the court structure in your state and determine in which court you would appeal a decision from your state's trial level.
2. Refer to the U.S. Constitution in Appendix I and read the article that sets up our judicial system.
3. Determine which federal circuit your state is in and how many judicial districts are in your state.
4. List all the trial-level courts in your state and their jurisdictional requirements.

CHAPTER 2 The Case Brief

OUTLINE

COMMENTARY

Your supervising attorney has an upcoming court hearing. One of her partners has brought to her attention a relevant case, *Davis v. Gomez*, 207 Cal.App.3d 1401, 255 Cal.Rptr. 743 (Cal. Ct. App., 1989). You have been provided with a copy of the case (see Figure 2–2) and asked by your supervising attorney to highlight the important points for her review. She wants the complicated opinion crystallized into a straightforward summary.

Accomplishing this task requires the preparation of a "case brief." In the last chapter, you learned how to find the law. In this chapter, you will learn how to analyze it.

OBJECTIVES

In the pages that follow, you will learn how to summarize a single case into the concise format know as a case brief. After completing this chapter, you will be able to:

1. Distinguish between a case brief and a trial or appellate brief.
2. Describe the components of a printed opinion.
3. Explain the usefulness of star-paging.

4. Differentiate between a majority opinion and a dissent.
5. Describe the components of a case brief.
6. Identify the relevant facts in an opinion.
7. State the issues presented by a written opinion.
8. Trace the procedural history of a case as set forth in the opinion.
9. Identify the holding of the court and the disposition of the case.
10. Analyze and summarize the reasoning behind an opinion.

2–1 The Case Brief Distinguished

The word *brief* has two separate and distinct connotations in legal practice. First, it can refer to a document filed with a court to present the legal argument of one party in a lawsuit, citing as many cases, statutes, and other sources of law as are deemed necessary to support the argument. Such a brief is usually further identified by including the level of the court in which the brief is filed: if in the trial court, it is a *trial brief;* if an appellate court, it is an *appellate brief.* These briefs do not provide an objective discussion of the law, but rather a one-sided argument intended to persuade the court of the validity of the party's position. We discuss such briefs in some detail in later chapters.

The word *brief* also appears in the term *case brief.* A **case brief** is an objective summary of the important points of a single case. If properly prepared, it will provide the reader with a concise abstract of the reasoning of the opinion, as well as important collateral information such as case name, citation, and identity of the parties. The key word is *objective*—the case brief should accurately reflect the meaning of the case, whether that meaning is helpful to your client or harmful.

As you might have guessed, the case brief is not a document prepared for the eyes of the court, nor is it shared with opposing parties. It is an internal document, designed to help attorneys develop an objective understanding of the impact of existing case law on the viability of their client's position. Only when such an understanding is reached can persuasive strategies be developed.

In this chapter we address the components of a printed opinion, the components of a case brief, and some general comments on the meaning and use of a case brief.

2–2 The Components of a Printed Opinion

As you have learned, reporters are collections of printed opinions, or cases. A case brief is a summary of one of these cases. In order to understand the method of briefing a case, then, it is necessary to learn about the components of a printed opinion. You are already familiar with some of these components from the previous chapter.

Figure 2–1 on page 276 reprints a full page from volume 255 of the *California Reporter* (which, as you recall, is the West publication for additional California decisions beyond those already appearing in the *Pacific Reporter*). The page shown (page 743) is the first page of our subject case, *Davis v. Gomez,* and it contains a wealth of information.

Figure 2–1 From the *California Reporter*

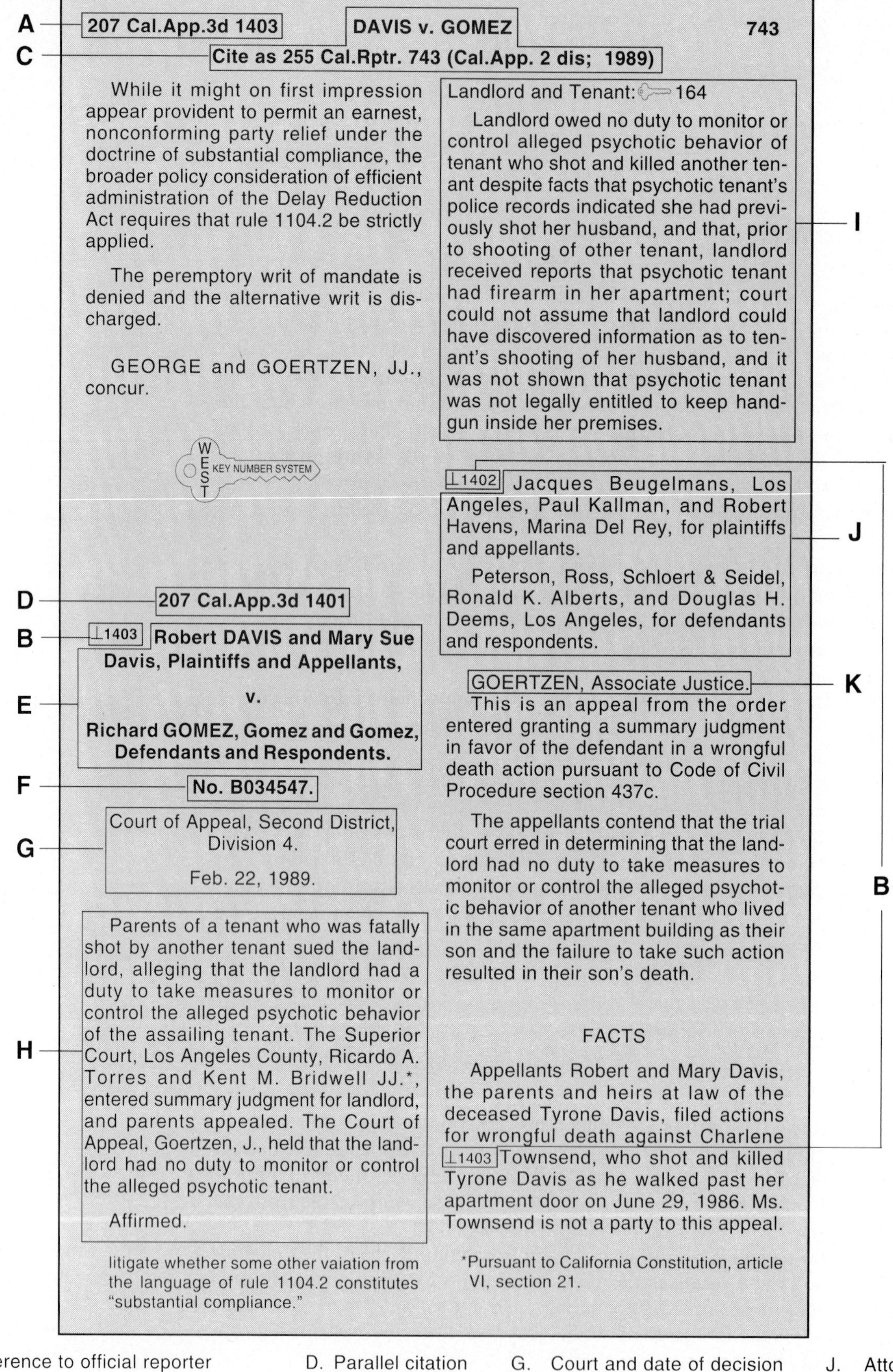

207 Cal.App.3d 1403 DAVIS v. GOMEZ 743

Cite as 255 Cal.Rptr. 743 (Cal.App. 2 dis; 1989)

While it might on first impression appear provident to permit an earnest, nonconforming party relief under the doctrine of substantial compliance, the broader policy consideration of efficient administration of the Delay Reduction Act requires that rule 1104.2 be strictly applied.

The peremptory writ of mandate is denied and the alternative writ is discharged.

GEORGE and GOERTZEN, JJ., concur.

WEST KEY NUMBER SYSTEM

207 Cal.App.3d 1401

⊥1403 **Robert DAVIS and Mary Sue Davis, Plaintiffs and Appellants,**

v.

Richard GOMEZ, Gomez and Gomez, Defendants and Respondents.

No. B034547.

Court of Appeal, Second District, Division 4.

Feb. 22, 1989.

Parents of a tenant who was fatally shot by another tenant sued the landlord, alleging that the landlord had a duty to take measures to monitor or control the alleged psychotic behavior of the assailing tenant. The Superior Court, Los Angeles County, Ricardo A. Torres and Kent M. Bridwell JJ.*, entered summary judgment for landlord, and parents appealed. The Court of Appeal, Goertzen, J., held that the landlord had no duty to monitor or control the alleged psychotic tenant.

Affirmed.

Landlord and Tenant: 🔑164

Landlord owed no duty to monitor or control alleged psychotic behavior of tenant who shot and killed another tenant despite facts that psychotic tenant's police records indicated she had previously shot her husband, and that, prior to shooting of other tenant, landlord received reports that psychotic tenant had firearm in her apartment; court could not assume that landlord could have discovered information as to tenant's shooting of her husband, and it was not shown that psychotic tenant was not legally entitled to keep handgun inside her premises.

⊥1402 Jacques Beugelmans, Los Angeles, Paul Kallman, and Robert Havens, Marina Del Rey, for plaintiffs and appellants.

Peterson, Ross, Schloert & Seidel, Ronald K. Alberts, and Douglas H. Deems, Los Angeles, for defendants and respondents.

GOERTZEN, Associate Justice.

This is an appeal from the order entered granting a summary judgment in favor of the defendant in a wrongful death action pursuant to Code of Civil Procedure section 437c.

The appellants contend that the trial court erred in determining that the landlord had no duty to take measures to monitor or control the alleged psychotic behavior of another tenant who lived in the same apartment building as their son and the failure to take such action resulted in their son's death.

FACTS

Appellants Robert and Mary Davis, the parents and heirs at law of the deceased Tyrone Davis, filed actions for wrongful death against Charlene ⊥1403 Townsend, who shot and killed Tyrone Davis as he walked past her apartment door on June 29, 1986. Ms. Townsend is not a party to this appeal.

litigate whether some other vaiation from the language of rule 1104.2 constitutes "substantial compliance."

*Pursuant to California Constitution, article VI, section 21.

A. Reference to official reporter
B. Star-paging notations
C. Short-form case name with citation
D. Parallel citation
E. Full case name
F. Docket number
G. Court and date of decision
H. Case synopsis
I. Headnote
J. Attorneys
K. Judge

Let's start with the left side of the top line, identified as *A* in Figure 2–1. The notation "207 Cal. App. 3d 1403" is a reference to a page from the official reporter, the *California Appellate Reports*, where *Davis v. Gomez* also appears. Page 1403 is the last page from that reporter, which is reproduced here on page 743 of the *California Reporter*. Private reporters often provide information as to the pagination in the official reporter.

Star-Paging

Pagination as it appears in the official reporter is reflected in a private reporter through the use of **star-paging**. Star-paging is a practice that enables us to identify the page breaks in one reporter by reviewing the decision as reprinted in another reporter. The three star-paging notations identified as *B* in Figure 2–1 identify the page breaks for pages 1401, 1402, and 1403 as they appear in the *California Appellate Reports*. By utilizing these star-paging notations when writing a brief, the drafter can reference the page and volume of important language as it appears in both West's *California Reporter* and the official *California Appellate Reports*, even though she only has the *California Reporter* at hand. Star-paging is often (but not always) found in private reporters; it is never found in official reporters, and thus constitutes an additional reason why private reporters can be superior to official reporters as research tools.

Shorthand Case Name

We next turn to the section we have labeled *C* in Figure 2–1. This is the **shorthand** form of the case name, with an instruction as to the appropriate citation. These instructions do not always conform to the rules set down in the bluebook; where there is a discrepancy, you should follow the bluebook (for example, the reference to "2 Dist." goes beyond the bluebook requirements). In any event, this citation will appear on alternate pages.

Parallel Citation

The *D* label shows the correct **parallel citation** for the case in *California Appellate Reports*, "207 Cal.App.3d 1401." Just as a reminder, this means that the case begins on page 1401 of volume 207 of the third series of that reporter.

Full Name of Case

E is the full name of the case, identifying all the parties and their roles (i.e., plaintiff or defendant; appellant or respondent). The full name, together with the docket number, court, and date of the decision, is called the **caption** (labels *E*, *F*, and *G* combined).

Docket Number, Court, and Date

The *F* identifies the docket number of the case. A **docket number** is assigned by the court to the case for its own administrative purposes. If you visited the appropriate courthouse and asked to see the file for this case, you would need to provide the docket number so that they could locate it in their files.

The *G* label provides the full name of the court that rendered the opinion, and the date of rendering. In this case the Court of Appeal, Second District, Division 4 handed down its decision on February 22, 1989.

Synopsis

Item *H* is called the **synopsis** of the case. It is an extremely short summary, prepared not by the court but by the publisher. It identifies the issue, the procedural history, and the ruling of the court in the instant case ("instant" is used in legal documents to mean *present* or *current*; this instant case is *Davis v. Gomez*). The synopsis is in a sense a preview; since it is an unofficial editorial addition, it should never be formally cited, but only informally reviewed.

Sometimes a synopsis is prepared by the official reporter of decisions. Such an "official" synopsis is called a **syllabus**, as you learned in Chapter 1's discussion of *United States Reports* (where each U.S. Supreme Court case is given a syllabus). Although "official," a syllabus is not part of the court's opinion and, like the synopsis, should never be formally relied upon or cited.

West Key Number and Headnote

I identifies the West key number and headnote. Since this case has only one headnote, there is no need to number it or reference it elsewhere in the opinion; if there were more than one headnote, each would be numbered and referenced as in the example of *Great Western v. Easley* in Figure 1–3 from the last chapter.

Attorneys and Judge

J identifies the attorney for the parties; *K* identifies the judge who wrote the opinion of the court, Associate Justice Goertzen.

Text and Disposition

The name of the judge who wrote the opinion is followed by the text of his or her opinion. The text or body of the decision contains the detailed reasoning by which the court reached its result. That result, which appears at the end of the opinion and is often simply a word or two telling the reader who won the lawsuit, is called the court's **disposition**. (For full text and disposition, see Figure 2–2.)

The text of an opinion generally sets forth the facts of the case and the procedural history. It then analyzes the issues presented and, citing precedent and drawing upon applicable legal principles and logic, reaches a conclusion. The text is the heart of a case; it is from the text that analogies can be drawn to pending controversies.

In *Davis v. Gomez* the court quotes at considerable length from the trial court's original opinion on the summary judgment motion at issue. Indeed, the quotation from that opinion is longer than the appellate court's first contribution. Although references to an underlying opinion are often seen in the text of an appellate opinion, such extended quoting is not a common practice.

Figure 2–2 The Court's Disposition

207 Cal.App.3d 1403 DAVIS v. GOMEZ 743

Cite as 255 Cal.Rptr. 743 (Cal.App. 2 dist., 1989)

While it might on first impression appear provident to permit an earnest, nonconforming party relief under the doctrine of substantial compliance, the broader policy consideration of efficient administration of the Delay Reduction Act requires that rule 1104.2 be strictly applied.

The peremptory writ of mandate is denied and the alternative writ is discharged.

GEORGE and GOERTZEN, JJ., concur.

207 Cal.App.3d 1401

⊥1403 Robert DAVIS and Mary Sue Davis, Plaintiffs and Appellants,

v.

Richard GOMEZ, Gomez and Gomez, Defendants and Respondents.

No. B034547.

Court of Appeal, Second District, Division 4.

Feb. 22, 1989.

Parents of a tenant who was fatally shot by another tenant sued the landlord, alleging that the landlord had a duty to take measures to monitor or control the alleged psychotic behavior of the assailing tenant. The Superior Court, Los Angeles County, Ricardo A. Torres and Kent M. Bridwell JJ.*, entered summary judgment for landlord, and parents appealed. The Court of Appeal, Goertzen, J., held that the landlord had no duty to monitor or control the alleged psychotic tenant.

Affirmed.

litigate whether some other variation from the language of rule 1104.2 constitutes "substantial compliance."

Landlord and Tenant ⚷ 164

Landlord owed no duty to monitor or control alleged psychotic behavior of tenant who shot and killed another tenant despite facts that psychotic tenant's police records indicated she had previously shot her husband, and that, prior to shooting of other tenant, landlord received reports that psychotic tenant had firearm in her apartment; court could not assume that landlord could have discovered information as to tenant's shooting of her husband, and it was not shown that psychotic tenant was not legally entitled to keep handgun inside her premises.

⊥1402 Jacques Beugelmans, Los Angeles, Paul Kallman, and Robert Havens, Marina Del Rey, for plaintiffs and appellants.

Peterson, Ross, Schloert & Seidel, Ronald K. Alberts, and Douglas H. Deems, Los Angeles, for defendants and respondents.

GOERTZEN, Associate Justice.

This is an appeal from the order entered granting a summary judgment in favor of the defendant in a wrongful death action pursuant to Code of Civil Procedure section 437c.

The appellants contend that the trial court erred in determining that the landlord had no duty to take measures to monitor or control the alleged psychotic behavior of another tenant who lived in the same apartment building as their son and the failure to take such action resulted in their son's death.

FACTS

Appellants Robert and Mary Davis, the parents and heirs at law of the deceased Tyrone Davis, filed actions for wrongful death against Charlene ⊥1403 Townsend, who shot and killed Tyrone Davis as he walked past her apartment door on June 29, 1986. Ms. Townsend is not a party to this appeal.

*Pursuant to California Consitution, article VI, section 21.

Figure 2–2 Cont.

Appellants also named as defendants in the actions the partnership which owned the apartment building where the shooting took place, respondents Richard Gomez, Rudy Gomez and Maria Gomez.

Carl McGill was the manager of the respondent's apartment building and a City of Los Angeles Police Officer. He claimed that in early April, 1986, Ms. Townsend's mental condition began to "deteriorate." By May 1986, it was apparent that Ms. Townsend was "losing her mind."

Ms. Townsend never threatened him or anyone in Mr. McGill's presence. But Mr. McGill heard Ms. Townsend "grumbling off as if she was talking to somebody" in a loud voice while she was alone in her apartment.

Other tenants complained to Mr. McGill that they felt threatened by her actions. The other tenants began avoiding the area in front of her apartment. Gerald Lewis told Mr. McGill that he had seen a gun in Ms. Townsend's living room. Bernadette Gillette came to him several times and told him Ms. Townsend was talking to herself out loud and was in the front window of her apartment moving her hands as if she was casting spells on those who walked by.

Jim Ross, another policeman who resided in the building, told Mr. McGill about the spell-casting behavior and said he was "worried about everybody's safety . . . because of her behavior." He also had seen the gun in her living room.

Mr. McGill stated that about a month before the shooting he telephoned Robert Gomez and told him that Ms. Townsend was "acting very peculiar and a lot of people are scared to go past her window to get downstairs." Mr. McGill also repeated the reports of the presence of the gun. Mr. Gomez replied that he "would check into it."

Richard Gomez did not take any action on the complaint before Tyrone was shot. There was also other evidence that the Gomez defendants did not investigate Ms. Townsend's background or references before renting the apartment to her and after the above complaints were reported to them by Mr. McGill.

The trial court's memorandum of ruling on the motion for summary judgment stated in pertinent part:

"It is well-established that the landlord of residential property owes certain duties not only to tenants, but also ⊥1404 third-party guests and visitors. (*See Uccello v. Laudenslayer* (1975) 44 Cal.App.3d 504, 118 Cal.Rptr. 741.) Under certain circumstances, that duty may be absolute, imposing 'strict liability' on the landlord for dangerous conditions of the rented premises. (*See Becker v. IRM Corp.* (1985) 38 Cal.3d 454, 213 Cal.Rptr. 213, 698 P.2d 116.)

"Still, it is not enough to surmise that the landlord should have done 'something' in response to a given situation. Instead, it is essential to define that 'something' in fairly precise terms. Otherwise, the law would be requiring adherence to an unknown standard of conduct, recognized only with 20-20 hindsight.

"Preliminarily, this Court does not believe that any landlord should be expected to check the references or background of a prospective tenant for reasons other than to protect the landlord's *own* interest. Nor was it within the reasonable province of either Mr. McGill or his employers to diagnose Ms. Townsend as 'psychotic.' What, then, should these defendants have done, and in what way was their failure to so act a proximate cause of plaintiff's loss? (Emphasis in original.)

"Plaintiffs argue that the Gomez defendants had both the power and the opportunity to evict Ms. Townsend on the basis of her reported behavior. (*See Uccello v. Laudenslayer, supra,* 44 Cal.App.3d at pp. 512-513, 118 Cal.Rptr. 741.) Certainly, a landlord owes a duty to preserve the quiet enjoyment of all tenants. In extreme cases, eviction of a troublesome tenant may provide the only practical means to abate a nuisance which affects other tenants. Notably, those other tenants would not share the power of eviction, and would otherwise be limited to remedies of a less certain nature.

"Still, the evicted tenant also has rights, and a landlord had better be

Fig. 2–2 cont.

extremely careful and sure of his/her grounds before instituting eviction proceedings. Under circumstances of the present variety, the landlord is often caught in the middle of competing tenant interests, and stands at risk no matter what course of action is decided upon. It is usually a classic 'no win' situation. Yet, if it were reasonably foreseeable that an innocent tenant might be killed, the possibility of legal laction by the evicted tenant obviously becomes of subordinate concern.

"Although the reported conduct of Ms. Townsend was perhaps disquieting, and while 'casting spells' may be considered aggressive behavior of sorts, none of it involved any physical violence or real threat to cause bodily harm (depending, perhaps, on whether one believes in the occult virulence of 'spells'). Nor did her open possession of a firearm necessarily invite ⊥1405 speculation that she was actually disposed to use it indiscriminately against another tenant.

"Consequently, while her conduct might have represented a common nuisance, it does not follow that anyone should have foreseen the escalation of that behavior into a fatal shooting. The reality is that persons exhibiting similarly 'bizarre' behavior are to be seen on the streets of every metropolitan community. Fortunately, few are ever actually dangerous.

"Although the issue of foreseeability is usually for the trier-of-fact to determine, the facts presented here simply do not support a finding that the shooting of plaintiff's decedent was reasonably foreseeable from the unusual and bothersome, but otherwise innocuous behavior reported.

"Certainly, the failure of these defendants to eliminate a mere nuisance is not the same as their failing to prevent a serious criminal act. This case is therefore distinguishable from the situation where a landlord neglects to provide adequate lighting or security in a *known* high-crime area. The mere failure to evict a 'nuisance' tenant, while representing a breach of duty to other tenants, would not be the proximate cause of a fatal shooting. A separate duty, touching upon different interests, would have to appear. (Emphasis in original.)

"Plaintiff Mary Sue Davis further suggests that the Gomez defendants should have requested a 72-hour psychiatric hold and observation. (See Welf. & Inst. Code, § 5000, et seq.) aside from the obvious legal repercussions of inducing the commencement of civil commitment proceedings (Welf. & Inst. Code, § 5150), the Court can discern no reason to impose this as the special duty of a landlord. Tenants are not so helpless that they must rely upon their landlord to pursue every alternative which is equally available (and equally risky) to all.

"Plaintiffs' most persuasive argument is that the Gomez defendants should at least have investigated further to determine whether Ms. Townsend posed a serious threat to the other tenants. They were certainly in a position to approach her and discuss the problem. Ostensibly, it might *then* have become reasonably foreseeable that Ms. Townsend was inclined toward actual violence. Yet, to assume that this failure to investigate was a proximate cause of the shooting represents a quantum leap in plaintiffs' logic. Clearly, investigation alone would at most have revealed the danger, although even that amounts to little more than speculation. It would not have alleviated the potential risk of harm. Something more would then have been required. Again, that 'something' is not easily defined. (Emphasis in original.)

⊥1406 "Based upon the facts presented, and resolving every conflict in favor of plaintiffs, this Court concludes as a matter-of-law that the Gomez defendants breached no legal duty that was a proximate cause of the tragic events which ultimately transpired. In reaching this decision, the Court draws upon much of the reasoning expressed in *Alva v. Cook* (1975) 49 Cal.App.3d 899, 123 Cal.Rptr. 166. Although that case involved somewhat different facts, and arose in a different procedural setting, the issues are remarkably similar."

DISCUSSION

Appellants' contention is dependent upon the assumption that Ms. Townsend was "brandishing and

Fig. 2–2 cont.

exhibiting a firearm for more than two months before Tyrone Davis' murder." We have reviewed the record and find no evidence whatsoever of the "brandishing and exhibiting" to which appellants refer.

As the trial court stated: "Plaintiff's most persuasive argument is that the Gomez defendants should at least have investigated further to determine whether Ms. Townsend posed a serious threat to the other tenants." We cannot assume, however, that the landlord could have discovered the information Mr. McGill belatedly obtained from another police officer after the fatal shooting, that Ms. Townsend's criminal records showed that she had shot her husband.

As was stated in *Leakes v. Shamoun* (1986) 187 Cal.App.3d 772, 776, 232 Cal.Rptr. 171, "an injured person must also show that the landlord had the right and ability to cure the condition. [Citations.]" The trial judge focused on this critical factor in granting the motion for summary judgment. We conclude that the trial court's decision was proper as a matter of law since appellants have also failed to establish what action the landlord could have taken, even with a reasonable investigation, with respect to Ms. Townsend's deteriorating mental condition. Nor have appellants shown that Ms. Townsend was not legally entitled to keep a handgun inside her premises. Other than the handgun's possession, Ms. Townsend had shown no dangerous tendencies. (See *Id.*, at p. 788, 232 Cal.Rptr. 171.)

The trial court carefully analyzed all the factors properly considered under *Rowland v. Christian* (1968) 69 Cal.2d 108, 113, 70 Cal.Rptr. 97, 443 P.2d 561. It determined, as a matter of law, that there was no duty owed by the landlord to the tenant. There is no error.

⊥1407 THE JUDGMENT IS AFFIRMED.

ARLEIGH M. WOODS, P.J., and GEORGE, J., concur.

Turning to the end of the opinion, you will see the disposition. The decision of the lower court was **affirmed**, meaning that the appellate court agreed with the trial court. If the appellate court had disagreed, the decision of the lower court would have been **reversed**. Sometimes an appellate court agrees with some parts of an appealed decision but disagrees with other parts, resulting in a disposition in which the decision is "affirmed in part and reversed in part." Sometimes the disposition requires that the case be sent back to the lower court for further consideration, as would have been the case if the appellate court had reversed the trial court in *Davis v. Gomez*. Such decision has been reversed and **remanded**.

Sometimes an appellate court simply voids the decision of the lower court. The disposition under these circumstances uses the term **vacated**.

Most appellate cases are decided by a panel of several judges. If all the judges agree on the correct disposition of the case, the decision is rendered ***per curiam***. Occasionally the judges on the panel disagree about the proper disposition. In such a case the majority rules, hence the majority judges issue the binding decision of the court, written as a **majority opinion**. A judge who agrees with the majority opinion is said to **concur**. A judge who agrees with the ultimate result but wishes to apply different reasoning from that in the majority opinion can file a **concurring opinion**, which sets forth the alternative reasoning (in *Davis v. Gomez,* Justice Woods and Justice George concurred; since they wrote no separate opinion, they presumably agreed with the reasoning of Justice Goertzen's opinion).

If a judge disagrees with the result reached by the majority, he or she is said to **dissent**. An opinion outlining the reasons for the dissent often critiques the majority and concurring opinions, and is known as a **dissenting opinion**.

It is possible that an individual judge agrees with part of the majority decision and disagrees with part. He or she is then said to "concur in part and dissent in part," and this judge, too, can set forth his or her reasoning in a separate opinion.

Some decisions, particularly those of the U.S. Supreme Court, may have several written opinions with various coalitions of judges concurring and dissenting on different points. It sometimes requires a fair amount of analysis to unravel the meaning of the court's disposition in such a case. In any event, a written opinion always identifies which judges concurred and which dissented.

Although most of this analysis relates to appellate opinions, trial court opinion can also be published in reporters. If a trial court opinion relates to a decision on a pending motion, the disposition will either **grant** or **deny** the motion. If the opinion is a final decision after trial, the disposition will indicate that judgment was entered for either plaintiff or defendant.

In analyzing the disposition and the text, you should keep in mind the concepts of **holding** and ***dictum*** (plural *dicta*). The court's holding is that aspect of the decision which directly affects the outcome of the case; it is composed of the reasoning necessary and sufficient to reach the disposition. *Dicta,* on the other hand, are statements made by the court that are beyond what is necessary to reach the disposition. For example, if a court suggests that a different result might have been reached if certain facts had been different, such a statement is *dictum* (as you read *Davis v. Gomez,* you will see an example of *dictum*). The difference between holding and *dictum* is important: a holding carries the precedential force of *stare decisis,* whereas *dictum* serves as a nonbinding guidance to future courts.

2–3 The Components of a Case Brief

Rather than simply recite and define the components of a case brief, in this section we take you step-by-step through the preparation of a comprehensive case brief for *Davis v. Gomez* (the finished product appears as Figure 2–3 at the end of this section).

Reading the Case

You cannot brief a case until you understand it, and you cannot understand it until you read it. Furthermore, when you read it, you should read the entire case, from start to finish. This might seem obvious, and indeed it should be, but it is a basic rule too often honored in the breach. Resist the temptation to skim, to rely on the editor's synopsis, to rely on the headnotes, or to search for the disposition without reading the court's underlying reasoning. There are problems ahead for those who think that they don't have the time to read the whole case or can get everything they need from the first and last page. Indeed, as we discuss, in *Davis v. Gomez* you will see excellent examples of the sorts of peculiarities a close reading can reveal.

Remember also that one reading is rarely enough for anyone, and certainly not enough for a beginning paralegal. At a minimum, you should read the case once to develop a general understanding of the obvious points and a second time to pick out the more subtle points. You should probably read it a third time to verify the points you found in the first two readings, then constantly refer back for specifics as you prepare your case brief. Before proceeding with this chapter, read *Davis v. Gomez* with care.

Identification of the Case

The first component of a case brief is, of course, to identify the case. This is done in our case brief both at the top of the page and in the citation section:

Case Brief — Davis v. Gomez

Citation:
Davis v. Gomez, 207 Cal.App.3d 1401, 255 Cal.Rptr. 743
(Cal.Ct.App., 1989)

Parties

The parties section of our case brief will reveal the peculiarities we referred to earlier. It is not entirely clear from this decision just who the parties are:

Parties:
Robert Davis (plaintiff/appellant); Mary Sue Davis (plaintiff/appellant); Charlene Townsend (defendant); Robert Gomez (defendant/respondent); Gomez and Gomez (defendant/respondent). [Note: The identity of the respondents is not entirely clear. The caption of the case identifies only the two defendants listed here, Richard Gomez individually, and some entity named "Gomez and Gomez." The opinion refers to a "partnership," presumably "Gomez and Gomez," but identifies three individuals (Richard Gomez, Rudy Gomez, and Maria Gomez) as "respondents." There is also a reference to a "Robert" Gomez at page 744. It will be assumed herein that the "Gomez defendants," regardless of their individual identity, and regardless of the nature of their partnership, were all co-owners. The confusion does not appear to have an impact on the decision of the court.]

The identities of the plaintiffs are clear. Both in the caption of the case and in the text, the plaintiffs are identified as the parents of the decedent (*decedent* is a legal term referring to a deceased person, in this case Tyrone Davis, the tenant who was killed), Robert Davis and Mary Sue Davis. It is also clear that these two plaintiffs are also the appellants.

It is not clear, however, exactly who are defendants. First look at the caption of the case. It would seem from the caption that there are two defendants—Richard Gomez and some entity called "Gomez and Gomez." Then, in the first paragraph on page 744 of the decision, the court refers to the defendant "partnership," which one might assume to be "Gomez and Gomez." But in the same sentence the court seems to equate the concept of "partnership" with individual "respondents" Richard Gomez, Rudy Gomez, and Maria Gomez. Suing a partnership is procedurally different from suing the partners themselves as individuals, but the court seems to skirt and confuse this distinction. Finally, to make matters even more confusing, further down in the same column on page 744 the court makes a reference to a "Robert" Gomez, although from the context it appears it should read "Richard" Gomez, since the very next paragraph indicates that "Richard Gomez did not take any action on the complaint before Tyrone was shot."

As it turns out, these discrepancies do not have any impact on the court's decision. Nevertheless, two lessons should be taken. First, as we emphasize at great length in later chapters, it is extremely important to express yourself clearly in every legal document you draft. The ambiguity in this decision could have been eliminated had the court used more care in draftsmanship. Second, you have to read with great attention to detail. A discrepancy like this can give you an opening to distinguish a case cited by your opponent; conversely, it could be used by your opponent to discredit a case cited by you. You must analyze opinions with great care.

In any event, since the discrepancies did not affect the court's decision, the case brief deals with the problem by identifying the "Gomez defendants" as a group. Incidentally, the "Gomez defendants" are also the respondents; that is to say, they are responding to the appeal brought by the plaintiff-appellants.

As to defendant Charlene Townsend, there is no indication of the lower court's action with regard to the claims brought by plaintiffs against her, nor is she a party to the appeal. This information is duly noted in the case brief.

Issues

The **issues** in the appeal are those points on which the appeal was based. Our case brief identifies them as follows:

> *Issues:*
> 1. Under California law, does the landlord of a multiple-unit dwelling owe a duty to the tenants therein to monitor or control the alleged psychotic behavior of a fellow tenant in the same building, or to warn the other tenants of dangers associated with such alleged psychotic behavior?
> 2. To the extent such duty exists, was it breached in this case?

The derivation of these issues is straightforward. The plaintiffs assert that the trial court was wrong in finding, as a matter of law, that the Gomez defendants had breached no duty by failing to protect their son from the attack of the allegedly psychotic Charlene Townsend. The court must address and decide this issue. The concept of making a finding "as a matter of law" will be discussed further in our analysis of the case brief's section on prior proceedings.

One quick and easy method of drafting the issues section is to determine the holding, then turn the holding into a question. This method is not recommended, however, because it requires working backwards.

Facts

The **facts** that should be included in a case brief are those which are necessary to gain a full and accurate understanding of the impact of the court's decision. Our case brief reads as follows:

> *Facts:*
> On June 29, 1986, Tyrone Davis, a tenant in a building owned by the Gomez defendants, was shot and killed by a fellow tenant in the same building, Charlene Townsend.
>
> Prior to the shooting, Townsend had been exhibiting symptoms of allegedly psychotic behavior, of which the Gomez defendants were aware. In addition, Townsend possessed a gun, of which the Gomez defendants were also aware.
>
> The Gomez defendants took no action with regard to the Townsend situation prior to the incident in which she shot and killed Davis.
>
> Plaintiff Robert Davis and plaintiff Mary Sue Davis are the parents of the deceased Tyrone Davis.

The key facts in this decision are the awareness on the part of the Gomez defendants of Townsend's condition, their failure to investigate further, and their failure to take any action. The failure to investigate ultimately becomes significant because the decision seems to hint that, if investigation had been made and other facts (such as Townsend's criminal record, revealing that she had shot her husband) had come to the knowledge of the Gomez defendants, a duty to intervene might have arisen based on their expanded knowledge of potential dangers.

Other facts are less important. It is not necessary, for example, that the reader know that the name of the manager of the apartment building was Carl McGill, nor that at least two residents of the building were police officers. Thus these facts are absent from our case brief.

Important facts affecting the decision of the court are considered to be **relevant** and **material**. If a fact is unimportant, it is considered immaterial; if unnecessary to understand the court's decision, it is considered irrelevant. The concepts of relevancy and materiality are not entirely distinct; there is a certain amount of overlap in meaning and usage.

Prior Proceedings

In order to understand the meaning of an opinion, the reader must first understand the procedural history of the case. Often the procedural setting is a crucial consideration in evaluating the extent to which the opinion can be applied to your client's case. The **prior proceedings** section of our case brief for Davis v. Gomez reads as follows:

> *Prior proceedings:*
> Plaintiffs filed an action for wrongful death against Charlene Townsend, and also against the Gomez defendants as owners of the building. Summary judgment was granted in favor of the Gomez defendants in the Superior Court, Los Angeles County. Plaintiffs appealed the granting of summary judgment. There is no indication in this decision as to the disposition with regard to defendant Charlene Townsend; she is not a party to this appeal.

Thus the plaintiffs originally brought suit against both Charlene Townsend and the Gomez defendants. The Gomez defendant filed a motion for summary judgment, which is a document seeking to demonstrate that there are not material factual disputes to be decided, and that based on the facts as they are known they are entitled to judgment "as a matter of law" (the phrase *as a matter of law* is used in the context of summary judgment motions or other situations in which facts are not in dispute, indicating that there is no need to make further inquiry into the facts, and that since the facts have been established, one side is entitled to prevail under existing law). The trial court agreed and granted the motion. The plaintiffs appealed.

As for Charlene Townsend, there is no indication regarding disposition of the claims against her. It is possible that they were still pending in the trial court at the time this opinion was rendered, but there is no way to tell from the text of this opinion.

Holding

The holding of a case is, of course, the most important element. The holding establishes the precedent—the rule of law in the case. The holding section of our case brief reads as follows:

> *Holding:*
> Under the circumstances present in this case, the failure of the landlord to take action with regard to tenant Townsend's allegedly psychotic behavior was NOT a proximate cause of the shooting death of tenant Davis.

The wording of this section must be precise. You must carefully read the case and extract the meaning of the court's ruling, being careful neither to overextend nor underestimate the scope.

Let's look more closely at the language we've chosen, so that you can get a sense of the necessary precision. The first phrase, "Under the circumstances present in this case," should set off an alarm in the reader. By drawing attention to the specific circumstances present, the drafter of the case brief has tipped off the reader that the court has rendered a decision in which the facts were taken into consideration in reaching its result. In other words, given a different factual setting, the application of the same general legal principle might nevertheless result in a different holding. For example, in *Davis v. Gomez,* if the Gomez defendants had begun an investigation and discovered that Townsend had shot her husband in the past, a duty to take action to protect the other tenants might have arisen.

What does it mean when a court qualifies its decision by limiting it to the specific facts of the case before it? It means that future parties who seek to use the case to support their argument must show how the facts of their case are analogous. It also presents an opportunity for a party seeking to discredit the precedential value of the case to distinguish it based upon the facts.

The wording of the next portion of our holding section is important as well. It indicates that the "failure to take action" was "NOT the proximate cause" of the shooting (*proximate cause* means one that foreseeably resulted in the ultimate effect; it is a concept used in tort law to determine liability).

Again, you must be careful. Look back at the issues section. The question we asked was whether the landlord "owe[d] a duty to the tenants" to control the psychotic tenant, or to warn the tenants of the danger. The landlord won the case; why then can't we simply say that the court held that landlords have no duty to take action or warn?

We can't, because that's not the holding. The court held that given the facts present *here,* the landlord had no duty. So we know that under at least one set of circumstances (namely, those present in this case) no duty was found. But it is entirely possible that under another set of circumstances a duty to take action or warn could arise. The court clearly left open that possibility. So if our case brief read, "The court held that a landlord has no duty to take action against, or warn tenants about, a psychotic tenant," it would be inaccurate. The court simply held that, under the circumstances present in *Davis v. Gomez,* no such duty had arisen.

Reasoning

In the **reasoning** section of our case brief, we analyze the rationale behind the court's holding:

> *Reasoning:*
> The trial court found that, though a landlord has a "duty to preserve the quiet enjoyment of all tenants," and though the behavior of tenant Townsend might have represented a "common nuisance" which the landlord has some duty to abate, "it does not follow that anyone should have foreseen the escalation of that behavior into a fatal shooting." Therefore, as a matter of law, the court held that the landlord's failure to take action was NOT the proximate cause of the decedent's death.
>
> The appellate court adopted the reasoning of the trial court. It also pointed out that there was no evidence to support the contention that Townsend had been "brandishing and exhibiting" the gun, nor did plaintiffs establish what action the landlord allegedly "could have taken, even with a reasonable investigation, with respect to Ms. Townsend's deteriorating mental condition."
>
> There is *dictum* which indicates that if an investigation had been conducted by the Gomez defendants and had revealed reason to believe that tenant Townsend was dangerous, a duty to warn or take other action might have arisen.

The first paragraph clarifies the scope of the trial court's holding, which found that although the landlord does have certain duties with regard to a tenant's "quiet enjoyment" of the premises, including a duty to abate (lessen or do away with) a "common nuisance," the landlord's failure to take action under the circumstances present in this case was not a violation of any alleged duty to protect the safety of the decedent, and hence not the proximate cause of the accident "as a matter of law." This passage, then, explains why the trial court, in its holding, did not simply assert the absence of a duty as the reason the landlord won the case. There are duties owed by a landlord to a tenant, but there is no violation of such a duty that can be pointed to by plaintiffs as the proximate cause of the death of Tyrone Davis.

The second paragraph of the reasoning section analyzes the appellate court's rationale. It first points out that the appellate court adopted the trial court's reasoning. It then notes that the appellate court also relied, in reaching its conclusion, upon plaintiffs' lack of evidentiary support for one of their key contentions (that Townsend had been "brandishing and exhibiting the gun") as well as the inability of plaintiffs to identify steps that the landlord could or should have taken to avoid the shooting.

The final paragraph further clarifies the circumstances that the appellate court suggests might have caused a duty to arise on the part of the Gomez defendants. The court concluded that, had the Gomez defendants investigated the situation and found reason to believe that tenant Townsend was dangerous, a duty to warn other tenants might have arisen. However, since such an investigation did not take place, this conclusion is not part of the court's holding but merely *dictum.*

Disposition

The purpose of the disposition section of the case brief is to alert the reader to the outcome of the case. The key to drafting it is to be concise. In *Davis v. Gomez,* where the appellate court found that the trial court was correct in granting summary judgment in favor of the Gomez defendants, the disposition can be relayed in one word: "Affirmed." For a more complex disposition, it might be necessary to expand this section.

2-4 Practical Considerations

There you have it—a complete and concise case brief for *Davis v. Gomez*. Having followed the step-by-step logic behind that case brief, you have now gained the raw skills necessary to unravel the law that lurks within the thousands, indeed millions, of opinions that fill every law library.

Of course, you will need much practice to refine those skills, and you will learn much about the law along the way. Some things that you learn will surprise you—such as the fact that not all judges write with clarity. You will also learn that opinions are written assuming that readers are trained to understand legal concepts and decipher legalese. You must be prepared to overcome these obstacles. Keep your legal dictionary at hand, learn as much as you can about the substantive law, learn where to find the answers to questions that arise, persevere until you understand the problem at hand, and don't be afraid to ask for help.

As you gain experience in case briefing, you will develop your own techniques, or learn techniques preferred by your supervising attorney. For example, in order to conserve space, some firms prefer case briefs that identify the litigants (parties to a lawsuit) as *P* and *D* rather than as plaintiff and defendant, or sometimes by the Greek letters π (pi) for plaintiff and Δ (delta) for defendant. Another shorthand notation is the letter *K* for contract. No one technique is preferable; but whatever format or style you choose, remember that your brief must be thorough, accurate, and understandable to those who need to read and rely upon it.

Finally, in preparing a case brief you should always keep in mind the goal of the attorney for whom you are working. For some cases an extensive and detailed analysis will be necessary; for other cases, little more will be needed than a brief statement of the facts and holding. Some case briefs are thus long and formalized; others short. You and your supervising attorney are a team, and to function well as a team you must coordinate your goals.

These first two chapters have provided you with an introduction to the American legal system, the challenge of legal research, and basic case analysis. Now it's time to turn to the task of legal writing.

Figure 2–3 Case Brief

Case Brief - Davis v. Gomez

Citation:
Davis v. Gomez, 207 Cal.App.3d 1401, 255 Cal.Rptr. 743 (Cal.Ct.App., 1989)

Parties:
Robert Davis (plaintiff/appellant); Mary Sue Davis (plaintiff/appellant); Charlene Townsend (defendant); Robert Gomez (defendant/respondent); Gomez and Gomez (defendant/respondent). [Note: The identity of the respondents is not entirely clear. The caption of the case identifies only the two defendants listed here, Richard Gomez individually, and some entity named "Gomez and Gomez." The opinion refers to a "partnership," presumably "Gomez and Gomez," but identifies three individuals (Richard Gomez, Rudy Gomez, and Maria Gomez) as "respondents." There is also a reference to a "Robert" Gomez at page 744. It will be assumed herein that the "Gomez defendants," regardless of their individual identity, and regardless of the nature of their partnership, were all co-owners. The confusion does not appear to have an impact on the decision of the court.]

Issues:
1. Under California law, does the landlord of a multiple-unit dwelling owe a duty to the tenants therein to monitor or control the alleged psychotic behavior of a fellow tenant in the same building, or to warn the other tenants of dangers associated with such alleged psychotic behavior?
2. To the extent such duty exists, was it breached in this case?

Facts:
On June 29, 1986, Tyrone Davis, a tenant in a building owned by the Gomez defendants, was shot and killed by a fellow tenant in the same building, Charlene Townsend.

Prior to the shooting, Townsend had been exhibiting symptoms of allegedly psychotic behavior, of which the Gomez defendants were aware. In addition, Townsend possessed a gun, of which the Gomez defendants were also aware.

The Gomez defendants took no action with regard to the Townsend situation prior to the incident in which she shot and killed Davis.

Plaintiff Robert Davis and plaintiff Mary Sue Davis are the parents of the deceased Tyrone Davis.

Prior Proceedings:
Plaintiffs filed an action for wrongful death against Charlene Townsend, and also against the Gomez defendants as owners of the building. Summary judgment was granted in favor of the Gomez defendants in the Superior Court, Los Angeles County. Plaintiffs appealed the granting of summary judgment. There is no indication in this decision as to the disposition with regard to defendant Charlene Townsend; she is not a a party to this appeal.

Holding:
Under the circumstances present in this case, the failure of the landlord to take action with regard to tenant Townsend's allegedly psychotic behavior was NOT a proximate cause of the shooting death of tenant Davis.

Reasoning:
The trial court found that, though a landlord has a "duty to preserve the quiet enjoyment of all tenants," and though the behavior of tenant Townsend might have represented a "common nuisance" which the landlord had some duty to abate, "it does not follow that anyone should have foreseen the escalation of that behavior into a fatal shooting." Therefore, as a matter of law, the court held that the landlord's failure to take action was NOT the proximate cause of the decedent's death.

The appellate court adopted the reasoning of the trial court. It also pointed out that there was no evidence to support the contention that Townsend had been "brandishing and exhibiting" the gun, nor did plaintiffs establish what action the landlord allegedly "could have taken, even with a reasonable investigation, with respect to Ms. Townsend's deteriorating mental condition."

There is *dictum* which indicates that if an investigation had been conducted by the Gomez defendants and had revealed reason to believe that tenant Townsend was dangerous, a duty to warn or take other action might have arisen.

Disposition:
Affirmed.

SUMMARY

2–1

A case brief is an objective summary of the important points of a case. This is different from a trial brief or appellate brief, each of which is drafted not to be objective, but rather to persuade.

2–2

The typical printed opinion appearing in a reporter contains several characteristic components. Star-paging enables the reader to identify page references from other reporters. The shorthand case name identifies the case at the top of the page. The parallel citation provides references to other reporters in which the case text appears. The full name of the case identifies all the parties and their position in the litigation (for example, plaintiff or defendant). The docket number is assigned to the case by the court for administrative purposes, and is usually included along with the date the decision was rendered and the full name of the court. The synopsis is an extremely short summary of the case prepared not by the court, but by the publisher of the reporter. A syllabus is a summary prepared by the court. Key numbers and headnotes are included, as well as the attorneys and judges involved in the matter and, of course, the text and disposition of the case. Decisions can be affirmed or reversed or subject to some other disposition. There can be majority opinions, dissenting opinions, and concurring opinions. The holding of a court is that aspect of the decision which directly affects the outcome of the case; *dictum* is a statement made by the court that goes beyond what is necessary to reach the disposition.

2–3

When preparing a case brief, you must first read the relevant case, then follow several steps to produce a document with several components. First, identify the case. Second, describe the parties. Third, identify the issues that were before the court for decision. Fourth, set out the relevant facts. Fifth, trace the procedural history of the case. Sixth, identify the holding of the court, taking great care to reflect accurately the precise parameters of the court's decision. Seventh, analyze the court's reasoning, again taking great care to restate and summarize the court's rationale. Eighth, alert the reader to the outcome of the case with a concise, shorthand statement of the court's disposition.

2–4

In drafting case briefs, you must overcome obstacles such as poorly drafted or highly technical judicial opinions. Over time you will develop your own style or learn the characteristic style preferred by your firm. Alway keep in mind the goal that you and your supervising attorney are attempting to accomplish with the drafting of the case brief. This goal will influence length, formality, and general content.

REVIEW

Key Terms

Before proceeding, review the key terms listed below to be sure you understand each one. If necessary, read over the corresponding section of the chapter. When you are ready to test your understanding, answer the Review Questions.

case brief
star-paging
shorthand case name
parallel citation
caption
docket number
synopsis
syllabus
disposition
affirmed
reversed
remanded

vacated
per curiam
majority opinion
concur
concurring opinion
dissent
dissenting opinion
grant
deny
holding
dictum
issues
facts
relevant
material
prior proceedings
reasoning

Questions for Review and Discussion

1. What is the difference between a case brief and a brief written for a trial or appellate court?
2. What are the components of a printed opinion?
3. Why is star-paging useful?
4. What is the difference between a majority opinion and a dissent?
5. What are the components of a case brief?
6. How do you identify the relevant facts in an opinion?
7. How do you identify the issues presented by a written opinion?
8. How do you locate the procedural history of a case as set forth in the opinion?
9. What is a holding? What is a disposition?
10. What is the reasoning of an opinion?

Activities

1. Read *Tarasoff v. Regents of the University of California*, 551 P.2d 334 (California 1976) and *Thompson v. County of Alameda*, 614 P.2d 728 (California 1980) and answer the following questions:
   a) What is the holding in Tarasoff? In Thompson?
   b) Are the results different? If so, list the reasoning of each court for reaching its decision.
   c) Can these cases be reconciled?
2. In your law library, find *Trump v. Chicago Tribune*, 616 F.Supp. 1434 (S.D. N.Y. 1985) and answer the following questions:
   a) Name the parties to the case.
   b) Identify the court and the case reporter.
   c) List the West topics and keys in the case.
   d) Identify the objectives of the parties.
   e) List the prior proceedings.

NOTES

CHAPTER 3 Introduction to Legal Writing

OUTLINE

COMMENTARY

On Monday morning you receive a telephone call from a friend who is buying a new car. The language of the contracts, credit agreements, warranties, and disclaimers has left him in a panic—it's too complicated to understand! He wants to make an appointment to have you review and explain the various provisions.

Your supervising attorney suggests you obtain copies of the contracts, then draft a letter to your friend explaining them in everyday language. Simplifying complicated legal documents is a task you will perform as a paralegal.

OBJECTIVES

Up to this point, you've been learning background information and valuable research skills. Now you're ready for an introduction to legal writing. After completing this chapter, you will be able to:

1. Define "legalese."
2. Describe a "term of art."
3. List basic techniques for good legal writing.
4. Identify the audience for a legal document.

5. Describe the difference between an "objective" purpose and an "adversarial" purpose.
6. Apply the "IRAC" method for defining and researching a legal issue.
7. Balance time constraints.
8. Organize a legal document.
9. List several different types of legal documents.
10. Identify two different types of pleadings.

3–1 Tradition and Trend in Legal Writing

Most people have the same reaction as the friend in our Commentary to legal documents—panic. They consider legal writing to be complicated, cumbersome, and incomprehensible. Although some legal writers do, in fact, allow their writing to deteriorate, most are reasonably competent. Why, then, is the image of legal writing so negative?

One answer, oddly enough, is the importance of precision. As with all writing, good legal writing requires **clarity**, *conciseness*, *accuracy*, and *simplicity*—but above all else, it must be **precise**. It is essential that every person interpreting a document take the same meaning from the words chosen. This leads to an unwritten rule of law—namely, that once a given usage is agreed to have a given meaning, it should ever after be the accepted method of conveying that meaning. Any change from that usage necessarily implies that an alteration of that meaning is intended.

This unwritten rule has led to a reliance on archaic legal language. Terms that originated hundreds of years ago and which sound odd in the context of our modern language are still used in legal documents because their meaning is accepted. Legal **jargon**, often referred to as **legalese**, is characterized by the frequent use of Latin, French, and Old English terms unfamiliar to most present-day vocabularies. You have already seen such Latin terms as *in re* and *ex parte* as they are used in case names (*ex parte* also has another meaning, as we will note). Other terms commonly used include *res ipsa loquitor* (a Latin term from tort law meaning "the thing speaks for itself"), *voir dire* (a French term for the questioning of a potential juror for evidence of prejudice or unfitness), and *writ* (an Old English term for an order of a court, or the first written notice of a lawsuit). These are just a sampling. Other examples of legalese are listed in Table 3–1, but a complete list would be enormous.

Legalese is also characterized by usages rarely seen elsewhere. Such phrases as, "Hereof fail not but by these presents make due and proper return," or "Comes now James Jones, Plaintiff in the above-styled and numbered cause, who does by these presents make due complaint," are examples of archaic sentence structure seen in legal documents. Such words as *aforementioned* or *hereinafter*, seldom used in everyday language, clutter legal sentences. These practices are often a holdover from centuries of Anglo-Saxon jurisprudence.

Wordiness is another characteristic of legalese. Lawyers often use a phrase with a combination of synonymous, hence redundant, words. Such phrases as *cease and desist*, *null and void*, and *give, devise and bequeath* date back to a time when two or three similar words were used to ensure clarity. Documents had to interpreted correctly by people of different nationalities, in an era when language lacked the consistency of modern times. Although historically there may have been distinctions between the words used, current legal practice has for the most part erased them and rendered such phrases redundant.

Tradition has been a powerful force in the law, as you might expect from a system in which the concepts of precedent and *stare decisis* play so important

Table 3–1 Examples of Legalese

The following table provides examples of legal jargon with the corresponding definitions in plain English. One of the challenges of legal writing is to exercise good judgment in deciding whether to employ legal terminology (which may have value for its precision or its standing as a term of art) or plain English.

Legalese	Translation
a fortiori	for a stronger reason
certiorari	discretionary request to the U.S. Supreme Court or other appellate court for review of a case
demurrer	request by defendant for a dismissal of a cause of action
duces tecum	to bring with you; a form of writ or request
ex parte	1. concerning the application of; 2. independent contact with an official, usually the judge, without the presence of the opposing side
inter alia	among other things
laches	principle of equity in which the passage of time prohibits pursuit of a cause of action
remittitur	judicial review and revision of an excessive judgment
res ipsa loquitor	the thing speaks for itself; in tort law, a doctrine that allows a finding of negligence without proof thereof
sua sponte	by the judge's own motion
tort	civil wrongdoing to another person
voir dire	to speak the truth; in practice refers to the examination of prospective jurors
writ	an order of the court, or the first pleading filed in a lawsuit

a role. Things are done a certain way because that is how they have always been done; certain language is used because it has always been used. Thus, not only for the reason of precision, but also because of institutional custom and perhaps even out of sentiment, the legal profession has clung to traditional language at the expense of broader understanding. Therefore language that is clear to a trained lawyer or paralegal is unclear to the average citizen, leading to the negative image of "legalese."

More often than not, legalese is used from habit rather than necessity. The objective of precision can be better achieved by rigorous and exacting use of modern language than by reliance on anachronistic formulas. As Richard Wydick observes in his book *Plain English for Lawyers* (Durham, NC: Carolina Academic Press, 1985):

> [W]e use eight words to say what could be said in two. We use arcane phrases to express commonplace ideas. Seeking to be precise, we become redundant. Seeking to explain, we become verbose. Our sentences twist on, phrase within clause within clause, glazing the eyes and numbing the minds of our readers.

The modern trend in legal writing is to emphasize broader comprehensibility. Whenever possible, **plain English** should be used. Long, complicated sentences should be the exception, not the rule. Archaic terms and phrases should be replaced by equivalent modern language. When one word is sufficient, avoid redundant combinations.

Of course, the survival of some legalese is inevitable, and even justifiable. Just as it is easier for doctors to use certain medical terminology, so it is easier for lawyers to use certain shorthand **terms of art** despite their obscurity to the general public. For example, the concise term *voir dire* mentioned previously requires a lengthy explanation in plain English, as does the alternate meaning of *ex parte* (contact with an official of the court in the absence of the opposing party). You must, however, use good judgment when evaluating the desirability of using legalese, and more often than not, there is a better alternative in plain English.

Legal writing needs to be demystified. Many people are under the impression that legal documents must be complicated, and that quality is related to complexity. This is simply not so. Indeed, the best expression of an idea is often the simplest composition that accurately conveys the intended meaning. The use of archaic legal terms and phrases should be minimized and plain English used instead. In the next few chapters we focus on techniques that:

- employ short, succinct sentences;
- minimize legalese;
- avoid redundancy;
- emphasize simple language in simple form (subject-verb-object) using accepted rules of grammar; and
- remind us that writing is reading—and good writing will only develop when we reread what we have written.

3–2 Prewriting Considerations

Now you know why legal language often causes people to panic. You know that eliminating excess legalese can help to reduce that panic. You have learned that some legalese remains useful. You have also learned that certain rules which apply to all forms of writing, such as the superiority of short sentences and simple words, apply to legal writing as well. Before you refine your knowledge of legal writing techniques, however, you must address four preliminary considerations: identifying your **audience**; identifying your purpose; defining and researching the issues presented; and evaluating time constraints.

Identifying the Audience

Lawyers prepare a wide range of writings for a diverse group of recipients. Some will be read by highly trained judges; others by less sophisticated clients. Before beginning a writing task, a lawyer or paralegal must determine:

- to whom the document is directed;
- the level of legal expertise of that person or persons; and
- the degree of that person or persons' familiarity with the subject.

There may be particular problems in a given situation, for example, language barriers or physical or mental disability. As a paralegal, you have to learn how to overcome potential obstacles.

Don't make assumptions when determining the audience. For example, you might think that the audience for a demand letter is easy to identify: the person upon whom your client is making demand, or in other words, the person to whom the letter is addressed. Such an assumption could lead to a critical error if your demand letter must meet statutory requirements in order to be effective. Consider a demand letter to be sent to a physician accused of malpractice. There may be a statute that outlines specific requirements for you to put the physician "on notice" of the claim. In such a case, the demand letter is drafted for two audiences—the physician who is being notified, of course, and, equally important, the court that may eventually have to determine whether the requirements have been met. The court will not appear in the salutation, nor even, quite possibly, in the letter itself—yet the judge who may someday evaluate the letter is a crucial segment of the audience who must be considered.

Identifying the Purpose

In order to draft any effective writing, you must identify your purpose. Do you want to update a client on the status of a lawsuit? Do you want to convince a court that your client's position should prevail in a pending motion? Are you summarizing a deposition transcript? Depending on your purpose, your approach to the task will differ markedly. It is therefore critical that you identify this purpose before you begin drafting.

The purpose of most legal documents falls into one of two broad categories—**objective** or **adversarial**. Objective documents accurately convey information and avoid bias. A letter to your client estimating his chances for success would be an objective document, as would an interoffice memo summarizing the current state of the law that applies to a given set of facts. Adversarial documents, on the other hand, are argumentative, drafted to emphasize the strong points of your client's position and the weaknesses of the opposing party's. They are *not* objective; they are *not* designed to balance both sides. A demand letter written to press your client's opponent or a brief submitted to persuade an appellate court are examples of adversarial documents.

Some documents have both objective and adversarial elements. For example, when drafting a contract proposal you will be seeking to reflect accurately the agreement of the parties (an objective purpose), while at the same time construing all ambiguous aspects of the agreement in your client's favor (an adversarial purpose).

By determining your purpose, you establish a focus that will enable you to accomplish your objective in every document you draft. In Table 3–2 we identify some strategies for accomplishing different purposes.

Table 3–2 Strategies for Different Writing Purposes

Purpose	Strategy
To Inform	1. Identify audience 2. Determine extent of audience's knowledge 3. Research relevant information 4. Determine what you desire to communicate
To Persuade	1. Identify audience 2. Determine relevant information 3. Research relevant information 4. Emphasize positive information and present in most favorable light 5. Convince audience that your position is the better position
To Discover Information	1. Identify audience 2. Determine information you need 3. Research relevant sources 4. Determine information that audience may possess 5. Elicit information that is important without revealing your position
To Prepare Legal Documents	1. Identify audience 2. Determine legal requirements 3. Elicit client's needs

Defining and Researching the Issues

Once you've identified your audience and determined your purpose, are you ready to begin writing? The answer is "No." Before you begin writing, you must define the issues presented and conduct the research necessary to address these issues.

For some documents, this last prewriting consideration may be easy. If, for example, you are simply updating a client on recent developments in a case, the issue is identical to the purpose (informing the client) and the research may be as simple as reviewing the file or even relating from memory.

In much legal writing, however, you will have to analyze the issues implied by your purpose and address them so as to accomplish your objective. A commonly used technique is the **IRAC method:**

- Identify the *issue* involved;
- Determine the *rule of law;*
- *Apply* the rule of law to the facts of your matter; and
- Reach a *conclusion.*

Taking the first letter of the four key items yields the mnemonic (memorizing) device *IRAC*. Let's take a closer look at each of these items.

The Issue The **issue** is the legal problem presented. For example, the issue in our Commentary problem is the meaning of the documents involved in the purchase of a new car. You have to inform your friend of several things—what the documents mean, whether they meet all legal requirements, and whether he has any option to negotiate their content.

The Rule of Law Having determined the issue, you must research the law to identify relevant statutes, regulations, cases, and constitutional provisions. Those sources that apply constitute the **rule of law** controlling the issue. For example, taking our Commentary situation, a statute might require certain portions of the contract to be written in plain English or in oversized typeface, or a case might have held that certain financing disclosures are required.

Applying the Law to the Facts The rule of law is an abstract concept that must be analyzed in the context of the particular facts of your client's matter. Applying the law to the facts enables you to address the issue in a manner meaningful to your client. Suppose, for example, that your research on our Commentary problem has shown that a car dealership must orally inform a purchaser of the repossession provisions in a sales contract. After you apply this rule of law to the facts of your specific matter, the letter to your friend might read in part as follows:

> The dealership is required to inform all prospective purchasers of their rights in the event of nonpayment, and to have the prospective buyer initial the relevant provisions of the contract. Your initials, however, do not appear next to those provisions.

The letter thus takes the rule (which requires initialing) and applies it to the facts (your friend did not initial his contract).

The Conclusion The result of your analysis is your **conclusion**. Carrying forward the Commentary example to this final step, your letter to your friend might conclude:

> The dealership has failed to comply with the requirement that you initial provisions that explain your rights upon nonpayment. This is an important requirement of state law, and the contract is therefore rendered voidable at your discretion.

The conclusion is the summation of your analysis. It answers the questions raised by the issues.

Time Constraints

Deadlines are a fact of life in legal practice. Virtually every document filed with a court is governed by a time requirement. In addition, practical considerations often create unofficial deadlines (a client may need certain legal questions answered immediately to gain an edge on his competitors). Finally, as a paralegal you will be expected to complete tasks within the time assigned by your supervising attorney.

An important prewriting consideration is thus to evaluate the time available and allocate your efforts accordingly. A brief due in 48 hours will be prepared in a fashion and on a schedule quite different from one due in four weeks. You must learn to budget your time without affecting the quality of your writing—which can be accomplished by organizing efficiently and taking advantage of all available resources (for example, if an old case involved similar issues, you might use the research from that file as a starting point).

3–3 Organizing the Legal Document

Organizing the document might be considered your final prewriting consideration, but it is better to think of it as the first consideration in the writing stage itself. Your plan of organization provides the blueprint by which your document will be crafted.

Outlining

The best method of organizing a legal document is by outlining. An **outline** is the skeleton of a legal argument, advancing from the general to the specific. You have no doubt prepared outlines in other contexts in the past. A legal outline differs from these other outlines in content but not concept. It is intended to help you to critically examine your approach, leading to a document that flows logically to a conclusion which accomplishes your purpose. An outline will assist you in:

- focusing on logical development;
- preventing critical omissions; and
- evaluating how well you accomplish your purpose.

An outline may use a sentence format or a shorthand topic format. When using a topic format, be sure you include enough information to enable you to remember why you included each topic. Unless you are comfortable or familiar with a particular subject area, the fuller sentence format is preferable. An accepted format for an outline is illustrated in Figure 3–1, page 300.

Figure 3–1 Example of an Outline

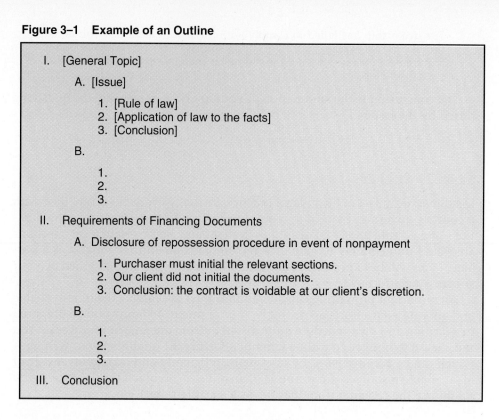

I. [General Topic]
   A. [Issue]
      1. [Rule of law]
      2. [Application of law to the facts]
      3. [Conclusion]
   B.
      1.
      2.
      3.
II. Requirements of Financing Documents
   A. Disclosure of repossession procedure in event of nonpayment
      1. Purchaser must initial the relevant sections.
      2. Our client did not initial the documents.
      3. Conclusion: the contract is voidable at our client's discretion.
   B.
      1.
      2.
      3.
III. Conclusion

Outlining is an effective method to focus and strengthen your document. It provides a guide that, carefully followed, leads to an organized and effective document.

An Alternative to Outlining

An alternative to a written outline is to separate your raw research into categories. This can be accomplished by using file cards or by grouping photocopies of related cases and statutes (for cases and statutes that overlap issues, place a separate copy in each group, or remind yourself with a post-it note). By ordering the cards or groups of photocopies in a logical sequence, you create in effect an unwritten outline—you have made decisions about organization and development. This method is somewhat unorthodox, but as you gain experience it may be a practical timesaver.

3–4 Types of Documents

There are many different types of legal documents, which we discuss in later chapters. Let's consider a few right now.

Letters

Correspondence is essential in virtually every legal matter. **Letters** to the client, to opposing counsel, to the court, to witnesses, to government agencies—the list is endless. Demand letters, opinion letters, retainer letters, settlement letters, update letters advising of case status or court date—some are objective, some adversarial, all important.

Internal Memoranda

An interoffice memorandum explains the law so as to inform and educate the attorneys. As mentioned, this memo is an objective writing that relates both good news and bad about the law as it applies to the client's case, and it can be used as a basis for strategy, as basic research for a brief, or as background when drafting pleadings or other documents.

Operative Documents

Many documents have, as a result of their language and content, legal effects beyond the mere transmission of information. Executed contracts, leases, wills, and deeds are examples of **operative documents** that lawyers and paralegals draft. Such documents serve to define property rights and performance obligations, and slight alterations in meaning can have great impact on the parties involved. Without minimizing the importance of precision in every document drafted, it is safe to say that you should be doubly attentive to accuracy in operative documents.

A Few Words About Forms

Many types of legal documents, particularly operative documents, incorporate **forms.** Forms are documents that set forth standard language which is the accepted format for accomplishing a given purpose. Recourse to a form is a decision to be made by your supervising attorney, although he or she may delegate some discretion to you.

The language in forms may be cumbersome and confusing, with excessive use of legalese and archaic construction. Forms are valuable, however, based upon their widespread acceptance. This is the paradox of precision—that a document confusing on its face due to peculiar language is actually precise as a result of years, even centuries, of accepted meaning.

There are forms for deeds, for wills, and for leases: indeed, there are multivolume sets of forms covering an enormous range of legal transactions. Most forms provide standard language with blank spaces where specific information from your case can be inserted; others provide the standard language with examples of information from other transactions, which must then be modified to fit your specific situations. The standard language in these forms, often referred to as **boilerplate**, should not be changed unless you are instructed to do so by your supervising attorney.

An example of a legal form is the promissory note found in Figure 3–2 on page 302.

Pleadings

Pleadings are documents filed with the court in a pending lawsuit that define the issues to be decided by the court at trial. The claims, counterclaims, defenses, and special defenses of the parties constitute the pleadings. The document that initiates a lawsuit is the **complaint**, filed by the plaintiff. The defendant

Figure 3–2 Sample of a Promissory Note Form

PROMISSORY NOTE

$ ________________ ____________, Texas A.D. 19___

For value received ______________________________ promises to pay to ________________ on order, the sum of ________________ dollars, with interest from date at the rate of ____________ per cent per annum, both principal and interest payable at ______________________________________ ________________.

This note payable in ______________________________ installments of ____ ____

All past due principal and interest on this note shall bear interest at the rate of ten per cent per annum.

It is understood and agreed that the failure to pay this note, or any installment as above promised, or any interest hereon, when due, shall at the option of the holder of said note, mature the full amount of said note, and it shall at once become due and payable.

And it is hereby especially agreed that if this note is placed in the hands of an attorney for collection, or collected by suit, or in probate or bankruptcy proceedings ____________ agree to pay a reasonable amount additional on the principal and interest then due thereon as attorneys' fees.

Address: ________________________ ________________________

Phone: ________________________ ________________________

responds to the complaint with an **answer**, replying to the claims of the plaintiff. There can be other pleadings as well. Pleadings are adversarial documents, drafted to place your client's position in the best light, and they must be prepared in the format prescribed by the court's rules of procedure.

Motions

A **motion** requests that the court take an action. It can be filed by either the plaintiff or the defendant in a lawsuit. A defendant might file a "motion to strike," asking the court to rule out part of the plaintiff's claim on the grounds that it fails to state a claim supported by the applicable rules of law. Either party might file a "motion *in limine*," seeking a preliminary ruling on an issue of evidence. Or either party might file a "motion for summary judgment," arguing that there are no disputed questions of fact and that the matter can be decided based on an application of the law to the undisputed facts. Indeed, the number of different motions is high, limited only by the imaginations of counsel. Motions are always adversarial documents, drafted to favor your client's position.

Briefs

A **brief** is a formal written argument presented to the court, usually countered by a brief written by the opposing party. Note the important difference between a case brief, which you studied in detail in Chapter 2 (an objective document) and the formal brief presented to a court, which is adversarial. A brief filed with the trial court is called a *trial brief;* if filed with an appellate court it is called an *appellate brief.* A close relative of the brief is the *memorandum of law to the court,* which performs exactly the same function as a brief, but is usually filed in support of a less significant motion. The difference between a formal brief and a memorandum of law to the court is more semantic than real.

Discovery Documents

The procedural rules governing lawsuits have liberal provisions that allow for **discovery**, when the opposing parties obtain information in the hands of the other party. Requests for documents or for responses to written questions (called **interrogatories**) are important adversarial documents that enable litigants to learn as much as possible about their opponent's case before trial. Although response to discovery requests must be honestly provided (hence they are objective), in fact an adversarial element often creeps into these responses, which can lead to time-consuming disputes in court.

3–5 Practical Considerations

Legal writing is an extremely varied subject area, with documents ranging from an informal client letter to a full-scale Supreme Court brief. There is room for both great eloquence and extreme brevity. There is a time for objectivity and a time for partisanship. There is a role for legalese and a role for plain English. Perhaps most important of all, there is a need for precision—a need to communicate ideas in a concise and unambiguous fashion.

A few practical considerations are universal. First, do all necessary background research. This includes the prewriting considerations outlined, as well as checking for technical requirements such as court rules on format. See Figure 3–3, which discusses some of the requirements of an appellate brief in Federal Court.

Second, always make your purpose clear by the use of a straightforward introduction. Readers do not enjoy guessing. Assuming too much about the expectations or knowledge of your audience can result in a document that confuses rather than enlightens.

Third, fully explain your position. Satisfy yourself that your points progress logically. Guide the reader through the subject matter. Avoid arriving at conclusions before exhausting your analysis.

Figure 3–3 Example of Federal Appellate Brief Requirements

Rule 28. Briefs

(a) Brief of the Appellant. The brief of the appellant shall contain under appropriate headings and in the order here indicated:

(1) A table of contents, with page references, and a table of cases (alphabetically arranged), statutes and other authorities cited, with references to the pages of the brief where they are cited.

(2) A statement of the issues presented for review.

(3) A statement of the case. The statement shall first indicate briefly the nature of the case, the course of proceedings, and its disposition in the court below. There shall follow a statement of the facts relevant to the issues presented for review, with appropriate references to the record (see subdivision (e)) . . .

(b) Length of Briefs. Except by permission of the court, or as specified by local rule of the court of appeals, principal briefs shall not exceed 50 pages, and reply briefs shall not exceed 25 pages, exclusive of pages containing the table of contents, tables of citations, and any addendum containing statutes, rules, regulations, etc.

Fourth, prepare a conclusion that concisely ties together the entire document. Again, be straightforward. As the introduction made your intent clear, so your conclusion should make the achievement of that purpose clear.

Finally, reread! Writing is nothing more than creating documents to be read. It is impossible to gauge how another person will read a document unless you yourself read it. By rereading you can see where your document succeeds and fails, then revise it into a precise, flowing finished product.

SUMMARY

3–1

Because of the long-standing and wide acceptance of the meaning of the words of which they are composed, legalese and anachronistic usages persist in legal writing. Although some terms of art remain useful, good legal writing is generally characterized by short, succinct sentences, a minimum of legalese, avoidance of redundancy, emphasis on simple language in simple form, and a recognition of the importance of rereading what you've written.

3–2

Prewriting considerations include identifying the audience and recognition that the sophistication of the audience will affect the nature of the language used; identification of the purpose, which will generally be either objective or adversarial; and a commitment to properly defining and researching the issues presented. A good method of analyzing the issues is the IRAC method, in which you identify the issue involved, determine the relevant rule of law, apply the rule of law to the facts of your matter, and reach a conclusion. The final prewriting step is to take into account the time constraints associated with your writing project.

3–3

Legal documents are often organized with the help of an outline, which is the framework of the proposed content, advancing from the general to the specific. An alternative to outlining is to group your raw research into categories, either by using file cards or by physically gathering related materials.

3–4

There are many different types of legal documents, including letters, internal memoranda, operative documents, forms, pleadings, motions, briefs, and discovery documents.

3–5

Writing is an extremely varied subject area. Keep in mind the following considerations: do all necessary background research; make your purpose clear with a straightforward introduction; fully explain your position; prepare a concise conclusion that ties your argument together; and finally, reread what you've written to ensure that you've accomplished your purpose.

REVIEW

Key Terms

Before proceeding, review the key terms listed below to be sure you understand each one. If necessary, read over the corresponding section of the chapter. When you are ready to test your understanding, answer the Review Questions.

clarity
precision
jargon
legalese
plain English
terms of art
audience
objective purpose
adversarial purpose
IRAC method
issue
rule of law
conclusion
outline
letters
internal memoranda
operative documents
forms
boilerplate
pleadings
complaint
answer

motion
brief
discovery
interrogatories

Questions for Review and Discussion

1. What is legalese?
2. What is a term of art?
3. What are some of the basic techniques associated with good legal writing?
4. What is the audience of a legal document?
5. What is the difference between an objective purpose and an adversarial purpose?
6. What is the IRAC method?
7. How can a paralegal effectively balance time constraints?
8. How does a writer go about organizing a legal document?
9. Name several different types of legal documents.
10. What are the two types of pleadings?

Activities

1. Review the promissory note in Figure 3–2.
   (a) Determine the purpose of the document and the audience.
   (b) Edit out all the legalese and unnecessary words.
2. Obtain a copy of your state's appellate brief requirements and identify all the constraints and legal requirements for filing a brief with your state.

CHAPTER 4 The Mechanics of Construction

OUTLINE

COMMENTARY

You have attended a deposition with your supervising attorney, taking notes on the questions posed and testimony given. Your notes reflect the rapid-fire context—scribbled sentence fragments, abbreviations, and jottings to jog your memory.

Afterward your supervising attorney informs you that, since that transcript is not expected for three weeks, she would like a summary of the deposition. She asks that you translate your notes into a written memorandum.

As you sit at your desk with your notes, you begin to ponder the basic principles of writing—words as the bricks of which a sentence is built, rules the mortar by which it is held together. Words and rules—language and grammar—provide the foundation from which good writing ascends.

OBJECTIVES

In this chapter we discuss some key elements of grammar—the rules of proper English—as they relate both to legal writing and to all writing. We analyze the basics: punctuation, sentence construction, and paragraphing. Then, in

Chapter 5, we turn to an examination of words—the pitfalls and possibilities of language.

After completing this chapter, you will be able to:

1. Set apart a parenthetical phrase.
2. Employ commas to provide clarity.
3. Identify two methods of combining the clauses of a compound sentence.
4. Inject certainty into a series with semicolons.
5. Format a block quotation.
6. Group passages with brackets and parentheses.
7. Separate sentence segments with a dash.
8. Distinguish simple, complex, and compound sentences.
9. Avoid sentence fragments and run-ons.
10. Draft a paragraph with a topic sentence, a body, and transitional language.

4–1 Punctuation

We affect the meaning of spoken language all the time—with the tone of our voice, by hesitating or speeding up, with facial expressions, hand movements, and the subtleties of body language. All these techniques are physical—and thus unavailable to writers. The writer must learn to recreate in the mind of the reader the impressions left by these embellishments. One way to accomplish this is by the artful use of punctuation. Let's consider some of its more significant aspects.

The Comma

Commas recreate verbal pauses. They separate distinct concepts and eliminate confusion, enabling the writer to establish a rhythm and maintain clarity. Commas often travel in pairs. They surround and set off phrases, as with the parenthetical phrase in Figure 4–1:

Figure 4–1 Use of Commas

> The plaintiff, who performed every act required of her by the terms of the contract, is seeking damages from the defendant.

The phrase set apart between commas could have been placed within parentheses, hence the term **parenthetical phrase**. Parenthetical phrases are often placed between commas, although it is not mandatory, as Figure 4–2 shows.

Figure 4–2 Use of Commas in Parenthetical Phrase

> **Between commas:**
>
> The plaintiff, James Jones, is assisting in the investigation of his case.
>
> **Without commas:**
>
> The plaintiff James Jones is assisting in the investigation of his case.

Where the parenthetical is short, as with "James Jones," the choice is largely a matter of personal style. You seek a document that "flows" (more about flow in the next chapter) and must decide whether the commas advance fluidity or impede it. If the parenthetical is long, as in Figure 4–1, it should be set off by commas. Remember that you may use two commas to set off a parenthetical, or none, but never use just one. Figure 4–3 shows two incorrect uses of commas.

Figure 4–3 Incorrect Use of Commas in Parenthetical Phrase

Incorrect:

The plaintiff, who performed every act required of her by the terms of the contract is seeking damages from the defendant.

The plaintiff who performed every act required of her by the terms of the contract, is seeking damages from the defendant.

How can you tell if a phrase is a parenthetical? One way is by reading the sentence without the phrase. If the sentence remains logical and grammatically correct, the phrase is likely a parenthetical. Parenthetical phrases supplement, or add information to, a thought that is already complete. Try reading the sentence in Figure 4–1 without the parenthetical phrase—it is less informative, but grammatical and logically complete.

If a phrase is **restrictive** (specifying or restricting the application of something), it is *not* parenthetical, and should not be set apart by commas, as Figure 4–4 shows.

Figure 4–4 Use of Commas in Restrictive Phrase

Correct:

Bankers who violate these statutes should go to jail.

Incorrect:

Bankers, who violate these statutes, should go to jail.

In the correct example, the phrase "who violate these statutes" specifies *which* bankers; it cannot be removed without changing the fundamental meaning of the sentence. The incorrect sentence creates the impression that *all* bankers violate the statutes (try reading it without the phrase).

We have noted that commas often travel in pairs. There are, of course, entirely proper sentences in which you will find only a single comma. A parenthetical, for example, may appear at the beginning of a sentence, as in Figure 4–5:

Figure 4–5 Parenthetical Phrase at Beginning of Sentence

Having performed every act required of him by the terms of the contract, the plaintiff is seeking damages from the defendant.

A single comma is also seen where a conjunction such as *but* or *and* joins two complete thoughts, as in Figure 4–6:

Figure 4–6 Use of Commas With Conjunction

The deposition transcript is lengthy, and its contents are fascinating.

or

Her eyesight is failing, but she heard the impact.

A common error in comma usage occurs when dealing with a series. There should be a comma after all but the last item in the series, as shown in Figure 4–7:

Figure 4–7 Use of Commas in Series

Correct:

The judge, jury, and prosecutor listened intently as defense counsel examined the witness.

Incorrect:

The judge, jury and prosecutor listened intently as defense counsel examined the witness.

This rule, however, does not necessarily apply to law firm names, something which, as a paralegal, you will be dealing with regularly, as in Figure 4–8:

Figure 4–8 Use of Commas in Law Firm Names

Correct:

Able, Baker & Charlie

Incorrect:

Able, Baker, & Charlie

There are many other specific rules governing the use of commas, some of the more important of which are set forth in Table 4–1. Once you have determined the message you intend, the comma can be a powerful means of avoiding confusion. As a paralegal drafting documents, you should be using commas to maximize clarity first, fluidity second.

The Semicolon

The **semicolon** is a close cousin of the comma. It is used to indicate a break in thought, though of a different sort than that indicated by a comma. Rather

Table 4–1 Some Examples of Comma Usage

Use Comma To:	Example:
set apart transitional language	Indeed, the statute is applicable and controlling.
set apart quotes	The defendant stated, "I'm innocent."
indicate an omission	The defendant went to Florida; his brother, to New Jersey; and his wife, to Florida.
clarify a date or number	1,000,000 January 1, 1992
set apart "yes" and "no"	Is the statute controlling? No, it is not.

than merely separating two thoughts, a semicolon also suggests a relationship between the two—making it a useful tool for an attorney or paralegal trying to make a point.

Semicolons are often used to join the components of a **compound sentence**. A compound sentence is one in which the clauses could stand separately, each ending with a period. In addition to using a semicolon or a period, a third method of expressing such a compound is with a comma and a conjunction, as we saw in Figure 4–6. In Figure 4–9 we express the first sentence from Figure 4–6 in these three different ways.

Figure 4–9 Expressions of Compound Sentences

With semicolon:

The deposition transcript is lengthy; its contents are fascinating.

As two sentences:

The deposition transcript is lengthy. Its contents are fascinating.

With conjunction and comma:

The deposition transcript is lengthy, and its contents are fascinating.

In this instance the original choice, with comma and conjunction, is probably the best choice, because the writer probably intended to imply no relationship between the two clauses (i.e., the length of the deposition is not what made it fascinating). Consider, however, the sentence in Figure 4–10:

Figure 4–10 Strategic Use of Semicolon

The defendant's blood alcohol level was twice the legal limit; his driving was erratic and led to the accident.

The use of the semicolon in this sentence implies the close relationship between the defendant's blood alcohol level and the erratic driving and subsequent accident. Although the two-sentence or comma-conjunction methods would convey the same information, the semicolon method conveys it with more force and is preferable.

A semicolon can also be useful in distinguishing separate elements in a series, particularly when commas are used in describing each individual element, as in Figure 4–11:

Figure 4–11 Use of Semicolon to Distinguish

Correct:

The witness identified defendant Jones, the butler; defendant Smith, the cook; and defendant Brown, the gardener.

Incorrect:

The witness identified defendant Jones, the butler, defendant Smith, the cook, and defendant Brown, the gardener.

The incorrect example would be correct if the witness had identified five separate people: (1) defendant Jones, (2) the butler, (3) defendant Smith, (4) the cook, and (5) defendant Brown (who was the gardener). However, if three witnesses were identified, the first sentence is clear and the second is confusing and misleading. Indeed, even if the second example were intended because there were five witnesses, it would still be preferable to separate all five by semicolons, so that confusion created by the lack of parallelism among the elements—some identified by name, some by occupation—would be eliminated.

Quotations

The use of quoted materials adds support to memoranda, briefs, letters, and any other legal writing in which the writer is trying to build an argument. Failing to follow the rules with regard to quotation marks, however, may distract the reader and detract from the force of your position.

When using a quote, should you include it in the body of the document or set it aside as a **block quote**? Although the context, and your ear for rhythm, will often dictate the better choice, a good rule of thumb is that any quote longer than 50 words (generally about three to five lines) should be set apart. This 50-word rule is incorporated into *A Uniform System of Citation* (the bluebook) for briefs and other court documents.

If the block quote format is chosen, the quoted passage is indented and single-spaced. Quotation marks are omitted at the beginning and end, but interior quotation marks should be kept. The citation appears on the line immediately following, at the original left margin. An example is shown in Figure 4–12.

Figure 4–12 Block Quote

It has been said that the case of *Swift v. Tyson* is based upon a fallacy:

> The fallacy underlying the rule declared in Swift v. Tyson is made clear by Mr. Justice Holmes. The doctrine rests upon the assumption that there is "a transcendental body of law outside of any particular state but obligatory within it . . .," [and] that federal courts have the power to use their judgment as to what the rules of common law are . . .

Erie Railroad v. Tompkins, 304 U.S. 64, 58 S.Ct. 817, 82 L.Ed. 1188 (1938), quoting from Holmes's dissent in *Black and White Taxicab and Transfer Co. v. Brown and Yellow Taxicab and Transfer Co.*, 276 U.S. 518, 533, 48 S.Ct. 404, 72 L.Ed. 681 (1928).

Note the use of brackets and ellipses (which we discuss further), as well as the use of a period to conclude the citation. Also note that the quote within the quote uses standard double quotation marks, since the outside quotation marks are omitted. If outside quotation marks are included, as when a quoted passage appears in the body of the text rather than in a separate block, the interior quotation marks would be single:

Figure 4–13 Interior Quotation

> The witness stated, "I heard the defendant shout, 'I didn't mean to kill her!'"

In addition to the standard purpose of attributing words to a specific source, quotation marks can also be used to indicate irony or sarcasm, or to identify or set apart a word or passage:

Figure 4–14 Use of Quotation Marks to Indicate Purpose

> **Irony:**
>
> Defendant argues that plaintiff benefited from defendant's partial performance of the obligations of the contract, but this "benefit" is hardly what was intended by the contract or anticipated by the plaintiff.
>
> **Sarcasm:**
>
> The alleged "witness" was not even present at the scene of the accident.
>
> **To identify:**
>
> In this contract the word "deliver" means to place in the plaintiff's hands, not send to him in the mail.

Using quotation marks to identify a word or phrase is common and acceptable. Using them for an ironic or sarcastic purpose is generally inappropriate in documents filed with a court, and under any circumstances should be done only after careful reflection.

A common source of confusion with regard to quotation marks is whether concluding punctuation goes inside the final quotation mark, or outside. Table 4–2 lists the rules for different punctuation marks.

Table 4–2 Concluding Punctuation

Placement of Quotation Marks

1. The period: A quotation mark appears *after* a period.
2. The comma: A quotation mark appears *after* a comma.
3. The question mark: A quotation mark appears *after* a question mark.
4. The semicolon: A quotation mark appears *before* a semicolon.
5. The colon: A quotation mark appears *before* a colon.

Parentheses, Brackets, and the Ellipsis

Clarity often demands grouping or special identification of text. This can be accomplished with punctuation: **parentheses** ( ) and brackets unite cohesive passages, **brackets** [ ] indicate changes or additions, and an **ellipsis** (...) indicates the elimination of text from an extended quote.

Parentheses are an alternative to the commas we used in Figure 4–1, as shown in Figure 4–15:

Figure 4–15 Use of Parentheses

> The plaintiff (who performed every act required of her by the terms of the contract) is seeking damages from the defendant.

The two figures, 4–1 and 4–15, are identical except that in 4–15 we've replaced the commas with parentheses. Since both are grammatically correct, how do you choose between parentheses and commas? In general, the closer the relationship between the parenthetical clause and the main sentence, the stronger the tendency to favor the commas. If the relationship is slight, parentheses are the better choice. The relationship in Figure 4–1 and 4–15 probably justifies commas (it is the plaintiff's performance that entitles her to damages), whereas the sentence in Figure 4–16 is better expressed with parentheses:

Figure 4–16 Use of Parentheses

> The plaintiff (who is eighty-five years old) is seeking damages from the defendant.

The choice is, in these instances, simply a matter of degree. When choosing a particular sentence construction, it is often wise to consider balance and variety in your document as a whole. The need for balance and variety or for parallel construction (discussed further in Chapter 5), will often dictate your choice where it would otherwise be a toss-up.

Some confusion may arise over using parentheses with other punctuation marks. As a general rule, you should leave out ending punctuation *within* the parentheses unless it is a question mark or an exclamation point; with regard to the remainder of the sentence, punctuate it exactly as you would if the material contained within the parentheses were missing (this means the final punctuation mark should be outside the final parentheses, as you see at the end of this sentence).

In Figure 4–12 we saw the word *and* in brackets. What do brackets signify? Generally speaking, brackets appearing in a quote identify some departure from the original text—in Figure 4–12 the addition of "and" to the original text makes the quote grammatical without changing the meaning. Brackets are also often used to change capitalization in a quoted passage to conform to the sentence in which it appears, as in Figure 4–17:

Figure 4–17 Use of Brackets to Identify Departure From Text

> The court noted that "[t]he fallacy underlying the rule in *Swift v. Tyson* is made clear by Mr. Justice Holmes."

Compare this to the block quote in Figure 4–12, and note how the bracketed lower-case *t* here incorporates the quote into the flow of the sentence.

Brackets have other uses as well. They may be used as parentheses within parentheses, and are used to enclose the word *sic,* a Latin term used to signify an error of spelling or usage in a quoted passage. In addition, brackets can be used to insert editorial comments or explanations into quoted materials, as in Figure 4–18:

Figure 4–18 Use of Brackets to Insert Editorial Comment

> The language of the will states, "Any member of the Jones family [there are four surviving members] alive at the time of my death shall be entitled to $1000 from my estate."

Another mark used to specially identify text is the ellipsis. Unlike brackets and parentheses, however, an ellipsis indicates the *omission* of text. It is formed by three dots (periods), as we saw in Figure 4–12. Punctuation that precedes or follows the omitted text may be included or excluded, depending on the needs of the sentence (the comma, for example, was retained after the ellipsis in Figure 4–12). A few simple rules govern the use of the ellipsis. First, there should be a space before the first dot, between each dot, and after the last dot. Second, when the words omitted follow a complete sentence, the sentence should end with the actual period, followed by the three spaced ellipsis points. Finally, when omitting a paragraph or more, the use of a line of dots is sometimes suggested (each spaced several spaces apart), although the three-dot device at the end of the last passage before the omission is also acceptable.

The ellipsis can be a valuable writing tool. Quotes are not always perfectly attuned to the context of your document. By judicious use of the ellipsis, you can eliminate extraneous passages and take your reader right to the heart of the matter.

Hyphens and Dashes

Hyphens are used to draw together groups of words to form a single idea—"up-to-date" is an example. As language evolves, accepted usage for such combinations often changes, and there is not always a consensus on proper form (for example: closeup/close-up; byproduct/by-product). In addition, although there are some standard rules (for example: hyphenate fractions such as one-half), they often have exceptions (don't hyphenate fractions when used as nouns, as in, "She wrote one half of the brief"). Perhaps it is best to forget the general rules about hyphens and, when in doubt, look it up in a dictionary. Hyphens are also used to divide words at the end of a line. The division must come between syllables, and it is wise to use a dictionary if the division is not obvious.

Dashes are longer than hyphens and are used for limited purposes. They can substitute for parentheses or parenthetical commas—as in this sentence—and can also be used to separate the segments of a two-part sentence, as in Figure 4–19:

Figure 4–19 Use of Dashes to Separate Two-Part Sentence

> His testimony was useless—biased, inconsistent, and obviously false.

Dashes are often used to indicate the word *to* when used with page numbers, dates, or other numerical references ("Earl Warren was Chief Justice from 1953–1969").

The Colon

Colons have several purposes. They follow the salutation in a letter, are used in expressions of time (for example: 10:48 p.m.), and can lead into a specified list:

Figure 4–20 Colons Preceding a List

> The statutory protection has three prerequisites: adequate notice, sufficient documentation, and a completed application.

Colons can also perform a function similar to a semicolon or period: joining together related phrases, as in this sentence. In general, a colon signifies a closer relationship than does a semicolon or a comma. Explanatory clauses are often preceded by a colon (for example, in Figure 4–19, a colon could substitute for the dash), as are quotations (see Figure 4–12).

Question Marks and Exclamation Points

Question marks are used in the ordinary manner in legal writing, with one caveat (warning): since the purpose of advocacy is to persuade, there is little place for rhetorical questions, hence little use for question marks in briefs or other documents filed with a court, other than formally stating the questions to be addressed.

Likewise, the **exclamation point** carries with it an air of informality that has little, if any, place in formal legal writing. Even if you find a certain fact extraordinary, it is better simply to state the fact than to emphasize it with an exclamation point.

The Apostrophe

Apostrophes arise primarily in two situations—contractions and possessives. As a general rule, contractions should be avoided in legal writing. "Cannot" is better than "can't"; "would not" than "wouldn't"; "it is" than "it's." Incidentally, it is unforgivable to confuse "it's" with "its"—the former is always a contraction of "it is," the latter always a possessive, as in "Its deadline is next week.")

Possessives are, of course, unavoidable. The general rule is to form a possessive for a singular noun by adding an apostrophe and an *s*. For a plural noun, you can usually simply add an apostrophe. The rule is the same for proper names. Although there are exceptions (e.g., men's, children's), in general you should follow this rule even when the result might seem odd:

Figure 4–21 Use of Apostrophe in Possessives

> Justice Stevens' opinion was lengthy.

4–2 Sentence Construction

A sentence uses words, punctuation, and rules of grammar to convey an idea. It is in the sentence that your writing begins to take form. Sentences should carry the reader through your document with a minimum of confusion. Let's turn now to the basics of sentence construction, then focus on a few things to watch out for.

The Simple Sentence: Subject/Verb/Object

Every sentence has a subject and a verb (also called a predicate). On occasion the subject is physically absent but implicit from the context; such usages, although acceptable in literature, have no place in legal writing. The simplest sentence structure is subject/verb:

Figure 4–22 Subject/Verb Sentence Structure

> The plaintiff won.

The subject in the sentence in Figure 4–22 is *The plaintiff* and the verb is *won*. Most sentences also contain an object that identifies the "receiver" of the subject's action:

Figure 4–23 Simple Sentence

> The plaintiff won the trial.

The object in this sentence—which tells what the plaintiff won—is *the trial*. This sentence format—subject/verb/object—is the most effective means of conveying ideas, and is known as the **simple sentence**. The further your writing departs from this level of simplicity, the weaker it may become.

Modifiers: Adjectives and Adverbs

The simple sentence may leave the reader asking questions. What kind of trial was it? How did the plaintiff win? To answer these questions, a writer can use **modifiers**—adjectives and adverbs—to add information. Adjectives modify nouns, adverbs modify verbs, as in Figure 4–24:

Figure 4–24 Use of Modifiers

> The plaintiff easily won the lengthy trial.

In Figure 4–24, "easily" is an adverb describing how the trial was won, and "lengthy" is an adjective describing the trial itself.

Beginning writers often make the mistake of equating lengthy descriptions with good writing. They may think that the more adverbs and adjectives they use, the better their writing will be. This is a false assumption. It is possible to create clear images in the mind of the reader and evoke powerful responses using nothing more than subjects and verbs. Indeed, more often than not, modifiers confuse rather than clarify. The sentence in Figure 4–24 may lead the reader to wonder—"lengthy" compared to what? "easily" as opposed to what? Although it is unfair to evaluate a sentence out of context (perhaps "length" and "ease" are essential to the writer's point), in general you should minimize the use of modifiers.

The Complex Sentence: Clauses

Although the simple subject/verb/object format is generally best, there are often circumstances that justify a departure. The addition of clauses creates a **complex sentence:**

Figure 4–25 Complex Sentence

> The plaintiff, who had spent a fortune in legal fees, won the trial.

In this sentence the phrase "who had spent a fortune in legal fees" is a **subordinate** (dependent) **clause** describing the subject of the sentence, and the rest of the sentence forms an **independent clause** that could stand on its own (i.e., without the subordinate clause) as a complete sentence.

Variety in sentence structure tends to create a more readable document, and the use of clauses to combine ideas contained in a succession of simple sentences can improve your writing. Your goal is to make your point in the simplest manner possible without becoming boring. Complex sentences give readers variety and interest.

The Compound Sentence

Compound sentences have two or more clauses, each of which is independent and could stand alone as a complete sentence. The clauses of a compound sentence are joined by either semicolons or conjunctions and commas to form a new sentence containing closely related ideas:

Figure 4–26 Compound Sentences

> **Comma and conjunction:**
>
> The plaintiff won the trial, and her triumph was the result of hard work by her attorney.
>
> **Semicolon:**
>
> The plaintiff won the trial; her triumph was the result of hard work by her attorney.

In a compound sentence, the semicolon is never followed by a coordinate conjunction such as and or but, but can be followed by certain subordinate conjunctions such as *however* or *although*. A comma, on the other hand, can never be used to separate compound clauses without a conjunction:

Figure 4–27 Separating Compound Clauses

Correct:

The defendant lost the trial; however, since he was thorough in his preparation and argued with eloquence, he should have no regrets.

The defendant lost the trial, but since he was thorough in his preparation and argued with eloquence, he should have no regrets.

Incorrect:

The defendant lost the trial; but since he was thorough in his preparation and argued with eloquence, he should have no regrets.

The defendant lost the trial, since he was thorough in his preparation and argued with eloquence, he should have no regrets.

Compound sentences, together with simple and complex sentences, lend welcome variety to your writing.

The Run-on Sentence and the Sentence Fragment

Run-on sentences have too many clauses for one grammatical sentence, **sentence fragments** too few. This is not the same as saying that run-ons are too long and fragments too short. A sentence can be too long or short stylistically, but grammatically correct. Run-ons and fragments are grammatically incorrect:

Figure 4–28 Run-ons and Fragments

Run-on Sentence (incorrect):

The plaintiff won the trial was long.

Correct:

The plaintiff won. The trial was long.

The plaintiff won the long trial.

Sentence Fragment (incorrect):

Testifying in great detail about the contract.

Correct:

The defendant is testifying in great detail about the contract.

The defendant was on the stand for two hours, testifying in great detail about the contract.

The run-on was eliminated by separating it into two sentences, or, alternatively, one grammatical sentence restructured to include two ideas. The fragment was corrected by identifying the subject who performed the action of "testifying." The second correct version is slightly more informative than the first. When choosing among alternative corrections, make sure the result is either a simple, complex, or compound sentence that expresses what the original, incorrect version intended.

Run-ons and fragments are indefensible in legal writing, where clarity is critically important. There is no excuse for allowing errors of sentence construction to muddle your point and confuse the reader.

4–3 Paragraphing

A paragraph is more than just a group of sentences—it is a group of related sentences. A paragraph uses sentences to convey an idea, which is introduced in the **topic sentence**, usually the first sentence of the paragraph. Having introduced the idea, the paragraph develops it in the **body**. Then, having developed the idea, the paragraph performs a **transitional function** that facilitates orderly progression through the entire document. Let's look at each of these individual areas—topic sentence, body, and transition.

The Topic Sentence

The topic sentence of a paragraph is necessary because, quite simply, a paragraph must have a topic. Each sentence in a paragraph must be tied to that topic and must advance it in some way. Sentences must avoid digressions, and even "essential" digressions should be tied somehow to the purpose of the paragraph. Otherwise, the digression belongs in a paragraph of its own.

That being said, let us consider the topic sentence. It generally appears at the beginning of a paragraph and, particularly in legal writing, typically states a proposition, which is then supported in the remainder of the paragraph.

Figure 4–29 Topic Sentence at Beginning of Paragraph

> The defendant's conduct with regard to the accident constituted negligence, and possibly recklessness. She was driving at a speed far beyond the speed limit. She was wearing neither glasses nor contact lenses, though her driver's license requires that she do so. She was weaving from lane to lane as a result of intoxication. Each of these offenses was a violation of her duty to drive with care, and therefore constitutes negligence. Taken together, they represent a blatant disregard for the rights of others that rises to the level of recklessness. In short, she was a threat to any driver unfortunate enough—as was plaintiff—to be on the same road.

The topic sentence in Figure 4–29 is underlined, and summarizes the argument to come. The sentences that follow support the point established by the topic sentence, culminating in the final two sentences which repeat the point dramatically.

Topic sentences do not always appear as the first sentence in a paragraph. Sometimes they don't even appear at all—they may be implicit. But the writer who omits the topic sentence is asking a favor of the reader—to store the information provided, sentence by sentence, until the purpose is revealed and the information can be logically fitted into the overall argument. This requires patience on the part of the reader, which constitutes a risk on the part of the writer—a risk that the reader will lose interest before the purpose has been made plain. It may be a risk worth taking—the drama or tension created may add to the overall impact—but it remains a risk nonetheless. In Figure 4–30 we see a paragraph with topic sentence at the end:

Figure 4–30 Topic Sentence at End of Paragraph

> The defendant was driving at a speed far beyond the speed limit. He was wearing neither glasses nor contact lenses, though his driver's license requires that he do so. He was weaving from lane to lane as a result of intoxication. In short, his conduct at the time of the accident constituted negligence and possibly recklessness: he was a threat to any driver unfortunate enough, as was plaintiff, to be on the same road.

The patience required of the reader, and the problems this might pose, should be immediately apparent. In general then, place your topic sentences at the beginning of each paragraph—and when you depart from this structure, do so with care.

The Body

The body of the paragraph contains the material that you claim supports the contention raised in the topic sentence. In Figure 4–29, for example, the sentences describing the defendant's excessive speed, failure to wear corrective lenses, and lane-weaving as a result of intoxication all support the assertion of the topic sentence that defendant was negligent and possibly reckless.

Paragraph development in legal writing often uses basic principles of argumentation. Having stated a proposition in the topic sentence, the writer endeavors to defend or support it in the succeeding sentences using one of several techniques. The proposition can be compared to similar situations; it can be contrasted with, or distinguished from, different situations; it can be explained or illustrated by a straightforward definition or example; it can be demonstrated logically, reasoning from basic principles; or it can be arrived at by some combination of these techniques, or related variants. Whatever technique is used, remember to tie your argument to the topic sentence. In Figure 4–31 on page 322, we show a topic sentence with various alternative follow-ups.

That there is relationship and overlap between and among these techniques is evident. The last two alternatives (explaining and reasoning), for example, are obviously closely related.

You should note that it is possible to use more than one technique in the same paragraph. For example, it is easy to imagine a paragraph that both compares analogous cases and distinguishes dissimilar cases, combining the methods of the first two alternatives.

Figure 4–31 Topic Sentence With Follow-Up

Topic sentence:

The defendant is not legally responsible for the injuries suffered by the plaintiff, who fell in defendant's store.

Compare and analogize:

Like the storekeeper in the case of *Jones v. Smith* (who was found to have used due care), she had placed large warning signs in prominent positions.

Contrast and distinguish:

Unlike the negligent storekeeper in *Brown v. Blue*, who allowed his employees to leave a freshly washed floor unattended and unidentified, the defendant stationed a clerk by the wet floor to warn customers, and provided a large sign that read,"Caution: Wet Floor!"

Explain or illustrate:

Legal responsibility requires a showing of negligence, and negligence requires the existence of a duty owed to the injured party. Because plaintiff was a burglar trespassing on the premises after hours, no duty was owed.

Reason or demonstrate through logic:

Only the owner of the premises can be held liable under the facts as proven by plaintiff. Defendant herself was not the owner of the premises in question; the building was owned by a corporation. Therefore defendant cannot be held responsible for the injuries suffered by the plaintiff.

Transitional Language

Transitional language provides signals to readers about the material they are reading. It reassures readers that there is a relationship between the writer's various points, and it serves to clarify that relationship. It is important, particularly in legal writing, that the reader follow, step-by-step, the progression of the argument. You can accomplish this by, quite simply, telling the reader what the argument is, as we discuss further in Chapter 5. It is this "telling" function that transitional language performs.

Figure 4–32 Transitional Language

Next, we will consider the cases that are distinguishable.

Since the cases all support the plaintiff's position, the conclusion is inevitable.

For example, the plaintiff in *Jones v. Smith* was held liable on facts similar to those in the instant matter.

Table 4–3 Transitional Words and Phrases

Passing of Time	Contrast or Opinion	Introduction	Summary/ Conclusion	Addition
Meanwhile	However	Initially	Therefore	Furthermore
Still	Notwithstanding	To begin	Accordingly	Moreover
Since	On the contrary	In order that (to)	Hence	Similarly
Ultimately	In contrast	Primarily	Consequently	Additionally
Presently	Although	First	In conclusion	In addition to
	Nevertheless		Finally	

The transitional language used—*next, since,* and *for example*—ties each sentence to other sentences in the writing, signalling the reader that there is a connection. See Table 4–3 for other examples of transitional language.

The transitional function can also be performed by using parallel construction or repetition, as in Figure 4–33:

Figure 4–33 Parallel Construction or Repetition

> The corporate statutes do not apply because *the business is not a corporation*; the partnership statutes do not apply because it is not a partnership; and the public utility statutes do not apply because it is not a public utility.
>
> *The business is not a corporation* because stock has never been sold nor corporate filings completed.

In the first paragraph, the parallel construction using the phrase *do not apply* ties the paragraph together; in the second paragraph, the phrase *The business is not a corporation* repeats a phrase taken from the first paragraph, providing the reader with an implicit indication that the sentences to come will explain the proposition first stated in the first paragraph. Repetition and parallel construction are in many instances (as here) virtually identical concepts. We consider them further in the next chapter.

4–4 Practical Considerations

The use of proper punctuation, sentence structure, and paragraphing techniques enables you to communicate ideas clearly. After mastering these basics you can begin to apply more subtle and complicated techniques.

A first draft often contains inconsistencies that will distract the reader and undercut your arguments. The first step in eliminating these problems is to review your draft for errors in the basics. A slight revision to a basic element often leads to dramatic improvement. By eliminating misleading punctuation, or adding punctuation to clarify, you ensure that your sentences accurately convey your ideas. When you vary sentence structure and eliminate run-ons and fragments, your paragraphs combine these ideas into a coherent argument. Finally, by structuring your paragraphs into logical units with clearly defined transitions, you carry the reader along the path to your conclusion.

SUMMARY

4–1

Punctuation embellishes writing and removes ambiguity. Commas can be used to set apart parenthetical phrases; semicolons can join the components of a compound sentence or clarify the elements in a list or series. Quotations add support to memoranda and briefs; parentheses, brackets, and ellipses group or identify special passages of text or omitted text. Hyphens draw words together, whereas dashes separate parenthetical clauses or disparate elements of a two-clause sentence. Colons can introduce quotes or lead into specified lists. Question marks and exclamation points are informal usages, and should be used sparingly in formal or legal writing (although question marks are acceptable for use in "questions presented" sections of memoranda or briefs). Apostrophes indicate contractions (although contractions are generally considered informal and should be avoided in legal writing) and possessives.

4–2

Simple sentences contain a subject and verb, and may contain an object and modifiers. Complex sentences contain a subordinate clause, and compound sentences contain at least two clauses that could stand alone as complete grammatical sentences. Simple sentences are preferable, although the need for variety (which prevents writing from becoming monotonous) suggests that complex and compound sentences be used as well. Excessive use of modifiers (adjectives and adverbs) undercuts your writing. A run-on sentence fails to join its component clauses grammatically; a sentence fragment lacks a subject or verb.

4–3

A paragraph needs a topic sentence to introduce its subject matter to the reader. The topic sentence is usually at the beginning of the paragraph. The body of the paragraph develops the subject matter introduced by the topic sentence. Transitional language helps guide the reader through the various paragraphs and sections of the document, carrying the reader smoothly from the beginning of the document to the end.

4–4

The first step in eliminating inconsistencies in a first draft is to review the draft for errors in the basics—punctuation, sentence structure, and paragraphing.

REVIEW

Key Terms

Before proceeding, review the key terms listed below to be sure you understand each one. If necessary, read over the corresponding section of the chapter. When you are ready to test your understanding, answer the Review Questions.

commas
parenthetical phrase
restrictive phrase
series
semicolon
compound sentence
block quote
parentheses
brackets
ellipsis
hyphen
dash
colon
question mark
exclamation point
apostrophe
simple sentence
modifiers

complex sentence
subordinate clause
independent clause
run-on sentence
sentence fragment
topic sentence
body
transitional function

Questions for Review and Discussion

1. What is a parenthetical phrase, and how can it be set apart?
2. Describe one way in which commas can bring clarity into a sentence.
3. How can compound clauses be combined?
4. How do semicolons inject clarity into a series?
5. Briefly describe the format for a block quotation.
6. How are parentheses and brackets used to group passages in a sentence?
7. When should a dash be used to separate segments of a sentence?
8. Describe: a simple sentence; a complex sentence; and a compound sentence.
9. What is a sentence fragment? What is a run-on sentence?
10. Describe the function of a topic sentence; define *body* in the context of paragraph structure; and explain what is meant by *transitional language*.

Activities

1. Rewrite the following passage:
   The Supreme Court, held that a "subject to legal documentation" provision in a hand-written document executed by parties after they had agreed on material terms of sale did not establish, as a matter of law, that no sales agreement had been reached.
2. Proofread and edit the following paragraph:
   I direct that my just and and legal debts and funneral expenses and all federal and state estate and inheratance taxes imposed upon my estate or any beneficiary therof including the portion of any such tax attributable to the proceeds of policies of insurance on my life or other property not constituting a part of my probate estate, be paid in fall out of my residuary estate as soon as convenient. This direction s not obligatory upon my Executrix and he is specifically given the right or renew and extend, in any form that she deems beast, any debt or charge existing at the time of my death, including any morgage on my home and similarly my Executrix shall have the right and power to incur indebtedness and to borrow money for the purpose of paying any or all of the aforesaid debts, expenses and taxes.

NOTES

CHAPTER 5 Effective and Persuasive Legal Writing

OUTLINE

5–1 Writing Is Reading
5–2 The Possibilities of Language
  Brevity, Clarity, and Precision
  Voice
  Similes and Metaphors
5–3 Pitfalls in Language
  Ambiguity
  Sexism
  Cliche's and Slang
  Failure of Subject and Verb to Agree
  Jargon
  Redundancy and Verbosity
5–4 Tell Them!
  Topic Sentences and Transitions
  Active Voice versus Passive Voice
  Structured Enumeration
  Take a Positive and Definitive Approach
5–5 Logical Development
  IRAC Method
  Strongest Argument First
  Chronological Development
  Outlining and Subheading
5–6 Practical Considerations

COMMENTARY

Your supervising attorney has asked that you prepare a draft memorandum in support of a motion he will be filing with the trial court. You perform the necessary research and return to your office, with pages of notes and a small pile of photocopied cases and statutes. You're now confident in your knowledge of punctuation, sentence structure, and paragraphing, but you want to bring more than just grammatical correctness to this memorandum—you want to prepare a document that will persuade the court. Now that you know the rules, you want to learn to evaluate words—to use language effectively to accomplish your purpose.

OBJECTIVES

Now that you've learned basic rules of grammar, sentence construction, and paragraphing, it's time to address some of the finer elements of writing. After completing this chapter, you will be able to:

1. Inject clarity and precision into your writing.
2. Define rhythm, flow, and voice.
3. Use similes and metaphors to make a colorful point.
4. Avoid ambiguity and redundancy.
5. Make subjects and verbs agree.
6. Use a simple method to eliminate obscurity in your writing.
7. Compare and contrast periodic sentences and cumulative sentences.
8. Differentiate active voice from passive voice, and know when to use each.
9. Use structured enumeration to identify the items in a list.
10. Logically develop your arguments.

5–1 Writing Is Reading

A writer strings together words to be read. The audience may be merely the writer him- or herself, as with a diary; one other person, as with a letter; or many thousands, as with a newspaper article or book, but in all cases the words written are intended, ultimately, to be read.

Writing, then, as we noted in Chapter 3, is *reading*.

This might seem simplistic. Of course writing is reading, you're saying to yourself. Everybody knows that—what's the big deal?

The big deal is simply that, although most people understand the connection, they fail to make use of it to improve their writing.

The point might be clearer if stated this way: "Writing is *re*reading." Too many novice writers fail to understand that to create "good writing," they must reread what they've written—placing themselves in the position of the reader—and improve it through revision. Not even the best writers are above the constant need to refine and perfect their drafts.

This person we've referred to before—"the reader"—is the key to the whole writing process. Good writers get inside the reader's head. They analyze the quality of the words they've chosen by analyzing their impact upon the reader. Only after such analysis can they be sure that their point has been successfully conveyed.

The process of writing is perhaps best illustrated by a comparison. A sculptor starts with a block of granite, which he then chips and shapes until it matches his vision. A writer must *create* her block of granite, called a first draft. Only then can she go about the business of "chipping and shaping" her writing by **rereading, editing**, and revising to match her vision. Let's investigate this process.

5–2 The Possibilities of Language

In Chapter 4 we identified words as the bricks of good writing and rules as the mortar, but we confined our discussion to rules. In this section we turn to words to explore the possibilities of language.

Brevity, Clarity, and Precision

Brevity leads to strong, tight writing. To be brief is to be forceful. A writer must be stingy with words; he must be efficient and focused.

Brevity, of course, requires work. An old story is illustrative: when asked why she had composed such a long piece, a writer responded, "I didn't have time to make it shorter." Editing takes time; expressing complex concepts in concise packages requires perseverance.

Brevity does not imply the elimination of detail. The writer need not reduce the argument's scope. Rather, the argument must be stated succinctly. This is demonstrated in Figure 5–1:

Figure 5–1 Being Brief

Incorrect:

The defendant's conduct was clearly wrong, in that the careless manner in which he maintained the subject premises, combined with the fact that he failed to issue a warning of any kind, certainly violated the duty that he owed to the plaintiff, and hence this court should find that the defendant was negligent.

Correct:

The defendant's negligence is established by his failure to maintain the subject premises and his failure to warn the plaintiff.

The two examples convey the same message; the correct version, however, does so with force and brevity.

Clarity is likewise key. Good writing accurately conveys its intended message—no more, no less. Every passage less than clear is a passage over which the reader stumbles, hesitates, or worse, loses interest. The writer must make her message plain:

Figure 5–2 Being Clear

Incorrect:

The witness testified about the accident only on the second day of the trial.

Correct:

Only on the second day of the trial did the witness testify about the accident.

On the second day of the trial, the witness testified only about the accident.

The first version is incorrect because it can be interpreted as having either of the meanings of the two correct versions.

Closely related to clarity is **precision**. Clarity requires that your writing be open to no more than one interpretation; precision requires that this one interpretation represent the point you seek to convey:

Figure 5–3 Being Precise

<u>Incorrect:</u>

The testimony establishes that the defendant had the unique habit of walking around his block at 3:00 a.m.

<u>Correct:</u>

The testimony establishes that the defendant had the unusual habit of walking around his block at 3:00 a.m.

It is unlikely that defendant is the only person ever to demonstrate such a habit (the most common meaning of the word *unique*), and even more unlikely that such a meaning was intended by the writer. Choose your words with care.

Brevity, clarity, and precision are essential characteristics of good writing. By analyzing and editing your writing to assure that it is succinct, clear, and precise, you gain an added benefit—a deeper, clearer understanding of your own argument.

Voice

Writing **voice**, in general, is a concept that is easy to define but difficult to analyze. It can be defined as the sound heard in the mind of the reader, or the impression created by virtue of the words chosen. Analyzing this sound, the "voice," is challenging because a writer can only "hear" her own mind, not that of the reader.

Defined more loosely, voice is the poetic aspect of prose writing—the flow and rhythm, the tone, the lyrical quality of the words. Such considerations might seem out of place in legal writing, but not if viewed as means rather than ends. The point is not to create a document that reads like a poem; the point is first to determine the tone you seek, then use voice to help achieve such a tone.

In the last chapter, we touched upon **flow.** A document flows when the reader moves easily through the text from point to point and from argument to argument. The reader's expectations are fulfilled because the writer has provided the elements that the reader needs to understand the content. Establishing flow is the first element of voice.

How is flow established? By using effective transitions (which we've touched on before and will discuss further) and by employing logical development (which we also discuss further), a writer creates a document that carries the reader along. Rereading is once again the key, followed by editing. Improving flow often requires "cutting and pasting": moving paragraphs around. Having placed raw information in a first draft, the writer sets about the task of logical ordering. It also helps to set aside your writing for a time, *then* reread it—the flaws are often readily apparent, since you are not so immersed in the details of your argument.

Rhythm is an important element of voice as well. A sentence has, so to speak, peaks and valleys and plateaus. A good writer manipulates the terrain, so that major points sit atop the peaks. Suppose you want to emphasize the believable nature of the testimony of an anxious witness. Consider Figure 5–4:

Figure 5–4 Rhythm in Voice

<u>Incorrect:</u>

The witness was credible, though nervous.

<u>Correct:</u>

The witness, though nervous, was credible.

The high points in a sentence often come at the beginning and at the end, as in this simple example. In the incorrect version the reader is left with the lingering impression that the nervousness undercut the credibility. In the correct version, the impression left is that, despite the nervousness, the witness was credible.

Analysis of rhythm is not so easy as simply making your strongest points first and last in a sentence or paragraph, however. It requires an analysis of style in general, and style in writing is a concept difficult to pin down. Consider the following two examples, both grammatically correct, but one more effective than the other:

Figure 5–5 Rhythm to Increase Impact

<u>Ineffective:</u>

The defendant's car had nonfunctional headlights, as well as barely audible horn and insufficient brakes.

<u>Effective:</u>

The defendant's car had neither functional headlights, nor an audible horn, nor sufficient brakes.

The effective example conveys the same information, but does so with impact.

Several techniques can be used to increase impact. In Figure 5–5, the power of a series that lists three items is apparent. The rhythm inherent in a list of three is more effective than a series of two or four or any other number:

Figure 5–6 Rhythm Inherent in Lists

<u>Two-item series:</u>

The defendant's car had neither functional headlights nor an audible horn.

<u>Four-item series:</u>

The defendant's car had neither functional headlights, nor an audible horn, nor sufficient brakes, nor adequate steering.

The list of two is acceptable, although its abrupt ending is a less powerful construction than a list of three. (Note that this analysis is in terms of *rhythm*, not the fact that the sheer evidentiary weight of three items is superior to two.) The list of four simply goes on too long. If it is essential to pass along all the information, the list of four might have been better stated as in Figure 5–7:

Figure 5–7 Four-Item List

Defendant's car had neither functional headlights, nor an audible horn, nor sufficient brakes. Indeed, it even lacked adequate steering.

The four-item sentence has been broken into two sentences, the first of which uses the rhythmic power of three.

The effective example from Figure 5–5 also works well because it uses **parallel construction**. Parallel construction means repeating usages to make a point, to suggest either a connection or a contrast. Certain word combinations naturally fall into parallel structures—the "neither/nor" combination, for example, or the "former/latter" combination:

Figure 5–8 Parallel Construction

The judge addressed the accused juvenile in her chambers, then, separately, the juvenile's parents. To the former, she urged the need for maturity; to the latter, the need for discipline.

Parallel construction in Figure 5–8 and in the effective sentence from Figure 5–5 requires that grammatical usage be consistent. Compare the two examples in Figure 5–9:

Figure 5–9 Agreement in Parallel Construction

Incorrect:

Legal writers should communicate in a clear manner, concisely, and be effective.

Correct:

Legal writers should communicate clearly, concisely, and effectively.

In the correct example, all three modifiers are adverbs relating back to and agreeing with the verb *communicate*. In the incorrect example, the relationship and agreement are muddled. Novice writers often shy away from parallel construction, believing that variety is always better than parallelism. Don't make this mistake—parallel construction has impact.

Under other circumstances, however, variety is an important element of good writing. To give just one such example, consider the following: although simple sentences (subject/verb/object) are often the most powerful, used exclusively they can lead to a monotonous, droning voice that actually drains the power from your words. A mixture of simple, complex, and compound sentences adds texture to the presentation of your thoughts. Thus, whereas variety should be avoided in parallel comparisons, it is desirable in other contexts.

We have noted that the point of establishing voice is not to make your document read like a poem, but rather to achieve the desired tone. But what *is* the desired tone? In legal writing, you generally seek to evoke a formal, assertive tone. To achieve such a tone, avoid light, familiar language; be straightforward without being ponderous. Your writing should be neither stuffy nor conversational. Stay away from the flip comment; keep your analysis sharp and your language focused.

Similes and Metaphors

Similes and metaphors are figures of speech useful to legal writers. A **simile** is a direct comparison of dissimilar objects, for the purpose of emphasizing a common characteristic. A **metaphor** also links dissimilar objects, but it is more powerful than a simile in that it equates, rather than compares, the objects:

Figure 5–10 Simile and Metaphor

Simile:

A good simile is like a good after-dinner speech: short and to the point.

Metaphor:

Metaphors are valuable weapons in the legal writer's arsenal.

When using metaphors, be careful of that entertaining but ineffective species, the mixed metaphor:

Figure 5–11 Mixed Metaphor

Metaphors are valuable tools in the legal writer's arsenal.

Until soldiers shower their enemies with hammers and screwdrivers, tools are not to be found in an arsenal!

Used selectively, metaphors and similes make a vivid impression in the mind of the reader. Be wary, however, of overuse, which can erode an otherwise effective argument.

5–3 Pitfalls in Language

Language presents potential problems, as well as possibilities. When drafting legal documents, there are several pitfalls to avoid.

Ambiguity

Ambiguity exists when a writer has failed in the obligation to provide precision and clarity. In the law, as in perhaps no other subject area, ambiguity can have devastating consequences. At best, ambiguity creates hardships and confusion for the reader; at worst, it can adversely affect your client's essential rights. The legal writer's words must convey her intended message—no more, no less. Consider the following example:

Figure 5–12 Pronoun Ambiguity

> Neither plaintiff nor defendant knew he had executed the contract without authority.

The sentence in Figure 5–12 is ambiguous because the reader is left wondering: who is "he?" Was it the plaintiff who had executed the contract without authority? Was it the defendant? Did *both* plaintiff and defendant unknowingly execute the contract without authority? Were both plaintiff and defendant unaware that some third party had executed the contract without authority? Because she is left wondering, the reader's inquiry is interrupted and perhaps inhibited. She loses the point of the argument, and she may abandon it altogether. Although the broader context from which this sentence was drawn may clear up some of the confusion, it might have been better stated in one of the following ways:

Figure 5–13 Unambiguous Alternative

> Example 1:
>
> Neither plaintiff not defendant knew that plaintiff had executed the contract without authority.
>
> Example 2:
>
> Neither plaintiff nor defendant knew that plaintiff's agent had executed the contract without authority.
>
> Example 3:
>
> Both plaintiff and defendant were unaware that each had executed the contract without authority.

Figure 5–12 provides an example of **pronoun ambiguity**. Pronoun ambiguity results from an unclear indication about the noun to which the pronoun refers back—in Figure 5–12, the pronoun "he."

Another form of ambiguity arises when the placement of a modifying clause obscures the object of the modification:

Figure 5–14 Object Ambiguity

> The testimony of the accounting expert led to the vindication of the corporation's accounting process as a result of its accuracy.

Was it the testimony that was accurate, or the accounting process? Both, we hope, but you see the problem. The placement of the clause obscures the reference of the pronoun "its." Two alternatives appear in Figure 5–15:

Figure 5–15 Unambiguous Alternative

The accurate testimony of the accounting expert vindicated the corporation's accounting process.

or

The accounting expert vindicated the corporation's accounting process by testifying to its accuracy.

Sexism

Sexist references and gender-based differentiation, which reinforce sexual stereotypes, have no place in legal writing. Consider the question of sexism when choosing pronouns that relate back to occupational nouns. For example, you should not always use the pronoun *he* when referring to a judge, or *she* when referring to a paralegal. One solution to this problem is to use "he or she," although this can be awkward, particularly when used repeatedly. Another alternative is to make a conscious effort to vary or alternate the pronouns used. This latter alternative has been employed in this book.

Another option is to make your original noun plural, enabling you to use a plural (hence gender-neutral) pronoun:

Figure 5–16 Relating Back to Occupational Nouns

Gender-specific:

When a judge considers a brief, she reviews form as well as substance.

Gender-neutral:

When judges consider briefs, they review form as well as substance.

The use of plurals eliminates the gender differentiation, but, like the "he or she" construction, can also create an awkward feel to the sentence. You will have to use your judgment abut the best means of eliminating sexist references.

Cliche's and Slang

Cliche's are, by definition, overused figures of speech. Legal writing should be crisp and fresh, with points made in clear, logical language that avoids vague references and shopworn phrases. In Figure 5–17, we identify a few of the many cliche's to be avoided:

Figure 5–17 Clichés

Slow as molasses
Kill two birds with one stone
Birds of a feather
The blind leading the blind

If a seasoned writer were to use a cliché to make a point, she would generally set off the cliché with quotation marks. However, after careful reflection, most such usages, although perhaps seeming clever at first, will be seen to be stylistically weak:

Figure 5–18 Setting Off the Cliché

To say that defendants are "birds of a feather" is to commit an injustice to birds.

Similarly, slang should be avoided. Defendant did not "rip off" the plaintiff; damages are not "30,000 bucks." Legal documents can be undermined by sloppy, colloquial usages.

Note that avoiding clichés and slang should not dampen your enthusiasm for the occasional simile or metaphor. But remember that tired, overused similes or metaphors such as "clear as mud" or "beating around the bush" don't inspire anyone.

Failure of Subject and Verb to Agree

Nothing confuses the reader or undermines a sentence more quickly than failure to use the proper verb form. The verb must always agree with its subject. Consider, for example, the compound subject:

Figure 5–19 Subject/Verb Agreement

Incorrect:
The traffic and weather was terrible on the day of the accident.
Correct:
The traffic and weather were terrible on the day of the accident.

Although both traffic and weather are singular, the subject of the sentence is "traffic *and* weather," which has two elements and hence requires a plural verb (were).

Certain phrases introduced by subordinate conjunctions are not considered part of the subject, despite their obvious relation to the subject, and thus are not taken into consideration when determining verb form:

Figure 5–20 Phrases Introduced by Subordinate Conjunctions

<u>Correct:</u>

The judge, as well as plaintiff's counsel, was stunned by the verdict.

<u>Incorrect:</u>

The judge, as well as plaintiff's counsel, were stunned by the verdict.

The subject is "judge" and the verb is "was"; "plaintiff's counsel" is not considered to be part of the subject.

A descriptive prepositional phrase that itself contains a noun can be misleading. Be sure that the verb form agrees with the subject, not the descriptive phrase's noun:

Figure 5–21 Prepositional Phrases With Nouns

<u>Incorrect:</u>

The lineup of defendants were a sorry sight.

<u>Correct:</u>

The lineup of defendants was a sorry sight.

The first example is incorrect because the verb was made to agree with the noun "defendants," although that noun is not the subject of the sentence. In the correct example, the verb agrees with the true subject, "lineup." The noun "defendants" is part of the prepositional phrase "of defendants," which merely describes the lineup.

A question often arises with regard to verb usage when the subject is "jury." Is a jury a group of individuals, requiring a plural verb, or a single entity, requiring a singular verb? The answers is, it depends: when a jury is acting in unison, use the singular; when acting individually, use the plural:

Figure 5–22 Verb Usage With "Jury"

<u>Correct use of singular:</u>

The jury was unanimous in its verdict of acquittal.

<u>Correct use of plural:</u>

The jury were hopelessly divided on the issue of defendant's negligence.

The second example is accepted usage, despite the strange sound. It might be better to use the following clearer version:

Figure 5–23 Correct Use of Plural

The jurors were hopelessly divided on the issue of defendant's negligence.

Jargon

Legal **jargon** or "**legalese**" is useful if used in moderation, and if the audience understands it. We discussed some of the problems and benefits of legalese in Chapter 3. To summarize, if you can say it in plain English, say it that way; if your audience is sophisticated legal professionals (as with, for example, an appellate brief), use language that the audience expects and understands, including "terms of art"; and if you feel compelled to use legalese in a document intended for a layman to read (for example, in a letter explaining a technical legal problem to a client), be sure to explain carefully any terms that the average person might not understand.

Redundancy and Verbosity

Just as ambiguity is the result when clarity and precision are disregarded, so redundancy and verbosity are the result when brevity is lost. That is a slightly verbose way of saying: "Get to the point! And don't repeat yourself!"

Redundancy exists when the writer has made the same point over and over. Say it *once*. Say it *forcefully*, but say it *once*. (Is this paragraph now redundant?) Don't underestimate the intelligence of the reader. You have to use your own judgment in particular instances, but generally speaking, repeated hammering on the same point can offend or bore the reader, and actually weaken an otherwise powerful argument.

Verbosity is simply the use of an excessive number of words, or excessively complicated words, to make a point. Some novice writers mistake verbosity for impressive analysis; in fact, it seems pompous and often indicates a lack of command of the subject matter. Keep your sentences as short as possible (given the need for variety) and use the simplest words you can: the defendant was "insensitive," not "obtuse"; the departure was "hasty," not "precipitate"; the road was "slippery," not "lubricious."

5–4 Tell Them!

A writer begins with an advantage: he knows what he wants to say. But this knowledge can turn into a disadvantage. Why? The reason is simple—because the reader doesn't share the same foreknowledge. The reader doesn't know what the writer wants to say until he says it. And if a writer gets so caught up in the particulars of his argument that he loses touch with this fact, the quality of his writing begins to plummet. He will fail to provide the hints and signals that the reader needs and wants. His message will become obscure.

How do you do away with the obscurity? Often you can cure it by simply telling the reader what you're talking about. Even an excellent writer can become so wrapped up in the details of her argument that she fails to put them in proper perspective. The solution is to step back and review the overall argument for the reader's benefit.

Topic Sentences and Transitions

By rereading an obscure passage, summarizing its importance in your mind, then reintroducing it with the summary, you provide the introduction that the reader needs. In Figure 5–24, note the improvement from the addition of a simple sentence that merely states, up front, the intended message:

Figure 5–24 Providing an Introduction

Without a lead-in:

In *Jones v. Smith*, the plaintiff claimed that the will was invalid because one of the alleged witnesses had been blind at the time of the will's execution. The court found, however, that the witness had been blind in one eye only. In the present case before the court, the witness in question was blind in both eyes at the time of execution, was partially deaf as well, and hence could not have properly witnessed the testator's signature.

With an informative lead-in:

The case of *Jones v. Smith* is distinguishable, and does not support the plaintiff's contention that the will was properly witnessed. In *Jones v. Smith*, the plaintiff claimed that the will was invalid because one of the alleged witnesses had been blind at the time of the will's execution. The court found, however, that the witness had been blind in one eye only. In the present case before the court, the witness in question was blind in both eyes at the time of execution, was partially deaf as well, and hence could not have properly witnessed the testator's signature.

Simply by telling the reader, at the outset, what will be addressed, the whole passage becomes easier to understand.

This concept of telling the reader what to expect is directly related to the concept of the **topic sentence**, which we discussed in Chapter 4. Indeed, what we've done in Figure 5–24 is nothing more than add a topic sentence. Our approach in this subsection is different from our previous discussion of topic sentences and **transitions**, however. In the last chapter, we were building a paragraph from the ground up, that is, **drafting**. In this subsection, think about it from a different perspective—think about it as **troubleshooting**. You've written a document, and you've reread it, and you know something's wrong. You've corrected all the punctuation and grammatical errors, you've removed the clichés, you've been succinct—and still something's missing. What can it be?

Think back for a moment to our discussion, near Figure 4–29, of a paragraph that holds back the topic sentence until the end. We noted that such paragraph structure requires patience on the part of the reader, and creates the risk that the reader will lose interest. Now imagine an entire *document* requiring such patience—it's *inevitable* that the reader will lose interest in such a document. A little of this technique might create useful tension, but a reader should not be kept waiting from beginning to end to find out the writer's point in a brief. Provide topic sentences and transitions to eliminate obscurity—in short, *tell them*!

The problem can exist even within an individual sentence. Some sentences, called **periodic sentences**, force the reader to store information until the end (analogous to the paragraph with topic sentence at the end). Contrast such a periodic sentence with the **cumulative** (also called "loose") **sentences** in Figure 5–25:

Figure 5–25 Periodic and Cumulative Sentences

<u>**Periodic sentence:**</u>

The treasurer of the corporation, who was elected by unanimous consent of the board of directors, who had been publicly acclaimed by both the corporation's chief executive officer and the local business media, and who in fifteen years of service had never missed a single day of work, has been missing for three weeks, was last seen at the Los Angeles airport, and is believed to have flown to South America with a substantial amount of embezzled funds.

<u>**Cumulative sentences:**</u>

The treasurer of the corporation is believed to have flown to South America with a substantial amount of embezzled funds. Missing for three weeks, and last seen at the Los Angeles airport, he had never missed a day of work in fifteen years of service. He had been elected by the unanimous consent of the board of directors, and had been publicly acclaimed by both the corporation's chief executive officer and the local business media.

The point is obvious. The periodic example makes the reader work, whereas the cumulative example requires the writer to work harder so that the reader need not.

When "something's missing," improving topic sentences and transitions so as to minimize the work the reader must do will often help cure the problem. But remember, even periodic sentences can have dramatic impact, used sparingly:

Figure 5–26 Dramatic Impact of Periodic Sentence

The witness, unruffled in demeanor, untroubled by conscience, and unaffected by the presence of the victim's relatives, testified about her role in the murder.

Like so many other aspects of writing, the final decision on sentence structure is a judgment call. But now you have a foundation on which to base your judgment.

Active Voice versus Passive Voice

We've discussed "voice" as a stylistic aspect of writing. One important element of voice is the active/passive split. In **active voice**, the subject of the sentence performs the action; in **passive voice**, the subject of the sentence is the object of the action:

Figure 5–27 Active vs Passive

<u>**Active:**</u>

The defendant violated the law.

<u>**Passive:**</u>

The law was violated by the defendant.

In the first example, the subject ("defendant") performed the action ("violated"), and the grammatical object ("the law") is also the object of the action. In the second example, "the law" remains the object of the action that the sentence describes, but grammatically it has taken the role of the subject.

Active voice is generally preferable to passive voice. Novice legal writers sometimes adopt a passive voice, since it sounds formal, but this usually weakens the power of their words. Again, *tell them*. It is generally better to describe the action than the result. Dull writing can often be enlivened by rewriting passive passages in the active voice.

Passive construction should not be entirely abandoned, however. If the point of the sentence focuses on the object, passive construction may be preferred. In Figure 5–28, the passive example would be preferable if the writer were discussing the difficulty of enforcing certain laws, whereas the active example would be preferable if the writer were discussing the habits of pedestrians:

Figure 5–28 Active/Passive Preference

Active voice:

Pedestrians have repeatedly violated the jaywalking law, with no enforcement action taken.

Passive voice:

The jaywalking law has been repeatedly violated by pedestrians, with no enforcement action taken.

Structured Enumeration

Sequential points are often difficult to follow if not clearly labeled. **Structured enumeration**, which specifically identifies each point, can eliminate the difficulty. Again, the purpose is to tell the reader precisely what is meant:

Figure 5–29 Structured Enumeration

Without structured enumeration:

The elements of negligence are all present here. The defendant owed a duty to the plaintiff, and the duty was breached. This breach was the proximate cause of the plaintiff's injury. The plaintiff suffered damage as a result.

With structured enumeration:

The elements of negligence are all present here. First, the defendant owed a duty to the plaintiff. Second, the duty was breached. Third, this breach was the proximate cause of the plaintiff's injury. Fourth, the plaintiff suffered damage as a result.

The structured enumeration makes the paragraph easier to follow and understand. Legal analysis often requires lists of complex factors; structured enumeration helps the reader to comprehend such lists.

Take a Positive and Definitive Approach

Positive statements are almost always more forceful than negative ones.

Figure 5–30 Negative/Positive Statements

Negative:

The club did not accept his application.

Positive:

The club rejected his application.

If you are trying to make a point, use the positive approach. If you are trying to deemphasize a point, use the negative approach. For example, suppose the person whose application was rejected in the preceding example sued the club alleging racial discrimination. The club's counsel might use the following sentence in her statement of facts:

Figure 5–31 Muting the Negative

Although plaintiff was not accepted for membership in the club, the club was unbiased in reaching its decision.

This sentence mutes the impact of the rejection, which is the goal of the club's counsel.

You should also be **definitive** when taking a position. There are few words more useless, for example, than "clearly":

Figure 5–32 Being Definitive

Incorrect:

The defendant was clearly negligent.

Correct:

The defendant was negligent.

An assumption is built into the incorrect example—an assumption that there are factors to be weighed, and that, based upon these factors, a "clear" conclusion can be reached. Using the word "clearly" in this way actually invites the reader to challenge the main proposition, to weigh the evidence and determine for himself just how "clear" it is that defendant was negligent.

The correct example simply states a proposition: "defendant was negligent." Period. It assumes no analysis, it simply provides the conclusion. This is the best way to present your points—forthrightly, with confidence, and without qualification. Vague, qualifying words such as "quite," "very," and "rather" have no place in legal writing. The road was not "very slippery," it was "slippery"; the defendant is not "unquestionably guilty," she is "guilty."

This is not to say that you should not support your conclusions with analysis. Such analysis is, of course, essential. By all means, point out the testimony that the road was slippery; by all means, point out that the fingerprints left on the gun were the defendant's. Nor is it to say that no one will challenge your conclusions if you state them forthrightly—they surely will. But in stating the propositions upon which your argument rests, don't undercut them by your own word usage. State them conclusively. You want your audience to know something—so *tell them*!

5–5 Logical Development

It takes more than bricks and mortar to build a house; there must be an architect as well. So it is with good writing: there must be central organizing principles within a document, so that the individual components work together to accomplish the overall objective. There must be structure and a plan.

The key to organization is logical development. Logical development is present in a writing when each point follows naturally from its predecessor. You have learned that you can use topic sentences, transitions, and structured enumeration to ensure that the reader has a reasonable understanding of where the argument is going. In addition to these techniques, you should also analyze your document on a larger scale, as an organic whole.

Several methods can be used to achieve logical development.

IRAC Method

We discussed the **IRAC method** in Chapter 3. It involves: (1) identifying the issue; (2) determining the rule of law; (3) applying the rule of law to the facts of your case; and (4) reaching a conclusion. This structure can be applied to a paragraph or to a series of paragraphs constituting a single argument. By using the IRAC format, the development of each individual argument will be logical. If your documents involve multiple arguments, you have to order them according to one of the overriding principles that follow.

Strongest Argument First

Writers often place their strongest argument first. By opening with their strength, they can then build on this foundation. Weaker points may be buttressed by association.

Chronological Development

Sometimes arguments are best ordered chronologically, particularly when they fit in a complex factual context, or when the order of events is crucial to the analysis. For example, in a business dispute over the performance of an electronic component built by defendant and purchased by plaintiff, there may be many letters, test reports, and field results that touch upon the knowledge of the parties and the positions taken and the risks assumed by the parties. The legal arguments may build upon the chronological development. In such a case, chronological assessment is essential, particularly with regard to your statement of facts.

When ordering your arguments chronologically, you must take special care that your strongest argument not get lost. One possible solution is a preliminary summary that emphasizes your important points, followed by the detailed chronological analysis.

Outlining and Subheading

Outlining has already been identified as a preliminary step in writing. By starting with an outline, the writer has a framework within which to work. The outline also provides a shorthand format in which the larger argument can be grasped, and against which the logic of its development can be measured.

Subheadings are useful both as transition tools (more will be said about this in future chapters) and as a form of outline. By reviewing your subheadings, you can analyze how the elements of your argument fit into the organic whole. If the progression, as seen through the subheads, does not seem logical, then the body of the argument is probably not logically developed.

5–6 Practical Considerations

A novice writes a paragraph. He rereads it. It isn't good. It fails to make the point he wanted to make. The logic doesn't follow from beginning to end. Is he a bad writer?

He might think he is—but he isn't.

He isn't, at least, if he recognized the cardinal rule of writing: that almost no one gets it right on the first try.

He isn't a bad writer if he recognizes the weaknesses in his paragraph and then takes out the tools of an editor—a pencil, eraser, scissors, and tape (or their word-processing equivalents)—to begin the task of improving it. Rereading, editing, revising, reworking, shifting paragraphs, substituting words, inserting explanations, deleting redundant elements, eliminating grammatical errors, crossing out, inserting, rereading, rereading, *rereading*—these are the elements that go into good writing.

Nothing you've learned about rules, style, design, and persuasiveness will be of any use if you fail to understand that writing is reading.

Nor is the process easy. "A writer is someone for whom writing is more difficult than it is for other people," said Thomas Mann. Writing is hard work, designed, ironically, to create the appearance of effortlessness—and, in the case of legal writing, to persuade.

SUMMARY

5–1

A good writer recognizes that writing is reading, and that she must reread what she has written, placing herself in the position of the reader, and improve it through revision.

5–2

Good writing requires brevity, clarity, and precision. Include necessary details, but be succinct. Accurately convey your intended message, no more and no less, and make sure the words you have chosen are open to no more than one interpretation. Writing voice is the "sound" that the reader hears in his mind; defined more loosely, it is the poetical or lyrical aspect of writing. Flow is established by combining logical development with a commitment to rereading and editing, so that the reader moves easily from point to point in the finished product. Rhythm in a sentence refers to the varying levels of emphasis of the words—the high points and the low points. Good sentence rhythm can be obtained by employing such techniques as placing the points you wish to emphasize at the beginning or end of a sentence, not hidden in the middle; recognizing the rhythmic power inherent in a series or list of three points; and using parallel construction to emphasize and clarify your points. Similes compare dissimilar objects, metaphors equate them. Both are useful figures of speech that a writer can employ to make a colorful point.

5–3

Legal writers must avoid ambiguity. Two things to look out for are pronoun ambiguity and unclear placement of modifying clauses. Sexist references have no place in legal writing, and can be eliminated by using plural forms, by using "he or she," or by alternating male and female pronouns. Clichés and slang are overused or excessively informal usages, which are out of place in legal writing. A good writer makes sure her verbs agree with her subjects, which requires a careful evaluation of which nouns constitute the subject and which perform some other function in the sentence. Never be redundant, since repetition can undercut, rather than emphasize, your strong points. Don't mistake verbosity for persuasive analysis; it is almost always better to keep your sentences short, your analysis brief, and your words simple.

5–4

Obscurity can often be cured simply by telling the reader what you are talking about. Use topic sentences and transitions to make your writing flow easily for the reader. Emphasize the active voice (in which the subject performs the action), but don't eliminate the passive voice entirely. It can be useful where the object of the action is the important point. Structured enumeration enables the reader to follow sequential points easily. Emphasize the strengths of your argument with positive language; deemphasize the weaknesses by stating them in a negative manner. Always be definitive.

5–5

Use the IRAC method as a foundation for logical development. State your strongest arguments first, and use chronological development, preliminary outlining, and explanatory subheadings as devices to improve the manner in which your document develops, so that the reader more easily grasps your arguments.

5–6

Almost no one gets writing right on the first try. Reread, edit, and revise until you are satisfied that your points have been presented in the best manner possible.

REVIEW

Key Terms

Before proceeding, review the key terms listed below to be sure you understand each one. If necessary, read over the corresponding section of the chapter. When you are ready to test your understanding, answer the Review Questions.

rereading
editing
brevity
clarity
precision
voice
flow
rhythm
parallel construction
similes
metaphors
ambiguity
pronoun ambiguity
verb agreement
jargon
legalese
redundancy
verbosity
topic sentence
transition
drafting
troubleshooting
periodic sentence
cumulative sentence
active voice
passive voice
structured enumeration
definitive
IRAC method
chronological development
outlining
subheadings

Questions for Review and Discussion

1. How can writing be made clear and precise?
2. What do rhythm, flow, and voice mean in the writing context?
3. How are similes and metaphors used?
4. How are ambiguity and redundancy avoided?
5. How are subjects and verbs made to agree?
6. Describe a simple method to eliminate obscurity in your writing.
7. Describe the difference between a periodic sentence and a cumulative sentence.
8. What is the difference between active voice and passive voice, and when should each be used?
9. What is structured enumeration?
10. How can arguments be logically developed?

Activities

1. Rewrite the following passage from *Cooley v. Board of Wardens* (1851) using proper punctuation and plain English.

   That the power to regulate commerce includes the regulation of navigation, we consider settled. And when we look to the nature of the service performed by pilots, to the relations which that service and its compensations bear to navigation between the several States, and between the ports of the United States and foreign countries, we are brought to the conclusion, that the regulation of the qualifications of pilots, of the modes and times of offering and rendering their services, of the responsibilities which shall rest upon them, of the powers they shall possess, of the compensation they may demand, and of the penalties by which their rights and duties may be enforced, do constitute regulations of navigation, and consequently of commerce, within the just meaning of this clause of the Constitution.

2. Identify the trouble spots in sentence structure in the following passage from *Ranta v. McCarney*, (Supreme Court–North Dakota, 1986).

   We believe a fair reading of Section 27-1101 and *Christianson* indicate a preference by both the Legislature and our Court of furthering the strong policy consideration underlying the prohibition against the unauthorized practice of law that occurs in this State by barring compensation for any such activities.

3. Rewrite the following passage from *United States v. Nixon* (1974) by simplifying the sentences and word choice.

[In this case] the traditional contempt avenue to immediate appeal is peculiarly inappropriate due to the unique setting in which the question arises. To require a President of the United States to place himself in the posture of disobeying an order of a court merely to trigger the procedural mechanism for review of the ruling would be unseemly, and would present an unnecessary occasion for constitutional confrontation between two branches of the Government. Similarly, a federal judge should not be placed in the posture of issuing a citation to a President simply in order to invoke the review. The issue whether a President can be cited for contempt could itself engender protracted litigation, and would further delay both review on the merits of his claim of privilege and the ultimate termination of the underlying criminal action for which his evidence is sought. These considerations lead us to conclude that the order of the District Court was an appealable order. The appeal from that order was therefore properly "in" the Court of Appeals, and the case is now properly before this Court on the writ of certiorari before judgment.

CHAPTER 6 The Initial Client Interview and the Internal Memorandum of Law

OUTLINE

COMMENTARY

Your supervising attorney calls you into her office to tell you about a telephone call she just received from the friend of a client. The friend, whose name is Mr. Giles, has briefly described a problem he is experiencing with regard to a power of attorney document. The problem appears to be urgent, but your supervising attorney could not discuss the details with Mr. Giles because she is in a rush to get to court for a trial.

Your assignment: Call Mr. Giles, schedule an appointment today for an initial client interview, conduct the interview yourself, then prepare an internal memorandum summarizing the facts of, and law relating to, Mr. Giles's problem.

OBJECTIVES

The first five chapters introduced you to writing and research in the American legal system. In Chapter 6, you begin to put your knowledge to use. After completing this chapter, you will be able to:

1. Identify preliminary considerations in a client interview.
2. Accomplish the practical and technical objectives of a client interview.
3. Prepare a postinterview memorandum.
4. Describe the objective nature of an internal memorandum of law.
5. List several purposes of an internal memorandum of law.
6. Identify the information that should be included in the heading section of a memorandum of law.

7. Explain the importance of the "issues presented" section.
8. Identify the purpose of the "short summary of the conclusion" section.
9. Prepare an appropriate statement of facts.
10. Identify key elements in the "discussion" section.

6–1 The Initial Client Interview

The **initial client interview** if the first stage of any writing project. This does not mean that, after receiving a writing assignment, the first thing you should do is schedule an interview. You shouldn't—this would often be wastefully duplicative.

It does mean, however, that the initial client interview affects every subsequent writing assignment. The information you obtain, with updates and supplementation, provides the foundation upon which the matter proceeds.

Preliminary Considerations

Although our focus in this section is on the interview's impact on the writing process, a few preliminaries must be considered.

First, before beginning your investigation into the facts of the matter, be sure to identify yourself as a paralegal. You are not someone who is authorized to practice law, and the interviewee should understand this. You are, however, someone whose knowledge of the case is protected under the **attorney/client privilege** (assuming the interviewee is a client or prospective client; if a nonclient, such as an eyewitness, the privilege does not apply). Privilege is important because it enables the interviewee to speak freely and honestly, without fear of self-incrimination of fear that you could be compelled by subpoena to reveal the information provided. You should also make the client aware that you are trained as a paraprofessional; this should be emphasized to cultivate the client's confidence.

Second, the matter off fees may also arise, particularly if the interviewee is a new or potential client, as in the Commentary to this chapter. You should consult your supervising attorney about how to field questions on fee structure. The client is entitled to a precise understanding of this structure, but the responsibility to inform him is ultimately the attorney's.

Finally, you should prepare all documents that will be required during the interview, including retainer letters, authorization to obtain medical or employment records, and other documents. You should also review any materials already in your firm's file on the matter. If you are aware of any of the details of the client's problem, you should perform some background research to familiarize yourself with the substantive areas of law that seem to be applicable.

The Interview

The interview itself has a practical purpose and a technical purpose. The practical purpose is to establish a positive relationship with the client. You want to impress upon the client the firm's professional approach and commitment to her matter.

The technical aspect relates to the primary purpose of the interview—fact gathering—and brings into focus the relationship between the interview and the writing process.

It is in the initial interview that you begin to develop an understanding of the factual context of the client's problem. This investigation sets the stage for future writing projects, whether related to litigation, drafting of operative documents to construct a deal, or some other purpose.

The investigation conducted in an initial interview should be thought of as proceeding in distinct segments. First, you need to get a broad overview of the situation. An interviewer who does not know the "big picture" will initially be unable to fit the facts he learns into a coherent framework, adrift, like a reader analyzing a paragraph with no topic sentence. The overview is also important because the client may not convey the details in a logical manner, resulting in confusion if the interviewer (that is, you) lacks a framework. Thus you should start by asking for (1) the client's basic problem, in broad terms, and (2) the result the client seeks.

Once you have obtained this information, you have the framework needed to collect and correlate the details. In the second segment of the interview, then, you allow the client to recite the specifics of the problem. You may need to prod the client, or you may need to ask focused questions to obtain facts that are legally significant, but which the client may not realize are important. In this segment of the interview you should ask the client open-ended questions. In essence, you are saying to the client: "Tell me what happened."

After the client has told her story you should begin to ask detailed questions. By using your knowledge of the area of law involved, you can obtain the specific information you and your supervising attorney need.

Finally, at the end of the fact-gathering segment, review the entire matter with the client. By going over the same ground a second time (more quickly, of course, than before), you will catch any inconsistencies between your interpretation of the client's statements and the client's intended meaning.

There is a substantial literature on interviewing techniques, and an in-depth review is beyond the scope of this book. If you keep in mind your goal, however—to get the client's story—and avoid putting words in the client's mouth (for example, don't use leading questions, which suggest a response), you will have a head start on perfecting your own style.

Note Taking and the Postinterview Memorandum

During the interview you should be taking comprehensive notes. Don't let your note taking interfere with the progression of the interview, but make sure you keep an accurate record of the client's statements. You will be referring to these notes in the final segment of the interview, when you review the entire account with the client.

After the interview, you should prepare a memorandum relating the client's statement in detail. This is not the internal memorandum of law that we discuss in the remainder of this chapter; it is simply a review of the content of the client interview, for the case file. This memorandum should be prepared immediately after the interview, when the details remain fresh in your mind and the references in your notes (including abbreviations and summaries) are still familiar to you. If you wait too long, your own notes may become incomprehensible.

6–2 The Internal Memorandum of Law

Once a client interview is completed, the resources of a law office are brought to bear on attending to the client's needs. The first step in this process is often the preparation of an internal memorandum of law.

An **internal memorandum of law** is a document that provides an objective analysis of the issues presented by the client's matter. Although memoranda differ in completeness, complexity, and the stage of the matter at which they are prepared, the purpose is always the same: to *inform*, to *explain*, and to *evaluate*. Internal memoranda analyze the law as it relates to the client's matter for such purposes as

- deciding whether to take the case;
- determining how to proceed on the case;
- providing a summary of the facts and the law;
- preparing for a hearing; and
- drafting appropriate operative documents.

The key to understanding the internal memorandum of law is in understanding its point of view—objective. The internal memorandum is not intended to advocate the client's position; it is intended to provide an objective assessment of the client's position. It is thus prepared only for review by the members of your law firm, and perhaps the client's inner circle. This differentiates the internal memorandum from a brief filed with a court, which is written from an advocate's perspective.

The format of the internal memorandum may vary from project to project, from firm to firm, and even from lawyer to lawyer (or department to department) within the same firm, depending on personal style preferences. When preparing a memorandum, you should make sure that you understand the format preferred by your supervising attorney. In general, however, most internal memoranda have the following components:

- heading;
- statement of issues presented;
- short summary of the conclusion;
- statement of facts;
- discussion and analysis of the law and facts, with citations to applicable authorities; and
- conclusion.

In the next several subsections we discuss each of these components in turn. As we do so we make reference to figures drawn from an internal memorandum.

The Heading

The **heading** identifies the party for whom the memorandum was prepared; by whom it was prepared; the date of preparation; and the subject matter. The heading for our memorandum appears in Figure 6–1.

The person for whom the memorandum is prepared is usually the attorney who gave you the assignment, and the person actually preparing the memorandum is usually you. This standard scenario may differ in an individual case, however. For example, an associate attorney may ask you to prepare a draft of a memorandum that he will ultimately submit to a partner under his own name (or with both your names). Make sure you understand this circumstance from the outset.

Figure 6–1 Example of Heading

```
                         MEMORANDUM

TO:         J. Mark, Senior Partner
FROM:       R. Lang, Paralegal
DATE:       June 1, 1992
RE:         Giles v. Harris
            The validity of a transfer of a joint venture
            interest with a blank power of attorney.
```

The next element of a heading is the date. If it takes more than one day to prepare a memorandum, do not identify the date when you started the memorandum, nor all the dates on which you worked on it, but rather the date on which you submit it. You should take care that shepardizing (or other updating) has been completed through that date.

Finally, the heading must identify the subject matter of the memorandum. This usually involves a brief capsule description of the legal issues presented, and possibly identification of the client as well. Although this information may be well known at the time of preparation both to you and the memorandum's recipient, it helps, for future reference, to label it. Such labeling also greatly assists in indexing when the memorandum is placed in the firm's permanent research files, which many firms maintain to avoid duplicating research.

The Statement of Issues Presented

The statement of issues presented identifies the legal and factual issues to be discussed in your memorandum. In framing these issues, be concise and direct, and number each issue (unless there is only one).

Figure 6–2 shows an example of appropriate form for a statement of issues presented. Each issue should be no longer than one or two sentences, and should generally be drafted to be answerable with a "yes" or "no" response.

Although the statement of issues presented is short, the time needed to prepare it may not be. In order to frame the issues properly, you must understand the facts and the relevant substantive law. Often your research will be well underway before you have adequate understanding even to draft a proper statement of issues presented. This may be true even if the ultimate statement amounts to a single short sentence summarizing a single simple issue. Take care in your analysis.

Often your supervising attorney will provide you with a preliminary statement of the issues that she wants investigated, or which she believes are relevant. If that is the case, then your memorandum should be limited to these points. If, however, your research indicates that other areas are more relevant, or at least worthy of consideration, you should consult with your supervising attorney and determine whether further research is warranted. Be careful not to go far afield from the original assignment without authorization; you may

Figure 6–2 Statement of Issue Presented

```
Under Texas law, is the transfer of a joint venture inter-
est with a blank power of attorney valid?
```

waste valuable time and money. Your supervising attorney should provide you with an understanding of the limits of your research; often, as your working relationship is established, you will develop an intuitive understanding of the requirements of a given project. When in doubt, however, ask.

Short Summary of the Conclusion

The purpose of the **short summary of the conclusion** is to provide the reader with a quick answer to the "yes or no" questions raised by the issues. It is always short, but rarely quite as simple in actuality as a mere "yes" or "no." There are generally qualifiers needed to provide a response representative of the analysis and conclusion to follow.

The short summary of the conclusion is useful for two purposes. First, to the attorney too busy to review the memorandum completely, it provides a capsule summary; second, to those who will study the memorandum in detail, it provides a preview of the end result, helping to place the analysis in perspective. An example is found in Figure 6–3.

Figure 6–3 Short Summary of the Conclusion

Yes. Since the power of attorney presented was devoid of any terms, it did not contain the necessary elements to be a valid power of attorney. The acts of the agent exercised under such an invalid power of attorney are not binding on the principal. However the cases hold that, if the principal received any personal benefits from the transaction, the issue of ratification might be sufficient to validate the acts of the agent.

Statement of Facts

The **statement of facts** sets forth the significant facts obtained in the client interview or provided to you by your supervising attorney, or otherwise present in the client's file. Individual facts are deemed legally significant if they are necessary for an understanding of or have an impact upon the conclusion drawn, with regard to the issues addressed in the memorandum. Although the intended scope and depth of the memorandum is a factor to consider in deciding whether to include specific facts, as a general rule you should lean toward inclusiveness.

Facts should be neither embellished nor downplayed, nor interpreted in the "best light." Rather, they should be objectively and accurately portrayed so that the reader can assess the situation presented. After your review of available materials, you may determine that further investigation is needed for a fair presentation; if so, discuss it with your supervising attorney and proceed if authorized.

A simple, logical, and understandable presentation of the facts is crucial, so that the reader has a clear understanding of the context in which the issues are analyzed and the conclusion reached. Chronological development is often best; sometimes it may be useful to emphasize crucial facts first, then demonstrate how they fit into the chronological whole. Figure 6–4 illustrates a clear, concise statement of facts.

Figure 6–4 Statement of Facts Section

Statement of Facts:

Mr. Giles went to a pre-Thanksgiving party at the home of Mr. Swan. Swan had been his friend and attorney for approximately two years.

At the party, Giles and Swan discussed Giles's desire to purchase a piece of real estate before the end of the year. Giles indicated that he was going out of town for Thanksgiving, and would not be back until on or about January 1. Swan stated that he could close the real estate transaction if Giles would execute a power of attorney. Giles then signed a document entitled "Power of Attorney," which Swan kept. Giles then left the party, and departed on his trip.

While Giles was away, Swan was contacted by Giles's partner, Mr. Harris, regarding a joint venture transaction completely unrelated to the real estate transaction. Harris told Swan that Giles was supposed to assume all of Harris's interest in the joint venture before January 1. Swan told Harris he had a power of attorney to close a real estate transaction, but did not know how he could help Harris out. Harris suggested to Swan that he could use the power of attorney to facilitate the transfer of the joint venture interest. Swan hesitated, but Harris indicated that Giles would not receive the tax benefits attendant to the transfer if he did not close the deal before December 31. Swan finally agreed to execute the transfer of the joint venture interest using the power of attorney, and shortly thereafter the deal was completed.

When Giles came back to town, he was furious, and told Swan that he did not want to assume the entire joint venture interest, and wanted the transaction voided.

Discussion and Analysis

The **discussion and analysis** section is the heart of the memorandum. In this section you will be:

- identifying points of law and supporting them with citations;
- quoting from relevant cases, statutes, and other sources; and
- relating your research to the facts of your matter.

Always remember that your purpose is to discuss objectively the strengths and the weaknesses of your case. You must view the issues not only from your client's perspective, but also from that of your opponent. The negative side of your client's position will surface eventually; the internal memorandum prepares your firm to deal with such weaknesses. Discuss both those points that operate to your client's advantage, and those likely to be cited against him; identify counterpoints to your own strong arguments and counterpoints to the opponent's. The reader should get a sense of how an objective observer might look at the matter.

As with the statement of facts, and indeed the other components of a memorandum as well, the scope and depth of your discussion will vary with the intended use. In some cases, your assignment will be to prepare an exhaustive survey of the law in a given area, citing all possibly relevant cases and statutes, and perhaps even providing separate copies or abstracts of these primary sources. In other cases, the assignment will be to obtain a quick answer, citing only the most relevant cases. Know your assignment, and hence your goal, from the outset.

Quotations from cases can be as useful in a memorandum as they are in other projects (and they are often incorporated into later briefs), and references to secondary sources can give added support to your arguments. All these possibilities should be discussed with your supervising attorney, and you should be sure that you understand her expectations before you begin.

Discuss the cases, statutes, and other material *favoring* your client first. Describe how they support your argument, and how they may be attacked. Then discuss the materials that go *against* your client's position, stating how they are harmful, and whether and how they can be distinguished.

Emphasize primary sources over secondary, and mandatory precedents over merely persuasive precedents. If the issues involved are state law issues, emphasize research in state law sources; if federal issues, emphasize federal sources.

You should constantly integrate the law and the facts. Don't do this at the expense of an extended discussion of a complicated legal concept, however; by all means, make the status and meaning of the law clear. But make sure the reader understands throughout the discussion, and particularly at the end, how the law affects the specific facts of the client's matter.

An example of a proper discussion section appears in Figure 6–5. Note how bluebook citation form is used. You should not deviate from proper citation form just because the memorandum is to be used internally, rather than filed with a court. Your text may someday to incorporated into a brief; the more accurate its form and substance, the more valuable the memorandum will be.

Figure 6–5 Discussion Section

Discussion:

A power of attorney creates an agency relationship whereby one person, the principal, appoints another person, the agent, to act on the principal's behalf. *Lawler v. Federal Deposit Insurance Corp.*, 538 S.W. 2d 245 (Tex. Civ. App., Dallas 1976, writ refd n.r.e.). The relationship is consensual. *Texas Processed Plastics, Inc. v. Gray Enterprises, Inc.*, 592 S.W. 2d 412 (Tex. Civ. App., Tyler 1979, no writ); *Green v. Hanon*, 367 S.W. 2d 853 (Tex. Civ. App., Texarkana 1963, no writ). The law specifically defines a power of attorney as "(A)n instrument by which the authority of one person to act in the place and stead of another as attorney in fact is set forth." *Olive-Sternberg Lumber Co. v. Gordon*, 143 S.W. 2d 694 (Tex. Civ. App., Beaumont 1940, no writ). The document in this case identified neither the principal, nor the agent, nor the extent of the authority of the agent. The document's validity is thus questionable.

However, before one can determine the validity of the document, it must be interpreted. Under Texas law, certain rules of construction and interpretation must be followed. The rules of construing a document date back as far as 1889, to the leading case of *Gouldy v. Metcalf*, 75 Tex. 455, 12 S.W. 830 (1889). In *Gouldy*, the Texas Supreme Court set out the rules of construction for a power of attorney:

> [W]hen an authority is conferred upon an agent by a formal instrument, as by a power of attorney, there are two rules of construction to be carefully adhered to:
>
> 1. The meaning of general words in the instrument will be restricted by the context, and construed accordingly.
>
> 2. The authority will be construed strictly, so as to exclude the exercise of any power which is not warranted, either by the actual terms used or as a necessary means of executing the authority with effect. *Id.* at 245.

Figure 6–5 cont.

Expanding the guidelines set forth in *Gouldy*, case law establishes that "all powers conferred upon an agent by a formal instrument are to receive a strict interpretation, and the authority is never extended by intendment or construction beyond that which is given in terms, or is necessary for carrying the authority into effect, and the authority must be strictly pursued." See *Bean v. Bean*, 79 S.W. 2d 652 (Tex. Civ. App., Texarkana 1935, writ refused); *Dockstader v. Brown*, 204 S.W. 2d 352 (Tex. Civ. App., Fort Worth 1947, writ refd n.r.e.).

In applying the rules of construction, for a power of attorney to be valid certain elements must be contained within the document. The necessary elements are the name of the principal, the name of the agent, and the nature and extent of the authority granted. *Sun Appliance and Electric, Inc. v. Klein*, 363 S.W. 2d 293 (Tex. Civ. App., Eastland 1962, no writ).

The power of attorney in the present matter contained only the signature of the principal and nothing else. In analyzing the power of attorney under the strict considerations, the essential terms of the power of attorney were missing. As such, it appears that the document does not comply with the legal definition of a power of attorney.

The facts further indicate that the power of attorney was executed for a specific purpose, although not stated. Giles had orally instructed Swan to use the power of attorney to consummate a real estate transaction only. As stated in *Giddings, Neiman-Marcus v. Estes*, 440 S.W. 2d 90 (Tex. Civ. App., Eastland 1969, no writ):

> The authority will be construed strictly, so as to exclude the exercise of any power which is not warranted either by the actual terms used or as a necessary means of effecting the authority with effect.

Since no authority was conferred to Swan by the document, he could not have acted on Giles's behalf. Consequently, any acts performed by Swan for Giles under the power of attorney are invalid.

However, the facts reveal that Swan had acted as Giles's attorney on a number of occasions. This may give rise to an implication that Swan was acting with apparent authority. This is defined as "such authority as a reasonably prudent man, using diligence and discretion in view of the principal's conduct, would naturally and reasonably suppose the agent to possess." *Great American Casualty Company v. Eichelberger*, 37 S.W. 2d 1050 (Tex. Civ. App., Waco 1931, writ refd). Thus, as the Houston Court of Civil Appeals stated in its dicta:

> (A)n agency may arise with respect to third persons if acts or appearances reasonably lead third persons to believe that an agency in fact has been created. And . . . apparent authority of an agent to bind a principal, by want of ordinary care, clothes the agent with such indicia of authority as to lead a reasonably prudent person to believe that he actually has such authority. *Hall v. Hallamicek*, 669 S.W. 2d 368 (Tex. App., Houston 14th Dist. 1984, no writ).

Harris may try to use apparent authority as a means to validate the transfer, as Giles has the burden of proof that Swan did not have the authority to act on Giles's behalf: *Dockstader v. Brown*, 204 S.W. 2d 352 (Tex. Civ. App., Fort Worth 1947, writ refd n.r.e.).

There is a problem with the apparent authority argument, however. Harris knew that the power of attorney was for a specific purpose: to close the real estate transaction. The law is very

Figure 6–5 cont.

clear in that a third party has a duty to inquire into the scope and fact of the agency, and the burden is on the third party to "ascertain at his peril the nature and scope of the authority of such agent." *Lawrie v. Miller*, 2 S.W. 2d 561 (Tex. Civ. App., Texarkana 1928, no writ); *Eliot Valve Repair v. Valve*, 675 S.W. 2d 555 (Tex. App. Houston 1st Dist. 1984, no writ; *Boucher v. City Paint & Supply*, 398 S.W. 2d 352 (Tex. Civ. App., Tyler 1966, no writ).

Mr. Harris neither investigated nor examined the extent of Swan's authority. As such, Giles cannot be held responsible for the acts of Swan and their effect.

In analyzing the facts and the law, it is apparent that the document that purports to be a power of attorney is not a valid one and that Swan did not have the authority to act on Giles's behalf under any circumstance. Consequently, the power of attorney is valueless and any action resulting from the use of the document is void.

Although the case law appears to be in our client's favor, there is an issue that may be raised by the defense which weakens our case substantially. The issue is the principal's ratification of the transaction. Ratification requires that the principal have full and complete knowledge of all material facts pertaining to the transaction prior to any affirmation of the act. *Leonard v. Hare*, 161 Tex. 28, 336 S.W. 2d 619 (1960). For ratification to occur, the principal must retain the benefits and "the critical factor in determining whether a principal has ratified an unauthorized act by his agent is the principal's knowledge of the transaction and his actions in light of such knowledge." *Land Title Company of Dallas, Inc. v. Stigler*, 609 S.W. 2d 754, 756 (Tex., 1980); *First National Bank in Dallas v. Kinnabrew*, 589 S.W. 2d 137 (Tex. Civ. App., Tyler 1979, writ refd n.r.e.). In the event that it is determined that Giles took benefits from Swan's actions, specifically tax benefits, the transaction may be valid, regardless of whether the initial power of attorney was legally sufficient.

Conclusion

Although the discussion section forms the heart of your memorandum, the **conclusion** is the culmination. In a few sentences you summarize what your research has shown about the law relating to your client's problem. You may even recommend a course of action, if that was part of your assignment.

Though coming to a conclusion generally means stating your opinion about how the legal issues will be resolved, it does not imply that you should become an advocate when drafting your conclusion. If you have strong reservations about your conclusion, or believe that a court could easily justify a different ruling, say so. Once again, you must keep in mind the most important rule of the internal memorandum of law—*objectivity*!

An example of a good conclusion is found in Figure 6–6 on page 358.

Figure 6–6 Conclusion Section

Conclusion:

Since the power of attorney did not grant specific authority to the agent, the power of attorney is void. Based upon the strict construction doctrine, one cannot construe a grant of authority which is nonexistent. The power of attorney contained neither the name of the agent, nor the purpose of the agency, nor the grant of authority to the agent, and therefore could not confer any powers upon the agent. The acts of the agent were improper, and the principal is not legally responsible for the effects of those acts. However, as noted, if the principal received any benefits from the transaction, the acts of the agent may be ratified, which would validate any acts of the agent. This would make the transaction valid.

6–3 Practical Considerations

An internal memorandum will inevitably involve at least some of your own opinions, since you must reach a conclusion based upon your research. It is important, however, that you let neither your opinions nor your conclusion color your analysis—which is to say, you must also include in your memorandum those portions of your research that go against your conclusion. The memorandum is designed to *inform* your supervising attorney, so that he is prepared to advocate on behalf of your client; it should not itself advocate a position.

In drafting your memorandum, remember the many basic rules you've learned in previous chapters. Use punctuation, sentence structure, and paragraphing to make your points clear; write with precision and forcefulness; avoid ambiguity, use logical development, and be sure your writing tells the reader what you want her to know.

MEMORANDUM

TO: J. Mark, Senior Partner
FROM: R. Lang, Paralegal

DATE: June 1, 1992

RE: Giles v. Harris
The validity of a transfer of a joint venture interest with a blank power of attorney.

Issue Presented:

Under Texas law, is the transfer of a joint venture interest with a blank power of attorney valid?

Answer to the Issue:

Yes. Since the power of attorney presented was devoid of any terms, it did not contain the necessary elements to be a valid power of attorney. The acts of the agent exercised under such a limited power of attorney are not binding on the principal. However the cases hold that, if the principal received any personal benefits from the transaction, the issue of ratification might be sufficient to validate the acts of the agent.

Statement of Facts:

Mr. Giles went to a pre-Thanksgiving party at the home of Mr. Swan. Swan had been his friend and attorney for approximately two years.

At the party, Giles and Swan discussed Giles's desire to purchase a piece of real estate before the end of the year. Giles indicated that he was going out of town for Thanksgiving, and would not be back until on or about January 1. Swan stated that he could close the real estate transaction if Giles would execute a power of attorney. Giles then signed a document entitled "Power of Attorney," which Swan kept. Giles then left the party, and departed on his trip.

While Giles was away, Swan was contacted by Giles's partner, Mr. Harris, regarding a joint venture transaction completely unrelated to the real estate transaction. Harris told Swan that Giles was supposed to assume all of Harris's interest in the joint venture before January 1. Swan told Harris he had a power of attorney to close a real estate transaction, but did not know how he could help Harris out. Harris suggested to Swan that he could use the power of attorney to facilitate the transfer of the joint venture interest. Swan hesitated, but Harris indicated that Giles would not receive the tax benefits attendant to the transfer if he did not close the deal before December 31. Swan finally agreed to execute the transfer of the joint venture interest using the power of attorney, and shortly thereafter the deal was completed.

When Giles came back to town he was furious, and told Swan that he did not want to assume the entire joint venture interest, and wanted the transaction voided.

Discussion:

A power of attorney creates an agency relationship whereby one person, the principal, appoints another person, the agent, to act on the principal's behalf. Lawler v. Federal Deposit Insurance Corp., 538 S.W. 2d 245 (Tex. Civ. App., Dallas 1976, writ refd n.r.e.). The relationship is consensual. Texas Processed Plastics, Inc. v. Gray Enterprises, Inc., 592 S.W. 2d 412 (Tex. Civ. App., Tyler 1979, no writ); Green v. Hanon, 367 S.W. 2d 853 (Tex.

Civ. App., Texarkana 1963, no writ). The law specifically defines a power of attorney as "[A]n instrument by which the authority of one person to act in the place and stead of another as attorney in fact is set forth." Olive-Sternberg Lumber Co. v. Gordon, 143 S.W. 2d 694 (Tex. Civ. App., Beaumont 1940, no writ). The document in this case identified neither the principal, nor the agent, nor the extent of the authority of the agent. The document's validity is thus questionable.

However, before one can determine the validity of the document, it must be interpreted. Under Texas law, certain rules of construction and interpretation must be followed. The rules of construing a document date back as far as 1889, to the leading case of Gouldy v. Metcalf, 75 Tex. 455, 12 S.W. 830 (1889). In Gouldy, the Texas Supreme Court set out the rules of construction for a power of attorney:

> [W]hen an authority is conferred upon an agent by a formal instrument, as by a power of attorney, there are two rules of construction to be carefully adhered to:
>
> 1. The meaning of general words in the instrument will be restricted by the context, and construed accordingly.
>
> 2. The authority will be construed strictly, so as to exclude the exercise of any power which is not warranted, either by the actual terms used or as a necessary means of executing the authority with effect. Id. at 245.

Expanding the guidelines set forth in Gouldy, case law establishes that "all powers conferred upon an agent by a formal instrument are to receive a strict interpretation, and the authority is never extended by intendment or construction beyond that which is given in terms, or is necessary for carrying the authority into effect, and the authority must be strictly pursued." See Bean v. Bean, 79 S.W. 2d 652 (Tex. Civ. App., Texarkana 1935, writ refused); Dockstader v. Brown, 204 S.W. 2d 352 (Tex. Civ. App., Fort Worth 1947, writ refd n.r.e.).

In applying the rules of construction, for a power of attorney to be valid certain elements must be contained within the document. The necessary elements are the name of the principal, the name of the agent, and the nature and extent of the authority granted. Sun Appliance and Electric, Inc. v. Klein, 363 S.W. 2d 293 (Tex. Civ. App., Eastland 1962, no writ).

The power of attorney in the present matter contained only the signature of the principal, and nothing else. In analyzing the power of attorney under the strict considerations, the essential terms of the power of attorney were missing. As such, it appears that the document does not comply with the legal definition of a power of attorney.

The facts further indicate that the power of attorney was executed for a specific purpose, although not stated. Giles had orally instructed Swan to use the power of attorney to consummate a real estate transaction only. As stated in Giddings, Neiman-Marcus v. Estes, 440 S.W. 2d 90 (Tex. Civ. App., Eastland 1969, no writ):

> The authority will be construed strictly, so as to exclude the exercise of any power which is not warranted either by the actual terms used or as a necessary means of effecting the authority with effect.

Since no authority was conferred to Swan by the document, he could not have acted on Giles's behalf. Consequently, any acts performed by Swan for Giles under the power of attorney are invalid.

However, the facts reveal that Swan had acted as Giles's attorney on a number of occasions. This may give rise to an implication that Swan was acting with apparent authority. This is defined as "such authority as a reasonably prudent man, using diligence and discretion in view of the principal's conduct, would naturally and reasonably suppose the agent to possess." Great American Casualty Company v. Eichelberger, 37 S.W. 2d 1050 (Tex. Civ. App., Waco 1931, writ refd). Thus, as the Houston Court of Civil Appeals stated in its dicta:

> [A]n agency may arise with respect to third persons if acts or appearances reasonably lead third persons to believe that an agency in fact has been created. And . . . apparent authority of an agent to bind a principal, by want of ordinary care, clothes the agent with such indicia of authority as to lead a reasonably prudent person to believe that he actually has such authority. Hall v. Hallamicek, 669 S.W. 2d 368 (Tex. App., Houston 14th Dist. 1984, no writ).

Harris may try to use apparent authority as a means to validate the transfer, as Giles has the burden of proof that Swan did not have the authority to act on Giles's behalf: Dockstader v. Brown, 204 S.W. 2d 352 (Tex. Civ. App., Fort Worth 1947, writ refd n.r.e.).

There is a problem with the apparent authority argument, however. Harris knew that the power of attorney was for a specific purpose: to close the real estate transaction. The law is very clear in that a third party has a duty to inquire into the scope and fact of the agency, and the burden is on the third party to "ascertain at his peril the nature and scope of the authority of such agent." Lawrie v. Miller, 2 S.W. 2d 561 (Tex. Civ. App., Texarkana 1928, no writ); Eliot Valve Repair v. Valve, 675 S.W. 2d 555 (Tex. App. Houston 1st Dist. 1984, no writ; Boucher v. City Paint & Supply, 398 S.W. 2d 352 (Tex. Civ. App., Tyler 1966, no writ).

Mr. Harris neither investigated nor examined the extent of Swan's authority. As such, Giles cannot be held responsible for the acts of Swan and their effect.

In analyzing the facts and the law, it is apparent that the document that purports to be a power of attorney is not a valid one and that Swan did not have the authority to act on Giles's behalf under any circumstance. Consequently, the power of attorney is valueless and any action resulting from the use of the document is void.

Although the case law appears to be in our client's favor, there is an issue that may be raised by the defense which weakens our case substantially. The issue is the principal's ratification of the transaction. Ratification requires that the principal have full and complete knowledge of all material facts pertaining to the transaction prior to any affirmation of the act. Leonard v. Hare, 161 Tex. 28, 336 S.W. 2d 619 (1960). For ratification to occur, the principal must retain the benefits and "the critical factor in determining whether a principal has ratified an unauthorized act by his agent is the principal's knowledge of the transaction and his actions in light of such knowledge." Land Title Company of Dallas, Inc. v. Stigler, 609 S.W.

2d 754, 756 (Tex., 1980); First National Bank in Dallas v. Kinnabrew, 589 S.W. 2d 137 (Tex. Civ. App., Tyler 1979, writ refd n.r.e.). In the event that it is determined that Giles took benefits from Swan's actions, specifically tax benefits, the transaction may be valid, regardless of whether the initial power of attorney was legally sufficient.

Conclusion:

Since the power of attorney did not grant specific authority to the agent, the power of attorney is void. Based upon the strict construction doctrine, one cannot construe a grant of authority which is nonexistent. The power of attorney contained neither the name of the agent, nor the purpose of the agency, nor the grant of authority to the agent and therefore could not confer any powers upon the agent. The acts of the agent were improper, and the principal is not legally responsible for the effects of those acts. However, as noted, if the principal received any benefits from the transaction, the acts of the agent may be ratified, which would validate any acts of the agent. This would make the transaction valid.

SUMMARY

6–1

Prepare all necessary documents ahead of time, and do preliminary background research. Before commencing the initial client interview, be sure to identify yourself as a paralegal. Be prepared to discuss fees. In the interview itself, establish a positive relationship with the client, and proceed in stages to gather the facts. Ask focused questions after the client has told his story, and review the entire fact pattern before he leaves. Then immediately prepare a postinterview memorandum.

6–2

The internal memorandum of law is designed to inform, to explain, and to evaluate. It is intended to assist with such things as deciding whether to take a case or determining how to proceed on a case. Its purpose is objective. The heading identifies the parties preparing and receiving the memorandum, the date of submission, and the subject matter covered. The statement of issues presented identifies the legal and factual issues to be discussed. The short summary of the conclusion provides a quick answer to the questions raised by the statement of issues presented. The statement of facts presents an accurate picture of the facts. The discussion and analysis section identifies applicable points of law and supports them with citations to, and quotes from, relevant cases, statutes, and other sources, always relating the research to the facts of the specific matter. The conclusion is the culmination of the research, summarizing the implications of your analysis and possibly including a recommended course of action.

6–3

Although an internal memorandum of law necessarily involves some of the writer's own opinions (since she must reach a conclusion), these opinions should not be allowed to color the analysis. The writer must remain objective, including in the text both those references that support her conclusions and those which go against it.

REVIEW

Key Terms

Before proceeding, review the key terms listed below to be sure you understand each one. If necessary, read over the corresponding section of the chapter. When you are ready to test your understanding, answer the Review Questions.

initial client interview
attorney/client privilege
postinterview memorandum
internal memorandum of law
heading
statement of issues presented
short summary of conclusion
statement of facts
discussion and analysis
conclusion

Questions for Review and Discussion

1. What are some factors that should be considered prior to conducting a client interview?
2. What are the practical and technical objectives of a client interview?
3. What is the importance of a postinterview memorandum?
4. What does it mean when we describe an internal memorandum of law as "objective?"
5. What are some of the purposes of an internal memorandum of law?
6. List the information that should be included in the heading section of an internal memorandum of law.
7. What is the importance of the "issues presented" section?

8. What is the purpose of the "short summary of the conclusion" section?
9. What factors should be considered in preparing an appropriate "statement of facts?"
10. What are the key elements of the "discussion" section?

Activities

1. Read *American Heritage Life Insurance Company v. Koch*, 721 S.W. 2d 611 (Tex. App., Tyler 1986, no writ) and draft the issue presented.
2. Draft the statement of facts as you would present it to your attorney in a memorandum of law by reading *First Texas Savings Association v. Jergins*, 705 S.W. 2d 390 (Tex. App., Fort Worth 1986, no writ).
3. Prepare a memorandum of law on the status of law in your state regarding the comparative negligence statute.

NOTES

CHAPTER 7 The Basics of Legal Correspondence

OUTLINE

COMMENTARY

For over three months your client, Management Company Inc., has been attempting to collect overdue rent from a difficult tenant. Phone calls to the tenant and several meetings have accomplished nothing. A week ago, an officer of the client firm sought your firm's advice. His initial consultation with your supervising attorney was completed shortly thereafter.

As a result of the consultation, a decision was made to take immediate action. You have just been assigned to draft a letter to the tenant on behalf of the client, demanding payment of an overdue rent.

Preparing basic correspondence, including demand letters, is a task often performed by paralegals.

OBJECTIVES

In Chapter 7 we discuss different types of legal correspondence and the strategies behind them. After completing this chapter, you will be able to:

1. Identify three functions of legal correspondence.
2. Prepare appropriate letters for clients, opposing counsel, and the court.
3. State the purpose of using letterhead.
4. Identify the importance of an accurate date.
5. Prepare a reference line.
6. Prepare a blind carbon copy.
7. Prepare a demand letter.
8. Prepare a client opinion letter.
9. Prepare a third party opinion letter.
10. Use a letter to request information.

7–1 The Function of Legal Correspondence

Although letter writing is something of a lost art in social communication, having been replaced by the telephone call, in business and legal matters it remains important. Letters form a permanent written record that can be relied upon later to reconstruct events. Used and drafted correctly, they help to prevent misunderstandings, broken agreements, and missed deadlines.

The legal profession relies on letters for three main purposes—to inform, to advise, and to confirm.

The Informative Letter

Letters that transmit information are known as **informative letters**, also called "for your information" or "FYI" letters. Such a letter might be sent to a client to inform him of the progress of a case, the status of billing and payment, or the need for information to prepare a deposition. An informative letter might also be sent to opposing counsel (for example, to provide dates of availability to schedule a deposition or trial), or to anyone to whom the attorney or paralegal need provide information.

The Advisory Letter

Advisory letters are more formal than informative letters. They offer legal opinions. This might be in the form of an objective analysis of the case at issue, as a detailed letter to a client. Or it might be written in a persuasive style from an advocate's perspective, as when an attorney writes to opposing counsel proposing settlement. Whatever form it takes, an advisory letter is detailed and formal. Research may be involved, and it must be done with the same care as any other research project. There may be statutory requirements to follow or questions of law that must be resolved. If the letter is incomplete or otherwise flawed, the result may harm your client.

Although the advisory letter is certainly informative, its content goes beyond that of an informative letter. The content and style often resemble more sophisticated legal writing, such as an internal memorandum or a brief.

The Confirmation Letter

In the course of a legal matter, information is often shared orally, by telephone or in person. In order to create a permanent record of the passing of such information, a **confirmation letter** is often sent, restating the content of the original oral communication. For example, when an attorney orally advises a client of a court date, a follow-up confirmation letter should immediately be sent. That way, there is no excuse for confusion.

A confirmation letter not only restates orally transmitted information, it also protects the attorney (and the paralegal) from future problems or repercussions. By establishing in writing the date of a court appearance, for example, or the terms of an orally agreed-upon settlement, there is a permanent record which can be referred to in the event of a disagreement.

7–2 Evaluating the Audience

The tone and style of a letter vary not only with the purpose, but also with the audience. Correspondence with your client, for example, may be less formal than a letter to the court, and less technical than a letter to opposing counsel. A different audience requires a different focus, attention, and style.

The Client

Regular contact with your clients is important, both to keep them informed and to minimize the anxiety they may feel because of their unfamiliarity with the legal system. In corresponding with clients, you should keep in mind several considerations.

First, provide concrete answers. Clients dislike lawyers and paralegals who hedge with vague language. This does not mean that you should misrepresent the state of affairs if it really is indefinite, but rather that you explain the indefinite state with concrete, clear language. If the law in your case is subject to several interpretations, say so clearly and identify the possible interpretations.

Second, write to the client's level of understanding. Avoid legalese or, if you must use it, *explain* it. Don't try to impress the client with your technical vocabulary; write in plain English. To do this is not to patronize or condescend—if a client, even an intelligent and educated client, has no legal training, there is no reason to subject her to difficult jargon.

Third, always be respectful and courteous to your clients. They have hired you because they have a legal problem, and it is probably a difficult time for them. Your compassion and understanding in your legal correspondence and face-to-face contacts can help them cope, whereas a harsh or pompous tone would cause more anxiety and ill will.

Finally, choose your words carefully. In litigation, a result is never certain; in a business deal or real estate transaction, the outcome is often unpredictable;

in negotiations, the other party is always an uncontrollable factor. Yet clients are always looking for certainties. They want to be told that everything will be all right. You must make it clear that your opinions are not *guarantees*. Avoid the temptation to act like an all-knowing legal forecaster; be accurate and honest, and communicate the uncertainties.

Opposing Counsel

Opposing counsel is not your friend in the case at hand, even if he is your friend in other contexts. Always remember that information shared with opposing counsel will be available to the opposing client (or might even be brought to the court's attention), and can be used against your client. Thus you must choose carefully what you communicate to opposing counsel. Be courteous in your correspondence with opposing counsel, but be cautious as well.

The Court

Correspondence directed to the court usually comes in one of three forms: either a cover letter accompanying documents to be filed; or a letter requesting a hearing date or other procedural assistance; or a formal letter to a judge stating a legal position.

Cover letters accompanying documents are usually standard form letters. They simply identify the documents and the date of filing. Such letters fulfill the confirmation function of correspondence—they provide a written record establishing that the documents were filed, and when. Copies generally need not be sent to opposing counsel.

A letter requesting a hearing date or other procedural assistance is similarly straightforward in its text—it simply makes a direct request. If such a letter is addressed to a judge, however, opposing counsel should receive a copy. If addressed to a clerk, the copy is optional.

A letter to a judge stating a legal position is less commonly seen, usually outside the standard course of a lawsuit, and it involves risks. If such a letter is sent, needless to say a copy should be sent to opposing counsel, and it should be prepared in a formal manner, as if it were a brief. Be concise, direct, and respectful to judges. Such a communication between one party in a lawsuit and the judge is called an ***ex parte*** communication (recall this term from our discussion of legalese in Chapter 3). Only under limited circumstances is such communication acceptable. The problem with *ex parte* communications is that the other side's opportunity to respond is limited. In any event, no such communication should ever be attempted by you without express authorization from your supervising attorney.

7–3 The Components of a Letter

The format of different types of letters varies, and different firms or attorneys may have different preferences, but the following are generally accepted as the standard components of most letters:

- letterhead;
- date;
- addressee;
- reference line;
- salutation;
- body;
- headers;
- closing; and
- carbon copy and blind carbon copy.

We consider each of these in turn in the following subsections.

The Letterhead

Most law firms and businesses have standard stationery, called **letterhead**, with the firm or company name, address, telephone number, and other relevant information. Law firm letterhead often lists, just below the firm name, all the attorneys in the firm.

When writing on behalf of your firm, use letterhead. It shows that you are associated with the firm, making the significance of the letter clear. It may even be relevant for professional liability insurance coverage.

Letterhead is used for the first page of a multiple-page letter. The other pages should be on matching paper, but without the letterhead.

The Date

The date appears below the letterhead. It is important for establishing an accurate chronology in a legal matter. Letters often go through several drafts over a period of several days; make sure the date on the letter matches the date of mailing.

The Addressee

The name of the person to whom the letter is written appears at the top left margin, just below the letterhead. If the letter is sent by other than U.S. mail (for example, by FAX or overnight delivery), the method of delivery should be indicated above the address block. Use titles, if applicable (for example, "Chairman William Jones"), and note that all attorneys should be addressed with the suffix "Esquire" or its abbreviation, "Esq." (as in "William Jones, Esq."). A typical address block is found in Figure 7–1.

Figure 7–1 Address Block

HAND DELIVERED

Ms. Susan Windsor, President
AACME SERVICE COMPANY, INC.
465 Commerce Blvd.
Lincoln, Nebraska 54321

The Reference Line

The **reference line** appears below the address block, and identifies the subject matter of the letter. It provides a quick (*very* quick) introduction for the reader, and helps your secretary to determine where to file the copy without reading the whole letter.

The detail in the reference line sometimes depends on the stage of the matter. The parties involved are always identified, along with a brief description of the matter. Some firms also include their internal file number and, if a lawsuit has been filed, the docket number is often included as well. If the parties are involved in several matters, or if only one aspect of a complex matter is addressed in the letter, there may be even more detailed identification. Figure 7–2 shows two examples of reference lines, one prior to litigation and the other afterward.

Figure 7–2 Reference Lines

Prelitigation:

Re: Our Client: Anytime Builders
Our File #91-325
Sale of Aacme Service Company, Inc.

Litigation pending:

Re: Anytime Builders, Inc. v. Aacme Service Company, Inc.
Cause No. 91-00576-X
Our File #91-325

The Salutation

The **salutation** appears below the reference line. It usually begins with the word ``Dear," even in formal correspondence. Use "Mr.," "Ms.," "Mrs.," or "Miss," unless you know the persc n to whom you are writing, and follow the name with a colon, which is more formal than a comma.

The Body

The **body** of a letter contains the information you wish to communicate. It may be as short as one or two sentences (if the purpose, for example, is simply to indicate that you have enclosed documents), or as long as several pages (for an in-depth legal analysis, such as an opinion letter).

As in most effective legal writing, the opening sentence and paragraph of your letters should summarize what you want to say and why. You should make it clear that you are representing the client, unless you have done this already in prior letters. You should use all the writing techniques you've learned—correct sentence structure, parallelism, conciseness, and so on.

Be sure to be complete. Cover all the material you need to communicate, both positive and negative. Avoid a pompous or arrogant tone. In fact, in letters to clients or other friendly parties, you may use a relatively informal tone, although you should be careful that the message is not distorted nor its importance undermined.

When you write an advisory letter, the tone should be formal and authoritative, just as you would write a brief or internal memorandum.

Figure 7–3 shows the body of a letter concerning the resolution of a dispute. In subsequent sections, we discuss the content of other types of letters.

Figure 7–3 Body of Confirmation Letter

> This letter will confirm our agreement regarding the sale of the Aacme Service Company, Inc. to Anytime Builders, Inc. As a result of our meeting of May 5, 1992, we agreed that Mr. Allen will provide my clients with books and records of the business. Once we have had an opportunity to review the books and records, we will be able to determine whether the sale of the business will be completed.
>
> I have received the weekly installment payment to Mr. Allen in the amount of $1,203.54. As I indicated to you at the meeting, I will be holding all future checks in trust until we can resolve the question of the purchase and sale of the business.
>
> It is my further understanding that some time next week we will meet again to determine whether the business will be sold to my clients, or whether Mr. Allen will reimburse all monies tendered for the purchase of the business to my clients.
>
> I hope we will be able to resolve this matter quickly.

The Header

As we stated, letterhead is used only for the first page of multipage letters. However, subsequent pages have identifying information as well, in the form of a **header**. A header appears at the top left margin of all subsequent pages, and identifies three elements: the person to whom the letter is addressed; the date of the letter; and the page number. A practical note: we indicated earlier that the date on the front of the letterhead page should be the date of mailing; this is obviously also true for the date appearing in headers. If the date on your letterhead and headers fails to match the postmark, you will seem disorganized; if different dates appear on the letterhead and headers in the same letter, you will look sloppy and careless. The amount of time it takes to check these details is minor; the impact of an error on your reputation can be great.

The Closing

A letter is generally concluded by one or two sentences at the end. A concluding message often contains such courteous statements as, "Please do not hesitate to call if you have any questions." Following the concluding message is the **closing**. In legal correspondence, the typical closing is "Very truly yours," followed by a comma. Note that the *V* in *Very* is capitalized, but the other words are not.

Examples of correct and incorrect concluding messages and closings are seen in Figure 7–4. Note that the correct concluding message ends with a peri-

Figure 7–4 Correct and Incorrect Closings of Letters

> <u>Correct closing of letter:</u>
>
> Thank you for your attention and courtesies.
>
> Very truly yours,
>
> P. R. Lang
>
> <u>Incorrect closing of letter:</u>
>
> Thanking you for your attention and courtesies, I remain,
>
> Very truly yours,
>
> P. R. Lang

od. It is outdated to end the concluding message with a comma leading into the closing, as in the incorrect example.

Most of the letters you prepare will be for the signature of your supervising attorney. Remember that it is improper, and indeed illegal, for a paralegal to give legal advice. If you do sign a letter, identify yourself as a paralegal or legal assistant (see Figure 7–5).

Figure 7–5 Appropriate Closing by a Paralegal

Very truly yours,

Mary Doe
Legal Assistant

Carbon Copy and Blind Carbon Copy

Copies of correspondence are often sent to parties other than the addressee. The client, for example, is often sent copies of letters to opposing counsel or the court. This fact is denoted at the end of the original letter by the notation **cc**, which stands for *carbon copy*. Although carbons have largely been replaced by photocopies, the reference has survived and can indicate either carbon copies or photocopies. After the *cc* come the names of any persons to whom the copy is sent. Thus the original addressee also knows who else has received copies.

Under certain circumstances the author of the letter may want to conceal from the original addressee who else has received a copy. The original letter, then, contains no notation about copies (i.e., no *cc*), but your file copy will contain the notation ***bcc*** (**blind carbon copy**), followed by the name of the blind copy recipient. The blind copy recipient's copy will also have the *bcc* designation, so that she will know it was a blind copy. Proper use of the *cc* and *bcc* designations requires good communication among the attorney, paralegal, and secretary; it is often wise, for example, to clip a note to the original with an instruction such as "bcc John Doe."

7–4 The Demand Letter

Many disputes are resolved through discussion and negotiation, but some are not. As negotiations stall, a client may need to make demands upon the opposing party. Sometimes clients want to make demands even before negotiations have begun. In your role as a paralegal, you will be drafting **demand letters** on behalf of your clients.

The purpose of a demand letter is to motivate a desired response—often, though not exclusively, the payment of a debt. In the following subsections we discuss several categories of demand letter, as well as some guidelines for preparing a response.

The Collection Letter

A **collection letter** demands payment of an amount claimed to be owed to your client. It is not, however, as simple as a "pay up or else" letter—in practice, the concept is more subtle than that. To prepare an effective collection letter, several considerations should be kept in mind.

First, understand your purpose. Again, this is not as simple as it may seem. Are you seeking immediate payment in full? Are you seeking partial payment? Are you seeking to create a written record of the amount claimed due? Are you trying to satisfy statutory notice requirements? Are you trying to accomplish some combination of these? Are you following up earlier client demands, or is your letter the first demand made upon the opposing party? As you can see, there are many factors to consider.

Second, determine if there are statutory rules or common law principles that affect your demand letter. If you fail to satisfy any applicable requirements, not only will your letter be faulty, but you may actually undermine your client's ability to collect.

Third, your letter should set forth your client's version of disputed events, and possibly undisputed events as well. State your claim in a concise, authoritative manner, setting forth the amount of the original debt, the date it was incurred, amounts already paid, interest due, the present amount due, and any other relevant terms. In addition, you should probably include supporting evidence, such as invoices, leases, promissory notes, or relevant correspondence.

Fourth, you should make your demand clear. Do not just demand payment, for example; demand payment by a certain date, called the **deadline date**. Tell the recipient what she can expect if she does not comply by that date, and be prepared to follow through—if your threats are exposed as empty, your credibility is damaged and your future ability to negotiate is undercut.

Fifth, if the opposing party is represented by counsel, be sure that you write to the attorney and not the party himself. It is a violation of codes of professional responsibility to write directly to a party who you know is represented by a lawyer.

The Fair Debt Collection Statutory Letter

The federal Fair Debt Collection Practices Act, 15 U.S.C. Sec. 1692–1692(o), regulates collection of debts owed by consumers. When preparing a collection letter that must comply with this statute's requirements, you should include the following information:

- the amount of the debt;
- the name of the creditor to whom the debt is owed;
- a statement that you assume the debt to be valid, unless the validity is disputed within 30 days;
- a statement that, if the consumer notifies the attorney in writing within the 30-day period that the debt or any part of it is disputed, verification of the debt will be obtained and sent to the consumer;
- a statement that, upon written request within the 30-day period, the attorney will provide the consumer with the name and address of the original creditor, if different from the current creditor; and
- a statement that the attorney is attempting to collect the debt, and that any information received will be used for that purpose.

Unless the federal statute is complied with, your collection letter may be faulty, and your attempt to collect for your client may fail. You should be familiar with this statute, and any similar legislation that is applicable in your state or region.

Figure 7–6 Example of a Minimally Aggressive Collection Letter

May 24, 1992

Mr. Travis Rande
CD'S UNLIMITED
1617 Concord Street
San Diego, CA 90404

Re: Our Client: MOULDE PRODUCTIONS, INC.
Balance Due and Owing: $5,325.87

Dear Mr. Rande:

The law firm of Helman & Jones represents Moulde Productions, Inc. in the above-referenced matter. On or about January 4, 1992, Moulde Productions, Inc. provided you with production services and air time for a commercial advertisement on the "Music Review" television program. For these services and air time, you agreed to pay Moulde Productions, Inc. the total amount of $5,325.87. Presently, there is a balance due and owing of $5,325.87.

In order to alleviate any additional costs and expenses, your prompt attention to this matter is advisable. It is expected that the entire amount will be paid within 30 days. Please contact me to discuss the matter immediately. If we have not received a satisfactory response from you within the time specified above, we will have no alternative but to pursue further remedies.

Very truly yours,

Jeanne J. Carr

Figure 7–6 shows a collection letter with a slightly aggressive tone. Figure 7–7 shows a more formal collection letter, written to collect a consumer debt in compliance with the federal Fair Debt Collection Practices Act.

The Consumer Protection Letter

Many states have created a statutory method for a consumer to file suit against a business that conducts its affairs in a deceptive or unfair manner. When drafting a demand letter setting forth a claim under such a statute, it is important to mention the statute in your letter, and to comply with all its requirements. As with other demand letters, the facts of your claim should be stated, as well as the amount of the demand; indeed, these things may be prerequisites to making a claim for punitive or other damages under the statute.

The basic requirements for a demand letter under the Texas statute appear in Figure 7–8, and a letter drafted to meet these requirements appears in Figure 7–9. If a statute has been passed in your state you should obtain a copy and review it.

Figure 7–7 Collection Letter Prepared in Compliance with the Federal Fair Debt Collection Practices Act

April 28, 1992

Ms. Linda Starr CERTIFIED MAIL #P117784262
Burgers, Etc. RETURN RECEIPT REQUESTED
645 Elm Street
Houston, Texas 77204

Re: Our Client: AAA Equipment
Amounts Due on Account: $8,847.58

Dear Ms. Starr:

This law firm has been retained to represent AAA Equipment in the above-referenced matter to effect collection of the amount owed by your company, Burgers, Etc. On or about February 4, 1992, our client provided Burgers, Etc. with restaurant equipment for use in its hamburger business. The cost of the equipment was $9,747.58, for which you paid $1,700 as a down payment, leaving a balance of $8,047.58. As per the contract, the balance was due on or before March 15, 1992. The balance is now past due. If $8,847.58 (constituting the original $8,047.58 plus an additional sum of $800.00 as attorneys' fees) is not received in this office within thirty (30) days from the date of this letter, we will have no alternative but to pursue whatever legal remedies are available to protect our client's interests, including the filing of a lawsuit.

Pursuant to the Fair Debt Collection Practices Act, 15 U.S.C. §§1692–1692(o), any such action could subject you to additional liability for attorneys' fees and costs of suit.

If the above amount is not disputed by you within thirty (30) days from the date hereof, it will be presumed valid. If the debt is disputed, verification of the debt will be provided by my client. Further, any information that you provide the undersigned will be used in the collection of the debt.

Please be assured this is not the beginning of a series of collection letters. If we have not received a satisfactory response from you within the time specified above, we will have no alternative than to proceed to litigation. In order to alleviate any additional costs and expenses, your prompt attention to this matter is advised.

Sincerely,

Joseph Johnson

Figure 7–8 Texas Deceptive Trade Practices Act Basic Requirements for Demand Letter

§17.505 Notice: Offer of Settlement

(a) As a prerequisite to filing a suit seeking damages under Subdivision (1) of Subsection (b) of Section 17.50 of this subchapter against any person, a consumer shall give written notice to the person at least 60 days before filing the suit advising the person in reasonable detail of the consumer's specific complaint and the amount of actual damages and expenses, including attorneys' fees, if any, reasonably incurred by the consumer in asserting the claim against the Defendant. During the 60-day period a written request to inspect, in a reasonable manner and at a reasonable time and place, the goods that are the subject of the consumer's action or claim may be presented to the consumer. If the consumer unreasonably refuses to permit the inspection, the court shall not award the two times actual damages not exceeding $1,000, as provided in Subsection (b) of Section 17.50 of this subchapter.

Figure 7–9 Consumer Demand Letter

April 25, 1992

Mr. Bryan Henley
Office Manager
SMITHTON CHIROPRACTIC CENTER
1487 Orange Grove Blvd.
Galveston, TX 77553

Re: Your letter to Deborah Lee Jones dated March 20, 1992

Dear Mr. Henley:

The undersigned law firm has been retained to represent Ms. Deborah Lee Jones in the matter of her account with Smithton Center. Ms. Jones purchased services from and made use of therapeutic equipment in Smithton Center during the summer of 1991.

This letter is being sent pursuant to Section 17.505 of the Texas Business and Commerce Code, hereinafter referred to as the Deceptive Trade Practices Act ("DTPA"), which requires that such a letter be sent sixty (60) days prior to the initiating of litigation. The DTPA specifically provides that you may tender a written offer of settlement within this sixty (60) day period of time, and further provides that your offer of settlement must include an agreement to reimburse Ms. Jones for her attorneys' fees incurred to date. To date, Ms. Jones has incurred $1,000 in attorneys' fees.

After receiving medical treatment rendered by your clinic on August 26, 1991, Ms. Jones experienced severely painful muscle spasms as a direct result of that treatment.

Ms. Jones attempted on several occasions to contact your office without success.

At no time was Ms. Jones informed by your clinic that charges continued to mount even though she no longer subscribed to therapy. Ms. Jones was told that aside from an initial $150.00 charge, she would incur no further cost as a result of her treatment.

Ms. Jones' specific complaints are as follows:

(i) you represented that goods and services had sponsorship, approval, characteristics, ingredients, uses, benefits, or qualities which they did not have;

(ii) you advertised goods and services with no intent to sell them as advertised;

(iii) you failed to disclose information that you knew at the time of the transaction, and such failure to disclose was intended to induce Ms. Jones into a transaction that she would not otherwise have entered into, in that you represented to Ms. Jones that the services would be rendered at no cost to her after payment of an initial $150.00;

(iv) you engaged in an unconscionable action or course of action, by taking advantage of the lack of knowledge, ability, experience, or capacity of Ms. Jones to a grossly unfair degree; and

(v) you charged Ms. Jones for services never rendered.

As a result of your false, misleading, and deceptive acts and practices and unconscionable conduct, Ms. Jones was deceived into executing a purported agreement you now claim obligates her to pay medical fees of $2,000.00. Not only does she not owe this amount, but she has suffered damages in the amount of at least $325.00 and has incurred attorneys' fees in the amount of $1,000.00, as a result of your wrongful acts. We urge you to make a written offer of settlement pursuant to Section 17.505 of the Texas Deceptive Trade Practices Act. If settlement cannot be reached within sixty(60) days, please take note that my client has authorized me to initiate a lawsuit on her behalf, to seek (1) rescission of any agreements procured by your fraud, and (2) the full measure of allowable damages, which can be three times actual damages, plus attorneys' fees and court costs.

As an additional cause of action, Ms. Jones has instructed me to initiate a lawsuit based upon your breach of contract, common law fraud, negligent entrustment, and medical malpractice for misdiagnosing her condition and causing her personal injury. Ms. Jones has instructed me to request rescission of any agreements procured by your fraud, and to seek punitive damages based upon the aforementioned fraudulent representations made knowingly by Smithton Center and its agents.

If I may be of any service to you or answer any of your questions, please contact me either personally or through your attorney.

Very truly yours,

Peter R. Moore

The Letter Notifying of Intention to Litigate

A special type of demand letter is the letter that places an opposing party or counsel on notice that your client intends to initiate a lawsuit. This may be combined with an ordinary letter demanding payment of an unpaid bill, or may relate to a claim where the amount of damage is not immediately quantifiable, as in a personal injury action or an action seeking an injunction.

Most parties, including insurance companies, like to avoid litigation where possible; your intention to go to court, if perceived as realistic, may spur settlement talks. It may also backfire, however, creating a hostile reaction that actually scuttles settlement talks. The risk involved is a matter of concern and interest to you, but the decision on how to proceed will be made by your supervising attorney and the client.

When preparing a letter notifying of intention to litigate, you should:

- accurately state the facts;
- state the specific damages you claim, even if the amount is only an estimate (as with a personal injury suit);
- state, if the claim is for other than money damages (as, for example, where the proposed lawsuit seeks an injunction to remove toxic waste), the specific relief sought;
- emphasize your good faith and desire to work out the disagreement, if possible; and
- keep the tone courteous, not belligerent; this is more likely to lead to settlement.

These factors are general considerations; in a specific case, they may or may not apply. Consult with your supervising attorney for your strategy, but keep these things in mind. Figure 7–10 is an example of a letter notifying of intention to take a lawsuit to court.

As with other demand letters, an important concern is whether it should be sent under the attorney's name or the client's. If under the attorney's, the recipient may believe that it is too late to settle because the decision to start a lawsuit has already been made. Depending on the circumstances, you may want to send it under the client's name. Consult with your attorney on the proper procedure; and, even if you decide to send it under the client's name, you and your firm should still review (and probably actually draft) the letter.

Figure 7–10 Letter Notifying of Intention to Litigate

April 28, 1992

Ms. Carly Ford
AAA Equipment
645 Elm Street
Houston, Texas 77204

CERTIFIED MAIL #P117784262
RETURN RECEIPT REQUESTED

Re: Gourmet Services, Inc.

Dear Ms. Ford;

Please be advised that the undersigned has been retained by Gourmet Services, Inc. to represent them concerning their dispute with you on the equipment auctioned out of the New Orleans Restaurant. Please direct any future correspondence or communication to the undersigned.

It is our understanding that you sold equipment owned by Gourmet Services, Inc. without their knowledge or permission. As previously communicated to you in a letter of December 12, 1991 from Gourmet Services, Inc., our client is prepared to settle this matter for the sum of $5,000.12. Demand is hereby made for payment in full of that amount in the form of a cashier's check or money order payable to Gourmet Services, Inc. and sent to the undersigned on or before ten (10) days from the date of this letter. Your failure to do so may result in litigation based upon wrongful conversion of the equipment, and possible other causes of action, which may result in the imposition of court costs, attorneys' fees, and interest. Our client does not desire to pursue this remedy, but is ready to do so if it is made necessary through your failure to comply with this demand.

Unless you dispute the validity of this debt, or any portion thereof within thirty (30) days after receipt of this letter, the debt will be assumed to be valid. Should you dispute the validity of the debt within thirty (30) days from the date of receipt of this communication, a verification of the debt will be obtained and mailed to you.

If you have any questions concerning our client's intention or wish to discuss this matter, please contact me.

Sincerely,

Lois J. Jackson

Responding to Demand Letters

When responding to a demand letter, the first step is to review the demand carefully with the client, pointing out the meaning and implications of the offer, and discussing what you believe to be the options for a response. When you begin to draft the response, be careful about reciting details. You should identify your position early, and counter any inaccurate factual claims made by the opposing side. You may want to avoid appearing aggressive, since this may do further harm to what may be a deteriorating situation; again, this is a judgment call.

One option almost always available is to request further information. This may "buy time" while the opposing party decides how to handle your request.

If you deny the claim, identify the reasons for your denial. If there are relevant cases or statutes that favor you, you may want to cite them. If there are documents that aid your cause, you may want to enclose copies. There may be strategic reasons to avoid such disclosure, however — so check with your supervising attorney first.

The best type of response to a demand letter, in general, is one that makes your position clear, but keeps the door open for negotiation. Be firm, though courteous in your denial, and try to provide a reason for keeping the dialogue open (for example, the request for further documentation). Remember that sometimes a forceful, aggressive approach may be necessary—for example, to threaten a counterclaim.

Figure 7–11 is a letter designed to maintain channels of communication. In Figure 7–12 appear a series of letters which ultimately resulted in the filing of a lawsuit.

Figure 7–11 Response to Notice of Litigation

May 4, 1992

Ms. Lois J. Jackson CERTIFIED MAIL #P117784263
Attorney at Law RETURN RECEIPT REQUESTED
2350 Alliance Street
Houston, Texas 77204

Re: Our Client: AAA Equipment
Your Client: Gourmet Services, Inc.

Dear Ms. Jackson:

The undersigned represents AAA Equipment in the above-referenced matter. The matter that you have addressed in your letter dated April 28, 1992 is disputed. I do not know the basis of your claims, nor the substance of the claims. Consequently, pursuant to the Fair Debt Collection Statute, we are hereby placing you on notice that we do dispute the validity of any claims that you are alleging in your letter and request further investigation into this alleged debt.

Thank you for your attention and courtesies.

Very truly yours,

Sue R. Miller

Figure 7–12 Series of Letters in Medical Malpractice Case

(a) Notice of Claim

February 21, 1992

Dr. Ned Radcliffe
18015 15th Street, Suite 310
Goodnight, Texas 75020

CERTIFIED MAIL 3P117784223
RETURN RECEIPT REQUESTED

Re: Lynn Murray
Health Care Liability Claim

Dear Dr. Radcliffe:

The undersigned represents Lynn Murray in the above-referenced matter. NOTICE IS HEREBY GIVEN that my client, Lynn Murray, has a "health care liability claim" against you, as the quoted term is defined in Article 4590i, §1.03, Subdivision (a), Paragraph (4) of the Revised Civil Statutes of Texas. This claim is based on the fact that you negligently administered and cared for Ms. Murray upon giving anesthesia on November 12, 1991, in the course of treating her to fill two abscessed teeth. As a result of your negligence, Ms. Murray suffered a sensitivity reaction to the anesthesia, including violent shaking of arms and legs, chattering of teeth, and convulsions.

Due to your negligence, Ms. Murray also contracted a severe skin reaction, triggered by the anesthesia. This condition has caused substantial rashes on her arms and upper body, and could in the future affect her entire body.

As a result of her reaction, Ms. Murray has had to engage the services of medical specialists and undergo and incur expenses for examination and diagnosis of the condition, for psychological consultation and for medication to help her condition, and she will have to continue various treatments, consultations, and medications in the future, and incur expenses therefor.

Prior to your negligence hereinabove referred to, Ms. Murray was twenty-eight (28) years old, in good health, and employed as a representative with MBI Corporation. As a result of your negligence, she has had to miss work at her job and has, therefore, lost wages and will be required in the future to lose further time from her job for an as-yet-undetermined period. As a further result of your negligence, she has suffered severe mental and physical pain and anguish, and in all probability will continue to suffer such mental and physical pain and anguish for the rest of her life, all to her further damage. To date, the amount of damages is $12,587.37, and continues to grow.

YOU ARE FURTHER NOTIFIED that this claim is given pursuant to the provisions of Article 4590i, Section 4.01, Subdivision (a) of the Revised Civil Statutes of Texas, and that, if it is not settled within sixty (60) days from the date this notice is given, the undersigned will commence an appropriate legal action against you to recover her damages.

Your prompt attention to this matter is advised.

Very truly yours,

Emma M. Costello

Figure 7–12 cont.

(b) Reply from Insurance Carrier

March 10, 1992

Ms. Emma M. Costello
Attorney at Law
6301 Marley Avenue
Anyplace, TX 75311

Re: Lynn Murray vs. Dr. Ned Radcliffe

Dear Ms. Costello:

Your notice letter addressed to Dr. Radcliffe has been referred to us as the professional carrier for the doctor. It is my understanding that Dr. Radcliffe has previously forwarded your client's medical records to you, along with a release executed by your client on December 7, 1991. Thus, not only is there no liability on the part of Dr. Radcliffe, your client has signed a release.

I personally guarantee that if you file a lawsuit with regard to this matter, it will be countered with a lawsuit against your client for breach of contract and a Motion for Sanctions, since the matter is a frivolous claim.

Please address any further correspondence or inquiries to my attention. Do not call or write the doctor with regard to this matter.

Sincerely,

Edward Z. Plant
MEDICAL INSURANCE COVERAGE COMPANY

(c) Response to Insurance Company's Letter

March 18, 1992

Mr. Edward Z. Plant
MEDICAL INSURANCE COVERAGE COMPANY
1601 Ohio Avenue, 5th Floor
Sandy, Illinois 42930

Re: Lynn Murray vs. Dr. Ned Radcliffe

Dear Mr. Plant:

This is in response to your letter dated March 10, 1992. I do not appreciate the statement in your letter regarding the filing of frivolous lawsuits. Perhaps you should investigate the facts of this matter, as well as the law in Texas.

If you are trying to make threats to me regarding any claims Ms. Murray has against Dr. Radcliffe, those threats are so noted. However, let me assure you that I am well aware of the Texas Rules of Procedure. I can further assure you that I intend to pursue this matter, and will shortly be filing a lawsuit.

Let me encourage you, in the future, to investigate and examine the facts of your cases before you begin threats of Motions for Sanction.

If you choose to discuss this matter in a civil and professional manner, I would be happy to do so. Otherwise, you can expect to be hearing from me with a lawsuit.

Your prompt attention to this matter is advised.

Very truly yours,

Emma M. Costello

7–5 The Opinion Letter

An **opinion letter** renders legal advice. Based upon specific facts, and applying information gained through research, it analyzes a legal problem and reaches a conclusion about the resolution of the problem. In the subsections that follow, we first discuss an opinion letter directed to your client, then address some separate considerations when the opinion letter is directed to a third party.

The Client Opinion Letter

A comprehensive client opinion letter should contain several distinct elements. Let's consider these elements.

Date The date listed at the top of the letter is important. Your research must be accurate through that date. You cannot be held responsible for changes in the law, or new cases or statutes, that arise *after* that date, but you are responsible for all changes in the law *up to* that date.

Introductory Paragraph An introductory paragraph should identify the issue or problem that the letter will address. Included in this paragraph should be a **disclaimer** (limiting claim or denial) indicating that the analysis that follows is based upon the facts as they are set forth in the letter. If a different version of the facts develops, the analysis may change as well. It is important that you emphasize this to protect yourself and your firm from liability—and it is important to emphasize to the client the need to provide accurate and complete factual information.

Facts and Background The next section should set forth the facts and background that have been developed through client conferences and independent investigation. It should again be emphasized that the analysis is based upon these facts. You should take great care in gathering and presenting these facts. Remember that clients may have selective memories, concentrating on their strong points and forgetting their weak points. Thus, as with other writing projects, a good client interview is the foundation for a good opinion letter.

Conclusion A brief statement of your conclusion may precede the analysis. This will help the client, or other reader, to follow the arguments to come. The scope of the conclusion should be indicated here, including any limitations or qualifications.

Analysis This section is like the discussion section of the internal memorandum. In it you analyze the applicable case law, statutes, and other sources. Both strengths and weaknesses of your client's position should be discussed. Remember that you are balancing two goals here—informing the client, and accurately stating the law. This balance requires that you both (1) accurately present complicated legal concepts, and (2) present them in language the client can understand. Don't misrepresent by oversimplifying; take the time and effort necessary to make the document both accurate and understandable. This may, on occasion, require explaining things twice—once using terms of art or other complicated language, and a second time, describing what these terms and language mean in plain and practical language.

Be sure, again, to identify the limitations upon, and qualifications of, the analysis. Define all terms that might create confusion; identify the extent of your investigation; and indicate any and all assumptions on which the analysis is based.

Recommendation In reaching her conclusion, an attorney rendering an opinion generally makes a recommendation to the client about the best approach to resolving the problem presented. This is perhaps the most important section of the opinion letter—where the attorney takes a position based upon his research. Again, emphasize that the opinion is based upon the facts as they are known to the attorney. If the attorney needs to qualify her position, or indicate problems, she should do so here as well as in earlier sections. Do not use qualifiers to make your position ambiguous, however—use them to describe precisely what you have concluded to be an ambiguous situation.

Directive Your last paragraph should be an instruction or directive to the client to contact the attorney after reviewing the letter. This contact is important, because it will enable you, your supervising attorney, and the client to discuss and clarify any questions that the client has regarding the facts, the conclusion, and the recommendations.

Remember that, as a paralegal, you can *never* sign an opinion letter—only an attorney can render legal advice. However, you may be drafting these letters for an attorney to review. Figure 7–13 shows an example of a client opinion letter.

The Third Party Opinion Letter

There are occasions when a third party will require that your client provide a legal opinion, so that he can complete a transaction. For example, a client seeking a mortgage may need to provide the bank with a legal opinion regarding a title question. If you are called upon to draft such a letter, there are several points to remember. First, be sure to identify in the letter your relationship with the client. Second, indicate that, despite this relationship, your opinion is based upon honest and unbiased analysis. Third, use language that restricts the applicability of the opinion, for liability purposes—for example, stating, "This opinion has been prepared for the benefit of First National Bank only, and no other party may rely on the representations contained herein." Fourth, identify the reason for the opinion—for example, "This opinion has been requested by First National Bank in connection with a mortgage sought by my client, William Doe." Fifth, be sure that you clearly identify your opinion or conclusion. This can be done with plain, unequivocal language: "Based on the above, it is our opinion that . . ."; or "We hereby render the following opinions based upon the preceding analysis: . . . ." Finally, clearly identify who is rendering the opinion. For example, on the signature line, the signer (who, as we have noted, will always be an attorney) should probably sign not on his own behalf, but on behalf of his firm.

Figure 7–13 Client Opinion Letter

July 21, 1992

Mr. Neil Crosby
9250 Kingsley Road
Aurora, Colorado 80011

Re: Evaluation of Insurance Claims

Dear Mr. Crosby:

You have retained me to review the law regarding the responsibility of insurance companies to provide coverage for preexisting medical conditions.

I have reviewed the documentation that you have supplied to me. Based on the medical response from Dr. Stills, it appears that you did not have a preexisting condition at the time you applied for medical insurance. The problem is convincing the insurance company of that fact.

The most logical first step would be to send a letter to the insurance company detailing our position, namely that you did not have a preexisting condition at the time you applied for insurance. However, before a letter is sent, it would be appropriate for us to meet so that I may discuss with you the result of my research on the legal meaning of preexisting condition.

Briefly, the case law on this issue is unsettled. The courts generally look to the definition of "preexisting condition" in your insurance policy, then apply this to your medical history. There is no generally accepted definition of preexisting condition; it is determined by a judge or jury as a question of fact.

This means that estimating our chances for success will be difficult. Unfortunately, unless the insurance company willingly agrees with our position, the most logical next step would be to file a lawsuit against the insurance company for failing to pay your claims.

As we had discussed in our first meeting, this may be quite costly, with the results uncertain. Please call me in the next ten days so we can decide how to pursue this matter: whether to send the letter to the insurance company based on your medicals and my research, or not pursue the matter at all. I look forward to hearing from you.

Thank you for your attention and courtesies.

Very truly yours,

Steven N. Young

Most of these points are designed to define clearly the areas, and the limits, of your firm's liability for the opinion rendered, since in the third party situation, they may not be immediately clear. Figure 7–14 shows an example of a third party opinion letter.

Figure 7–14 Third Party Opinion Letter

September 18, 1992

Ms. Roberta McMillan, Examiner
Individual Benefit Department
UNITED INSURANCE AGENCY
716 Milton Drive
Richmond, VA 32187

Re: Our Client: Mr. Neil Crosby
Health Coverage Due and Owing Under
Policy number 718465023GB8A dated December 2, 1990

Dear Ms. McMillan:

The undersigned represents Mr. Neil Crosby in the above-referenced matter. You have requested a legal opinion of the law in the state of Texas on preexisting conditions as it relates to my client. A brief synopsis of the facts is necessary.

On December 2, 1990, Mr. Crosby became insured with United Insurance Agency for health insurance with a quarterly premium of $187.60. A copy of the policy is attached hereto as Exhibit A. The policy contained certain contractual obligations, one of which was to pay medical expenses, over and above the noted deductible, for the insured in the event of the occurrence of any health problems. In January, 1992, your company failed and refused to pay Mr. Crosby for his health care costs, stating that he had a preexisting condition before the policy was issued and therefore was not covered under your company's policy. A representative contended that Mr. Crosby did not properly and accurately inform your company of his medical history in answers supplied by him on your company's application for insurance. This application, with the responses, is attached hereto as Exhibit B. As noted on the application, Mr. Crosby had not been diagnosed as having any type of disease condition within the five (5) years prior to applying for insurance with United Insurance Agency.

His policy was conditioned upon the information contained within the application being "to the best of my [Mr. Crosby's] knowledge and belief . . . complete and true." Mr. Crosby's information was in fact a truthful representation of his condition.

United Insurance Agency never followed up his application with any type of medical examination by its own physicians. This was a condition that your company would have had to so follow up as a condition precedent to justify any denial of coverage.

The Texas Administrative Code, Section 3.3018 defines preexisting illness as:

> The existence of symptoms which could cause an ordinarily prudent person to seek diagnosis, care, or treatment within a five-year period preceding the effective date of the coverage of the insured person or a condition for which medical advice or treatment was recommended by a physician or received from a physician within a five-year period preceding the effective date of the coverage of the insured person.

My client had no knowledge of any preexisting illness that would preclude coverage as defined in the Texas statute. Further, the law requires knowledge of a preexisting condition, or that the insurer make independent investigation. My client did not have any latent symptoms that were intentionally ignored. Your company had an affirmative duty to investigate independently my client's representation of "good health." Due to your company's failure to investigate my client's health history, my client is not precluded from coverage. Mr. Crosby does fall within the protected class covered under your health insurance application.

United Insurance Agency knew of all medical records pertaining to the medical history of Mr. Crosby, based upon the completed information and history. As a result, you are contractually bound and responsible to pay his health expenses.

Based on my evaluation of the law, it is my opinion that there should be complete reimbursement of all medical expenses of my client from the inception of the policy to the present, as well as the payment of any future medical expenses.

This opinion is based on the present state of the law, as well as the documentation that has been supplied by my client, which included the insurance policy and application. Please contact me at your earliest convenience so that we may discuss this matter.

Thank you for your attention to this matter.

Very truly yours,

Steven N. Young

7–6 General Legal Correspondence

Legal correspondence comes in many forms. You've just learned about the demand letter and the opinion letter, but there are other categories as well. Earlier we touched briefly on the **transmittal letter**, a type of confirmation letter that accompanies information sent to a designated party. Sometimes documents sent with a transmittal letter must be signed or filed and returned; if that is the case, a return envelope with proper address and postage should be included, and the transmittal letter should contain instructions about what the receiver should do. Two examples of proper transmittal letters are found in Figure 7–15.

Figure 7–15 Transmittal Letters

(a) Transmittal Letter Forwarding Document to Opposing Counsel

May 15, 1992

Mr. Jeffrey Smith
Attorney at Law
701 Lawnview Avenue
Tulsa, OK 78910

Re: No. 91-432-A
O.K. Binding, Inc. vs. Southern Paper Co.

Dear Mr. Smith:

Enclosed is a copy of Plaintiff's First Amended Original Petition in the above-referenced matter, which has been filed with the Court this date.

Thank you for your attention and courtesies.

Very truly yours,

P.R. Lang

PRL/sst

(b) Transmittal Letter Forwarding Document to Court and Requesting Return of Document

May 15, 1992

Clerk of the Court
201st District Court
Tulsa, Oklahoma 78910

Re: No. 91-432-A
O.K. Binding, Inc. vs. Southern Paper Co.

Dear Clerk:

I enclose the original and two copies of Plaintiff's First Amended Original Petition. Please file the original with the court's records and return a file-stamped copy to this office in the enclosed self-addressed, stamped envelope.

Thank you for your attention and courtesies.

Very truly yours,

P. R. Lang

PRL/sst

Another type of correspondence is a letter requesting information. Such requests must be specific. By sending such a letter, you not only obtain information, but also create a record that the request was made. Typically the letter will request medical records, employment records, or other investigative materials. Figure 7–16 shows an example of a letter requesting medical information, and Figure 7–17 shows a letter requesting an administrative transcript.

Figure 7–16 Letter Requesting Medical Records

October 23, 1992

CERTIFIED MAIL #P117824932
RETURN RECEIPT REQUESTED

Dr. Martin Banks
603 East 21st Street
Houston, TX 77015

Re: Mrs. Beth Windsor

Dear Dr. Banks:

Enclosed is an authorization for release of medical records signed by my client. At this time, I would request that you forward to my office copies of all medical records in your possession regarding Mrs. Windsor. Please have this information forwarded to me by November 3, 1992.

Thank you for your cooperation in this matter.

Very truly yours,

Colleen O. Hayward

COH/bng

Figure 7–17 Letter Requesting Administrative Transcript

February 1, 1992

HAND DELIVERED

Office of the City Secretary
City Hall
Minneapolis, MN 75201

Re: Certified Copy of Transcript of Hearings Held on April 1, 1991 and June 3, 1991 before the Urban Rehabilitation Standards Board
Property located at 7042 Rocky Road

Board Members:

I hereby request that a certified transcript of the Urban Rehabilitation Standards Board hearings on April 1, 1991 and June 3, 1991 on the property located at 7042 Rocky Road, Minneapolis, Minnesota, be prepared by the City Secretary of the City of Minneapolis. This transcript is now requested for the purpose of an appeal to the District Court of Minneapolis County, Minnesota. Please advise when the certified copies of the record will be ready for transmission to the court, and I will have a courier transport them.

Thank you for your prompt attention and courtesies.

Very truly yours,

Mark O. Walker

A **retainer letter** is a form of correspondence important in the practice of law, for it sets forth the agreement and relationship between the attorney and the client. Such things as fees and a description of the matter are included.

In an **authorization letter**, the client provides the attorney with official permission to contact her employers, doctors, or other individuals who have records that relate in some way to the matter at hand. The attorney drafts the authorization letter for the client's signature; the client reviews and signs it.

The list could go on and on. When preparing general legal correspondence, you should keep the following factors in mind:

- determine the purpose of your letter;
- identify to whom your letter is directed;
- communicate in plain English;
- if you use legalese or terms of art, explain your meaning unless the audience is trained in legal matters;
- be specific when requesting information;
- follow the guidelines we've discussed for demand and opinion letters;
- be polite and courteous; and
- send copies to the appropriate parties.

7–7 Practical Considerations

We end this chapter with one practical consideration: When framing correspondence, keep the ball in *your* court!

What does this mean? It's quite simple, and the best way to demonstrate is by example. Assume that your client has a dispute with a customer to whom he has supplied building materials, but from whom he has received no payment. You take the trouble to write a comprehensive demand letter, setting forth the terms on which you would be willing to settle the matter. The following are two possible closings to your letter (Figure 7–18); or consider the following comments from letters trying to schedule a deposition (Figure 7–19).

Figure 7–18 Closings to Your Letter

Closing 1: Ball in *opponent's* court:

Please advise as soon as possible if the enclosed terms are acceptable to you.

Closing 2: Ball in *your* court:

If we have not heard from you by September 1, 1992, we will assume the terms are unacceptable and immediately institute suit.

Figure 7–19 Closings to Your Letter

Comment 1: Ball in *opponent's* court:

Please advise whether September 1, 1992 is an acceptable date for the deposition of John Doe.

Comment 2: Ball in *your* court:

The deposition will be held on September 1, 1992, unless you advise that this date is unacceptable.

The point is this: when you leave the ball in your court, you have control over the situation, and inaction on the part of the other party will not impede your ability to take action. When you pass the ball to the other side's court, you place yourself in the position of having to wait for acceptance of an offer, or some other matter. Thus, you needlessly handicap your ability to respond to events as you see fit.

So, in drafting correspondence, use language that keeps your side in control of events. Keep the ball in your court!

SUMMARY

7–1

The legal profession uses correspondence to inform, to advise, and to confirm. Informative letters transmit information; advisory letters are more formal than informative letters and offer legal opinions; and confirmation letters create a permanent record of the oral sharing of information.

7–2

The tone of a letter varies with the audience as well as the purpose. Letters to clients should contain concrete answers and be written to the client's level of understanding. They should be drafted so as to avoid unreasonable expectations in the mind of the client. Letters to opposing counsel should be written with caution, since they may be used against your client. Letters to the court should be written with respect. You should generally send copies to opposing counsel, and be aware of the pitfalls of *ex parte* communications.

7–3

A letter generally contains the following components: a letterhead; the date on which the letter is sent; identification of the addressee; a brief, descriptive reference line; a salutation opening with "Dear" and followed by a colon; a body containing the message of the letter, which may be short or long, but which should always be written clearly; headers, which identify subsequent pages; a closing, often "Very truly yours" followed by the signer's name and position. Note that paralegals can *never* sign letters rendering legal advice. Finally, letters show the parties to whom copies have been sent; only your file copy should show those parties to whom blind carbon copies have been sent.

7–4

The demand letter is designed to motivate a desired response—often (though not exclusively) the payment of a debt. Demand letters can be in the form of a standard collection letter; a "Fair Debt Collection" letter designed to comply with statutory requirements; a consumer protection letter; or a notice of intention to sue. In drafting a demand letter, you should state your purpose, clarify the action you expect the recipient to take, establish a deadline date, and, under most circumstances, maintain a tone that will keep channels of communication open. In responding to a demand letter, you should review and discuss the situation with your client and identify reasons why you deny the claim. The letter should deny inaccurate factual statements made by the opposition, make your position clear, and, as with a demand letter, keep the channels of communication open.

7–5

An opinion letter renders legal advice. In a client opinion letter, work to balance two competing considerations: (1) accurately presenting legal concepts; and (2) presenting them in language the client can understand. Make it clear that your analysis is based upon the facts as you understand them, and make your recommendations clear as well. A third party opinion letter must indicate your relationship with the client; the purpose of the letter; any limitations for liability purposes; and a clear statement of the bounds of the opinion.

7–6

Transmittal letters accompany information, confirming its nature and the fact that it was sent. Letters requesting information should be specific, and serve two purposes: to obtain information, and to create a record that the request was made. A retainer letter sets forth the agreement between attorney and client on fees and services to be rendered. An authorization letter enables the attorney to pursue an investigation for the client's benefit into records maintained by third parties.

7–7

An important practical point in drafting legal correspondence is to keep the ball in your court, which means that whenever possible, you should maintain control over subsequent events.

REVIEW

Terms

Before proceeding, review the key terms listed below to be sure you understand each one. If necessary, read over the corresponding section of the chapter. When you are ready to test your understanding, answer the Review Questions.

informative letter
advisory letter
confirmation letter
cover letter
ex parte
letterhead
reference line
salutation
body
header
closing
cc
bcc
blind carbon copy
demand letter
collection letter
deadline date
opinion letter
disclaimer
transmittal letter
retainer letter
authorization letter

Questions for Review and Discussion

1. Name three functions of legal correspondence.
2. List some characteristics of letters addressed to: clients; opposing counsel; and the court.
3. What is the purpose of using letterhead?
4. What is the importance of an accurate date?
5. How is a reference line prepared?
6. What is a blind carbon copy?
7. What is the purpose of a demand letter?
8. What is the purpose of a client opinion letter?
9. How does a third party opinion letter differ from a client opinion letter?
10. List two possible purposes of a letter that requests information, and describe its most important characteristic.

Activities

1. Your law firm has just been retained to represent a woman who has been injured in an industrial accident. Your attorney has instructed you to request the client's medical history. Draft the letter requesting the information.
2. A client has a claim against an insurance company for nonpayment of medical bills. Draft the representation letter to the insurance company.
3. Prepare a transmittal letter to the court sending the Defendant's Original Answer. (Remember to state that the opposing counsel has been notified of this transmittal.)

NOTES

CHAPTER 8 The Basics of Pleadings

OUTLINE

8–1 Pleadings in General
- Types of Pleadings
- Fact Pleading and Notice Pleading Distinguished
- The Caption
- Title of the Pleading
- Signature
- Certificate of Service

8–2 The Complaint
- The Caption
- Introduction
- The Body of the Complaint
- The Prayer for Relief
- The Signature Block and the Verification
- Service of Process
- Checklist

8–3 The Answer
- The Components of an Answer
- Checklist

8–4 Additional Pleadings

8–5 Amending and Supplementing Pleadings
- Amended Pleadings
- Supplemental Pleadings

8–6 Practical Considerations

COMMENTARY

Your firm's client, Mary Mackey, is 51 years old. After 30 years of continuous employment with XYZ Corporation, and despite a personnel file that contains exceptional performance reviews and no hint of misconduct, she was recently fired with no explanation and for no apparent reason. Based on conversations she has since had with former coworkers, she believes that she was replaced by a 23-year-old woman who came in at a higher salary despite minimal qualifications.

Your supervising attorney believes that Mrs. Mackey's termination constitutes age discrimination. He has written to XYZ Corporation, demanding that Mrs. Mackey be reinstated and that she be reimbursed for the weeks of salary missed since the firing. The corporation has rejected this demand, and refuses to discuss the situation further.

Your supervising attorney has decided that litigation can no longer be avoided. You have been assigned to draft a complaint on behalf of Mrs. Mackey.

OBJECTIVES

Drafting pleadings is a basic litigation skill important to master, both as a means of defining the issues in a lawsuit and as a means to develop a deeper understanding of the litigation process. After completing this chapter, you will be able to:

1. Differentiate fact pleading from notice pleading.
2. Prepare a caption.
3. Identify a certificate of service.
4. Explain why preliminary research is important to the proper drafting of a complaint.
5. Describe a count.
6. Identify a benefit and a pitfall of using form books and models to assist in the preparation of pleadings.
7. Explain what is meant by "service of process."
8. Define the term *affirmative defense*, and identify several affirmative defenses.
9. Explain the difference between a counterclaim and a cross-claim.
10. Describe the purpose of a Motion for a More Definite Statement.

8–1 Pleadings in General

When a lawsuit is begun, it is important for the court and the litigants—the competing parties—to identify the issues in dispute. If the issues are unclear, the plaintiff will be unable to prepare for trial; the defendant will be unable to prepare a defense; and the court will be unable to evaluate the competing positions. The problem is solved by the filing of pleadings. **Pleadings** are formal documents filed with the court that establish the claims and defenses of the parties to the lawsuit.

Types of Pleadings

There are several different types of pleadings. They are filed in sequence, in a manner specified by procedural rules. Some are filed by a plaintiff, some by a defendant.

The **complaint** is the first pleading filed by any party to a lawsuit. It is the filing of the complaint that actually commences the lawsuit; before the complaint reaches the court, no lawsuit is pending. The complaint tells the defendant who is suing him and why, and also identifies the nature and extent of the damages claimed.

The **answer** is filed by the defendant in response to the complaint. It generally denies the plaintiff's claim, sets forth the reasons for the denial, and identifies affirmative defenses that the defendant asserts.

A **counterclaim** or **cross-claim** may also be included in the pleadings in a particular case. A counterclaim is made by the defendant against the plaintiff—not a defense, but a new claim for damages, as if the defendant were the plaintiff in a separate suit. A cross-claim is made in a suit where there are two or more defendants, one of whom also acts like a plaintiff in a separate suit. But rather than making her claim against the plaintiff (as in the counterclaim), she makes it against another defendant.

In addition to the complaint, answer, counterclaim, and cross-claim, there are also several motions considered to be pleadings. For example, a party who believes that the claims made in the pleadings of another party are unclear can file a **Motion for More Definite Statement**. A party who believes his opponent has "failed to state a claim" for which the court can grant relief can file a **Motion to Dismiss**, which, if granted by the court, dismisses the claim. There may be available other motions with other names, or similar motions with variant names, depending on the rules of your jurisdiction; you should become familiar with the rules that apply in your area.

In this chapter we use the complaint and the answer as a backdrop for exploring the drafting of pleadings by the legal writer. We then briefly consider the other types of pleadings. Where procedural rules are mentioned, we often discuss the Federal Rules of Civil Procedure (FRCP), since they are uniform throughout the United States. Remember, however, that our purpose is to teach you how to draft a pleading, as opposed to mastering the rules. Although the two concepts are connected, teaching you to master the rules of civil procedure, whether the FRCP or state rules, is beyond the scope of this book.

We cannot, however, overemphasize the importance of learning the rules. Even when the FRCP are applicable, for example, there will be additional local rules that govern certain technical matters. Failure to follow *all* applicable rules and to file pleadings in the manner and in the order that the rules require can waive (forfeit) your clients' rights and lead to a disastrous result.

Fact Pleading and Notice Pleading Distinguished

There are two broad styles of pleading—fact pleading and notice pleading. You should always determine which style is required in the jurisdiction in which your lawsuit is pending.

Fact pleading requires that you identify all the facts necessary to allege a valid cause of action. In other words, the pleading must include, at a minimum, those facts which must be proved in order to win on the claims made.

Notice pleading, which has been incorporated into the FRCP, requires only a short, plain statement of the grounds on which a party is basing her claim, and a showing of why the party is entitled to relief. The party need not allege all the facts needed to support the claim, but only such facts as are needed to put the opposing party on notice of the claim. The text of FRCP 8(a), which sets out the requirements of notice pleading for a complaint filed in federal court, appears in Figure 8–1.

The rationale behind the less strict requirements of notice pleading is that the facts will be developed by the parties through the **discovery** process, which is the investigation aspect of pretrial procedure (which we discuss further in Chapter 9). Parties often, however, include significant detail in their pleadings anyway, for two reasons: (1) to make their claims clear from the start, and (2) because the jurors can take the pleadings into the jury room, so that the added detail helps to clarify the party's position.

Figure 8–1 Rule 8(a), Federal Rules of Civil Procedure

(a) Claims for Relief. A pleading which sets forth a claim for relief, whether an original claim, counterclaim, cross-claim, or third-party claim, shall contain (1) a short and plain statement of the grounds upon which the court's jurisdiction depends, unless the court already has jurisdiction and the claim needs no new grounds of jurisdiction to support it, (2) a short and plain statement of the claim showing that the pleader is entitled to relief, and (3) a demand for judgment for the relief the pleader seeks. Relief in the alternative or of several different types may be demanded.

You should note the exceptions to notice pleading in federal court, set forth in FRCP 9. For example, when a plaintiff is alleging a fraud committed by a defendant, rule 9 requires that the facts surrounding the alleged fraud be stated with "particularity," that is, in detail. This is to protect defendants from unsubstantiated allegations of fraud, which can damage reputations.

The Caption

All pleadings filed with the court require a **caption**. The caption goes at the top of the first page of the pleading, and identifies (l) the name of the case; (2) the court in which the case is pending; (3) the docket number of the case; and

Figure 8–2 Variations of Captions

(a) UNITED STATES DISTRICT COURT FOR THE SOUTHERN DISTRICT OF CALIFORNIA

Civil Action, File Number __________

MICHAEL BUFFETT, et al. Plaintiffs	§ §	
	§	ANSWER
vs.	§ §	
CARMEN BROWN, et al. Defendants	§ §	

(b) UNITED STATES DISTRICT COURT FOR THE EASTERN DISTRICT OF NEW JERSEY

XTC CORPORATION, Plaintiff vs.	§ §	
SMITH, INC., Defendant and Third-Party Plaintiff	§ §	THIRD-PARTY COMPLAINT
vs.	§	CIVIL ACTION NO. ______
FRANÇOIS BENET, Third-Party Defendant	§	

(c) UNITED STATES DISTRICT COURT FOR THE NORTHERN DISTRICT OF ILLINOIS, CHICAGO DIVISION

Civil Action, File Number __________

XTC CORPORATION, Plaintiff vs.	§ §	
SMITH, INC., Defendant	§	INTERVENER'S ANSWER
FRANÇOIS BENET, Intervener	§	

(d)

		NO. 89-7786-J
XTC CORPORATION,	)	IN THE DISTRICT COURT OF
	)	
Plaintiff	)	
	)	
vs.	)	DALLAS COUNTY, TEXAS
	)	
SMITH, INC.,	)	
	)	
Defendant	)	191st JUDICIAL DISTRICT

(4) the date on which the pleading is filed. The caption is identical for all parties in the case, whether plaintiffs or defendants. Captions vary slightly in style and format from one jurisdiction to another, as can be seen from the examples shown in Figure 8–2.

Title of the Pleading

It is necessary to identify the type of pleading with a title appearing below the caption. With multiple parties it is often helpful to include enough information in the title to clearly differentiate the pleading from other, potentially similar pleadings (for example, "Defendant Johnson's Motion to Dismiss the Second Count").

Signature

Someone must sign all pleadings, usually the attorney for the party filing the pleading. The signature constitutes a pledge by the person signing that the contents have been prepared in good faith. If it can be shown that this is not the case, a lawyer can be sanctioned (see, for example, FRCP 11).

Certificate of Service

Almost every jurisdiction requires some form of certification or guarantee by an attorney (or a party, if the party does not have an attorney) that copies of the pleading have been sent to all other parties. This certification is very important, because unless the other parties are aware that the pleading has been filed, they cannot make appropriate responses in accordance with the applicable rules and deadlines. The certification usually consists of an attesting signature of the attorney preparing the complaint to a pledge like the following:

Figure 8–3 Certificate of Service

Certification

I, Mary Attorney, hereby certify that a copy of the foregoing Motion to Dismiss was mailed to all counsel of record on this 15th day of June, 1992.

____
Mary Attorney

8–2 The Complaint

As noted, the complaint is the pleading that commences the lawsuit. In addition to the caption and signature block, a complaint prepared in accordance with the FRCP includes an introduction, an identification of the parties, a statement of the basis for jurisdiction, numbered paragraphs containing the allegations (including damages) and causes of action, and a prayer for relief. It does *not* include an ordinary certificate of service, because a complaint must be served according to its own special rules. Let's take a look at each of these areas.

The Caption

The caption that appears on the complaint includes the same information which appears on every other caption, with the exception of the docket number. The court clerk assigns the docket number after the filing of the complaint; subsequent pleadings will show it, but the complaint cannot until the clerk assigns it (more about the sequence of events later).

Introduction

Although the trend is to eliminate the introductory paragraph of pleadings, it is still used in many jurisdictions. The introductory paragraph identifies the party filing the pleading and the nature of the pleading. Figure 8–4 shows several examples of introductory paragraphs in a complaint.

The Body of the Complaint

The body of the complaint consists of the identification of the parties, the basis for jurisdiction, and the numbered paragraphs containing the allegations and cause of action.

The parties are identified by name and status (i.e., whether an individual, corporation, or some other status), state of citizenship, and street address. These characteristics can be important; their significance is discussed in the subsection on "service of process." Figure 8–5 shows examples of paragraphs identifying various parties.

Complaints prepared under the FRCP must also identify the basis for the alleged jurisdiction of the federal court. This usually requires identifying the substantive federal statutes that apply to the facts to form the basis of the

Figure 8–4 Introductory Paragraphs

Simple, General Clause:

Plaintiff alleges . . .

Comes Now, Plaintiff in the above-styled cause, and complains of Defendant and would show unto the Court as follows:

Single Claim Stated:

Plaintiff for his claim alleges . . .

Plaintiff for its complaint alleges . . .

Claims Made in Separate Counts:

Plaintiff for a first count alleges . . .

Alternate Forms:

The Plaintiff, for his complaint against the Defendant through Miranda Carr, his attorney, alleges . . .

The Plaintiffs bring their complaint against the Defendants and for their claims would respectfully show . . .

Figure 8–5 General Jurisdictional Allegations in the Body of Complaint

Natural Persons—Single Parties

Plaintiff is a citizen of the State of Minnesota, and resides in the City of Owatana. Defendant is a citizen of the State of Minnesota and resides in the City of Owatana. The matter in controversy, exclusive of interest and costs, exceeds fifty thousand dollars ($50,000.00).

Multiple Plaintiffs

Plaintiff, ALBERT CROSS, is a citizen of the State of Rhode Island, Plaintiff, SANDRA CROSS, is a citizen of the State of Rhode Island, and Defendant, CHRISTOPHER VAIL, is a citizen of the State of Rhode Island. The matter in controversy exceeds, exclusive of interest and costs, the sum of fifty thousand dollars ($50,000.00).

Corporations

Plaintiff is a corporation incorporated under the laws of the State of Delaware, having its principal place of business in the State of New Hampshire, and Defendant is a corporation incorporated under the laws of the State of New Hampshire, having its principal place of business in a State other than the State of New Hampshire. The matter in controversy exceeds, exclusive of interest and costs, the sum of fifty thousand dollars ($50,000.00).

jurisdiction, or, if no substantive statute is the basis for the jurisdiction, then the applicable federal jurisdictional statute (usually relating to diversity of citizenship) is cited, with a statement showing that its requirements have been satisfied. Figure 8–6 shows some examples of jurisdictional paragraphs.

Following the identifying and jurisdictional paragraphs come the allegations. The allegations set forth the claims of the party. Asserted as a group, they form the plaintiff's cause of action, which is the particular legal theory upon which plaintiff claims a right to judicial relief, or recovery of damages, against the defendant. The complaint should include all claims that plaintiff has against the defendant that arise from the same facts and circumstances. If there is more than one claim, each separate claim or cause of action is set forth in a separate **count.** Figure 8–7 on page 398 shows FRCP 8(e) regarding multiple causes of action.

The allegations are the substantive heart of the complaint. It is here that legal writing considerations come into play. The drafter cannot simply state facts and claim damages. Preliminary research must be conducted to determine what elements the law requires the plaintiff to prove. All such elements must then be pleaded, or else plaintiff has "failed to state a claim" on which relief can be granted, leaving himself open to the Motion to Dismiss discussed already. Careful drafting often requires that certain specific language be used

Figure 8–6 Statutory Jurisdictional Allegations in the Body of Complaint

General Form

The section arises under the Constitution of the United States, Article II, Section 8, and the 14th Amendment to the Constitution of the United States, U.S.C., Title 28 § 1 et seq.

Diversity of Citizenship and Federal Question

The jurisdiction of this Court is based upon diversity of citizenship and Title 15, U.S.C.A. Sections 1, et seq. The matter in controversy, exclusive of interest and costs, exceeds the sum of fifty thousand dollars ($50,000.00).

Figure 8–7 Guideline for Pleading Multiple Causes of Actions.

8(e) Pleading to be Concise and Direct; Consistency.

(1) Each averment of a pleading shall be simple, concise, and direct. No technical forms of pleading or motions are required.

(2) A party may set forth two or more statements of a claim or defense alternately or hypothetically, either in one count or defense or in separate counts or defenses. When two or more statements are made in the alternative and one of them, if made independently, would be sufficient, the pleading is not made insufficient by the insufficiency of one or more of the alternative statements. A party may also state as many separate claims or defenses as the party has, regardless of consistency and whether based on legal, equitable, or maritime grounds. All statements shall be made subject to the obligations set forth in Rule 11.

to comply with statutory or common law requirements; the sufficiency of the complaint depends on it. The extent of detail required varies, of course, depending on whether the jurisdiction requires fact pleading or notice pleading.

Case law is never cited in the complaint, but statutes and regulations relied upon are generally identified. For example, the complaint based on the facts in the Commentary to this chapter would identify the federal age-discrimination statute on which the claim is based.

The allegations are contained in consecutively numbered paragraphs. Sometimes the identification of the parties is included in these numbered paragraphs. Each paragraph should be limited to one concise idea or statement. The language used should be accurate but adversarial—telling the plaintiff's story from the plaintiff's perspective, and sympathetic to the plaintiff for the wrong allegedly committed against her. The writer should strike a balance between mundane, unemotional language and excessively expressive language; the reader should be able to visualize events without sensing that they have been exaggerated or embellished.

Often the requirements of a later count require a restatement of allegations already set forth as paragraphs in an earlier count. If this is the case, it is not only acceptable but indeed important to eliminate redundancy by using a phrase such as the following:

Figure 8–8 Restatement of Allegations

Second Count

1. Paragraphs 1–8 of the First Count are hereby set forth as paragraphs 1–8 of this, the Second Count.

By thus eliminating redundancy, the writer minimizes the risk that the reader will become bored or miss the significant points as a result of wading through repetitions.

The allegations should also identify the damages suffered by the plaintiff. The recovery of damages in the form of money is a **legal remedy**. If such legal damages are sought, you should be as specific as possible. Sometimes this is difficult, as with a personal injury situation where the nature of the damage defies precise evaluation. If the remedy sought is equitable relief (which resolves a lawsuit by directing the wrongdoer either to perform a certain act, or to refrain from performing a certain act), the specific nature of the equitable remedy sought should be identified as well.

When you begin drafting complaints, and even when you are more

Figure 8–9 Example of Body of Complaint

TO THE HONORABLE JUDGE OF SAID COURT:

1. Plaintiff Robert Andrews is an individual residing in Travis County, Texas, and is the natural parent of Francis Andrews, the minor Plaintiff. Defendant George Peters is an individual residing in Jollyville, Oklahoma, and service of process may be had at 8362 Longhorn Drive, Jollyville, Oklahoma. Defendant D.C. Computers, Inc. is a corporation duly formed and existing under the laws of the State of Texas and may be served with process by serving its agent for service, David Clark at 287 South Main, Austin, Texas 75853.

2. On the 4th day of June, 1991, Plaintiff Francis Andrews was a passenger in a vehicle driven by Plaintiff Robert Andrews, which was traveling eastbound in the 8700 block of Elm Street in Austin, Travis County, Texas.

3. Defendant Peters attempted to make a left turn in front of the Andrews' vehicle. As a result, the Andrews vehicle and the vehicle driven by Defendant Peters collided, causing injuries to Plaintiff, Francis Andrews. At the time of the collision, the vehicle driven by Defendant Peters was owned by Defendant D.C. Computers, Inc.

4. As a result of the negligent conduct of Defendant Peters, Plaintiff Francis Andrews suffered the damages and injuries set out hereinafter.

5. Plaintiffs would show that Defendant Peters was guilty of the following acts and omissions of negligence, each of which, separately or concurrently, was a proximate cause of the damages and injuries sustained by the Plaintiff, Francis Andrews:

1) Failure to yield right of way;
2) Failure to keep a proper lookout;
3) Failure to take proper evasive action;
4) Failure to apply brakes.

6. At the time of the collision described above, Defendant Peters was the agent, servant, and employee of Defendant D.C. Computers, Inc. and was acting within the scope of his authority as such agent, servant, and employee.

7. Defendant Peters was incompetent and unfit to safely operate a motor vehicle on the public streets and highways.

8. Defendant D.C. Computers, Inc. knew, or in the exercise of due care should have known, that Defendant Peters was an incompetent and unfit driver and would create an unreasonable risk of danger to persons and property on the public streets and highways of Texas.

9. Plaintiff Francis Andrews was severely injured as a proximate result of the negligent conduct of the Defendants. Plaintiff Francis Andrews has suffered physical pain and mental anguish in the past and in reasonable probability will suffer from such in the future. Plaintiff Francis Andrews has sustained physical impairment and in reasonable probability will sustain such impairment in the future.

10. Plaintiffs have sustained reasonable medical expenses in the amount of $52,000.00 as a result of the Defendants' negligence in the past and in reasonable probability will sustain additional medical expenses in the future.

11. At the time of this collision, Defendant Peters was under the influence of an alcoholic beverage. The conduct of Defendant Peters in driving the vehicle while under the influence of an alcoholic beverage constitutes gross negligence. As a result of such conduct, the Plaintiffs are entitled to recover exemplary damages.

experienced, it is often helpful to refer to form books and models. **Form books** are publications that contain complete or partial sample complaints, with sample factual situations and various alternative methods of stating the legal basis for the cause of action. **Models** are copies of actual complaints, obtained from your firm's files, that have a similar factual foundation. These sources are useful in that they give you a basic framework within which to begin drafting your complaint. In the case of a model, you have an actual complaint that has withstood scrutiny; in the case of a form book, a sample complaint that has withstood editorial scrutiny by a panel of experts. You must be careful, however, when using models and form books. There are problems which can arise. If the law has changed since the model or form book was prepared, for example, or if you fail to recognize the significance of a twist in your particular factual situation, you may make critical drafting errors. Thus, you should use models and form books to supplement your research, not in place of it.

In general, when drafting the body of the complaint you should keep in mind the many factors we've discussed in previous chapters about effective legal writing—concise sentences, a minimum of legalese, good punctuation and grammar. Figure 8–9 on page 399 shows an example of the body of a complaint.

The Prayer for Relief

The **prayer for relief** sets out the specific demands that the plaintiff has against the defendant. It requests judgment in favor of the plaintiff on the causes of action alleged, and identifies the damages (legal and/or equitable) the plaintiff asserts judgment should allow (including interest and attorneys' fees). In essence, the plaintiff is telling the court what he seeks to gain from the lawsuit.

Since the prayer for relief often begins with the phrase "Wherefore, the plaintiff claims . . . ," followed by a statement of the relief sought, it is often called the "wherefore clause." The current trend toward simplifying pleadings has streamlined the language in some jurisdictions, however, eliminating the archaic term "wherefore."

Almost all prayers for relief have a "catch-all" provision, which states that the plaintiff also seeks "such other and further relief as the court may deem proper or appropriate." By using this or a similar catch-all clause, the plaintiff gives the court discretion on the relief it may grant, even allowing it to go beyond the plaintiff's specified requests.

You should note that in some jurisdictions, the prayer for relief is also the location for a jury-trial request. You should also note that some jurisdictions require a prayer for relief at the end of every count, not just at the end of the complaint.

Examples of a prayer for relief are shown in Figure 8–10.

The Signature Block and the Verification

The attorney preparing the complaint must sign it and, as we noted earlier, Rule 11 of the FRCP states that the signature constitutes a written affirmation that she has a good-faith basis for filing it (protecting against frivolous or harassing suits). Usually the attorney's name, address, and telephone number are typed below the signature; check the rules in your jurisdiction.

Some complaints require a brief affidavit, called a **verification**, in which the plaintiff swears to the truth of the contents. By signing the verification, the plaintiff shows that he (1) has read the complaint, (2) understands the contents, and (3) pledges that, to the best of his personal knowledge, the allegations are true. The purpose of the verification is to protect further against false claims. Often the requirement applies where the allegations of the complaint are particularly

FIGURE 8–10 Prayer for Relief Section of Complaint

WHEREFORE, PREMISES CONSIDERED, Plaintiffs pray that the Defendants be cited to appear and answer herein and further pray that upon final hearing, Plaintiff have final judgment against each Defendant, jointly and severally, for damages in excess of the minimum jurisdictional limits of this Court, for exemplary damages, for prejudgment and post-judgment interest as allowed by law, for costs of court and for such other and further relief, both general and special, at law and in equity, to which the Plaintiffs may show themselves justly entitled.

OR

WHEREFORE:

The Plaintiffs, Robert Andrews and Francis Andrews, demand judgment against the Defendant in the sum of Fifty-Two Thousand Dollars ($52,000.00).

The Plaintiff demands a trial by jury.

OR

The Plaintiffs demand judgment . . .

strong, as where fraud is claimed. Signing an untruthful verification can lead to criminal prosecution, and the possible results should be explained to the plaintiff before he signs. An example of a verification appears as Figure 8–11.

Service of Process

The certificate of service is not needed in a complaint because, since the complaint is the first notice of a lawsuit that a defendant receives, the service requirements are actually much stricter than merely requiring a certificate of service. **Service of process** is the procedure by which a defendant is notified by a **process server** (a person statutorily authorized to serve legal documents such as complaints) that she is being sued. Among the papers that a defendant receives is a summons, ordering her to appear in court at a certain time or suf-

Figure 8–11 Verification

STATE OF NEW JERSEY §
COUNTY OF CUMBERLAND §

BEFORE the undersigned Notary Public for the State of New Jersey, at large, personally appeared, ROBERT ANDREWS, Plaintiff in the above-styled cause, who, being by me first duly sworn, deposes and says that the averments contained in the foregoing Complaint are true and correct.

This the ___ day of August, 1992.

____
ROBERT ANDREWS

Sworn to and subscribed before me, this ____ day of August, 1992.

____
NOTARY PUBLIC IN AND FOR THE
STATE OF NEW JERSEY
My Commission Expires: ________

fer the consequences. Service of process is accomplished by delivery of the complaint and **summons**; the procedure has many technical requirements, which vary from one jurisdiction to another. The *status* of the defendants is also significant for the purpose of service of process. Rules of service differ depending on whether the defendant is an individual, a corporation, or of some other status.

In some jurisdictions the complaint is filed with the court, *then* served on the defendants, whereas in other jurisdictions it is served first, then filed. If filed before service, the procedure is as follows: (l) original is filed with the court; (2) the clerk assigns a docket number to the case; then (3) copies are returned to the plaintiff for service on the defendants. Make sure you find out and follow the proper sequence in your jurisdiction. In general, you should learn the specific rules of service for all the courts in your area, and always review questions with your supervising attorney.

Checklist

The full text of a complaint appears as Appendix A on page 177. Here, however, is a checklist for preparation of a complaint:

- ___ Determine the parties who will be sued.
- ___ Identify the court in which suit will be filed, and verify that the court has jurisdiction.
- ___ Research and determine the necessary elements for the causes of action you intend to allege, including the applicable statutes.
- ___ Identify the necessary and useful facts, and determine whether yours is a fact- or notice-pleading jurisdiction.
- ___ Identify the damages suffered and the relief sought.
- ___ Prepare the caption and the introduction.
- ___ Check the applicable procedural rules, form books, and models to determine the proper style of pleading.
- ___ Draft concise, effective statements that establish the cause of action in a light which favors your client.
- ___ Draft the prayer for relief.
- ___ Prepare the summons and determine the proper procedure to complete service of process.
- ___ Review and edit your draft.

8–3 The Answer

The complaint has been correctly served. Under FRCP 12(a), the defendant must file a response within 20 days of receipt of the complaint; you should always check the rules of your jurisdiction to verify such a deadline.

If the defendant believes that some aspect of the plaintiff's allegations is inadequate, he may file one of the motions described in the next section. If, however, no such motion is filed, then the defendant files his response, called an answer.

The Components of an Answer

An **answer** comprises several distinct parts. First, it contains a section responding specifically to the plaintiff's numbered paragraphs. It either admits an allegation, denies it, or pleads that the defendant "lacks sufficient knowledge or information to form a belief as to the truth or falsity" of the allegation. This last category would apply to those of the plaintiff's allegations that relate to issues of her own status or conduct, necessarily outside the knowledge of the defendant. Each and every allegation must be addressed and responded to by the defendant; failure to respond can be taken as an admission.

Figure 8–12 Answer with General and Affirmative Defenses Alleged

DEFENDANT'S ORIGINAL ANSWER

1. Defendant admits the allegations of Paragraph 1 of the complaint.
2. Defendant denies the allegations of Paragraph 2 of the complaint.
3. Defendant denies the allegations of Paragraph 3 of the complaint, but has no knowledge of information sufficient to form a belief regarding the ownership of the vehicle.
4. Defendant denies the allegations of Paragraph 4 of the complaint.
5. Defendant denies the allegations of Paragraph 5 of the complaint.
6. Defendant admits the allegations of Paragraph 6 of the complaint.
7. Defendant denies the allegations of Paragraph 7 of the complaint.
8. Defendant D.C. Computers, Inc. has no knowledge or information sufficient to form a belief regarding the truth of the allegations of Paragraph 8 of the complaint.
9. Defendant D.C. Computers, Inc. has no knowledge or information sufficient to form a belief regarding the truth of the allegations of Paragraph 9 of the complaint.
10. Defendant D.C. Computers, Inc. has no knowledge or information sufficient to form a belief regarding the truth of the allegations of Paragraph 10 of the complaint.
11. Defendant denies the allegations of Paragraph 11 of the complaint.

GENERAL DENIALS

12. This court lacks personal jurisdiction pursuant to Federal Rule 12(b).
13. Plaintiff has failed to state a claim upon which relief can be granted.

AFFIRMATIVE DEFENSES

14. Plaintiff was contributorally negligent in operating his automobile and is barred from recovery.
15. Plaintiff was traveling at an excessive speed and the alleged accident was unavoidable due to Plaintiff's negligence.

WHEREFORE, Defendant requests that this matter be dismissed and that Defendant be reimbursed its costs and attorneys' fees expended in the defense of this matter.

Rule 8 of the FRCP does not allow for a "general denial" disputing all of plaintiff's claims in one generalized statement; rather, each allegation must be identified and responded to. Most jurisdictions follow this rule; Texas and California are two notable exceptions.

General defenses are sometimes included in the complaint. These are items which, under the FRCP, can also be made by motion; we discuss them further in section 8–4. They cover such things as an assertion that the court lacks jurisdiction, or that the plaintiff has failed to state a claim on which relief can be granted.

The next section of the answer contains the **affirmative defenses**, which are also called **special defenses**. Affirmative defenses are those which go beyond mere denial of the plaintiff's claims; because of a separate affirmative fact, the defendant asserts that a defense exists even if plaintiff's allegations are true. Such defenses are usually waived unless specifically pleaded, which means that the defendant can only introduce evidence to prove an affirmative defense if he has included it in his answer. The affirmative or special defenses that must be included in the pleadings are often identified by statute or rule, as with Rule 8(c) of the FRCP. Examples of affirmative defenses are such issues as contributory negligence, "last clear chance" (a tort defense), assumption of risk, or statute of limitations.

Figure 8–12 on page 403 is an example of an answer with general and affirmative defenses.

Under some circumstances, the defendant includes a counterclaim after her defenses. A counterclaim may be filed with the answer or separately. It may arise out of the same facts as the complaint or be unrelated. Whatever the context, a counterclaim can be thought of as a separate lawsuit within a lawsuit, in which the defendant sues the plaintiff. The drafting considerations are similar to those for a complaint.

There are two types of counterclaims—compulsory and permissive. A **compulsory counterclaim** is one in which the facts relate to the same transaction as that set forth in the original complaint. It is *compulsory* because, if it is not included in the pending lawsuit, it is waived forever (see FRCP 13(a)). The purpose of making this sort of counterclaim compulsory is to conserve judicial resources: the court is able to adjudicate in one trial all claims arising out of the same set of facts, so that repetitive trials can be avoided. A **permissive counterclaim** (also discussed in FRCP 13) arises out of different facts. It may be filed in the pending lawsuit, but if it is not, it may be filed at a later date in a separate lawsuit. That is, no rights are waived by failing to include it. If filed as a counterclaim a plaintiff may move to sever it if its presence serves to cloud or confuse the original issues.

Figure 8–13 is an example of a counterclaim in a negligence action.

To complicate matters even more, a cross-claim, (which we discussed as a type of pleading) can be brought within the original lawsuit. A cross-claim is filed against a co-party, almost always by one defendant against another defendant, and must relate to the cause of action in the main complaint. The circumstances justifying a cross-claim often arise when a plaintiff sues two defendants who themselves have a business relationship—for example, when a person falls down in rented premises, then sues both the owner of the property and the tenant.

Although the terminology we have used applies in all federal jurisdictions, you should take great care in reviewing your state and local rules, because state and local terminology can vary dramatically. In California, for example, what we have just described as a "counterclaim" is referred to as a "cross-complaint."

Figure 8–13 Counterclaim in a Negligence Action

The Defendant, counterclaiming against Plaintiff, says:

1. On September 17, 1991, the Defendant was driving an automobile in a southerly direction on Highway 42 in Cumberland County, New Jersey, and entered the intersection of that highway and Atlantic County Road.

2. At the same time, Plaintiff was driving an automobile in a general easterly direction and entered said intersection after the Defendant was well within the intersection.

3. At about the same time Wesley Whittaker was driving an automobile in a general westerly direction upon the same highway.

4. The automobiles driven by Plaintiff and by Defendant came into contact within the intersection, and in the collision, the Defendant suffered damages to his property and injuries to his person.

5. At and about the time and place of the collision and just prior to it, Plaintiff negligently managed and operated the automobile he was driving. Plaintiff was negligent in the following respects: (1) In carelessly driving at an excessive rate of speed contrary to the statute; (2) In failing to use ordinary care to keep a proper lookout; (3) In failing to use ordinary care to have the automobile he was driving under proper control.

6. As a proximate result of the negligence of Plaintiff, the Defendant suffered the following damage and injuries: defendant's automobile front end was demolished; the left side of his ribs were broken; he was forced to incur expense for medical treatment and hospitalization; he suffered great pain and suffering, and was prevented from pursuing his business, thus suffering economic loss.

7. Defendant will be partially disabled for a long period and unable to attend his usual occupations, and to his damage in the sum of fifty-five thousand dollars ($55,000.00).

WHEREFORE, the Defendant demands judgment as follows:

(1) Dismissing Plaintiff's complaint;

(2) Against Plaintiff for Defendant's damages in the sum of fifty-five thousand dollars ($55,000.00) together with costs and disbursements; and

(3) For such other and further relief as Defendant is justly entitled.

____

Bonnie Hiatt
Attorney for Defendant
8201 South Broadway
Charleston, MO 40387
(304) 786-4873

Checklist

The full text of an answer appears as Appendix B on pages 411–412. The following is a checklist that you can follow in drafting an answer:

___ Check the rules to verify the deadline for filing the answer.

___ Admit or deny each allegation of the complaint, or allege that you have insufficient information to respond.

- Check to be sure that every paragraph and allegation of the complaint has been responded to.
- Allege any affirmative or general defenses that apply.
- Set forth any applicable counterclaim or cross-claim.
- Review and edit your draft.

8–4 Additional Pleadings

In the previous section we mentioned general defenses, which can be raised either in the answer, or by a separate motion. Rule 12(b) of the FRCP identifies the following defenses, any one or more of which may be made by motion:

1. Lack of jurisdiction over the subject matter.
2. Lack of jurisdiction over the person.
3. Improper venue (which is an assertion that plaintiff has filed the complaint in the wrong court).
4. Insufficiency of process (which means the summons or some aspect of the papers served by the process server was not correct).
5. Insufficiency of service of process (which means that the process server did not follow the rules in delivering the lawsuit).
6. Failure to state a claim on which relief can be granted.

If a party chooses to assert these defenses in a motion, the motion is called a Motion to Dismiss. It is generally supported by a brief, to which plaintiff responds and on which the court renders a decision. Before making its decision, the court often allows oral argument. An example of a Motion to Dismiss appears as Figure 8–14.

As we noted earlier, the complexities of procedural rules are beyond the scope of this discussion. Nevertheless, as you review the six defenses listed, you should keep in mind the following points:

Figure 8–14 Rule 12(b) Motion to Dismiss

MOTION TO DISMISS

The Defendant, RAINEY, INC., moves the court to dismiss Plaintiff's complaint on the following grounds:

1. That there is no actual controversy between the parties under the provisions of Title 42 U.S.C. §2000(e), as Plaintiff is not within the protected class under Title VII of the Civil Rights Act of 1964.

2. The court lacks jurisdiction of the subject matter of the complaint.

3. The complaint fails to state a claim against the Defendant upon which relief can be granted, since Plaintiff is male, thirty-nine (39) years of age, and not subject to protection under 42 U.S.C. §2000(e).

____

Katherine Haley
Attorney for Defendant
333 E. Denton Drive
Richardson, Texas 75221
(214)763-9736

- A defendant in a lawsuit has numerous options available to attack the claims in a complaint, in addition to admission, denial, or claim of insufficient knowledge.
- The six defenses listed constitute a sampling of these options, by no means exhaustive.
- There is great variety between and among jurisdictions as to the manner and timing of the filing of defenses, and the names of the related motions.
- It is necessary to study and master the applicable rules.
- When in doubt, discuss questions and problems with your supervising attorney.

A special kind of response, which we have referred to previously as the Motion for More Definite Statement, is authorized by FRCP 12(e) and merits brief additional mention. The filing of this motion is an assertion by the defendant that more information must be provided by the plaintiff before an intelligent response can be prepared. In some jurisdictions this pleading is called a "Request to Revise" or a "Request for More Definite Statement," or some similar name. Such a motion or request is often useful to pin down a plaintiff who has made vague allegations, and it can set the stage for the assertion of other defenses.

Strategy lies behind the filing of pleadings. Because they define the issues before the court, and because they are provided to the jury, if the matter is a jury trial, great care must be taken to ensure that the issues presented are the issues intended by the parties. The strategist/drafter should always strive to limit the issues, to the extent possible, to those most favorable to her client, and draft them in language sympathetic to her client.

8–5 Amending and Supplementing Pleadings

Although pleadings must be prepared in good faith, and hence should be prepared fully and to the best of the drafter's knowledge and ability, often information arises after filing that a party may wish to add. In addition, a party may be *required* to add information when a Motion for More Definite Statement is granted. A drafter may also have forgotten to include some information. Such additions (or analogous deletions) are made by filing amended or supplemented pleadings.

Amended Pleadings

An **amended pleading** changes, corrects, revises, or deletes information from a prior pleading. Information from the original pleading that is not changed remains in force, but information which is superseded is no longer in force. It is critically important to distinguish that which is changed from that which remains as before—your skills of writing with clarity become important in this regard. It is generally best to file an entirely new pleading, identifying it as "amended" in the title (for example, "Amended Complaint") incorporating all the old and new provisions in one place.

If an optional amended pleading (i.e., one not required by the granting of a motion) is not filed within a certain number of days of the original pleading, it generally can be filed thereafter only with the permission of the court. Check the applicable rules to verify such a deadline.

Supplemental Pleadings

A **supplemental pleading** adds to a pleading without deleting prior information. The prior pleading remains intact and is read in conjunction with the supplement. A supplemental pleading is usually filed when additional facts become known after the filing of the original pleading, perhaps after information is learned through a deposition or other discovery procedure (discussed in the next chapter). Court permission may also be required prior to the filing of a supplemental pleading.

8–6 Practical Considerations

Pleading is both a science and an art. It is a science in that specific rules must be strictly followed, or the pleading fails on technical grounds. It is an art in that the pleader must use creative skills to plot a strategic course and draft pleadings that assist in reaching the intended destination.

It is difficult to separate the science from the art, and this chapter has talked as much about rules as about writing. Mastering the rules is essential to mastering pleadings, and hence you should take the time to thoroughly review both the Federal Rules of Civil Procedure and the state and local rules applicable in your jurisdiction. We have only touched on these considerations; you should go much further.

But remember that drafting pleadings requires more than merely knowing and following rules, and more than mechanically adapting the facts of your case to the formats suggested in a form book. Pleadings define your case for yourself, the opposition, the court, and (if a jury matter) the jury. But *you* define the pleadings, by careful and effective drafting.

UNITED STATES DISTRICT COURT FOR THE SOUTHERN
DISTRICT OF CALIFORNIA

Civil Action, File Number ______

MELANIE COLEMAN,	§	
Plaintiff	§	
	§	COMPLAINT
vs.	§	
	§	
PRODUCTS OF AMERICA, INC.	§	
Defendant	§	

Plaintiff alleges:

1. Defendant is a Pennsylvania corporation, doing business in the State of Delaware. The address of its principal place of business is Philadelphia, Pennsylvania.
2. At all times relevant, Defendant was an "employer" as defined by 29 U.S.C. § 640(b) and is thus covered by and subject to the Age Discrimination in Employment Act of 1967 ("ADEA"), 29 U.S.C. § 621 et seq. This court has jurisdiction under 29 U.S.C. 640 (b).
3. As of July 15, 1991, Plaintiff was fifty-five years and two months of age and is an individual protected by tbe ADEA.
4. As of December 1, 1991, Plaintiff was employed by Defendant in the capacity of "project manager."
5. Plaintiff had been employed in various positions by Defendant from approximately October, 1982 until December, 1991.
6. Plaintiff was discharged by Defendant on December 2, 1991.
7. Plaintiff's discharge was because of Plaintiff's age in violation of the ADEA.
8. Defendant's violation of the ADEA was willful.
9. Plaintiff has satisfied all of the procedural and administrative requirements set forth in 29 U.S.C.§ 626.
   a. Plaintiff has filed a timely charge with the appropriate state fair employment practice office.
   b. Plaintiff has filed a timely charge with the Equal Employment Opportunity Commission.
   c. These charges were filed more than sixty (60) days prior to the filing of this action.
10. Proper venue is in this court as the unlawful action occurred within this jurisdiction where Defendant is doing business.
11. Plaintiff has suffered, is now suffering, and will continue to suffer irreparable injury as a result of Defendant's actions.

Appendix A cont.

WHEREFORE, Plaintiff hereby demands a trial by jury and prays for the following legal and equitable remedies:

a. Defendant be ordered to employ and reemploy the Plaintiff to the position from which she was discharged, together with all benefits incident thereto, including but not limited to wages, benefits, training, and seniority.

b. Defendant be required to compensate Plaintiff for the full value of wages and benefits that Plaintiff would have received had it not been for Defendant's unlawful treatment of the Plaintiff, with interest thereon, until the date Plaintiff is offered reemployment into a position substantially equivalent to the one Plaintiff occupied on December 2, 1991.

c. That a final judgment in favor of Plaintiff and against Defendant be entered for liquidated damages in an amount equal to the amount of wages due and owing Plaintiff as provided by 29 U.S.C. §§ 626(b) and 216(b)

d. That defendant be enjoined from discriminating against Plaintiff in any manner that violates the Age Discrimination in Employment Act.

e. That Plaintiff be awarded against the Defendant the costs and expenses of this litigation and reasonable attorneys' fees.

f. That Plaintiff be granted such other and further legal and equitable relief as the court may deem just and proper.

KETCHUM AND WYNN

By______________________________
Cynthia Goodman
Attorney for Plaintiff
1801 S. Main St., Suite 104
Philadelphia, PA 40987

UNITED STATES DISTRICT COURT FOR THE EASTERN
DISTRICT OF NEW JERSEY

XTC CORPORATION, Plaintiff	§	
	§	
	§	DEFENDANT'S ORIGINAL
vs.	§	ANSWER
	§	
	§	CIVIL ACTION NO.____
FRANÇOIS BENET, Defendant	§	

1. Defendant admits the allegations contained in paragraph 1 of the complaint.
2. Defendant admits that Plaintiff seeks to bring a cause of action under Title 29 U.S.C. § 640(b), but denies that Plaintiff is entitled to relief.
3. Defendant has no knowledge of information sufficient to form a belief regarding the truth of allegations of paragraph 3 of the complaint.
4. Defendant admits the allegations contained in paragraph 4 of the complaint.
5. Defendant admits the allegations contained in paragraph 5 of the complaint.
6. Defendant admits that Plaintiff was relieved of job responsibilities but denies that Plaintiff was discharged unlawfully under Title 29 U.S.C. § 640(b).
7. Defendant denies the allegations contained in paragraph 7 of the complaint.
8. Defendant denies the allegations contained in paragraph 8 of the complaint.
9. Defendant admits that he received a charge filed by Plaintiff but denies that the charge was filed timely.
10. Defendant denies the allegations contained in paragraph 10 of the complaint.
11. Defendant denies the allegations contained in paragraph 11 of the complaint.

GENERAL DEFENSES

12. Plaintiff has failed to state a claim upon which relief can be granted.
13. Plaintiff's suit is barred by virtue of statute of limitations.

AFFIRMATIVE DEFENSES

14. Plaintiff failed to file the complaint in this court within ninety (90) days following Plaintiff's right to sue notice as required by the statute.

WHEREFORE, Defendant requests that this matter be dismissed and that Defendant be reimbursed its costs and attorneys' fees expended in the defense of this matter.

Respectfully submitted,

____

Bonnie Hiatt
Attorney for Defendant
8201 South Broadway
Charleston, MO 40387
(304)786-4873

SUMMARY

8–1

Pleadings are formal documents filed with the court that establish the claims and defenses of the parties. The complaint is filed by the plaintiff, and commences the lawsuit. The answer is filed by the defendant in response to the complaint. There may also be counterclaims and cross-claims, and motions directed to the content of the pleadings. In filing pleadings, it is critical to know and understand the applicable procedural rules. Fact-pleading jurisdictions require more detail in their pleadings than notice-pleading jurisdictions. The caption, title, signature, and certificate of service are common components of pleadings.

8–2

The complaint begins with a caption and an introduction, followed by the body of the complaint, with a statement of the jurisdiction of the court (if in federal court), identification of the parties, and numbered paragraphs containing the allegations of the plaintiff. The language of the complaint is adversarial; the story it tells is sympathetic to the plaintiff. Each cause of action is stated in a separate count. Form books and models can be used to supplement the drafter's preliminary research, but should not be used as a substitute for such research. The prayer for relief identifies the remedy sought by the plaintiff. A complaint must be signed, and sometimes a verification is required. Rather than a certificate of service, delivery of the complaint is made by the more complicated procedure of service of process.

8–3

The answer responds to the allegations of the complaint by admitting them, denying them, or pleading insufficient information to respond. General defenses, affirmative defenses, counterclaims and cross-claims are also often included. A general defense can be made by motion as well as in the answer; an affirmative defense must be stated in the answer, or is waived. A counterclaim is filed by a defendant against a plaintiff; a cross-claim is filed by one co-party against another, usually by a defendant against another defendant. A compulsory counterclaim must be filed or the claim is waived; a permissive counterclaim can be filed as a counterclaim, or can be filed in the future in a separate lawsuit.

8–4

A Motion to Dismiss is a means to assert certain specified defenses, including (in a federal lawsuit) an assertion that the plaintiff has failed to state a claim on which relief can be granted. A Motion for More Definite Statement seeks more information from the other party about the details of their pleading, as a means of pinning down vague allegations; it can set the stage for other defenses.

8–5

An amended pleading changes, corrects, revises, or deletes information from a prior pleading. Amendments should be carefully identified to avoid confusion; the best practice is to file an entirely new pleading, labeled as an amended pleading, that includes both the still-accurate parts of the original content and the newly drafted changes. A supplemental pleading adds to a pleading without deleting prior information. Court permission may be required for amended and supplemental pleadings.

8–6

Pleading is both a science and an art: science in that rules must be strictly followed; art in that creative skills are required for writing and strategy. Pleadings define your case, but you define the pleadings.

REVIEW

Key Terms

Before proceeding, review the key terms listed below to be sure you understand each one. If necessary, read over the corresponding section of the chapter. When you are ready to test your understanding, answer the Review Questions.

pleadings
complaint
answer
counterclaim
cross-claim
Motion for More Definite Statement
Motion to Dismiss
fact pleading
notice pleading
discovery
caption
certificate of service
count
legal remedy
form book
model
prayer for relief
verification
service of process
process server
summons
answer
general defenses
affirmative defenses
special defenses
compulsory counterclaim
permissive counterclaim
amended pleading
supplemental pleading

Questions for Review and Discussion

1. What is the difference between fact pleading and notice pleading?
2. What is a caption?
3. What is a certificate of service?
4. Why is preliminary research important to the proper drafting of a complaint?
5. What is a count?
6. Describe a benefit and a pitfall of using form books and models to assist in the preparation of pleadings.
7. What is meant by service of process?
8. What does the term *affirmative defense* mean? List several affirmative defenses.
9. What is the difference between a counterclaim and a cross-claim?
10. What is the purpose of a Motion for More Definite Statement?

Activities

1. Draft a complaint on behalf of the Crandalls, based on the following facts:

   Mr. and Mrs. Crandall are from Maine and were traveling cross-country in their new automobile. While en route to their destination of Cheyenne, Wyoming, they traveled through Illinois. Harry Hart of New Town, Illinois was crossing through the town square in New Town and hit the Crandall's car. Mrs. Crandall was thrown against the windshield, and Mr. Crandall hit the steering wheel. Mr. Hart was barely scratched, because his car had airbags, but his car was completely destroyed. The medical and hospital expenses for the Crandalls were $78,000.00, and repairs to their car were $6,000.

2. Using the facts in Activity 1, draft the answer of Mr. Hart and allege general and affirmative defenses.
3. Go to the library and find your state's procedural requirements for complaints, answers, and defenses.

NOTES

CHAPTER 9 Discovery

OUTLINE

9–1 Discovery in General
9–2 Interrogatories
- The Caption
- Title
- The Introductory Paragraphs
- Instructions
- Definitions
- Interrogatories
- Signature Block and Certificate of Service
- Responses to Interrogatories

9–3 Requests for Admissions
- The Introduction of a Request for Admission
- Text of a Request for Admission
- Responses to Requests for Admission

9–4 Request for Production of Documents and Things
9–5 Request for Medical Examination
9–6 The Deposition
- Notice of Intention to Take Oral Deposition
- Applicability of a Subpoena
- Production of Documents in Conjunction With a Deposition
- Deposition Preparation
- Digesting a Deposition

9–7 Discovery Motions
- The Motion for Protective Order
- The Motion to Compel Discovery
- The Motion for Sanctions

9–8 Practical Considerations

COMMENTARY

A complaint has been prepared and served in the matter of *Ascot v. Widget Company*. Your firm represents Mr. Ascot. The attorney for Widget Company has filed an answer, denying the claim.

Your supervising attorney wants to take the deposition of Henry Widget, the president of Widget Company. Before he does so, however, he wants to do some preliminary investigation to determine the understanding of Widget Company about the chronology of events. He has asked you to prepare interrogatories, requests for admission, and requests for production of documents and things, all of which are to be answered by Widget Company.

Discovery is an important aspect of almost every lawsuit. As a paralegal, you will often be involved in preparing and responding to discovery requests.

OBJECTIVES

Involvement in the discovery process is often an important segment of a paralegal's responsibilities. After completing this chapter, you will be able to:

1. Explain why a discovery process is needed.
2. List some characteristics of a properly drafted interrogatory.
3. Explain the importance of instructions and definitions in discovery requests.
4. List appropriate areas of inquiry as to the opposition's consultation with experts.
5. Explain what is meant by the "continuing duty to respond."
6. Explain the usefulness of a request for admissions.
7. Draft requests for production that are sufficiently specific.
8. Explain who a "deponent" is.
9. Define "subpoena."
10. Explain the difference between a Motion for Protective Order and a Motion to Compel Discovery.

9–1 Discovery in General

The "surprise witness" who arrives to testify at the eleventh hour of a trial, turning certain defeat into stunning victory, is a character still seen in television or movie courtrooms, but not in reality. The days of "trial by ambush," where one side or the other held back key information until unleashing it in front of a jury, have been replaced by the era of discovery.

Discovery is the pretrial investigation process, authorized and governed by the rules of civil procedure. Discovery rules are broad, so that parties have the ability to pursue information in the hands of other parties to a lawsuit.

To be "discoverable," information must be relevant and not protected by attorney-client privilege. The party requesting the information need not show that it will be admissible at trial, however, but only that it "appears reasonably calculated to lead to the discovery of admissible evidence" (Rule 26(b) of the FRCP; see Figure 9–1). Discovery requests may be directed to other parties, but not to nonparties, except that nonparties are subject to deposition (and related production of documents) if subpoenaed (more about subpoenas later).

Figure 9–1 Rule 26(b)

> (b) Discovery Scope and Limits. Unless otherwise limited by order of the court in accordance with these rules, the scope of discovery is as follows:
>
> (1) In General. Parties may obtain discovery regarding any matter, not privileged, which is relevant to the subject matter involved in the pending action, whether it relates to the claim or defense of the party seeking discovery or to the claim or defense of any other party, including the existence, description, nature, custody, condition and location of any books, documents, or other tangible things and the identity and location of person having knowledge of any discoverable matter. It is not ground for objection that the information sought will be inadmissible at the trial if the information sought appears reasonably calculated to lead to the discovery of admissible evidence.

In Chapter 8 we discussed the Motion for More Definite Statement. You may now be wondering: If more information about a party's claim is needed, why not simply file that motion? The reason that a distinct and separate discovery process is needed, at least in part, is this: there are limits on the detail that a party can be required to place in her pleadings. Indeed, a court will often deny a Motion for More Definite Statement on the grounds that the detail requested is more appropriately sought through the discovery process, and goes beyond the requirements of even a fact-pleading jurisdiction. Pleadings are intended to be straightforward summaries, not all-inclusive tracts. Furthermore, there may be strategic reasons why one party wishes to learn information about another *without* having it placed in the pleadings. Finally, such forms of discovery as a deposition or a medical examination are of a character entirely different from mere written information—they supply not just words, but also the personal characteristics or condition of the person deposed or examined.

There are, in fact, five different types of discovery: interrogatories; requests for admission; requests for production of documents and things; requests for medical examination; and depositions. Some aspects are common to all; some unique to each. In the sections that follow, we discuss each form in turn, highlighting format, drafting, and strategy requirements.

9–2 Interrogatories

An **interrogatory** is a written question submitted by one party to another, to be answered under oath. Rule 33 of the FRCP sets out the requirements governing the use of interrogatories in the federal courts. Most states have adopted a similar rule; check the rules that apply in your jurisdiction.

By following certain preliminary procedures, you will be able to prepare more effective interrogatories. First, review the case file and pleadings to become thoroughly familiar with the facts and allegations. Identify the information you need to fill in gaps or increase your understanding. Make lists of areas of appropriate inquiry. Next, as with pleadings, you can use form books and models for assistance. Again, be wary of relying on them exclusively. Also consult the rules, and review any questions you have with your supervising attorney. Form books and models will also be helpful in drafting documents associated with the other discovery methods to be discussed.

When you draft your interrogatories, use specific and detailed language that precisely identifies the information you seek. Use short sentences in simple language. Avoid the phrase "and/or," or a large number of colons and semicolons, which can confuse the reader and lead to an unsatisfactory response. Avoid multiple subtopics and sections in the interrogatory, which can also cause confusion. Such subtopics may even be prohibited in some jurisdictions, or each subtopic may be counted as a separate interrogatory in a jurisdiction that limits the total number of interrogatories allowed.

Take care in choosing verb tenses. If an interrogatory is phrased in the present tense, the information received may be different than if worded in the past tense. Who *has* possession of the records of Widget Company, for example, may be a different party than who *had* those records.

Interrogatories should also be drafted to avoid a response of "yes" or "no." The request should require the respondent to present additional information. If all that is desired is a "yes" or "no" response, another form of discovery, such as the request for admissions, might be the better method.

Certain interrogatories are common to many different types of cases, seeking such information as identification of the person responding to the interrogatories (if the party to whom the request is directed is a corporation or other form of business); the names of witnesses and experts who will testify; and identification of documents that are relevant, such as correspondence or contracts. The format of such questions is often similar, even for different types of cases. Other interrogatories must be tailored to reflect the peculiar circumstances of the particular case at hand.

To add to the precision of individual interrogatories, the drafter often includes **instructions** and **definitions** that precede the interrogatories and define terms to avoid confusion. The drafter can often anticipate and eliminate potential problems by clarifying ambiguous terms with precise definitions. Instructions often serve to eliminate evasive answers, as, for example, an instruction that if a party objects to one subpart of a question, he should still respond to the remaining subparts.

Although you should be sure to check the rules of your jurisdiction for specific guidance in the drafting of interrogatories, the following subsections discuss elements common to all sets of interrogatories.

The Caption

Just as with pleadings, discovery requests, including interrogatories, must be identified by case name, court, docket number, and date of filing. Although jurisdictions differ on the precise documents that are filed with the court (some courts require notice of filing interrogatories, for example, but not the interrogatories themselves until answers are provided), you should always put the caption of your case at the top of the first page of your interrogatories.

Title

Also as with pleadings, discovery requests require a title. Again, the value of the title is in its capacity to differentiate documents. Thus, in a case with multiple parties and extensive discovery, it is useful to use a title that identifies the requesting party, the party from whom a response is sought, and whether the request is the first such request or a subsequent, supplemental set. For example, a proper title might be, "Plaintiff Ascot's Second Set of Interrogatories to Defendant Widget Company."

The Introductory Paragraphs

The introduction directs the interrogatories to the party from whom a response is sought, often showing that the request is made through that party's attorney of record. Figure 9–2 illustrates an acceptable introduction.

Figure 9–2 Introduction

```
TO: Irene Miller, by and through her attorney of record,
    Malcolm Anders, 1776 Declaration Drive, Boston,
    Massachusetts 20185
```

After the introduction, another introductory paragraph identifies the appropriate state or federal rule that governs the interrogatories. It also identifies the oath requirement, which mandates that the person responding attests to the truth of the responses. Figure 9–3 shows such a paragraph.

Figure 9–3 Introductory Paragraph

COMES NOW, the Defendant in the above-entitled and numbered cause pursuant to Rule 33 of the Federal Rules of Civil Procedure, and propounds the attached Interrogatories. You are advised that your answers to such Interrogatories must be answered fully in writing and under oath and served on the undersigned within thirty (30) days from the date of service thereof.

You are further notified that these Interrogatories and your sworn Answers to them may be offered in evidence at the time of trial of the above cause.

Instructions

Following the introduction are the **instructions**, which, as mentioned, provide guidelines to the party responding. Figure 9–4 shows an example of common instructions found in interrogatories.

Definitions

Following (or sometimes combined with) the instructions is a section defining terms and abbreviations used in the interrogatories. The meanings established

Figure 9–4 Instructions Section

INSTRUCTIONS

In answering these interrogatories, defendant is required to set out each responsive fact, circumstance, act, omission, or course of conduct, whether or not admissible in evidence at trial, known to defendant or about which he has or had information, which is or will be the basis for any contentions made by defendant with respect to this lawsuit. If you are unable to answer any Interrogatory completely, so state, and to the extent possible, set forth the reasons for your inability to answer more fully, and state whatever knowledge or information you have concerning the unanswered portion.

These Interrogatories are deemed to have continuing effect to the extent that if, after filing your responses to these interrogatories, you obtain information upon the basis of which you know that a response was incorrect when made, or you know that a response though correct when made is no longer true, you are required to amend your response in accordance with Rule 33 of the Federal Rules of Civil Procedure. In addition, defendant is required to supplement his responses with respect to any question directly addressed to the identity and location of persons having knowledge of discoverable matters, and with respect to the identity of each person expected to be called as an expert witness at trial, the subject matter on which he or she is expected to testify, and the substance of his or her testimony.

in this section eliminate ambiguity, which in turn eliminates the justification for many potential objections. Also eliminated is the need to define terms repeatedly within the interrogatories. Figure 9–5 shows an example of a definition section.

Figure 9–5 Definition Section

DEFINITIONS

The following terms have the meanings stated wherever used in these interrogatories, unless otherwise indicated:

"You" and "your" means Gilda Murray.
"Patient" means Gilda Murray.
"This Defendant" means Dr. Ned Radcliffe.

"Identify" means to state the person's full name, date of birth, marital status and spouse's name, social security number, present or last known residence and business addresses and telephone number, occupation, employer, and business address at the date of the event or transaction referred to, present or last known position and business affiliation, present or last known employer and business address. If a person is identified more than once, only the name need be provided after the first identification.

"Health care provider" means any person involved in the examination, care, or treatment of injuries, illnesses, or other health-related conditions, both physical and mental. This term includes, but is not limited to, physicians, dentists, podiatrists, chiropractors, nurses, therapists, psychologists, counselors, home care attendants, and special education instructors.

"Health care facility" means any organization or institution involved in the examination, care or treatment of injuries, illnesses, or other health-related conditions, both physical and mental. This term includes, but is not limited to, hospitals, clinics, health maintenance organizations, outpatient facilities, testing facilities, laboratories, nursing homes, and pharmacies from which medications were obtained.

"Person" means, in the plural as in the singular, any natural person, corporation, firm, association, partnership, joint venture, or other form of legal or official entity, as the case may be.

Interrogatories

After the definitions come the interrogatories themselves. They are numbered, and enough space is generally left between interrogatories for the party responding to type in her response. The detail in the questions should be enough to make them clear and precise, and will vary depending on the detail already set forth in the instructions and definitions. For example, if the term "identify" is defined to mean "provide the full name, residence address and phone number, business address and phone number, age, and marital status of," then a proper interrogatory designed to elicit all this information would simply state: "Identify Mr. Widget." If no such definition is provided, then the information must be requested specifically.

We next discuss interrogatories relating to five areas: background information; specific case information; information about experts consulted; content of the pleadings; and generalized conclusory information.

Figure 9–6 Interrogatory That Elicits Background Information

INTERROGATORY NO. 1: Please state:

a. Your full legal name and any other names by which you have ever been known;
b. Your date and place of birth;
c. Your social security number;
d. Your driver's license number; and
e. Each address where you have lived in the past ten years.

ANSWER

INTERROGATORY NO.2:

Please state the name, address, telephone number, and employer of each and every person known to you or your attorneys who has or may have knowledge, directly or indirectly, of any facts relevant to this case. For each such person, state generally the subject matter of the facts which may be known to him or her. NOTE: This interrogatory includes, but is not limited to, any person who may be called by you as a witness at the trial of this cause.

ANSWER:

Background Information It is important to develop general background information about the person responding to the interrogatories. If the person is an individual defendant, it will be important to have a current address if a subpoena needs to be served in the future; other information such as past and present employers, educational background, prior medical history, marital status, age, or other general facts may become significant as well. In addition, if the person responding is an employee of a defendant corporation, it is important to know the person's job title and the scope of the person's knowledge about the events in question, as well as the person's authority to speak on behalf of the corporation. Examples of a background interrogatory appear in Figure 9–6.

Specific Case Information After requesting background information, the drafter should begin a more focused, customized inquiry. Information specific to the case should be requested about witnesses (names, addresses, and other pertinent facts should be sought), documents (volume, description of contents, and current location should be sought), and any other facts or matters that bear on the outcome. Figure 9–7 shows examples of specific interrogatories.

Figure 9–7 Examples of Case-Specific Interrogatories

6. Identify all employees of Widget Company with whom Henry Widget has discussed his meeting of March 15, 1992, with John Ascot.

7. Identify all correspondence in the possession of Widget Company, including copies of correspondence, which in any way references, describes, or relates to the meeting of March 15, 1992, at which Henry Widget and John Ascot were present.

8. List the dates of every in-person meeting between Henry Widget and John Ascot between January 1, 1992 and April 30, 1992.

9. Provide the date and time of day of every phone call between Henry Widget and John Ascot that occurred between January 1, 1992 and April 30, 1992.

Figure 9–8 Interrogatories Regarding Expert Witness

INTERROGATORY NO. 3

Please state the following information for each person who may be called by you to testify as an expert witness at the trial of this cause:

a. name, address, telephone number, and employer;
b. the date on which the witness was first contacted in connection with this case;
c. the subject matter on which the expert is expected to testify;
d. the qualifications of the expert to give testimony on that subject;
e. the specific opinions and conclusions of the expert regarding the matters involved in this case, and the factual basis for each;
f. the name, address, and telephone number of each person whose work forms a basis, in whole or in part, of the opinions of the expert.

ANSWER:

INTERROGATORY NO. 4:

Identify each individual with whom you have consulted or your attorneys have consulted as an expert, indicating whether a decision has been reached about whether: (1) said individual(s) may testify in this lawsuit; and (2) written reports were made or requested, in connection with the incidents made the basis of this lawsuit. For each expert listed, please also identify the following:

a. complete educational background of such individual, beginning with the year in which said individual graduated from high school and continuing through completion of the formal education process of such expert;
b. his or her occupation and field of specialization, as well as qualifications to act as an expert;
c. all published writings of the individual expert, listing the titles of any article(s) or book(s), the name(s) of the publication(s), the year(s) of publication(s), volume and page number.
d. for what remuneration Defendant has employed said individual:
e. whether said individual has ever been a witness in any other lawsuit, and, if so, for each lawsuit give the name of the suit, the name of the court, the date of the filing, and the name and address of the other party for whom said individual provided evidence or testimony;
f. all mental impressions and opinions held by the expert relating to the lawsuit in question;
g. all facts known to the expert (regardless of when the factual information was acquired) that relate to or form the basis of the mental impressions and opinions held by the expert; and
h. the complete employment history of such expert for the preceding five (5) years, including the name and address of the employer, and the general nature of the expert's work for such employer.

Information About Experts Consulted In cases involving technical issues, expert testimony is often crucial. If such issues are present in your case, one or more interrogatories should be included that inquire into the identity and qualifications of the opposition's experts, the nature of their inquiry and intended areas of testimony, and the existence of any written reports. Figure 9–8 illustrates interrogatories drafted to gain information about experts consulted. Note that these interrogatories are submitted to the other *party*, not to the expert; interrogatories, as we noted earlier, can only be served on other parties.

Content of the Pleadings Pleadings present factual allegations and legal contentions. It is very important to explore the basis for these allegations and contentions. Interrogatories should be drafted to uncover the facts behind the pleadings.

Consider, for example, a complaint that contains the following paragraph: "The president of Widget Company, Henry Widget, forged the signature of John Ascot on the Modification of the contract between the parties." From the perspective of Henry Widget and Widget Company, this is a very strong allegation, which must be investigated. Widget Company should file an interrogatory similar to the following: "State the facts upon which you rely, in paragraph 6 of the complaint, for the allegation that Henry Widget forged the signature of John Ascot."

Similarly, if a plaintiff states a legal claim that has several prerequisites the defendant may want to inquire into the facts behind each of the prerequisite elements. However, be careful in this regard—if a plaintiff has failed to allege one or more prerequisite elements, there may be strategic reasons to avoid inquiry in discovery (it might alert the plaintiff to the deficiency) so that you can later attack the deficiency by a Motion to Dismiss.

Generalized Conclusory Information It is wise to conclude your interrogatories with generalized questions that inquire broadly into areas which may have been overlooked or omitted. An interrogatory with such a purpose is a "catch-all" designed to prevent a surprise at trial. The trick in drafting such an interrogatory is to devise language that can survive an objection that it is so broad as to constitute an unjustifiable "fishing expedition." An example of a potential concluding interrogatory appears in Figure 9–9.

Signature Block and Certificate of Service

In most jurisdictions the interrogatories are signed by the attorney preparing them, but not by the party she represents (in contrast to the *responses*, which must be signed not only by the attorney but also by the party responding; more about that later). To verify the date that the interrogatories were sent to opposing counsel, a certificate of service is required (see Figure 9–10 on page 424).

Responses to Interrogatories

Responses to interrogatories must be prepared within the time established by the applicable procedural rules. Under Rule 33 of the FRCP, the time limit is 30

Figure 9–9 Common "Catch-all" Interrogatory

```
INTERROGATORY NO. 5:

State any additional information relevant to the subject of
this action not previously set out in your answers above.
```

Figure 9–10 Signature Block and Certificate of Service

Respectfully submitted,

____
Bonnie Hiatt
Attorney for Defendant
8201 South Broadway
Charleston, MO 40387
(304)786-4837

CERTIFICATE OF SERVICE

I certify that a true copy of this Plaintiff's First Set of Written Interrogatories was served on Katherine Haley, Attorney for Defendant, 333 E. Denton Drive, Richardson, Texas 75221, by certified mail, return receipt requested, in accordance with the Texas Rules of Civil Procedure on November 29, 1992.

____
BONNIE HIATT

days. Extensions can be requested by motion; at least in the early stages of the discovery process, the court will probably be lenient about granting such requests, and few opposing counsel will object to reasonable extensions.

Responses must be signed and verified by the client. The attorney preparing them signs them as well, but the client must attest to their accuracy. Figure 9–11 shows an example of a **verification**.

The response can be either a presentation of the information requested, or an

Figure 9–11 Verification Used with Interrogatories

THE STATE OF NEW YORK §
§
COUNTY OF SUFFOLK §

NED RADCLIFFE, being duly sworn upon his oath deposes and says: I am the Defendant in the above-entitled action and have read the interrogatories served upon me by the Plaintiff, Gilda Murray; and the foregoing answers to those interrogatories are true according to the best of my knowledge, information and belief.

____
NED RADCLIFFE

SUBSCRIBED AND SWORN to before me this ____ day of September, 1992

____
NOTARY PUBLIC IN AND FOR THE STATE OF NEW YORK
My Commission Expires: _______

objection. Objections should be addressed to individual interrogatories; it is not proper to object to *all* the interrogatories, and it remains necessary to provide responses for all those interrogatories not objected to (which is to say that the presence of one or more objectional interrogatories does not poison the entire set of interrogatories).

As you might expect, wide-ranging requests are often met with objection. Common objections include contentions that: the instructions or definitions are overbroad, or include requirements that go beyond the scope of the rules; the information requested is privileged; the information requested is irrelevant; the request is unduly burdensome; the request is so broad as to be meaningless (an objection often raised to the generalized conclusory interrogatories); or the request is ambiguous or unintelligible.

It is important to identify and comply with time requirements in making objections. If not raised in time, objections may be waived, or dismissed.

It is also important to note that, in the federal courts and many state and local jurisdictions, there is a "continuing duty to respond" to interrogatories. This means that if new information arises *after* responses are filed that would have been included in the original responses had it been known at the time of filing, it must be forwarded to the other side as a **supplemental response**. If such supplement is not made, the court at trial can refuse to allow the presentation of evidence that includes or relates to the undisclosed materials. Such supplementation is often necessary in a case where medical treatment of an injured plaintiff is ongoing—so make sure you have provided copies of all relevant medical materials to the other side before trial.

A party is required to make reasonable good-faith efforts to locate materials and information responsive to a discovery request. Be wary of a client who has a selective memory, or who wishes to avoid the difficulty of complying with a lengthy discovery request. You may wish to file objections claiming the request is unduly burdensome; but if such objections are not sustained, your client must turn over the requested materials or information, however unpleasant and time-consuming the task may be.

In addition to filing objections, a responding party can obstruct the information-gathering efforts of the opposition by filing a Motion for Protective Order. This motion will be discussed further.

9–3 Requests for Admissions

The **request for admissions**, authorized under Rule 36 of the FRCP, provides the drafter with the opportunity to conclusively establish selected facts prior to trial. A proposition is presented to the opposing party for admission or denial; if admitted, no further evidence need be presented on the point; the trial court accepts it as fact, at least with regard to the party who admitted it. Admissions serve to limit the complexity and expense of trials.

The caption, signature of the preparing attorney, and certificate of service are the same for a request for admissions as for a set of interrogatories. The introductory paragraph and the text of the requests are discussed in the next subsections, followed by a few words about preparing responses.

The Introduction of a Request for Admission

The introductory paragraph of a request for admissions includes an identification of the party to whom the request is directed, the rule providing for the

Figure 9–12 Introductory Paragraph for Request for Admissions

> Plaintiffs in the above-entitled action request pursuant to Rule 36 of the Federal Rules of Civil Procedure that Defendant, within thirty (30) days after service of this request, admit for the purpose of this action that the following facts are true:

request, and the time period allowed for response. Figure 9-12 shows an example of an appropriate introductory paragraph for a request for admission.

Text of a Request for Admission

The requests themselves consist of statements that are to be admitted or denied by the recipient. The statements are numbered sequentially.

An effective technique for drafting the requests is to move through the case point by point, from general points to those more specific. Alternative versions can appear as different numbered statements, and consecutive questions can feature finely drawn distinctions; the responses to such a pattern of requests can assist the drafter in reaching an understanding about the nuances of the other party's position. An example of this technique is shown in Figure 9–13.

Several different formats are acceptable for requests for admission, three of which appear in Figure 9–14. The most important consideration in drafting requests for production is that they be so straightforward that they avoid an evasive response. The more detail added to the sentence, the greater the tendency to elicit a qualified response. Although the responding party retains some freedom to explain the response (as we discuss further) your goal as a drafter should be to minimize the responder's ability to hedge, assuring a straightforward admission or denial.

A common use of requests for admission is to establish the authenticity of documents. A copy of a document can be appended to the set of requests, and the requests can ask for an admission or denial that the copy is an exact copy of the original. Figure 9–15 shows an example of a request for admission inquiring into the genuineness of a document.

Figure 9–13 Technique for Drafting Request for Admissions

<u>Alternative requests for admission:</u>

Admit or deny the following:

1. On June 1, 1992, defendant Jones executed the contract that is attached as Exhibit A.
2. On June 2, 1992, defendant Jones executed the contract that is attached as Exhibit A.
3. On June 3, 1992, defendant Jones executed the contract that is attached as Exhibit A.

<u>Requests for admission with finely drawn distinctions:</u>

1. On March 15, 1992, defendant Jones attended a meeting at which was discussed the terms of a contract with Mr. Smith.
2. On March 15, 1992, defendant Jones and plaintiff Smith attended a meeting at which was discussed the terms of a contract with Mr. Smith.
3. On March 15, 1992, defendant Jones and plaintiff Smith attended a meeting at which they executed the contract that is attached hereto as Exhibit A.

Figure 9–14 Formats for Request for Admission

```
(a) Admit or deny that you requested a refund on March 6,
    1992 for the car repairs performed by Defendant.
(b) Do you admit or deny that you requested a refund on March
    6, 1992 for the car repairs performed by Defendant?
(c) Do you admit that you requested a refund on March 6, 1992
    for the car repairs performed by Defendant?
(d) Admit or deny the following facts:
    (1) That you requested a refund on March 6, 1992 for the
        car repairs performed by Defendant.
```

Figure 9–15 Request for Admission Regarding Genuineness of Document

```
Admit or deny that the document marked "Exhibit A" and
attached hereto is a true and genuine copy of the Lease
dated June 17, 1992.
```

Responses to Requests for Admission

Requests for admission must be answered with great care, because of the impact of an admission. If a request is impossible to respond to with a flat admission or denial, but is not otherwise objectionable, a qualified response is acceptable. A qualified response should not be used for the purpose of evading, however.

Another possible response is a motion for protective order, to be discussed. Be sure to keep in mind the deadline for a response—failure to file a timely response can, as noted, be deemed to be an admission.

9–4 Request for Production of Documents and Things

Under Rule 34 of the FRCP, a party can request the other side to produce for inspection documents or objects in its possession. The materials requested need not be specifically identified, nor need they even be known to exist; but the description in the request should be sufficiently specific so that the opposing party can reasonably determine whether a document is responsive. It would not, for example, be acceptable to ask the other side to produce "all relevant documents"; it *would*, however, be acceptable to request "all correspondence between Henry Widget and John Ascot." The request for production allows for the evaluation and assessment of the physical evidence that is available for presentation at trial.

As with other forms of discovery, the request for production has a caption, title, introductory paragraphs, the requests themselves, the signature of the attorney making the request, and a certificate of service. In preparing requests, the drafter should take care that all relevant documents have been requested; this generally requires a review of the pleadings and facts of the case. In responding, you must take care that all requests not objected to are fully complied with; failure to produce a document requested is grounds for excluding that document, even if otherwise admissible, at trial.

Figure 9–16 Introductory Paragraph for Request for Production

Pursuant to Rule 34 of the Federal Rules of Civil Procedure, Plaintiff requests that Defendants make available for inspection and copying the documents described herein at a time and place to be arranged by counsel, but in no event later than thirty (30) days from the date of service of this request.

If a document is no longer in possession of or subject to the control of Defendant, state when such document was most recently in the possession of defendant or subject to the defendant's control and what disposition was made of it. If documents have been destroyed, please identify when they were destroyed, the person who destroyed the documents, the person who directed that they be destroyed, the reason(s) for such action, and any communications or documents that relate or refer to the destruction of the documents.

This request is continuing in character and requires defendant to provide any supplemental documents if, prior to trial, defendant should obtain any additional or supplemental documents that are responsive to this request.

As a practical matter, where documents are requested compliance is usually made by providing a set of copies of the requested documents. Tangible objects may not be able to be copied, requiring you to arrange a convenient time and location for them to be inspected.

An acceptable introductory paragraph for a request for production appears in Figure 9–16. An example of general requests for production of documents and things appears in Figure 9–17.

Figure 9–17 General Request for Production of Documents

1. All documents pertaining to or reflecting any damages for which you are seeking recovery in this suit.

2. All correspondence, notes, memoranda, recordings, or other documents evidencing or reflecting any communication, conversation, transaction, or dealing between Plaintiff and this Defendant (including Defendant's agents, employees, or representatives), or between the Plaintiff's family and Defendant (including Defendant's agents, employees, and representatives).

3. All documents and tangible things prepared by any person whose work product forms a basis, in whole or in part, of the opinions of the expert witness.

4. The expert's entire file pertaining to this case.

9–5 Request for Medical Examination

Preparing a **request for medical examination** involves issues of litigation strategy almost exclusively, with little emphasis or importance on writing other than to make the request clear and to conform to the rules that establish the right. Because an examination is a substantial invasion of the opposing party's person, it will likely be granted only in cases where the physical or mental condition is an issue, as in a personal injury case.

9–6 The Deposition

In a deposition, a party or witness is placed under oath and questioned by attorneys, and the content of the examination is recorded in a transcript prepared by a certified court reporter. The party or witness who is questioned is referred to as a **deponent**.

There are three types of deposition: the oral deposition; the deposition on written questions; and the video deposition. The nature of each varies somewhat.

The **oral deposition**, in which the witness responds to questions from an attorney, is by far the most common. Depending on the answers to the questions, the attorney generally frames **follow-up questions** that explore an area in detail.

In the **deposition on written questions**, questions are submitted in advance; only those questions are answered, with no follow-up questions allowed. Often, no attorney is even present; the court reporter swears the witness and records the responses to the prepackaged questions.

Video depositions are simply videotaped versions of the oral deposition; the videotape serves as an additional method of preserving the testimony, in addition to the transcript. If a witness is going to be unavailable for trial because he is beyond the subpoena power of the court (more about subpoenas later) or is aged or ill, a video deposition is a good means of preserving the immediacy of real testimony for trial.

There are few limitations on the areas of questioning at a deposition; objections can (and generally should) be stated by the attorneys present, but rulings on the objections are generally reserved until trial, and thus the witness answers despite the objection. A witness can be instructed not to answer by an attorney, but this is usually a dramatic step, evidence of an exceedingly bitter, contentious deposition. When a deposition grows so quarrelsome that excessive objections and instructions not to answer erode the ability of the parties to continue, the parties can file motions to the court to rule on the objections before the deposition proceeds. Courts generally frown on this, however, and costs can be imposed against the party adjudged to have caused the problem.

Depositions are useful means of learning about the demeanor of a party or witness when subjected to questioning. They are also useful as a means of immediate follow-up when answers suggest further lines of inquiry—the follow-up question can be posed on the spot. This distinguishes depositions from interrogatories, which give no opportunity for immediate follow-up. Although subsequent sets of interrogatories can be filed that follow up initial answers, they lack the immediacy of a follow-up question at a deposition. Indeed, interrogatories and requests for production are often most useful as a means of gathering information in preparation for a deposition.

Notice of Intention to Take Oral Deposition

A formal document must be drafted to notify all parties that a deposition is to be taken. This is called a Notice of Intention to Take Oral Deposition (or often simply Notice of Deposition). In addition to a caption, title, and introductory information, the notice identifies the deponent, the location of the deposition, often the rule under which the deposition is authorized, and the fact that it will be taken before a certified court reporter or official authorized to administer oaths. An example of the body of a deposition notice appears in Figure 9–18.

Figure 9–18 The Body of a Notice of Oral Deposition

```
TO: Dr. Ned Radcliffe, by and through his attorney of
    record, Matthew Brockton, Suite 850, 3265 Montclaire
    Avenue, Waco, Texas 75683

  PLEASE TAKE NOTICE that on October 12, 1992, at ten
o'clock (10:00) a.m. at the law office of Emma M. Costello,
6301 Marley Avenue, Waco, Texas 75204, Plaintiff, GILDA
MURRAY will take the deposition of DR. NED RADCLIFFE. The
deposition will be taken on oral examination pursuant to
Rule 200 of the Texas Rules of Civil Procedure before an
officer authorized to administer oaths, and will continue
from day to day until completed.
```

Applicability of a Subpoena

If a *party* is identified as the deponent, the party is required to appear at the time and place identified, unless a Motion for Protective Order is filed (more about such a motion later). This requirement can be enforced because parties are subject to the rules of the court. Plaintiffs have submitted to them voluntarily; defendants have been brought under the control of the court by effective service of process. The deponent need not necessarily be a party, however— she may be merely a witness. A witness has not submitted to nor been brought under the control of the court; a witness might simply refuse or neglect to appear for the deposition.

The solution to this potential problem is the subpoena. A **subpoena** is a document similar to a summons, in that it is served upon an individual under authority of the court, and orders the person to appear at a certain place and certain time, or suffer the consequences. Subpoenas are often used to ensure the presence of a witness at a deposition; the subpoena and deposition notices are served simultaneously. Subpoenas can also be used to compel a witness to testify at a trial.

Production of Documents in Conjunction With a Deposition

It is possible to combine a request for production of documents with a deposition notice. In this case, the deposition notice contains an additional sentence, referring to the request for production attached to the notice. The Latin term ***duces tecum*** signifies a deposition notice or subpoena requiring the deponent/witness to "bring with him" specified documents or things. Figure 9–19 shows an example of a Notice of Intention to Take Oral Deposition *Duces Tecum*.

Deposition Preparation

Because a deposition is generally an oral exercise, the need for writing skills to prepare formal documents is minimal. Nevertheless, it is important to apply your organizational skills—outlining, focusing on key factual points, identifying the secondary elements of legal arguments—in order to prepare to conduct the deposition, covering all necessary areas of inquiry. For the deposition on written questions (which, as noted, is a format rarely employed), you will of course draft questions ahead of time. The key to drafting such written questions is to keep them short and precise, so as to avoid evasive answers.

Figure 9–19 Notice of Intention to Take Oral Deposition *Duces Tecum*

TO: Dr. Ned Radcliffe, by and through his attorney of record, Matthew Brockton, Suite 850, 3265 Montclaire Avenue, Waco, Texas 75683.

PLEASE TAKE NOTICE that on October 12, 1992, at ten o'clock (10:00) a.m. at the law office of Emma M. Costello, 6301 Marley Avenue, Waco, Texas 75204, Plaintiff, GILDA MURRAY will take the deposition of DR. NED RADCLIFFE. The deposition will be taken on oral examination pursuant to Rule 200 of the Texas Rules of Civil Procedure before an officer authorized to administer oaths, and will continue from day to day until completed.

Please take notice that the deponent identified above will be required to produce at the taking of his deposition all the materials described in Exhibit A attached hereto and incorporated herein. The definitions and instructions included in Exhibit A shall control the production of the materials requested in Exhibit A.

Digesting a Deposition

After a deposition is completed, the court reporter who recorded the questions and testimony prepares the **transcript**, which is a written account of the entire proceeding. The transcript of a deposition can run to many hundreds of pages or more, and a complex case can require many depositions. It is often helpful for the attorneys handling the matter to have a **digest** of the deposition, which is a summary of the testimony indexed with references to the corresponding page numbers of the deposition. (This type of digest is not to be confused with the digest we discussed in Chapter l, which contains research topics and headnotes from reported judicial opinions.) There is no standard method of digesting a deposition; if you are given such an assignment, you should strive to be accurate, using the writing techniques we have discussed to avoid ambiguity, and you should ask your supervising attorney the appropriate format and degree of detail desired.

9–7 Discovery Motions

In previous sections we have touched upon some factors to consider in responding to discovery requests. Although these factors, coupled with the desire to protect your client, give you some flexibility in drafting responses to discovery requests, the good-faith requirement that governs discovery responses implies a duty to provide all reasonable information requested. Nevertheless, parties often try to evade in the discovery process by making indefensible requests, failing to respond to reasonable requests, or otherwise abusing the process. This may lead to the filing of motions designed to resolve disputed issues. The three principal motions seen in discovery practice are the **Motion for Protective Order**, filed by a party upon whom a discovery request has been made; the **Motion to Compel Discovery**, filed by a party seeking to force compliance with a discovery request, and the **Motion for Sanctions**, filed by any party to counter alleged violations by another. Each of these motions generally includes attachments consisting of the discovery requests objected to or sought to be enforced; check the rules for format and special requirements. Each is discussed in the subsections that follow.

Figure 9–20 Motion for Protective Order

COMES NOW, Dr. Ned Radcliffe, Defendant in the above-entitled and numbered cause, and files this his Motion for Protective Order, and in support of this Motion would show unto the Honorable Court as follows:

1. On or about September 17, 1992, Plaintiff issued upon this Defendant Plaintiff's First Set of Written Interrogatories and Request for Production of Documents. In responding to said discovery requests, this Defendant objected to Interrogatory Nos. 4, 11, 13, and 15 and Request for Production Nos. 1, 2, and 4, as well as making general objections. Said Objections are attached hereto and incorporated herein as Exhibit A by reference for all purposes.

WHEREFORE, PREMISES CONSIDERED, Defendant hereby requests that upon final hearing and trial hereof, that the Court enter an Order sustaining his objections to the discovery requests of the Plaintiff, and for such other and further relief, in law or in equity, to which this Defendant may show himself to be justly entitled.

The Motion for Protective Order

When the party upon whom a discovery request has been filed contends that the request oversteps the bounds of the rules, she can file a Motion for Protective Order. Such a motion argues that the information sought is irrelevant or privileged, or that the request is unduly burdensome or overly broad or ambiguous. It may argue that a deposition is inappropriate at the location suggested. Whatever the argument, the purpose is to obstruct the other side. Figure 9–20 shows an example of a Motion for Protective Order opposing certain interrogatories and a request for production of documents.

The Motion to Compel Discovery

The Motion to Compel Discovery is the reverse of the Motion for Protective Order—it seeks not to obstruct discovery, but to force it.

Simply because a party chooses not to disclose information, or has objected to its disclosure, does not mean it isn't discoverable. The party seeking the information must notify the court of the failure to respond, and the need to have the court rule on the dispute. This can be done through a Motion to Compel Discovery, which identifies the information sought, notes that it is relevant, unprivileged, and not otherwise subject to protection, and argues that it should be supplied. Such a motion can also be supported by a brief. A Motion to Compel Discovery is often filed in response to a Motion for Protective Order, or sometimes simply as a means of prodding a party who has allowed the deadline for discovery response to pass without having filed the response. An example of a typical Motion to Compel Discovery is found in Figure 9–21.

The Motion for Sanctions

A Motion for sanctions is filed when there have been attempts to force cooperation, but based upon alleged deliberate inaction or gross indifference of one party, discovery has been stalled. Failure to appear at a duly noticed deposition,

Figure 9–21 Motion To Compel Discovery

Now Comes the Defendant by her attorney and moves the Court as follows:

1. On October 14, 1992, Defendant, after commencement of the above-entitled action, served on the Plaintiff in this cause ten interrogatories in writing pursuant to Rule 33 of the Federal Rules of Civil Procedure (28 U.S.C.A.), which interrogatories are attached hereto.

2. Plaintiff answered Interrogatories 1, 2, 3, 4, 5, and 10, but did not answer such interrogatories under oath as required by Rule 33 of the Federal Rules of Civil Procedure (28 U.S.C.A.).

3. Plaintiff failed to answer Interrogatories 6, 7, 8, and 9.

WHEREFORE, Defendant moves that this court enter an order directing and requiring Plaintiff to answer all of said interrogatories under oath.

Defendant further moves the court for an order awarding Defendant the reasonable expenses, including attorneys' fees incurred in this motion.

without making an objection or indicating the intention not to attend, would be an example of behavior that might justify a Motion for Sanctions, since time and resources were wasted (a court reporter had to be paid to attend) with no justification. Another example would be a failure to follow the order of the court on a Motion to Compel Discovery. The granting of a Motion for Sanctions often includes an award of attorneys' fees and expenses incurred in its preparation.

Sometimes, if the circumstances justify, a party files a Motion for Sanctions at the same time as a Motion for Protective Order or a Motion to Compel Discovery. Sanctions are an extreme remedy, however, and Motions for Sanctions should be filed only after a cautious review of the facts.

9–8 Practical Considerations

The role of paralegals in discovery is often an important one. Complex cases may involve hundreds or thousands of documents, which must be tracked, reviewed, evaluated, disclosed, requested, and catalogued. Numerous depositions may be needed; numerous areas inquired into with interrogatories; multiple medical examinations may be necessary, and lengthy medical records may require interpretation. Much time-consuming work is involved—work that can be tedious, but that requires a sharp and trained mind nevertheless. By refining your skills at organizing the discovery process, you can heighten your value as an essential member of your firm's litigation team.

The following is a checklist of items to keep in mind when formulating discovery requests and responses:

—— Review the rules of procedure to determine the applicable bounds of discovery.

—— Make a point of identifying and remaining alert to all applicable deadlines. Review your client's file and make notes about the areas of the case in which discovery is desirable or necessary.

- Prepare discovery requests that are detailed and specific.
- Draft requests that will survive the opposition's efforts to object.
- Organize materials so that confusion is minimized and access maximized.
- Coordinate with your supervising attorney at every step.
- Analyze your client's position and determine whether objections to discovery requests are in order.
- Evaluate discovery responses to determine whether they are in compli ance with the requirements of the rules and fully responsive to the corresponding requests. Evaluate both responses that you receive from the other side and responses that you prepare.
- If the discovery process breaks down, prepare all necessary motions.

SUMMARY

9–1

Discovery is the pretrial investigatory process authorized and governed by the rules of civil procedure. To be discoverable, information requested must be reasonably calculated to lead to the discovery of admissible evidence. Discovery requests may be directed to parties but not to nonparties, except that it is acceptable to take the deposition of a nonparty.

9–2

An interrogatory is a written question submitted by one party to another to be answered under oath. Interrogatories should be specific and precise. Definitions and instructions can be included to reduce ambiguity. Titles should be sufficiently specific as to distinguish one set of interrogatories from another, particularly in cases with multiple parties on either side. Basic background information can be sought with interrogatories, as well as specific information about the case at hand, information about experts consulted, and information about the content of the pleadings. The truth of the responses must be attested to by the signature of the party on whose behalf the responses are filed. Objections to interrogatories can be justified on several grounds, including a contention that the information sought is privileged or that the request is overbroad. There is a continuing duty to respond to interrogatories, which means that a supplemental response must be filed if new information is uncovered.

9–3

The request for admissions allows the filing party to conclusively establish contested issues prior to trial. This serves to limit the complexity and expense of the ensuing trial. A common use of requests for admission is to authenticate documents. Requests should be drafted to minimize the potential for a qualified response; responses should be made with great care due to the impact of an admission.

9–4

A request for production of documents and things enables one party to inspect the physical and documentary evidence of the other party. The responding party must be reasonably able to determine whether a given document or thing is responsive.

9–5

The request for medical examination should be drafted clearly and in conformity with the rules. The issues associated with such a request are largely issues of litigation strategy, not legal writing.

9–6

In a deposition, the deponent (who can be a party or a witness) provides testimony that is transcribed by a court reporter. The deposition can be taken in response to oral or written questions, and can also be videotaped. The opportunity for follow-up questions makes the oral deposition a useful form of discovery. A notice of intention to take deposition must be filed by the party seeking to take the deposition; if the intended deponent is a witness rather than a party, a subpoena can be served to ensure the witness's attendance. A document request can be combined with a deposition notice. Lengthy deposition transcripts can be summarized in a deposition digest.

9–7

A Motion for Protective Order can be filed by a party in opposition to a discovery request that it believes oversteps the acceptable bounds of the discovery rules. The Motion to Compel Discovery is filed by a party seeking to force compliance with a discovery request. A Motion for Sanctions can be filed by a party who believes that the opposing party's discovery conduct is particularly uncooperative or unlawful.

9–8

Complex cases often involve an extended and complex discovery process. Paralegals can heighten their value by using organizational skills to assist in the workings of that process.

REVIEW

Key Terms

Before proceeding, review the key terms listed below to be sure you understand each one. If necessary, read over the corresponding section of the chapter. When you are ready to test your understanding, answer the Review Questions.

discovery
interrogatory
instructions
definitions
verification
supplemental response
request for admissions
request for production of documents and things
request for medical examination
deponent
oral deposition
follow-up question
deposition on written questions
video deposition
subpoena
duces tecum
transcript
digest
Motion for Protective Order
Motion to Compel Discovery
Motion for Sanctions

Questions for Review and Discussion

1. Why is the discovery process needed?
2. What are some of the characteristics of a properly drafted interrogatory?
3. Why are instructions and definitions important to include with discovery requests?
4. What are appropriate areas of inquiry about the opposition's consultation with experts?
5. What is meant by the continuing duty to respond?
6. How is a request for admissions useful?
7. How can requests for production be made sufficiently specific to avoid objection?
8. Who is a deponent?
9. What is a subpoena?
10. What is the difference between a Motion for Protective Order and a Motion to Compel Discovery?

Activities

1. Based on the facts of Figure 8–13 in Chapter 8, draft seven interrogatories, five requests for admission, and five requests for production of documents.
2. Draft a motion for protective order, based on the fact that the information sought in the request for production of documents is overly broad and unduly burdensome.
3. Check your state rules of procedure and compare and contrast your rules for interrogatories, admissions, and production of documents. Determine the differences or similarities to the Federal Rules in your jurisdiction's discovery requirements.

NOTES

CHAPTER 10 The Memorandum of Law to the Trial Court

OUTLINE

COMMENTARY

Your firm's client, Dr. Williams, has been served with a subpoena *duces tecum*, commanding her to testify at a deposition and to produce all medical records of an identified patient. Neither Dr. Williams nor her patient wishes to disclose these records.

The doctor has consulted with your supervising attorney, and a decision has been made to file a motion for protective order asserting the existence of a patient/physician privilege. Since the law on this point in your state is not entirely clear, a supporting memorandum that argues in favor of the motion must be prepared. You have been assigned the task of drafting this memorandum.

The memorandum of law to the trial court is an important document in the litigation process, commonly seen and often instrumental in defining the scope and nature of the trial and its outcome. In your role as a paralegal, you will likely be called upon to participate in the preparation of such memoranda.

OBJECTIVES

A properly prepared memorandum of law to the trial court can have substantial impact on the outcome of a lawsuit. After you have completed this chapter, you will be able to:

1. Identify the two audiences for a trial memorandum.
2. Explain how to prepare a trial memorandum so as to assist the trial judge.
3. Draft your trial memorandum so as to minimize the impact of the attack of opposing counsel.

4. Describe the characteristics of a trial memorandum in regard to a motion.
5. Identify the reasons why a judge might request a trial memorandum.
6. Explain the potential importance of an unsolicited trial memorandum that anticipates issues.
7. Understand the importance of the caption and the title of a trial memorandum.
8. Explain the perspective from which the "issues presented" section is drafted.
9. List four objectives of a statement of facts.
10. Describe the difference between the discussion section of an internal memorandum and the argument section of a trial memorandum.

10–1 The Nature and Purpose of the Memorandum of Law to the Trial Court

The **memorandum of law to the trial court** (which we will refer to as a **trial memorandum**) is an adversarial document filed with the trial court and written to persuade the trial court that one party's position on a disputed point of law is superior to the opposing party's position. It may be written in support of or in opposition to a motion; it may be written at the request of a judge to assist her in rendering a decision; or it may be an unsolicited memorandum filed at trial in order to persuade the judge on anticipated legal questions. Whatever the reason, the content should be one-sided, or *partisan*.

We have already used two names, trial memorandum and memorandum of law to the trial court, for this. There are still other names that refer to the same type of document: memorandum of points and authorities, memorandum in opposition to motion, brief in support of motion, trial brief in opposition to motion, and others. These titles all refer to the same basic document—an adversarial document setting forth legal arguments to the trial court. The title depends upon the jurisdiction, and even on individual attorneys and judges. Different courts and individuals have different styles. It is important to remember that, regardless of the name applied, the factors to take into account are essentially the same.

One potential area of confusion should, however, be cleared up at the outset. In some areas, the term *trial brief* refers to the materials that an attorney prepares, not for filing with the court, but rather to assist him with the conduct of the trial—such things as witness lists, summaries of pleadings, an outline of his opening statement, copies of important cases, possible jury instructions, and so on. In this book, such preparatory materials will be called a *trial notebook*, which we discuss in Chapter 11. Thus, we consider a trial brief to be the same as a trial memorandum.

Although some trial courts have specific requirements for the format of a trial memorandum, in general these requirements are less formal than those for an appellate brief (which we discuss in Chapter 12). You should learn your jurisdiction's requirements for a trial memorandum.

It is important to take into consideration the audience for the trial memorandum. Although your client may read your trial memorandum, and should certainly be consulted about the factual background, she is *not* part of the audience for whom the trial memorandum is written. The audience is composed of two segments—the judge, whom you must convince, and the opposing counsel, whom you must refute and whose attack your arguments must survive. Let's take a moment and consider these two audiences.

First, the judge. Unlike appellate judges, who sit in judgment only on appeals, trial judges handle varied responsibilities, from overseeing courtroom personnel, to deciding motions, to conducting trials. Often their schedules are busy, and time is short. Whereas an appellate judge may have the time and the responsibility to read and research enough to render appropriate decisions (which have broad impact), a trial judge generally only needs to know how the higher courts have dealt with the issues presented, or analogous situations. This is not to say that trial judges are not thoughtful, or do not take their responsibilities seriously; they are and they do. It is simply a warning that a trial memorandum needs to get to the point. Tell the judge what you want, why you want it, and why you are legally entitled to it, as concisely as you can. If you must make a complicated argument, by all means make it—but if it can be done more simply, it is a mistake to write a lengthy explanation. Keep your memoranda short, concise, and direct.

Opposing counsel are the second audience. Unlike judges, who will give your arguments a fair reading, opposing counsel are the enemy. They scour your arguments looking for logical holes and unjustified analytical leaps, in an effort to refute your arguments and prove that your client's position is not supported by law. You must, therefore, write *accurately*. Do not overstate your arguments, and never misstate or misrepresent the law. If you are honest in your interpretations (partisan, yes, but nevertheless honest), and if you shepardize with care, your arguments should survive the attack of opposing counsel. Indeed, by recognizing the threat posed by opposing counsel, you may well be saved from making the type of borderline argument that, if read and rejected by a judge, might tend to poison your other, more logical arguments in the eyes of the court.

10–2 Types of Trial Memoranda

All legal memoranda argue a point of law in an adversarial manner. Each of the three broad categories we identified earlier, however—a **memorandum in regard to a motion,** a **memorandum at the request of a judge,** and an **unsolicited memorandum anticipating legal issues**—presents its own unique considerations for the drafter. Let's take a look at each.

Memorandum in Regard to a Motion

Many issues arise in the course of a lawsuit—issues about the content of the pleadings, the propriety of discovery requests, the sufficiency of responses, the right of a party to file amendments, and on and on. Such issues must be resolved before the case is ready for trial. Sometimes they are resolved by mutual agreement of the parties, but often they are not. When agreement is not possible, a motion is generally made to the court in which one party requests that the court resolve the dispute in its favor, so that the case can move to trial. The motion itself generally identifies the nature of the dispute and the order or relief that the filing party seeks, but generally does *not* contain any legal analysis or arguments. These analyses and arguments are reserved for the trial memoranda filed in regard to the motion.

The trial memorandum of the party that filed the motion is drafted, of course, in support of it, whereas the opposing party files a trial memorandum in opposition. For example, in conjunction with the motion for protective order filed on behalf of Dr. Williams from our Commentary problem, a supporting trial memorandum would discuss the issues of physician/patient privilege that are posed by the motion and argue that they justify withholding the information requested; a trial memorandum in opposition, arguing for disclosure, would be filed by the party that requested the deposition. The issues discussed in the two memoranda are limited to the issues raised by the motion.

During the course of a lawsuit, there may be several motions pending and, hence, several trial memoranda in regard to these motions. Each should have a title that identifies the party filing it and the motion to which it relates. We discuss format further in the following subsections.

Memorandum at the Request of a Judge

Contested issues continually arise during the course of a lawsuit, both during the pretrial stage and during the trial itself. During oral argument on a motion, for example, the judge may raise a point that the parties had not anticipated or addressed in their trial memoranda. Or an objection to the introduction of a piece of evidence at trial may present a novel legal problem that neither the judge nor the parties have ever considered. Under such circumstances the judge, rather than ruling immediately on the issue at hand, may request that the parties submit trial memoranda setting forth their positions on the disputed issue before he makes his decision.

The response of the attorneys is the memorandum at the request of the judge. This memorandum will be adversarial, like a memorandum in regard to a motion, and will be limited to the issue that the judge raised. It is designed to provide the judge with guidance on the issue presented, in the form of legal support for the position favoring your client. Your goal is to predispose the judge to your client's position, and downplay the opponent's position. The memorandum should be direct and concise, particularly at trial, where time is short.

The judge may even request an additional memorandum on a given point *after* the trial is completed, but *before* her decision is rendered. Again, you will be emphasizing the superiority of your client's position on the issue raised.

Unsolicited Memorandum Anticipating Legal Issues

By the conclusion of a trial, the legal issues that control the trial's outcome are clear. It is often useful to prepare a trial memorandum that identifies these issues, then argues in favor of a resolution which benefits your client. By clarifying the issues and identifying your strongest arguments at the conclusion of trial and for the benefit of the judge, you can establish a foundation on which the judge can render a decision in which your client prevails.

An unsolicited trial memorandum should be straightforward, identifying the issues at the outset and presenting arguments that are clear and direct. You should highlight the issues that are most important to you, and include every issue which you believe has bearing on the result. In other words, if you are going to file an unsolicited memorandum, you should be thorough; prepare it correctly. If, for strategic reasons, you want to emphasize only a particular aspect of the contested issues, then make that absolutely clear. Otherwise, you may leave the impression that you are conceding on the points left unaddressed.

10–3 The Components of a Memorandum of Law to the Trial Court

The format of trial memoranda varies from jurisdiction to jurisdiction, and from judge to judge. The following comments are offered as a general frame of reference; you should check the rules applicable in your jurisdiction for more specific guidance.

The Caption or Heading

As with pleadings and discovery requests, trial memoranda must have captions identifying the court, parties, date, and docket number. The title of the pleading may be included as well. Figure 10–1 shows two alternative captions.

Title

If the title of the pleading is not included in the caption, it must appear below it. As mentioned earlier, the title should be specific enough to identify the party filing it and, if in regard to a motion, the title of the motion. If not in regard to a motion, it should identify the context—for example, "Plaintiff's Memorandum Regarding Admissibility of Contract X" or "Plaintiff's Trial Brief" (if an unsolicited summary of the issues after trial.)

Figure 10–1 Examples of Caption Set-Ups

```
(a)                                   No. 12344
STEPHEN GILES,              §     IN THE DISTRICT COURT OF
                            §
  Plaintiff                 §
                            §
vs.                         §     DALLAS COUNTY, TEXAS
                            §
GEORGE HARRIS,              §
                            §
  Defendant                 §     _____JUDICIAL DISTRICT
                           OR
(b)          IN THE UNITED STATES DISTRICT COURT
              FOR THE NORTHERN DISTRICT OF TEXAS
STEPHEN GILES,              §
                            §
  Plaintiff                 §
                            §
vs.                         §     CIVIL ACTION NO. 90-12387
                            §
GEORGE HARRIS,              §     Plaintiff's Memorandum in
                            §     Support of Motion to
  Defendant                 §     Dismiss
```

Figure 10–2 Introduction to the Court

```
(1)

TO THE HONORABLE JUDGE OF SAID COURT:

  COMES NOW STEPHEN GILES Plaintiff and files this
Memorandum of Law to the Trial Court in Support of
Plaintiff's Motion for Summary Judgment and would show unto
the Court as follows:

                          or

(2)

Plaintiff STEPHEN GILES submits this Memorandum of Law in
Support of this Motion for Summary Judgment in this matter:
```

Introduction to the Court

A formal introductory section is still required in some jurisdictions, although others, such as California, have done away with the requirement. The introduction seen in Figure 10–2 illustrates the formal tone associated with a document filed with a court. For example, the opening phrase, "To the Honorable Judge . . . ," is a means of showing respect to the court. The trend today, however, is toward the elimination of such introductions.

Issues or Questions Presented

Although similar to the analogous section of an internal memorandum, the **issues presented** section of a trial memorandum should be slanted toward your client's position. The issues should be stated accurately, but the outcome you seek should be implied in the questions.

Several styles for this section are commonly seen. The issue can be stated commencing with the word "Whether," followed by a statement of your client's position. The issue can also be drafted as a positive statement, or as an ordinary question. Figure 10–3 shows three numbered alternative formats for stating the issue presented; the (*A*) section of each alternative is drafted from a plaintiff's perspective, and the (*B*) section from the defendent's perspective.

Statement of Facts

The trial memorandum, like the internal memorandum, contains a **statement of facts** that relates the factual context of the issue posed. The critical difference between the facts as stated in an internal memorandum and those stated in a trial memorandum, however, is in the point of view of the drafter. In the internal memorandum (which is drafted to be objective) the facts are set out in straightforward fashion. In a trial memorandum, the facts should be set out accurately, but drafted so as to favor your client's position.

Facts should be presented chronologically. You seek to develop sympathy for your client's position, using descriptive words and emotional facts to predispose the court toward accepting your client's position. You have four objectives in drafting a statement of facts:

1. Introduce your client's case to the court.
2. Provide an accurate presentation of the events.

Figure 10–3 Forms of the Issues Presented Section

Alternative 1

(A)
Issue Presented. Whether a transaction using a blank power of attorney is valid when agent was not authorized to act on behalf of Plaintiff, the principal.

(B)
Issue Presented. Whether Plaintiff's acts of accepting tax benefits ratified the transaction of an agent, where a blank power of attorney was used.

Alternative 2

(A)
Issue Presented. A transaction using a blank power of attorney is not valid when an agent was not authorized to act on behalf of the Plaintiff, the principal.

(B)
Issue presented. A transaction using a blank power of attorney is valid when the allegedly unauthorized act was ratified.

Alternative 3

(A)
Issue Presented. Is a transaction using a blank power of attorney valid when an agent was not authorized to act on behalf of the Plaintiff, the principal?

(B)
Issue Presented. Is a transaction valid when the Plaintiff, the principal, ratified the unauthorized acts of his agent?

3. Minimize those facts which favor your opponent.
4. Paint a memorable picture of your client's position.

Although you are writing from your client's perspective, do not misstate, misrepresent, or ignore key facts that are detrimental to your case. A misrepresentation of damaging facts will be pointed out to the court by the opposition; ignoring them allows the other side an unchallenged opportunity to emphasize their importance. Rather, identify them, attempt to minimize their importance in your statement of facts, then, in your argument section, show why you contend that they are unimportant.

Figure 10–4 on page 444 shows a statement of facts written from the plaintiff's perspective.

The Argument

The **argument** of a legal memorandum presents your client's position; it is the heart of the memorandum. You present the results of your research in an adversarial form intended to persuade the court of the superiority of your client's contentions. The partisan purpose and slant of the argument section differentiate it from the discussion section of an internal memorandum, where the legal analysis is objective, not adversarial. In the trial memorandum, your purpose is to have your position prevail.

Effective writing techniques are essential for this section. Outline for logical organization. Be definitive. Write to convince, not simply to inform. Use lan-

Figure 10–4 Statement of Facts

The facts in the case are undisputed. Mr. Giles went to a holiday party on November 20, at the home of Mr. Swan, a business associate. Mr. Swan had been Mr. Giles's friend and attorney for some time. Giles was going out of town for Thanksgiving and would not be back until the first of the new year. Giles wanted to purchase a piece of real estate before the end of the year, but was going out of town. The only business discussion that evening concerned the real estate transaction.

Swan suggested that Giles could execute a power of attorney, with Swan as Giles's representative. The gentlemen went into Swan's study and Giles signed a document entitled "Power of Attorney." Neither man filled in any information in the document. Swan's name did not appear anywhere on the document. Swan kept the Power of Attorney in his top desk drawer. Giles went on his trip.

While Giles was on his trip, one of his partners, Mr. Harris, contacted Swan regarding a joint venture transaction completely unrelated to the real estate transaction. Giles and Harris had been discussing dissolving the joint venture, with Giles acquiring Harris's interest. Swan knew nothing about this transaction.

Harris stated to Swan that Giles was supposed to assume all Harris's interest in the joint venture before January 1. Harris inquired whether Swan could help him. Swan told Harris that he had a power of attorney to close a real estate transaction, but did not know how he could help Harris out.

Harris asked Swan to use the power of attorney to transfer the joint venture interest. Harris told Swan this would save his friend some money. Swan continued to tell Harris that he only had authority to close a real estate transaction. Harris however, was able to persuade Swan to execute the transfer of the joint venture interest, using the power of attorney, on December 29.

When Giles came back to town, Swan informed him of the transfer from Harris and told him that he had used the power of attorney. Giles was enraged and told Swan he had no authority to transfer the interest. Giles wanted the transaction rescinded.

guage that is positive and forceful. Make the court believe that your position is correct.

Move from general points to those more specific, applying the law to the facts and using the IRAC model as your guide. Emphasize your strong points and facts; deemphasize and attack the opposition's strong points and facts. Most of all, avoid obscurity—tell the court your position clearly and effectively. An example of an argument section is provided in Figure 10–5.

Conclusion

The conclusion section is a summary of the legal position taken in the trial memorandum. It informs the court of the finding and relief sought. Although a one-sentence conclusion requesting relief is sometimes acceptable, particularly for a short trial memorandum, a better approach summarizes the entire argument, crystallizing the legal contentions. Figure 10–6 on page 446 shows a conclusion that summarizes the argument, and identifies the relief requested.

Signature Block and Certificate of Service

As with all other documents filed with a court, the trial memorandum must be signed by the responsible attorney. As we have noted before, you as a paralegal are not authorized to sign a court document on behalf of a client. The name of the attorney and firm name, address, telephone number, and sometimes a state bar identification number are among the items to be included in a signature block. Figure 10–7 on page 447 shows an example of an acceptable signature block.

Likewise, a certificate of service attesting to the fact that copies of the trial memorandum have been sent to other attorneys of record (or parties) must be included. The method of service—ordinary mail, certified mail, hand delivery, or other accepted means—is identified. A simple statement certifying delivery is adequate for the purposes of the certificate, but remember that if service ever comes into question, proof will become important. Hence the certified mail option (with a return receipt proving delivery) is better than, say, ordinary mail. Check the rules and practices of your jurisdiction to determine applicable rules and requirements. A typical certificate of service is seen in Figure 10–8 on page 447.

Figure 10–5 Argument Section

A power of attorney must set forth the authority and the name of the principal and agent. The document before this court does neither.

To determine the validity of the power of attorney and the extent of the authority granted, certain rules of construction and interpretation must be addressed. The leading case of *Gouldy v. Metcalf*, 75 Tex. 455, 12 S.W. 830 (1889) sets out the rules of construction for a power of attorney, which are:

> [W]hen an authority is conferred upon an agent by a formal instrument, as by a power of attorney, there are two rules of construction to be carefully adhered to:
>
> 1. The meaning of general words in the instrument will be restricted by the context, and construed accordingly.
>
> 2. The authority will be construed strictly, so as to exclude the exercise of any power which is not warranted, either by the actual terms used or as a necessary means of executing the authority with effect.

Id. at 458.

Expanding the guidelines set forth in *Gouldy*, case law establishes that "all powers conferred upon an agent by a formal instrument are to receive a strict interpretation, and the authority is never extended by intendment or construction beyond that which is given in terms, or is necessary for carrying the authority into effect, and the authority must be strictly pursued." See *Bean v. Bean*, 79 S.W. 2d 652 (Tex. Civ. App., Texarkana 1935, writ refused); *Dockstader v. Brown*, 204 S.W. 2d 352 (Tex. Civ. App., Fort Worth 1947, writ refd n.r.e.).

Giles and Swan had a specific conversation about Swan closing a real estate transaction. No mention of a joint venture

Figure 10–5 cont.

ever took place. Swan did not have the authority to use the power of attorney for the joint venture transfer. As stated in *Giddings, Neiman-Marcus v. Estes*, 440 S.W. 2d 90 (Tex. Civ. App., Eastland 1969, no writ), "(T)he authority will be construed strictly, so as to exclude the exercise of any power which is not warranted either by the actual terms used or as a necessary means of effecting the authority with effect." Since no authority was conferred on Swan by the document, he could not have acted on Giles's behalf. Consequently, any acts performed by Swan for Giles under the power of attorney are invalid, especially ones (like the joint venture transfer) not anticipated by the Grantor.

Swan told Harris that the power of attorney was for a specific purpose, which was to close the real estate transaction. The law is clear that a third party has a duty to inquire into the scope and fact of the agency, and the burden is on the third party to "ascertain at his peril the nature and scope of the authority of such agent." See *Lawrie v. Miller*, 2. S.W. 2d 561 (Tex. Civ. App., Texarkana 1928, no writ); *Eliot Valve Repair v. Valve*, 675 S.W. 2d 555 (Tex. App., Houston [1st Dist.] 1984, no writ); *Boucher v. City Paint & Supply*, 398 S.W. 2d 352 (Tex. Civ. App., Tyler 1966, no writ).

It was Harris's responsibility to investigate the extent of Swan's authority. Harris indeed knew the purpose of the power of attorney, but chose to coerce Swan to sign the document under the guise of "friendship." Any acts resulting from Harris's coercion and Swan's misuse of his authority cannot be imputed to Giles, and thus cannot be his responsibility.

The document that Harris is relying upon to effectuate the transfer of the joint venture interest is useless and invalid. The power of attorney does not comply with the requirements for a valid power of attorney, and Swan's actions violated Giles's instructions and interests.

Figure 10–6 Conclusion and Requested Relief

Since the purported power of attorney from Giles to Swan did not contain specific authority granted to the agent, the power of attorney is void. Based upon the strict construction doctrine, one cannot construe a grant of authority that is nonexistent. The power of attorney contained neither the name of the agent, nor the purpose of the agency, nor the authority of the agent; therefore, it could not confer any powers upon the agent. Swan's acts were therefore improper, and Giles is not legally responsible for the effects of those acts. Giles requests that the Motion for Summary Judgment be granted upon the court's finding, as a matter of law that the transfer of the joint venture interest was invalid and the power of attorney void.

Figure 10–7 Signature Block

Respectfully submitted,

____

R.T. LANG
State Bar #12344567
1234 Main Street, #10030
Dallas, Texas 75202
(214)555-1212
Attorney for Plaintiff

Figure 10–8 Certificate of Service

CERTIFICATE OF SERVICE

I certify that a true copy of the Memorandum of Law in Support of Plaintiff's Motion for Summary Judgment was served on Jane Smith, Assistant District Attorney, at 111 Elm Street, Suite 123, Ft. Worth, Texas, by certified mail, return receipt requested, in accordance with the Minnesota Rules of Civil Procedure on May 12, 1992.

____

R.T. LANG

10–4 Practical Considerations

A trial memorandum is an important document in the litigation process, because if properly drafted it can resolve issues in your favor and begin to turn the lawsuit toward your client. Furthermore, since the amount at issue in many cases will not justify the expense of an extended appeals process, prevailing at the trial level is often the guarantee of prevailing once and for all.

An example of a completed trial memorandum appears as Figure 10–9. In general, you should keep in mind the following points when preparing a trial memorandum:

- Check for local jurisdictional requirements about format or content.
- Identify your purpose.
- Always draft from your client's perspective.
- Present the law honestly and accurately, but with a partisan slant.
- Identify all significant facts, and present them in a manner that minimizes the opposition's strong points and paints a memorable picture of your client's position.
- Write convincingly, using effective and persuasive writing techniques.
- Be clear, precise, and concise.
- Tell the judge what result and relief you seek.

Figure 10–9 Memorandum of Law to the Trial Court

		No. 12344
STEPHEN GILES	§	IN THE DISTRICT COURT OF
	§	
Plaintiff	§	
	§	
vs.	§	DALLAS COUNTY, TEXAS
	§	
GEORGE HARRIS	§	
	§	
Defendant	§	_____JUDICIAL DISTRICT

MEMORANDUM OF LAW IN SUPPORT OF
PLAINTIFF'S MOTION FOR SUMMARY JUDGMENT

TO THE HONORABLE JUDGE OF SAID COURT:

COMES NOW STEPHEN GILES Plaintiff and files this Memorandum of Law to the Trial Court in Support of Plaintiff's Motion for Summary Judgment and would show unto the Court as follows:

Issue Presented

Whether a transaction using a blank power of attorney is valid when agent was not authorized to act on behalf of Defendant, the principal.

Statement of Facts

The facts in the case are undisputed. Mr. Giles went to a holiday party on November 20, at the home of Mr. Swan, a business associate. Mr. Swan had been Mr. Giles's friend and attorney for some time. Giles was going out of town for Thanksgiving and would not be back until the first of the new year. Giles wanted to purchase a piece of real estate and wanted to do so before the end of the year, but was going to be out of town. The only discussion that evening concerned the real estate transaction.

Swan suggested that Giles could execute a power of attorney with Swan as Giles's representative. The gentlemen went into Swan's study and Giles signed a document entitled "Power of Attorney." Neither man filled in any information in the document. Swan's name did not appear anywhere on the document. Swan kept the power of attorney in his top desk drawer. Giles went on his trip.

While Giles was on his trip, one of his partners, Mr. Harris, contacted Swan regarding a joint venture transaction completely unrelated to the real estate transaction. Giles and Harris had been discussing dissolving the joint venture, with Giles acquiring Harris's interest. Swan knew nothing about this transaction.

Harris stated to Swan that Giles was supposed to assume all Harris's interest in the joint venture before January 1. Harris inquired whether Swan could help him. Swan told Harris he had a power of attorney to close a real estate transaction, but did not know how he could help Harris out.

Harris asked Swan to use the power of attorney to transfer the joint venture interest. Harris told Swan this would save his friend some money. Swan indicated that he had no way of contacting his friend. Swan continued to tell Harris that he only had authority to close a real estate transaction. Harris, however, was able to persuade Swan to execute the transfer of the joint venture interest, using the blank power of attorney, on December 29.

Figure 10–9 cont.

When Giles came back to town, Swan informed him of the transfer from Harris and told Giles that he had used the power of attorney. Giles was enraged and told Swan he had no authority to transfer the interest, and Giles wanted the transaction rescinded.

<u>Argument</u>

A power of attorney must set forth the authority and the name of the principal and agent. The document before this court does neither.

To determine the validity of the power of attorney and the extent of the authority granted, certain rules of construction and interpretation must be addressed. The leading case of *Gouldy v. Metcalf*, 75 Tex. 455, 12 S.W. 830 (1889) sets out the rules of construction for a power of attorney, which are:

> [W]hen an authority is conferred upon an agent by a formal instrument, as by a Power of Attorney, there are two rules of construction to be carefully adhered to:
>
> 1. The meaning of general words in the instrument will be restricted by the context, and construed accordingly.
>
> 2. The authority will be construed strictly, so as to exclude the exercise of any power which is not warranted, either by the actual terms used or as a necessary means of executing the authority with effect.

Id. at 458.

Expanding the guidelines set forth in *Gouldy*, case law establishes that "all powers conferred upon an agent by a formal instrument are to receive a strict interpretation, and the authority is never extended by intendment or construction beyond that which is given in terms, or is necessary for carrying the authority into effect, and the authority must be strictly pursued." See *Bean v. Bean*, 79 S.W. 2d 652 (Tex. Civ. App., Texarkana 1935, writ refused); *Dockstader v. Brown*, 204 S.W.2d 352 (Tex.Civ.App., Fort Worth 1947, writ refd n.r.e.).

Giles and Swan had a specific conversation about Swan closing a real estate transaction. No mention of a joint venture ever took place. Swan did not have the authority to use the power of attorney for the joint venture transfer. Since the document did not contain any specifics, it is questionable whether the power of attorney was even proper for Swan to use to execute the real estate transaction. As stated in *Giddings, Neiman-Marcus v. Estes*, 440 S.W. 2d 90 (Tex. Civ. App., Eastland 1969, no writ), "[T]he authority will be construed strictly, so as to exclude the exercise of any power which is not warranted either by the actual terms used or as a necessary means of effecting the authority with effect." Since no authority was conferred on Swan by the document, he could not have acted on Giles's behalf. Consequently, any acts performed by Swan for Giles under the power of attorney are invalid, especially ones (like the joint venture transfer) not anticipated by the Grantor.

Swan told Harris that the power of attorney was for a specific purpose, which was to close the realestate transaction. The law is clear that a third party has a duty to inquire into the scope and fact of the agency, and the burden is on the third party to "ascertain at his peril the nature and scope of the authority of such agent." *Lawrie v. Miller*, 2. S.W. 2d 561 (Tex. Civ. App., Texarkana 1928, no writ.);

Figure 10–9 cont.

Eliot Valve Repair v. Valve, 675 S.W. 2d 555 (Tex. App., Houston [1st Dist.] 1984, no writ); *Boucher v. City Paint & Supply*, 398 S.W. 2d 352 (Tex. Civ. App., Tyler 1966, no writ).

It was Harris's responsibility to investigate the extent of Swan's authority. Harris indeed knew the purpose of the power of attorney, but chose to coerce Swan to sign the document under the guise of "friendship." Any acts resulting from Harris's coercion and Swan's misuse of his authority cannot be imputed to Giles, and thus cannot be his responsibility.

The document that Harris is relying upon to effectuate the transfer of the joint venture interest is useless and invalid. The power of attorney does not comply with the requirements for a *valid* power of attorney, and Swan's actions violated Giles's instructions and interests.

Conclusion and Requested Relief

Since the purported power of attorney from Giles to Swan did not contain any specific authority granted to the agent, the power of attorney is void. Based upon the strict construction doctrine, one cannot construe a grant of authority that is nonexistent. The power of attorney contained neither the name of the agent, nor the purpose of the agency, nor the authority of the agent, and therefore it could not confer any powers upon the agent. Swan's acts were therefore improper, and Giles is not legally responsible for the effects of those acts. Giles requests that the motion for Summary Judgment be granted upon the court's finding, as a matter of law, that the transfer of the joint venture interest was invalid and the power of attorney void.

Respectfully submitted,

____

R.T. LANG
State Bar #12344567
1234 Main Street, #10030
Dallas, Texas 75202
(214)555-1212
Attorney for Plaintiff

CERTIFICATE OF SERVICE

I certify that a true copy of the Memorandum of Law in Support of Plaintiff's Motion for Summary Judgment was served on Jane Smith, Assistant District Attorney, at 111 Elm Street, Suite 123, Fort Worth, Texas, by certified mail, return receipt requested, in accordance with the Minnesota Rules of Civil Procedure on May 12, 1992.

SUMMARY

10–1

The memorandum of law to the trial court is an adversarial document written to persuade a trial court on a disputed issue of law. It is also known as a trial memorandum, and other similar names, depending on the jurisdiction. The audience for a trial memorandum consists of the judge, who will read it fairly but must be convinced, and opposing counsel, who will read it looking to attack logical holes and unjustified analytical leaps. Be accurate but partisan in drafting a trial memorandum.

10–2

There are three broad categories of trial memoranda: the memorandum in regard to a motion; the memorandum prepared at the request of a judge; and the unsolicited memorandum that anticipates and addresses key legal issues. All are drafted with an adversarial purpose, designed to persuade a judge that a dis-puted question of law should be resolved in favor of a particular party.

10–3

There are several components to a trial memorandum. First come the caption, title, and introduction to the court. Next, in the "issues presented" section, the drafter presents the legal questions raised in a manner that suggests a resolution in favor of the client on whose behalf the drafter is working. Similarly, the statement of facts should state all events accurately, but with a slant toward the position of the client. The argument is the heart of the trial memorandum, presenting the results of the drafter's research in an adversarial argument designed to persuade the court of the superiority of the client's contentions. The conclusion summarizes the argument and identifies the relief sought. It is followed by a signature block and a certificate of service.

10–4

A properly drafted trial memorandum is an important part of the litigation process. Indeed, since appeals are often too expensive for clients to pursue, drafting effective trial memoranda can lead to a victory in the trial court that stands once and for all.

REVIEW

Key Terms

Before proceeding, review the key terms listed below to be sure you understand each one. If necessary, read over the corresponding section of the chapter. When you are ready to test your understanding, answer the Review Questions.

memorandum of law to the trial court
trial memorandum
memorandum in regard to a motion
memorandum at the request of a judge
unsolicited memorandum anticipating legal issues
issues presented
statement of facts
argument

Questions for Review and Discussion

1. Who are the two audiences for a trial memorandum?
2. How should a trial memorandum be prepared so as to assist a judge?
3. How should a trial memorandum be drafted so as to minimize the impact of the attack of opposing counsel?
4. What are the characteristics of a trial memorandum prepared in regard to a motion?
5. Why might a judge request a trial memorandum?
6. What is the potential importance of an unsolicited trial memorandum that anticipates issues?

7. What is the importance to a trial memorandum of the caption and the title?
8. From what perspective is the "issues presented" section of a trial memorandum prepared?
9. What are the four objectives of a statement of facts?
10. What is the difference between the discussion section of an internal memorandum and the argument section of a trial memorandum?

Activities

1. Assume that your attorney has been served with a request to produce tax returns in a personal injury case in your jurisdiction. Go to the library and research whether the tax returns are protected information, then prepare the argument section of the memorandum of law to the trial court, requesting an order that the documents not be produced.
2. Determine for your jurisdiction the format for a memorandum of law to the trial court. Check both the state and federal requirements.

NOTES

CHAPTER 11 Settlement and Trial

OUTLINE

COMMENTARY

It has been over three years since your firm filed suit on behalf of its client, Mrs. Hudson, against her surgeon. The claim—that the operation which she underwent was not only incorrectly performed, but unnecessary in the first place—has led to extensive discovery (including several depositions of expert witnesses) and numerous bitterly contested motions. All pretrial matters were finally resolved six months ago; since that time you've been waiting for the court to schedule trial.

Finally the day has arrived. The parties, their attorneys, assisting paralegals, and witnesses are sitting at the counsel tables, awaiting the judge. Suddenly lead defense counsel motions to your supervising attorney that she would like to speak for a moment in the hallway.

It soon becomes apparent that settlement is a possibility. Counsel send word to the judge that they would like him to mediate discussions. A conference room is located; hours of negotiation ensue.

Will the case settle? Perhaps; most cases do. But negotiations may break down; the case may have to be tried. Attorneys and paralegals must be prepared for both eventualities.

OBJECTIVES

The pace of a lawsuit quickens as trial approaches—it may be the last chance for settlement discussions, and if settlement proves impossible, the parties must prepare for trial. After you have completed this chapter, you will be able to:

1. Describe what a settlement agreement is.
2. Explain what is meant by consideration.
3. Identify the importance of a release.
4. Prepare a document for execution by a corporate party.
5. Explain the difference between an order of dismissal, a withdrawal, and a stipulated judgment.

6. Identify the two assertions made by a party filing a Motion for Summary Judgment.
7. Explain the difference between a jury trial and a bench trial.
8. Explain the function of a trial notebook.
9. Identify what is meant by jury instructions.
10. Explain the difference between a judgment and a verdict.

11–1 Settlement

Trials are expensive—it's an unfortunate fact of life. Hours of lawyer and paralegal time to prepare, hours in court, preparation of exhibits, payment of experts—the costs can quickly mount up. As the litigation process comes closer to trial, then, parties tend to be more willing to negotiate, with agreements often reached "on the courthouse steps."

Agreement alone is not sufficient to bring the matter to a close, however. In addition, the lawsuit itself must be concluded in some manner. A paralegal must be prepared to assist in the drafting of documents that accomplish these objectives.

The Settlement Agreement

A **settlement** is a compromise and agreement between the parties to resolve all disputed issues. A high percentage of all lawsuits filed in the United States end by settlement. The document that contains the terms of the compromise is called the **settlement agreement**. There is no one accepted format for a settlement agreement; like any other contract, it varies with the complexities of the issues and the needs of the parties. It may even be incorporated into the documents that are filed with the court to conclude the lawsuit. Most settlement agreements, however, contain at least some of the components examined in the following subsections. As a paralegal, you will be gathering and organizing the information needed to prepare these agreements, and you may even assist in the drafting.

Introductory Paragraphs The opening paragraphs of a settlement agreement generally identify the parties to the agreement and the basic facts of the case. If the settlement is reached before a lawsuit has been filed, no lawsuit will be referenced; if suit was started, the name of the case, the court in which it was filed, and the docket number should all be included.

Parties often include a paragraph stating that their willingness to settle should not be construed as an admission of fault or liability. This is done to minimize any precedent-setting implications; neither party wants to admit that it was wrong.

Figure 11–1 illustrates a typical introductory paragraph in a settlement agreement.

Recital of Consideration The law of contracts generally requires that, for an agreement to be binding between the parties, there must be **consideration**. Consideration is an exchange of value—in other words, each side must receive something of value in exchange for what it relinquishes under the terms of the

Figure 11–1 Introductory Paragraphs in Settlement Agreement

This Settlement Agreement (the "Agreement") is made and entered into by and between WINWOOD LEASING, INC., hereinafter referred to as "Plaintiff," and STEVEN ROBERTS, Individually, hereinafter referred to as "Defendant."

1. Plaintiff filed suit against Defendant on July 14, 1992, seeking recovery of the amount owed, such suit being styled WINWOOD LEASING, INC. vs. STEVEN ROBERTS, Individually, Number 90-11223-Z in the 100th Judicial District Court, Harris County, Texas (hereinafter referred to as "Litigation"), and

2. The Parties have agreed that settlement of all the disputes between the Parties relating to the litigation is the most economical, efficient, and desirable disposition for all concerned.

3. This agreement is executed by the Parties for the sole purpose of compromising and settling the matters involved in this dispute, and it is expressly understood and agreed, as a condition of the signing of this agreement, that this agreement shall not constitute or be construed to be an admission on the part of Defendant as to the claims asserted by Plaintiff.

contract. In a settlement agreement, usually the value received by one party is money; the value received by the other party (which paid the money) is an enforceable promise by the first party not to pursue the claim further.

The consideration for a settlement agreement is usually explicitly identified by the terms. Nevertheless, the parties often include some language stating that the agreement has been reached based upon the exchange of "good and valuable consideration," or some similar phrase. An example of a clause reciting consideration is shown in Figure 11–2.

Figure 11–2 Recital of Consideration

For good and valuable consideration, and in consideration of the mutual promises, covenants, and agreements set forth herein, Winwood and Roberts (sometimes herein referred to collectively as the "Parties") agree as follows:

Terms of Settlement A settlement agreement can be as short as one paragraph or as long as hundreds of pages, depending upon the nature of the dispute. Figure 11–3 on page 456 sets out the terms of a typical settlement agreement.

Included among the terms is usually found a release provision. A **release** is a clause by which the parties expressly abandon the right to pursue further the claims forming the basis for the dispute at hand (and, often, any other claims, known or unknown, that may exist at that time).

In other words, each party *releases* the other from further liability, thereby acting on the desire to settle the suit. Figure 11–4 shows two examples (one formal, one less formal) of a release clause.

Sometimes the release is a separate document. A separate release is commonly used where the terms of the settlement are so simple as to eliminate the need for a separate settlement agreement document (as where a release is given in exchange for a check for the agreed-upon amount, with no other terms to the settlement).

Figure 11–3 Terms of Settlement

1. Roberts shall pay to Winwood the sum of FORTY-TWO THOUSAND DOLLARS ($42,000.00) to be paid under the following terms and conditions:

a. On or before December 1, 1992, Roberts shall pay the sum of TWENTY THOUSAND DOLLARS ($20,000.00) to Winwood in the form of certified or cashier's check, or money order; thereafter, Roberts shall make monthly payments in the amount of $2,000.00 each month thereafter until payment of the full amount is paid to Winwood by Roberts.

b. All payments set forth in paragraph 1 are due on the first day of each month. If the required monthly payments are not received by Winwood by the 4th of the month, it shall be deemed a default entitling Winwood to pursue his available remedies.

c. Payment of the amounts set forth in paragraph 1 above will render a total payment of $42,000.00 to Winwood from Roberts.

2. Roberts agrees to make the payments required by Paragraph 1 hereinabove to WINWOOD LEASING, INC., and to send them to the law offices of Frederick Gabriel, Attorney at Law, 1710 Oak Street, Suite 130, Houston, Texas 79222.

3. Roberts agrees that in the event of default of any or all of the obligations contained in this Agreement, Roberts also shall be responsible for all costs and attorneys' fees incurred in the collection of the remaining balance due under this Agreement.

Figure 11–4 Examples of Release Clause

Paragraph Regarding Release—Formal

7. Except for the respective covenents, promises, and agreements contained in and provided for by this Agreement, Roberts does hereby release, relinquish, remit, and discharge Winwood, its successors, legal representatives, employees, servants, agents, representatives, heirs, and assigns (collectively "Winwood"), of and from any and all liabilities, damages, debts, costs, obligations, responsibilities, covenants, agreements, expenses, and attorneys' fees, claims, demands, or causes of action, of any nature whatsoever, both known and unknown, matured or contingent, liquidated or unliquidated, direct or derivative, that now exist or that might hereafter accrue based upon any and all facts, claims, or events occuring up through the last date of signing of this Agreement, relating in any way to the Lease, the premises demised by the Lease, and the relationship between the Parties arising as a result of the Lease, including but not limited to, any and all claims that Roberts might assert against Winwood in the Litigation and/or that Roberts has asserted against Winwood to date.

Paragraph Regarding Release—Informal

Plaintiff releases the Defendant from any claims arising from the pending litigation and forever discharges Defendant from all claims, demands, damages, and causes of actions that may arise from the claims of Plaintiff.

Another paragraph commonly seen among the terms of a settlement agreement is the default provision. The default provision identifies the options of each party should the other party fail to perform its obligations under their settlement agreement. Figure 11– 5 shows a typical default provision.

Figure 11–5 Default Provision

Failure to pay the sums when due shall constitute default. In the event of such default, all remaining unpaid payments due under this agreement shall become immediately due and payable. All such unpaid payments shall bear interest, from the date of default until paid, at the maximum rate permitted by law.

Claimant may exercise any other rights that claimant may have at law or in equity against the defaulting party.

Standard Provisions Certain paragraphs containing background information are drafted into virtually every settlement agreement. These paragraphs generally include the addresses of the parties, the venue where suit may be filed in the event of breach of the settlement agreement's terms, definitions of words and phrases, and possibly other requirements imposed by the jurisdiction in which the agreement is made. Figure 11–6 shows some standard provisions found in a settlement agreement.

Figure 11–6 Standard Provisions for Settlement

11. This Agreement states the entire agreement of the Parties hereto with regard to the subject matter of the Agreement. This Agreement supersedes all prior and contemporaneous negotiations and agreements, oral or written, with regard to the subject matter of the Agreement, and all prior and contemporaneous negotiations and agreements with regard to the subject matter of the Agreement are deemed to have been abandoned if not incorporated into this Agreement.

12. This Agreement may be amended only by a written agreement signed by all the Parties to this Agreement, and a breach of this Agreement may be waived only a written waiver signed by the party granting the waiver. The waiver of any breach of this Agreement shall not operate or be construed as a waiver of any other similar or prior or subsequent breach of this Agreement.

13. This Agreement shall be governed by the laws of the State of Texas and venue for its enforcement shall be exclusively in Harris County, Texas.

14. This Agreement shall bind and inure to the benefit of the respective successors and assigns of the Parties.

15. The persons signing this Agreement represent and warrant that they are authorized to do so.

Date and Signatures The date that appears on a settlement agreement is significant, particularly where the terms include a release that relinquishes any and all claims which the parties have against each other "from the beginning of the world to the date of this document" (a colorful phrase often seen in release clauses). Make sure the date reflects the understanding of the parties about the effective date of the settlement.

Problems can arise when a settlement agreement is revised prior to execution (putting into effect). The drafter may neglect to change dates in the text of the document, or dates identified in the text may conflict with the date of final execution. A similar problem can occur when parties execute the document on different dates (as where originals have to be mailed to geographically distant parties). Take care to choose language that ensures that after execution is complete there will be no confusion about the operative and effective date of the agreement.

Figure 11–7 Examples of Jurats

(a) Form of Jurat—Corporate

EXECUTED effective this ____day of November, 1992.

WINWOOD LEASING, INC.

By:____________________________
Deborah Patterson, President

THE STATE OF TEXAS)
)
COUNTY OF HARRIS)

BEFORE ME, the undersigned authority, on this day personally appeared DEBORAH PATTERSON, known to me to be the person and officer whose name is subscribed to the foregoing instrument and acknowledged to me that the same was the act of the said WINWOOD LEASING, INC., a Texas Corporation, and that she executed the same as the act of such corporation for the purposes and consideration therein expressed and in the capacity therein stated.

GIVEN under my hand and seal of office this ____day of November, 1992.

____
NOTARY PUBLIC IN AND FOR THE STATE OF TEXAS

My Commission Expires:____

(b) Form of Jurat—Partnership

EXECUTED effective this ____day of November, 1992.

PETERSON & SWAN

By:____________________________
Daon Peterson, Partner

THE STATE OF TEXAS)
)
COUNTY OF HARRIS)

BEFORE ME, the undersigned authority, on this day personally appeared DAON PETERSON, known to me to be the person and partner whose name is subscribed to the foregoing instrument and acknowledged to me that the same was the act of the said PETERSON & SWAN, a Texas Partnership, and that he executed the same as the act of such partnership for the purposes and consideration therein expressed and in the capacity therein stated.

GIVEN under my hand and seal of office this ____ day of November, 1992.

____
NOTARY PUBLIC IN AND FOR THE STATE OF TEXAS

My Commission Expires:____

Figure 11–7 Cont.

(c) Form of Jurat—Individual

```
EXECUTED effective this _____ day of November, 1992.

              ______________________________
              STEVEN ROBERTS, Individually

DATED:November ______, 1992
THE STATE OF TEXAS  )
                    )
COUNTY OF HARRIS    )

   BEFORE ME, the undersigned authority, on this day per-
sonally appeared STEVEN ROBERTS, Individually, known to me
to be the person whose name is subscribed to the foregoing
instrument and acknowledged to me that he executed the same
for the purposes and consideration therein expressed.
   GIVEN under my hand and seal of office this _____day of
November, 1992.

           ___________________________________
      NOTARY PUBLIC IN AND FOR THE STATE OF TEXAS

        My Commission Expires:_____
```

Signatures are, of course, a critically important aspect of the settlement agreement. The only parties bound by the settlement agreement are the parties who sign. If a corporation is a party, for example, and an individual officer is signing on behalf of the corporation, it is absolutely essential to make it clear that he is signing on behalf of the corporation, and not as an individual. This can be done by crafting a signature block identifying the corporation and indicating that the corporation is signifying its agreement by the signature of its president of other officer (see Figure 11–7).

It is often appropriate to have the signature to the agreement notarized or acknowledged. If this is necessary, the drafter must be sure to include the proper **jurats** at the end of the document. A jurat is a clause following the signature that identifies when, where, and before whom the signature was sworn or affirmed (Figure 11–7 also shows examples of jurats).

Concluding the Lawsuit

If the suit had already been filed at the time agreement was reached, the parties must conclude the lawsuit in a manner acceptable to all concerned. There are generally three methods of concluding a lawsuit after settlement—by dismissal, by withdrawal, or by stipulated judgment.

Conclusion by Dismissal A dismissal occurs when the court concludes the case by entering an **order of dismissal**. This occurs in one of two ways. The parties can *jointly* draft it, making reference to their settlement agreement and the fact that neither objects to entry of the order. The order is then signed by the parties (or their attorneys), signed by the judge, and placed in the court file. This abruptly ends the lawsuit at whatever stage it has reached. In the alternative method, one party can file a Motion to Dismiss, which also references the settlement agreement and indicates to the court that neither party objects to the dismissal. The court then orders the motion granted, which also terminates the lawsuit.

The most important point in drafting an order of dismissal or a Motion to Dismiss is to indicate whether the dismissal is "with prejudice" or "without prejudice." A case dismissed *with* prejudice is a final resolution of the claims raised by the complaint; those same claims can never be brought before a court again. If dismissal is *without* prejudice, the same claims can be refiled in another lawsuit, as long as the claim is still within the statute of limitations (the time limit within which a claim must be filed, or else expire). In most cases that are settled, the dismissal entered is with prejudice; the same claims can never be refiled, although if the settlement agreement is breached, a contract claim can be brought alleging breach of the agreement.

Figure 11–8 shows the body of a Motion to Dismiss, prepared with an accompanying order for the court to enter.

Conclusion by Withdrawal The parties can also conclude the matter by **withdrawal**. A withdrawal is a document filed by the party who originally filed a claim against another, by which the claim is abandoned. The party filing would be either a plaintiff who is giving up one or more of the claims in the complaint, or a defendant who is abandoning a counterclaim or cross-claim. For a lawsuit to be effectively concluded, all claims by the plaintiff, or counterclaims and cross-claims by the defendant, must be concluded. It is possible for one party to file a

Figure 11–8 Body of Motion to Dismiss

Motion to Dismiss

PLAINTIFF, WINWOOD LEASING, INC. files this Motion to Dismiss Defendant STEVEN ROBERTS, Individually, with prejudice as follows:

Plaintiff and Defendant have reached an agreement to compromise and settle this litigation. Therefore, Plaintiff does not desire to prosecute its cause of action against Defendant STEVEN ROBERTS, Individually.

WHEREFORE, Plaintiff, WINWOOD LEASING, INC., requests that its cause of action against Defendant STEVEN ROBERTS, Individually, be dismissed with prejudice.

Respectfully submitted,

____

FREDERICK GABRIEL
State Bar #2209900
1710 Oak Street, Suite 130
Houston, Texas 79222
(713)455-1234

Order of Dismissal

On this day, the Court considered Plaintiff's Motion to Dismiss all causes of action against STEVEN ROBERTS, Individually, and concluded that the Motion should be granted. It is therefore,

ORDERED, ADJUDGED AND DECREED that all causes of action asserted herein against Defendant STEVEN ROBERTS, Individually, are hereby dismissed with prejudice.

SIGNED this _____ day of November, 1992.

____
JUDGE PRESIDING

Figure 11–9 Stipulated Judgment

```
    On November 24, 1992, came on to be heard the announce-
ment of counsel for Plaintiff, WINWOOD LEASING, INC. and
counsel for Defendant STEVEN ROBERTS, Individually, to the
effect that the parties have agreed and desire to have entered
in this cause a judgment in favor of WINWOOD LEASING, INC.
against STEVEN ROBERTS, Individually, as indicated by the
approval of the parties below. The Court is of the opinion
that the judgment should be granted. It is, therefore,
    ORDERED, ADJUDGED AND DECREED that WINWOOD LEASING, INC.
have and recover judgment of and from STEVEN ROBERTS,
Individually, for the principal sum of FIFTY-THREE THOUSAND
DOLLARS ($53,000.00); for postjudgment interest at the rate
of ten percent (10%) per annum on all amounts awarded here-
in until paid; and for all costs and attorneys' fees in col-
lection of the judgment.

    Signed this _____ day of _____, 1992.

                  ____________________
                  JUDGE PRESIDING

AGREED AS TO FORM AND CONTENT:
```

withdrawal of one claim in a lawsuit, with other claims proceeding; but a settlement generally involves resolution of *all* outstanding claims (although when there are multiple parties in a lawsuit, it is more common to see piecemeal settlements).

As with the Motion to Dismiss, an important point in a withdrawal is whether it is with or without prejudice. If not expressly stated in the withdrawal, the effect can vary, depending on the jurisdiction and the nature of the matter. Be sure that the documents you file are drafted with language that carries out the intent of the parties.

Conclusion by Stipulated Judgment A third alternative is to conclude the matter by **stipulated judgment**. This is the equivalent of a decision of the court on the merits, except that the parties indicate to the court that they have agreed to the terms of the stipulated judgment by signing, along with the judge, at the bottom. A stipulated judgment constitutes a conclusion with prejudice, in that it is a final decision that precludes the parties from ever again making the same claims. An example of a stipulated judgment appears in Figure 11–9. You will learn more about judgments in the sections that follow.

11–2 Summary Judgment

Another pretrial resolution of a lawsuit flows out of the **summary judgment** motion, which, if granted, ends the lawsuit by the entry of a judgment in favor of one side. The granting of a summary judgment motion differs from settlement in that it is not the result of an agreement between the opposing parties; rather, it involves a decision of the court on a contested motion in which one party asserts (1) that there is "no genuine issue of material fact," and (2) that it is entitled to judgment in its favor "as a matter of law" (see Rule 56 of the FRCP). To explain these concepts fully, a brief discussion is in order.

There are two aspects to every legal controversy—the *facts* and the controlling *law*. When a lawsuit is filed, the parties involved are in essence saying to the court, "We will each present our version of the facts and our interpretation of the law; you decide who is right." The presentation of evidence in the form of documents, exhibits, and witness testimony is designed to enable the trier-of-fact (the jury or the judge; more about this later) to weigh the competing positions and determine whose version of the facts is accurate. Once the facts have been established by the trier-of-fact, the judge applies the controlling law and renders a decision.

Sometimes there is no dispute as to the facts, or at least one party *asserts* that there is no significant and genuine controversy over important facts. If the court finds this assertion to be true, no trial is necessary. The only matter left for the court is to apply the controlling law to these facts. When one party files a Motion for Summary Judgment, the other party can contest it by asserting (1) that there *is* a genuine factual dispute that needs to be decided by the court, or (2) that, although there is no factual dispute, the court should nevertheless find against the moving party based on the controlling law. Sometimes both parties file Motions for Summary Judgment simultaneously, agreeing to stipulate as to the facts. Then the only things necessary to resolve the lawsuit are for the parties to file trial memoranda stating their competing legal arguments, and for the court to decide the contested legal issues.

Motions for Summary Judgment are not readily granted by courts. Where the nonfiling party contends that there *are* contested issues and can show even a slight amount of evidence (physical evidence or deposition testimony) that supports its version of the facts, a court will not grant the motion but will, rather, allow the factual issues to be decided after the full presentation of evidence at trial.

The Motion for Summary Judgment should include a brief statement of the basis for the motion, and you should attach all documentary evidence and deposition passages that support your position. A brief in support of the motion, arguing that there is no contested factual issue and developing the filing party's legal position, is generally filed as well (and sometimes the attachments are appended to this brief rather than to the motion).

Rule 56 of the FRCP, quoted previously, governs the procedure for Motions for Summary Judgment filed in federal court. You should check your local jurisdiction for its requirements. The body of a Motion for Summary Judgment in a case involving a lease agreement, and the ensuing order granting the motion, are shown in Figure 11–10.

11–3 The Scope and Nature of a Trial

The level of disagreement in some matters is so great that nothing short of trial will resolve the dispute. The parties then proceed in one of the two basic types of trial, which differ with regard to the identity of the trier-of-fact mentioned in the last section. The two types are the **jury trial**, and the **trial before the court**, or **bench trial**.

In a jury trial, selected citizens act as jurors. These jurors hear all the evidence, then, after receiving instructions from the judge, go to the jury room, where they deliberate until they have decided all contested issues of *fact*. Issues of *law* are always decided by the judge, who also makes rulings during the trial on the admissibility of evidence and other procedural disputes that arise. Usually all issues of law have been settled by the point at which the jury begins its deliberations—indeed, the instructions provided to the jury by the judge usually incorporate the decisions she has made with regard to contested legal issues.

Figure 11–10 Summary Judgment: Body of Motion and Order

Body of Motion for Summary Judgment

1. Plaintiff's Complaint has been filed and served on Defendant VICTRONIC, INC. Defendant has appeared and answered herein. Plaintiff's action is based upon a lease agreement.

2. The pleadings on file herein, together with all the pretrial discovery documents on file herein, the official records of the Court, and the Affadavits of Victor Brennan and Amelia Johnson, attached hereto, all show that there is no genuine issue to any material fact and that the Defendant, as moving party herein, is entitled to judgment in its favor as a matter of law.

3. Defendant asks the Court that, on hearing of this Motion, judgment be entered against Plaintiff.

4. If the Court grants this Motion for Summary Judgment, Defendant requests that immediately after hearing of the Motion, the Court shall award Defendant its attorney fees and costs of suit.

Order Granting Summary Judgment

The motion of the Defendant for summary judgment pursuant to Rule 56(c) of the Federal Rules of Civil Procedure, having been presented, and the court being fully advised,

The court finds that the Defendant is entitled to a summary judgment as a matter of law.

IT IS THEREFORE ORDERED, ADJUDGED AND DECREED that the Defendant's motion for summary judgment be, and the same hereby is granted, that Plaintiffs have and recover nothing by their suit, that the Defendant, VICTRONIC, INC., be dismissed, and that Defendant recover its costs and charges in this behalf expended and have execution therefor.

In a bench trial, there is no jury. The judge decides not only issues of law, but issues of fact as well. The presentation of evidence is conducted in a manner identical to that in a jury trial (except that attorneys may slightly alter their style or technique for strategic reasons), and at the conclusion the judge renders a decision that incorporates both his findings of fact and his conclusions of law.

Whether before a jury or before the bench, a trial requires a great deal of preparation and work. Let's turn to some of the legal writing assignments you may face in connection with a trial.

The Trial Notebook and the Course of Trial

There are many practical and technical matters that need to be addressed by attorneys and paralegals prior to trial. In the **trial notebook**, each party gathers together in one central location as much useful information as is reasonable and efficient. Although the layout and content of the trial notebook vary from one attorney to the next, the following elements are generally addressed or included in one form or another:

- copies of all pleadings, with summaries;
- list of the elements to be proven;
- copies of relevant cases, statutes, and regulations;
- pretrial motions and decisions thereon;
- internal memoranda and other research on legal issues;

- questions to ask potential jurors in *voir dire*;
- outline of the opening argument;
- list of witnesses with addresses and phone numbers;
- key passages from deposition transcripts;
- digests of all depositions;
- list of exhibits and copies of key documents;
- outlines of questions for witnesses;
- outline of closing argument;
- proposed jury instructions; and
- drafts of potential posttrial motions.

As can be seen from this list, the trial notebook provides a blueprint for the trial to come. The lawyer can follow through the sections, step by step, when in the courtroom trying the case. Unanticipated situations almost always arise during trial, but by preparing the trial notebook with care, counsel can minimize surprises. You should study the list, and use it when preparing a trial notebook according to your firm's accepted format. Legal writing considerations for the preparation of the trial notebook include proper indexing for ease of reference and drafting subsections (for example, the internal memoranda) using the guidelines we have discussed in previous chapters.

Some of the references in the list refer to items we have yet to discuss, for example, the questions to witnesses or the outline of opening argument. These items should be drafted in a clear manner with an adversarial tone. Their content, however, delves into areas of trial strategy that go beyond the scope of this book. In any event, as a paralegal, if you have occasion to assist in the preparation of these items, you will be acting under the direction and guidance of your supervising attorney, and should be closely following her preferences.

The last two items in the list, jury instructions and posttrial motions, refer to trial documents that may be needed at the conclusion of the evidence. For example, a **Motion for Directed Verdict** can be prepared ahead of time.

Such a motion can be made in a jury trial; it requests that the judge enter an order finding that the other side failed to offer sufficient evidence to make its case, hence the jury should be directed to find in favor of the moving party. An example of the body of a Motion for Directed Verdict is seen in Figure 11–11.

Jury instructions are another item that can and should be prepared ahead of time. At the end of a jury trial, the judge must instruct the jury on the legal principles or rules that it must follow in reaching its conclusions. Such instructions take into account the manner in which the judge has interpreted the law. Prior to the submission of instructions to the jury, each side presents to the judge its version of proposed jury instructions, prepared in an adversarial manner to influence the jury in its favor. The judge weighs the competing proposals in light of the controlling law, and submits what he determines to be the appropriate instructions (either one party's version, or the judge's own original draft) to the jury.

Some jury instructions are in the form of questions that must be answered "yes" or "no" depending on the jury's conclusions. Some are direct statements. To prepare jury instruction proposals, the parties may have to conduct legal research on the status of the law in the relevant area. Most jurisdictions have relatively standardized instructions for questions that commonly arise (such as in an ordinary negligence claim), which must be tailored to the facts of the specific case. Figure 11–12 shows some typical jury questions.

We discuss some other posttrial motions in a later subsection.

Figure 11–11 Body of Motion for Directed Verdict

Now comes the Defendant, CHAPMAN, INC., at the close of Plaintiff's case, and moves the court to withdraw the evidence from the consideration of the jury and to instruct the jury to find the Defendant not liable, instruction to that effect being attached hereto.

As grounds for the allowance of this motion and the giving of the attached instruction, the Defendant avers that:

(1) no evidence has been offered or received upon the trial of the above entitled cause to sustain the allegations of negligence contained in Plaintiff's complaint;

(2) no evidence has been offered or received upon the trial proving or tending to prove that the Defendant was guilty of any negligence whether alleged or not;

(3) the proximate cause of the occurrence in question was not the negligence of the defendant;

(4) by the uncontroverted evidence, the decedent was guilty of contributory negligence, which was the sole cause of her death; and

(5) no evidence was offered or received on the trial proving or tending to prove that the decedent was engaged in interstate transportation immediately before and at the time of her death.

Figure 11–12 Sample Jury Questions

Question No. 1

"Do you find from a preponderance of the evidence that the Defendant CHAPMAN, INC., was guilty of negligence in performing any one or more of the specific acts of negligence alleged by the Plaintiff?"

ANSWER: Yes __ or No __

Question No. 2

"Do you find from a preponderance of the evidence that the negligence of the Defendant CHAPMAN, INC., was either the sole proximate cause or a contributing proximate cause of the injuries and death of Roslyn Shearson?"

Answer: Yes__ or No __

Question No. 3

"Do you find from a preponderance of the evidence that Roslyn Shearson, deceased, was guilty of negligence in performing any one or more of the specific acts of negligence alleged by the Defendants?"

Answer: Yes__ or No __

Judgment

The decision rendered in a bench trial is called a **judgment**. The decision rendered by a jury is called a **verdict**; however, it must also be incorporated into a subsequent judgment. For both jury and bench trials, then, the judgment is the official, written decision of the court reciting the relief, if any, that is granted and the damages, if any, allowed.

Upon the signing of the judgment, the time for appeal or posttrial motions begins to run. The judgment, which may be prepared by the prevailing party for the court to execute, or by the court itself, contains a caption, title, introductory paragraphs, an identification of the findings of fact, an identification of the rulings of law, often a discussion of the legal principles and analysis

Figure 11–13 Completed Judgment

On May 10, 1992, came on to be heard the above-entitled cause. All parties appeared both in person and by and through their counsels and announced ready for trial. A jury was thereupon selected, composed of twelve qualified persons, and such jury was impaneled and sworn. After hearing the pleadings, evidence, and argument of counsel, the jury did receive the charge of the court, and return into open court on May 12, 1992, its verdict resolving all issues in favor of the Plaintiff's contentions, and awarding the sum of TWENTY THOUSAND DOLLARS ($20,000.00) to Plaintiff as compensation for his injuries, the sum of TEN THOUSAND FIVE HUNDRED TWENTY-NINE DOLLARS AND SEVENTEEN CENTS ($10,529.17) as compensation for hospital and medical expenses incurred by reason of treatment of Plaintiff, together with the sum of FIVE THOUSAND DOLLARS ($5,000.00), being the difference between the reasonable cash market value of his 1990 Chrysler automobile immediately before and immediately after such collision.

The verdict of the jury was received and filed by the court, and in consonance therewith,

IT IS ORDERED, ADJUDGED, AND DECREED by the Court that the Plaintiff have and recover from Defendant the sum of TWENTY THOUSAND DOLLARS ($20,000.00) for his personal injuries, the sum of TEN THOUSAND FIVE HUNDRED TWENTY-NINE DOLLARS AND SEVENTEEN CENTS ($10,529.17) for hospital and medical bills, together with the sum of FIVE THOUSAND DOLLARS ($5,000.00) for damage to his vehicle, making in all the sum of THIRTY-FIVE THOUSAND FIVE HUNDRED TWENTY-NINE DOLLARS AND SEVENTEEN CENTS ($35,529.17).

IT IS FURTHER ORDERED, ADJUDGED, AND DECREED that this judgment bear interest at the rate of ten percent (10%) per annum from date hereof until paid, and that Plaintiff recover his costs of suit.

involved, the specification of relief, including damages allowed, and generally ends with a concise statement of the judgment, such as "judgment for plaintiff." An example of a judgment appears in Figure 11–13.

When a defendant fails to respond to a complaint within the time allowed for a response, or if one party fails to comply properly with procedural deadlines or requirements, a **default** may occur and be followed, ultimately, by a **default judgment**. The default judgment is entered without a trial or hearing against the party who failed to respond or follow proper procedures. An example of a default judgment is shown in Figure 11–14.

Posttrial Practice

The issuance of the judgment does not end the lawsuit. The parties can still exercise one or more of several options at this point.

If new evidence is found, or if errors on evidentiary or other procedural matters prejudiced one or the other of the parties, a **Motion for a New Trial** (governed by Rule 59 of the FRCP) can be filed that, if granted, negates the result of the first trial and allows a second to proceed. The grounds for a new trial, as they are stated in Rule 59 of the FRCP, are set forth in Figure 11–15; an example of the body of a Motion for New Trial appears in Figure 11–16.

Figure 11–14 Default Judgment

CAME ON to be heard this day the above-entitled and numbered cause wherein FRAME CONSTRUCTION, INC. is Plaintiff and BERNIE'S DRYWALL, INC., is Defendant; and

It appearing to the Court that Defendant BERNIE'S DRYWALL, INC., having been duly and legally cited to appear and answer, and wholly made default; and Plaintiff having announced ready for trial, and no jury being demanded and it further appearing that this is a suit upon a credit purchase offered in evidence, and the Court having read the pleadings and heard the evidence and argument of counsel, is of the following opinion;

The wrong done by Defendant was aggravated by that kind of willfulness, wantonness, and malice for which the law allows the imposition of exemplary damages. The Defendant acted with an evil and deliberate intent to harm Plaintiff. Its conduct was intentional, willful, and wanton, and without justification or excuse, and it acted with gross indifference to the rights of the Plaintiff. Plaintiff therefore seeks exemplary damages in the amount of $8,547.00, three times the actual amount of damages the Plaintiff incurred. The Court is further of the opinion that Plaintiff should have the relief for which it prays, it is therefore,

ORDERED, ADJUDGED AND DECREED, that Plaintiff, FRAME CONSTRUCTION, INC., do have and recover from the Defendant BERNIE'S DRYWALL, INC. the sum of TWO THOUSAND EIGHT HUNDRED FORTY-NINE DOLLARS ($2,849.00), together with interest at the rate of six percent per annum on the outstanding balance from September 1, 1992, until judgment, plus EIGHT THOUSAND FIVE HUNDRED FORTY-SEVEN DOLLARS ($8,547.00) in exemplary damages, plus reasonable attorneys' fees in the amount of $2,000.00, plus interest at ten percent (10%) per annum from the date of judgment until paid, plus all costs of Court expended.

SIGNED THIS _____DAY OF __________, 19__.

____

JUDGE PRESIDING

Figure 11–15 Federal Rules of Civil Procedure—Rule 59

New Trials; Amendments of Judgments

(a) Grounds. A new trial may be granted to all or any of the parties and on all or part of the issues (1) in an action in which there has been a trial by jury, for any of the reasons for which new trials have heretofore been granted in actions at law in the courts of the United States; and (2) in an action tried without a jury, for any of the reasons for which rehearings have heretofore been granted in suits in equity in the courts of the United States. On a motion for a new trial in an action tried without a jury, the court may open the judgment if one has been entered, take additional testimony, amend findings of fact and conclusions of law or make new findings and conclusions, and direct the entry of a new judgment . . .

Figure 11–16 Body of Motion for New Trial with Statement of Grounds

The defendant, CHAPMAN, INC., moves that the verdict of the jury in the above-entitled cause be set aside and that the judgment entered on the verdict be vacated and set aside and that a new trial be granted to the defendant for one or more of the following reasons:

1. The verdict is contrary to law.
2. The verdict is contrary to the evidence.
3. The verdict is contrary to the law and the evidence.
4. The verdict is contrary to the weight of the evidence.
5. There is no substantial evidence that the Defendant is guilty of negligence.
6. The evidence shows that the sole proximate cause of the decedant's death was his own contributory negligence.
7. The court erred in denying Defendant's motion to direct a verdict in his favor at the close of Plaintiff's case.
8. The court erred in denying Defendant's motion to direct a verdict in his favor at the close of all the evidence.
9. There is no sufficient or substantial evidence tending to support the amount of the jury's verdict.
10. The verdict is excessive and appears to have been given under the influence of passion and prejudice.

Figure 11–17 Motion for Judgment Notwithstandng the Verdict

Plaintiff, by his attorney, moves the court for judgment in favor of Plaintiff and against Defendant for SIXTY THOUSAND DOLLARS ($60,000.00) principal, interest thereon at ten percent (10%) per year from June 4, 1991, and Plaintiff's costs, notwithstanding the general verdict of the jury in favor of the Defendant returned herein on February 4, 1992, on the grounds and for the reasons that:

1. the general verdict is wholly contrary to and cannot be reconciled with the findings of the jury on all the special issues submitted to the jury; and
2. the findings on the special issues are all consistent with each other and fully support judgment as prayed for in Plaintiff's complaint, and as herein requested, and negate and deny the defense asserted by the Defendant.

This motion is based on all the records, papers, pleadings, and files of this action, including the full record of the trial.

Another type of posttrial motion is the Motion for Judgment Notwithstanding the Verdict (also known as a judgment n.o.v., or non obstante veredicto) pursuant to Rule 50 of the FRCP. This motion is filed when the losing party in a jury trial contends that the evidence presented is not sufficient to support the verdict that the jury rendered (an example of the body of such a motion, in which it is alleged that the specific findings of fact made by the jury are not consistent with its general verdict, is shown in Figure 11–17.) It often follows on the heels of a Motion for Directed Verdict that was denied. The following sequence is not unusual: (1) at the close of evidence, Party A concludes the evidence is insufficient to allow a verdict for Party B, and makes a Motion for Directed Verdict; (2) Judge denies Motion for Directed Verdict; (3) jury returns verdict in favor of Party B; (4) Party A files motion for Judgment Notwithstanding the Verdict. Since the judge denied the Motion for Directed Verdict, she will probably deny the Motion for Judgment Notwithstanding the Verdict as well; this brings us to the appeal, a common posttrial practice.

Figure 11–18 Express Findings of Fact and Conclusions of Law

The above-styled and numbered cause came for trial before the court without a jury on June 20, 1992. All parties and their attorneys were present. After considering the pleadings, the evidence, the argument, and briefs of counsel, the Court in response to a request from DENTAL CLINICS OF THE WORLD, INC. ("Dental Clinics"), Plaintiff, makes its findings of fact and conclusions of law as follows:

FINDINGS OF FACT

1. On or about November 17, 1991, Defendant voluntarily resigned his employment with Plaintiff.
2. Defendant became a Vice President of DENTAL CLINICS on or about February, 1986.
3. Defendant had access to the books and records of DENTAL CLINICS.
4. Defendant was an employee and Vice President of DENTAL CLINICS.

CONCLUSIONS OF LAW

1. Plaintiff had the burden of proving a probable right and a probable injury in gaining a temporary injunction.
2. Defendant was a fiduciary of Plaintiff.
3. Defendant was in a confidential relationship with Plaintiff.
4. Even in the absence of an employment contract, a former employee may not breach a confidential relationship.
5. Even in the absence of an employment contract, a former employee may not disclose trade secrets to use his competitive advantage to the Plaintiff's detriment.

An **appeal** is a demand by the losing party that a higher court review the decision of the trial court. The party that loses on a Motion for Judgment Notwithstanding the Verdict can appeal; indeed, the losing party almost always has some recourse to appeal, regardless of whether any posttrial motions are filed (although the decisions in certain matters, such as small claims actions, may not be appealable; check the statutes in your jurisdiction). The most important consideration in filing an appeal is to do so within the time limitations allowed by the rules. It is also sometimes necessary to request express findings of fact and conclusions of law from the court, if the judgment is vague. An example of express findings of fact and conclusions of law appears in Figure 11–18. Check the rules of your local jurisdiction, and consult with your supervising attorney if this situation arises.

11–4 Practical Considerations

The surest way to settle a case is to convince the other side that you are fully prepared to go to trial. And the surest way to win a case that can't be settled is, likewise, to be fully prepared.

The key, then, to both settlement and trial is preparation. The attorney and paralegal who have done their homework—who have digested the depositions, researched the law, painstakingly prepared the trial notebook, prepped the witnesses, organized the exhibits, anticipated potential problems and made contingency plans, drafted jury instructions and posttrial motions ahead of time—make a team that will be able to negotiate from strength and, if necessary, engage the opposition with focused precision. Ask any experienced trial attorney, any successful litigation firm, any seasoned trial judge, and they will tell you that preparation is the most important factor for success in the courts.

As a paralegal, you will likely have a central role in trial preparation. By honing your writing skills and organizational abilities, you will contribute to each client's prospects for a successful resolution of her matter.

SUMMARY

11–1

A settlement is a compromise and agreement between the parties to resolve all disputed issues. A settlement agreement is a document that incorporates the terms of a settlement. The settlement agreement recites the consideration, and generally contains a release and default provisions. A lawsuit that is settled is terminated by a dismissal, a withdrawal, or a stipulated judgment.

11–2

A summary judgment motion is granted where the court finds that (1) there is no genuine issue as to any material fact and (2) the moving party is entitled to judgment as a matter of law. Motions for summary judgment are usually supported by a brief; the opposing brief can argue either that (1) there is a genuine dispute as to a material fact, of (2) even if there is no such dispute, the court should find against the moving party based on the controlling law.

11–3

In a jury trial, the jury is the trier-of-fact. In a bench trial, the judge is the trier-of-fact. A trial notebook includes a great deal of basic information, such as an exhibit list, proposed witness questions, copies of pleadings, and an outline of opening and closing arguments, which helps the attorney who is trying the case. A Motion for Directed Verdict is filed when the moving party asserts, at the end of the evidence, that the other party has offered insufficient evidence to support a verdict in its favor. Jury instructions are provided by the judge to the jury to inform the jurors of the legal principles and rules that they must follow in reaching their conclusions. A verdict is the decision reached by a jury; a judgment is the official, written decision of the court (which, in a jury trial, incorporates the verdict). After the trial, a losing party can file a Motion for a New Trial or a Motion for Judgment Notwithstanding the Verdict. The losing party can also appeal.

REVIEW

Key Terms

Before proceeding, review the key terms listed below to be sure you understand each one. If necessary, read over the corresponding section of the chapter. When you are ready to test your understanding, answer the Review Questions.

settlement
settlement agreement
consideration
release
default provision
jurat
order of dismissal
withdrawal
stipulated judgment
summary judgment
jury trial
trial before the court
bench trial
trial notebook
Motion for Directed Verdict
jury instructions
judgment
verdict
default
default judgment
Motion for a New Trial
Motion for Judgment Notwithstanding the Verdict
appeal

Questions for Review and Discussion

1. What is a settlement agreement?
2. What is meant by consideration?
3. What is the importance of a release?
4. How does a corporation execute a document?
5. Explain the difference between an order of dismissal, a withdrawal, and a stipulated judgment.

6. What are the two basic assertions that are made by a party filing a Motion for Summary Judgment?
7. What is the difference between a jury trial and a bench trial?
8. What is the function of a trial notebook?
9. What are jury instructions?
10. What is the difference between a judgment and a verdict?

Activities

1. Review the facts in the Internal Memorandum of Law from Chapter 6 and draft a Motion for Summary Judgment as submitted by the Client.
2. Negotiate a settlement based on the facts in the Appellate Brief in Chapter 12 and draft the settlement agreement that is the result of your negotiation.

NOTES

CHAPTER 12 The Appellate Brief

OUTLINE

COMMENTARY

Closing arguments have concluded a court trial in which you have been the assisting paralegal, and the judge informs counsel that a decision will be rendered after trial briefs are submitted. Briefs are then filed and both sides nervously await the result.

Within a week the decision arrives in your office mail. The judge has denied the permanent injunction sought by your supervising attorney—in short, your client has lost. The supervising attorney reviews the opinion, determines that there are valid reasons to question the judge's reasoning, consults with the client, and decides that she will file an appeal.

The next morning there is a memorandum on your desk. You have been assigned to assist in the legal research and preparation of the appellate brief.

OBJECTIVES

In Chapter 10 you learned how to prepare a brief (or memorandum of law) to the trial court. In this chapter we consider the briefs that are filed with the appellate court if the decision of the trial court is appealed. After completing this chapter, you will be able to:

1. Explain the importance of following the appellate rules.
2. Explain the function of the appellate brief.
3. Identify the components of the record on appeal.
4. Differentiate errors of fact from errors of law.
5. Describe the jurisdictional statement section of an appellate brief.
6. Explain the "road map" function of the table of contents.
7. Identify two key points to remember in drafting the statement of facts section.
8. Use point headings to divide the body of your brief into distinct segments.
9. Make a public policy argument.
10. Distinguish between an appellant's brief, an appellee's brief, a reply brief, and an *amicus curiae* brief.

12–1 A Preliminary Note About Procedural Rules

Although this chapter addresses the preparation of the appellate brief, a proper examination of that subject requires that we consider two preliminary steps essential to *all* phases of an appeal, from its initiation through the briefing phase, and even beyond. These preliminary steps relate to the content of the rules of your specific jurisdiction.

Appealing the decision of a trial court is a complicated process. It involves extensive technical requirements. Before the appellate court will review your client's arguments, it must be satisfied that posttrial motions, briefs, and other filings comply with specific, detailed criteria. This is true in every appellate court, state or federal.

Fortunately, these criteria are spelled out in the **appellate rules** of each jurisdiction. Although there are many broad similarities among the rules of various appellate courts, a word of caution is in order. There are often significant differences on specific formats, filing deadlines, and other particulars. Furthermore, the rules can be strict in their requirements (see Figure 12–1, which reproduces sections of Rule 32 of the Federal Rules of Appellate Procedure and Rule 33 of the U.S. Supreme Court Rules). Failure to follow with precision the rules that apply to your jurisdiction can be fatal to your appeal. Never assume anything; check to make sure.

The *first step* in pursuing an appeal, then, is to obtain a copy of the applicable rules of your jurisdiction, and to verify that they are current.

The *second step*, having obtained the current rules, is obvious but commonly disregarded. Simply stated, you must read the rules, and make sure you understand them.

The importance of the two steps cannot be overemphasized for the preparation of the appellate brief as well as every other aspect of an appeal. They are critical. Although the attorney for whom you work is ultimately responsible for compliance with the rules, your value as an assisting paralegal is directly related to your ability to follow the detailed requirements that govern the appeal process.

Figure 12–1 Appellate Brief Requirements

Federal Rules

Rule 32. Form of Briefs, the Appendix, and Other Papers

(a) Form of Briefs and the Appendix. Briefs and appendices may be produced by standard typographic printing or by any duplicating or copying process which produces a clear black image on white paper. Carbon copies of briefs and appendices may not be submitted without permission of the court, except in behalf of parties allowed to proceed in forma pauperis. All printed matter must appear in at least 11 point type on opaque, unglazed paper. Briefs and appendices produced by the standard typographic process shall be bound in volumes having pages 6 1/8 by 9 1/4 inches and type matter 4 1/6 by 7 1/6 inches. Those produced by any other process shall be bound in volumes having pages not exceeding 8 1/2 by 11 inches and type matter not exceeding 6 1/2 by 9 1/2 inches, with double spacing between each line of text. In patent cases the pages of briefs and appendices may be of such size as is necessary to utilize copies of patent documents. Copies of the reporter's transcript and other papers reproduced in a manner authorized by this rule may be inserted in the appendix; such pages may be informally renumbered if necessary.

If briefs are produced by commercial printing or duplicating firms, or, if produced otherwise and the covers to be described are available, the cover of the brief of the appellant should be blue; that of the appellee, red; that of an intervenor or *amicus curiae*, green; that of any reply brief, gray. The cover of the appendix, if separately printed, should be white. The front covers of the briefs and of appendices, if separately printed, shall contain: (1) the name of the court and the number of the case; (2) the title of the case (see Rule 12(a)); (3) the nature of the proceeding in the court (e.g., Appeal; Petition for Review) and the name of the court, agency, or board below; (4) the title of the document (e.g., Brief for Appellant, Appendix); and (5) the names and addresses of counsel representing the party on whose behalf the document is filed.

Rules of the Supreme Court

Rule 33 Printing Requirements

1. (a) Except for papers permitted by Rules 21, 22, and 39 to be submitted in typewritten form (see Rule 34), every document filed with the Court must be printed by a standard typographic printing process or be typed and reproduced by offset printing, photocopying, computer printing, or similar process. The process used must produce a clear, black image on white paper. In an original action under Rule 17, 60 copies of every document printed under this Rule must be filed; in all other cases 40 copies must be filed.

(b) The text of every document, including any appendix thereto, produced by standard typographic printing must appear in print as 11-point or larger type with 2-point or more leading between lines. The print size and typeface of the United States Reports from Volume 453 to date are acceptable. Similar print size and typeface should be standard throughout. No attempt should be made to reduce or condense the typeface in a manner that would increase the content of a document. Footnotes must appear in print as 9-point or larger type with 2-point or more leading between lines. A document must be printed on both sides of the page.

(c) The text of every document, including any appendix thereto, printed or duplicated by any process other than standard typographic printing shall be done in pica type at no more than 10 characters per inch. The lines must be double spaced. The right-hand margin need not be justified, but there must be a margin of at least three-fourths of an inch. In footnotes, elite type at no more than 12 characters per inch may be used. The document should be printed on both sides of the page, if practicable. It shall not be reduced in duplication. A document which is photographically reduced so that the print size is smaller than pica type will not be received by the Clerk.

What follows is a discussion of those elements of an appellate brief that are in large measure uniform across all jurisdictions. This discussion is intended to provide you with the background and insight necessary to follow your own local rules. Mastering the elements described will prepare you to assist in preparation of an appellate brief. But remember: there is no substitute for a thorough understanding of the precise requirements of the specific appellate court in which your brief will be filed.

Know the rules!

12–2 The Appellate Brief Defined

In order to understand the purpose of an appellate brief, and thus properly prepare it to achieve your objective, it is necessary to consider the context in which the brief is drafted and the role it plays in the appellate process.

An **appellate brief** is a legal document filed with an appellate court and drafted so as to persuade that court to decide contested issues in favor of the filing party. The appellate court uses the appellate briefs filed by the parties to gain familiarity with the facts and controlling law of the case. The appellate brief that you and your supervising attorney prepare will not present this information objectively, however, but will argue from your client's viewpoint, with the goal of convincing the court of the validity of your client's position. An example of an appellate brief appears as the Appendix to this chapter.

After reviewing the arguments set forth in the briefs, the appellate court often allows the parties to elaborate on their positions in oral argument. The attorneys appear before the court and verbally present their competing positions, emphasizing the strong points and clarifying any complex or confusing points. The oral argument stage also enables the appellate judges to directly question the attorneys on specific points that require further explanation.

The appellate court will not always allow oral argument, however. Thus, you must prepare the appellate brief as if it is your only opportunity to present your client's position. Use skill and care; each word must count.

There are two key elements of the context in which the appellate brief is filed: (1) the records; and (2) the standard of review.

The Record

At trial, having defined the disputed issues in the pleadings, the parties began the presentation of evidence with a blank slate. They could bring to the attention of the court any and all facts that were relevant and material, and were free to cite to any and all legal authorities deemed applicable. With a few technical exceptions, such as failure to disclose information during the discovery stage (which need not concern us here), there were generally no prior restraints on the introduction of evidence, nor was there any limitation on the right to formulate legal arguments.

The situation is quite different on appeal. The parties do not start with a blank slate in an appellate court. *No* new evidence is presented on appeal. The appellate court considers only whether, based upon the evidence and legal arguments already offered in the trial court, the trial court in fact reached the correct conclusion. If a particular piece of evidence or legal argument was not at least offered in the trial court, as a rule it will not be considered by the appellate court.

This brings us to consideration of the **record**. The record is the documentation of the trial, including pleadings; briefs; physical evidence introduced; a transcript of the proceedings, including all witness testimony and judge's rulings on admissibility of evidence and testimony; and the decision of the trial court.

It is the record on which the appellate court will rely in evaluating the appeal. A consideration of the individual components of the record is worthwhile.

Pleadings The **pleadings** appearing in the record include the complaint, which defines the underlying claim; the answer and special defenses, which define the response to the complaint; and all cross-claims and responses thereto. The pleadings establish the bounds of the lawsuit.

Briefs The briefs filed by the parties in the lower court are often part of the record as well, and can set the stage for the legal arguments addressed in the appellate court.

Physical Evidence All exhibits admitted into evidence by the trial court, as well as those exhibits offered into evidence but denied admission by the trial court, are part of the record. The issues on appeal often result from the trial court's rulings on admissibility of the **physical evidence**.

Transcript The **transcript** is a written account of all proceedings in the trial court, including questions and comments of the attorneys; witness testimony; and the judge's rulings and comments. The transcript is usually a stenographic record created by a **court reporter** (who is a court employee certified to record and transcribe court proceedings).

Decision of the Trial Court The decision of the trial court, and any written opinion of the judge explaining her reasoning, is always a part of the record.

The Standard of Review

As stated, the issue on appeal is whether, based on the evidence and legal arguments presented at trial, the trial court decided the case correctly. You and your supervising attorney will be scouring the record to determine whether the lower court made any errors in reaching its conclusion. If errors are found and an appeal taken, the appellate court must then evaluate these alleged errors and determine whether reversal of the lower court is justified or, rather, that the lower court be upheld. The guideline that the court applies in evaluating the alleged errors is called the **standard of review**.

There are two types of error to which a standard of review must be applied: errors of fact and errors of law.

Errors of Fact The parties at trial often present competing versions of the facts. The trial court must sift through the evidence and decide which version of the facts is correct. The party whose version was not accepted by the trial court has the right to appeal the decision, on the ground that the facts as found by the trial court are not supported by the evidence that was admitted—in other words, that there was an **error of fact**. The standard of review by which the appellate court evaluates such an appeal, however, is extremely difficult to satisfy. In general, an appellate court shows great deference to the trial court's judgment with regard to fact finding. Only if the facts found by the court are wholly unsupported by the record can a decision be overturned based on errors of fact. For example, a trial court's factual findings with regard to an injunction application (as in our Commentary problem) will be overturned in most jurisdictions only if the appellate court finds that the trial court's interpretation of the facts constituted an **abuse of discretion**, meaning that it was completely unreasonable and not logically based upon the facts.

Errors of Law The more common basis of appeal is an **error of law**. Errors of law include procedural errors, in which the trial court allowed the lawsuit to proceed in a manner not authorized by the rules; evidentiary errors, where the court admitted evidence that should have been excluded, or excluded evidence which should have been admitted; and substantive errors, where the court incorrectly interpreted the specific rules of law applicable to the facts of the case. Procedural or evidentiary errors must be shown to have caused harm to the appellant's position for a reversal to be granted (another term for this is that the appellant was "prejudiced" by the error). Otherwise it is considered to be **harmless error**, and the original decision is allowed to stand. Where errors are substantive, the appellate court will generally reverse if its interpretation of the law differs from that of the trial court.

12–3 The Sections of an Appellate Brief

There are several basic sections to an appellate brief required by the rules of virtually all appellate courts. Though the precise title of each section, as well as its order of appearance in the finished brief, may differ between jurisdictions, the substantive content is universal. Keeping in mind, then, that you should refer to your own local rules for specific guidance, what follows is a general discussion of the sections:

- Title or Cover Page
- Certificate of Interested Parties
- Table of Contents
- Table of Authorities
- Jurisdictional Statement
- Statement of the Case
- Questions Presented
- Statement of Facts
- Argument
- Conclusion
- Signature Block
- Certificate of Service
- Appendix

Title or Cover Page

The first page of an appellate brief is called the **title page** or the cover page. The title page identifies:

- the *court* in which the appeal is pending;
- the *lower court* in which the case originated;
- the *names of the parties* involved in the appeal;
- the *docket number* of the case;
- the name of the *party on whose behalf* the brief is being filed;
- the name of the *attorney* or *law firm* filing the brief; and
- the *date* of filing.

Some courts also require that, if oral argument is desired, it be requested on the title page. If your appeal is pending in such a court, failure to include this request may waive your client's right to demand oral argument at a later stage. This can damage the outcome of the appeal. Part of your responsibility as a paralegal, then, is to know your jurisdiction's rule for requesting oral argument.

When the list of parties involved in an appeal is long, some jurisdictions allow the use of the abbreviation *et al.*, which means "and others," to substitute for a full listing. Again, check your local rules.

A question always arises as to the order in which parties are listed in the appellate caption. In the past, the party making the appeal was generally listed first. This could lead to confusion when a defendant was making the appeal, however, since a case known as *Smith v. Jones* in the trial court (with Smith being the plaintiff and Jones the defendant) would become *Jones v. Smith* in the appellate court. The modern practice is to retain the caption order as it appeared in the lower court and simply identify the parties as appellant or appellee. Of course, you must check your own local rules on this point.

Some courts require that the color of the title page correspond to the status of the filing party. Thus, an appellant might have a light blue title page, an appellee a red title page, and an ***amicus curiae*** (literally, "friend of the court," discussed further in section 12–4) a green title page. Jurisdictions are not consistent on this practice, so again you must check.

A title page appears in Figure 12–2, (see page 480) with various components identified.

The Certificate of Interested Parties

The **certificate of interested parties** identifies all those parties to the case who have an interest in the outcome. It appears immediately after the title page (see chapter Appendix) and is intended to provide the appellate judge with an opportunity to determine the existence of a conflict between her own financial and personal interests and those of a party to the appeal.

If the judge determines that a conflict exists, she will exercise the **recusal** option. A recusal occurs when the judge voluntarily disqualifies herself from further participation in the disposition of the case.

Some jurisdictions do not require the certificate of interested parties. Check your local rules.

Table of Contents

Although the **table of contents** exists primarily to identify section headings with corresponding page numbers, it is far more than just an index. It is, rather,

Figure 12–2 Format of Title Page

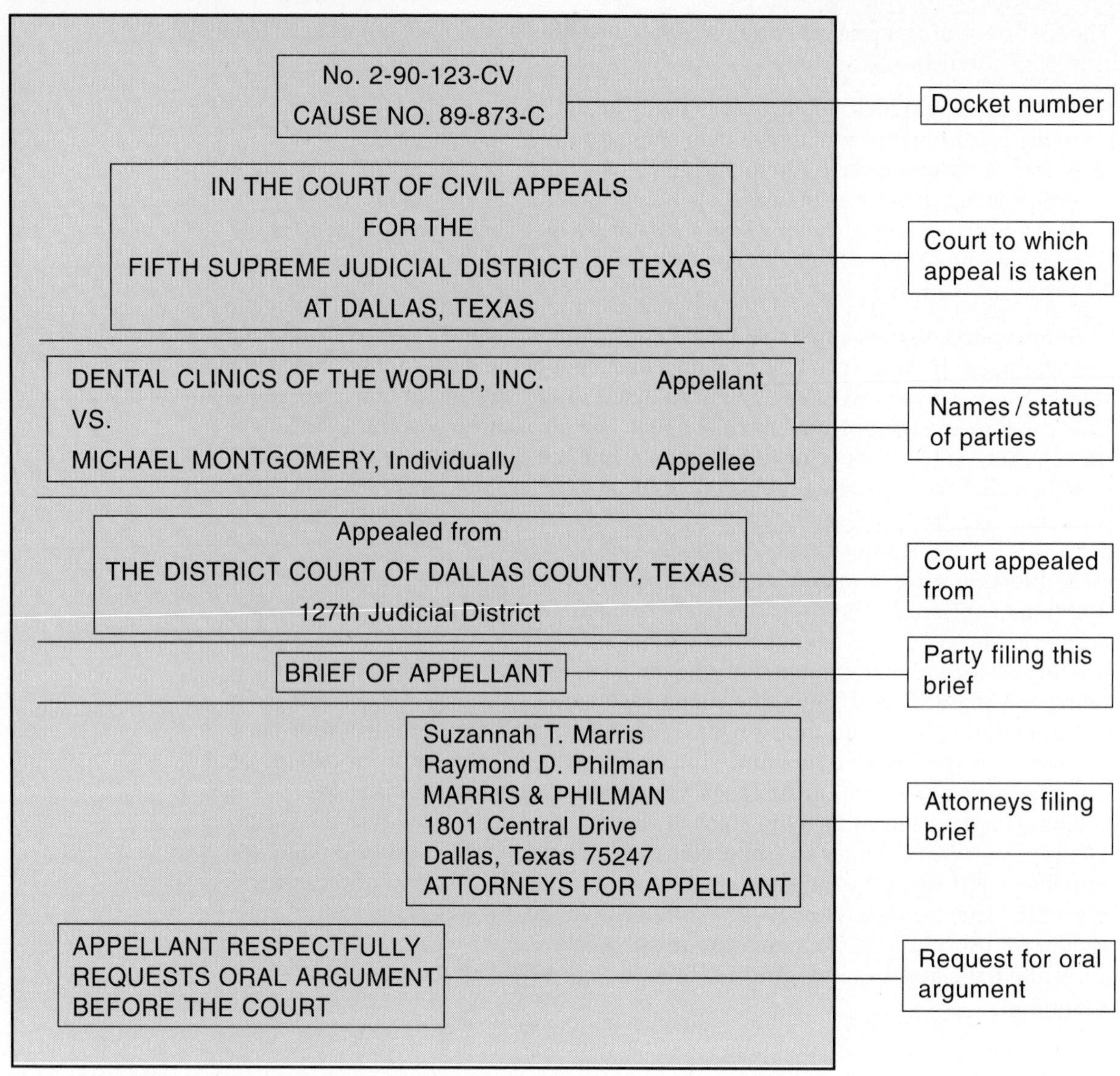

a concise outline of your client's contentions, the road map by which the court will follow the path of your argument.

No. 2-90-123-CV
CAUSE NO. 89-873-C
Docket number
IN THE COURT OF CIVIL APPEALS
FOR THE
FIFTH SUPREME JUDICIAL DISTRICT OF TEXAS
AT DALLAS, TEXAS
Court to which appeal is taken
DENTAL CLINICS OF THE WORLD, INC. Appellant
VS.
MICHAEL MONTGOMERY, Individually Appellee
Names / status of parties
Appealed from
THE DISTRICT COURT OF DALLAS COUNTY, TEXAS
127th Judicial District
Court appealed from
BRIEF OF APPELLANT
Party filing this brief
Suzannah T. Marris
Raymond D. Philman
MARRIS & PHILMAN
1801 Central Drive
Dallas, Texas 75247
ATTORNEYS FOR APPELLANT
Attorneys filing brief
APPELLANT RESPECTFULLY
REQUESTS ORAL ARGUMENT
BEFORE THE COURT
Request for oral argument

The "road map" objective is achieved through expanded reference to the "argument" section. As will be discussed further, point headings and subpoint headings in the argument section identify, in an orderly and logical fashion, the rationale behind your client's position on appeal. In the table of contents, the complete text of each of these headings is set forth. Thus, simply by referring to the table of contents the court will be able to learn the broad parameters of your argument before exploring the details. Review the table of contents that appears in Figure 12–3.

Although the table of contents is one of the first sections to appear in your brief, it is one of the last sections you will draft. This is because page numbers, and perhaps even the text of the point headings, will not be finalized until you approach completion of the project.

Figure 12–3

Table of Contents

Table of Authorities

The term **table of authorities** refers to the cases, statutes, constitutional provisions, and all other primary and secondary sources that are cited in your brief. Since both the court and opposing parties will be examining these sources in detail, is is useful to have an easily referenced list. Although the requirements for the table of authorities may vary in different jurisdictions, Table 12–1 on page 482 provides a common format. References appearing in the table of authorities should be drafted in conformity with the rules of *A Uniform System of Citation* (discussed in Chapter 1 and commonly known as the bluebook) unless your appellate court has its own special requirements. The table should also reference every page on which each authority appears in the brief. (See chapter Appendix.)

As with the table of contents, the table of authorities is one of the last sections prepared. Accuracy in both is important. If inaccurate and sloppy, they will undermine the court's confidence in the credibility of your arguments.

Preparing these tables is a task often left to paralegals. Great care should be taken.

Jurisdictional Statement

The **jurisdictional statement** identifies the legal authority that grants to the appellate court jurisdiction over the appeal. It usually makes reference to the statute establishing the right of appeal. The jurisdiction conferred by such a statute is a prerequisite to the appeal. (See chapter Appendix.)

Table 12–1 Table of Authorities

Case Opinions	Judicial decisions are listed first and *alphabetically* (some states require cases ranked by court: The U.S. Supreme Court, the U.S. Courts of Appeal, etc.). List each page number where case appears.
Constitutional Provisions	Federal constitutional provisions are listed first, with state constitutional provisions to follow. List the provisions in descending numerical order.
Statutory Provisions	Federal statutory provisions are listed after constitutional provisions; state statutes follow. As with the constitutional provisions, list in descending numerical order.
Secondary Authority	Secondary authorities are listed last, alphabetically by author. Secondary authorities range from legal periodicals to treatises, and include all other sources that are neither case decisions, constitutional provisions, nor statutes.

Statement of the Case

The **statement of the case** sets forth the procedural history of the case. It identifies the lower court or courts in which the case has been heard and the decision of each. It is analogous to the "prior proceedings" section of a case brief. (See chapter Appendix.)

There are several different titles in use for this section besides "statement of the case." Others include "preliminary statement," "nature of the action," or "nature of the case." The case history information is also frequently incorporated into the statement of facts.

Your statement of the case should include the following items:

- a concise statement of the nature of the cause of action (one or two sentences), not to be confused with the detailed statement of facts;
- whether the appeal is from a court trial, a jury trial, or a hearing;
- the name of the court whose decision is being appealed;
- the name of other courts that have had jurisdiction over the case, and the nature of their disposition; and
- the party bringing the appeal.

Questions Presented

In the **questions presented** section of the brief, you provide the appellate court with a convenient, concise statement of the grounds upon which the decision of the trial court is being questioned. For each ground, there should be a separately numbered question.

Although at first glance it might appear that drafting these questions is an objective task, in fact, you should be applying your persuasive skills. The questions should be framed so as to suggest an answer that favors your client. Useful techniques include:

- identifying the erroneous ruling of the lower court and suggesting, in question form, the result you seek;
- keeping the questions short, clear, and succinct;
- presenting separate issues in separate questions; and
- identifying the applicable standard of review.

Figure 12–4 Examples of Contrasting Versions of a "Question Presented"

From the appellant's perspective:

Did the District Court err and abuse its discretion by denying appellant's application for a temporary injunction, since appellant proved a probable right and probable injury and thereby established sufficient grounds to impose an injunction and preserve the status quo?

From the appellee's perspective:

Was the District Court correct in denying plaintiff's request for an injunction?

The "questions presented" section is sometimes referred to as "points of error," "issues presented," or "assignments of error." As always, check your local rules.

In Figure 12–4, two questions are set forth that were drafted by opposing sides on the same appeal. Note the manner in which the appellant and appellee have stated the same basic issue in a contrasting, and partisan, fashion.

Statement of Facts

The **statement of facts** is the first of the two major sections of the appellate brief, the other being the argument. In it you set forth the background information and significant facts of your client's case, so that the appellate court has a clear factual framework within which to consider the legal questions presented. (See chapter Appendix.)

The statement of facts is not based upon your memory of events in the case, nor is it based upon those facts which you believe you can prove, since there is no opportunity to "prove" facts on appeal. It is based, rather, on the record of the case. If a fact is not contained in the record of the case, then, for the purposes of the appellate court, that fact simply doesn't exist.

There are two key points to remember in drafting your statement of facts:

- every fact set forth should be followed by a reference in parentheses to that portion of the record in which the fact appears; and
- the statement of facts should be drafted in a persuasive fashion, setting forth the facts in a light most favorable to your client, while at the same time remaining accurate, straightforward, and faithful to the record.

The first of these points, making reference to the record, is easy to understand but often difficult to accomplish. The record of a trial court can be bulky. Many trials are lengthy, and the transcript can run to hundreds of pages or more, with a large number of exhibits. Sometimes the exhibits themselves are lengthy and complicated documents, the meaning of which is disputed by the parties.

There is no magic solution to mastering the record. Simply stated, you must study the transcript and exhibits until you develop a full understanding of their content. It is likely that, in your role as a paralegal, you will be responsible for having a good working knowledge of the record. You will be expected to locate references quickly. Your supervising attorney may draft a statement of facts without parenthetical references, and then expect you to provide the missing information.

One method that is useful for mastering the record is the **indexing method**. By preparing an index to the transcript—for example, identifying (1) the party testifying, (2) the attorney conducting the examination, (3) the content of the testimony, and (4) the transcript page on which the testimony appears, you will have a useful shorthand reference enabling you to locate specific items quickly. An index can also be used to summarize documentary exhibits.

Indexes are sometimes also called "digests." Although some might say that a "digest" suggests a summary more detailed than an index, the difference is largely semantic, and the purpose of each is identical—namely, to summarize a lengthier document.

Different appellate courts have different rules with regard to referencing the record. For example, references to the transcript might be identified by "(T-78)," meaning "page 78 of the transcript," or a variation such as "(R-78)," meaning "page 78 of the record." You should check your local rules for the appropriate style in your jurisdiction.

Though a tedious task, providing comprehensive parenthetical references is very important to the success of your brief. By identifying all those portions of the record that support your factual claims, you not only provide a useful summary of the record but also establish credibility in the eyes of the court. A thorough and well-referenced statement of facts provides the foundation on which you build your arguments and persuade the appellate court.

The second point requires that your statement of facts be not only honest and accurate but also partisan. Although on the face of it this might seem to be inconsistent, in fact it goes to the essence of persuasive legal writing. In order to set the stage for your legal arguments, you want the court to interpret the facts in a light most favorable to your client. At the same time, you do not want the court to think that you are distorting the record. In order to accomplish these objectives, you should employ several techniques:

- set forth the facts in chronological order, which is the easiest and most logical to follow;
- emphasize those facts which support your client's position; and
- when negative facts are essential to an accurate presentation, resist the temptation to omit them, since this will erode your credibility in the eyes of the court (you can be sure that the other side will draw such facts to the court's attention anyway). You should address these negative facts in such a way that their impact is minimized.

Argument

The most important section of the appellate brief is known as the **argument**. In this section you analyze the legal issues raised by the "questions presented" section and interpret the applicable cases and statutes to demonstrate that your client's position should prevail on appeal.

The argument section of an appellate brief is the highest point of persuasive legal writing. Its preparation represents the climax of all your training in written advocacy. The success or failure of your appeal will turn in large measure on your ability to state logically and forcefully, in writing, your client's position. Every stylistic decision has an impact; every substantive choice a consequence; every word an effect.

The argument section comprises two components, the point headings and the body. (See chapter Appendix.)

Point Headings **Point headings** are brief synopses of the argument to follow, set apart from the body of the brief by underlines or type style. (See chapter Appendix.) They perform both a stylistic function, in that they divide the brief into distinct sections for easier reading, and a substantive function, in that they separate the argument into logical components. They provide concise answers to the questions posed in the "questions presented" section, thus giving the court a preview of the detailed argument, and in general, introduce the complex reasoning to follow.

The level of complexity of the brief determines the number of point headings. Isolate the distinct legal issues presented, and begin the discussion of each separate issue with a new point heading.

If the discussion of a given legal issue is complex, you may need subpoint headings as well. In deciding whether subpoint headings are needed, you must keep in mind that too many subpoint headings may actually confuse the reader. If you decide that subpoint headings are justified, choose a format or type style that clearly distinguishes subpoint headings from point headings, so as to maintain clarity.

The brief in the Appendix shows both point headings and subpoint headings. In reviewing this brief, note both the substantive content of the headings and the manner in which capitalization, indenting, spacing, and underlining are used to differentiate headings from the body, and point headings from subpoint headings.

Body The **body** of the argument is the section in which the main text is set forth. (See the chapter Appendix.) It is here that you inform the court of the detailed arguments that support your client's position.

The sole purpose of the body of the brief is to present the law so as to persuade the court. Although this purpose may appear obvious, many attorneys and paralegals lose sight of this consideration when drafting a brief. The problem arises as a result of the interpretation that the drafter attaches to the term "detailed argument." Appellate courts often see briefs that exhaustively document the issue presented, but fail to persuade. You must keep in mind that your job is not to draft a treatise on the issues raised, but rather to persuade the court to resolve the issues in favor of your client. This requires that you cite essential sources and discuss relevant concepts, hence the word "detailed." It does not require that you cite every source, nor discuss every concept, that might arguably be deemed relevant to your brief.

If the issue presented is not complex (or even in many cases where it *is* complex), it is possible that one or two controlling cases and one or two applicable statutes may adequately define and support your argument. If you address such a context in an excessively complicated manner, you dilute the impact of these essential authorities.

Remember that deciding upon the final content of a brief is often a balancing act between simplifying the issues for ease of understanding on the one hand, and accurately reflecting the state of the law on the other. Your goal is a brief that is easy to understand, thorough, and an accurate and defensible representation of the law—in a word, *persuasive*. In achieving this goal, you should follow the basic rules and techniques of writing that we addressed in previous chapters, including clarity and brevity. In addition, keep in mind the following points:

- Place your strongest point first.
- The court will be relying on precedent, not your personal theories. When the law is on your side, *tell* the court. When it is not, distinguish the precedents by pointing out factual or other differences between their context and that of your appeal. It is almost always advisable to avoid the temptation to improvise theory.
- Where the case law is against you, argue that "justice and fair play"

compel the court to find for your client and reverse the precedents. This is the so-called **equitable argument**.

- *Never* misrepresent facts or case law to the court.
- A court is often persuaded by **public policy arguments**. Whether your case is supported by precedent or not, it is always useful to show the court how a decision in your favor will benefit the public interest.
- **String citations** (long lists of cases that you claim support your point) may actually undercut your argument, if the significance of the most important precedent is diluted. The trend is to cite the one best and/or most recent case for your point.

Conclusion

The **conclusion** is a brief statement appearing after the "argument" section. It does not summarize your argument, but rather "respectfully submits" that, based upon the logic of your argument, the court must grant the relief you desire. In other words, the appellant concludes that the trial court should be reversed, whereas the appellee concludes that it should be upheld.

The key here is to be specific. Do not leave the court to guess at the relief you seek—*tell* the court. (See chapter Appendix.)

Signature Block

The **signature block** provides a line for the signature of the attorney who is ultimately responsible for the brief. His name, address, and telephone number are typed below the signature. The client on whose behalf the brief is filed is also identified, and sometimes other information as well. (See chapter Appendix.) Check your local rules for the specific requirements in your jurisdiction.

Certificate of Service

The **certificate of service** is an acknowledgment at the end of any court-filed document, including an appellate brief, that verifies delivery of the document to all persons entitled to a copy, and identifies the date and type of service. (See chapter Appendix.) Mail delivery is usually sufficient.

Those entitled to service generally include the attorneys in the case, as well as parties who represent themselves without the assistance of an attorney. Sometimes the certification must also verify that a copy was served upon the court.

The certificate of service is attested to by the attorney filing the brief. Your local rules will provide specific guidance.

Appendix

Appellate briefs often contain an **appendix**, which is a supplementary collection of primary source materials. Most of these materials are taken from the record. In many jurisdictions it is mandatory to include certain portions of the record in the appendix, for example, those pages from the transcript that are referenced in the text of the appellate brief.

The appendix appears as the last section in the brief. In addition to transcript pages, it often contains relevant passages from pleadings, evidentiary exhibits introduced at trial, and the lower court's judgment and opinion.

12-4 The Four Categories of Appellate Briefs

All appellate briefs share the same basic characteristics outlined. The approach to drafting a specific appellate brief, however, varies somewhat with the procedural status of your client. An appellant, for example, takes a different approach than an appellee, whereas the brief filed by an *amicus curiae* has its own unique emphasis. The stage at which a brief is filed also affects its content, a reply brief being a different creature altogether from an opening brief. It is worthwhile to take a moment and review the differences in emphasis among the four categories of appellate brief: appellant's; appellee's; the reply brief, and that of the *amicus curiae*.

Appellant's Brief

The appellant, as you recall, is the party making the appeal. It is the appellant who asserts that the decision of the trial court must be overturned. Almost without exception, the **appellant's brief** will be filed first. Thus the appellant has the opportunity to set the tone of the appeal and define the issues that will be brought before the appellate court. Although this might appear to be an advantage, any edge inferred is offset by the fact that the appellant is seeking to overturn the judgment of a trial court that has carefully considered the issues and found for the other side. The burden of proving the trial court wrong is on the appellant.

Appellee's Brief

The **appellee's brief** is filed in response to the appellant's brief. Thus the appellee has the appellant's brief in hand as the response is prepared. This enables the appellee to review and attack the specific arguments made by the appellant. In addition to attacking the arguments of the appellant, the appellee should also set forth independent reasons that demonstrate why the lower court should be upheld.

Reply Brief

The term *reply brief* could be attached to any brief filed by a party in response to an earlier brief filed by an opposing party. The appellee's opening brief is thus technically a reply brief, since it is filed after, and in response to, the appellant's brief. In general, however, the term **reply brief** refers to a brief filed by the appellant in response to the appellee's opening brief.

The justification for allowing such a reply brief is simple. It would be unfair to deny the appellant an opportunity to respond to the arguments of the appellee, since the appellee had the opportunity to review and attack the arguments set forth in the appellant's first brief. Hence the appellant is authorized to file a reply brief.

When preparing a reply brief, the appellant should resist the temptation to restate arguments already set forth in the first brief. The court will not forget these earlier arguments. Rather, the appellant should concentrate on addressing issues raised for the first time in the appellee's brief. It is similarly inappropriate (although probably prudent) for the appellant to raise points in the reply brief that it failed, through negligence or oversight, to address in the opening brief. If such points are raised in the reply brief, the court may allow the appellee another chance to respond, or disregard the new points entirely.

Amicus Curiae Brief

An *amicus curiae* is a person or organization that was not directly involved in the lawsuit between the parties, but which has an interest in the outcome of the appeal and has succeeded in petitioning the court for the right to file a brief on the issues presented. An ***amicus* brief** (as it is often called) may correspond to any of the other three categories of brief, depending on whose interest the *amicus* brief mirrors and what stage the appeal has reached. One difference between the *amicus* brief and others is that the *amicus* brief argues from a public policy viewpoint.

12–5 Practical Considerations

An appellate brief is not prepared in a day. Unlike briefing schedules in the trial court, often characterized by tight deadlines imposed by the trial judge, an appellate briefing schedule is generally established by specific rules that set reasonable minimum time periods.

Thus the most important practical consideration in preparing an appellate brief is twofold: first, you have ample time to polish your brief; second, because of this appellate judges *expect* a polished product. You must schedule sufficient time to perform the tasks that go into every appellate brief—reviewing the record; researching the issues; writing a draft; editing; finalizing your draft; preparing the tables of contents and authorities, as well as all other supplements; and reviewing the final version to ensure that it is as polished as you can make it. It's easy to delude yourself into thinking, "The brief's not due for four weeks—I'll do other things first." If you fall into this trap, you'll end up with a major headache—a brief due in a week or less, and insufficient time to prepare it correctly.

There is one other important practical consideration. Remember that this chapter is only an *introduction* to writing the appellate brief, and is not the final word. There are as many opinions on appellate advocacy, briefing strategies, and brief writing as there are on trial advocacy. But all good briefs have a few common characteristics—they are thorough, yet concise; accurate, yet partisan; and most of all, they are *persuasive*.

APPENDIX

1

No. 2-90-123-CV
CAUSE NO. 89-873-C
IN THE COURT OF CIVIL APPEALS
FOR THE
FIFTH SUPREME JUDICIAL DISTRICT OF TEXAS
AT DALLAS, TEXAS

DENTAL CLINICS OF THE WORLD, INC. Appellant

vs.

MICHAEL MONTGOMERY, Individually Appellee

Appealed from
THE DISTRICT COURT OF DALLAS COUNTY, TEXAS
127th Judicial District

BRIEF OF APPELLANT

Suzannah T. Marris
Raymond D. Philman
MARRIS & PHILMAN
1801 Central Drive
Dallas, Texas 75247

ATTORNEYS FOR APPELLANT

APPELLANT RESPECTFULLY
REQUESTS ORAL ARGUMENT
BEFORE THE COURT

Refer to the corresponding key numbers to identify each element of this Brief.

1 — Title or Cover Page
2 — Certificate of Interested Parties
3 — Table of Contents
4 — Table of Authorities
5 — Jurisdictional Statement
6 — Statement of the Case
7 — Questions Presented
8 — Statement of Facts
9 — Argument
10 — Point Heading
11 — Body
12 — Conclusion
13 — Signature Block
14 — Certificate of Service

2

CERTIFICATE OF INTERESTED PARTIES

The following are all the interested parties in this Appeal:

1. Dental Clinics of the World, Inc.
2. Michael Montgomery
3. Joseph Dean

(i)

Table of Contents

(ii)

4

Table of Authorities

UNITED STATES SUPREME COURT

E.I. DuPont De Nemours Power Co. v. Masland, 244 U.S. 100 (1917)

TEXAS SUPREME COURT

City of Spring v. Southwestern Bell Telephone Company, 484 S.W. 2d, 579 (Tex. 1974)

Hyde Corp. v. Huffines, 158 Tex. 566, 314 S.W. 2d 763 (1958)

International Bankers Life Ins. Co. v Holloway, 368 S.W. 2d 567 (Tex. 1963)

K & G Oil Tool & Service Co. v. G & G Fishing Tool Service, 158 Tex. 594, 314 S.W. 2d 782 (1958)

Southland Life Insurance Co. v. Egan, 126 Tex. 160, 86 S.W. 2d 722 (1935)

Texas Foundries, Inc. v. International Moulding & Foundry Workers Union, 151 Tex. 239, 248 S.W. 2d 460 (1952)

Transport Co. of Texas v. Robertson Transports, 152 Tex. 551, 261 S.W. 2d 549 (1953)

TEXAS COURT OF APPEALS

Green v. Stratoflex, Inc., 596 S.W. 2d 305 (Tex. Civ. App., Ft. Worth 1980, no writ)

Jeter v. Associated Rack Corp. 607 S.W. 2d 272 (Tex. Civ. App., Texarkana 1980, writ ref'd n.r.e.) cert. denied, 454 U.S. 965 (1980)

Lamons Metal Gasket Co. v. Traylor, 361 S.W. 2d 211, (Tex. Civ. App., Houston, 1962, writ ref'd n.r.e.)

Morgan v. City of Humble, 598 S.W. 2d 364, (Tex. Civ. App., Houston [14th Dist.] 1980, no writ)

Plagge v. Gambino, 570 S.W. 2d 106 (Tex. Civ. App., Houston [1st Dist.] 1978, no writ)

Texas Shop Towel, Inc. v. Haine, 246 S.W. 2d 482 (Tex. Civ. App., San Antonio 1952, no writ)

Weed Eater v. Dowling, 562 S.W. 2d 898 (Tex. Civ. App., Houston [1st Dist.] 1978, writ ref'd n.r.e.)

JURISDICTIONAL STATEMENT

This court has jurisdiction of this appeal pursuant to the Texas Constitution Art. 5 § 6 and Tex. Civ. Prac. & Rem. Code Ann. § 51.014 5
(Vernon 1986).

STATEMENT OF THE CASE

This case is an appeal from the denial of a temporary injunction. DENTAL CLINICS OF THE WORLD, INC. ("DENTAL CLINIC" or "Appellant") filed suit against MICHAEL MONTGOMERY ("MONTGOMERY" or "Appellee") alleging that Appellee used Appellant's confidential and proprietary information and trade secrets. MONTGOMERY used information that he gained through his employment with DENTAL CLINIC to bid on a servicing dental clinic's contract with Health Care, Inc., Dallas, Texas. The information was DENTAL 6
CLINIC's proprietary, confidential information and trade secrets, which MONTGOMERY acquired and used in violation of his obligations to DENTAL CLINIC. MONTGOMERY also contacted other persons to attempt to establish a business that would compete with Appellant, using DENTAL CLINIC'S information. A temporary injunction hearing was held by the 127th Judicial District Court, Dallas, Texas. On June 20, 1992, the Court entered an Order denying the temporary injunction.

Question Presented

Did the District Court err and abuse its discretion by denying appellant's application for a temporary injunction, since appellant proved a 7
probable right and probable injury and thereby established sufficient grounds to impose an injunction and preserve the status quo?

Fact Statement

DENTAL CLINIC is a Texas corporation specializing in dental clinic services. DENTAL CLINIC offers personnel and equipment (for example, drills, x-ray machines, and other equipment; Tr. 47) to dental clinics in Texas.

In 1980, DENTAL CLINIC employed MICHAEL MONTGOMERY as a salesperson. MONTGOMERY became Vice President of the company in 1986. (Tr. 36) While Vice President, MONTGOMERY had many responsibilities, including hiring employees, purchasing equipment, compiling marketing data, selling the company's services, and dealing with customers. (Tr. 38) Throughout his tenure with DENTAL CLINIC, MICHAEL MONTGOMERY gained confidential knowledge and information.

DENTAL CLINIC's business is service-oriented. Through contracts with its customers, DENTAL CLINIC provides equipment and personnel. The customers are normally small clinics or health centers. (Tr. 45) DENTAL CLINIC 8
installs the equipment and provides the technicians. Only three other companies provided a similar service in Texas. (Tr 31)

To determine whether an area is appropriate for a dental clinic, a sizable amount of research and development takes place. This research and development takes years. (Tr. 51) If competitors obtained this information, thousands of research dollars could be saved, as well as the time spent researching. Having this information would allow a competitor to set up a clinic in an area or forego an area based on DENTAL CLINIC's research.

DENTALCLINIC treated this information as confidential,proprietary data and trade secrets.This information was kept from employees unless needed in their job functions.(Tr. 55) MONTGOMERY was one of the few employees of DENTAL CLINIC who had access to all Company information. (Tr. 55) This information included, but was not limited to, customer lists, supplier lists, pricing lists, clinics, and manufacturers. As an employee and fiduciary of the Company, MONTGOMERY knew this information was confidential and proprietary. (Tr. 56)

MONTGOMERY worked directly with DENTAL CLINIC's customers. In fact, MONTGOMERY worked with clinic administrators and found out that one of DENTAL CLINIC's customers had received a bid from another company. MONTGOMERY was asked to revise DENTAL CLINIC's prior contract and gave the information to the President of DENTAL CLINIC. (Tr. 71) The new bid was resubmitted to the clinic with MONTGOMERY's new prices. (Tr. 72) MONTGOMERY gained all this information while employed with the Company.

On November 17, 1991, MONTGOMERY resigned and terminated his employment with DENTAL CLINIC.(Tr. 95) Not more than one month after he left DENTAL CLINIC, MONTGOMERY formed his own company, DENTAL HEALTH CARE. This company offered the same services as DENTAL CLINIC. (Tr. 98)

8 MONTGOMERY contacted one of DENTAL CLINIC's customers regarding a dental services contract.(Tr. 101) The clinic turned out to be the same clinic MONTGOMERY had revised the pricing for while employed with DENTAL CLINIC. MONTGOMERY did not contact anyone for pricing information. In fact, MONTGOMERY knew his bid would be lower than DENTAL CLINIC's since he had access to the information while employed with DENTAL CLINIC.(Tr. 107) Months later, in January 1992, DENTAL CLINIC was notified that its contract with the clinic would be cancelled and that MONTGOMERY's company would receive the contract. (Tr. 158) MONTGOMERY also contacted other customers of DENTAL CLINIC and attempted to gain their contracts. Clearly, MONTGOMERY knew all DENTAL CLINIC customers, the services performed for them, and the prices charged. This information could only be gained from MONTGOMERY's employment. DENTAL CLINIC sued MONTGOMERY for misappropriation of trade secrets and confidential proprietary information and requested a temporary injunction. This injunction was denied, and the denial has been appealed.

9 ARGUMENT AND AUTHORITIES

10 I. THE TRIAL COURT ABUSED ITS DISCRETION BY NOT GRANTING THE TEMPORARY INJUNCTION.

11 The standard of review for an appeal in a temporary injunction hearing is whether the trial court abused its discretion in granting or denying the temporary injunction. Texas Foundries, Inc. v. International Moulding & Foundry Workers Union, 151 Tex. 239, 248 S.W. 2d 460 (1952); City of Spring v. Southwestern Bell Telephone Company, 484 S.W. 2d 579 (Tex. 1974). In determining whether the granting or denial of a temporary injunction is proper, this Court must look to the record in the trial court and determine whether the party requesting relief is entitled to preservation of status quo of the subject matter pending trial on the merits. Green v. Stratoflex, Inc., 596 S.W. 2d 305 (Tex. Civ. App., Ft. Worth 1980, no writ). In evaluating whether or not the trial court abused its discretion in granting or denying a temporary injunction, this Court must consider whether the trial court erroneously applied the law to undisputed facts, where pleadings and evidence presented a probable right and probable injury. Southland Life Insurance Co. v. Egan, 126 Tex. 160, 86 S.W. 2d 722 (1935); Plagge v. Gambino, 570 S.W. 2d 106 (Tex. Civ. App., Houston [1st Dist.] 1978, no writ); Morgan v. City of Humble, 598 S.W. 2d 364 (Tex. Civ. App., Houston [14th Dist.] 1980, no writ).

2

The purpose of the temporary injunction is to preserve the status quo of a matter in controversy until final hearing on the merits of the case. For a temporary injunction to be issued by a trial court, a party need show only a probable right and a probable injury, and is not required to establish that he will finally prevail in the litigation. Therefore, the burden in a temporary injunction hearing is substantially different than it is in a trial on the merits. The movant has to prove there is a probable right to recovery at a trial on merits, but does not have the burden to prove that he would ultimately prevail at a final hearing. 11
Transport Co. of Texas v. Robertson Transports, 152 Tex. 551, 261 S.W. 2d 549 (1953). At the temporary injunction hearing, DENTAL CLINIC proved that a probable injury was suffered and that DENTAL CLINIC had a probable right to recovery. MONTGOMERY took information from his employer, DENTAL CLINIC, and used the information to injure DENTAL CLINIC. The misappropriation of this information was wrongful, for which DENTAL CLINIC was entitled to relief in the form of a temporary injunction. The trial court abused its discretion by failing to properly apply the law to the facts. DENTAL CLINIC made a proper showing to meet the standards necessary for issuance of an injunction.

II. TEXAS PROHIBITS THE USE OF TRADE SECRETS AND CONFIDENTIAL PROPRIETARY INFORMATION WHEN MISAPPROPRIATED BY A CORPORATE OFFICER. 10

MONTGOMERY was a Vice President of DENTAL CLINIC. The Supreme Court of Texas has held that corporate officers are fiduciaries of the corporation. International Bankers Life Ins. Co. v. Holloway, 368 S.W. 2d 567 (Tex. 1963). Not only do the courts impose a general fiduciary obligation on officers, but additionally, the courts have articulated a specific rule that an employee has a duty not to disclose the confidential matters of its employer. Lamons Metal Gasket Co. v. Traylor, 361 S.W. 2d 211 (Tex. Civ. App., Houston 1962, writ ref'd n.r.e.); Jeter v. Associated Rack Corp., 607 S.W. 2d 272 (Tex. Civ. App., Texarkana 1980, writ ref'd n.r.e.), cert. denied, 454 U.S. 965 (1980). Certain information was considered confidential by DENTAL CLINIC. The undisputed testimony of the President shows that DENTAL CLINIC considered customer lists, renewal dates, and pricing as confidential. (Tr. 57-59) 11

MONTGOMERY disregarded his fiduciary responsibilities to further his own personal endeavors. But for MONTGOMERY's relationship to DENTAL CLINIC, he would not have known the trade secrets and confidential and proprietary information. The law is clear that Texas prohibits the use of confidential information by a former corporate officer. Weed Eater v. Dowling, 562 S.W. 2d 898 (Tex. Civ. App., Houston [1st Dist.] 1978, writ ref'd n.r.e.)

A. A trade secret by definition may be a compilation of information, including a customer list.

In defining a trade secret, the Texas Supreme Court has adopted the Restatement of Torts, 2nd § 757, which defines a trade secret as follows:

> A trade secret may consist of any formula, pattern, device, or compilation of information which is used in one's business and which gives him an opportunity to obtain an advantage over competitors who do not know or use it. It may be a formula for a chemical compound, a process of manufacturing, treating or preserving materials, a pattern for a machine, or other device, or a list of customers.* * * Trade secret is a process or device

> for continuous use in the operation of the business. Hyde Corp. v. Huffines, 158 Tex. 566, 314 S.W. 2d 763 (1958) (emphasis supplied).
>
> The Restatement of Torts § 757 further states that:
>
> One who discloses or uses another's trade secrets, without a privilege to do so, is liable to the other if (a) he discloses the secret by improper means, or (b) his disclosure or use constitutes a breach of confidence reposed in him by the other in disclosing the secret to him. Hyde Corp. v. Huffines, supra (emphasis supplied).

DENTAL CLINIC had developed confidential and proprietary information that it used in its business. This information gave it an advantage over competitors. For years DENTAL CLINIC compiled information. The information included but was not limited to customer lists, contact persons at clinics, pricing information, financial information, and market planning strategies. (Tr. 57) Information had been exclusively developed through DENTAL CLINIC's financial investment and research and was not readily accessible to outsiders of DENTAL CLINIC without substantial monetary and time investment. This compilation of information is DENTAL CLINIC's trade secrets and proprietary and confidential information, which it uses in the development of its business activities.

MONTGOMERY had access to trade secrets and confidential and proprietary information of DENTAL CLINIC by virtue of his position of confi-
11 dence and trust with the President, Joseph Dean. As the testimony showed, Joseph Dean and MONTGOMERY worked together in the development of DENTAL CLINIC. MONTGOMERY had access to all the information regarding DENTAL CLINIC. The information that MONTGOMERY acquired is a valuable asset of DENTAL CLINIC. A temporary injunction is the only remedy that will protect DENTAL CLINIC's investment. A temporary injunction will preserve the status quo pending a trial on the merits. Without the injunction, DENTAL CLINIC will continue to suffer harm and injury. MONTGOMERY admitted he took information that he gained while employed with DENTAL CLINIC to contact other dental clinics. He made offers and submitted proposals to the clinics. (Tr. 88) Specifically, MONTGOMERY contacted Dental Resources of the Southwest, with whom DENTAL CLINIC had been negotiating a renewal of its contract. MONTGOMERY breached his fiduciary relationship with DENTAL CLINIC by using its proprietary and confidential information and trade secrets. When a vice president breaches his fiduciary duty, it is proper under Texas law to grant a temporary injunction. Weed Easter v. Dowling, 562 S.W. 2d 898 (Tex. Civ. App., Houston [1st Dist.] 1978, writ ref'd n.r.e.).

In any analysis of trade secrets and confidential and proprietary information, the Court must evaluate how the information was acquired. Although it may be argued by MONTGOMERY the information was generally available for someone with time and money to accumulate the information, the fact is clear that the data which MONTGOMERY utilized to compete with his former employer came from DENTAL CLINIC's investment of hundreds of hours and substantial sums of money to accumulate and develop the data. Even if MONTGOMERY could acquire the information, that does not mean that he is entitled, through a breach of confidence, to gain the "information in usable form and escape the efforts of inspection and analysis." K & G

Oil Tool & Service Co. v. G & G Fishing Tool Service, 158 Tex. 594, 314 S.W. 2d 782 (1958). The law in Texas imposed equitable measures against an individual who has breached a fiduciary relationship through a temporary injunction. As the court in its dicta in Weed Eater, Inc. v. Dowling, supra, recognized,

> [W]here an employee will acquire trade secrets by virtue of his employment, the law permits greater restrictions to be imposed on the employee than in other contracts of employment.
>
> Confidential business information is not given protection merely as a reward to its accumulator. The courts condemn employment of improper means to procure trade secrets. The fact that a trade secret is of such a nature that it can be discovered by experimentation or other fair and lawful means does not deprive its owner of the right to protection from those who would secure possession by unfair means (emphasis supplied).

Texas law clearly imposes a responsibility on a corporate officer such as MONTGOMERY not to disclose information gained during employment. The responsibility of the corporate fiduciary is implied and is part of a contract of employment.

Although the appellee would suggest that liability can be imposed only if a written contract existed, this is not the law. In confidential and proprietary information actions, a contract of employment is not necessary to create the right. As Texas Shop Towel, Inc. v. Haine points out:

> [A]n owner may protect a trade secret even in the total absence of any contract with his employees, and the agents and employees who learn of the trade secret or secret formula are prohibited 11
> from its use. In the case of a trade secret, a contract does not create the right, for the right exists by reason of the confidence. It will exist in the total absence of a contract. A contract may be additional evidence of the existence of the trade secret but an owner's rights in his secrets do not depend upon a contract (emphasis supplied). Texas Shop Towel, Inc. v. Haine, 246 S.W.2d 482 (Tex. Civ. App., San Antonio 1952, no writ).

No employment contract is necessary to hold MONTGOMERY legally responsible for his actions.

The testimony and the evidence before this Court are undisputed. MONTGOMERY received DENTAL CLINIC's confidential, proprietary, and trade secret information in confidence as DENTAL CLINIC's employee, and MONTGOMERY was an officer of DENTAL CLINIC and as such was a fiduciary of the corporation. In E.I. DuPont De Nemours Power Co. v. Masland, 244 U.S. 100 (1917), the Supreme Court of the United States recognized the importance of a fiduciary duty and the consequence of a breach of that duty. The Supreme Court in dicta made the following observation:

> [W]hether the Plaintiffs have any valuable secret or not, the Defendant knows the facts, whatever they are, through a special confidence that he accepted. The property may be denied, but the confidence cannot be. Therefore, the starting point for the present matter is not property or due process of law, but that

> the Defendant stood in confidential relations with the Plaintiff, or one of them. These have given place to hostility, and the first thing to be made sure of is that the Defendant shall not fraudulently abuse the trust reposed in him. It is the usual incident of confidential relations. If there is any disadvantage in the fact that he knew the Plaintiff's secrets, he must take the burden with the good. Id., at 102.

The U.S. Supreme Court recognized the rights of an employer over fifty years ago. It is a right that continues today. The only remedy DENTAL CLINIC has is a temporary injunction.

B. An injunction is an appropriate remedy for misappropriation of trade secrets and for the breach of a fiduciary relationship.

The evidence is clear that MONTGOMERY acquired trade secrets and confidential and proprietary information from DENTAL CLINIC while an employee. After his resignation, MONTGOMERY used the trade secrets and confidential and proprietary information of DENTAL CLINIC to his own benefit. Though the information may have been available to a competitor, that availability did not give MONTGOMERY the right to violate his confidential relationship with DENTAL CLINIC. Texas Shop Towel, Inc. v. Haine, supra.

11 By not issuing a temporary injunction and preserving the status quo, the trial judge abused his discretion. The facts in this case are undisputed by the evidence and the testimony.

By applying the undisputed facts to the law, DENTAL CLINIC was entitled to a temporary injunction to preserve the status quo. DENTAL CLINIC proved through the testimony and evidence that it had a probable injury, which would result from (1) MONTGOMERY's utilizing information to undercut DENTAL CLINIC's contract bid, and (2) MONTGOMERY's contacting users of DENTAL CLINIC services. DENTAL CLINIC also showed that there was a probable right to recovery since the information was admittedly gained from MONTGOMERY's employment with DENTAL CLINIC. MONTGOMERY admitted that he learned the information that he utilized to prepare that clinic's contract from his employment with DENTAL CLINIC. The trial court abused its discretion by not granting the temporary injunction as the court did not properly apply the law to the undisputed facts. In Weed Eater v. Dowling, supra, the Houston Court of Appeals recognized that a temporary injunction is a proper remedy when there is a breach of confidence and a misuse of proprietary information and trade secrets. The facts in this case support such a conclusion of probable injury and probable right and the law dictates the issuance of an injunction.

CONCLUSION

In a temporary injunction hearing, DENTAL CLINIC had to show only a probable right to recovery and a probable injury and that there was not an adequate remedy at law. In applying the law to the facts, DENTAL CLINIC showed an injury, MONTGOMERY's interference with a business contract, and a right to recovery arising from MONTGOMERY's use of information gained
12 while employed with DENTAL CLINIC. As a matter of law, this information was confidential and proprietary and trade secrets of DENTAL CLINIC. By not granting the temporary injunction, the trial court erred and abused its discretion by misapplying the law to the facts. DENTAL CLINIC requests that this court instruct the trial court to issue and enter a temporary injunction to preserve the status quo in this case until a final trial on the merits can be heard.

6

DENTAL CLINIC requests that this Honorable Court instruct the trial court to issue and enter a temporary injunction against MONTGOMERY to preserve the status quo until a final trial on the merits by ordering MONTGOMERY not to contact any customers or dentists who are customers of DENTAL CLINIC during the pendency of the litigation.

Respectfully submitted,

____

SUZANNAH T. MARRIS
State Bar #18769283

RAYMOND D. PHILMAN 13
State Bar #27619317

MARRIS & PHILMAN
1801 Central Drive
Dallas, Texas 75247
(214)512-0927

ATTORNEYS FOR APPELLANT

CERTIFICATE OF SERVICE

I certify that a true and correct copy of the foregoing Brief of Appellant has been forwarded to Appellee, by and through their attorney of record, 14 C. J. Coldaway at 617 Renewal Tower, Dallas, Texas, 76202, by certified mail, return receipt requested, on this______day of__________, 1992.

____

Suzannah T. Marris.

SUMMARY

12–1

The first step in pursuing an appeal is to obtain a copy of the current appellate rules applicable in your jurisdiction. The second step is to read and understand them.

12–2

An appellate brief is a legal document filed with an appellate court and drafted so as to persuade that court to decide contested issues in favor of the filing litigant. An appeal is based on the record, which is the written documentation of the trial. The guideline that the court applies in evaluating an appeal is called the standard of review. There are two types of errors to which a standard of review is applied: errors of fact and errors of law.

12–3

There are several basic sections to an appellate brief, which may vary slightly in designation or content from one jurisdiction to the next, but are otherwise always required. The title page identifies the parties and court, and usually also contains the request for oral argument. The certificate of interested parties identifies those parties with a direct interest in the outcome of the case. The table of contents provides section headings with corresponding page numbers, and performs a "road map" function. The table of authorities identifies references cited. The jurisdictional statement identifies the legal authority that grants the appellate court authority over the appeal. The statement of the case sets forth the procedural history of the case. The questions presented section provides a convenient and concise statement of the grounds of the appeal. The statement of facts is based upon the record, and should be both accurate and partisan. The argument is the most important section of an appellate brief, comprised of point headings and the main text or body, and containing the legal and factual positions of the party preparing it. The conclusion identifies the relief sought. A signature block and certificate of service are also included, as well as an appendix containing source materials from the record.

12–4

An appellant's brief is filed first, and sets the tone and defines the issues. The appellee's brief is filed in response to the appellant's brief, and both attacks the appellant's arguments and makes its own arguments. The reply brief is filed by the appellant in response to the appellee's brief. An *amicus curiae* brief is filed by a nonparty presenting public policy arguments.

12–5

Because of the nature of appellate briefing schedules, you have ample time to prepare an appellate brief. However, this means that judges expect a polished product, so make sure that you leave yourself adequate time to do your best work.

REVIEW

Key Terms

Before proceeding, review the key terms listed below to be sure you understand each one. If necessary, read over the corresponding section of the chapter. When you are ready to test your understanding, answer the Review Questions.

appellate rules
appellate brief
record
pleadings
physical evidence
transcript
court reporter

standard of review
errors of fact
abuse of discretion
errors of law
harmless error
title page
amicus curiae
certificate of interested parties
recusal
table of contents
table of authorities
jurisdictional statement
statement of the case
questions presented
statement of facts
indexing method
argument
point headings
body
equitable argument
public policy argument
string citation
conclusion
signature block
certificate of service
appendix
appellant's brief
appellee's brief
reply brief
amicus brief

Questions for Review and Discussion

1. Why is it important to follow the applicable appellate rules?
2. What is the function of the appellate brief?
3. What are the components of the record on appeal?
4. Explain the difference between errors of fact and errors of law.
5. What is a jurisdictional statement?
6. What is the "road map" function of the table of contents?
7. What are two key points to remember when drafting the statement of facts?
8. What are point headings?
9. What is a public policy argument?
10. Describe the different characteristics of the appellant's brief, the appellee's brief, the reply brief, and the *amicus curiae* brief.

Activities

1. Check the federal, state, and local appellate court rules for your jurisdiction and answer the following questions:
   a) When must an appeal be filed?
   b) When must the record be filed? The transcript?
   c) How much time does the appellant have to prepare and file the appellant's brief? The appellee?
   d) List the page length, the paper size, color of cover page, and binding requirements.
2. Compare your state rules of appellate procedure and the Federal Rules of Appellate Procedure, and list the differences in the rules.

CHAPTER 13 Drafting Operative Documents

OUTLINE

COMMENTARY

Your client, Mr. Hardrive, has spent months in his basement developing a computer program that will forecast stock market trends. His program must really work, because a major software manufacturer has expressed an interest in buying and marketing the program.

Mr. Hardrive recently contacted your supervising attorney. He needs help in negotiating a contract with the software company. After a lengthy conference with Mr. Hardrive, your supervising attorney provides you with a list of preliminary terms that Hardrive would like to see in the ultimate contract, copies of two contract forms from a form book, and a letter and proposed contract that Hardrive received from the software manufacturer. She asks you to draft a contract proposal that reflects Hardrive's position, rather than the manufacturer's.

Preparing contracts and other operative documents is a task for which a paralegal must be able to lend his training and assistance.

OBJECTIVES

Legal writing is not limited to correspondence, research memoranda, and litigation documents. After completing this chapter, you will be able to:

1. Explain what is meant by operative documents.
2. Identify the importance of determining client intent.
3. Explain how an operative document becomes a fifth source of law.
4. Explain the usefulness of a form.
5. Identify a possible pitfall when using a model.

6. Explain what a contract is.
7. List several important considerations in a lease.
8. Explain the importance of an accurate property description.
9. Identify who a testator is.
10. Explain the importance of a residuary clause in a will.

13–1 Operative Documents in General

In Chapter 3 we identified a category of documents called **operative documents**. We defined operative documents as those documents which, as a result of their language and content, serve to define property rights and performance obligations. They are drafted to express the intent of the parties who execute them—be they multiple parties with competing interests, as with a contract; or a single party with individual interests, as with a will.

In this section we discuss some characteristics and considerations that apply across the spectrum of operative documents. In the succeeding sections we address specific considerations for contracts, leases and deeds, and wills, then conclude with a few practical considerations.

Client Intent and Approval

The first step in drafting any operative document is to determine the intent of the client. The purpose for, and importance of, determining client intent is quite simple—it is the *client's* rights that will be affected by the operative document. Determining the client's intent is often not as easy as it might sound, however. The client may not be quite sure about what she wants, or the controlling law may prevent the client from obtaining the precise result desired in the manner envisioned.

Two possible situations illustrate the dilemma. First, consider the client who comes to you with a fully negotiated agreement, a transaction complete except for documentation. This client simply wants you to commit to paper, in proper and binding legal form, details already worked out. Be wary in this situation—the client may not fully understand the implications of his agreement; it is for you and your supervising attorney to unravel the mysteries of the substantive law as it applies to the proposed transaction, and determine whether the language of proposed operative documents best reflects the intent and interests of your client.

Second, consider the client who comes to your firm with a wholly different problem—she is seeking representation in negotiating a contract. This client has certain goals in mind, but understands that, in the ebb and flow of negotiation, compromise and flexibility may be necessary. Once again, the substantive law must be sorted and explained; this time legal consideration may vary as the negotiation proceeds into new areas, and the client must be made aware of shifting options and possibilities. Only after receiving full explanation of all alternatives can the client determine and transmit her true intent.

In explaining the meaning of a draft operative document, an attorney or paralegal should explain the need to balance technical legal requirements with practical client needs. The possibility of changed future circumstances, and the effect such changes may impose on the usefulness of a given draft, should be explored as well. Potential risks should be explored and explained, both as they exist on the face of the draft and as they might exist under these changed circumstances.

After determining the client's purpose, informing him of options, and explaining the meaning of a proposed draft, the attorney and paralegal must obtain the client's approval for the finished product. It is often wise to explain the draft in some permanent written form, such as an extended cover letter with an enclosed copy of the draft, both to assist the client in understanding the draft and to protect the law firm if the client later claims to have been misinformed.

The Importance of Clarity

An operative document, as we have noted, creates rights and obligations. It is, in some sense, a law unto itself—for although a court, in considering whether to enforce an operative document, will follow general rules in construing its content, if the format is acceptable and the content within the bounds of the law, then the court will also follow the specific guidelines established by the parties.

For this reason, it is extremely important that an operative document reflect the intent of the parties. Clarity in drafting is essential; the words used must accomplish the purpose sought.

The need for clarity doesn't mean that there isn't sometimes a place for ambiguous language, however odd it may seem. There are situations where the parties to a contract, for example, struggle to reach agreement on certain issues but simply can't. In the manner of the maxim "agreeing to disagree," the parties may intentionally leave the contract ambiguous as to one or more terms, hoping the need to resolve the ambiguity never arises but, in any event, leaving such resolution for another day. They have sacrificed clarity for the sake of commerce—they have made a deal that would otherwise have been impossible. If you are faced with such a situation, there are two factors to keep in mind: first, be sure to explain carefully the implication of the ambiguity to the client; second, be sure that the ambiguous expression accurately reflects the intent of the parties (in other words, state the ambiguity *clearly*!). An example of an intentionally ambiguous clause is shown in Figure 13–1.

Boilerplate and Form Books

We spoke briefly about **boilerplate** and **forms** in Chapter 3. Many operative documents have common language that must always be used to achieve a desired intent. Hence forms, boilerplate and **form books** (which we touched on briefly, in the context of pleadings, in Chapter 8) can be very helpful in the

Figure 13–1 Example of an Intentionally Ambiguous Clause in a Contract

"The widgets shall be guaranteed against failure for a commercially reasonable period of time, under all the circumstances present herein."

Explanation: The parties to this contract were unable to reach agreement as to the period during which the widgets (which were being sold under the terms of the contract) were to be guaranteed. The seller did not anticipate that his widgets would fail, but was hesitant to commit a specific period to writing; the buyer insisted on a guarantee against failure. The parties compromised on the above clause, which left open and ambiguous the issue of what was a "commercially reasonable period of time."

preparation of operative documents. But there are also pitfalls that need to be avoided.

Forms, as you recall, are printed documents incorporating standardized language and leaving blank spaces for specific information. Boilerplate is a term applied to the standard language in operative documents; to some extent, a form can be thought of as entirely boilerplate, with specific information to be filled in when available. Form books are collections of forms, often from many jurisdictions or covering many areas of the law. Form books can be multivolume collections with an enormous variety of sample provisions.

The usefulness of forms, form books, and boilerplate is apparent. By providing standardized language that reflects the controlling law, they represent a valuable means of shortcutting what could be time-consuming and repetitive research. For example, a simple lease of residential property will likely require virtually the identical boilerplate (and general format) as prior residential leases.

The problem with forms and boilerplate, however, lies in a phrase lurking in the previous paragraph—"reflecting the controlling law." Forms and boilerplate are only valuable as long as they do reflect the controlling law. If the controlling law changes, and the drafter uses an outdated form, the result could be disastrous.

The bottom line: never rely on a form over knowledge of the substantive area addressed. What does this imply in practical terms? Basically, two things: first, understand *why* the form or boilerplate uses the language it does (in other words, research the statutes, regulations, and case law that dictate the requirements in the subject area at issue). Second, keep up with developments in the subject area to assure yourself that the form or boilerplate remains reflective of the controlling law. An example of a problem that might occur when using a form is shown in Figure 13–2.

Figure 13–2 Example of Potential Problem When the Drafter Relies on a Model

Circumstance: Formerly the mechanic's lien statute required that a mechanic's lien had to be filed within 90 days after a job for which services had been performed or materials supplied was completed. If not filed within 90 days, the claim was lost forever. The legislature recently amended the time limit to 60 days.

Clause from preexisting form: "The above-referenced party who is filing this mechanic's lien hereby affirms that the services and/or materials for which payment has not been made were performed and/or supplied for a job that was completed within the 90 days immediately preceding the date of filing of this mechanic's lien."

Explanation: If the drafter relies on the form she may be led to believe that she can wait up to 90 days from the date the work was completed to file the mechanic's lien. Research would have revealed the amendment to a 60-day time limit; the form should have been modified and the lien filed within 60 days.

A special kind of form is a **model**, which we also touched on briefly in Chapter 8. A model is a copy of a completed document taken from one of your firm's files, and which was formerly used to accomplish the same purpose you wish to accomplish with the document you are drafting. By using the model as a guide, you can copy the boilerplate and insert your own specific information where needed. Three factors need to be considered when using a model: first, is it attempting to accomplish the same objective you are seeking to accomplish now? A slight difference in objective can lead to significant differences in content. This is a factor to consider with regard to forms as well; see Figure 13–3.

Figure 13–3 Example of Difference in Objective Requiring Different Model

> **Drafter's intent:** The drafter wants to initiate a lawsuit by filing a complaint that includes a request for attachment.
>
> **Basic law:** A plaintiff who shows "probable cause" of success is entitled to file an attachment on real estate owned by the defendant. The attachment can be made either at the beginning of the suit or after suit is commenced. The petition that demonstrates probable cause must include a copy of the complaint and an affidavit attesting to its truth.
>
> **Problem:** The drafter used as his model a set of papers that were used to obtain an attachment *after* suit had earlier been initiated. The model contained a copy of the complaint, as the law required, but did not contain a summons to court, since the lawsuit had already started. The drafter's papers, based on this model, failed to contain a summons and, when served on the defendant, were defective; hence the suit was not commenced and no attachment was granted.
>
> If the drafter had recognized that his objective, namely commencing suit and obtaining an attachment, was different from the objective of the model (namely, obtaining an attachment *after* suit was started), he would either have used another model, or modified his draft to account for the difference in objective.

Second, did it succeed in accomplishing that objective? Third, has the law changed since the model was used?

Substantive Law

In the following sections on contracts, leases and deeds, and wills, we touch upon some aspects of substantive law in these areas. You should be aware, however, that these subjects, and others that may be the subject of operative documents, are far more complex than represented herein. In drafting operative documents (or for that matter, legal documents of any kind) legal writing skills are never sufficient to overcome lack of understanding of the substantive law.

13–2 Contracts

What is a contract? The question is not easy to answer, but we will try. A **contract** is an enforceable agreement. There you have it—a nice, tidy definition, the implications and complexities of which have filled volumes and require an entire course, and more, in law school.

The law of contracts is filled with words like "consideration" (which we addressed briefly in our discussion of settlement agreements in Chapter 11), "offer and acceptance," "third-party beneficiary," "performance," "breach," and so on. The meaning of most of these terms is readily apparent, at least in a general sense; their specific and detailed quirks in the context of contract law are beyond the scope of this book. But in your role as a paralegal it is almost certain that you will have, from time to time, either the opportunity to draft a contract, or the need to interpret a contract already drafted. In either event, the following comments should be useful.

The meaning of a contract must be clear. To say this is, perhaps, repetitious of comments already made, but in the repetition you may gain a sense of its importance. Since a contract defines the rights and obligations of the parties, its intent should be unambiguous (or ambiguous only as expressly intended by the parties). Furthermore, it must be clear not only to the parties to the agreement, but also to the court that may someday search its provisions to determine that intent.

Beware of using models for drafting contracts. Provisions and laws vary from state to state; circumstances vary from matter to matter. You must be very careful to perform adequate research to assure that a model or form is adequate.

Be sure your document is internally consistent. Particularly when ongoing negotiation changes provisions from draft to draft, it is critical that all provisions affected by a change are altered to reflect the new basis for agreement. Dates, terms of payment, character of performance, and other key terms must be checked and rechecked for consistency.

Terms should be defined. Even if you believe a definition to be widely accepted, it is better to be safe than sorry. Redundancy is less of an evil in contract drafting than in other forms of legal writing; your concern is not that the reader might get bored, but only that the contract represent without doubt the intentions of your client. If you believe it is necessary to state the same basic proposition twice to make the point clear, by all means do so, but make sure that the redundant statement doesn't lead to confusion (as when the person interpreting the contract presumes that every word has an independent meaning, and searches for a new meaning from a phrase you intended as mere restatement).

Another point to ponder is the value of submitting your draft for review by others. It can be very useful to have another person, either another paralegal or another attorney, read your draft at various stages of preparation. Their differing interpretations can assist you in determining where ambiguities lie.

13–3 Leases and Deeds

A **lease**, which relates to the rental of property, is really just a special kind of contract. A **deed** is also, in a sense, a contract—it documents the exchange of land for money (or some other form of consideration). Let's turn to an analysis of these two areas.

Leases

Leases involve two parties: the owner of property, and a party desiring to use that property in some way. By entering into a lease, the parties are able to pursue mutually beneficial interests. The owner receives a payment while retaining ownership of the property, and the other party is able to use the property. The owner is typically referred to as a **landlord** or **lessor**; the user of the property is typically referred to as a **tenant** or **lessee**. Leases can involve material items, such as a car, or **real property**, which is defined to mean *land*.

There are several considerations that are important to the drafter of a lease of real property. In general, the following items should be addressed:

- the agreed-upon rent;
- the manner in which rent payments will be made (for example, mailed or hand-delivered to the landlord's residence);
- the term of the lease (i.e., how long it is for);
- a description of the property (we discuss the legal description of a parcel of real estate further in the next subsection on deeds);
- who is responsible for repairs, maintenance, and damage to the premises;
- whether either party may assign its rights under the lease, and whether the tenant may sublet;

- the right of the landlord to inspect or enter the premises; and
- the rights of the parties should the other party default on the agreement.

Deeds

A deed is a document by which an interest in land is passed. There are several different kinds of deeds: a **quitclaim deed**, which makes no warranty as to title but only passes such interest as the seller is ultimately shown to have (in other words, the buyer is accepting the risk of a defective title); a **general warranty deed**, in which the seller pledges that the title is good; or a **special warranty deed**, in which a seller warrants the title against defects arising during her period of ownership, but not those that may exist from an earlier time.

Figure 13– 4 Sample of General Warranty Deed

General Warranty Deed

KNOW ALL MEN BY THESE PRESENTS, that John Q. Public, of the Town of Anytown, State of North Anywhere, in consideration of eighty-five thousand dollars ($85,000.00) to me paid by Henry Doe, the receipt of which is hereby acknowledged, do hereby give, grant, convey, sell, and transfer unto the said Henry Doe a certain parcel of land situated at 123 Main Street in Anytown and more particularly described as follows:

> Beginning at a brass plate known as "Plate 171" at the corner of Main Street and Jones Street, proceeding north exactly 101.2 feet; east along land now or formerly owned by Elmer Johnson, 96.3 feet; south along land now or formerly owned by Agnes Miller, 101.2 feet; and west along Main Street 96.3 feet back to the same brass plate; and being the same premises and parcel conveyed in a deed from Eleanor Public to John Q. Public dated April 1, 1960 and recorded at page 65 of volume 1501 of the land records of the Town of Anytown.

To have and to hold the said premises, with all the privileges and appurtenances thereto, by the said Henry Doe, his heirs and assigns, from this day forward and forevermore.

And I hereby, for myself and my heirs, executors, and administrators, do hereby covenant and warrant with the said Henry Doe and his heirs and assigns that I am the lawfully seised owner of a fee simple interest in said premises, that they are free from any and all encumbrances except as set forth in the deed of Eleanor Public to John Q. Public hereinbefore referenced, that I have the full right and power to transfer title to said premises, and that I, my heirs, executors, and administrators shall warrant and defend the said Henry Doe, his heirs and assigns against the claims of any person at any time, forever.

In witness whereof we set our hands and signature this ____day of ________, 1992.

____
Witness

____
Witness

____
John Q. Public

Sworn and acknowledged before me, the undersigned________, Notary Public in and for the town of Anytown, North Anywhere, on this ________ day of ____________1992.

____
Notary Public

An example of a general warranty deed, the most common form seen, is shown in Figure 13–4. Note the property description (which is contained in the indented section). It is very important to make sure that this property description accurately reflects the description on an earlier deed. In other words, in Figure 13–4, the description should be identical to the description that appeared on the earlier deed referenced therein (identified as being "from Eleanor Public to John Q. Public dated April 1, 1960 . . . "). Accuracy as to the property description is important because if the description is inaccurate, there may be confusion over precisely what parcel of property was, in fact, transferred by the deed.

The language appearing in Figure 13–4 is fairly standard. However, when preparing a deed for your jurisdiction, you must make sure that the format used conforms to the applicable requirements. This will require research, as well as consultation with your supervising attorney.

13–4 Wills

When a person dies, he may leave behind property; a system generally referred to as the **probate system** has developed to regulate the distribution of this property. If the deceased person, called a **decedent**, left no instructions for the distribution, she is said to have died **intestate**, and the property passes according to the intestate laws. In addition to distribution under the intestate laws, the probate system offers another means of distribution by which an individual can avoid the automatic distribution of the intestate laws—by specifically identifying, in a formal document, the parties to whom distribution should be made at death. The formal document is called, of course, a **will**. The person who makes the will is called the **testator**.

A will is yet another type of operative document. The law of wills is significantly intertwined with substantive tax law, trust law, and the law of future interest (which regulate, in general, how long after the decedent's death his testamentary wishes can continue to encumber his property). Legal writing considerations, however, play an important role as well.

The first step in drafting a will is to obtain as complete a background as possible on the client's property, family structure, potential beneficiaries, and **testamentary intent** (which means, simply, her intentions about disposition of her property after death). An example of a checklist for information about preparation of a will appears in Figure 13–5 on page 510. Once all information is obtained, a will can be prepared. It must be prepared according to the requirements of your jurisdiction; this can get tricky, particularly where an individual retires to another jurisdiction, or lives in a jurisdiction different from the one in which his will is being prepared. Be sure to do adequate research to ensure that your format is proper.

Forms and models are often useful in preparing wills, particularly simple wills. By using the format and boilerplate of previous wills that have succeeded in their purpose, and by researching for any subsequent changes in the law, you will be able to prepare a document that is both time-tested and in compliance with current law.

An extremely simple will appears in Figure 13–6. It contains a title and introductory clause; an appointment of executor and instructions; bequests and devises; a residuary clause; and signature, witness, and acknowledgment blocks. These provisions, or similar ones, are commonly seen, but you must

Figure 13–5 Sample Checklist of Information for Will Preparation

- ___ Name
- ___ Other names by which known
- ___ Address
- ___ Name of spouse
- ___ Name of children
- ___ Employer's name and address
- ___ Employer-provided insurance
- ___ Employer pension plan or profit-sharing plan
- ___ Medical insurance
- ___ Life insurance
- ___ Property insurance
- ___ Automobiles and boats owned
- ___ Other personal property
- ___ Real estate, with reference to specific deeds (and with original cost and present value)
- ___ Bank accounts (including name and address of bank, contact person, and account numbers)
- ___ Stocks; stock certificates with numbers; stock options held
- ___ Jewelry and art (original cost and present value)
- ___ Leases held
- ___ Mineral rights
- ___ Debts and liabilities, including mortgages

verify that the format you use is adequate to satisfy the requirements of your jurisdiction. The format shown in Figure 13–6 is simply to illustrate. With that cautionary note in mind, let's briefly consider each of these segments of a will.

Title and Introductory Clause

The title identifies the document as the "Last Will and Testament of John Q. Public." The introductory paragraph following the title (below the double bar in Figure 13–6) is important for the purpose of specifically identifying the testator. Enough information should be provided to make it clear who is making the will. If a father and son share the same name, for example, or if the name is a common one, such information as address, date of birth, or other facts needed to distinguish the testator from other individuals with the same or similar names should be included.

In addition, some effort should be made to indicate any other names by which the testator was known (particularly if he owns property in those names that he seeks to transfer through this will). For example, depending on the law of your jurisdiction, the name "John Q. Public" may be problematically different from "John Public." This becomes more an issue of substantive estate law than legal writing; the point for our purpose is simply to be sure to adequately identify the testator.

It is also important , again, to specifically identify this document as the Last Will and Testament of the testator, and to specifically revoke all wills and codicils previously made (a **codicil** is an amendment to a will).

Figure 13–6 Last Will and Testament

Last Will and Testament
of
John Q. Public

I, the undersigned John Q. Public, of 123 Main Street, Anytown, North Anywhere, U.S.A., being of sound mind, do hereby make and execute this document as my Last Will and Testament, revoking and superceding any and all wills and codicils previous executed.

Article I. I hereby appoint the First National Bank of Anytown as my Executor, to pay all debts justly owed at my death, and to perform all the duties of an Executor as specified in the laws of the State of North Anywhere, U.S.A.

Article II. At my death, I wish to be buried in the Town Cemetery of Anytown. It is my wish that funeral expenses not exceed the sum of $4000.00 (Four Thousand Dollars and no cents).

Article III. To my son, John Q. Public, Jr., I leave the sum of $10,000.00 (Ten Thousand Dollars and no cents).

Article IV. To my daughter, Mary Public Doe, I leave the sum of $10,000.00 (Ten Thousand Dollars and no cents).

Article V. If either or both my son or daughter predecease me, their shares under Articles III and IV shall pass to their children, *per stirpes.*

Article VI. To my wife, Mary Public, I give, devise, and bequeath all my interest in the real property located at 123 Main Street and identified in a certain deed from Eleanor Public to John Q. Public dated April 1, 1960.

Article VII. All the rest, residue, and remainder of my estate, in whatsoever form and wheresoever situate, I leave to my wife, Mary Public. If the specific provisions of Articles III, IV, and V of this Last Will and Testament shall fail, then it is my wish and intent that the bequests identified in those Articles pass under this residuary clause to my wife, Mary Public.

The undersigned acknowledged this to be his Last Will and Testament by signing by his own hand in our presence on this _____ day of _____, 1992.

____
Witness

____
Witness

I hereby set my hand and signature to this my Last Will and Testament on the ____ day of ________, 1992.

____
John Q. Public
Anytown, North Anywhere, U.S.A.

Sworn and acknowledged before
me, the undersigned _________,
Notary Public in and for the town
of Anytown, North Anywhere, on this
_____ day of _______, 1992.

____
Notary Public

Appointment of Executor and Instructions

In Articles I and II of Figure 13–6, the testator has appointed a bank as his executor, has called for the payment of all debts justly owed, and has established a spending limit for his funeral. Sometimes these items all appear in one article, sometimes they are combined with the bequests, sometimes they all appear in different articles—again, it depends upon the jurisdiction. The requirement to "pay all justly owed debts" is probably superfluous, since it would be required anyway, but it is a holdover still frequently seen in wills. From a drafting standpoint, the key is to accurately reflect the testator's wishes in a manner consistent with the controlling law.

Bequests and Devises

A gift under a will is called a **bequest**; if the gift is real estate, it is called a **devise**. The important thing to remember when drafting sections that make bequests and devises is, once again, to accurately reflect the testator's wishes. Clarity and precision are essential; a slight error in drafting may invalidate or confuse the ultimate effect of the will. For example, does a bequest "to my children" made in 1985 apply to children born after the will was executed? You must understand the substantive law in order to reflect, in your draft, the client-testator's intent.

Property that is bequeathed should be accurately identified. Account numbers of bank accounts, serial numbers of stock certificates, and references to deeds all assist in clarifying the intent of the will.

The phrase *per stirpes* appears in Article V. This term indicates an intention that, should a person identified as a beneficiary die, then her descendants should divide the share that she would have received had she lived.

Residuary Clause

Most deeds contain a **residuary clause** by which that portion of the deceased's estate which is not specifically identified in the will is bequeathed. Often the party identified in the residuary clause is the principal beneficiary under the will—a few specific items are bequeathed to others, with the "rest, residue, and remainder" going to that party. Make sure the testator understands the impact of the residuary clause.

Witness, Signature, and Acknowledgment Blocks

Once again, the primary consideration as to signature format, witnesses, and acknowledgments is not a legal writing consideration, but rather a formal, substantive one. Be sure your will is witnessed and signed as required by the applicable jurisdiction; the format shown in Figure 13–6 is simply by way of example.

13-5 Practical Considerations

You've seen a message repeated over and over in this chapter—to reflect the client's intent. There is no more important advice to give with regard to the drafting of operative documents.

But the client's intent is not the only consideration. You must make sure the client understands what he is doing, and you must make sure that what you have done meets all the requirements of the controlling law.

Drafting operative documents is an art form different from the drafting of correspondence or litigation documents. If two competing parties are involved, as with a contract or a lease, the adversarial aspect has been concluded through negotiation. If a will, where there is only one party's intent to consider, there is no adversarial purpose at all. The sole purpose of drafting operative documents, then, is, after determining the intent of the parties, to *accurately reflect* that intent in the language of the operative document. To the extent that you are able to do this, you will succeed as a draftsperson.

SUMMARY

13–1

Operative documents define property rights and performance obligations in and of themselves, as a result of their content and language. It is important to determine the client's intent for an operative document, and obtain his approval for the finished product. Clarity is critical. Forms and models may be of assistance in drafting operative documents. Writing technique cannot substitute for knowledge of the substantive area of law to which an operative document relates.

13–2

A contract is an enforceable agreement. A contract's meaning must be clear from the language used. Since circumstances vary from matter to matter, be wary of using models for contracts. Keep the contract internally consistent; be particularly careful where ongoing negotiation leads to frequent revised drafts. Define terms clearly. Be redundant if necessary, and have others review your draft for clarity.

13–3

By entering into a lease, one party (the owner) allows another to use her property. The owner of the property is referred to as the lessor or landlord; the person using the property is referred to as the lessee or tenant. Among the items addressed by a lease of real property are the rent, the term of the lease, and the rights of the parties upon a default. A deed transfers ownership of real property. There are three basic types of deed: a quitclaim deed; a general warranty deed; and a special warranty deed. The property description is an important element of a deed. It must be accurate in order to avoid confusion over the parcel of property transferred.

13–4

The probate system governs the disposition of a person's property after death. If an individual dies without a will, he is said to have died intestate. A will is a formal document by which an individual can avoid the automatic distribution of the intestate laws. It often has an introductory clause that precisely identifies the testator, who is the person making the will. The testator can appoint an executor in his will, leave instructions as to his funeral, and make bequests and devises. Property not specifically mentioned in the will often passes through a residuary clause.

13–5

If you can accurately reflect the interest of the parties when you draft operative documents, you will be a successful drafter.

REVIEW

Key Terms

Before proceeding, review the key terms listed below to be sure you understand each one. If necessary, read over the corresponding section of the chapter. When you are ready to test your understanding, answer the Review Questions.

operative documents
boilerplate
forms
form books
model
contract
lease
deed
landlord
lessor
tenant
lessee
real property
quitclaim deed
general warranty deed
special warranty deed

probate system
decedent
intestate
will
testator
testamentary intent
codicil
bequest
devise
residuary clause

Questions for Review and Discussion

1. What is meant by operative documents?
2. What is the importance of determining client intent when drafting an operative document?
3. How can a form be used to assist in drafting an operative document?
4. Identify one possible pitfall of relying too heavily on a model.
5. What is a contract?
6. What are some important items that should be addressed by the text of a lease?
7. Why is an accurate property description important in a deed?
8. To whom does the term *testator* refer?
9. What is the importance of the residuary clause in a will?

Activities

1. Find the case *Frigaliment Importing Co. v. B.N.S. International Sales Corp.*, 190 F. Supp. 116 (S.D.N.Y., 1960), and read Judge Henry Friendly's fine decision, which indicates the confusion that can result from contract language.
2. Go to your local land records and try to find a quitclaim deed; a general warranty deed; and a special warranty deed (you may have trouble finding the latter).
3. Review the probate statutes that apply to your jurisdiction.

APPENDIX I The Constitution of the United States

WE THE PEOPLE of the United States, in Order to form a more perfect Union, establish Justice, insure domestic Tranquility, provide for the common defence, promote the general Welfare, and secure the Blessings of Liberty to ourselves and our Posterity, do ordain and establish this Constitution for the United States of America.

ARTICLE I

Section 1. All legislative powers herein granted shall be vested in a Congress of the United States, which shall consist of a Senate and House of Representatives.

Section 2. **[1]** The House of Representatives shall be composed of Members chosen every second Year by the People of the several States, and the Electors in each State shall have the Qualifications requisite for Electors of the most numerous Branch of the State Legislature.

[2] No Person shall be a Representative who shall not have attained to the Age of twenty-five Years, and been seven Years a Citizen of the United States, and who shall not, when elected, be an Inhabitant of that State in which he shall be chosen.

[3] Representatives [and direct Taxes] {see 16th Amendment} shall be apportioned among the several States which may be included within this Union, according to their respective Numbers, [which shall be determined by adding to the whole Number of free Persons, including those bound to Service for a Term of Years, and excluding Indians not taxed, three fifths of all other Persons.] {See 14th Amendment.} The actual Enumeration shall be made within three Years after the first Meeting of the Congress of the United States, and within every subsequent Term of ten Years, in such Manner as they shall by Law direct. The Number of Representatives shall not exceed one for every thirty Thousand, but each State shall have at Least one Representative; and until such enumeration shall be made, the State of New Hampshire shall be entitled to choose three, Massachusetts eight, Rhode Island and Providence Plantations one, Connecticut five, New York six, New Jersey four, Pennsylvania eight, Delaware one, Maryland six, Virginia ten, North Carolina five, South Carolina five, and Georgia three.

[4] When vacancies happen in the Representation from any State, the Executive Authority thereof shall issue Writs of Election to fill such Vacancies.

[5] The House of Representatives shall chuse their Speaker and other Officers; and shall have the sole Power of Impeachment.

Section 3. **[1]** The Senate of the United States shall be composed of two Senators from each State, [chosen by the Legislature thereof,] {see 17th Amendment} for six Years; and each Senator shall have one Vote.

[2] Immediately after they shall be assembled in Consequence of the first Election, they shall be divided as equally as may be into three Classes. The Seats of the Senators of the first Class shall be vacated at the Expiration of the Second Year, of the second Class at the Expiration of the fourth Year, and of the third Class at the Expiration of the sixth Year, so that one third may be chosen every second Year; and if Vacancies happen by Resignation, or otherwise, during the Recess of the Legislature of any State, the Executive thereof may make temporary Appointments until the next Meeting of the Legislature, which shall then fill such Vacancies. {See 17th Amendment.}

[3] No person shall be a Senator who shall not have attained to the Age of thirty Years, and been nine Years a Citizen of the United States, and who shall not, when elected, be an Inhabitant of that State for which he shall be chosen.

[4] The Vice President of the United States shall be President of the Senate, but shall have no Vote, unless they be equally divided.

[5] The Senate shall choose their other Officers, and also a President pro tempore, in the Absence of the Vice President, or when he shall exercise the Office of the President of the United States.

[6] The Senate shall have the sole Power to try all Impeachments. When sitting for that Purpose, they shall be on Oath or Affirmation. When the President of the United States is tried, the Chief Justice shall preside: And no Person shall be convicted without the Concurrence of two thirds of the Members present.

[7] Judgment in Cases of Impeachment shall not extend further than to removal from Office, and disqualifications to hold and enjoy any Office of honor, Trust or Profit under the United States: but the Party convicted shall nevertheless be liable and subject to Indictment, Trial, Judgment, and Punishment, according to Law.

Section 4. [1] The Times, Places and Manner of holding Elections for Senators and Representatives, shall be prescribed in each State by the legislature thereof; but the Congress may at any time by Law make or alter such Regulations, except as to the Places of chusing Senators.

[2] The Congress shall assemble at least once in every Year, and such Meeting shall be on the first Monday in December, {see 20th Amendment} unless they shall by Law appoint a different Day.

Section 5. [1] Each House shall be the Judge of the Elections, Returns and Qualifications of its own Members, and a Majority of each shall constitute a Quorum to do Business; but a smaller Number may adjourn from day to day, and may be authorized to compel the Attendance of absent Members, in such Manner, and under such Penalties as each House may provide.

[2] Each House may determine the Rules of its Proceedings, punish its Members for disorderly Behavior, and, with the Concurrence of two thirds, expel a Member.

[3] Each House shall keep a Journal of its Proceedings, and from time to time publish the same, excepting such Parts as may in their Judgment require Secrecy; and the Yeas and Nays of the Members of either House on any question shall, at the Desire of one fifth of those Present, be entered on the Journal.

[4] Neither House, during the Session of Congress, shall, without the Consent of the other, adjourn for more than three days, nor to any other Place than that in which the two Houses shall be sitting.

Section 6. [1] The Senators and Representatives shall receive a Compensation for their Services, to be ascertained by Law, and paid out of the Treasury of the United States. They shall in all Cases, except Treason, Felony and Breach of the Peace, be privileged from Arrest during their Attendance at the Session of their respective Houses, and in going to and returning from the same; and for any Speech or Debate in either House, they shall not be questioned in any other Place.

[2] No Senator or Representative shall, during the Time for which he was elected, be appointed to any civil Office under the Authority of the United States, which shall have been created, or the Emoluments whereof shall have been increased during such time; and no Person holding any Office under the United States shall be a Member of either House during his Continuance in Office.

Section 7. [1] All Bills for raising Revenue shall originate in the House of Representatives; but the Senate may propose or concur with Amendments as on other Bills.

[2] Every Bill which shall have passed the House of Representatives and the Senate, shall, before it becomes a Law, be presented to the President of the United States; if he approve he shall sign it, but if not he shall return it, with his Objections to that House in which it shall have originated, who shall enter the Objections at large on their Journal, and proceed to reconsider it. If after such Reconsideration two thirds of that House shall agree to pass the Bill, it shall be sent together with the Objections, to the other House, by which it shall likewise be reconsidered, and if approved by two thirds of that House, it shall become a Law. But in all such Cases the Votes of both Houses shall be determined by Yeas and Nays, and the Names of the Persons voting for and against the Bill shall be entered on the Journal of each House respectively. If any Bill shall not be returned by the President within ten Days (Sundays excepted) after it shall have been presented to him, the Same shall be a Law, in like Manner as if he had signed it, unless the Congress by their Adjournment prevent its Return, in which Case it shall not be a Law.

[3] Every Order, Resolution, or Vote to Which the Concurrence of the Senate and the House of Representative may be nec-

essary (except on a question of Adjournment) shall be presented to the President of the United States; and before the Same shall take Effect, shall be approved by him, or being disapproved by him, shall be repassed by two thirds of the Senate and House of Representatives, according to the Rules and Limitations prescribed in the Case of a Bill.

Section 8. The Congress shall have the Power

[1] To lay and collect Taxes, Duties, Imposts and Excises, to pay the Debts and provide for the common Defence and general Welfare of the United States; but all Duties, Imposts and Excises shall be uniform throughout the United States;

[2] To borrow money on the credit of the United States;

[3] To regulate Commerce with foreign Nations, and among the several States, and with the Indian Tribes;

[4] To establish a uniform Rule of Naturalization, and uniform Laws on the subject of Bankruptcies throughout the United States;

[5] To coin Money, regulate the Value thereof, and of foreign Coin, and fix the Standard of Weights and Measures;

[6] To provide for the Punishment of counterfeiting the Securities and current Coin of the United States;

[7] To Establish Post Offices and Post Roads;

[8] To promote the Progress of Science and useful Arts, by securing for limited Times to Authors and Inventors the exclusive Right to their respective Writings and Discoveries;

[9] To constitute Tribunals inferior to the supreme Court;

[10] To define and punish Piracies and Felonies committed on the high Seas, and Offenses against the Law of Nations;

[11] To declare War, grant Letters of Marque and Reprisal, and make Rules concerning Captures on Land and Water;

[12] To raise and support Armies, but no Appropriation of Money to that Use shall be for a longer Term than two Years;

[13] To provide and maintain a Navy;

[14] To make Rules for the Government and Regulation of the land and naval Forces;

[15] To provide for calling forth the Militia to execute the Laws of the Union, suppress Insurrections and repel Invasions;

[16] To provide for organizing, arming, and disciplining the Militia, and for governing such Part of them as may be employed in the Service of the United States, reserving to the States respectively, the Appointment of the Officers, and the Authority of training the Militia according to the discipline prescribed by Congress;

[17] To exercise exclusive Legislation in all Cases whatsoever, over such District (not exceeding ten Miles square) as may, by Cession of particular States, and the Acceptance of Congress, become the Seat of the Government of the United States, and to exercise like Authority over all Places purchased by the Consent of the Legislature of the State in which the Same shall be, for the Erection of Forts, Magazines, Arsenals, dock-Yards, and other needful Buildings;—And

[18] To make all Laws which shall be necessary and proper for carrying into Execution the foregoing Powers, and all other Powers vested by this Constitution in the Government of the United States, or in any Department or Officer thereof.

Section 9. **[1]** The Migration or Importation of Such Persons as any of the States now existing shall think proper to admit, shall not be prohibited by the Congress prior to the Year one thousand eight hundred and eight, but a Tax or duty may be imposed on such Importation, not exceeding ten dollars for each Person.

[2] The privilege of the Writ of Habeas Corpus shall not be suspended, unless when in Cases of Rebellion or Invasion the public Safety may require it.

[3] No Bill of Attainder or ex post facto Law shall be passed.

[4] No Capitation, or other direct, Tax shall be laid, unless in Proportion to the Census or Enumeration herein before directed to be taken. {See 16th Amendment.}

[5] No Tax or Duty shall be laid on Articles exported from any State.

[6] No Preference shall be given by any Regulation of Commerce or Revenue to the Ports of one State over those of another: nor shall Vessels bound to, or from, one State be obliged to enter, clear, or pay Duties in another.

[7] No money shall be drawn from the Treasury, but in Consequence of Appropriations made by Law; and a regular Statement and Account of the Receipts and Expenditures of all public Money shall be published from time to time.

[8] No Title of Nobility shall be granted by the United States: And no Person holding any Office of Profit or Trust under them, shall, without the Consent of the Congress, accept of any present, Emolument, Office, or Title, of any kind whatever, from any King, Prince, or foreign State.

Section 10. **[1]** No State shall enter into any Treaty, Alliance, or Confederation; grant Letters of Marque and Reprisal; coin Money; emit Bills of Credit; make any Thing but gold and silver Coin a Tender in Payment of Debts; pass any Bill of Attainder, ex post facto Law, or Law impairing the Obligation of Contracts, or grant any Title of Nobility.

[2] No State shall, without the Consent of the Congress, lay any Imposts or Duties on Imports or Exports, except what may be absolutely necessary for executing its inspection Laws; and the net Produce of all Duties and Imposts laid by any State on Imports or Exports, shall be for the Use of the Treasury of the United States; and all such Laws shall be subject to the Revision and Control of the Congress.

[3] No State shall, without the Consent of the Congress, lay any Duty of Tonnage, keep Troops, or Ships of War in time of Peace, enter into any Agreement or Compact with another State, or with a foreign Power, or engage in War, unless actually invaded, or in such imminent Danger as will not admit of delay.

ARTICLE II

Section 1. **[1]** The executive Power shall be vested in a President of the United States of America. He shall hold his Office during the Term of four Years, and, together with the Vice President, chosen for the same Term, be elected as follows:

[2] Each State {see 23rd Amendment} shall appoint, in such Manner as the Legislature thereof may direct, a Number of Electors, equal to the whole Number of Senators and Representatives to which the State may be entitled in the Congress: but no Senator or Representative, or Person holding an Office of Trust or Profit under the United States, shall be appointed an Elector.

[3] [The Electors shall meet in their respective States, and vote by Ballot for two Persons, of whom one at least shall not be an Inhabitant of the same State with themselves. And they shall make a List of all the Persons voted for, and of the Number of Votes for each; which List they shall sign and certify, and transmit sealed to the Seat of the Government of the United States, directed to the President of the Senate. The President of the Senate shall, in the Presence of the Senate and House of Representatives, open all the Certificates, and the Votes shall then be counted. The Person having the greatest Number of Votes shall be the President, if such Number be a Majority of the whole Number of Electors appointed; and if there be more than one who shall have such Majority, and have an equal Number of Votes, then the House of Representatives shall immediately chuse by Ballot one of them for President; and if no Person have a Majority, then from the five highest on the List the said House shall in like Manner chuse the President. But in chusing the President, the Votes shall be taken by States, the Representation from each State having one Vote; a quorum for this Purpose shall consist of a Member or Members from two thirds of the States, and a Majority of all the States shall be necessary to a Choice. In every Case, after the Choice of the President, the Person having the greatest Number of Votes of the Electors shall be the Vice President. But if there should remain two or more who have equal Votes, the Senate shall chuse from them by Ballot the Vice President.] {See 12th Amendment.}

[4] The Congress may determine the Time of chusing the Electors, and the Day on which they shall give their Votes; which Day shall be the same throughout the United States.

[5] No person except a natural born Citizen, or a Citizen of the United States, at the time of the Adoption of this Constitution, shall be eligible to the Office of President; neither shall any Person be eligible to that Office who shall not have attained to the Age of thirty-five Years, and been fourteen Years a Resident within the United States.

[6] In case of removal of the President from Office, or of his Death, Resignation or Inability to discharge the Powers and Duties of the said Office, the Same shall devolve on the Vice President, and the Congress may by Law provide for the Case of Removal, Death, Resignation or Inability, both of the President and Vice President, declaring what Officer shall then act as President, and such Officer shall act accordingly, until the Disability be removed, or a President shall be elected. {See 25th Amendment.}

[7] The President shall, at stated Times, receive for his Services a Compensation, which shall neither be increased nor diminished during the Period for which he shall have been elected, and he shall not receive within that Period any other Emolument from the United States, or any of them.

[8] Before he enter on the Execution of his Office, he shall take the following Oath or Affirmation:—"I do solemnly swear (or affirm) that I will faithfully execute the Office of President of the United States, and will to the best of my Ability, preserve, protect and defend the Constitution of the United States."

Section 2. **[1]** The President shall be Commander in Chief of the Army and Navy of the United States, and of the militia of the several States, when called into the actual Service of the United States; he may require the Opinion, in writing, of the principal Officer in each of the Executive Departments, upon any Subject relating to the Duties of their Respective Offices, and he shall have Power to grant Reprieves and Pardons for Offenses against the United States, except in Cases of Impeachment.

[2] He shall have Power, by and with the Advice and Consent of the Senate, to make Treaties, provided two thirds of the Senators present concur; and he shall nominate, and by and with the Advice and Consent of the Senate, shall appoint Ambassadors, other public Ministers and Consuls, Judges of the supreme Court, and all other Officers of the United States, whose Appointments are not herein otherwise provided for, and which shall be established by Law: but the Congress may by Law vest the Appointment of such inferior Officers, as they think proper, in the President alone, in the Courts of Law, or in the Heads of Departments.

[3] The President shall have Power to fill up all Vacancies that may happen during the Recess of the Senate, by granting Commissions which shall expire at the End of their next Session.

Section 3. He shall from time to time give to the Congress Information of the State of the Union, and recommend to their Consideration such Measures as he shall judge necessary and expedient; he may, on extraordinary Occasions, convene both Houses, or either of them, and in Case of Disagreement between them with Respect to the Time of Adjournment, he may adjourn them to such Time as he shall think proper; he shall receive Ambassadors and other public Ministers; he shall take Care that the Laws be faithfully executed, and shall Commission all the Officers of the United States.

Section 4. The President, Vice President, and all civil Officers of the United States, shall be removed from Office on Impeachment for, and Conviction of, Treason, Bribery, or other high Crimes and Misdemeanors.

ARTICLE III

Section 1. The judicial Power of the United States shall be vested in one supreme Court, and in such inferior Courts as the Congress may from time to time ordain and establish. The Judges, both of the supreme and inferior Courts, shall hold their Offices during good Behavior, and shall, at stated Times, receive for their Services, a Compensation, which shall not be diminished during their Continuance in Office.

Section 2. **[1]** The judicial Power shall extend to all Cases, in Law and Equity, arising under this Constitution, the Laws of the United States, and Treaties made, or which shall be made, under their Authority;—to all Cases affecting Ambassadors, other public Ministers and Consuls;—to all Cases of admiralty and maritime Jurisdiction;—to Controversies to which the United States shall be a Party;—to Controversies between two or more States;—between a State and Citizens of another State; {see 11th Amendment}—between Citizens of different States;—between Citizens of the same State claiming Lands under Grants of different States, and between a State, or the Citizens thereof, and foreign States, Citizens or Subjects.

[2] In all Cases affecting Ambassadors, other public Ministers and Consuls, and those in which a State shall be a Party, the supreme Court shall have original Jurisdiction. In all the other Cases before mentioned, the supreme Court shall have appellate Jurisdiction, both as to Law and Fact, with such Exceptions, and under such Regulations as the Congress shall make.

[3] The trial of all Crimes, except in Cases of Impeachment, shall be by Jury; and such Trial shall be held in the State where the said Crimes shall have been committed; but when not committed within any State, the Trial shall be at such Place or Places as the Congress may by law have directed.

Section 3. **[1]** Treason against the United States shall consist only in levying War against them, or, in adhering to their Enemies, giving them Aid and Comfort. No Person shall be convicted of Treason unless on the Testimony of two Witnesses to the same overt Act, or on Confession in open Court.

[2] The Congress shall have Power to declare the Punishment of Treason, but no Attainder of Treason shall work Corruption of Blood, or Forfeiture except during the Life of the Person attained.

ARTICLE IV

Section 1. Full Faith and Credit shall be given in each State to the public Acts, Records, and judicial Proceedings of every other State. And the Congress may by general Laws prescribe the Manner in which such Acts, Records, and Proceedings shall be proved, and the Effect thereof.

Section 2. **[1]** The Citizens of each State shall be entitled to all Privileges and Immunities of Citizens in the several States. {See 14th Amendment.}

[2] A Person charged in any State with Treason, Felony, or other Crime, who shall flee from Justice, and be found in another State, shall on demand of the executive Authority of the State from which he fled, be delivered up to be removed to the State having Jurisdiction of the Crime.

[3] No Person held to Service or Labor in one State under the Laws thereof, escaping into another, shall, in Consequence of any Law or Regulation therein, be discharged from such Service or Labor, but shall be delivered up on Claim of the Party to whom such Service or Labor may be due. {See 13th Amendment.}

Section 3. **[1]** New States may be admitted by the Congress into this Union; but no new State shall be formed or erected within the Jurisdiction of any other State; nor any State be formed by the Junction of two or more States, or Parts of States, without the Consent of the Legislatures of the States concerned as well as of the Congress.

[2] The Congress shall have Power to dispose of and make all needful Rules and Regulations respecting the Territory or other Property belonging to the United States; and nothing in this Constitution shall be so construed as to Prejudice any Claims of the United States, or of any particular State.

Section 4. The United States shall guarantee to every State in this Union a Republican Form of Government, and shall protect each of them against Invasion; and on Application of the Legislature, or of the Executive (when the Legislature cannot be convened) against domestic Violence.

ARTICLE V

The Congress, whenever two thirds of both Houses shall deem it necessary, shall propose Amendments to this Constitution, or, on the Application of the Legislatures of two thirds of the several States, shall call a Convention for proposing Amendments, which in either Case, shall be valid to all Intents and Purposes, as part of this Constitution, when ratified by the Legislatures of three fourths of the several States, or by Conventions in three fourths thereof, as the one or the other Mode of Ratification may be proposed by Congress; Provided that no Amendment which may be made prior to the year One thousand eight hundred and eight shall in any Manner affect the first and fourth Clauses in the Ninth Section of the first Article; and that no State, without its Consent, shall be deprived of its equal Suffrage in the Senate.

ARTICLE VI

[1] All Debts contracted and Engagements entered into, before the Adoption of this Constitution, shall be valid against the United States under this Constitution, as under the Confederation.

[2] This Constitution, and the Laws of the United States which shall be made in Pursuance thereof; and all Treaties made, or which shall be made, under the Authority of the United States, shall be the supreme Law of the Land; and the Judges in every State shall be bound thereby, any Thing in the Constitution or laws of any State to the Contrary notwithstanding.

[3] The Senators and Representatives before mentioned, and the Members of the several State Legislatures, and all executive and judicial Officers, both of the United States and of the several States, shall be bound by Oath or Affirmation, to support this Constitution; but no religious Test shall ever be required as a Qualification to any Office or public Trust under the United States.

ARTICLE VII

The Ratification of the Conventions of nine States shall be sufficient for the Establishment of this Constitution between the States so ratifying the Same.

DONE in Convention by the Unanimous Consent of the States present the Seventeenth Day of September in the Year of our Lord one thousand seven hundred and Eighty-seven, and of the Independence of the United States of America the Twelfth. IN WITNESS whereof we have hereunto subscribed our Names.

[AMENDMENTS]

ARTICLE I [1791]

Congress shall make no law respecting an establishment of religion, or prohibiting the free exercise thereof; or abridging the freedom of speech, or of the press; or the right of the people peaceably to assemble, and to petition the Government for a redress of grievances.

ARTICLE II [1791]

A well regulated Militia, being necessary to the security of a free State, the right of the people to keep and bear Arms, shall not be infringed.

ARTICLE III [1791]

No Soldier shall, in time of peace be quartered in any house, without the consent of the Owner, nor in time of war, but in a manner to be prescribed by law.

ARTICLE IV [1791]

The right of the people to be secure in their persons, houses, papers, and effects, against unreasonable searches and seizures, shall not be violated, and no Warrants shall issue, but upon probable cause, supported by Oath or affirmation, and particularly describing the place to be searched, and the person or things to be seized.

ARTICLE V [1791]

No person shall be held to answer for a capital, or otherwise infamous crime, unless on a presentment or indictment of a Grand Jury, except in cases arising in the land or naval forces, or in the Militia, when in actual service in time of War or public danger; nor shall any person be subject for the same offence to be twice put in jeopardy of life or limb; nor shall be compelled in any criminal case to be a witness against himself, nor be deprived of life, liberty, or property, without due process of law; nor shall private property be taken for public use, without just compensation.

ARTICLE VI [1791]

In all criminal prosecutions, the accused shall enjoy the right to a speedy and public trial, by an impartial jury of the State and district wherein the crime shall have been committed, which district shall have been previously ascertained by law, and to be informed of the nature and cause of the accusation; to be confronted with the witnesses against him; to have compulsory process for obtaining witnesses in his favor, and to have the Assistance of Counsel for his defence.

ARTICLE VII [1791]

In Suits at common law, where the value in controversy shall exceed twenty dollars, the right of trial by jury shall be preserved, and no fact tried by jury, shall be otherwise re-examined in any Court of the United States, than according to the rules of the common law.

ARTICLE VIII [1791]

Excessive bail shall not be required, nor excessive fines imposed, nor cruel and unusual punishments inflicted.

ARTICLE IX [1791]

The enumeration in the Constitution, of certain rights, shall not be construed to deny or disparage others retained by the people.

ARTICLE X [1791]

The powers not delegated to the United States by the Constitution, nor prohibited by it to the States, are reserved to the States respectively, or to the people.

ARTICLE XI [1798]

The Judicial power of the United States shall not be construed to extend to any suit in law or equity, commenced or prosecuted against one of the United States by Citizens of another State, or by Citizens or Subjects of any Foreign State.

ARTICLE XII [1804]

The Electors shall meet in their respective states and vote by ballot for President and Vice-President, one of whom, at least, shall not be an inhabitant of the same state with themselves; they shall name in their ballots the person voted for as President, and in distinct ballots the person voted for as Vice-President, and they shall make distinct lists of all persons voted for as President, and of all persons voted for as Vice-President, and of the number of votes for each, which lists they shall sign and certify, and transmit sealed to the seat of the government of the United States, directed to the President of the Senate;—The President of the Senate shall, in the presence of the Senate and House of Representatives, open all the certificates and the votes shall then be counted;—The person having the greatest number of votes for President, shall be the President, if such number be a majority of the whole number of Electors appointed; and if no person have such majority, then from the persons having the highest numbers not exceeding three on the list of those voted for as President, the House of Representatives shall choose immediately, by ballot, the President. But in choosing the President, the votes shall be taken by states, the representation of each state having one vote; a quorum for this purpose shall consist of a member or members from two-thirds of the states, and a majority of all the states shall be necessary to a choice. And if the House of Representatives shall not choose a President whenever the right of choice shall devolve upon them before the fourth day of March {see 20th Amendment} next following, then the Vice-President shall act as President, as in the case of the death or other constitutional disability of the President.—The person having the greatest number of votes as Vice-President, shall be the Vice-President, if such number be a majority of the whole number of Electors appointed, and if no person have a majority, then from the two highest numbers on the list, the Senate shall choose the Vice-President; a quorum for the purpose shall consist of two-thirds of the whole number of Senators, and a majority of the whole number shall be necessary to a choice. But no person constitutionally ineligible to the office of President shall be eligible to that of Vice-President of the United States.

ARTICLE XIII [1865]

Section 1. Neither slavery nor involuntary servitude, except as a punishment for crime whereof the party shall have been duly convicted, shall exist within the United States, or any place subject to their jurisdiction.

Section 2. Congress shall have power to enforce this article by appropriate legislation.

ARTICLE XIV [1868]

Section 1. All persons born or naturalized in the United States, and subject to the jurisdiction thereof, are citizens of the United States and of the State wherein they reside. No State shall make or enforce any law which shall abridge the privileges or immunities of citizens of the United States; nor shall any State deprive any person of life, liberty, or property, without due process of law; nor deny to any person within its jurisdiction the equal protection of the laws.

Section 2. Representatives shall be apportioned among the several States according to their respective numbers, counting the whole number of persons in each State excluding Indians not taxed. But when the right to vote at any election for the choice of electors for President and Vice President of the United States, Representatives in Congress, the Executive and Judicial officers of a State, or the members of the Legislature thereof, is denied to any of the male inhabitants of such State, being twenty-one years of age, and citizens of the United States, or in any way abridged, except for participation in rebellion, or other crime, the basis of representation therein shall be reduced in the proportion which the number of such male citizens shall bear to the whole number of male citizens twenty-one years of age in such State.

Section 3. No person shall be a Senator or Representative in Congress, or elector of President and Vice President, or hold any office, civil or military, under the United States, or under any State, who having previously taken an oath, as a member of Congress, or as an officer of the United States, or as a member of any State legislature, or as an executive or judicial officer of any State, to support the Constitution of the United States, shall have engaged in insurrection or rebellion against the same, or given aid or comfort to the enemies thereof. But Congress may by a vote of two-thirds of each House, remove such disability.

Section 4. The validity of the public debt of the United States, authorized by law, including debts incurred for payment of pensions and bounties for services in suppressing insurrection or rebellion, shall not be questioned. But neither the United States nor any State shall assume or pay any debt or obligation incurred in aid of insurrection or rebellion against the United States, or any claim for the loss or emancipation of any slave; but all such debts, obligations and claims shall be held illegal and void.

Section 5. The Congress shall have power to enforce, by appropriate legislation, the provisions of this article.

ARTICLE XV [1870]

Section 1. The right of citizens of the United States to vote shall not be denied or abridged by the United States or by any State on account of race, color, or previous condition of servitude.

Section 2. The Congress shall have power to enforce this article by appropriate legislation.

ARTICLE XVI [1913]

The Congress shall have power to lay and collect taxes on incomes, from whatever source derived, without apportionment among the several States, and without regard to any census or enumeration.

ARTICLE XVII [1913]

[1] The Senate of the United States shall be composed of two Senators from each State, elected by the people thereof, for six years; and each Senator shall have one vote. The electors in each State shall have the qualifications requisite for electors of the most numerous branch of the State legislatures.

[2] When vacancies happen in the representation of any State in the Senate, the executive authority of such State shall issue writs of election to fill such vacancies: Provided, That the legislature of any State may empower the executive thereof to make temporary appointments until the people fill the vacancies by election as the legislature may direct.

[3] This amendment shall not be so construed as to affect the election or term of any Senator chosen before it becomes valid as part of the Constitution.

ARTICLE XVIII [1919]

[repealed by 21st Amendment]

Section 1. After one year from the ratification of this article the manufacture, sale, or transportation of intoxicating liquors within, the importation thereof into, or the exportation thereof from the United States and all territory subject to the jurisdiction thereof for beverage purposes is hereby prohibited.

Section 2. The Congress and the several States shall have concurrent power to enforce this article by appropriate legislation.

Section 3. This article shall be inoperative unless it shall have been ratified as an amendment to the Constitution by the legislatures of the several States, as provided in the Constitution, within seven years from the date of the submission hereof to the States by the Congress.

ARTICLE XIX [1920]

[1] The right of citizens of the United States to vote shall not be denied or abridged by the United States or by any State on account of sex.

[2] Congress shall have power to enforce this article by appropriate legislation.

ARTICLE XX [1933]

Section 1. The terms of the President and Vice President shall end at noon on the 20th day of January, and the terms of Senators and Representatives at noon on the 3d day of January, of the years in which such terms would have ended if this article had not been ratified; and the terms of their successors shall then begin.

Section 2. The Congress shall assemble at least once in every year, and such meeting shall begin at noon on the 3d day of January, unless they shall by law appoint a different day.

Section 3. If, at the time fixed for the beginning of the term of the President, the President elect shall have died, the Vice President elect shall become President. If the President shall not have been chosen before the time fixed for the beginning of his term, or if the President elect shall have failed to qualify, then the Vice President elect shall act as President until a President shall have qualified; and the Congress may by law provide for the case wherein neither a President elect nor a Vice President elect shall have qualified, declaring who shall then act as President, or the manner in which one who is to act shall be selected, and such person shall act accordingly until a President or Vice President shall have qualified.

Section 4. The Congress may by law provide for the case of the death of any of the persons from whom the House of Representatives may choose a President whenever the right of choice shall have devolved upon them, and for the case of the death of any of the persons from whom the Senate may choose a Vice President whenever the right of choice shall have devolved upon them.

Section 5. Sections 1 and 2 shall take effect on the 15th day of October following the ratification of this article.

Section 6. This article shall be inoperative unless it shall have been ratified as an amendment to the Constitution by the legislatures of three-fourths of the several States within seven years from the date of its submission.

ARTICLE XXI [1933]

Section 1. The eighteenth article of amendment to the Constitution of the United States is hereby repealed.

Section 2. The transportation or importation into any State, Territory, or possession of the United States for delivery or use therein of intoxicating liquors, in violation of the laws thereof, is hereby prohibited.

Section 3. This article shall be inoperative unless it shall have been ratified as an amendment to the Constitution by conventions in the several States, as provided in the Constitution, within seven years from the date of the submission hereof to the States by the Congress.

ARTICLE XXII [1951]

Section 1. No person shall be elected to the office of the President more than twice, and no person who has held the office of President, or acted as President, for more than two years of a term to which some other person was elected President shall be elected to the office of President more than once. But this Article shall not apply to any person holding the office of President when this Article was proposed by the Congress, and shall not prevent any person who may be holding the office of President, or acting as President, during the term within which this Article becomes operative from holding the office of President or acting as President during the remainder of such term.

Section 2. This article shall be inoperative unless it shall have been ratified as an amendment to the Constitution by the legislatures of three-fourths of the several States within seven years from the date of its submission to the States by the Congress.

ARTICLE XXIII [1961]

Section 1. The District constituting the seat of Government of the United States shall appoint in such manner as the Congress may direct:

A number of electors of President and Vice President equal to the whole number of Senators and Representatives in Congress to which the District would be entitled if it were a State, but in no event more than the least populous state; they shall be in addition to those appointed by the states, but they shall be considered, for the purposes of the election of President and Vice President, to be electors appointed by a state; and they shall meet in the District and perform such duties as provided by the twelfth article of amendment.

Section 2. The Congress shall have power to enforce this article by appropriate legislation.

ARTICLE XXIV [1964]

Section 1. The right of citizens of the United States to vote in any primary or other election for President or Vice President, for electors for President or Vice President, or for Senator or Representative in Congress, shall not be denied or abridged by the United States, or any State by reason of failure to pay any poll tax or other tax.

Section 2. The Congress shall have power to enforce this article by appropriate legislation.

ARTICLE XXV [1967]

Section 1. In case of the removal of the President from office or of his death or resignation, the Vice President shall become President.

Section 2. Whenever there is a vacancy in the office of the Vice President, the President shall nominate a Vice President who shall take office upon confirmation by a majority vote of both Houses of Congress.

Section 3. Whenever the President transmits to the President pro tempore of the Senate and the Speaker of the House of Representatives his written declaration that he is unable to discharge the powers and duties of his office, and until he transmits to them a written declaration to the contrary, such powers and duties shall be discharged by the Vice President as Acting President.

Section 4. Whenever the Vice President and a majority of either the principal officers of the executive departments or of such other body as Congress may by law provide, transmit to the President pro tempore of the Senate and the Speaker of the House of Representatives their written declaration that the President is unable to discharge the powers and duties of his office, the Vice President shall immediately assume the powers and duties of the office as Acting President.

Thereafter, when the President transmits to the President pro tempore of the Senate and the Speaker of the House of Representatives his written declaration that no inability exists, he shall resume the powers and duties of his office unless the Vice President and a majority of either the principal officers of the executive department or of such other body as Congress may by law provide, transmit within four days to the President pro tempore of the Senate and the Speaker of the House of Representatives their written declaration that the President is unable to discharge the powers and duties of his office. Thereupon Congress shall decide the issue, assembling within forty-eight hours for that purpose if not in session. If the Congress, within twenty-one days after receipt of the latter written declaration, or, if Congress is not in session, within twenty-one days after Congress is required to assemble, determines by two-thirds vote of both Houses that the President is unable to discharge the power and duties of his office, the Vice President shall continue to discharge the same as Acting President; otherwise, the President shall resume the powers and duties of his office.

ARTICLE XXVI [1971]

Section 1. The right of citizens of the United States, who are eighteen years of age or older, to vote shall not be denied or abridged by the United States or by any State on account of age.

Section 2. The Congress shall have power to enforce this article by appropriate legislation.

ARTICLE XXVII [1992]*

No law, varying the compensation for the services of the Senators and Representatives, shall take effect, until an election of Representatives shall have intervened.

*This amendment was certified by the Archivist of the United States on May 18, 1992.

APPENDIX II Table of Parallel Volume References, U.S. Supreme Court Reporters

Term or Year of Decision	Government Printing Office	Nominative Reporters & West	LCP
1790	1 U.S.	1 Dall.	1 L. Ed.
1791	2 U.S.	2 Dall.	1 L. Ed.
1794	3 U.S.	3 Dall.	1 L. Ed.
1799	4 U.S.	4 Dall.	1 L. Ed.
1801	5 U.S.	1 Cranch	2 L. Ed.
1804	6 U.S.	2 Cranch	2 L. Ed.
1805	7 U.S.	3 Cranch	2 L. Ed.
1807	8 U.S.	4 Cranch	2 L. Ed.
1809	9 U.S.	5 Cranch	3 L. Ed.
1810	10 U.S.	6 Cranch	3 L. Ed.
1812	11 U.S.	7 Cranch	3 L. Ed.
1814	12 U.S.	8 Cranch	3 L. Ed.
1815	13 U.S.	9 Cranch	3 L. Ed.
1816	14 U.S.	1 Wheat.	4 L. Ed.
1817	15 U.S.	2 Wheat.	4 L. Ed.
1818	16 U.S.	3 Wheat.	4 L. Ed.
1819	17 U.S.	4 Wheat.	4 L. Ed.
1820	18 U.S.	5 Wheat.	5 L. Ed.
1821	19 U.S.	6 Wheat.	5 L. Ed.
1822	20 U.S.	7 Wheat.	5 L. Ed.
1823	21 U.S.	8 Wheat.	5 L. Ed.
1824	22 U.S.	9 Wheat.	6 L. Ed.
1825	23 U.S.	10 Wheat.	6 L. Ed.
1826	24 U.S.	11 Wheat.	6 L. Ed.
1827	25 U.S.	12 Wheat.	6 L. Ed.
1828	26 U.S.	1 Pet.	7 L. Ed.
1829	27 U.S.	2 Pet.	7 L. Ed.
1830	28 U.S.	3 Pet.	7 L. Ed.
1830	29 U.S.	4 Pet.	7 L. Ed.
1831	30 U.S.	5 Pet.	8 L. Ed.
1832	31 U.S.	6 Pet.	8 L. Ed.
1833	32 U.S.	7 Pet.	8 L. Ed.
1834	33 U.S.	8 Pet.	8 L. Ed.
1835	34 U.S.	9 Pet.	9 L. Ed.
1836	35 U.S.	10 Pet.	9 L. Ed.
1837	36 U.S.	11 Pet.	9 L. Ed.
1838	37 U.S.	12 Pet.	9 L. Ed.
1839	38 U.S.	13 Pet.	10 L. Ed.
1840	39 U.S.	14 Pet.	10 L. Ed.
1841	40 U.S.	15 Pet.	10 L. Ed.
1842	41 U.S.	16 Pet.	10 L. Ed.
1843	42 U.S.	1 How.	11 L. Ed.
1844	43 U.S.	2 How.	11 L. Ed.
1845	44 U.S.	3 How.	11 L. Ed.
1846	45 U.S.	4 How.	11 L. Ed.

Term or Year of Decision	Government Printing Office	Nominative Reporters & West	LCP
1847	46 U.S.	5 How.	12 L. Ed.
1848	47 U.S.	6 How.	12 L. Ed.
1849	48 U.S.	7 How.	12 L. Ed.
1850	49 U.S.	8 How.	12 L. Ed.
1850	50 U.S.	9 How.	13 L. Ed.
1850	51 U.S.	10 How.	13 L. Ed.
1850	52 U.S.	11 How.	13 L. Ed.
1851	53 U.S.	12 How.	13 L. Ed.
1851	54 U.S.	13 How.	14 L. Ed.
1852	55 U.S.	14 How.	14 L. Ed.
1853	56 U.S.	15 How.	14 L. Ed.
1853	57 U.S.	16 How.	14 L. Ed.
1854	58 U.S.	17 How.	15 L. Ed.
1855	59 U.S.	18 How.	15 L. Ed.
1856	60 U.S.	19 How.	15 L. Ed.
1857	61 U.S.	20 How.	15 L. Ed.
1858	62 U.S.	21 How.	16 L. Ed.
1859	63 U.S.	22 How.	16 L. Ed.
1859	64 U.S.	23 How.	16 L. Ed.
1860	65 U.S.	24 How.	16 L. Ed.
1861	66 U.S.	1 Black	17 L. Ed.
1862	67 U.S.	2 Black	17 L. Ed.
1863	68 U.S.	1 Wall.	17 L. Ed.
1864	69 U.S.	2 Wall.	17 L. Ed.
1865	70 U.S.	3 Wall.	18 L. Ed.
1866	71 U.S.	4 Wall.	18 L. Ed.
1866	72 U.S.	5 Wall.	18 L. Ed.
1867	73 U.S.	6 Wall.	18 L. Ed.
1868	74 U.S.	7 Wall.	19 L. Ed.
1868	75 U.S.	8 Wall.	19 L. Ed.
1869	76 U.S.	9 Wall.	19 L. Ed.
1869	77 U.S.	10 Wall.	19 L. Ed.
1870	78 U.S.	11 Wall.	20 L. Ed.
1870	79 U.S.	12 Wall.	20 L. Ed.
1871	80 U.S.	13 Wall.	20 L. Ed.
1871	81 U.S.	14 Wall.	20 L. Ed.
1872	82 U.S.	15 Wall.	21 L. Ed.
1872	83 U.S.	16 Wall.	21 L. Ed.
1872	84 U.S.	17 Wall.	21 L. Ed.
1873	85 U.S.	18 Wall.	21 L. Ed.
1873	86 U.S.	19 Wall.	22 L. Ed.
1873	87 U.S.	20 Wall.	22 L. Ed.
1874	88 U.S.	21 Wall.	22 L. Ed.
1874	89 U.S.	22 Wall.	22 L. Ed.
1874	90 U.S.	23 Wall.	23 L. Ed.
1875	91 U.S.		23 L. Ed.
1875	92 U.S.		23 L. Ed.
1876	93 U.S.		23 L. Ed.
1876	94 U.S.		24 L. Ed.
1877	95 U.S.		24 L. Ed.
1877	96 U.S.		24 L. Ed.
1878	97 U.S.		24 L. Ed.
1878	98 U.S.		25 L. Ed.
1878	99 U.S.		25 L. Ed.
1879	100 U.S.		25 L. Ed.
1879	101 U.S.		25 L. Ed.
1880	102 U.S.		26 L. Ed.
1880	103 U.S.		26 L. Ed.
1881	104 U.S.		26 L. Ed.
1881	105 U.S.		26 L. Ed.
1882	106 U.S.	1 S. Ct.	27 L. Ed.
1882	107 U.S.	1 S. Ct.	27 L. Ed.
1882	107 U.S.	2 S. Ct.	27 L. Ed.

Term or Year of Decision	Government Printing Office	Nominative Reporters & West	LCP
1882	108 U.S.	2 S. Ct.	27 L. Ed.
1883	109 U.S.	3 S. Ct.	27 L. Ed.
1883	110 U.S.	3 S. Ct.	28 L. Ed.
1883	110 U.S.	4 S. Ct.	28 L. Ed.
1883	111 U.S.	4 S. Ct.	28 L. Ed.
1884	112 U.S.	5 S. Ct.	28 L. Ed.
1884	113 U.S.	5 S. Ct.	28 L. Ed.
1884	114 U.S.	5 S. Ct.	29 L. Ed.
1884	115 U.S.	5 S. Ct.	29 L. Ed.
1885	115 U.S.	6 S. Ct.	29 L. Ed.
1885	116 U.S.	6 S. Ct.	29 L. Ed.
1885	117 U.S.	6 S. Ct.	29 L. Ed.
1886	118 U.S.	7 S. Ct.	30 L. Ed.
1886	119 U.S.	7 S. Ct.	30 L. Ed.
1886	120 U.S.	7 S. Ct.	30 L. Ed.
1886	121 U.S.	7 S. Ct.	30 L. Ed.
1887	122 U.S.	7 S. Ct.	30 L. Ed.
1887	123 U.S.	8 S. Ct.	31 L. Ed.
1887	124 U.S.	8 S. Ct.	31 L. Ed.
1887	125 U.S.	8 S. Ct.	31 L. Ed.
1887	126 U.S.	8 S. Ct.	31 L. Ed.
1887	127 U.S.	8 S. Ct.	32 L. Ed.
1888	128 U.S.	9 S. Ct.	32 L. Ed.
1888	129 U.S.	9 S. Ct.	32 L. Ed.
1888	130 U.S.	9 S. Ct.	32 L. Ed.
1888	131 U.S.	9 S. Ct.	33 L. Ed.
1889	132 U.S.	10 S. Ct.	33 L. Ed.
1889	133 U.S.	10 S. Ct.	33 L. Ed.
1889	134 U.S.	10 S. Ct.	33 L. Ed.
1889	135 U.S.	10 S. Ct.	34 L. Ed.
1889	136 U.S.	10 S. Ct.	34 L. Ed.
1890	137 U.S.	11 S. Ct.	34 L. Ed.
1890	138 U.S.	11 S. Ct.	34 L. Ed.
1890	139 U.S.	11 S. Ct.	35 L. Ed.
1890	140 U.S.	11 S. Ct.	35 L. Ed.
1891	141 U.S.	11 S. Ct.	35 L. Ed.
1891	141 U.S.	12 S. Ct.	35 L. Ed.
1891	142 U.S.	12 S. Ct.	35 L. Ed.
1891	143 U.S.	12 S. Ct.	36 L. Ed.
1891	144 U.S.	12 S. Ct.	36 L. Ed.
1891	145 U.S.	12 S. Ct.	36 L. Ed.
1892	146 U.S.	13 S. Ct.	36 L. Ed.
1892	147 U.S.	13 S. Ct.	37 L. Ed.
1892	148 U.S.	13 S. Ct.	37 L. Ed.
1892	149 U.S.	13 S. Ct.	37 L. Ed.
1893	150 U.S.	14 S. Ct.	37 L. Ed.
1893	151 U.S.	14 S. Ct.	38 L. Ed.
1893	152 U.S.	14 S. Ct.	38 L. Ed.
1893	153 U.S.	14 S. Ct.	38 L. Ed.
1893	154 U.S.	14 S. Ct.	38 L. Ed.
1894	155 U.S.	15 S. Ct.	39 L. Ed.
1894	156 U.S.	15 S. Ct.	39 L. Ed.
1894	157 U.S.	15 S. Ct.	39 L. Ed.
1894	158 U.S.	15 S. Ct.	39 L. Ed.
1895	159 U.S.	15 S. Ct.	40 L. Ed.
1895	159 U.S.	16 S. Ct.	40 L. Ed.
1895	160 U.S.	16 S. Ct.	40 L. Ed.
1895	161 U.S.	16 S. Ct.	40 L. Ed.
1895	162 U.S.	16 S. Ct.	40 L. Ed.
1895	163 U.S.	16 S. Ct.	41 L. Ed.
1896	164 U.S.	17 S. Ct.	41 L. Ed.
1896	165 U.S.	17 S. Ct.	41 L. Ed.
1896	166 U.S.	17 S. Ct.	41 L. Ed.

Term or Year of Decision	Government Printing Office	Nominative Reporters & West	LCP
1896	167 U.S.	17 S. Ct.	42 L. Ed.
1897	168 U.S.	18 S. Ct.	42 L. Ed.
1897	169 U.S.	18 S. Ct.	42 L. Ed.
1897	170 U.S.	18 S. Ct.	42 L. Ed.
1898	171 U.S.	18 S. Ct.	43 L. Ed.
1898	171 U.S.	19 S. Ct.	43 L. Ed.
1898	172 U.S.	19 S. Ct.	43 L. Ed.
1898	173 U.S.	19 S. Ct.	43 L. Ed.
1898	174 U.S.	19 S. Ct.	43 L. Ed.
1899	175 U.S.	20 S. Ct.	44 L. Ed.
1899	176 U.S.	20 S. Ct.	44 L. Ed.
1899	177 U.S.	20 S. Ct.	44 L. Ed.
1899	178 U.S.	20 S. Ct.	44 L. Ed.
1900	178 U.S.	21 S. Ct.	44 L. Ed.
1900	179 U.S.	21 S. Ct.	45 L. Ed.
1900	180 U.S.	21 S. Ct.	45 L. Ed.
1900	181 U.S.	21 S. Ct.	45 L. Ed.
1901	182 U.S.	22 S. Ct.	45 L. Ed.
1901	183 U.S.	22 S. Ct.	46 L. Ed.
1901	184 U.S.	22 S. Ct.	46 L. Ed.
1901	185 U.S.	22 S. Ct.	46 L. Ed.
1901	186 U.S.	22 S. Ct.	46 L. Ed.
1902	186 U.S.	23 S. Ct.	46 L. Ed.
1902	187 U.S.	23 S. Ct.	47 L. Ed.
1902	188 U.S.	23 S. Ct.	47 L. Ed.
1902	189 U.S.	23 S. Ct.	47 L. Ed.
1902	190 U.S.	23 S. Ct.	47 L. Ed.
1903	190 U.S.	24 S. Ct.	47 L. Ed.
1903	191 U.S.	24 S. Ct.	48 L. Ed.
1903	192 U.S.	24 S. Ct.	48 L. Ed.
1903	193 U.S.	24 S. Ct.	48 L. Ed.
1903	194 U.S.	24 S. Ct.	48 L. Ed.
1903	195 U.S.	24 S. Ct.	49 L. Ed.
1904	195 U.S.	25 S. Ct.	49 L. Ed.
1904	196 U.S.	25 S. Ct.	49 L. Ed.
1904	197 U.S.	25 S. Ct.	49 L. Ed.
1904	198 U.S.	25 S. Ct.	49 L. Ed.
1904	199 U.S.	25 S. Ct.	50 L. Ed.
1905	199 U.S.	26 S. Ct.	50 L. Ed.
1905	200 U.S.	26 S. Ct.	50 L. Ed.
1905	201 U.S.	26 S. Ct.	50 L. Ed.
1905	202 U.S.	26 S. Ct.	50 L. Ed.
1906	203 U.S.	27 S. Ct.	51 L. Ed.
1906	204 U.S.	27 S. Ct.	51 L. Ed.
1906	205 U.S.	27 S. Ct.	51 L. Ed.
1906	206 U.S.	27 S. Ct.	51 L. Ed.
1907	207 U.S.	28 S. Ct.	52 L. Ed.
1907	208 U.S.	28 S. Ct.	52 L. Ed.
1907	209 U.S.	28 S. Ct.	52 L. Ed.
1907	210 U.S.	28 S. Ct.	52 L. Ed.
1908	211 U.S.	29 S. Ct.	53 L. Ed.
1908	212 U.S.	29 S. Ct.	53 L. Ed.
1908	213 U.S.	29 S. Ct.	53 L. Ed.
1908	214 U.S.	29 S. Ct.	53 L. Ed.
1909	215 U.S.	30 S. Ct.	54 L. Ed.
1909	216 U.S.	30 S. Ct.	54 L. Ed.
1909	217 U.S.	30 S. Ct.	54 L. Ed.
1909	218 U.S.	30 S. Ct.	54 L. Ed.
1910	218 U.S.	31 S. Ct.	54 L. Ed.
1910	219 U.S.	31 S. Ct.	55 L. Ed.
1910	220 U.S.	31 S. Ct.	55 L. Ed.
1910	221 U.S.	31 S. Ct.	55 L. Ed.
1911	222 U.S.	32 S. Ct.	56 L. Ed.

Term or Year of Decision	Government Printing Office	Nominative Reporters & West	LCP
1911	223 U.S.	32 S. Ct.	56 L. Ed.
1911	224 U.S.	32 S. Ct.	56 L. Ed.
1911	225 U.S.	32 S. Ct.	56 L. Ed.
1912	226 U.S.	33 S. Ct.	57 L. Ed.
1912	227 U.S.	33 S. Ct.	57 L. Ed.
1912	228 U.S.	33 S. Ct.	57 L. Ed.
1912	229 U.S.	33 S. Ct.	57 L. Ed.
1912	230 U.S.	33 S. Ct.	57 L. Ed.
1913	231 U.S.	34 S. Ct.	58 L. Ed.
1913	232 U.S.	34 S. Ct.	58 L. Ed.
1913	233 U.S.	34 S. Ct.	58 L. Ed.
1913	234 U.S.	34 S. Ct.	58 L. Ed.
1914	235 U.S.	35 S. Ct.	59 L. Ed.
1914	236 U.S.	35 S. Ct.	59 L. Ed.
1914	237 U.S.	35 S. Ct.	59 L. Ed.
1914	238 U.S.	35 S. Ct.	59 L. Ed.
1915	239 U.S.	36 S. Ct.	60 L. Ed.
1915	240 U.S.	36 S. Ct.	60 L. Ed.
1915	241 U.S.	36 S. Ct.	60 L. Ed.
1916	242 U.S.	37 S. Ct.	61 L. Ed.
1916	243 U.S.	37 S. Ct.	61 L. Ed.
1916	244 U.S.	37 S. Ct.	61 L. Ed.
1917	245 U.S.	38 S. Ct.	62 L. Ed.
1917	246 U.S.	38 S. Ct.	62 L. Ed.
1917	247 U.S.	38 S. Ct.	62 L. Ed.
1918	248 U.S.	39 S. Ct.	63 L. Ed.
1918	249 U.S.	39 S. Ct.	63 L. Ed.
1918	250 U.S.	39 S. Ct.	63 L. Ed.
1919	250 U.S.	40 S. Ct.	63 L. Ed.
1919	251 U.S.	40 S. Ct.	64 L. Ed.
1919	252 U.S.	40 S. Ct.	64 L. Ed.
1919	253 U.S.	40 S. Ct.	64 L. Ed.
1920	254 U.S.	41 S. Ct.	65 L. Ed.
1920	255 U.S.	41 S. Ct.	65 L. Ed.
1920	256 U.S.	41 S. Ct.	65 L. Ed.
1921	257 U.S.	42 S. Ct.	66 L. Ed.
1921	258 U.S.	42 S. Ct.	66 L. Ed.
1921	259 U.S.	42 S. Ct.	66 L. Ed.
1922	260 U.S.	43 S. Ct.	67 L. Ed.
1922	261 U.S.	43 S. Ct.	67 L. Ed.
1922	262 U.S.	43 S. Ct.	67 L. Ed.
1923	263 U.S.	44 S. Ct.	68 L. Ed.
1923	264 U.S.	44 S. Ct.	68 L. Ed.
1923	265 U.S.	44 S. Ct.	68 L. Ed.
1924	266 U.S.	45 S. Ct.	69 L. Ed.
1924	267 U.S.	45 S. Ct.	69 L. Ed.
1924	268 U.S.	45 S. Ct.	69 L. Ed.
1925	269 U.S.	46 S. Ct.	70 L. Ed.
1925	270 U.S.	46 S. Ct.	70 L. Ed.
1925	271 U.S.	46 S. Ct.	70 L. Ed.
1926	272 U.S.	47 S. Ct.	71 L. Ed.
1926	273 U.S.	47 S. Ct.	71 L. Ed.
1926	274 U.S.	47 S. Ct.	71 L. Ed.
1927	275 U.S.	48 S. Ct.	72 L. Ed.
1927	276 U.S.	48 S. Ct.	72 L. Ed.
1927	277 U.S.	48 S. Ct.	72 L. Ed.
1928	278 U.S.	49 S. Ct.	73 L. Ed.
1928	279 U.S.	49 S. Ct.	73 L. Ed.
1929	280 U.S.	50 S. Ct.	74 L. Ed.
1929	281 U.S.	50 S. Ct.	74 L. Ed.
1930	282 U.S.	51 S. Ct.	75 L. Ed.
1930	283 U.S.	51 S. Ct.	75 L. Ed.
1931	284 U.S.	52 S. Ct.	76 L. Ed.

Term or Year of Decision	Government Printing Office	Nominative Reporters & West	LCP
1931	285 U.S.	52 S. Ct.	76 L. Ed.
1931	286 U.S.	52 S. Ct.	76 L. Ed.
1932	287 U.S.	53 S. Ct.	77 L. Ed.
1932	288 U.S.	53 S. Ct.	77 L. Ed.
1932	289 U.S.	53 S. Ct.	77 L. Ed.
1933	290 U.S.	54 S. Ct.	78 L. Ed.
1933	291 U.S.	54 S. Ct.	78 L. Ed.
1933	292 U.S.	54 S. Ct.	78 L. Ed.
1934	293 U.S.	55 S. Ct.	79 L. Ed.
1934	294 U.S.	55 S. Ct.	79 L. Ed.
1934	295 U.S.	55 S. Ct.	79 L. Ed.
1935	296 U.S.	56 S. Ct.	80 L. Ed.
1935	297 U.S.	56 S. Ct.	80 L. Ed.
1935	298 U.S.	56 S. Ct.	80 L. Ed.
1936	299 U.S.	57 S. Ct.	81 L. Ed.
1936	300 U.S.	57 S. Ct.	81 L. Ed.
1936	301 U.S.	57 S. Ct.	81 L. Ed.
1937	302 U.S.	58 S. Ct.	82 L. Ed.
1937	303 U.S.	58 S. Ct.	82 L. Ed.
1937	304 U.S.	58 S. Ct.	82 L. Ed.
1938	305 U.S.	59 S. Ct.	83 L. Ed.
1938	306 U.S.	59 S. Ct.	83 L. Ed.
1938	307 U.S.	59 S. Ct.	83 L. Ed.
1939	308 U.S.	60 S. Ct.	84 L. Ed.
1939	309 U.S.	60 S. Ct.	84 L. Ed.
1939	310 U.S.	60 S. Ct.	84 L. Ed.
1940	311 U.S.	61 S. Ct.	85 L. Ed.
1940	312 U.S.	61 S. Ct.	85 L. Ed.
1941	313 U.S.	61 S. Ct.	85 L. Ed.
1941	314 U.S.	62 S. Ct.	86 L. Ed.
1941	315 U.S.	62 S. Ct.	86 L. Ed.
1942	316 U.S.	62 S. Ct.	86 L. Ed.
1942	317 U.S.	63 S. Ct.	87 L. Ed.
1942	318 U.S.	63 S. Ct.	87 L. Ed.
1942	319 U.S.	63 S. Ct.	87 L. Ed.
1943	320 U.S.	63 S. Ct.	87 L. Ed.
1943	320 U.S.	63 S. Ct.	88 L. Ed.
1943	320 U.S.	64 S. Ct.	88 L. Ed.
1943	321 U.S.	64 S. Ct.	88 L. Ed.
1943	322 U.S.	64 S. Ct.	88 L. Ed.
1944	323 U.S.	65 S. Ct.	89 L. Ed.
1945	324 U.S.	65 S. Ct.	89 L. Ed.
1945	325 U.S.	65 S. Ct.	89 L. Ed.
1945	326 U.S.	65 S. Ct.	89 L. Ed.
1945	326 U.S.	65 S. Ct.	90 L. Ed.
1945	326 U.S.	66 S. Ct.	90 L. Ed.
1946	327 U.S.	66 S. Ct.	90 L. Ed.
1946	328 U.S.	66 S. Ct.	90 L. Ed.
1946	329 U.S.	67 S. Ct.	91 L. Ed.
1947	330 U.S.	67 S. Ct.	91 L. Ed.
1947	331 U.S.	67 S. Ct.	91 L. Ed.
1947	332 U.S.	67 S. Ct.	91 L. Ed.
1947	332 U.S.	67 S. Ct.	92 L. Ed.
1947	332 U.S.	68 S. Ct.	92 L. Ed.
1948	333 U.S.	68 S. Ct.	92 L. Ed.
1948	334 U.S.	68 S. Ct.	92 L. Ed.
1948	335 U.S.	68 S. Ct.	92 L. Ed.
1948	335 U.S.	69 S. Ct.	93 L. Ed.
1949	336 U.S.	69 S. Ct.	93 L. Ed.
1949	337 U.S.	69 S. Ct.	93 L. Ed.
1949	338 U.S.	69 S. Ct.	93 L. Ed.
1949	338 U.S.	69 S. Ct.	94 L. Ed.
1949	338 U.S.	70 S. Ct.	94 L. Ed.

Term or Year of Decision	Government Printing Office	Nominative Reporters & West	LCP
1950	339 U.S.	70 S. Ct.	94 L. Ed.
1950	340 U.S.	71 S. Ct.	95 L. Ed.
1951	341 U.S.	71 S. Ct.	95 L. Ed.
1951	342 U.S.	72 S. Ct.	96 L. Ed.
1952	343 U.S.	72 S. Ct.	96 L. Ed.
1952	344 U.S.	73 S. Ct.	97 L. Ed.
1953	345 U.S.	73 S. Ct.	97 L. Ed.
1953	346 U.S.	73 S. Ct.	97 L. Ed.
1953	346 U.S.	74 S. Ct.	98 L. Ed.
1954	347 U.S.	74 S. Ct.	98 L. Ed.
1954	348 U.S.	75 S. Ct.	99 L. Ed.
1955	349 U.S.	75 S. Ct.	99 L. Ed.
1955	350 U.S.	76 S. Ct.	100 L. Ed.
1956	351 U.S.	76 S. Ct.	100 L. Ed.
1956	352 U.S.	77 S. Ct.	1 L. Ed. 2d
1957	353 U.S.	77 S. Ct.	1 L. Ed. 2d
1957	354 U.S.	77 S. Ct.	1 L. Ed. 2d
1957	355 U.S.	78 S. Ct.	2 L. Ed. 2d
1958	356 U.S.	78 S. Ct.	2 L. Ed. 2d
1958	357 U.S.	78 S. Ct.	2 L. Ed. 2d
1958	358 U.S.	78 S. Ct.	3 L. Ed. 2d
1958	358 U.S.	79 S. Ct.	3 L. Ed. 2d
1959	359 U.S.	79 S. Ct.	3 L. Ed. 2d
1959	360 U.S.	79 S. Ct.	3 L. Ed. 2d
1959	361 U.S.	80 S. Ct.	4 L. Ed. 2d
1960	362 U.S.	80 S. Ct.	4 L. Ed. 2d
1960	363 U.S.	80 S. Ct.	4 L. Ed. 2d
1960	364 U.S.	80 S. Ct.	4 L. Ed. 2d
1960	364 U.S.	81 S. Ct.	5 L. Ed. 2d
1961	365 U.S.	81 S. Ct.	5 L. Ed. 2d
1961	365 U.S.	81 S. Ct.	6 L. Ed. 2d
1961	366 U.S.	81 S. Ct.	6 L. Ed. 2d
1961	367 U.S.	81 S. Ct.	6 L. Ed. 2d
1961	368 U.S.	82 S. Ct.	7 L. Ed. 2d
1962	369 U.S.	82 S. Ct.	7 L. Ed. 2d
1962	369 U.S.	82 S. Ct.	8 L. Ed. 2d
1962	370 U.S.	82 S. Ct.	8 L. Ed. 2d
1962	371 U.S.	83 S. Ct.	9 L. Ed. 2d
1963	372 U.S.	83 S. Ct.	10 L. Ed. 2d
1963	373 U.S.	83 S. Ct.	10 L. Ed. 2d
1963	374 U.S.	83 S. Ct.	10 L. Ed. 2d
1963	375 U.S.	84 S. Ct.	11 L. Ed. 2d
1964	376 U.S.	84 S. Ct.	11 L. Ed. 2d
1964	376 U.S.	84 S. Ct.	12 L. Ed. 2d
1964	377 U.S.	84 S. Ct.	12 L. Ed. 2d
1964	378 U.S.	84 S. Ct.	12 L. Ed. 2d
1964	379 U.S.	85 S. Ct.	13 L. Ed. 2d
1965	380 U.S.	85 S. Ct.	13 L. Ed. 2d
1965	380 U.S.	85 S. Ct.	14 L. Ed. 2d
1965	381 U.S.	85 S. Ct.	14 L. Ed. 2d
1965	382 U.S.	86 S. Ct.	15 L. Ed. 2d
1966	383 U.S.	86 S. Ct.	15 L. Ed. 2d
1966	383 U.S.	86 S. Ct.	16 L. Ed. 2d
1966	384 U.S.	86 S. Ct.	16 L. Ed. 2d
1966	385 U.S.	87 S. Ct.	17 L. Ed. 2d
1967	386 U.S.	87 S. Ct.	17 L. Ed. 2d
1967	386 U.S.	87 S. Ct.	18 L. Ed. 2d
1967	387 U.S.	87 S. Ct.	18 L. Ed. 2d
1967	388 U.S.	87 S. Ct.	18 L. Ed. 2d
1967	389 U.S.	88 S. Ct.	19 L. Ed. 2d
1968	390 U.S.	88 S. Ct.	19 L. Ed. 2d
1968	390 U.S.	88 S. Ct.	20 L. Ed. 2d
1968	391 U.S.	88 S. Ct.	20 L. Ed. 2d

Term or Year of Decision	Government Printing Office	Nominative Reporters & West	LCP
1968	392 U.S.	88 S. Ct.	20 L. Ed. 2d
1968	393 U.S.	89 S. Ct.	21 L. Ed. 2d
1969	393 U.S.	89 S. Ct.	22 L. Ed. 2d
1969	394 U.S.	89 S. Ct.	22 L. Ed. 2d
1969	394 U.S.	89 S. Ct.	23 L. Ed. 2d
1969	395 U.S.	89 S. Ct.	23 L. Ed. 2d
1969	396 U.S.	90 S. Ct.	24 L. Ed. 2d
1970	397 U.S.	90 S. Ct.	25 L. Ed. 2d
1970	398 U.S.	90 S. Ct.	26 L. Ed. 2d
1970	399 U.S.	90 S. Ct.	26 L. Ed. 2d
1970	400 U.S.	91 S. Ct.	27 L. Ed. 2d
1971	401 U.S.	91 S. Ct.	27 L. Ed. 2d
1971	401 U.S.	91 S. Ct.	28 L. Ed. 2d
1971	402 U.S.	91 S. Ct.	28 L. Ed. 2d
1971	402 U.S.	91 S. Ct.	29 L. Ed. 2d
1971	403 U.S.	91 S. Ct.	29 L. Ed. 2d
1971	404 U.S.	92 S. Ct.	30 L. Ed. 2d
1971	404 U.S.	92 S. Ct.	31 L. Ed. 2d
1972	405 U.S.	92 S. Ct.	30 L. Ed. 2d
1972	405 U.S.	92 S. Ct.	31 L. Ed. 2d
1972	406 U.S.	92 S. Ct.	31 L. Ed. 2d
1972	406 U.S.	92 S. Ct.	32 L. Ed. 2d
1972	407 U.S.	92 S. Ct.	32 L. Ed. 2d
1972	407 U.S.	92 S. Ct.	33 L. Ed. 2d
1972	408 U.S.	92 S. Ct.	33 L. Ed. 2d
1972	409 U.S.	93 S. Ct.	34 L. Ed. 2d
1973	409 U.S.	93 S. Ct.	35 L. Ed. 2d
1973	410 U.S.	93 S. Ct.	35 L. Ed. 2d
1973	410 U.S.	93 S. Ct.	36 L. Ed. 2d
1973	411 U.S.	93 S. Ct.	36 L. Ed. 2d
1973	412 U.S.	93 S. Ct.	36 L. Ed. 2d
1973	412 U.S.	93 S. Ct.	37 L. Ed. 2d
1973	413 U.S.	93 S. Ct.	37 L. Ed. 2d
1973	414 U.S.	94 S. Ct.	38 L. Ed. 2d
1974	414 U.S.	94 S. Ct.	39 L. Ed. 2d
1974	415 U.S.	94 S. Ct.	39 L. Ed. 2d
1974	416 U.S.	94 S. Ct.	39 L. Ed. 2d
1974	416 U.S.	94 S. Ct.	40 L. Ed. 2d
1974	417 U.S.	94 S. Ct.	40 L. Ed. 2d
1974	417 U.S.	94 S. Ct.	41 L. Ed. 2d
1974	418 U.S.	94 S. Ct.	41 L. Ed. 2d
1974	419 U.S.	95 S. Ct.	42 L. Ed. 2d
1975	420 U.S.	95 S. Ct.	42 L. Ed. 2d
1975	420 U.S.	95 S. Ct.	43 L. Ed. 2d
1975	421 U.S.	95 S. Ct.	43 L. Ed. 2d
1975	421 U.S.	95 S. Ct.	44 L. Ed. 2d
1975	422 U.S.	95 S. Ct.	44 L. Ed. 2d
1975	422 U.S.	95 S. Ct.	45 L. Ed. 2d
1975	423 U.S.	96 S. Ct.	46 L. Ed. 2d
1976	424 U.S.	96 S. Ct.	46 L. Ed. 2d
1976	424 U.S.	96 S. Ct.	47 L. Ed. 2d
1976	425 U.S.	96 S. Ct.	47 L. Ed. 2d
1976	425 U.S.	96 S. Ct.	48 L. Ed. 2d
1976	426 U.S.	96 S. Ct.	48 L. Ed. 2d
1976	426 U.S.	96 S. Ct.	49 L. Ed. 2d
1976	427 U.S.	96 S. Ct.	49 L. Ed. 2d
1976	428 U.S.	96 S. Ct.	49 L. Ed. 2d
1976	429 U.S.	97 S. Ct.	50 L. Ed. 2d
1977	429 U.S.	97 S. Ct.	51 L. Ed. 2d
1977	430 U.S.	97 S. Ct.	51 L. Ed. 2d
1977	430 U.S.	97 S. Ct.	52 L. Ed. 2d
1977	431 U.S.	97 S. Ct.	52 L. Ed. 2d
1977	431 U.S.	97 S. Ct.	53 L. Ed. 2d

Term or Year of Decision	Government Printing Office	Nominative Reporters & West	LCP
1977	432 U.S.	97 S. Ct.	53 L. Ed. 2d
1977	433 U.S.	97 S. Ct.	53 L. Ed. 2d
1977	434 U.S.	98 S. Ct.	54 L. Ed. 2d
1978	434 U.S.	98 S. Ct.	55 L. Ed. 2d
1978	435 U.S.	98 S. Ct.	55 L. Ed. 2d
1978	435 U.S.	98 S. Ct.	56 L. Ed. 2d
1978	436 U.S.	98 S. Ct.	56 L. Ed. 2d
1978	437 U.S.	98 S. Ct.	57 L. Ed. 2d
1978	438 U.S.	98 S. Ct.	57 L. Ed. 2d
1978	439 U.S.	99 S. Ct.	58 L. Ed. 2d
1979	439 U.S.	99 S. Ct.	59 L. Ed. 2d
1979	440 U.S.	99 S. Ct.	59 L. Ed. 2d
1979	441 U.S.	99 S. Ct.	60 L. Ed. 2d
1979	442 U.S.	99 S. Ct.	60 L. Ed. 2d
1979	442 U.S.	99 S. Ct.	61 L. Ed. 2d
1979	443 U.S.	99 S. Ct.	61 L. Ed. 2d
1979	444 U.S.	100 S. Ct.	62 L. Ed. 2d
1980	444 U.S.	100 S. Ct.	63 L. Ed. 2d
1980	445 U.S.	100 S. Ct.	63 L. Ed. 2d
1980	446 U.S.	100 S. Ct.	64 L. Ed. 2d
1980	447 U.S.	100 S. Ct.	64 L. Ed. 2d
1980	447 U.S.	100 S. Ct.	65 L. Ed. 2d
1980	448 U.S.	100 S. Ct.	65 L. Ed. 2d
1980	449 U.S.	101 S. Ct.	66 L. Ed. 2d
1981	450 U.S.	101 S. Ct.	67 L. Ed. 2d
1981	451 U.S.	101 S. Ct.	67 L. Ed. 2d
1981	451 U.S.	101 S. Ct.	68 L. Ed. 2d
1981	452 U.S.	101 S. Ct.	68 L. Ed. 2d
1981	452 U.S.	101 S. Ct.	69 L. Ed. 2d
1981	453 U.S.	101 S. Ct.	69 L. Ed. 2d
1981	454 U.S.	102 S. Ct.	70 L. Ed. 2d
1982	455 U.S.	102 S. Ct.	70 L. Ed. 2d
1982	455 U.S.	102 S. Ct.	71 L. Ed. 2d
1982	456 U.S.	102 S. Ct.	71 L. Ed. 2d
1982	456 U.S.	102 S. Ct.	72 L. Ed. 2d
1982	457 U.S.	102 S. Ct.	72 L. Ed. 2d
1982	457 U.S.	102 S. Ct.	73 L. Ed. 2d
1982	458 U.S.	102 S. Ct.	73 L. Ed. 2d
1982	459 U.S.	103 S. Ct.	74 L. Ed. 2d
1983	460 U.S.	103 S. Ct.	74 L. Ed. 2d
1983	460 U.S.	103 S. Ct.	75 L. Ed. 2d
1983	461 U.S.	103 S. Ct.	75 L. Ed. 2d
1983	461 U.S.	103 S. Ct.	76 L. Ed. 2d
1983	462 U.S.	103 S. Ct.	76 L. Ed. 2d
1983	462 U.S.	103 S. Ct.	77 L. Ed. 2d
1983	463 U.S.	103 S. Ct.	77 L. Ed. 2d
1983	463 U.S.	104 S. Ct.	77 L. Ed. 2d
1983	464 U.S.	104 S. Ct.	78 L. Ed. 2d
1984	465 U.S.	104 S. Ct.	79 L. Ed. 2d
1984	466 U.S.	104 S. Ct.	80 L. Ed. 2d
1984	467 U.S.	104 S. Ct.	81 L. Ed. 2d
1984	468 U.S.	104 S. Ct.	82 L. Ed. 2d
1984	468 U.S.	105 S. Ct.	82 L. Ed. 2d
1984	469 U.S.	105 S. Ct.	83 L. Ed. 2d
1985	470 U.S.	105 S. Ct.	84 L. Ed. 2d
1985	471 U.S.	105 S. Ct.	85 L. Ed. 2d
1985	472 U.S.	105 S. Ct.	86 L. Ed. 2d
1985	473 U.S.	105 S. Ct.	87 L. Ed. 2d
1985	473 U.S.	106 S. Ct.	87 L. Ed. 2d
1985	474 U.S.	106 S. Ct.	88 L. Ed. 2d
1986	475 U.S.	106 S. Ct.	89 L. Ed. 2d
1986	476 U.S.	106 S. Ct.	90 L. Ed. 2d
1986	477 U.S.	106 S. Ct.	91 L. Ed. 2d

Term or Year of Decision	Government Printing Office	Nominative Reporters & West	LCP
1986	478 U.S.	106 S. Ct.	92 L. Ed. 2d
1986	478 U.S.	107 S. Ct.	92 L. Ed. 2d
1986	479 U.S.	107 S. Ct.	93 L. Ed. 2d
1987	480 U.S.	107 S. Ct.	94 L. Ed. 2d
1987	481 U.S.	107 S. Ct.	95 L. Ed. 2d
1987	482 U.S.	107 S. Ct.	96 L. Ed. 2d
1987	483 U.S.	107 S. Ct.	97 L. Ed. 2d
1987	484 U.S.	108 S. Ct.	98 L. Ed. 2d
1988	485 U.S.	108 S. Ct.	99 L. Ed. 2d
1988	486 U.S.	108 S. Ct.	100 L. Ed. 2d
1988	487 U.S.	108 S. Ct.	101 L. Ed. 2d
1988	488 U.S.	109 S. Ct.	102 L. Ed. 2d
1989	489 U.S.	109 S. Ct.	103 L. Ed. 2d
1989	490 U.S.	109 S. Ct.	104 L. Ed. 2d
1989	491 U.S.	109 S. Ct.	105 L. Ed. 2d
1989	492 U.S.	109 S. Ct.	106 L. Ed. 2d
1989	493 U.S.	110 S. Ct.	107 L. Ed. 2d
1990	494 U.S.	110 S. Ct.	108 L. Ed. 2d
1990	495 U.S.	110 S. Ct.	109 L. Ed. 2d
1990	496 U.S.	110 S. Ct.	110 L. Ed. 2d
1990	497 U.S.	110 S. Ct.	111 L. Ed. 2d
1990	498 U.S.	111 S. Ct.	112 L. Ed. 2d
1991	499 U.S.	111 S. Ct.	113 L. Ed. 2d
1991	500 U.S.	111 S. Ct.	114 L. Ed. 2d
1991	501 U.S.	111 S. Ct.	115 L. Ed. 2d

APPENDIX III Table of Selected State Law Sources

ALABAMA (AL) {Ala.}†

Federal Circuit: Eleventh {11th Cir.} (Atlanta, GA)
Federal Districts: Northern, Middle, Southern
All Courts:
    West Region: Southern Reporter {So. 2d.}
    On LEXIS: ALA;CASES
    On WESTLAW: AL-CS
High Court:
*Supreme Court {Ala.}
    Official Reporter: Southern Reporter {So. 2d}
Intermediate Courts:
*Court of Civil Appeals {Ala. Civ. App.}
    Official Reporter: Southern Reporter {So. 2d}
*Court of Criminal Appeals {Ala. Crim. App.}
    Official Reporter: Southern Reporter {So. 2d}
Statutory Code:
*Code of Alabama (Michie) {Ala. Code § x (19xx)}
    On LEXIS: ALA;ALCODE
    On WESTLAW: AL-ST-ANN
Administrative Code:
*Alabama Administrative Code {Ala. Admin. Code r. x (19xx)}

ALASKA (AK) {Alaska}

Federal Circuit: Ninth {9th Cir.} (San Francisco, CA)
Federal District: Alaska
All Courts:
    West Region: Pacific Reporter {P.2d}
    On LEXIS: ALAS;CASES
    On WESTLAW: AK-CS
High Court:
*Supreme Court {Alaska}
    Official Reporter: Pacific Reporter {P.2d}
Intermediate Court:
*Court of Appeals {Alaska Ct. App.}
    Official Reporter: Pacific Reporter {P.2d}
Statutory Code:
*Alaska Statutes (Michie) {Alaska Stat. § x (19xx)}
    On LEXIS: ALAS;AKCODE
    On WESTLAW: AK-ST-ANN
Administrative Code:
*Alaska Administrative Code {Alaska Admin. Code tit. x, § x (month 19xx)}

†{ } = *The Bluebook: A Uniform System of Citation* Abbreviation

ARIZONA (AZ) {Ariz.}

Federal Circuit: Ninth {9th Cir.} (San Francisco, CA)
Federal District: Arizona
All Courts:
West Region: Pacific Reporter {P.2d}
On LEXIS: ARIZ;CASES
On WESTLAW: AZ-CS
High Court:
*Supreme Court {Ariz.}
Official Reporter: Arizona Reports {Ariz.}
Intermediate Court:
*Court of Appeals {Ariz. Ct. App.}
Official Reporter: Arizona Reports {Ariz.}
Statutory Codes:
*Arizona Revised Statutes
On LEXIS: ARIZ;AZCODE
*Arizona Revised Statutes Annotated (West) {Ariz. Rev. Stat. Ann. § x (19xx)}
On WESTLAW: AZ-ST-ANN
Administrative Code:
*Official Compilation Administrative Rules and Regulations {Ariz. Comp. Admin. R. & Regs. x (19xx)}

ARKANSAS (AR) {Ark.}

Federal Circuit: Eighth {8th Cir.} (St. Louis, MO)
Federal Districts: Eastern, Western
All Courts:
West Region: South Western Reporter {S.W.2d.}
On LEXIS: ARK;CASES
On WESTLAW: AR-CS
High Court:
*Supreme Court {Ark.}
Official Reporter: Arkansas Reports {Ark.}
Intermediate Court:
*Court of Appeals {Ark. Ct. App.}
Official Reporter: Arkansas Appellate Reports {Ark. App.}
Statutory Code:
*Arkansas Code of 1987 Annotated, Official Edition (Michie) {Ark. Stat. Ann. § x (19xx)}
On LEXIS: ARK;ARCODE
On WESTLAW: AR-ST-ANN
Administrative Code: none

CALIFORNIA (CA) {Cal.}

Federal Circuit: Ninth {9th Cir.} (San Francisco, CA)
Federal Districts: Central, Eastern, Northern, Southern
All Courts:
West Region: Pacific Reporter {P.2d.},
California Reporter {Cal. Rptr.}
On LEXIS: CAL;CASES
On WESTLAW: CA-CS
High Court:
*Supreme Court {Cal.}
Official Reporter: California Reports {Cal. 3d}

Intermediate Court:
*Court of Appeal {Cal. Ct. App.}
Official Reporter: California Appellate Reports {Cal. App. 3d}
Statutory Codes:
*Deering's Annotated California Code (BW) {Cal. [subject] Code § x (Deering 19xx)}
On LEXIS: CAL;CACODE
*West's Annotated California Code {Cal. [subject] Code § x (West 19xx)}
On WESTLAW: CA-ST-ANN
Administrative Code:
*California Administrative Code {Cal. Admin. Code tit. x, § x (19xx)}
Encyclopedia: California Jurisprudence 3d (LCP)

COLORADO (CO) {Colo.}

Federal Circuit: Tenth {10th Cir.} (Denver, CO)
Federal District: Colorado
All Courts:
West Region: Pacific Reporter {P.2d}
On LEXIS: COLO;CASES
On WESTLAW: CO-CS
High Court:
*Supreme Court {Colo.}
Official Reporter: Pacific Reporter {P.2d}
Intermediate Court:
*Court of Appeals {Colo. Ct. App.}
Official Reporter: Pacific Reporter {P.2d}
Statutory Codes:
*Colorado Revised Statutes (Bradford) {Colo. Rev. Stat. § x (19xx)}
On LEXIS: COLO;COCODE
*Colorado Revised Statutes Annotated (West)
On WESTLAW: CO-ST-ANN
Administrative Code:
*Code of Colorado Regulations {x Colo. Code Regs. § x (19xx)}

CONNECTICUT (CT) {Conn.}

Federal Circuit: Second {2d Cir.} (New York, NY)
Federal District: Connecticut
All Courts:
West Region: Atlantic Reporter {A.2d}
On LEXIS: CONN;CASES
On WESTLAW: CT-CS
High Court:
*Supreme Court {Conn.}
Official Reporter: Connecticut Reports {Conn.}
Intermediate Court:
*Appellate Court {Conn. App. Ct.}
Official Reporter: Connecticut Appellate Reports {Conn. App.}
Statutory Codes:
*Connecticut General Statutes Annotated (West) {Conn. Gen. Stat. Ann. § x (West 19xx)}
On WESTLAW: CT-ST-ANN
*General Statutes of Connecticut {Conn. Gen. Stat. § x (19xx)}
On LEXIS: CONN;CTCODE
Administrative Code:
*Regulations of Connecticut State Agencies {Conn. Agencies Regs. § x (19xx)}

DELAWARE (DE) {Del.}

Federal Circuit: Third {3d Cir.} (Philadelphia, PA)
Federal District: Delaware
All Courts:
West Region: Atlantic Reporter {A.2d}
On LEXIS: DEL;CASES
On WESTLAW: DE-CS
High Court:
*Supreme Court {Del.}
Official Reporter: Atlantic Reporter {A.2d}
Intermediate Court: none
Statutory Code:
*Delaware Code Annotated (Michie) {Del. Code. Ann. tit. x, § x (19xx)}
On LEXIS: DEL;DECODE
On WESTLAW: DE-ST-ANN
Administrative Code: none

DISTRICT OF COLUMBIA (DC) {D.C.}

Federal Circuit: District of Columbia {D.C. Cir.}
Federal District: District of Columbia
All Courts:
West Region: Atlantic Reporter {A.2d}
On LEXIS: DC;DCAPP
On WESTLAW: DC-CS
High Court:
*Court of Appeals {D.C.}
Official Reporter: Atlantic Reporter {A.2d}
Intermediate Court: none
Statutory Code:
*District of Columbia Code (Michie) {D.C. Code Ann. § x (19xx)}
On WESTLAW: DC-ST-ANN
Administrative Code: none

FLORIDA (FL) {Fla.}

Federal Circuit: Eleventh {11th Cir.} (Atlanta, GA)
Federal Districts: Northern, Middle, Southern
All Courts:
West Region: Southern Reporter {So. 2d}
On LEXIS: FLA;CASES
On WESTLAW: FL-CS
High Court:
*Supreme Court {Fla.}
Official Reporter: Southern Reporter {So. 2d}
Intermediate Court:
*District Courts of Appeals {Fla. Dist. Ct. App.}
Official Reporter: Southern Reporter {So. 2d}
Statutory Codes:
*Florida Statutes {Fla. Stat. § x (19xx)}
On LEXIS: FLA;FLCODE
*West's Florida Statutes Annotated {Fla. Stat. Ann. § x (West 19xx)}
On WESTLAW: FL-ST-ANN
Administrative Code:
*Florida Administrative Code Annotated {Fla. Admin. Code Ann. r. x (19xx)}
Encyclopedia: Florida Jurisprudence 2d (LCP)

GEORGIA (GA) {Ga.}

Federal Circuit: Eleventh {11th Cir.} (Atlanta, GA)
Federal Districts: Northern, Middle, Southern
All Courts:
West Region: Southern Reporter {So. 2d}
On LEXIS: GA;CASES
On WESTLAW: GA-CS
High Court:
*Supreme Court {Ga.}
Official Reporter: Georgia Reports {Ga.}
Intermediate Court:
*Court of Appeals {Ga. Ct. App.}
Official Reporter: Georgia Appeals Reports {Ga. App.}
Statutory Codes:
*Official Code of Georgia Annotated (Michie) {Ga. Code Ann. § x (19xx)}
On LEXIS: GA;GACODE
*Code of Georgia Annotated (Harrison) {Ga. Code Ann. § x (Harrison 19xx)}
On WESTLAW: GA-ST-ANN
Administrative Code:
*Official Compilation: Rules and Regulations of the State of Georgia {Ga. Comp. R. & Regs. r. x (19xx)}

HAWAII (HI) {Haw.}

Federal Circuit: Ninth {9th Cir.} (San Francisco, CA)
Federal District: Hawaii
All Courts:
West Region: Pacific Reporter {P.2d}
On LEXIS: HAW;CASES
On WESTLAW: HI-CS
High Court:
*Supreme Court {Haw.}
Official Reporter: Hawaii Reports {Haw.}
Intermediate Court:
*Intermediate Court of Appeals {Haw. Ct. App.}
Official Reporter: Hawaii Appellate Reports {Haw. App.}
Statutory Code:
*Hawaii Revised Statutes Annotated (Michie) {Haw. Rev. Stat. § x (19xx)}
On LEXIS: HAW;HICODE
On WESTLAW: HI-ST-ANN
Administrative Code: none

IDAHO (ID) {Idaho}

Federal Circuit: Ninth {9th Cir.} (San Francisco, CA)
Federal District: Idaho
All Courts:
West Region: Pacific Reporter {P.2d}
On LEXIS: IDA;CASES
On WESTLAW: ID-CS
High Court:
*Supreme Court {Idaho}
Official Reporter: Idaho Reports {Idaho}

Intermediate Court:
*Court of Appeals {Idaho Ct. App.}
    Official Reporter: Idaho Reports {Idaho}
Statutory Code:
*Idaho Official Code (Michie) {Idaho Code § x (19xx)}
    On LEXIS: IDA;IDCODE
    On WESTLAW: ID-ST-ANN
Administrative Code: none

ILLINOIS (IL) {Ill.}

Federal Circuit: Seventh {7th Cir.} (Chicago, IL)
Federal Districts: Northern, Central, Southern
All Courts:
    West Region: North Eastern Reporter {N.E.2d}
    On LEXIS: ILL;CASES
    On WESTLAW: IL-CS
High Court:
*Supreme Court {Ill.}
    Official Reporter: Illinois Reports {Ill. 2d}
Intermediate Court:
*Appellate Court {Ill. App. Ct.}
    Official Reporter: Illinois Appellate Reports {Ill. App. 3d}
Statutory Codes:
*Illinois Revised Statutes {Ill. Rev. Stat. ch. x, para. x (19xx)}
    On LEXIS: ILL;ILCODE
*Smith-Hurd Illinois Annotated Statutes (West) {Ill. Ann. Stat. ch. x, para. x (Smith-Hurd 19xx)}
    On WESTLAW: IL-ST-ANN
Administrative Code:
*Illinois Administrative Code {Ill. Admin. Code tit. x, § x (19xx)}
Encyclopedia: Illinois Law and Practice (West)

INDIANA (IN) {Ind.}

Federal Circuit: Seventh {7th Cir.} (Chicago, IL)
Federal Districts: Northern, Southern
All Courts:
    West Region: North Eastern Reporter {N.E.2d}
    On LEXIS: IND;CASES
    On WESTLAW: IN-CS
High Court:
*Supreme Court {Ind.}
    Official Reporter: North Eastern Reporter {N.E.2d}
Intermediate Court:
*Court of Appeals {Ind. Ct. App.}
    Official Reporter: North Eastern Reporter {N.E.2d}
Statutory Codes:
*Burns Indiana Statutes Annotated (Michie) {Ind. Code Ann. § x (Burns 19xx)}
    On LEXIS: IND;INCODE
    On WESTLAW: IN-STB-ANN
*Indiana Code {Ind. Code Ann. § x (19xx)}
*West's Annotated Indiana Code {Ind. Code Ann. § x (West 19xx)}
    On WESTLAW: IN-ST-ANN
Administrative Code:
*Indiana Administrative Code {Ind. Admin. Code tit. x, r. x (19xx)}

IOWA (IA) {Iowa}

Federal Circuit: Eighth {8th Cir.} (St. Louis, MO)
Federal Districts: Northern, Southern
All Courts:
 West Region: North Western Reporter {N.W.2d}
 On LEXIS: IOWA;CASES
 On WESTLAW: IA-CS
High Court:
*Supreme Court {Iowa}
 Official Reporter: North Western Reporter {N.W.2d}
Intermediate Court:
*Court of Appeals {Iowa Ct. App.}
 Official Reporter: North Western Reporter {N.W.2d}
Statutory Codes:
*Code of Iowa {Iowa Code § x (19xx)}
 On LEXIS: IOWA;IACODE
*Iowa Code Annotated (West) {Iowa Code Ann. § x (West 19xx)}
 On WESTLAW: IA-ST-ANN
Administrative Code:
*Iowa Administrative Code {Iowa Admin. Code r. x-x.x (19xx)}

KANSAS (KS) {Kan.}

Federal Circuit: Tenth {10th Cir.} (Denver, CO)
Federal District: Kansas
All Courts:
 West Region: Pacific Reporter {P.2d}
 On LEXIS: KAN;CASES
 On WESTLAW: KS-CS
High Court:
*Supreme Court {Kan.}
 Official Reporter: Kansas Reports {Kan.}
Intermediate Court:
*Court of Appeals {Kan. Ct. App.}
 Official Reporter: Kansas Court of Appeals Reports {Kan. App.}
Statutory Codes:
*Kansas Statutes Annotated {Kan. Stat. Ann. § x (19xx)}
 On LEXIS: KAN;KSCODE
*Vernon's Kansas Statutes Annotated (West) {varies}
Administrative Code:
*Kansas Administrative Regulations {Kan. Admin. Regs. x (19xx)}

KENTUCKY (KY) {Ky.}

Federal Circuit: Sixth {6th Cir.} (Cincinnati, OH)
Federal Districts: Eastern, Western
All Courts:
 West Region: South Western Reporter {S.W.2d}
 On LEXIS: KY;CASES
 On WESTLAW: KY-CS
High Court:
*Supreme Court {Ky.}
 Official Reporter: South Western Reporter {S.W.2d}
Intermediate Court:

*Court of Appeals {Ky. Ct. App.}
Official Reporter: South Western Reporter {S.W.2d}
Statutory Codes:
*Baldwin's Official Edition, Kentucky Revised Statutes Annotated (Banks-Baldwin) {Ky. Rev. Stat. Ann. § x (Baldwin 19xx)}
On LEXIS: KY;KYCODE
On WESTLAW: KY-ST-ANN
*Kentucky Revised Statutes Annotated, Official Edition (Michie) {Ky. Rev. Stat. Ann. § x (Michie/Bobbs-Merrill 19xx)}
On LEXIS: KY;KYSTAT
Administrative Code:
*Kentucky Administrative Regulations Service {x Ky. Admin. Regs. x:x (19xx)}
Encyclopedia: Kentucky Jurisprudence (LCP)

LOUISIANA (LA) {La.}

Federal Circuit: Fifth {5th Cir.} (New Orleans, LA)
Federal Districts: Eastern, Middle, Western
All Courts:
West Region: Southern Reporter {So. 2d}
On LEXIS: LA;CASES
On WESTLAW: LA-CS
High Court:
*Supreme Court {La.}
Official Reporter: none {cite to So. 2d}
Intermediate Court:
*Court of Appeal {La. Ct. App.}
Official Reporter: none {cite to So. 2d}
Statutory Codes:
*Louisiana Statutes
On LEXIS: LA;LACODE
*West's Louisiana Statutes Annotated {La. Rev. Stat. Ann. § x (West 19xx)}
On WESTLAW: LA-ST-ANN
Administrative Code:
*Louisiana Administrative Code {La. Admin. Code tit. x, § x (19xx)}

MAINE (ME) {Me.}

Federal Circuit: First {1st Cir.} (Boston, MA)
Federal District: Maine
All Courts:
West Region: Atlantic Reporter {A.2d}
On LEXIS: ME;ME
On WESTLAW: ME-CS
High Court:
*Supreme Judicial Court {Me.}
Official Reporter: Atlantic Reporter {A.2d}
Intermediate Court: none
Statutory Codes:
*Maine Revised Statutes
On LEXIS: ME;MECODE
*Maine Revised Statutes Annotated (West) {Me. Rev. Stat. Ann. tit. x, § x (19xx)}
On WESTLAW: ME-ST-ANN
Administrative Code: none

MARYLAND (MD) {Md.}

Federal Circuit: Fourth {4th Cir.} (Richmond, VA)
Federal District: Maryland
All Courts:
West Region: Atlantic Reporter {A.2d}
On LEXIS: MD;CASES
On WESTLAW: MD-CS
High Court:
*Court of Appeals {Md.}
Official Reporter: Maryland Reports {Md.}
Intermediate Court:
*Court of Special Appeals {Md. Ct. Spec. App.}
Official Reporter: Maryland Appellate Reports {Md. App.}
Statutory Code:
*Annotated Code of Maryland (Michie) {Md. [subject] Code Ann. § x (19xx)}
On LEXIS: MD;MDCODE
On WESTLAW: MD-ST-ANN
Administrative Code:
*Code of Maryland Regulations {Md. Regs. Code tit. x, § x (19xx)}
Encyclopedia: Maryland Law and Practice (West)

MASSACHUSETTS (MA) {Mass.}

Federal Circuit: First {1st Cir.} (Boston, MA)
Federal District: Massachusetts
All Courts:
West Region: North Eastern Reporter {N.E.2d}
On LEXIS: MASS;CASES
On WESTLAW: MA-CS
High Court:
*Supreme Judicial Court {Mass.}
Official Reporter: Massachusetts Reports {Mass.}
Intermediate Court:
*Appeals Court {Mass. App. Ct.}
Official Reporter: Massachusetts Appeals Court Reports {Mass. App. Ct.}
Statutory Codes:
*Annotated Laws of Massachusetts (LCP) {Mass. Ann. Laws ch. x, § x (Law. Co-op. 19xx)}
*General Laws of the Commonwealth of Massachusetts (LCP) {Mass. Gen. L. ch. x, § x (19xx)}
*Massachusetts General Laws Annotated (West) {Mass. Gen. Laws Ann. ch. x, § x (West 19xx)}
On WESTLAW: MA-ST-ANN
Administrative Code:
*Code of Massachusetts Regulations {Mass. Regs. Code tit. x, § x (19xx)}

MICHIGAN (MI) {Mich.}

Federal Circuit: Sixth {6th Cir.} (Cincinnati, OH)
Federal Districts: Eastern, Western
All Courts:
West Region: North Western Reporter {N.W.2d}
On LEXIS: MICH;CASES
On WESTLAW: MI-CS

High Court:
*Supreme Court {Mich.}
Official Reporter: Michigan Reports {Mich.}
Intermediate Court:
*Court of Appeals {Mich. Ct. App.}
Official Reporter: Michigan Appeals Reports {Mich. App.}
Statutory Codes:
*Michigan Compiled Laws {Mich. Comp. Laws § x (19xx)}
On LEXIS: MICH;MICODE
*Michigan Compiled Laws Annotated (West) {Mich. Comp. Laws Ann. § x (West 19xx)}
On WESTLAW: MI-ST-ANN
*Michigan Statutes Annotated (Callaghan) {Mich. Stat. Ann. § x (Callaghan 19xx)}
Administrative Code:
*Michigan Administrative Code {Mich. Admin. Code r. x (19xx)}
Encyclopedia: Michigan Law and Practice (West)

MINNESOTA (MN) {Minn.}

Federal Circuit: Eighth {8th Cir.} (St. Louis, MO)
Federal District: Minnesota
All Courts:
West Region: North Western Reporter {N.W.2d}
On LEXIS: MINN;CASES
On WESTLAW: MN-CS
High Court:
*Supreme Court {Minn.}
Official Reporter: North Western Reporter {N.W.2d}
Intermediate Court:
*Court of Appeals {Minn. Ct. App.}
Official Reporter: North Western Reporter {N.W.2d}
Statutory Codes:
*Minnesota Statutes {Minn. Stat. § x (19xx)}
On LEXIS: MINN;MNCODE
*Minnesota Statutes Annotated (West) {Minn. Stat. Ann. § x (West 19xx)}
On WESTLAW: MN-ST
Administrative Code:
*Minnesota Rules {Minn. R. x.x (19xx)}

MISSISSIPPI (MS) {Miss.}

Federal Circuit: Fifth {5th Cir.} (New Orleans, LA)
Federal Districts: Northern, Southern
All Courts:
West Region: Southern Reporter {So.2d}
On LEXIS: MISS;MISS
On WESTLAW: MS-CS
High Court:
*Supreme Court {Miss.}
Official Reporter: Southern Reporter {So. 2d}
Intermediate Court: none
Statutory Code:
*Mississippi Code Annotated (LCP) {Miss. Code Ann. § x (19xx)}
Administrative Code: none

MISSOURI (MO) {Mo.}

Federal Circuit: Eighth {8th Cir.} (St. Louis, MO)
Federal Districts: Eastern, Western
All Courts:
West Region: South Western Reporter {S.W.2d}
On LEXIS: MO;CASES
On WESTLAW: MO-CS
High Court:
*Supreme Court {Mo.}
Official Reporter: South Western Reporter {S.W.2d}
Intermediate Court:
*Court of Appeals {Mo. Ct. App.}
Official Reporter: South Western Reporter {S.W.2d}
Statutory Codes:
*Missouri Revised Statutes {Mo. Rev. Stat. § x (19xx)}
On LEXIS: MO;MOCODE
*Vernon's Annotated Missouri Statutes (West) {Mo. Ann. Stat. § x (Vernon 19xx)}
On WESTLAW: MO-ST-ANN
Administrative Code:
*Missouri Code of State Regulations {Mo. Code Regs. tit. x, § x-x.x (19xx)}

MONTANA (MT) {Mont.}

Federal Circuit: Ninth {9th Cir.} (San Francisco, CA)
Federal District: Montana
All Courts:
West Region: Pacific Reporter {P.2d}
On LEXIS: MONT;CASES
On WESTLAW: MT-CS
High Court:
*Supreme Court {Mont.}
Official Reporter: Montana Reports {Mont.}
Intermediate Court: none
Statutory Code:
*Montana Code Annotated {Mont. Code Ann. § x (19xx)}
On LEXIS: MONT;MTCODE
Administrative Code:
*Administrative Rules of Montana {Mont. Admin. R. x (19xx)}

NEBRASKA (NE) {Neb.}

Federal Circuit: Eighth {8th Cir.} (St. Louis, MO)
Federal District: Nebraska
All Courts:
West Region: North Western Reporter {N.W.2d}
On LEXIS: NEB;NEB
On WESTLAW: NE-CS
High Court:
*Supreme Court {Neb.}
Official Reporter: Nebraska Reports {Neb.}
Intermediate Court: none

Statutory Code:
*Revised Statutes of Nebraska {Neb. Rev. Stat. § x (19xx)}
On LEXIS: NEB;NECODE
On WESTLAW: NE-ST
Administrative Code:
*Nebraska Administrative Rules & Regulations {Neb. Admin. R. & Regs. x (19xx)}

NEVADA (NV) {Nev.}

Federal Circuit: Ninth {9th Cir.} (San Francisco, CA)
Federal District: Nevada
All Courts:
West Region: Pacific Reporter {P.2d}
On LEXIS: NEV;NEV
On WESTLAW: NV-CS
High Court:
*Supreme Court {Nev.}
Official Reporter: Nevada Reports {Nev.}
Intermediate Court: none
Statutory Codes:
*Nevada Revised Statutes {Nev. Rev. Stat. § x (19xx)}
On WESTLAW: NV-ST-ANN
*Nevada Revised Statutes Annotated (Michie) {Nev. Rev. Stat. Ann. § x (Michie 19xx)}
On LEXIS: NEV;NVCODE
Administrative Code:
*Nevada Administrative Code {Nev. Admin. Code ch. x, § x (19xx)}

NEW HAMPSHIRE (NH) {N.H.}

Federal Circuit: First {1st Cir.} (Boston, MA)
Federal District: New Hampshire
All Courts:
West Region: Atlantic Reporter {A.2d}
On LEXIS: NH;CASES
On WESTLAW: NH-CS
High Court:
*Supreme Court {N.H.}
Official Reporter: New Hampshire Reports {N.H.}
Intermediate Court: none
Statutory Code:
*New Hampshire Revised Statutes Annotated (Equity) {N.H. Rev. Stat. Ann. § x (19xx)}
On WESTLAW: NH-ST-ANN
Administrative Code:
*New Hampshire Code of Administrative Rules {N.H. Code Admin. R. [abbrev. dep't name] x.x (19xx)}

NEW JERSEY (NJ) {N.J.}

Federal Circuit: Third {3d Cir.} (Philadelphia, PA)
Federal District: New Jersey

All Courts:
West Region: Atlantic Reporter {A.2d}
On LEXIS: NJ;CASES
On WESTLAW: NJ-CS
High Court:
*Supreme Court {N.J.}
Official Reporter: New Jersey Reports {N.J.}
Intermediate Court:
*Appellate Division, Superior Court {N.J. Super. Ct. App. Div.}
Official Reporters:*New Jersey Superior Court Reports {N.J. Super.}
*New Jersey Equity Reports {N.J. Eq.}
Statutory Codes:
*New Jersey Statutes {N.J. Rev. Stat. § x (19xx)}
On LEXIS: NJ;NJCODE
*New Jersey Statutes Annotated (West) {N.J. Stat. Ann. § x (West 19xx)}
On WESTLAW: NJ-ST-ANN
Administrative Code:
*New Jersey Administrative Code {N.J. Admin. Code tit. x, § x-x.x (19xx)}

NEW MEXICO (NM) {N.M.}

Federal Circuit: Tenth {10th Cir.} (Denver, CO)
Federal District: New Mexico
All Courts:
West Region: Pacific Reporter {P.2d}
On LEXIS: NM;CASES
On WESTLAW: NM-CS
High Court:
*Supreme Court {N.M.}
Official Reporter: New Mexico Reports {N.M.}
Intermediate Court:
*Court of Appeal {N.M. Ct. App.}
Official Reporter: New Mexico Reports {N.M.}
Statutory Code:
*New Mexico Statutes Annotated (Michie) {N.M. Stat. Ann. § x (19xx)}
On LEXIS: NM;NMCODE
On WESTLAW: NM-ST-ANN
Administrative Code: none

NEW YORK (NY) {N.Y.}

Federal Circuit: Second {2d Cir.} (New York, NY)
Federal Districts: Eastern, Northern, Southern, Western
All Courts:
West Region: North Eastern Reporter {N.E.2d},
West's New York Supplement {N.Y.S.2d}
On LEXIS: NY;CASES
On WESTLAW: NY-CS
High Court:
*Court of Appeals {N.Y.}
Official Reporter: New York Reports {N.Y.}
Intermediate Court:
*Appellate Division, Supreme Court {N.Y. App. Div.}
Official Reporter: Appellate Division Reports {A.D.2d}

Statutory Codes:
*McKinney's Consolidated Laws of New York Annotated (West) {N.Y. [subject] Law § x (McKinney 19xx)}
On WESTLAW: NY-ST-ANN
*New York Consolidated Laws (Michie) {N.Y. [subject] Law § x (Consol. 19xx)}
On LEXIS: NY;NYCODE
*New York Consolidated Laws Service (LCP) {N.Y. [subject] Law § x (Consol. 19xx)}
Administrative Code:
*Official Compilation of Codes, Rules & Regulations of the State of New York {N.Y. Comp. Codes R. & Regs. tit. x, § x (19xx)}
Encyclopedia: New York Jurisprudence 2d (LCP)

NORTH CAROLINA (NC) {N.C.}

Federal Circuit: Fourth {4th Cir.} (Richmond, VA)
Federal Districts: Eastern, Middle, Western
All Courts:
West Region: South Eastern Reporter {S.E.2d}
On LEXIS: NC;CASES
On WESTLAW: NC-CS
High Court:
*Supreme Court {N.C.}
Official Reporter: North Carolina Reports {N.C.}
Intermediate Court:
*Court of Appeals {N.C. Ct. App.}
Official Reporter: N.C. Court of Appeals Reports {N.C. App.}
Statutory Code:
*General Statutes of North Carolina (Michie) {N.C. Gen. Stat. § x (19xx)}
On LEXIS: NC;NCCODE
On WESTLAW: NC-ST-ANN
Administrative Code:
*North Carolina Administrative Code (microfiche) {N.C. Admin. Code tit. x, r. xx.xxxx (month 19xx)}

NORTH DAKOTA (ND) {N.D.}

Federal Circuit: Eighth {8th Cir.} (St. Louis, MO)
Federal District: North Dakota
All Courts:
West Region: North Western Reporter {N.W.2d}
On LEXIS: ND;CASES
On WESTLAW: ND-CS
High Court:
*Supreme Court {N.D.}
Official Reporter: North Western Reporter {N.W.2d}
Intermediate Court: none
Statutory Code:
*North Dakota Century Code Annotated (Michie) {N.D. Cent. Code § x (19xx)}
Administrative Code:
*North Dakota Administrative Code {N.D. Admin. Code § x (month 19xx)}

OHIO (OH) {Ohio}

Federal Circuit: Sixth {6th Cir.} (Cincinnati, OH)
Federal Districts: Northern, Southern

All Courts:
West Region: North Eastern Reporter {N.E.2d.}
On LEXIS: OHIO;CASES
On WESTLAW: OH-CS
High Court:
*Supreme Court {Ohio}
Official Reporter: Ohio Official Reports {Ohio St. 3d}
Intermediate Court:
*Court of Appeals {Ohio Ct. App.}
Official Reporter: Ohio Official Reports {Ohio App. 3d}
Statutory Codes:
*Baldwin's Ohio Revised Code Annotated (Banks-Baldwin) {Ohio Rev. Code Ann. § x (Baldwin 19xx)}
On LEXIS: OHIO;OHCODE
*Page's Ohio Revised Code Annotated (Anderson) {Ohio Rev. Code Ann. § x (Anderson 19xx)}
On WESTLAW: OH-ST-ANN
Administrative Code:
*Ohio Administrative Code {Ohio Admin. Code § x (19xx)}
On LEXIS: OHIO;OHADMIN
Encyclopedia: Ohio Jurisprudence 3d (LCP)

OKLAHOMA (OK) {Okla.}

Federal Circuit: Tenth {10th Cir.} (Denver, CO)
Federal Districts: Eastern, Northern, Western
All Courts:
West Region: Pacific Reporter {P.2d.}
On LEXIS: OKLA;CASES
On WESTLAW: OK-CS
High Courts:
*Supreme Court {Okla.}
Official Reporter: Pacific Reporter {P.2d}
*Court of Criminal Appeals {Okla. Crim. App.}
Official Reporter: Pacific Reporter {P.2d}
Intermediate Court:
*Court of Appeals {Okla. Ct. App.}
Official Reporter: Pacific Reporter {P.2d}
Statutory Codes:
*Oklahoma Statutes {Okla. Stat. tit. x, § x (19xx)}
On LEXIS: OKLA;OKCODE
*Oklahoma Statutes Annotated (West) {Okla. Stat. Ann. tit. x, § x (West 19xx)}
On WESTLAW: OK-ST-ANN
Administrative Code: none

OREGON (OR) {Or.}

Federal Circuit: Ninth {9th Cir.} (San Francisco, CA)
Federal District: Oregon
All Courts:
West Region: Pacific Reporter {P.2d}
On LEXIS: ORE;CASES
On WESTLAW: OR-CS
High Court:
*Supreme Court {Or.}
Official Reporter: Oregon Reports {Or.}

Intermediate Courts:
*Court of Appeals {Or. Ct. App.}
Official Reporter: Oregon Reports, Court of Appeals {Or. App.}
*Tax Court {Or. T.C.}
Official Reporter: Oregon Tax Reports {Or. Tax}
Statutory Code:
*Oregon Revised Statutes {Or. Rev. Stat. § x (19xx)}
On LEXIS: ORE;ORCODE
On WESTLAW: OR-ST
Administrative Code:
*Oregon Administrative Rules {Or. Admin. R. x (19xx)}

PENNSYLVANIA (PA) {Pa.}

Federal Circuit: Third {3d Cir.} (Philadelphia, PA)
Federal Districts: Eastern, Middle, Western
All Courts:
West Region: Atlantic Reporter {A.2d}
On LEXIS: PA;CASES
On WESTLAW: PA-CS
High Court:
*Supreme Court {Pa.}
Official Reporter: Pennsylvania State Reports {Pa.}
Intermediate Courts:
*Commonwealth Court {Pa. Commw. Ct.}
Official Reporter: Pennsylvania Commonwealth Court Reports {Pa. Commw.}
*Superior Court {Pa. Super. Ct.}
Official Reporter: Pennsylvania Superior Court Reports {Pa. Super.}
Statutory Codes:
*Pennsylvania Consolidated Statutes {x Pa. Cons. Stat. § x (19xx)}
On LEXIS: PA;PACODE
*Purdon's Pennsylvania Statutes Annotated and Consolidated Statutes Annotated (Bissel/West) {x Pa. Cons. Stat. Ann. § x (Purdon 19xx)}
On WESTLAW: PA-ST-ANN
Administrative Code:
*Pennsylvania Code {x Pa. Code § x (19xx)}

RHODE ISLAND (RI) {R.I.}

Federal Circuit: First {1st Cir.} (Boston, MA)
Federal District: Rhode Island
All Courts:
West Region: Atlantic Reporter {A.2d}
On LEXIS: RI;RI
On WESTLAW: RI-CS
High Court:
*Supreme Court {R.I.}
Official Reporter: Atlantic Reporter {A.2d}
Intermediate Court: none
Statutory Code:
*General Laws of Rhode Island (Michie) {R.I. Gen. Laws § x (19xx)}
On LEXIS: RI;RICODE
On WESTLAW: RI-ST-ANN
Administrative Code: none

SOUTH CAROLINA (SC) {S.C.}

Federal Circuit: Fourth {4th Cir.} (Richmond, VA)
Federal District: South Carolina
All Courts:
    West Region: South Eastern Reporter {S.E.2d}
    On LEXIS: SC;CASES
    On WESTLAW: SC-CS
High Court:
*Supreme Court {S.C.}
    Official Reporter: South Carolina Reports {S.C.}
Intermediate Court:
*Court of Appeals {S.C. Ct. App.}
    Official Reporter: South Carolina Reports {S.C.}
Statutory Code:
*Code of Laws of South Carolina Annotated (LCP) {S.C. Code Ann. § x (Law. Co-op. 19xx)}
Administrative Code:
*Code of Laws of South Carolina Annotated, Code of Regulations (LCP) {S.C. Code Regs. x (19xx)}

SOUTH DAKOTA (SD) {S.D.}

Federal Circuit: Eighth {8th Cir.} (St. Louis, MO)
Federal District: South Dakota
All Courts:
    West Region: North Western Reporter {N.W.2d}
    On LEXIS: SD;SD
    On WESTLAW: SD-CS
High Court:
*Supreme Court {S.D.}
    Official Reporter: North Western Reporter {N.W.2d}
Intermediate Court: none
Statutory Code:
*South Dakota Codified Laws Annotated (Michie) {S.D. Codified Laws Ann. § x (19xx)}
    On LEXIS: SD;SDCODE
    On WESTLAW: SD-ST-ANN
Administrative Code:
*Administrative Rules of South Dakota {S.D. Admin. R. x (19xx)}

TENNESSEE (TN) {Tenn.}

Federal Circuit: Sixth {6th Cir.} (Cincinnati, OH)
Federal Districts: Eastern, Middle, Western
All Courts:
    West Region: South Western Reporter {S.W.2d}
    On LEXIS: TENN;CASES
    On WESTLAW: TN-CS
High Court:
*Supreme Court {Tenn.}
    Official Reporter: South Western Reporter {S.W.2d}
Intermediate Courts:
*Court of Appeals {Tenn. Ct. App.}
    Official Reporter: South Western Reporter {S.W.2d}

*Court of Criminal Appeals {Tenn. Crim. App.}
Official Reporter: South Western Reporter {S.W.2d}
Statutory Code:
*Tennessee Code Annotated (Michie) {Tenn. Code Ann. § x (19xx)}
On LEXIS: TENN;TNCODE
On WESTLAW: TN-ST-ANN
Administrative Code:
*Official Compilation: Rules & Regulations of the State of Tennessee {Tenn. Comp. R. & Regs. tit. x, ch. x (19xx)}

TEXAS (TX) {Tex.}

Federal Circuit: Fifth {5th Cir.} (New Orleans, LA)
Federal Districts: Eastern, Northern, Southern, Western
All Courts:
West Region: South Western Reporter {S.W.2d}
On LEXIS: TEX;CASES
On WESTLAW: TX-CS
High Courts:
*Supreme Court {Tex.}
Official Reporter: none {cite to S.W.2d}
*Court of Criminal Appeals {Tex. Crim. App.}
Official Reporter: none {cite to S.W.2d}
Intermediate Court:
*Court of Appeals {Tex. Ct. App.}
Official Reporter: none {cite to S.W.2d}
Statutory Codes:
*Texas Statutes and Codes
On LEXIS: TEX;TXCODE
*Vernon's Annotated Texas Statutes and Codes (West) {Tex. [subject] Code Ann. § x (Vernon 19xx)}
On WESTLAW: TX-ST-ANN
Administrative Code:
*Texas Administrative Code {Tex. Admin. Code tit. x, § x (19xx)}
Encyclopedia: Texas Jurisprudence 3d (LCP)

UTAH (UT) {Utah}

Federal Circuit: Tenth {10th Cir.} (Denver, CO)
Federal District: Utah
All Courts:
West Region: Pacific Reporter {P.2d}
On LEXIS: UTAH;CASES
On WESTLAW: UT-CS
High Court:
*Supreme Court {Utah}
Official Reporter: none {cite to P.2d}
Intermediate Court:
*Court of Appeals
Official Reporter: none {cite to P.2d}
Statutory Code:
*Utah Code Annotated (Michie) {Utah Code Ann. § x (19xx)}
On LEXIS: UTAH;UTCODE
On WESTLAW: UT-ST-ANN

Administrative Code:
*Administrative Rules of the State of Utah {Utah Admin. R. x (19xx)}

VERMONT (VT) {Vt.}

Federal Circuit: Second {2d Cir.} (New York, NY)
Federal District: Vermont
All Courts:
West Region: Atlantic Reporter {A.2d}
On LEXIS: VT;CASES
On WESTLAW: VT-CS
High Court:
*Supreme Court {Vt.}
Official Reporter: Vermont Reports {Vt.}
Intermediate Court: none
Statutory Code:
*Vermont Statutes Annotated (Equity) {Vt. Stat. Ann. tit. x, § x (19xx)}
On WESTLAW: VT-ST-ANN
Administrative Code:
*Vermont Administrative Procedures Compilation {Vt. Admin. Proc. Comp. [agency] r. [or §] x (19xx)}

VIRGINIA (VA) {Va.}

Federal Circuit: Fourth {4th Cir.} (Richmond, VA)
Federal Districts Eastern, Western
All Courts:
West Region: South Eastern Reporter {S.E.2d}
On LEXIS: VA;CASES
On WESTLAW: VA-CS
High Court:
*Supreme Court {Va.}
Official Reporter: Virginia Reports {Va.}
Intermediate Court:
*Court of Appeals {Va. Ct. App.}
Official Reporter: Virginia Court of Appeals Reports {Va. App.}
Statutory Code:
*Code of Virginia Annotated (Michie) {Va. Code Ann. § x (19xx)}
On LEXIS: VA;VACODE
On WESTLAW: VA-ST-ANN
Administrative Code: none

WASHINGTON (WA) {Wash.}

Federal Circuit: Ninth {9th Cir.} (San Francisco, CA)
Federal Districts Eastern, Western
All Courts:
West Region: Pacific Reporter {P.2d.}
On LEXIS: WASH;CASES
On WESTLAW: WA-CS
High Court:
*Supreme Court {Wash.}
Official Reporter: Washington Reports {Wash. 2d}

Intermediate Court:
*Court of Appeals {Wash. Ct. App.}
    Official Reporter: Washington Appellate Reports {Wash. App.}
Statutory Codes:
*Revised Code of Washington {Wash. Rev. Code § x (19xx)}
    On LEXIS: WASH;WACODE
*West's Revised Code of Washington Annotated {Wash. Rev. Code Ann. § x (19xx)}
    On WESTLAW: WA-ST-ANN
Administrative Code:
*Washington Administrative Code {Wash. Admin. Code § x (19xx)}

WEST VIRGINIA (WV) {W. Va.}

Federal Circuit: Fourth {4th Cir.} (Richmond, VA)
Federal Districts: Northern, Southern
All Courts:
    West Region: South Eastern Reporter {S.E.2d}
    On LEXIS: WVA;CASES
    On WESTLAW: WV-CS
High Court:
*Supreme Court {W. Va.}
    Official Reporter: South Eastern Reporter {S.E.2d}
Intermediate Court: none
Statutory Code:
*West Virginia Code Annotated (Michie) {W. Va. Code § x (19xx)}
    On LEXIS: WVA;WVCODE
    On WESTLAW: WV-ST-ANN
Administrative Code: none

WISCONSIN (WI) {Wis.}

Federal Circuit: Seventh {7th Cir.} (Chicago, IL)
Federal Districts: Eastern, Western
All Courts:
    West Region: North Western Reporter {N.W.2d}
    On LEXIS: WISC;CASES
    On WESTLAW: WI-CS
High Court:
*Supreme Court {Wis.}
    Official Reporter: Wisconsin Reports {Wis. 2d}
Intermediate Court:
*Court of Appeals {Wis. Ct. App.}
    Official Reporter: Wisconsin Reports {Wis. 2d}
Statutory Codes:
*West's Wisconsin Statutes Annotated {Wis. Stat. Ann. § x (West 19xx)}
    On WESTLAW: WI-ST-ANN
*Wisconsin Statutes {Wis. Stat. § x (19xx)}
    On LEXIS: WISC;WICODE
Administrative Code:
*Wisconsin Administrative Code {Wis. Admin. Code § [agency] x (month 19xx)}

WYOMING (WY) {Wyo.}

Federal Circuit: Tenth {10th Cir.} (Denver, CO)
Federal District: Wyoming
All Courts:
  West Region: Pacific Reporter {P.2d}
  On LEXIS: WYO;CASES
  On WESTLAW: WY-CS
High Court:
*Supreme Court {Wyo.}
  Official Reporter: Pacific Reporter {P.2d}
Intermediate Court: none
Statutory Code:
*Wyoming Statutes Annotated (Michie) {Wyo. Stat. § x (19xx)}
  On LEXIS: WYO;WYCODE
  On WESTLAW: WY-ST-ANN
Administrative Code: none

APPENDIX IV Law Library Classification

A **library,** by definition, is an organized collection of books and other media kept for their use. As a practical matter, books and other media in a library can be used only if they can be found in the collection. A library, to be worthy of the name, must be organized to facilitate the finding of books and other media.

A **law library** is an organized collection of law books and other media. Legal research is the art of the effective use of law books and other media generally found in a law library. To find books and other media in a law library, a legal researcher must have a basic understanding of the organization of books and other media in a law library.

The arrangement of books and other media in a library is known as **classification.** Classification brings related books and other media together in sequence from general to specific. Classification is usually according to the predominant subject of an item, then to its form, then to its most useful place in the collection. Over the years, many different systems of classification have been developed, but almost every library in the United States uses either the Dewey Decimal system or the Library of Congress system. In addition, government publications are usually organized according to the Superintendent of Documents system.

The **Dewey Decimal Classification** system was devised by Melvil Dewey in 1876. Dewey's system, entirely numerical, was devised around standard divisions and subdivisions, with the social sciences classified in the 300s, and law starting at 340. The Dewey system is generally used in public, primary school, and secondary school libraries.

The **Library of Congress Classification** system was devised in the early 1900s by Librarian of Congress Herbert Putnam and his Chief Cataloger, Charles Martel, replacing the previous system, which had become inadequate. Their letter-number classification system reflected the actual content of the Library of Congress at the time. After preparing the main classifications, they called in subject specialists to prepare the subclassifications. The resulting classification schedules are periodically reviewed by committees and are published as needed. Many of the classification schedules have gone through several editions. Because of its expansive and flexible format, the Library of Congress Classification is generally used in large government, university, and research libraries, including law school and other law libraries. It is used in the U.S. Supreme Court Library, and, of course, in the Library of Congress Law Library.

The **Superintendent of Documents Classification** system is often used for collections of governmental documents. Its essential feature is the grouping of publications by the issuing governmental agency. The issuing governmental agency is indicated by a letter or letter combination prefix. Numbers follow indicating the subordinate bureau within the agency, the title designation, and the year of publication (e.g., C 61.34:987). Common prefixes include:

A	Agriculture Department
C 3.	Census Bureau (Commerce Department)
D	Defense Department
E	Energy Department
ED	Education Department
GA	General Accounting Office
GS	General Services Administration
HE	Health and Human Services Department
I	Interior Department
I 19.	U.S. Geological Survey (Interior Department)
J	Justice Department
JU	Judiciary
L	Labor Department
LC	Library of Congress
NAS	National Aeronautics and Space Administration
S	State Department
SI	Smithsonian Institution
T 22.	Internal Revenue Service (Treasury Department)
X, Y	Congress
Y 4.	Congressional Committees

The LC Classification Scheme

Because it is the classification system used in most law libraries, legal researchers should have an intimate knowledge of the Library of Congress Classification system (LC). There are 21 main classifications, lettered from A to Z (except for I, O, W, X, and Y). A second letter, or a second and third letter, each from A to Z, is used to indicate a subclassification. The Library of Congress Classification includes published schedules covering the following subjects:

A	General Works; Polygraphy
B-BJ	Philosophy; Psychology
BL-BX	Religion
C	Auxiliary Sciences of History
D	General and Old World History
E-F	American History
G	Geography; Maps; Anthropology; Recreation
H-HJ	Economics
HM-HX	Sociology
J	Political Science
K	Law (General)
KD	Law of the United Kingdom and Ireland
KDZ, KG-KH	Law of the Americas, Latin America, and the West Indies
KE	Law of Canada

KF	Law of the United States
KK-KKC	Law of Germany
L	Education
M	Music
N	Fine Arts
P	Language
Q	Science
R	Medicine
S	Agriculture
T	Technology
U	Military Science
V	Naval Science
Z	Bibliography; Library Science

Note that political science (which includes international law) is covered in the J classification, law is covered in the K classification, and law of the United States is covered in the KF subclassification.

KF Subclassification

The KF subclassification covers the law of the United States in general. The law of each state, alphabetically by state, is covered in subclasses KFA-KFW. The law of each city, alphabetically by city, is covered in subclass KFX. The law of each territory, alphabetically by territory, is covered in subclass KFZ.

The KF subclassification is broken down numerically from 1 to 9760. The class number assignments may be summarized as follows:

KF	Law of the United States.
1– 8	Bibliography.
16– 49	Legislative documents.
50– 90	Statutes and administrative regulations.
101– 152	Law reports and related materials.
154	Encyclopedias.
156	Law dictionaries. "Words and Phrases."
159	Legal maxims. Quotations.
165	Uniform State laws.
170	Form books.
175	Periodicals.
178	Yearbooks.
180– 185	Judicial statistics.
190– 195	Directories.
200	Society and bar association journals and yearbooks.
202	Congresses.
209– 224	Collections.
209	-Monographic series.
210– 211	-Several authors.
213	-Individual authors.

220– 224	-Criminal trials.
228	Records and briefs of individual civil suits.
240– 246	Legal research. Legal bibliography.
250– 251	Legal composition and draftsmanship.
255	Law reporting.
260	Cases and materials.
262– 292	Legal education.
294	Law societies, A–Z.
297– 334	The legal profession.
320	Legal Assistantship/Paralegalism.
336– 337	Legal aid. Legal aid societies.
338	Lawyer referral services.
350– 375	History.
379– 384	Jurisprudence and philosophy of American law.
384	Criticism. Legal reform. General "administration of justice."
385– 391	General and comprehensive works.
394– 395	Common law in the U.S.
398– 400	Equity.
410– 418	Conflict of laws.
420	Retroactive law.
425– 435	General principles and concepts.
445– 450	Concepts applying to several branches of law.
465– 553	Persons.
465– 485	-General. Status. Capacity.
501– 550	-Domestic relations. Family law.
553	-Guardian and ward.
560– 720	Property.
560– 562	-General. Ownership.
566– 698	-Real property. Land law.
701– 720	-Personal property.
726– 745	Trusts and trustees.
746– 750	Estate planning.
753– 780	Succession upon death.
801–1241	Contracts.
801– 805	-General and comprehensive works.
807– 839	-General principles.
841– 869	-Government contracts.
871–1241	-Particular contracts.
871– 890	--Comprehensive. Commercial law. Mercantile transactions.
894	--Contract of service. Master and servant.
898– 905	--Contract for work and labor. Independent contractors.
911– 935	--Sale of goods.
939– 951	--Contracts involving bailments.
956– 962	--Negotiable instruments.
966–1032	--Banking.

1033	--Foreign exchange brokerage.
1035–1040	--Loan of money.
1045	--Suretyship. Guaranty.
1046–1062	--Secured transactions.
1066–1083	--Marketing of securities. Investments. Stock exchange transactions.
1085–1086	--Commodity exchanges. Produce exchanges.
1091–1137	--Carriers. Carriage of goods and passengers.
1091	---General. Liability.
1092	---Carriage by land.
1093	---Carriage by air.
1096–1114	---Carriage by sea. Maritime commercial law. Admiralty.
1121–1132	---Maritime labor law.
1135–1137	---Marine insurance.
1146–1238	--Insurance.
1241	--Aleatory contracts.
1244	Restitution. Quasi contracts. Unjust enrichment.
1246–1327	Torts.
1341–1348	Agency.
1355–1480	Associations.
1355–1359	-General.
1361–1380	-Unincorporated associations.
1361–1362	--General.
1365–1380	--Business associations. Partnership.
1384–1480	-Corporations.
1384–1386	--General.
1388–1389	--Nonprofit corporations.
1396–1477	--Business corporations.
1480	--Government-owned corporations and business organizations.
1501–1548	Insolvency and bankruptcy. Creditors' rights.
1600–2940	Regulation of industry, trade, and commerce. Occupational law.
1600	-General and comprehensive.
1601–1666	-Trade regulation. Control of trade practices.
1601–1611	--General. Unfair trade practices.
1614–1617	--Advertising.
1619–1620	--Labeling.
1624–1625	--Restraint of trade.
1626–1629	--Price fixing.
1631–1657	--Monopolies. Antitrust laws.
1659	--"Small business."
1661	--Trade associations.
1663	--State jurisdiction. "Trade barriers."
1665–1666	--Weights and measures. Containers.
1681–1873	-Primary production. Extractive industries.
1681–1750	--Agriculture. Forestry.

1770–1773	--Fishery.
1801–1873	--Mining. Quarrying. Oil and gas.
1875–1893	-Manufacturing industries.
1900–1944	-Food processing industries.
1950	-Construction and building industry.
1970–2057	-Trade and commerce.
2076–2140	-Public utilities.
2161–2849	-Transportation and communication.
2901–2940	-The professions.
2971–3192	Intellectual property.
2971–2980	-General.
2986–3080	-Copyright.
3084	-Author and publisher. The publishing contract.
3086	-Design protection.
3091–3192	-Patent law and trade marks.
3195–3198	Unfair competition.
3300–3750	Social legislation.
3300	-General.
3301–3580	-Labor law.
3600–3686	-Social insurance.
3720–3745	-Public welfare. Public assistance.
3750	-Disaster relief.
3775–3813	Public health. Sanitation.
3821–3829	Medical legislation.
3832	Eugenics. Sterilization.
3835–3838	Veterinary laws. Veterinary hygiene.
3841–3845	Prevention of cruelty to animals.
3861–3894	Food. Drugs. Cosmetics.
3901–3925	Liquor control. Prohibition.
3941–3977	Public safety.
3941–3942	-Weapons. Firearms. Munitions.
3945–3965	-Hazardous articles and processes.
3970	-Accident control.
3975–3977	-Fire prevention and control. Explosives.
3985–3995	Control of social activities.
3985	-General.
3987	-Amusements.
3989	-Sports. Prize-fighting.
3992	-Lotteries.
3995	-Other.
4101–4258	Education.
4270–4330	Science and the arts. Research.
4270	-General.
4280	-Particular branches and subjects. A–Z.
4288–4302	-The arts.
4305	-Museums and galleries.
4310–4312	-Historical buildings and documents.

4315–4319	-Libraries.
4325	-Archives. Historical documents.
4330	-Educational, scientific, and cultural exchanges.
4501–5130	Constitutional law.
4501–4515	-Sources.
4520	-Works on legislative history of the constitution.
4525–4528	-Texts of the Constitution.
4530	-State constitutions (Collections).
4541–4545	-Constitutional history of the United States.
4546–4554	-General works (History, theory, and interpretation of constitutional law).
4555	-Amending process.
4558	-Particular amendments.
4565–4578	-Separation of powers. Delegation of powers.
4581–4583	-Sources and relationships of law.
4600–4629	-Structure of government. Federal and State relations. Jurisdiction.
4635	-National territory. Noncontiguous territories.
4650–4694	-Foreign relations.
4695	-Public policy. Police power.
4700–4856	-Individual and state.
4700–4720	--Nationality and citizenship.
4741–4783	--Civil and political rights and liberties.
4788	--Political parties.
4791–4856	--Control of individuals.
4791	---Identification.
4794	---Passports.
4800–4848	---Aliens.
4850–4856	---Internal security.
4865–4869	-Church and state.
4880–5130	-Organs of the government.
4880–4921	--The people. Election law.
4930–5005	--The legislature.
5050–5125	--The executive branch.
5130	--The judiciary. Judicial power.
5150	National emblems. Flag. Seal. Seat of government. National anthem.
5152	Patriotic customs and observances.
5153–5154	Decorations of honor. Awards.
5155–5156	Commemorative medals.
5300–5332	Local government.
5336–5398	Civil service. Government officials and employees.
5399	Police and power of the police.
5401–5425	Administrative organization and procedure.
5500–5865	Public property. Public restraints on private property.
5500–5501	-General.
5505–5508	-Conservation of natural resources.

5521–5536	-Roads.
5540–5541	-Bridges.
5551–5590	-Water resources. Watersheds. Rivers. Lakes. Water courses.
5594	-Weather control. Meteorology. Weather stations.
5599	-Eminent domain.
5601–5646	-Public land law.
5660–5662	-Indian lands.
5670–5673	-Homesteads.
5675–5677	-Land grants.
5691–5710	-Regional and city planning. Zoning. Building.
5721–5740	-Housing. Slum clearance. City development.
5750–5857	-Government property.
5750–5755	--Administration. Powers and controls.
5760–5810	--Land and real property.
5820–5857	--Personal property.
5865	-Public works.
5900–6075	Government measures in time of war, national emergency, or economic crisis. Emergency economic legislation.
6200–6795	Public finance.
6200	-General.
6201–6219	-Money. Currency. Coinage.
6221–6225	-Budget. Government expenditures.
6231–6236	-Expenditure control. Public auditing and accounting.
6241–6245	-Public debts. Loans. Bond issues.
6251–6708	-National revenue.
6251–6256	--History.
6260	--General.
6265–6708	--Particular sources of revenue.
6265	---Charges.
6271–6645	---Taxation.
6651–6708	---Tariff. Trade agreements. Customs.
6720–6795	--State and local finance.
7201–7755	National defense. Military law.
7201–7225	-Comprehensive. General.
7250–7680	-The military establishment. Armed Forces.
7250–7298	--General.
7305–7479	--Particular branches of service.
7485–7488	--Auxiliary services during war or emergency.
7590	--Military discipline.
7595–7596	--Law enforcement. Criminal investigation.
7601–7679	--Military criminal law and procedure.
7680	--Civil status of members of the Armed Forces.
7683	-Other defense agencies, A–Z.

7685	-Civil defense.
7695	-Other topics, A–Z.
7701–7755	-War veterans.
8201–8228	Indians.
8700–9075	Courts. Procedure.
8700–8707	-Administration of justice. Organization of the judiciary.
8711–8807	-Court organization and procedure.
8810–9075	-Civil procedure.
9085	Arbitration and award. Commercial arbitration.
9201–9461	Criminal law.
9601–9760	Criminal procedure.

Note that books on legal research are classified at KF240, and books on legal assistantship are classified at KF320 (more precisely: KF320.L4).

LC Cataloging

Books are cataloged in the Library of Congress Classification system beginning with the **class notation:** a main classification letter, then a subclassification may be indicated by additional letters, then a class number assignment (e.g., KF 320). Then comes a letter-number (and perhaps letter-number-letter-number) designation treated as a decimal, known as a **cutter number,** named after its originator, Charles Ammi Cutter. The tables for the assignment of cutter numbers are beyond the scope of this book, but generally a cutter number identifies a book's author by the initial letter of the author's last name, followed by a number representing the remaining letters of the author's last name (e.g., Carter is .C37).

In a library using the Library of Congress Classification system, the **call number** of a book, the place on the shelf where the book may be found, consists of the class notation, the cutter number, followed by the year of publication (e.g., KF320.C37 1990). Books are then shelved alpha-numeric-chronologically by their call number. The genius of the system is the idea that two books on the same subject are rarely written by two authors with the same name in the same year.

Interestingly, you don't need a Master's Degree in Library Science in order to arrange a small collection of books according to the Library of Congress Classification system. Skipping the details of (and, of course, the benefits of) true cataloging, you can engage in a portion of what is known as **copy cataloging,** whereby you pick up a book's call number by finding it, by whatever means, in a library using the Library of Congress Classification system, and copy the call number given it by the librarian.

Better yet, you can copy the preliminary call numbers used by the Library of Congress. More and more major publishers are participating in the **Library of Congress Cataloging-in-Publication Data** program. Manuscripts are sent to the Library of Congress just prior to publication. The Library of Congress librarians then catalog the book, and the publisher includes the preliminary data, including the call number, on the reverse side of the title page.

Using the Card Catalog

Like the card catalog in an ordinary library, the card catalog in a law library can be very useful in helping you find what you're looking for. Most libraries now have some type of on-line (i.e., computer) catalog. Nevertheless, three cards are usually inserted for each book: an author card, a title card, and a subject card. Thus, using a card catalog, you can search for a book by author, title, or subject. An on-line catalog may also allow you to search for particular terms in the catalog. From the appropriate card, you pick up the call number of the book. With the call number you then locate the book on the shelf. Of course, you can locate other books on your subject by scanning the books shelved next to the book you've located.

Key Terms

call number
class notation
classification
copy cataloging
cutter number
Dewey Decimal Classification
law library
library
Library of Congress Cataloging-in-Publication Data
Library of Congress Classification
Superintendent of Documents Classification

GLOSSARY

Abuse of discretion: Grounds for appeal: the appellant argues that the decision of the trial court was completely unreasonable and not logically based on the facts.

Act: Bill considered and passed by one house of the Congress of the United States.

Adjudication: Deciding of a case by judgment and/or decree.

Administrative agency: Generally, a specialized governmental entity. Narrowly, a governmental entity distinct from the branches of government, created to independently regulate a limited specialized area of law.

Administrative codes: Topical collections of regulations.

Administrative decision: Decision of, or written explanation of the decision of, an administrative law judge.

Administrative law judge: Generally, the decision maker in an administrative hearing.

Administrative order: Formal exercise of discretionary power by the administrator of an administrative agency.

Advance sheets: Temporary pamphlets of court opinions; they are paged exactly as they will be in the official reporter.

Adversarial documents: Argumentative documents, drafted to emphasize the strong points of your client's position and the weaknesses of the opposing party's.

Advisory letter: Letter that offers legal opinions.

Affirm: Decision of an appellate court that it agrees with the decision of the lower court and that the party who won in the lower court wins.

Affirmative defenses: A section of an answer or pleading in which the defendant asserts that a defense exists even if the plaintiff's allegations are true.

Affirmed: The appellate court agreed with the trial court.

Amended pleading: A pleading that changes information in a prior pleading.

***Amicus* brief:** A brief that argues from the public policy point of view; submitted by a person or organization not directly involved in the lawsuit.

Annotate: To note or to mark up.

Annotated: With a careful editorial compilation of the authorities on important points raised by the decisions.

Annotated code: Code containing case summaries of how the courts have interpreted each statute (e.g., cases that have construed a statute, law review articles that have discussed it, and its procedural history).

Annotated constitution: Version of a constitution containing case summaries of how the courts have interpreted it.

Annotation: Method of finding cases in a specialized collection of the law (e.g., an A.L.R. annotation).

Answer: Document filed by a defendant in response to a complaint; comprising specific responses to the defendant's allegations; general defenses; affirmative or special defenses; and counterclaims or cross-claims.

Appeal: A demand by the losing party that a higher court review the decision of the trial court.

Appellant: Party who appealed.

Appellant's brief: The brief filed first in an appeal, allowing the appellant the opportunity to define the issues that will be brought before the appellate court.

Appellate brief: A brief filed with the appellate court to persuade that court to decide contested issues in favor of the filing party.

Appellate rules: The criteria, different for each jurisdiction, governing the appellate procedure.

Appellee: Party who answered the appeal.

Appellee's brief: The brief filed in response to the appellant's brief.

Appendix: A supplementary collection of primary source materials.

Argument: The portion of a legal memorandum or appellate brief that presents your client's position, analyzing the legal issues raised by the "questions presented" section and demonstrating that your client's position should prevail.

Attorney/client privilege: The law that keeps communication between lawyers and their clients confidential, thus protecting clients from self-incrimination.

Attorney general: Chief lawyer for a sovereign.

Authorization letter: A letter in which the client provides the attorney with official permission to contact employers, doctors, or other individuals who have records that relate in some way to the matter at hand.

Bad law: Overruled (or otherwise discredited) precedent. Precedent without authority.

Bar journal: Law journal published by a bar association.

Bench trial: A trial with no jury.

Bequest: A gift under a will.

Bibliographic: Approach emphasizing detailed descriptions of the various books used.

Bill: Proposed permanent law introduced in a house of Congress.

Bill of Rights: First 10 amendments to the Constitution of the United States.

Binding authority: Authority that a court must follow.

Bluebook: Abbreviated form for *The Bluebook: A Uniform System of Citation*, 15th edition (1991), and earlier editions, recognized as the model of correct citation form.

Bluebook style: Citation style suggested by *The Bluebook*.

BNA: Acronym for the Bureau of National Affairs, Inc., of Washington, D.C.

Body: In an appellate brief, the section of the argument in which you set forth the main text and support your client's position with detailed arguments; or, in a complaint, the section consisting of the identification of the parties, the basis for jurisdiction, and numbered paragraphs of allegations and cause of action.

Boilerplate: Standardized language used in forms.

Brief: Formal written argument to a court.

BW: Acronym for the Bancroft-Whitney Company of San Francisco, California, a long-time subsidiary of the Lawyers Co-operative Publishing Company.

Call number: In Library of Congress Classification system, place on the shelf where a book may be found, consisting of the class notation, cutter number, and year of publication (e.g., KF320.C37 1990).

CALR: Acronym for computer-assisted legal research. Use of computer-modem systems to automate the search of legal materials.

Canned briefs: Guides to law school casebooks in which each major case is preanalyzed for the reader.

Caption: The part of the brief that identifies the name of the case, its docket number, the court in which it is pending, and the date on which the pleading is filed.

Case at bar: Actual legal controversy to be decided.

Case brief: An objective summary of the important points of a single case; internal to the law firm, not filed with the court.

Case history: Path, noted by citations, a legal controversy has taken through the court system.

Case in point: Previous case like the case at bar.

Case law: Law from the judicial branch.

Case method: Method of legal research whereby if you know at least one case like yours, you can search the law book's table of cases, if any, and go to the references.

Case of first impression: A case without precedent.

Casebook: Law school textbook containing a series of selected cases on each topic to be covered.

Casenotes: Case summaries in the *United States Code Service* (U.S.C.S.).

Cases: Actual legal controversies.

CCH: Acronym for the Commerce Clearing House, Inc., of Chicago, Illinois.

CD-ROM: Acronym for compact disk with read-only memory.

Certificate of interested parties: The document identifying all those parties to the case who have an interest in its outcome.

Certificate of service: An acknowledgment at the end of any court-filed document that verifies delivery of the document to all persons entitled to a copy, identifying the date and type of delivery.

***Certiorari,* writ of:** Written order of an appellate court with discretionary jurisdiction stating that it chooses to review a lower court decision and directing the lower court to produce its records for review.

Charter: Documents that form a government. The fundamental law of a local government.

Chronologically: In or by real-time sequence.

Citation: Reference to the location at which a case opinion may be found in a reporter. In dictionary making, a sample of the actual use of a word in context.

Citation-based: Standard for creating a dictionary in which a fair sample of actual uses of each word in context are collected, allowing the editor to authoritatively determine whether each word is current or archaic, and its spelling, etymology, meaning, and usage.

Citation search: Computer search made by entering a citation, rather than a word.

Citation style: How cited legal materials should be abbreviated to avoid confusing readers.

Citators: Books and other media that primarily list legal citations.

Cite: To point out the location of legal authority for the law that supports your case. Reference to the location at which a case opinion may be found in a reporter.

Cited case: Case being cited by other courts. The target case.

Citing cases: Cases that make reference to the cited case.

Class notation: In Library of Congress Classification system, beginning main classification letter, any subclassification indicated by additional letters, and a class number assignment (e.g., KF 320).

Classification: Arrangement of books and other media in a library.

Code: Topical collection of statutes.

Codification: Process of collecting permanent public statutes topically, adding amendments, and deleting expired, repealed, or superseded statutes.

Collection letter: A letter that demands payment of the amount claimed to be owed to your client.

COLR: Acronym for computer-organized legal research. Use of computers to automate the organization of search results.

Comments: Articles written by law professors, prominent practitioners, or outstanding students that are published in law reviews.

Common law: Rules of law common to all of medieval England. The law made by judges in deciding actual cases. A legal system emphasizing case law.

Complaint: The first pleading by any party to a lawsuit; defines the underlying claim.

Compulsory counterclaim: A counterclaim that must be brought in the pending lawsuit, or it will be waived.

Computer-assisted legal research (CALR): Use of computer-modem systems to automate the search of legal materials.

Computer-organized legal research (COLR): Use of computers to automate the organization of search results.

Conclusion: The section of an appellate brief, opinion letter, or internal memorandum of law in which you summarize your analysis, answering the questions raised by the issues.

Concordance: Index of words. A literal alphabetical listing of the principal words of a book, with precise references to where in the book each word is used.

Concur: Agree, as when a judge agrees with the majority opinion of a court.

Concurrent resolution: Proposed *administrative* (not legislative) statement of Congress.

Concurring opinion: Opinion of a justice who agrees with the decision of the court, but does not fully agree with the opinion of the court.

Confirmation letter: A letter which restates the content of an oral communication in order to create a permanent record.

Congress: Two-year period in which the Congress of the United States meets, mirroring the two-year term of a representative.

Connectors: Codes used to indicate the desired logical and numerical relationships among the terms in a computer word search.

Considered *dicta*: Serious extra comment made by a court in its opinion, not necessary to the decision.

Constitution: Written fundamental law of a sovereign (e.g., the Constitution of the United States).

Constitution of the United States: Written fundamental law of the United States of America.

Constitutional law: Any aspect of law directly derived from the written fundamental law of a sovereign.

Contract: An enforceable agreement.

Copy cataloging: Mimicking the cataloging used by an existing library.

Count: The part of a claim setting forth a particular cause of action.

Counterclaim: Separate charges raised by the defendant against the plaintiff; raised in the answer.

Court reporter: An employee of the court who is certified to record and transcribe court proceedings.

Cover letter: A letter which accompanies a document.

Cross-claim: A counterclaim made against another defendant, rather than the plaintiff.

Cross-references: In an index, references to other entries.

Cutter number: In Library of Congress Classification system, after the class notation, the letter-number designation treated as a decimal (e.g., .C37).

Database: Generally, collection of information placed in a computer's memory and capable of being searched by the computer. Technically, collection of information especially organized for rapid computer search and retrieval.

Decedent: A deceased person.

Decision: Outcome of a case (i.e., who wins).

Decree: Determination of the rights and duties of the parties (e.g., in a divorce).

Deed: A contract documenting the exchange of land.

Default judgment: Decision entered without a trial or hearing against a party who fails to respond to a complaint or to follow proper procedures.

Defendant: Person or legal entity responding to the claim of a plaintiff.

Defendant/plaintiff table: Section of a digest listing cases alphabetically by first defendants. Contains parallel citations, but not procedural histories or key numbers.

Definitions: Meanings of a word.

Demand letter: A letter intended to motivate a desired response; often, though not exclusively, the payment of a debt.

Deponent: The party or witness who is questioned in a deposition.

Deposition: A party or witness is placed under oath and questioned by attorneys; the content of the deposition is recorded by a certified court reporter.

Deposition on written questions: A deposition in which questions have been submitted in advance.

Descriptive word index: Provides a quick survey of specific key numbers which apply to a given subject area.

Devise: A gift of real estate under a will.

Dewey Decimal Classification: Entirely numerical system of library classification devised by Melvil Dewey in 1876 (law starts at 340).

Dicta: Extra comments made by a court in its opinion, not necessary to the decision.

Dictionary: Book containing an alphabetical list of words, along with information about each word, usually including its spelling, pronunciation, etymology, definitions, forms, and uses.

Dictum: Single extra comment made by a court in its opinion, not necessary to the decision.

Digest: Specialized index of reported cases. Case summary used as an entry in such an index. In litigation support, extraction of significant information from a deposition transcript or other document.

Digest paragraphs: Case summaries used as entries in a digest.

Directory: List of names and certain other information, such as addresses, telephone numbers, and the like.

Disclaimer: The portion of an opinion letter that limits its claim or denial, indicating that its analysis is based upon the facts as they are set forth in the letter.

Discovery: The pretrial investigation process by which parties can pursue information in the hands of other parties.

Discussion and analysis: The section of the internal memorandum of law in which one identifies points of law, supports them with citations, quotes from relevant sources, and relates the research to the facts of the matter at hand.

Disposition The result of the court decision which appears at the end of the opinion.

Dissenting opinion: Opinion of a justice who disagrees with the decision of the court.

Docket number: A number assigned by a court to a case for administrative purposes.

Enabling act: Statute creating and/or empowering a local government or agency.

Enactment: Legislative process resulting in the making of a statute.

Encyclopedia: Comprehensive work, usually a narrative summary, that covers all of the subjects within a particular branch of knowledge (or all branches of knowledge).

Engrossed bill: Final, officially signed copy of an act.

Enrolled bill: Final, officially signed copy on parchment of a bill that has passed both houses of Congress.

Entries: In an index, words or phrases used to note key concepts, words, and phrases in the text indexed.

Equitable argument: The argument that "justice and fair play" compel the court to find for your client, even though case law is against you.

Error of fact: Ground for appeal: appellant charges that facts as found by the trial court are not supported by the evidence admitted.

Error of law: Ground for appeal: appellant cites procedural errors, arguing that the trial court allowed the lawsuit to proceed in a manner not authorized by the rules or that the court admitted evidence which should have been excluded, or excluded evidence which should have been included.

Et seq.: Latin for "and the following."

Etymology: Word origin.

***Ex parte* communication:** Communication between one party in a lawsuit and the judge.

Ex post facto: Latin for "after the fact." A criminal law with retroactive effect. Such laws are prohibited by the Constitution of the United States.

Executive: Branch of government that enforces the law.

Executive agreement: President's agreement with a foreign country that, because it is without the advice and consent of the Senate, is not nation-binding.

Executive departments: Under the executive branch, groups of specialists organized to assist the executive in carrying out the functions of the executive branch.

Executive order: Executive's formal announcement of the exercise of a discretionary power.

Exhaustive annotations: Annotations collecting every case on the point annotated.

Exhaustive search: A search through every source.

Fact pleading: A pleading requiring you to identify all the facts necessary to allege a valid cause of action.

Federal Depository Library: Library that gets copies of federal government publications at little or no cost. By federal law, such a library must be open to the public.

Federalism: Concept that the federal government of the United States is a limited sovereign, having only the powers explicitly or implicitly granted it in the Constitution; all other powers being retained by the states.

Feudalism: Legal system in medieval England in which the king parceled out the use of the land in exchange for services to his kingdom.

Fields: Defined categories of information in a database.

Form books: Collections of sample legal documents used by lawyers and paralegals. They contain sample situations and alternative method of stating the legal basis for the cause of an action.

General defenses: The various grounds upon which the defendant refutes the complaint; included in the answer.

General warranty deed: A deed in which the seller pledges that the title in question is good.

Good law: Case precedent that has not been overruled (or otherwise discredited). Precedent with authority.

Harmless error: An error that has neither harmed nor prejudiced the appellant.

Headnotes: Brief editor-made summaries of the major points of law in an opinion that appear before the court's opinion (and generally falling at the top or "head" of a page).

Holding: Rule of law found in a case.

Hornbook: One of a series of one-volume treatises for students published by West Publishing Company, named after teaching tablets with handles used from the late 1400s to the middle 1700s, which held a sheet of paper protected by a sheet of translucent horn.

House organ: In-house periodical.

In point: Case that covers an issue explicitly, or exactly.

Index: A-to-Z list that refers a reader to the location of concepts in a book or other text by short entries and page references.

Index method: Method of legal research using entry terms to search the law book's index, if any, and go to the references.

Informative letter: A letter that transmits information (but not legal advice).

Infra: Below or after this point in the text.

Initial client interview: The beginning of your investigation into a client's problem.

Instructions and definitions: Introductory material of interrogatories that clarifies ambiguous terms.

Internal memorandum of law: Document within a law firm that provides an objective analysis of a client's problem.

International law: Rules governing sovereign countries by their consent, the law of nations.

Interrogatories: Requests for documents or for responses to written documents, submitted by one party to another, to be answered under oath.

Intestate: Leaving no will or instructions for the distribution of one's estate.

IRAC method: Technique to analyze issues raised in a legal matter. *IRAC* stands for: Identify the *issue* involved; Determine the *rule of law; Apply* the rule of law to the facts of your matter; and Reach a *conclusion.*

Issues: The legal problems a case presents.

Joint resolution: Proposed temporary (time-oriented) law.

Judges: Individuals with the power to decide actual legal disputes in the name of the sovereign.

Judgment: Final decision of a court entered into its records.

Judicial: Branch of government that interprets the law.

Judicial review: Doctrine that the clauses of the Constitution, like statutes, are subject to interpretation by the courts, and in particular, by the U.S. Supreme Court.

Jump cite: Reference to a specific succeeding page, after the first page, of an opinion (also known as a pinpoint cite).

Jur table: "Table of Jurisdictions Represented" in an A.L.R. annotation.

Jurats: Clauses following the signature on a document, identifying when, where, and before whom the signature was sworn or affirmed.

Jurisdictional statement: Identifies the legal authority that grants to the appellate court jurisdiction over the appeal.

Jurisprudence: The philosophy of law. The law collectively.

Jury instructions: Information a judge gives the jury at the conclusion of a trial about the legal principles it must follow. Each party presents the judge with its own version beforehand.

Jury trial: A trial before a jury of selected citizens.

Justices: Appellate court judges.

Key Number: West Publishing Company's term for the numerical designation of a line in a Topic outline.

KWIC: Acronym for the "key word in context" display of the results of a word search on LEXIS.

Landlord or lessor: The owner of property.

Landmark case: First significant case, often the case of first impression for your issue, decided in your favor.

Law: The command of a sovereign.

Law dictionary: Book containing a list of words unique to the legal profession, words often used by the legal profession, and ordinary words with a legal meaning.

Law journal: Legal periodical emphasizing current events.

Law library: Organized collection of law books and other media.

Law review: Scholarly periodical published by a law school.

Lawyer: Legal expert.

LCP: Acronym for the Lawyers Co-operative Publishing Company, of Rochester, New York, which became the Lawyers Cooperative Publishing Division of Thomson Legal Publishing Inc.

Leading case: Case opinion that reads like an A.L.R. annotation or treatise, laying out all the precedent on your issue, pro and con, and deciding in your favor.

Lease: A contract that relates to the rental of property.

Legal directory: Guide to lawyers, law firms, and/or government agencies.

Legal encyclopedia: A multivolume compilation that provides in-depth coverage of every area of the law.

Legal forms: Samples of legally effective documents, such as contracts, deeds, and wills.

Legal remedy: The recovery of damages in the form of money.

Legislative: Branch of government that makes the law.

Legislative departments: Under the legislative branch, groups of specialists organized to assist the legislature in carrying out the functions of the legislative branch.

Legislative history: Committee reports, floor debates, and other information considered by the legislature in enacting a bill or joint resolution, which may be reviewed by a court in an attempt to determine the intent of the legislature in enacting a statute.

Letterhead: The standard stationery of a law firm, printed with the firm name, address, telephone number, and other relevant information.

LEXIS: Mead Data Central, Inc.'s computer-assisted legal research system, which includes access to A.L.R.

Library: Collection of books and other media kept for their use. An organized collection of books and other media.

Library of Congress Cataloging-in-Publication Data: Results of a program by which manuscripts are sent to the Library of Congress just prior to publication. Library of Congress librarians catalog them, and publishers include the preliminary data for each book, including the call number, on the reverse side of the title page.

Library of Congress Classification: Letter-number system of library classification devised in the early 1900s by Librarian of Congress Herbert Putnam and his Chief Cataloger, Charles Martel (law of the United States is subclassification KF).

Litigation support: Organization of case information, particularly from discovery, to aid an attorney in the trial of a case.

Local case: Most recent case from your local jurisdiction decided in your favor, pointing out that your local jurisdiction follows established precedent.

Looseleaf service: Law publication, usually a set of books, issued in notebook form.

Macro: User-made program of a series of commands and keyboard strokes in WordPerfect.

Majority opinion: Opinion of the court in which a majority of the justices join.

Mandatory authority: Authority that a court must follow.

MB: Abbreviated form for the Matthew Bender & Company of New York, New York.

MDC: Acronym for Mead Data Central, Inc., of Dayton, Ohio.

Memorandum at the request of a judge: A trial memorandum submitted by each of the parties to a lawsuit, setting forth a position on a disputed issue so the judge may render a decision.

Memorandum in regard to a motion: A memorandum submitted to the court in support of a motion.

Memorandum of law: Written discussion of a legal question, objectively reporting the law favoring each side in the fact pattern, as found after researching the topic.

Memorandum opinion: A brief opinion.

Michie: Abbreviated form for The Michie Company of Charlottesville, Virginia, now a subsidiary of Mead Data Central, Inc.

Microfiche: File-card-sized sheets of film containing miniature pictures of printed pages.

Microfilm: Reels or cassettes of film containing miniature pictures of printed pages.

Microforms: Reproductions of printed matter in greatly reduced size.

Models: Copies of actual complaints, obtained from your firm's files, that have a factual foundation similar to your complaint.

Motion: A request that the court take an action.

Motion for Directed Verdict: A motion requesting the judge to find that the other party failed to offer sufficient evidence to make its case, and so to find in favor of the moving party.

Motion for More Definite Statement: A motion requesting other party to make its pleadings clearer.

Motion for New Trial: Motion to negate the result of the present trial and allowing a second to proceed; based on the discovery of new evidence, or on the argument that evidentiary or other procedureal matters prejudiced one of the parties.

Motion for Protective Order: Motion filed by the party upon whom a discovery request has been made, contending that the request oversteps the bounds of the rules.

Motion for Sanctions: A motion filed by any party to counter alleged violations by another.

Motion to Compel Discovery: A motion filed by a party seeking to force compliance with a discovery request.

Motion to Dismiss: Motion filed to discontinue a trial by a party who believes the other party has failed to state a claim for which the court can grant relief; or motion filed to conclude a trial after settlement.

National Reporter System: System of reporters published by West Publishing Company covering all the appellate courts in the United States.

Noise words: Set of commonly used words that cannot be searched on LEXIS.

Nominative reporters: Reporter volumes compiled by individuals; especially the initial reporters who covered the U.S. Supreme Court.

Norman Conquest: Event in English history to which the U.S. legal system can be traced. In 1066, William the Conqueror, living on the Normandy coast of France, crossed the English Channel and deposed the reigning king, Harold.

Notes: Short book, case, or subject reviews that are published in law reviews.

Notice pleading: Pleading requiring only a short statement of the grounds upon which a party is basing a claim and showing why the party is entitled to relief.

Nutshells: Series of paperback textbooks published by West Publishing Company and offering brief introductions to issues.

Obiter dicta: Irrelevant extra comment made by a court in its opinion, not necessary to the decision.

Objective documents: Nonadversarial documents that accurately convey information and avoid bias.

Official reports: Reports designated by the high court (or the legislature) as the official version of its opinions.

On-line: Accessible by a modem-equipped computer using telephone lines. Available on a computer system.

On point: Case that covers an issue implicitly or by analogy, if not explicitly, or exactly.

Operative documents: Documents that lawyers and paralegals draft, such as executed contracts, leases, wills, and deeds, that define property rights and performance obligation.

Opinion: Court's written explanation of its decision.

Opinion letter: A letter that renders legal advice based upon specific facts, applying information from research to analyze a legal problem and reach a conclusion about its resolution.

Order: Preliminary decision of a court (e.g., a ruling on a motion).

Order of dismissal: Conclusion of a lawsuit after settlement. Either both parties jointly draft the order, or one party files a Motion to Dismiss and the other agrees.

Ordinance: Legislation of a local government.

Outline: Summary showing the pattern of subordination of one thought to another.

P-H: Acronym for Prentice-Hall, Inc., a division of Simon & Schuster, Inc., Paramus, New Jersey.

Page mode: Browsing by page feature on WESTLAW.

Parallel citation/cite: Alternate location reference for a case opinion.

***Per curiam* opinion:** "By the court" opinion. A joint anonymous opinion of the court.

Periodical: Work that is published at regular intervals.

Permissive counterclaim: A counterclaim that arises out of facts different from those in the complaint. May be filed in the pending lawsuit or in a separate lawsuit at a later date.

Persuasive authority: All nonmandatory primary authority.

Petitioner: Party who appealed. A plaintiff, especially a plaintiff expecting to be unopposed.

Physical evidence: All exhibits admitted into evidence by the trial court, as well as those exhibits offered but denied admission.

Pinpoint cite: Reference to a specific succeeding page, after the first page, of an opinion (also known as a jump cite).

Plaintiff: Person or legal entity that sought relief in the trial court.

Plaintiff in error: A defendant-appellant.

Pleadings: Documents filed with the court in a pending lawsuit that define the issues to be decided by the court at trial. These include the complaint; the answer and special defenses (the responses to the complaint); and all cross-claims and responses thereto.

Plurality opinion: Opinion of the court where a majority of the justices agree on a decision, but a majority is unable to agree on the reasoning behind it.

Pocket parts: Annual supplements to digests that fit into the back covers of the books.

Pocket veto: Untimely nonreturn of a bill presented to the President. Since, in such a case, the houses of Congress have adjourned, the veto cannot be overridden.

Positive law: Codified law passed as a statute. The law "actually enacted."

Practice pointers: Part of an A.L.R. annotation that contains "useful hints" on how to handle a case involving the point annotated.

Prayer for relief: Document which sets out the specific demands that the plaintiff has against the defendant, requests a judgment in favor of the plaintiff, and identifies the damages the plaintiff asserts judgment should allow.

Preamble: Introductory statement of legal intent (e.g., the "We the People . . ." portion of the Constitution of the United States).

Precedent: Preceding similar case. A case like yours.

Precedential value: The force that a cited authority exerts upon a judge's reasoning.

Prima facie: Accepted on its face, but not irrebuttably.

Primary authority: The law itself. The authoritative acts of the sovereign (e.g., the constitution, statutes, executive orders, court decisions, and administrative regulations).

Prior proceedings: The previous judicial considerations of a case.

Private law: Law that applies only to an individual or to a few individuals.

Probate system: The system that regulates the distribution of the property of a deceased person.

Proclamations: Executive orders having no continuing legal effect, such as declaring a certain day to be "National Whatever Day."

Promulgated: Made official and public.

Proximity search: CALR word search for one word within a specified number of words from another.

Public law: Law that applies to everyone.

Public policy argument: An argument to the court that a decision in your favor would be to the public good.

Query: A word search on WESTLAW.

Questions presented: The section of the appellate brief which states the grounds upon which the decision of the trial court is being questioned.

Quitclaim deed: A deed making no warranty as to the title but only passes such interest as the seller is ultimately shown to have.

Ratio decidendi: Distinction or point on which a case turns.

Real property: Land.

Record: The documentation of a trial: includes pleadings, briefs, physical evidence, a transcript of the proceedings, and the court's decision.

References: In an index, page numbers indicating the location in the text at which key concepts, words, or phrases appear.

Regional reporters: Seven reporters corresponding to the geographic areas of the country and containing decisions from all states.

Regulates: Makes regulations.

Regulations: Laws made by an administrative agency.

Related matters: Part of an A.L.R. annotation that lists similar, related annotations, along with a token sample of law review articles and treatises on the point annotated.

Relevant and material facts: Facts affecting the decision of the court.

Remand: Decision of an appellate court that the proceedings in a lower court were not fair or complete, returning the case to lower court for a new decision to be made after a fair and complete proceeding.

Reply brief: A brief filed by the appellant in response to the appellee's opening brief.

Reporters: Hardbound volumes of judicial opinions, published in a continuing series.

Request for admissions: Request to admit evidence prior to trial. Provides drafter with the opportunity to establish selected facts.

Residuary clause: Section of a will by which that portion of the estate which is not specifically identified is bequeathed.

Respondent: Party who answered the appeal. A defendant, especially a defendant opposing a petitioner.

Restatement: Systematic exposition of the common law as if it were a codified statutory code.

Retainer letter: A letter that sets forth the agreement and relationship between attorney and client.

Reversal: Decision of an appellate court that it disagrees with the decision of the lower court and that the party who lost in the lower court wins.

Reverse: Decision of an appellate court that it disagrees with the decision of the lower court, and that either the party who lost in the lower court wins or the case itself is dismissed.

RIA: Acronym for the Research Institute of America of New York, New York, a long-time subsidiary of the Lawyers Co-operative Publishing Company.

Rule of law: What the law says.

Rulemaking: Process of making administrative rules and regulations.

Scheme: Detailed logical section-numbered outline of an A.L.R. annotation.

Scope: Part of an A.L.R. annotation that states the purported contents of the annotation.

Secondary authority: Anything that is not primary authority. Any assertion about the law that is not the law itself.

Sections: Organizing subdivision of statutes under each title of a code.

Separation of powers: Concept that the powers of the federal government of the United States are divided by the Constitution into three branches—legislative, executive, and judicial—to avoid the tyranny of a king.

Service of process: Procedure by which the defendant is notified by a person statutorily authorized to serve legal documents (a process server) that the defendant is being sued.

Session: One of the yearly meeting periods of the Congress of the United States.

Session law: Bill or joint resolution that has become law during a particular session of the legislature.

Settlement: The compromise and agreement reached between the parties to resolve all disputed issues.

Settlement agreement: The document that sets out the terms of the compromise.

Setout: Paragraph sketch of a case in an A.L.R. annotation.

Shepardize: To review all the citing cases for a cited case using *Shepard's Citations* to make sure the cited case is not bad law or to help find other cases like the cited case. Also, to review all the cases cited in the brief or other legal writing using *Shepard's Citations* to make sure the brief or other legal writing does not cite bad law or to help find other cases like the case cited to use in a reply or revision.

Shepard's: Abbreviated form for any or all of the *Shepard's Citations* sets published by Shepard's/McGraw Hill, Inc., of Colorado Springs, Colorado. A book of tables listing all the citing cases for a cited case.

Short summary of the conclusion: Section of an internal memorandum of law that provides a quick overview of its analysis.

Shorthand form: The shorthand version of the case name; does not always conform to bluebook rules.

Signature block: The space on the appellate brief, compliant, or interrogatory for the signature of the attorney ultimately responsible for its contents.

Simple resolution: Proposed *administrative* (not legislative) statement of one house of Congress.

Slip law: Copy of a particular law passed during a session of the legislature.

Slip opinion: Individual court opinion published separately from bound volumes.

Sort: Put in alphanumeric order.

Sovereign: Entity with the power to command.

Special defenses: Those defenses that go beyond the mere denial of the plaintiff's claims; also called affirmative defenses.

Special warranty deed: A deed in which the seller warrants the title against defects arising during the seller's period of ownership only.

Standard of review: The guideline that the court applied in evaluating alleged errors.

Star pagination: Notation of the pagination of one text (e.g., an official reporter) in another text (e.g., an unofficial reporter).

Stare decisis: Custom or doctrine of following precedent.

Statement of facts: A major section of a legal document that sets forth the factual context of the case.

Statement of issues presented: Opening statement of an internal memorandum of law that identifies the legal and factual issues to be discussed therein.

Statement of the case: A statement setting forth the procedural history of the case, identifying all lower courts in which the case has been heard and the decision of each.

Statute edition: Volume of *Shepard's Citations* that lists all the citing cases for a statute or ordinance.

Statute method: Method of legal research whereby if you know at least one statute like yours, you can search the law book's code finding table, if any, and go to the references.

Statutes: Laws the legislative branch makes.

Statutory law: Law from the legislative branch.

Stipulated judgment: A conclusion of a trial that precludes the parties from ever again making the same claims.

Stop words: Set of commonly used words that cannot be searched on WESTLAW.

String citations: A long list of cases that you claim support your point, but they could dilute your argument.

Subpoena *duces tecum:* A deposition notice requiring the deponent to "bring with him" specified documents or things.

Summary judgment: Judgment without a trial when there is no dispute as to the facts.

Summons: The service of process accomplished by delivering the complaint.

Superintendent of Documents Classification: Letter-number system of library classification often used for collections of governmental documents.

Superseding annotation: Annotation that replaces another annotation.

Supplemental pleading: A document which adds to a pleading without deleting prior information.

Supplemental response: Statement of information pertinent to the response to an interrogatory but not known at the time of filing.

Supplementing annotation: Annotation that provides additional cases on a point already annotated.

Supra: Above or before this point in the text.

Syllabus: Official summary or list of the major legal points made in an opinion.

Synergistic: Having "a whole greater than the sum of its parts" effect.

Synopsis: Short paragraph summary of an entire case.

Table of authorities: List of all primary and secondary sources cited in your brief.

Table of cases: A section of a digest listing all cases whose texts appear in the associated volumes; cases are listed alphabetically by plaintiff.

Table of contents: The section of an appellate brief identifying section headings with corresponding page numbers.

TAPP Rule: Rule of thumb used by indexers at the Lawyers Co-operative Publishing Company for analyzing fact patterns and for generating entry terms. It is based on the premise that legal researchers should be able to find the law they are looking for by looking up terms representing the thing, act, person, or place involved.

TCSL Box: Part of an A.L.R. annotation that lists cross-references to other units of the LCP's Total Client Service Library.

Tenant or lessee: User of property.

Term mode: Browsing by search term feature on WESTLAW.

Terms of art: Shorthand terms necessary to the practice of law despite their obscurity.

Testamentary intent: The intentions of the testator.

Testator: The person who makes a will.

Textbook: Book that contains the principles of a given subject; thus it is useful in the study of that subject.

Thesauri: Books of words and their synonyms and near synonyms. The singular form is "thesaurus."

Title page: The cover or first page of an appellate brief.

Titles: Major topical division of a code (e.g., the 50 titles of the *United States Code*).

TLPI: Acronym for Thomson Legal Publishing Inc., of Rochester, New York, of which the Lawyers Cooperative Publishing division is the successor to the Lawyers Co-operative Publishing Company.

Topic method: Method of legal research whereby if you know the topic you want to search, you can search the law book's table of contents, if any, and go to all references, and scan the text for your topic.

Topically: By subject or by topic.

Topics: The central divisions, the subdivisions of the subdivisions of the seven main divisions, in the outline of the law used for digests published by West Publishing Company.

Total Client Service Library (TCSL): LCP's marketing slogan for its national law book sets, which are thoroughly cross-referenced with each other.

Transcript: A written account of all proceedings in the trial court, including questions and comments of the attorneys, witness testimony, and the judge's rulings and comments.

Transmittal letter: A type of confirmation letter that accompanies information sent to a designated party.

Treatise: Systematic scholarly discussion, or treatment, of the principles of a given subject; thus it is especially useful in the study of that subject.

Treaty: Nation-binding agreement with a foreign country.

Trial and practice books: Books that guide a lawyer or a paralegal through the proof of contentions at trial, often with samples of litigation aids and trial testimony.

Trial before the court: A trial with no jury. The judge decides issues of both law and fact.

Trial notebook: A collection made by each party of information relevant to the trial.

Unconstitutional: Fundamentally illegal.

Unofficial reports: Reports not designated by the high court (or the legislature) as the official version of its opinions.

Unsolicited memorandum anticipating legal issues: Memorandum filed at trial to try to persuade the judge on a particular issue.

User-friendly: A computer system that is easy to use.

Vacating: Decision of an appellate court that it disagrees with the decision of the lower court, and that the case is dismissed.

Verdict: A decision rendered by a jury; must be incorporated into subsequent judgments.

Verification: The plaintiff swears to the truth of the contents of an affadavit.

Veto: Return to Congress of a bill without the President's signature that had been presented to the President by Congress. A vetoed bill is not law unless the veto is overridden by a two-thirds vote of each house.

Video deposition: A videotaped record of an oral deposition.

West: Abbreviated form for West Publishing Company of St. Paul, Minnesota.

WESTLAW: West Publishing Company's computer-assisted legal research system, which includes access to West's case summaries.

Will: A formal document that identifies the parties to whom property should be distributed upon the death of the testator.

Withdrawal: A document abandoning a claim, filed by the party who originally filed the claim.

Word processing: Electronic display, correction, and revision of text before printing.

Word search: Computer search of the words likely to have been used to describe the information sought.

***Words and Phrases* index:** A section of the digest by means of which you can trace the cases in which a word or phrase is construed.

INDEX

Y